GET THE MOST FROM YOUR BOOK

VOUCHER CODE:

21F93BMV

Online Access

Your print purchase of *The Counseling Practicum and Internship Manual: A Resource for Graduate Counseling Students in a Dynamic, Global Era, Fourth Edition,* includes **online access via Springer Publishing Connect**™ to increase accessibility, portability, and searchability.

Insert the code at http://connect.springerpub.com/content/book/978-0-8261-6607-4 or scan the QR code and insert the voucher code today!

Having trouble? Contact our customer service department at cs@springerpub.com

Instructor Resource Access for Adopters

Let us do some of the heavy lifting to create an engaging classroom experience with a variety of instructor resources included in most textbooks SUCH AS:

Visit **https://connect.springerpub.com/** and look for the **"Show Supplementary"** button on your **book homepage** to see what is available to instructors! First time using Springer Publishing Connect?

Email **textbook@springerpub.com** to create an account and start unlocking valuable resources.

The Counseling Practicum and Internship Manual

Shannon Hodges, PhD, LMHC, ACS, is professor emeritus of clinical mental health counseling at Niagara University and currently an associate professor of counseling at the University of the Sunshine Coast near Brisbane, Australia. He has over 25 years of experience providing counseling in community agencies, university counseling centers, residential treatment centers, and overseas. He is a former director of a university counseling center and clinical director of a county mental health clinic and has 10 years of experience supervising and providing peer counseling in collegiate living groups. He has 33 years of experience in training school counselors, mental health counselors, and undergraduate psychology students. He has authored numerous professional publications, including books, book chapters, journal articles, and essays. He has also served on the editorial review boards of several journals including the *Journal of Counseling and Development, Journal of Counseling and Values, Journal of Mental Health Counseling, Journal of Professional Counseling,* and *Journal of College Counseling.* He has received awards both for his teaching and for his writing. Dr. Hodges is a longtime member of the American Counseling Association (ACA) and several ACA-affiliate divisions. His book *101 Careers in Counseling* is a popular text for counselors and those considering the counseling profession. His most recent book is *Creating a Meaningful Life: A Practical Guide for Counselors, Therapists, and Other Helping Professionals.* He has taught and counseled overseas and made regular service and volunteering trips to South African orphanages and remote Australian Aboriginal schools and communities.

The Counseling Practicum and Internship Manual

A Resource for Graduate Counseling Students in a Dynamic, Global Era

Fourth Edition

Shannon Hodges, PhD, LMHC, ACS

Copyright © 2025 Springer Publishing Company, LLC
All rights reserved.
First Springer Publishing edition 2011 (978-0-8261-1832-5); subsequent editions, 2016, 2020.

No part of this publication may be reproduced, stored in a retrieval system, or transmitted in any form or by any means, electronic, mechanical, photocopying, recording, or otherwise, without the prior permission of Springer Publishing Company, LLC, or authorization through payment of the appropriate fees to the Copyright Clearance Center, Inc., 222 Rosewood Drive, Danvers, MA 01923, 978-750-8400, fax 978-646-8600, info@copyright.com or at www.copyright.com.

Springer Publishing Company, LLC
902 Carnegie Center/Suite 140, Princeton, NJ 08540
www.springerpub.com
connect.springerpub.com

Acquisitions Editor: Mindy Okura-Marszycki
Compositor: Amnet
Production Editor: Diana Osborne

ISBN: 978-0-8261-6606-7
ebook ISBN: 978-0-8261-6607-4
DOI: 10.1891/9780826166074

SUPPLEMENTS:

A robust set of instructor resources designed to supplement this text is located at http://connect.springerpub.com/content/book/978-0-8261-6607-4. Qualifying instructors may request access by emailing **textbook@springerpub.com**.

Instructor Materials:
LMS Common Cartridge (All Instructor Resources and Instructions for Use) ISBN: 978-0-8261-6613-5
Instructor Manual ISBN: 978-0-8261-6608-1
Instructor PowerPoints ISBN: 978-0-8261-6609-8
Transition Guide ISBN: 978-0-8261-8962-2

Student Materials:
Documents for Practicum and Internship (Editable Forms) ISBN: 978-0-8261-6621-0

24 25 26 27 / 5 4 3 2 1

The author and the publisher of this Work have made every effort to use sources believed to be reliable to provide information that is accurate and compatible with the standards generally accepted at the time of publication. Because medical science is continually advancing, our knowledge base continues to expand. Therefore, as new information becomes available, changes in procedures become necessary. We recommend that the reader always consult current research and specific institutional policies before performing any clinical procedure or delivering any medication. The author and publisher shall not be liable for any special, consequential, or exemplary damages resulting, in whole or in part, from the readers' use of, or reliance on, the information contained in this book. The publisher has no responsibility for the persistence or accuracy of URLs for external or third-party Internet websites referred to in this publication and does not guarantee that any content on such websites is, or will remain, accurate or appropriate.

Library of Congress Cataloging-in-Publication Data
Names: Hodges, Shannon, author.
Title: The counseling practicum and internship manual : a resource for
  graduate counseling students in a dynamic, global era / Shannon Hodges.
Description: Fourth edition. | New York, NY : Springer Publishing Company,
  LLC, [2025] | Includes bibliographical references and index.
Identifiers: LCCN 2023050723 (print) | LCCN 2023050724 (ebook) | ISBN
  9780826166067 (paperback) | ISBN 9780826166081 (instructor manual) |
  ISBN 9780826166074 (ebook) | ISBN 9780826166098 (instructor chapter
  PowerPoints) | ISBN 9780826166135 (LMS Common Cartridge)
Subjects: MESH: Counseling | Internship, Nonmedical | Vocational Guidance | Education, Graduate
Classification: LCC BF636.65 (print) | LCC BF636.65 (ebook) | NLM WM 55 | DDC 361/.0607155—dc23/eng/20231207

LC record available at https://lccn.loc.gov/2023050723

LC ebook record available at https://lccn.loc.gov/2023050724

Contact sales@springerpub.com to receive discount rates on bulk purchases

Publisher's Note: New and used products purchased from third-party sellers are not guaranteed for quality, authenticity, or access to any included digital components.

Printed in the United States of America by Gasch Printing.

This text is dedicated to my spouse, Shoshanna Cogan,
who has been with me through the many journeys
we've taken together the past 28 years.
We have traveled down the street and to the far reaches of the globe.

I love you always!

Contents

Preface   *xi*
Acknowledgments   *xv*
Springer Publishing Resources   *xvii*

1. **INTRODUCTION TO THE COUNSELING PROFESSION AND THE PRACTICUM/INTERNSHIP EXPERIENCE**   *1*
   Introduction   *1*
   An Identity in Transition   *2*
   Professional Counseling Organizations in the United States
      and the International Community   *8*
   Counselor Licensure   *14*
   Occupational Outlook for Counselors   *16*
   Practicum Versus Internship   *17*
   Practicum/Internship Requirements   *18*
   Conclusion   *23*
   Lessons Learned   *23*
   References   *26*

2. **MULTICULTURAL ISSUES, COMPLEXITIES, AND CONSIDERATIONS**   *27*
   Introduction: Why Multiculturalism Is Important for Counselors   *27*
   Self-Awareness: The First Step   *29*
   Multicultural Competencies   *31*
   Developing Culturally Appropriate Skills   *34*
   Ethics and Multicultural Counseling   *36*
   Final Thoughts   *39*
   Conclusion   *40*
   Lessons Learned   *40*
   Recommended Resources   *43*
   References   *44*

3. **SELECTING AND APPLYING FOR A PRACTICUM/INTERNSHIP**   *47*
   Introduction   *47*
   Selecting a Practicum/Internship   *47*
   The Informational Interview   *59*

VIII • CONTENTS

Applying for the Practicum/Internship   *60*
The Practicum/Internship Contract   *66*
Final Issues to Consider   *67*
Conclusion   *70*
Lessons Learned   *70*
References   *72*

4.   **ETHICAL AND LEGAL ISSUES**   **75**
Introduction   *75*
Competent Ethical Practice for Counselors   *76*
Health Insurance Portability and Accountability Act   *77*
Informed Consent   *77*
Confidentiality and Privileged Communication   *82*
Technology and Client Records   *92*
Boundary Issues: Dual Relationships in Counseling   *93*
Sexual Intimacy With Clients   *97*
Liability Insurance   *101*
Conclusion   *102*
Lessons Learned   *102*
References   *107*

5.   **CLINICAL ISSUES IN PRACTICUM AND INTERNSHIP**   **109**
Introduction   *109*
Teletherapy   *110*
Building the Therapeutic Alliance   *110*
Initial Intake Form   *111*
Initial Assessment   *114*
Counseling Techniques   *120*
The Clinical Record   *122*
Closing the Session   *123*
Final Suggestions   *125*
Conclusion   *126*
Lessons Learned   *126*
References   *129*

6.   **CLINICAL WRITING AND DOCUMENTATION IN COUNSELING
     RECORDS**   *131*
Introduction   *131*
Client Records and the Standard of Care   *133*
Documenting Complicated End-of-Life Issues   *134*
Case Notes   *138*
Recommendations for Recordkeeping   *141*
General Recommendations for Writing Case Notes   *142*
The Subjective, Objective, Assessment, and Plan Format   *145*
Conclusion   *154*
Lessons Learned   *155*
Recommended Resources   *157*
References   *157*

7.   **MODELS OF SUPERVISION: CLASSROOM AND SITE SUPERVISION**   *159*
Introduction   *159*
Practicum/Internship Class   *160*
Models of Supervision and Critique   *167*

CONTENTS • IX

Written Feedback   *169*
Offering Feedback to Peers   *171*
Conclusion   *180*
Lessons Learned   *181*
References   *183*

8.   COUNSELOR SELF-CARE: MANAGING STRESSFUL DEMANDS DURING PRACTICUM/INTERNSHIP   185
Introduction   *185*
Developing and Maintaining a Healthy and Mindful Lifestyle   *186*
Conflict Management Skills   *203*
The Counseling Student as Client   *205*
Final Suggestions for Self-Care   *207*
Conclusion   *211*
Lessons Learned   *211*
Recommended Resources   *214*
References   *214*

9.   CRISIS INTERVENTION IN PRACTICUM/INTERNSHIP   217
Introduction   *217*
What Defines a Crisis?   *218*
The Duty to Warn   *218*
Suicidal Clients   *220*
Assessing Danger to Others   *233*
Child Abuse and Neglect   *239*
Conclusion   *241*
Lessons Learned   *241*
Recommended Resources for Suicide Prevention   *244*
Organizations for the Prevention of Suicide   *244*
Suicide Hotlines   *244*
References   *245*

10.   ENSURING SAFETY ON PRACTICUM AND INTERNSHIP   247
Introduction   *247*
Predictors of Client Violence   *249*
Dealing With Aggressive Behaviors   *252*
Defusing Violence   *254*
Self-Defense Training   *257*
Workplace Violence Prevention Plan   *258*
What to Do After an Assault   *259*
Conclusion   *260*
Lessons Learned   *261*
Recommended Resources   *264*
References   *264*

11.   ADDRESSING TRAUMA IN COUNSELING: INTERVENTIONS FOR VICTIMS, SURVIVORS, AND PRACTICUM AND INTERNSHIP STUDENTS   267
Introduction: Acknowledging the Tyrannosaurus Rex
   in the Therapeutic Encounter   *267*
Trauma Defined   *268*
Acute Stress Disorder and Posttraumatic Stress Disorder   *269*

X • CONTENTS

Posttraumatic Stress Disorder   269
Factors of Trauma   270
Assessing Trauma   272
Self-Medicating Trauma   286
Healing Rituals for Trauma Treatment   289
Conclusion   293
Lessons Learned   294
Recommended Resources   298
References   298

12. TERMINATION IN COUNSELING: HOW TO SAY GOODBYE   301

Introduction   301
When to Terminate a Counseling Relationship   303
Discussing Termination With the Client   305
The Termination Plan   307
Client Resistance to Termination   307
Counselor Resistance to Termination   310
Referrals and Follow-Up   312
Abandonment   314
Conclusion   316
Lessons Learned   317
Recommended Resources   321
References   321

13. COMPLETING THE PRACTICUM/INTERNSHIP AND PREPARING FOR THE FUTURE AS A PROFESSIONAL COUNSELOR   323

Introduction   323
Terminating the Field Supervisor–Intern Relationship   323
Preparing for the Job Search   333
The Visioning Process: Creating Your Dream Career   333
The Career Center   337
Professional Networking Sites   337
Requesting References   338
Developing a Résumé or Curriculum Vitae   340
Writing a Cover Letter   342
The Job Interview   346
Dealing With Rejection   351
Evaluating a Job Offer   354
Final Thoughts on Concluding Your Practicum/Internship,
    Graduation, and Beginning Your Career   358
Conclusion   359
Lessons Learned   360
Recommended Resource   363
References   363

Appendix A: List of Professional Counseling Organizations   365
Appendix B: State Licensure Boards and Requirements   373
Appendix C: Documents for Practicum and Internship   415
Index   445

Preface

This text originated from my interest in and commitment to promoting the counseling profession as separate and distinct from related fields, such as social work and psychology. Many practicum and internship texts combine discussions of these noble professions in an amalgamation that blurs the numerous boundaries that exist between them. My intention is to offer a counselor's practicum and internship manual targeted at and to be used specifically in graduate counselor education programs.

As a professional counselor and counselor educator who has supervised numerous professional counselors in the field as well as graduate counseling students, I believe it is essential that our profession maintain a distinction from the related fields of psychology and social work. Having made this statement regarding distinctiveness, I wish to emphasize that I have nothing but respect for professional psychologists and social workers and the excellent work they do in the mental health field. At the same time, the counseling profession must take the lead in educating, promoting, and advocating for itself. Of the three professions, counseling is the only one that trains students primarily in the practice of counseling. Although psychology and social work programs certainly do an excellent job in educating and training future psychologists and social workers, counseling is an ancillary, as opposed to a primary, function for professionals in those fields. This text is written by a counselor and counselor educator for students in graduate counseling programs.

I struggled to develop this book for several years, toying with various outlines before promptly consigning them to the recycle bin. Finally, in the winter of 2009, I became more serious and developed a prospectus for publication, and the people at Springer Publishing Company were interested enough to take me up on my desire to publish this book. As a child, I recall Reverend Stanley Cooper, our minister, preaching on the topic of "Be careful what you wish for." Brother Stanley was more accurate than I could ever have imagined, as writing a book was very hard work indeed (at least it was for me!). Recently, I have updated the text for this fourth edition and hope counselor educators and counseling students will find the text worthwhile.

Naturally, your practicum and internship experience will vary greatly depending on your specialization (e.g., school counseling, mental health counseling, rehabilitation counseling); the type of placement (e.g., inpatient, outpatient, public vs. private school); your particular supervisor; and the beliefs, attitudes, and experiences you bring to practicum and internship. Because the practicum/internship is the backbone of any counseling program, I encourage you to make the most of your experience by being proactive. Ask questions to your supervisor, take advantage of any training your practicum/internship site offers, and be willing to ask for assistance when you feel you need it. I also encourage my students to "make mistakes" because that suggests you are trying to stretch your skills and learn. It is crucial that you reflect on and learn from your mistakes so that you will be less likely to repeat them.

I would like to share my own practicum/internship experience in the hope that it proves illustrative. From the winter of 1986 through the late spring of 1987, I had a very challenging and rewarding practicum and internship at a small college health and counseling center at what was then known as Western Oregon State College (now Western Oregon University). The college, then with an enrollment of some 3,000 students, was a close-knit college community, where relationships were strong and virtually everyone knew everyone else. The practicum/internship provided a complete therapeutic experience involving providing individual, group, and the occasional couples counseling; career advising; psychoeducational workshops; resident advisor training; crisis intervention; guest speaking in undergraduate classes; and teaching a 2 credit-hour course for "reentry" students. (Reentry students were those returning to college after an extended absence.) The experience was often intense and required considerable reading, viewing of videos, attending meetings, and providing advocacy for students.

Each week, the director, Dr. Merlin Darby, who was a very skilled and encouraging supervisor, would lead a staff meeting wherein five interns would take turns presenting difficult cases. Everyone would critique the intern who presented the case. The director was popular, very experienced, and had a knack for coming up with key phrases that assisted my fellow interns and me in seeing angles previously hidden from view. Although we were not always comfortable in presenting cases, the director was very considerate and temperate in his critique. Each week, it seemed that I learned something constructive that I had previously lacked. The meeting would occasionally include a representative from the medical staff providing medical consultation.

In addition to operations within the counseling center, I was frequently called on to consult with faculty, student affairs staff, and parents. Our offices, although decidedly not fancy, were spacious, with ample bookshelves, comfortable furniture, and tasteful throw rugs to accent the décor. The support staff was generally very supportive and seemed to value our work. For me, the internship placement was almost ideal. I felt myself to be a key component of the campus and a valued member of the counseling staff. Then one day in late spring, I completed my internship and later graduated with my master's degree from the Oregon State University Counselor Education program.

My entry into full-time community counseling work was an abrupt wake-up call into the baser realities of the profession. Suddenly, I was working in a residential psychiatric center, on what was a swing shift during the week with a double shift on Saturdays. I had no real office, as we operated on milieu treatment, with an entirely group focus. As the newest member of the treatment team, I felt like an outsider, and although the staff was courteous, the center was not the homey, close-knit pleasant environment that the college counseling center was. Our clients, who were called *patients*, were typically of three types: adolescents placed in the center by their families for psychiatric care, those adjudicated by the juvenile court system, or children or adolescents discharged from the state psychiatric hospital. Unlike the college population, they were oppositional, often defiant—hardened by serious physical, sexual, and emotional abuse and parental neglect—unhappy to be there, and definitely uninterested in what treatment we could provide. To top it off, the psychiatric center forced me to work with a behavioral-type program when I considered myself a humanistic, person-centered counselor.

I was overwhelmed, frustrated, and unhappy with my job and wondering if I had made a mistake in entering the field. I longed for the comfy confines of a college campus, where I could be part of a learning environment dedicated to supporting students well on their way to fulfilling their dreams, not a residential center where much of my efforts involved confronting sex offenders and violent adolescents. Needing advice, I sought out my former supervisor, Dr. Darby, at the college counseling center. He listened patiently, then explained that most counselors do not begin by working in college centers but in treatment facilities like the one in which I currently worked. He encouraged me to stick the job out until I found something else and challenged me to see the potential in the tough kids I counseled. He also encouraged me to stretch my therapeutic skills by learning what I could from the psychiatric center's behavioral approach.

In a short time, I found my former supervisor's counsel very wise. Soon, I began to get along better with the staff and my relationships with many of the patients improved. I also came to feel that the job was far more demanding of me emotionally and psychologically and required far more therapeutic skills than my internship. In time, even the behavioral system began to make real sense to me, as it provided needed structure in the adolescents' lives. I still preferred working with college students (who can be quite challenging themselves), but I had learned the value of broader clinical experience. The entire experience forced me to grow and adapt in ways I could not have previously imagined. In fact, the seeds of my transition to cognitive behavioral therapy were planted during this time. While I have not jettisoned my humanistic side, I find clients often need specific skills, thought stoppage, reframing, scaling questions, and so forth to accompany genuineness, empathy, and unconditional positive regard.

I mention my personal story to illustrate a broader point, namely, many graduate counseling students complete their practicum/internship in an environment where they feel secure, challenged, respected, and safe. Then the experience abruptly ends and they are released into a broader, sometimes less certain, and perhaps "scarier" environment. In my nearly 25 years of experience in the field, I have discovered my own rocky beginnings are very common for many recent graduates of counseling programs.

A more salient point to my story is that I have come to see my former job at the psychiatric center as a critical link in my beginnings as a professional counselor. Had it not been for the intense struggles the job required, I wonder if I would have developed the resilience needed for more in-depth psychotherapeutic work. The demands of a residential psychiatric center counseling a population resistant to therapeutic intervention were likely the best thing that could have happened to my career. But at the time, because I was in the midst of such intense experiences and numerous struggles, I could not have known that, and I struggled with the opportunity and growth it offered. Looking back on my experience more than 30 years ago, everything looks so much different. What formerly was an unpleasant and unsatisfying experience, I now view as one of my most fulfilling professional experiences. My only advice, and I offer it with some trepidation knowing how unwelcome unsolicited advice can be, is even if you do not enjoy your practicum or internship, *do* learn from it, as such knowledge may be an unexpected asset later on.

The counseling profession has recently reached several longtime goals. On December 23, 2022, the Congress passed the Mental Health Access Improvement Act (S.828/H.R.432), signed into law by President Biden. The law provides LPCs, LMFTs, LMHCs, LPCCs, and others to enroll in the Centers for Medicare and Medicaid Services as Medicare providers. (Counselors already were billing Medicaid.) Counseling organizations in other countries may likely benefit from the U.S. counseling profession's legislative successes, and it is my belief that one day, counseling will be as global a profession as that of psychology.

Regardless of your own professional experiences, I hope you will find this text to be helpful and illuminating regarding your path toward becoming a professional counselor. Although we have many specialties and divisions in our field, we are indeed one unified counseling profession. So, welcome to the profession of counseling! I wish all of you a long, meaningful journey full of both challenge and fulfillment. Counseling is a career full of real-life challenges but also one intrinsically rewarding. Best of luck on your journey!

Shannon Hodges

Acknowledgments

A lot of work goes into writing a book. In my younger years, I imagined writing books, articles, and so forth to be exciting, exotic work (yes, I was *very* naïve!). The past 40 years, however, have taught me that writing involves far more perspiration than inspiration. Still, for those of us who write—regardless of *what* we write—there is something very rewarding in the process that makes the labor worthwhile. The topics for my books occur to me at odd moments—driving long hours through very remote deserts in the Australian Outback, camping in South Africa's Drakensberg Mountains, trekking through a Central American jungle, or simply sitting in my office—then take long periods of contemplation, then lots of work before the concepts emerge into full creations. While writing is very hard work, it brings me much satisfaction and the intrinsic rewards are priceless. To me, writing is far more a process journey than a destination, though completion remains important.

Writing a book involves many people behind the scenes, providing opportunity, encouragement, and critique. I wish to thank my wife, Shoshanna, for continuing to encourage me in my writing endeavors. She believed in me when there was little evidence to support her faith. I offer a hearty thanks to my colleagues at Springer Publishing Company for providing me the opportunity to write and publish this book. I hope you will find your faith in me well founded.

Author's Note: A percentage of the royalties from this text is donated to the Dr. Morgan Brooks–Rev. Michael T. Mazurchuk Memorial Scholarship fund at Niagara University. The scholarship will assist graduate students in the Clinical Mental Health Counseling program in continuing their studies. *Morgan and Maz, we hold your memory in the light.*

Springer Publishing Resources

All purchasers of this text have access to an editable version of the Documents for Practicum and Internship. This resource is located at http://connect.springerpub.com/content/book/978-0-8261-6607-4

 A robust set of instructor resources designed to supplement this text is located at http://connect.springerpub.com/content/book/978-0-8261-6607-4. Qualifying instructors may request access by emailing textbook@springerpub.com.

INSTRUCTOR RESOURCES

- **LMS Common Cartridge With All Instructor Resources and Instructions for Use**
- **Instructor Manual**:
  - Learning Objectives
  - Chapter Summary
  - Discussion Questions
- **Instructor PowerPoints**
- **Transition Guide: Third Edition to Fourth Edition**

Visit https://connect.springerpub.com/ and look for the "**Show Supplementary**" button on the **book homepage**.

XVII

CHAPTER 1

Introduction to the Counseling Profession and the Practicum/Internship Experience

INTRODUCTION

Congratulations! You have completed a portion of your graduate counseling program and are preparing for practicum and/or internship! The practicum and internship experience is the backbone of any counseling program. You have reached an exciting time in your academic career, and now you will begin working with actual clients as opposed to simply reading case studies from a textbook. If you are like most students I have taught and supervised, it is likely you are experiencing a variety of emotions: enthusiasm, anxiety, anticipation, uncertainty, and a myriad of others. Regardless of the amount of classroom preparation you already have, starting your initial practicum will be unlike any other academic experience.

Beginning a practicum/internship represents a major step in your development as a counselor. Although previously you may have practiced in-class techniques with peers and made recordings of mock counseling sessions with friends, you will now begin conducting actual counseling sessions with real, as opposed to mock, clients. In my experience, the initial practicum or internship tends to be the most challenging experience in the curriculum. Although students may have mastered individual techniques and performed well in mock counseling sessions, establishing a therapeutic relationship with real clients presenting serious issues requires a different skill set. The initial experience at the onset of practicum can leave the most resilient of students feeling overwhelmed by the demands of the counseling relationship. Fortunately, if you have reached this point, survival rates are high.

Practicum and internship are important in counselor development because instead of reading about, for example, depression, acting out behavior, alcoholism, and bipolar disorder, you will actually be assisting people struggling with these and other developmental and/or mental health issues. You will also receive an education in the inner workings of your field setting—whether a school, mental health, addictions, or residential psychiatric setting. You will encounter numerous counseling professionals who will demonstrate various approaches to their work (e.g., cognitive behavioral therapy [CBT], person-centered therapy, dialectical behavioral therapy [DBT], and integrated therapy). Ethical and legal issues will be paramount for success; you will receive training in crisis intervention, the chain of command in the event of a trauma, and how to deal with potentially litigious situations, among other issues.

You may be wondering, "How can I survive my practicum and internship?" The goal of this book is to provide orientation and guidance to help you successfully navigate your field placements. First, this chapter discusses various general issues regarding the counseling profession itself; then, it offers a brief overview of the practicum/internship process. Future chapters discuss many of these issues in more detail. However, as first things should come first, let us review some basics of the counseling profession.

AN IDENTITY IN TRANSITION

Since the origins of the counseling profession in 1952, the American Counseling Association (ACA; originally named the American Personnel and Guidance Association [APGA]) has been the flagship counseling organization. As an organization, the composition of the ACA has been mixed "like a ball of multicolored yarn," and sometimes within the ACA, there has been an emphasis within the specialties of counseling as opposed to the overall profession (Bradley & Cox, 2001, p. 39). "Other professions such as medicine have overcome the divisiveness that comes within a profession where there is more than one professional track that practitioners can follow. The ACA has not been as fortunate" (Gladding, 2009, pp. 26–27). Essentially, counseling specialty area organizations often came and went in different directions than the flagship organization, sometimes to the detriment of the ACA.

Fortunately, as the counseling profession has grown stronger, achieved licensure in all states and major territories, and become accepted by the public, the ACA has begun to benefit from this progression. The recent 20/20 initiative, *Principles for Unifying and Strengthening the Profession* (Kaplan & Gladding, 2011), involving 29 counseling organizations, represents a key step toward professional unity. The 20/20 initiative includes long-range planning and solidified leadership working toward common goals across all 29 counseling organizations. Although this major step toward unification has taken far longer than some would like, it provides a blueprint for future growth and continued unity. As a graduate student reading this text, you may play a major role in the development of a unified counseling profession. Although there are numerous choices and options beginning counselors can make to enhance the profession, this author recommends the following:

- As the ACA is *the* flagship organization, all counselors, regardless of counseling specialty (e.g., school counseling, clinical mental health counseling, or clinical rehabilitation counseling), should hold ACA membership their entire professional lifetime.
- All counselors should also hold a membership in their specialty area. For example, school counselors should maintain membership in the American School Counselor Association (ASCA), clinical mental health counselors should join the American Mental Health Counselors Association (AMHCA), and so forth.

- All counselors should join their respective state counseling organization. State organizations assist the ACA and other national affiliate organizations with lobbying on the state and local levels. This ensures a stronger counseling presence at the state level and helps strengthen the ACA, ASCA, AMHCA, and other national organizations.

If beginning counselors reading this text simply follow these three suggestions, they will help the counseling profession achieve increased parity across the board with their mental health colleagues in psychology and social work.

Because the counseling profession is broad—encompassing the ACA, 20 affiliate organizations, and other professional counseling organizations such as the National Board for Certified Counselors (NBCC), the Council for Accreditation of Counseling and Related Educational Programs (CACREP), and others—unity remains a work in progress. Still, as this text's readers are the counseling profession's future, I remain optimistic that the profession will be far more unified in the future. As an illustration of unity's success, the ACA's membership now exceeds 60,000 members, representing a continued membership increase in the last several years (David Kaplan, personal communication).

Definition of Professional Counseling

Though it is likely that most readers of this text have studied counseling in depth, some may not have come across a precise definition of *counseling*. Until recently, there was no consensus on how the term *counseling* was defined. Although most definitions of counseling likely were more similar than different, strength tends to come in precision, especially in defining the term forming the cornerstone of our profession (i.e., counseling). Fortunately, delegates of the groundbreaking 20/20: A Vision for the Future of Counseling arrived at the following succinct definition of *counseling* at the 2010 national conference of the ACA: "Counseling is a professional relationship that empowers diverse individuals, families, and groups to accomplish mental health, wellness, education, and career goals" (Linde, 2010, p. 5). Granted, any definition of a vocation as broad as the counseling profession is likely only scratching the surface with regard to professional functions and responsibilities.

Who we are as a profession is clearly crucial to our identity as professional counselors and having a common definition represents a very important step for the counseling profession.

An Identity in Transition

The counseling profession has experienced significant growth in membership, affiliate organizations, number of practicing counselors, and political influence since its founding in 1952 (Remley & Herlihy, 2020). Counselors now are the second largest mental health profession behind social workers and are poised to achieve even great growth in the near future (U.S. Bureau of Labor Statistics [BLS], 2023). Growth in numbers typically equates with a stronger position in the marketplace. As counselors as a profession are growing at a faster rate than their sibling mental health organizations, the professional and occupational outlook for the profession is bright. This is further exemplified by the recent passage of a bill in New York State, which will allow licensed mental health counselors (LMHC) to diagnose patients using the *DSM-5*, something previously denied to them (Moore, 2022). New York was one of the last states to restrict diagnostic privileges to psychiatrists, psychologists, and social workers. This expansion of the licensed counselor's scope of practice will likely lead to a much stronger profession in New York and beyond.

Ethical Practice

Professional ethics standards defining professional behavior are not unique to counselors. Counselors are guided in their professional conduct by ethical codes established by organizations like the *ACA Code of Ethics* (ACA, 2014). The 2014 edition of the Code, immediately following its Preamble, specifies that it serves six primary purposes (ACA, 2014, p. 3):

- The *Code* establishes the ethical obligations of ACA members and provides standards to inform the ethical practice for professional counselors.
- The *Code* identifies ethical considerations relevant to professional counselors and counselors-in-training.
- The *Code* provides standards to inform its members of the ethical responsibilities members are to follow.
- The *Code* serves as an ethical guide designed to assist members in developing a course of action that best serves those utilizing counseling services.
- The *Code* helps to support the ACA's mission.
- The ethical standards within the *Code* serve as the foundation for processing inquiries and ethical complaints concerning ACA members.

Diversity, Equity and Inclusion, and Cultural Strife

While the counseling profession has its roots in Western thought and philosophy, over the past 70+ years, society has witnessed numerous transitions, including the civil rights era, the U.S. Supreme Court upholding marriage equality (for LGBTQ persons), and record numbers of women and persons of color being elected to Congress and even the vice presidency. However, with recent transitions on the Supreme Court, *Roe v. Wade* (1973) has been overturned, resulting in many states rolling back abortion access. Critical race theory has become a battle cry for conservatives and a rallying point for progressives, resulting in some state legislatures passing laws prohibiting teaching CRT (Alfonseca, 2022). The reality is that higher education has become a pawn on the political and cultural chessboard. Graduate counseling interns in southern and mountain western states are those most affected. For example, if a counseling intern in a southern state has a client who discloses an unplanned pregnancy and wishes to seek counseling for the purposes of deciding to keep or terminate their pregnancy, such services would be illegal in some states (Carrillo & Salhorta, 2022).

In the era of highly politicized legislation, counselors serving in colleges and universities, secondary schools, hospitals, and community clinics face many professional, legal, and even personal risks (Wheeler & Bertram, 2019). The previous paragraph discusses the rationale for the *ACA Code of Ethics* (ACA, 2014). However, while the *Code* posits following all applicable state, territorial, and federal laws (ACA, 2014, I.1.c), doing so may cause great distress to the client (e.g., client is pregnant from a sexual assault, yet abortion counseling is illegal). Thus, a direct contradiction exists in select states between state laws and the counselor's primary role to ". . . respect the dignity and promote the welfare of clients' (ACA, 2014, A.1.a, p. 3). The political quagmire results in counselor educators, professional counselors, and counseling interns caught in the crosshairs of a divided nation.

Case Study 1.1 is precisely the type of real-life situation that is certain to occur in the near future. Without question, this type of unfortunate situation is unlikely to be resolved anytime in the near future. Counselors working in states with such restrictive laws have an even more challenging job than most.

Case Study 1.1

Lucia is a licensed counselor who has recently relocated to a conservative state from the Los Angeles area. She has been hired into a community clinic as a counselor. During her first month, Mary, a young female client, discloses that she has been date-raped and wishes to terminate the pregnancy. She informs Lucia that in their state, the law would require her to share custody with her rapist. She exclaims, "I cannot imagine having to co-parent with my rapist." Lucia explains she understands and begins assisting Mary in exploring her options for terminating the pregnancy. Mary is very emotional during the session, often crying while offering she is glad having a sympathetic professional like Lucia. Later that day while in supervision, her supervisor informs her that she has broken the law and that she may face prosecution, given that abortion counseling is against the law. Her supervisor then places her on paid administrative leave pending an investigation. Lucia is naturally distraught, explaining, "I was only following my professional, ethical responsibility of doing what is best for the client!" In this complex case, what is in the client's best interest? If you were Lucia's supervisor, how might you proceed?

Maturation of a Profession and Looking to the Future

The counseling profession has come a long way since its creation in 1952 as the APGA (interestingly enough, the term *counseling* was not included as part of the original title). The first state to pass a counselor licensure law was the state of Virginia in 1976. Currently, with the passage of California's counselor licensure in 2009, all 50 states, plus the territories of Washington, DC, Puerto Rico, and Guam, have enacted counselor licensure. This achievement, especially in the face of opposing established mental health professions, represents a major accomplishment. Regardless of the evident success, there remain goals that the counseling profession has targeted. Medicare reimbursement for licensed counselors has very recently been enacted, and soon, licensed counselors in the United States will be able to counsel and bill Medicare services. Medicare reimbursement represents the coming of age to the counseling profession. Counselors having graduated from CACREP-accredited counseling programs are also approved to work in the Department of Veterans Affairs (VA) hospitals. Unfortunately, the VA has been tediously slow at hiring professional counselors; however, this is likely to change over time, albeit slowly given the social work profession's historic presence in VA centers. Given political pressure on the VA to trim long wait lists and serve veterans more efficiently, counselors should see better employment numbers in the VA in the next 2 to 3 years.

Consensus on a counseling definition represented a critical tipping point for the profession. After all, what type of a profession cannot agree on how its namesake is defined? Cashwell (2010) refers to the 20/20: A Vision for the Future of Counseling initiative as "maturation of a profession" (p. 58) from adolescence into early adulthood. Cashwell (2010, p. 58) also breaks down this growth process into several recognizable benchmarks:

- The passage of California Senate Bill 788, resulting in California becoming the 50th U.S. state with counselor licensure.

- Regulations implementing the Mental Health Parity Act and Addiction Equity Act of 2008, essentially mandating that insurance companies use the same limits and cost-sharing requirements for mental health and addiction services as used for other services.

- Results of the Institute of Medicine's (IOM) TRICARE study, which recommended removing physician referral and supervision requirements for counselors' services, ultimately paving the way for independent practice for professional counselors under the Department of Defense's TRICARE program:

  o There is *one* organization, the ACA, that serves as our professional membership organization.

  o There is *one* accrediting body, the CACREP, that serves to promote professional counselor preparation. (CACREP is the national credentialing organization for counseling programs.)

  o There is *one* organization, the American Association of State Counseling Boards, involved in the organization of state licensure boards, which regulate the practice of counseling.

  o There is *one* national credentialing body, the NBCC, that monitors voluntary national certification of counselors. (Cashwell, 2010, p. 58)

As of this writing (2023), the number of CACREP-accredited counseling programs stands at 906 across 434 institutions (www.cacrep.org), with CACREP now integrated into the language of many state licensure laws. This number of accredited programs is a strong testament to CACREP accreditation's increasing strength and influence in the profession. Given CACREP's exponential expansion, there remains little doubt regarding the importance of accreditation.

Cashwell goes on further to express that there are still several marking points before the counseling profession reaches full adulthood. These are the following:

- Far too few professional counselors are members of the ACA. Counselor educators should encourage ACA membership among students as a commitment to lifelong learning and professional growth, not as a short-term requirement or a way to get liability insurance.
- Licensure regulations, often initially written in ways necessary to glean passage of laws in the face of oppositional lobbying, should be reviewed by state boards with a focus on strengthening professional identity. In many states, it is far too easy for people with professional identities other than that of counselor(s) to become licensed. Licensure regulations that ensure that licensees are trained and identify as professional counselors will greatly strengthen the counseling profession. (2010, p. 58)

Medicare: A Signature Accomplishment

Unquestionably, the biggest professional goal for the counseling profession was the privilege of billing Medicare. Licensed counselors, unlike licensed psychologists and social workers, previously were unable to bill Medicare for services provided to elderly clients. For well over a decade, the ACA and its affiliates had advocated for successful passage of the Mental Health Access Improvement Act (S.828/H.R. 432). Although the bill previously passed in both houses at separate times, it never passed at the same time to be sent to the president to sign into law. Due to consistent lobbying by the ACA, the AMHCA, and many partner organizations, including individual counselors, this monumental legislation passed both houses of Congress and was signed into law by President Biden in late December 2022!

The Mental Health Access Improvement Act will close the gap in federal law that had prevented licensed counselors from being recognized as Medicare providers. The legislation is projected to provide Medicare beneficiaries more access to qualified professionals and help close the widening treatment gap. The successful Medicare reimbursement strategy by the counseling profession carries the additional gravitas of creating parity with psychology and social work, both professions that have been billing Medicare since the early 1990s. Thus, readers of the text should realize just how far the profession has come.

For students in counseling programs outside the United States, Medicare success in the United States could serve as a foundation to lobby upon. With respect to all societies, that the United States would recognize counselors as a profession on equal footing to psychologists and social workers would seem to be a strong admission of support. As a counselor educator now teaching in Australia, my prediction is the profession's professional and legislative success in the United States will eventually work their way into other countries.

It bears mentioning that some counseling students on practicum or internship are supervised by a related mental health professional, such as a social worker, psychologist, marriage and family therapist, and so forth. Your supervisor may have opposed the counseling profession's effort to gain Medicare privileges. If your supervisors do oppose this effort, treat them with respect even though you will disagree with their position on this issue. Remember that you are in a vulnerable position with regard to your relationship with your field supervisor and will likely need a letter of reference when you are applying for a job. In addition, developing the ability to dialogue or, at the very least, to disagree respectfully is one of the most useful skills anyone can develop. So, support your national, regional, and state organizations' efforts to achieve Medicare reimbursement (e.g., ACA, ASCA, or AMHCA), but respect your supervisors' and colleagues' rights to disagree.

Once again, for counseling students in the United States, the ACA and the AMHCA provide lobbying information and access to contacting U.S. congressional representatives. Students may simply go to the website to send messages to their U.S. senator and representative. The ACA, AMHCA, and related professional organizations also provide a lobbying day for counselors and counseling students to demonstrate support for the profession and its legislative efforts. *Counseling Today*, ACA's monthly magazine, includes a regular column titled "Advocacy Update" to provide information on lobbying efforts. ACA's Governmental Affairs Officer author the column and coordinate lobbying efforts on behalf of the profession, along with other affiliate organizations.

PROFESSIONAL COUNSELING ORGANIZATIONS IN THE UNITED STATES AND THE INTERNATIONAL COMMUNITY

As a graduate student enrolled in a counseling program, it is important for you to understand that you are becoming a part of a larger profession. In addition to your graduate counseling department, there are local, state, national, and international counseling organizations that you may join. Professional activity is essential for the health and well-being of the counseling profession, and graduate students represent the lifeblood of these organizations and the profession. Many of these organizations also play an important role in the practicum and internship process. Some, such as the ACA and the AMHCA, provide graduate student liability insurance along with a professional journal, monthly magazine, continuing education credits, legislative updates, and international collaboration efforts with counseling organizations from other countries.

Throughout this book, I will mention organizations such as the ACA, ASCA, AMHCA, American Rehabilitation Counseling Association (ARCA), and others that represent the counseling profession. These professional organizations advocate and lobby for the profession, offer professional standards and guidance, and publish helpful journals, books, recordings, and more. For this reason, it is my strong opinion that all professional counselors and graduate students should purchase a membership in the ACA (and/or ASCA, AMHCA, ARCA, etc.). I will primarily advocate for ACA membership because the ACA is the national umbrella organization, and it is my belief that professions are as strong as their national organization (consider the American Psychological Association [APA] as an example). In addition, I would encourage counselors (and graduate counseling students) to maintain membership in their specialty area, whether that area is in school counseling, clinical mental health counseling, clinical rehabilitation counseling, or another field. Keeping an active membership with these organizations is an investment in the profession's future. Failure to maintain professional membership is akin to divesting in the professional stock of the very profession you—and thousands before you—have worked so hard to enter.

By maintaining active membership in the ACA and related counseling organizations, you are investing in your own professional future as well. So, keep your membership current; it will provide both you and the field important dividends.

In the following sections, I briefly describe some of the key organizations that you will likely encounter as a student or over the course of your professional career. I have also included international counseling organizations, as counseling is a global profession and many graduate counseling programs have international students enrolled. Recently, the ACA has co-sponsored international conferences with professional associations in other countries. The 6th Asia Pacific Rim Confederation of Counsellors Conference (APRCCC), held in Brisbane, Australia in 2019, was co-sponsored by the ACA and the Australian Counseling Association. The ACA and the Canadian Counselling and Psychotherapy Association (CCPA) have co-sponsored ACA-CCPA international conferences in Canada. Given the growth of the profession beyond international borders, increased growth and popularity in the international counseling profession is likely. Furthermore, joint conferences venues such as that of the ACA (United States) and ACA Australia will one day be commonplace, both in residential and virtual options.

American Counseling Association

The flagship organization for counseling is the ACA. The ACA was founded in 1952 as the APGA and much later was renamed to more accurately reflect the organization (Gladding, 2009). The ACA has some 60,000 members, making it the world's largest counseling organization. The ACA has 19 divisional affiliates, including the aforementioned ARCA, AMHCA, Association for Counselor Education and Supervision (ACES), and many more. For a complete list of ACA divisions, as well as other relevant counseling associations, see Appendix A. For students in a graduate counseling program, the *ACA Code of Ethics* (ACA, 2014) is the primary ethical code; however, the ASCA has a separate ethical code, as does the AMHCA, ARCA, and all ACA affiliate organizations. So, be facile with the ACA's ethical code as well as that of your own counseling organizations (e.g., ASCA, AMHCA, and ARCA). Likely, all such ethical codes will be congruent.

Although you may have studied ethical and legal issues in an ethics course, it has been my experience as a director of two clinics and a longtime counselor educator that graduate students cannot know enough about ethics. Therefore, throughout this book, I will refer to the *ACA Code of Ethics* (and occasionally those of the ASCA, AMHCA, Australian Counselling Association, CCPA, etc.). Furthermore, although other books may discuss the ethical codes of other professions (such as the APA or the National Association of Social Workers), it is my intent to keep the discussion specific to the counseling profession's codes of ethics. The current *ACA Code of Ethics* (ACA, 2014) is available for download on the ACA's website at www.counseling.org. Graduate counseling students are encouraged to read and regularly refer to their profession's code of ethics, as they are legally responsible for understanding and practicing within ethical parameters. ACA divisions, such as the ASCA, AMHCA, and so on, also have separate codes of ethics accessible through their respective websites. Again, as the flagship organization, my counsel is that the *ACA Code of Ethics* represents the flagship of the profession and all students should read and refer to it.

Professional ethical codes are not exact roadmaps but rather serve as a guide to assist counseling professionals in making decisions in the best interests of their clients (Wheeler & Bertram, 2019). For example, let us say you have been counseling Yvonne, a fourth-grade girl struggling with her parents' divorce. Her teacher inquires how Yvonne is doing in counseling, expressing that she wants to help. You feel caught between your desire to protect confidentiality and at the same time be helpful. Based on your understanding of the *ACA Code of Ethics* and/or *ASCA Code of Ethics* or *CCPA*, how would you proceed?

This is a common situation counseling students will face while on practicum and internship. In my experience, students frequently are dismayed to learn that ethical codes are not written in stone—rather, they are living documents, shaped by court decisions, legislative initiatives, technological advances, and professional evolution. Legal and ethical issues are covered in more detail in Chapter 4, "Ethical and Legal Issues."

Council for Accreditation of Counseling and Related Educational Programs

CACREP sets standards for many professional counseling education programs. CACREP guidelines include the required parameters for practicum and internships for counseling students in addiction counseling; career counseling; clinical mental health counseling; clinical rehabilitation counseling; marriage, couple, and family counseling; school counseling; student affairs and college counseling; and counselor education and supervision (CACREP, n.d.). For a complete list of CACREP-accredited counseling programs, go to www.cacrep.org/directory. As previously mentioned, the CACREP reports over 900 accredited counseling programs, with numerous more in the process of accreditation. Graduates of CACREP-accredited counseling programs are approved to work in VA hospitals and are able to bill Medicare, Medicaid, and TRICARE without physician referral, among other advantages. CACREP-accredited counseling programs have increased exponentially in the last decade, and the trend looks very likely to continue, especially as the Council on Rehabilitation Education (CORE) has merged with the CACREP, meaning CACREP will accredit rehabilitation counseling programs.

Some related programs are accredited by other accrediting organizations. The Commission on Accreditation for Marriage and Family Therapy Education (COAMFTE), established by the American Association for Marriage and Family Therapy, is the accrediting agency for clinical programs in marriage and family therapy, which are separate from the marriage and family counseling program accredited by the CACREP (for a complete list of COAMFTE-accredited programs, go to www.coamfte.org).

There has recently been an issue with master's-level psychology programs not being eligible either for accreditation by the APA (APA accredits only doctoral programs in psychology) or CACREP which accredits only counseling programs. The recent Master's in Psychology and Counseling Accreditation Council (MPCAC; www.mpcacaccreditation.org) currently lists just over 60 accredited programs as of this writing. It is likely that MPCAC-accredited programs will grow in number and scope of practice as master's in psychology programs desiring accreditation have no other option, at least currently. Counseling programs that do not meet CACREP accreditation—typically those housed in psychology departments—may choose to become MPCAC accredited and a perusal of the MPCAC website will verify such is occurring. The limitation is that MPCAC graduates are not yet eligible to work in VA hospitals and may have trouble billing TRICARE absent physician referral. Still, the MPCAC offers an option for many master's-level psychology programs and some master's counseling programs. While the CACREP's numbers dwarf the MPCAC's number, the MPCAC does provide an alternative option. Realistically, however, the MPCAC will need extended time to reach the type of maturation the CACREP has achieved. The MPCAC's playbook likely will follow CACREP's script and time will reveal how successful the organization will become.

National Board for Certified Counselors, Inc.

NBCC is a voluntary organization that credentials counselors. Most counselors who earn a credential from the NBCC are national certified counselors (NCC) or certified clinical mental health counselors (CCMHC; for a complete list of all NBCC certifications, go to www.nbcc.org).

National certification came during a period when counselors were not licensed to provide the profession with a national credential (Remley & Herlihy, 2020). Certification, unlike licensure, is an optional credential. However, students should be aware that most state licensure boards have adopted one of the NBCC's examinations as the state licensure examination. Some states use the National Counselor Examination (NCE), whereas others use the National Clinical Mental Health Counseling Examination (NCMHCE). A few states require passage both of the NCE and the NCMHCE for licensure. The Commission on Rehabilitation Counselor Certification (CRCC), a separate organization from the NBCC, administers the Certified Rehabilitation Counseling Examination (CRCE). Rehabilitation counselors passing the CRCE receive the certified rehabilitation counselor (CRC) credential.

The NBCC awards the designation of NCC to counseling professionals who successfully pass the NCE examination. (Applicants from a CACREP-accredited program may take the NCE or CCMHC in their final semester of their counseling program.) The NBCC was created in 1983 by the ACA, and currently over 63,000 hold an NBCC credential. An NCC is the prerequisite for all specialty certifications with the NBCC (see the following). The NBCC has become an independent entity from the ACA, although both organizations remain committed to the promotion of the counseling profession.

The NBCC also awards counseling credentials in specialty areas of mental health (CCMHC), addictions (master addictions counselor), and school counseling (national certified school counselor). These specialty area certifications require additional coursework and professional experience, as well as the passing of an examination. Counselors seeking certification in a counseling specialty area must first obtain the NCC certificate. Thereafter, counselors are eligible to pursue additional NBCC certifications.

Center for Credentialing and Education

The Center for Credentialing and Education (CCE) is an affiliate of NBCC and provides services to organizations, professionals, and the public (CCE, 2022). It provides specialty credentialing for counselors and related professionals in nine areas. The CCE specialty certifications are as follows:

Approved clinical supervisor (ACS): The CCE offers the ACS credential for counselors and related mental health professionals who have obtained licensure or certification and who have extended training and experience in clinical supervision. The ACS represents a recent standard in supervision. Likely, the ACS credential will become one of the more important certifications in the future, given that supervisor training is so critical. In fact, as supervisors carry more liability (Wheeler & Bertram, 2019), additional training and credentialing in supervision is likely a good idea.

Distance Credentialed Counselor (DCC): The DCC represents to employers and the public that credentialed holders have met established requirements to provide distance counseling. Given the increased popularity and ubiquity of distance counseling (i.e., teletherapy or telemedicine), the DCC credential is likely to become increasingly popular.

Educational and Vocational Guidance Practitioner (EVGP): EVGPs have international competencies for career professionals.

Human Services-Board Certified Practitioner (HS-BCP): Designed for human service professionals seeking to advance their careers by acquiring an independent credential, the HS-BCP holds wide applicability.

Virginia Substance Abuse Counselors: CCE administers the examination for Certified Substance Abuse Counselors (CSAC) in the Commonwealth of Virginia.

Board Certified Coach (BCC): The BCC credential likely is the most rapidly expanding certification the CCE offers, given numerous professionals advertise as "coaches." The BCC sets a standard for counselors and other professionals interested in professional coaching, a popular, currently unlicensed occupation.

Global Career Development Facilitator (GCDF): The GCDF is a relatively recent credential focusing on international work in the career and facilitation field.

Thinking for a Change (T4C) Certified Facilitator: The T4C was developed for corrections professionals, although it is open to counselors and other professionals.

Naturally, counselors likely will be interested in one or more of these certificates. Interested counselors or students will find more information on the CCE website at www.cce-global.org.

International Counseling Organizations

The following international counseling organizations do not represent a comprehensive list. Rather, they are professional counseling organizations I have had contact with during the past 20 years. Be aware that new professional counseling organizations will emerge in various countries. In some cases, organizations may merge. Students interested in working in the following various countries should visit the respective website for contact information. Hopefully, in the future, graduate counseling students will be more able to complete internships in countries beyond their nation of residence.

Exhibit 1.1 Divisions and Affiliates of the ACA

Association for Adult Development and Aging (AADA)
Association for Assessment and Research in Counseling (AARC)
Association for Child and Adolescent Counseling (ACAC)
Association for Creativity in Counseling (ACC)
American College Counseling Association (ACCA)
Association for Counselor Education and Supervision (ACES)
Association for Humanistic Counseling (AHC)
Association for Multicultural Counseling and Development (AMCD)
American Rehabilitation Counseling Association (ARCA)
Association for Spiritual, Ethical, and Religious Values in Counseling (ASERVIC)
Association for Specialists in Group Work (ASGW)
Counselors for Social Justice (CSJ)
International Association for Resilience and Trauma Counseling (IARTC)
International Association of Addictions and Offender Counselors (IAAOC)
International Association of Marriage and Family Counselors (IAMFC)
Military and Government Counseling Association (MGCA)
National Employment Counseling Association (NECA)
Society for Sexual, Affectional, Intersex, and Gender Expansive Identities (SAIGE)

Note: AMHCA and ASCA are now independent organizations from ACA. Many ASCA and AMHCA members will also hold membership in the ACA.
ACA, American Counseling Association

International internships are happening already (my own program has had them), but thus far, such remains a small part of the field.

- Asociacion Argentina de Counselors (AAC; https://www.aacounselors.org.ar/): The AAC serves the counseling profession in Argentina and advocates for the profession and the patients the profession serves.
- Australian Counseling Association (www.theaca.net.au): The ACA is Australia's largest single registration for counselors and psychotherapists.
- Association of Psychotherapists and Counselors Singapore (APCS; www.apacs .org.sg): The APACS is an association for all practitioners in the healthcare sector keen to be a part of this family of helping organizations.
- Botswana Counseling Association (BCA; https://vymaps.com/BW/Botswana -Counselling-Association-BCA-391248030991045/): The BCA is a professional organization dedicated to the professional development of the counseling practice.
- British Association for Counseling and Psychotherapy (BACP; www.bacp.co.uk): The BACP is the professional association for members of the counseling professions in the United Kingdom.
- Canadian Counseling and Psychotherapy Association (CCPA; www.ccpa-accp.ca): The CCPA is a national bilingual association that promotes the profession of counseling and psychotherapy and its contribution to the mental health and well-being of all Canadians.

- The EAC is a professional organization of counselors dedicated to serving the interests of all individuals who work in counseling settings.
- Hong Kong Professional Counseling Association (HKPCA; www.hkpca.org.hk): The HKPCA is the oldest and largest organization representing professional counsellors in Hong Kong.
- International Association for Counseling (IAC; www.iac-irtac.org): The IAC is an international NGO with UN consultative status. The IAC advances the development of counseling in order to improve people's lives.
- Irish Association for Counseling and Psychotherapy (IACP; www.iacp.ie): The IACP serves to promote the counseling and psychotherapy profession in Ireland and to establish and maintain professional standards.
- Indonesian Counseling Association (ICA; https://indo-counseling.org): The ICA is a professional organization that brings together all counselors in Indonesia.
- Korean Counseling Association (KCA; https://counselors.or.kr/KOR/ENG/intro.php): The KCA was established to promote the development of counseling theory, research, and global practice.
- Malta Association for the Counseling Profession (MAPC; http://macpamalta.org/): The MACP and its members strive to empower clients to feel more comfortable in their own skin, through the beautiful process of counseling.
- New Zealand Association of Counselors (NZAC; https://nzac.org.nz): The NZAC is the national professional association that acts for and with counselors to monitor and improve the services they provide.
- Psychotherapy and Counseling Federation of Australia (PACFA; www.pacfa.org.au): The PACFA is a national peak body for counselors and psychotherapists in Australia.
- The Counseling Association-South Africa (CASA; http://counselling-sa.co.za/index.html): The CASA has an aim to establish a platform for counselors in the private sector to provide an ethical service focusing on relationship counseling trauma counseling, and pastoral counseling and promoting mental and emotional well-being and health.

COUNSELOR LICENSURE

To protect public safety, states and major territories have established licensure for various mental health professionals, including social workers, marriage and family therapists, and, of course, counselors. All 50 U.S. states, the District of Columbia, Puerto Rico, and most recently, Guam have enacted counselor licensure. Licensure laws establish minimum standards for counseling and related mental health professions. Each state and territory has a licensure board responsible for reviewing applications and issuing licenses, handling ethical complaints regarding potential counselor malpractice, and enforcing state/territory regulations regarding the practice of counseling (Wheeler & Bertram, 2019). In some states, one board is responsible for overseeing the practice of counseling as well as social work, marriage and family therapy, and so forth.

Unlike certification, licensure is the most important credential for counselors. Licensure is required for professional practice, billing insurance, diagnosing and treating mental disorders, and other important functions of professional practice. The basic state licensure requirements are listed in Appendix B. For a complete list of state-by-state requirements, check the *Licensure Requirements for Professional Counselors*, published and updated annually by the ACA (2016), at www.counseling.org/knowledge-center /licensure-requirements/state-professional-counselor-licensure-boards.

U.S. states use a number of different titles to identify licensed professional counselors. Currently, state and territorial statutes to designate counselor licensure use six titles:

- licensed professional counselor (LPC; LPC is by far the most common licensure name and has been recommended by the American Association of State Counseling Boards as the preferred title)
- licensed mental health counselor (LMHC)
- licensed clinical professional counselor (LCPC)
- licensed professional clinical counselor (LPCC)
- licensed clinical mental health counselor (LCMHC)
- licensed mental health practitioner (LMHP)

Obtaining licensure is usually a three-step process. The first step involves completion of a master's degree in counseling. The second requires the accumulation of the state-required number of post-master's clock hours while supervised by a licensed mental health professional (e.g., licensed counselor, social worker, psychologist, and psychiatrist). Most states require individuals to accumulate between 2,000 and 3,000 supervised clock hours (ACA, 2016). Finally, the individual must pass the required counselor examination. Some of the examinations are the following:

- NCE—administered by the NBCC, this is the most common examination used by states for licensure.
- NCMHCE—also administered by the NBCC, this examination focuses more specifically on mental health practice and required by a smaller number of states as the licensure examination.
- Counselor Preparatory Comprehensive Examination (CPCE)—administered by the CCE, an affiliate of the NBCC; this is not a credentialing exam. More than 300 graduate counseling programs use the CPCE to assess student knowledge.
- CRCE—administered by the CRCC, passage of this examination is accepted in some states for licensure of rehabilitation counselors.
- Examination for Clinical Counselor Practice (ECCP)—also administered by the NBCC, passage of the ECCP is required to obtain the CCMHC credential issued by the NBCC (passage of the NCMHCE is also accepted). Currently, two states accept passage of the ECCP as their state licensure examination: Illinois and North Carolina.

Because of the many variations in counselor licensure among states, I recommend *Licensure Requirements for Professional Counselors* (ACA, 2016). This text provides licensure requirements for all 50 states and territories, including required counseling programs, credit hours, licensure examination, post-master's supervision hours, whether a temporary permit is required prior to licensure, and so forth.

Registered Counselor or Registered Psychotherapist

I have included the terms registered counselor (RC) and registered psychotherapist (RP) in this due to counseling being an international profession. My own university is located on the United States–Canada border and each year we graduate several Canadian students. The Canadian Province of Ontario's College of Registered Psychotherapists of Ontario (CRPO; www.crpo.ca) offers the RP for graduates of counseling and related programs. The Australian Counseling Association and the BACP offer the title of RC. Unlike the United States, counseling is a self-governing occupation in many countries (e.g., Australia, the United Kingdom, and New Zealand). While this text primarily focuses on counseling programs in the United States, counseling programs in Australia, Canada, and beyond use this book as well. Therefore, in the spirit of inclusiveness, I will make occasional references to global counseling concerns and issues.

OCCUPATIONAL OUTLOOK FOR COUNSELORS

The counseling profession has expanded considerably in the past 60-plus years. Originally, counselors worked primarily in schools, college career centers, and in public and private agencies devoted to career or vocational guidance. Today, counselors work in a broad variety of settings, including schools, addiction treatment centers, residential psychiatric centers and hospitals, college and university counseling centers, rehabilitation clinics, and many more. The BLS currently estimates a total of over 700,000 professional counselors in the areas tracked and this number will expand considerably by 2026 (BLS, 2023). Although all specialties of counseling are expected to grow, some will increase more dramatically than others (Table 1.1).

As you can see from Table 1.1, the future of employment in the counseling profession is very promising, although stronger in some specialty areas than others. My recommendation is that you stay current of the always-shifting employment landscape by regularly reviewing the employment outlook in your area, state, and region. The BLS updates occupational projections every 2 years (you can review their findings online at www.bls.gov and search on "counselors"). For counseling students in creative arts therapy programs (e.g., art therapists, dance therapists, and music therapists), check with your relevant professional organization for employment information. While the BLS does not yet track employment numbers and future projections for creative arts counseling fields, such occupations and jobs do indeed exist. Furthermore, the recommendation here is for the various creative arts organizations to unite and lobby the BLS to track their profession as well. Likely, it would be wise for the ACA, NBCC, and other counseling organizations to assist the creative arts professions and lobby the BLS as well.

Genetic counseling was also included in Table 1.1, despite the fact that most, if not all, genetic counseling graduate training programs are separate from traditional counseling departments and have a separate national organization. Genetic counseling, while different from, say, mental health counseling, arguably is a related counseling profession and as much so as, say, rehabilitation counseling and addictions counseling. As counseling occupations and roles can vary significantly,

TABLE 1.1 PROJECTIONS DATA FROM THE NATIONAL EMPLOYMENT MATRIX

Occupational Title	Employed in 2021	Projected Employed in 2031	% Change
Counselors (all)	783,103	903,303	+%15
Breakdown by specialty area			
Substance abuse and mental health counselors	351,000	428,500	+22%
School, educational, and vocational counselors	336,000	368,400	+10%
Rehabilitation counselors	93,200	103,000	+11%
Genetic counselors	2,900	3,030	+18%

Note: Genetic counselors are included due to BLS tracking and because it is a related field. BLS does not currently track creative arts counselors (e.g., art therapists, dance therapists). BLS only tracks Marriage and Family Therapists and not Marriage and Family Counselors. The former are a separate profession from counselors and the latter a much smaller number. Thus, the reason for not listing Marriage and Family Counselors.

Source: Data from Bureau of Labor Statistics. (2023). *Occupational outlook handbook.* U.S. Department of Labor. https://www.bls.gov/ooh/community-and-social-service/home.htm. (Be aware that BLS projections are periodically updated.)

genetic counseling would appear to fit as well as any other counseling specialty area. Perhaps in the future, the National Society of Genetic Counselors (a leading professional organization) and the American Board of Genetic Counselors (genetic counseling's credentialing board) will develop ties with the ACA and other counseling organizations. Regardless, genetic counseling likely will become a rapidly growing profession in the next decade.

PRACTICUM VERSUS INTERNSHIP

Faculty, counseling literature, field supervisors, and counseling students will often use the terms *practicum* and *internship* interchangeably. There are, however, some important distinctions between these terms and placements. In this text, we consider practicum to be the first field placement for counseling students (the CACREP also specifies differences). Compared to the internship, practicum typically requires fewer *clock hours* (the total number of hours the student is required to complete) and fewer *direct client contact hours* (hours where the student is in direct contact with clients). Because practicum is the initial placement, expectations will be more flexible than internship. Practicum is, in a sense, a "preinternship" to determine whether the student is appropriate to proceed to internship.

Internship, on the other hand, *usually* begins the semester after practicum completion and requires more clock hours and more direct client contact hours. Most counseling programs usually require one semester of practicum and two to three semesters of internship. (For counseling programs on the quarter system, internship may be spread over four to five quarters.) Naturally, this also depends on state licensure and certification laws. Mental health counseling programs, for example, sometimes require 800 to 1,000 hours of internship, whereas school counseling programs would seldom require more than 600 (ACA, 2016). (*Note:* CACREP accreditation standards require 600 hours of internship and 100 hours of practicum, although programs may exceed these requirements.)

Most of the guidance and information presented throughout this book applies equally to the practicum and/or internship; thus, the term *practicum/internship* typically refers to field placement. When a distinction between the two is necessary, the text specifically delineates between practicum and internship.

PRACTICUM/INTERNSHIP REQUIREMENTS

Because practicum and internship are so different from the typical classroom, graduate counseling students may naturally be confused regarding the requirements for successful completion. All CACREP-accredited counseling programs must follow specific guidelines for the practicum and internship experience (CACREP, 2023[1]).

For practicum, 2024 CACREP requirements are

- a clinical placement in a particular field setting (e.g., school, agency, or treatment center);
- a minimum of 100 clock hours over a minimum 15-week academic term;
- at least 40 clock hours of direct service with actual clients;
- weekly interaction that averages 1 hour per week of supervision throughout the practicum by a program faculty member, a student supervisor, or a site supervisor who is working in biweekly consultation with a program faculty member;
- an average of 1.5 hours per week of group supervision that is provided on a regular schedule throughout the practicum by a program faculty member or a student supervisor. A student must also be supervised by a properly credentialed field site supervisor (e.g., licensed or certified) in the agency, school, hospital, and so on; and
- evaluation of the student's counseling performance throughout the practicum, including a formal evaluation after the student completes the practicum (CACREP, 2023).

For the practicum experience, a triadic model of supervision, although not CACREP required, is often encouraged. The triadic model of supervision specifies three roles: the supervisor, the supervisee, and the role of an observer (Boylan & Scott, 2009). The field site supervisor, who directly observes the practicum student's work through co-counseling and/or reviewing recorded sessions, conducts the supervisor's role. The supervisor then provides ongoing feedback in a 1-hour weekly setting. Many counseling programs also use site-based supervision, with the students supervised 1 hour per week (individual or group setting) in the practicum or internship, then for at least 90 minutes in a weekly classroom environment. Given the popularity of Zoom and other distance technologies, these media are becoming more common for supervision.

---

[1] The 2024 CACREP standards were finalized and posted in July 2023 and will go into effect July 1, 2024. Additional resources will continue to be added. Be advised regarding changes.

Distance-based supervision is an area that is certain to grow steadily given the economics of time and distance.

For an internship, 2024 CACREP requirements are

- the same type of clinical placement as practicum;
- 600 clock hours, beginning after successful completion of the practicum;
- at least 240 clock hours of direct service, including experience leading groups;
- weekly interaction that averages 1 hour per week of supervision throughout the internship, usually performed by the on-site supervisor;
- an average of 1.5 hours per week of group supervision provided on a regular schedule throughout the internship and performed by a program faculty member; and
- evaluation of the student's counseling performance throughout the internship, including a formal evaluation after the student completes the internship by a program faculty member in consultation with the site supervisor (CACREP, 2023).

Again, some counselor education programs will exceed CACREP standards and may require additional clock hours and contact hours. A few states with two-tier licensure mandate more than 600 hours of practicum–internship during the graduate program for the higher tier license. Students should confer with their faculty advisor to ensure the placements they are considering can meet CACREP standards or any other standards the program is based upon. As mentioned earlier in the chapter, the COAMFTE is the accrediting agency for clinical programs in marriage and family therapy (separate from CACREP's accredited marriage and family counseling programs). COAMFTE's standards of accreditation require 500 direct contact hours and numerous other requirements (these can be accessed through www.coamfte.org). As might be inferred from the list, international counseling credentialing will likely be based on different standards. Such international standards may be organizations (e.g., BACP, Australian Counseling Association, or KCA) or the state, territorial, or national government of the particular country in which the counseling program resides.

Recently, the CORE and the CACREP merged organizations. The CACREP now accredits clinical rehabilitation counseling programs. Their practicum and internship requirements are stated in the Accreditation Manual for Rehabilitation Counselor Education Programs (these are available at www.cacrep.org/wp-content /uploads/2017/07/CORE-Standards-for-Rehabilitation-Counselor-Education -Programs.pdf). Since the merger of the CORE and the CACREP, a new credential was created, clinical rehabilitation counseling (CLRC). CLRC graduates will be able to sit for the NCE examination, as the program will hold dual accreditation as a CACREP CMCH program. CLRC program graduates thus may be eligible for employment in VA hospitals. Previously, CORE-accredited rehabilitation graduates were not eligible for employment in VA hospitals. The merger certainly provides stronger advocacy for the profession of rehabilitation counseling. While VA Medical Centers have yet to hire significant numbers of counselors, the future will likely prove fruitful for the counselors. Speaking as an individual, clinical rehabilitation counselors and clinical mental health counselors would appear natural professionals to address trauma-related injuries, be they physical or psychological.

We will now look at some of the practicum/internship requirements in more detail.

Contact Hours

For practicum, a minimum of 100 clock hours are required, but 40 of these must involve direct services to students or clients (CACREP, 2024). Direct contact hours most typically include counseling (individual, group, couples, and family), intakes, psychoeducational trainings, presentations to classes, and so on. Your graduate program should have forms available for documenting student clock and contact hours. (An example of such a documentation form can be found in Exhibit 1.2.) Naturally, the contract between the counseling program and the sponsoring agency should specify contact hours so that the student and the agency are clear as to program requirements for practicum and internship. Each counseling program should maintain a program manual and either print it for all students or make it available on the counseling program's website. The latter approach of a virtual handbook holds the advantage of accessibility, cost savings, and environmental sustainability and is the direction all publishing is moving toward.

Exhibit 1.2 Hourly Practicum/Internship Activities Log

Weekly Practicum/Internship Hours Log
Practicum: 100 Clock Hours (40 direct hours required within this total)
Internship: 300 Clock Hours (120 direct hours required within this total)

Date	Direct Hours[a]	Clock Hours[b]	Supervisor Signature

(continued)

Exhibit 1.2 Hourly Practicum/Internship Activities Log (*continued*)

Total direct hours
completed _____

Total clock hours
completed _____

_____
Student signature

_____
Date

_____
On-site supervisor signature

_____
Date

_____
University supervisor signature

_____
Date

Note: Counseling students need to track their practicum/internship hours in a log format to be signed by their on-site clinical supervisor and the university supervisor at the conclusion of each semester. The university supervisor keeps the log in the student's file.

[a]Direct Hours—Individual, group, couples, family counseling, co-counseling, intakes, assessment, phone crisis counseling, psychoeducational or support groups, and any direct contact with clients.

[b]Total Clock Hours—Any work activity that does not involve direct contact with clients. Practicum requires a minimum of 100 clock hours, of which 40 hours should be direct contact. Internship requires 300 clock hours, of which 120 hours should be direct contact.

For internship, counseling students need to record a minimum total of 600 clock hours with 240 hours of direct contact. Internship is typically split into two or three semesters, with the student documenting the same types of activities noted in the preceding practicum section. As a student proceeds from practicum to internship I and then internship II, they likely are given more responsibility.

Practicum/Internship Class

The practicum/internship class time (called *group* in CACREP guidelines) involves a review of counseling responsibilities. Classroom activities include the following:

- viewing and critiquing recordings of counseling sessions or mock counseling sessions
- providing and receiving critique from faculty and peers
- role-playing problematic scenarios encountered during the practicum/internship
- discussing various therapeutic approaches and interventions
- sharing by students of their practicum/internship experiences and receiving support and suggestions from the instructor and peers
- discussing ethical and legal issues that emerge during practicum or internship
- providing support for students during practicum and internship

Practicum/internship class is discussed further in Chapter 7, "Models of Supervision: Classroom and Site Supervision."

Academic and On-Site Supervision

Counseling students are required to spend an average of 1 hour per week in individual, on-site supervision at their placement throughout the practicum. In addition, practicum students must meet weekly in a small group format run by a program faculty, adjunct faculty, or counselor education doctoral student. During practicum, the practicum–internship coordinator or designee maintains biweekly consultation with field site supervisors. A brief explanation of the triadic supervision model was previously mentioned. Though not all counseling practicum programs in the United States will be utilizing triadic supervision, it has become a popular model for many counseling programs.

Site Supervision

The individual supervisor–counselor meetings provide an opportunity for more in-depth exploration of the counselor's skill, effectiveness, and professional ethics. The clinical supervisor or professor will generally be concerned with issues such as the following:

- What strengths does the student possess?
- What challenges does the student appear to be having?
- How is the student adapting to the demands of the school/agency?
- Can the student write effective, accurate, and concise case notes?
- Does the student display the required counseling knowledge, therapeutic skills, and professional dispositions necessary for a professional counselor-in-training?
- Can the student establish and facilitate the therapeutic encounter?
- Can the student develop adequate treatment plans?
- Does the student understand their current professional limits?
- Can the student manage the caseload they have been assigned?
- Can the student receive feedback without becoming defensive?
- Does the student understand how to apply the code of ethics?
- Can the student display both empathy and at the same time set appropriate boundaries with clients?
- Should a client suddenly disclose that they are in crisis, would the student know how to proceed?
- Does the student understand the seriousness of confidentiality?
- How well does the student understand cultural issues in counseling?
- Does the student get along well with agency/school staff?
- What kind of self-care plan does the student appear to have? How well is that self-care plan working?

The list of potential site supervisor questions and concerns is much longer than those listed here, but the list should give you a good idea of the types of issues you may discuss with your supervisor. Supervision is discussed in more detail in Chapter 7, "Models of Supervision: Classroom and Site Supervision."

CONCLUSION

Hopefully you now have a brief introduction to the counseling profession, professional counseling organizations, licensure and certification, theoretical approaches, and your practicum/internship experience. The counseling profession has experienced dramatic growth in the past 2 decades and the future suggests continued expansion, particularly for the areas of CMHC, addictions counseling, and CLRC. In the future, trauma treatment likely will become a dominant focus for master's degree training programs and for professional counselors in the field. In the next chapter, we look at how to select and evaluate a potential practicum/internship placement.

LESSONS LEARNED

My palms felt moist and my heart was beating a rhythm against my ribcage. The year was spring of 1986 and I was to begin seeing my first practicum clients. I had landed my preferred choice of a small college health center that provided both medical and counseling services to the undergraduate and graduate students. The director, also my supervisor, was a veteran of nearly 30 years of counseling and was an individual who seemed to possess supreme confidence. I worried as to whether I would be able to measure up to his exacting standards. During my interview, he seemed to be regarding me in an oddly curious manner. When he called to offer me the practicum and internship experience, I was very pleased, even excited. On my first day, however, excitement had transformed into anxiety.

Two of my classmates were doing their field experience with me and we had all gone through several days of training. Studying them, it quickly became evident that they seemed anxious as well. All three of us were to begin seeing clients the same day. My first ever client was for ten o'clock. As it was practicum and not internship, the director was only allowing us to counsel students with academic, career, and relationship issues, not depression, anxiety, substance abuse, or anything more serious. While our restricted patient list abated my anxiety somewhat, butterflies fluttered throughout my stomach. My spacious office, formerly an infirmary room, was comfortable and is still the best office I have had in my entire career. Yet, the pleasant, comfortable room offered little comfort as the old wall clock drained down the time, and the only sound louder to me than my heart was the clicking sound of the old clock on the wall. Finally, as 2 minutes until the appointed hour, I rose and walked unsteadily down the long hallway toward the joint medical-counseling waiting room.

The secretary handed me the file and indicated the client (I will refer to him as *Tom*, a pseudonym), who, unlike me, appeared very relaxed. I introduced myself and he smiled as we shook hands, and then I walked back to my office. After a brief intake, I reviewed his file again. He had made an appointment for *academic counseling*. After stumbling through my introduction and informed consent, he shook his head when I inquired whether he had any questions. I then asked, "Well, how might I be helpful?" He then offered something like "I am going to flunk out of school." As soon as his words reached my ears, my self-talk echoed throughout the chambers of my mind, "This is terrible!" Thus, I immediately slipped on my counselor-in-training cape and leapt into action.

My grandparents, who raised me, preached the gospel of education as a virtue listed above all other corporeal pursuits. My grandfather had even spent several years as a one-room schoolteacher prior to working as a rural county school supervisor. Unquestionably assuming this young man viewed a college education with the same reverence as myself, I commenced checking for hopelessness and suicide intention. Suddenly, looking very surprised, he denied any intent for self-harm. The most significant issue addressed, I then began elaborating how he might appeal academic dismissal (the college was very patient academically and offered continuances). This avenue led to yet another verbal cul-de-sac, so I tried another route. "So, might this be an issue of needing a more appropriate academic major?" I even suggested career assessment with the Strong Interest Inventory (SII) to discern his career interests. At this point, he was becoming visibly agitated with the process (and with me!). He crossed his arms and replied he needed neither a new major nor any assessment. Feeling totally lost, I asked, "So what would be helpful?" He thought for a long moment and then replied, "I was hoping you might tell me." He then rose and left the room.

I sat inert and in stunned silence. Finally, I got up from the chair and walked out the rear exit door just outside my office. Taking in the fresh, Pacific Northwest air, I stared at the Coast Range to the west, wondering just what in hell had happened! The supervisor was certain to kick me out of the field experience given my performance being so grossly incompetent. At some point, I returned to my office and began examining my next appointment scheduled for the noon hour. About 20 minutes into my preparation for the next client, the phone rang. The secretary was calling to say the client who had walked out of session stood at the desk requesting to see me. Taking a deep breath, I left to fetch my client. He stood at the reception desk, looking confused. After leading him back to the very office he had left a half-hour earlier, he sat down in the same chair and leaned forward.

"Look," he began, "here's the problem. See my dad is the reason I'm here at college . . ." He went to express that he had never really been interested in attending, but his father, who was a college graduate, believed a college education was a necessity. "Basically, I came here [college] to please him [dad]." He went on to say he had been unhappy for nearly 2 years and consequently had performed poorly in academic work.

I inquired whether he had spoken with his dad regarding his feelings. He shook his head and said his father had been so insistent regarding college that he simply shut down and did not assert himself on the subject of his future. Therapeutically dim-witted as the counseling neophyte I was, the important issue clearly was his relationship with his dad. "Okay, let's talk about your dad and how you plan to discuss the matter with him." At this point, therapy began. Tom nodded and then chronicled his relationship with his father. He elaborated that while he loved and respected his dad, he had realized during high school that the two of them held different values, particularly with regard to one's occupation. His dad had started college while working full time and raising two young children with Tom's mother. He reported that his dad was the first in his family to earn a college degree, and that despite working long hours, he managed to graduate with honors and land a lucrative job in a Portland area company. "I have long felt that dad was living his life through me. He never thought to ask me what I wanted."

Thereafter, a thoughtful silence descended, and we sat together in a companionable manner for several seconds, a long time in Western culture. "I need to talk with my dad but have been putting it off," he replied breaking the silence. "What will you tell him?" I inquired. He shook his head and explained it was difficult to contemplate. Then, taking in the surroundings, he offered, "I wish he were here in this room." "Well, what if he were?" I asked. Tom then gave me a bewildered look. I then explained what any counselor and other therapist would recognize as psychodrama founder Jacob Moreno's empty chair technique. Tom was initially hesitant about the intervention. "You want me to talk to that empty chair over there," he asked, pointing across the room, "as if my dad were sitting in it?" He had a bewildered look on his face. I nodded, encouraging him to try it. After another pause, he shrugged and agreed.

"Uh, look dad," he began, clearly uncomfortable with addressing the chair, his absent father, or both. He stumbled about verbally but soon began to articulate his own thoughts and feeling regarding his future. "Dad, I love and respect you and what you have done. . . . but don't want what you want for me . . . I just want to work in the trades, not some office job. I just don't want to be at college anymore. But, there's this great program at the community college where I can be trained to become a certified welder. Dad, I have always wanted to make you proud. I just can't do this [college]."

This seemed the perfect point to have him switch chairs and speak as his dad. I recall he rose and walked the short distance with some trepidation. However, when he sat, he began speaking with confidence. "Tom, I just wanted to best for you. I didn't want you to grow up in the poverty of my childhood. My education was the difference for me and I so badly wanted that for you." He paused. "Now, if you want to go to this program at the community college and become a welder . . . well . . . okay."

Naturally, exact words fade with time, especially after nearly 4 decades. What I do recall is that Tom then moved to his original chair and spoke the most impactful words of the session: "Dad, I love you. We never say it, but I feel it."

What had begun as a disastrous session had unexpectedly been transformed into a therapeutically powerful experience for both client and counselor. No doubt about it, I was initially awful. That this therapeutic encounter happened at all was due to Tom's diligence in returning to finish the abortive session. I am grateful Tom was able to get his needs met and equally thankful he gave me a second chance when I certainly had not earned one. A few weeks later, I received a card in the mail. Tom wrote that he and his dad had worked things out and that he would be starting his training at the community college in June. He thanked me for the help and joked he would need to remember that "empty chair thing."

I remain grateful to Tom and for the many Toms and Tommies (female) I have encountered in my long counseling and counselor education career. When I consider it, philosopher-theologian Martin Buber and his I-it and I-thou encounters have been most informative in my career. Most of my counseling sessions have begun as I-it encounters, with little meaningful connection. Once I can focus on presence over technique, my session have gone much better. While technique is very important, presence is what builds the relationship and leads to deeper I-thou experiences, as with Tom and I (and his father).

SPRINGER PUBLISHING CONNECT™ | A robust set of instructor resources designed to supplement this text is located at **http://connect.springerpub.com/content/book/978-0-8261-6607-4.** Qualifying instructors may request access by emailing **textbook@springerpub.com.**

REFERENCES

Alfonseca, K. (2022, March 24). *Map: Where anti-critical race theory efforts have reached*. ABC News. https://abcnews.go.com/Politics/map-anti-critical-race-theory-efforts-reached/story?id=83619715

American Counseling Association. (2014). *ACA code of ethics*. https://www.counseling.org/resources/aca-code-of-ethics.pdf

American Counseling Association. (2016). *Licensure requirements for professional counselors*. https://www.counseling.org/knowledge-center/licensure-requirements

Boylan, J. C., & Scott, J. (2009). *Practicum and internship: Textbook and resource guide for counseling and psychotherapy* (4th ed.). Routledge.

Bradley, R. W., & Cox, J. A. (2001). Counseling: Evolution of the profession. In D. C. Locke, J. E. Myers, & E. L. Herr (Eds.), *The handbook of counseling* (pp. 27–41). Sage.

Bureau of Labor Statistics. (2023). *Occupational outlook handbook*. U.S. Department of Labor. https://www.bls.gov/ooh/community-and-social-service/home.htm

Carrillo, S., & Salhorta, P. (2022, July 19). *Colleges navigate confusing legal landscapes as new abortion laws take effect. All things considered*. NPR. https://www.npr.org/2022/07/19/1112014281/abortion-laws-college-campus

Cashwell, C. S. (2010, May). Maturation of a profession. *Counseling Today, 52*(11), 58–59. http://www.cacrep.org/wp-content/uploads/2012/07/Maturation-of-a-profession-May-2010.pdf

Center for Credentialing and Education. (2022). *Credentials/resources/applications*. https://www.cce-global.org

Council for Accreditation of Counseling and Related Educational Programs. (2023). *2024 CACREP standards*. https://www.cacrep.org/wp-content/uploads/2023/06/2024-Standards-Combined-Version-6.27.23.pdf

Gladding, S. T. (2009). *Counseling: A comprehensive profession* (6th ed.). Merrill/Prentice Hall.

Kaplan, D. M., & Gladding, S. T. (2011). A vision for the future of counseling: The 20/20. *Principles for Unifying and Strengthening the Profession. Journal of Counseling & Development, 89*, 367. https://doi.org/10.1002/j1556-6678.2011.tb00101.x

Linde, L. (2010, May). From the president: Counseling is. . . . *Counseling Today, 52*(11), 5, 37.

Moore, K. (2022, July 12). Regents expand mental health professionals who can diagnose. *Times Union*. https://www.timesunion.com/news/article/Regents-vastly-expands-the-number-of-mental-17297374.php

Roe v. Wade, 410 U.S. 113 (1973).

Remley, T. P., Jr., & Herlihy, B. P. (2020). *Ethical, legal, and professional issues in counseling* (6th ed.). Pearson.

Wheeler, A. M., & Bertram, B. (2019). *The counselor and the law: A guide to legal and ethical practice* (8th ed.). American Counseling Association.

CHAPTER 2

Multicultural Issues, Complexities, and Considerations

INTRODUCTION: WHY MULTICULTURALISM IS IMPORTANT FOR COUNSELORS

In the early years of its existence, the counseling profession mirrored the society that encapsulated it—largely Caucasian, male dominated, and middle class (McIntosh, 1998). In 1962, the pioneering counselor C. Gilbert Wrenn suggested that "culturally encapsulated" counselors define reality according to one's set of cultural standards and fail to take into account other cultural frameworks (Lee, 2019; Remley & Herlihy, 2020). Culturally encapsulated counselors tend to judge other cultural practices through the lens of their own culture and may tend to ignore evidence at odds with their own cultural framework. Consequently, cultural encapsulation tends to lead to stereotyping and biased thinking against other cultures, often represented through microaggressions. Microaggressions are subtle messages that insult, demean, and invalidate persons and are routine occurrences for diverse people (Wing Sue & Wilson, 2020). Hook et al. (2016) found that among more than 2,000 clients of color surveyed, 81% indicated they experienced at least one microaggression from their counselor. Hook et al. found that a lack of counselor humility was a strong predictor in counselor–client dyads for both racially and nonracially matched pairs. The implications of these results highlight the need for counselors to develop a framework that addresses how power, privilege, and culture influence the counselor–client relationship. This chapter devotes much space to addressing cultural needs and influences in counseling. In doing so, the following page addresses the history of multiculturalism in the counseling profession.

Wrenn's (1962) writings dovetailed with other societal movements that hastened the recognition of multicultural viewpoints, including the Vietnam War and the resulting protests, the civil rights era, the beginning of the gay rights movement, and the women's movement. These civil and sociocultural movements changed the political and social landscape of the United States and the counseling profession as well (Wehrly, 1991). Counseling professionals finally, although slowly, began to offer multicultural viewpoints in counseling curricula, journal articles, and textbooks. In 1972, the Association of Non-White Concerns in Personnel and Guidance (now known as the Association for Multicultural Counseling and Development [AMCD]) was chartered by the American Counseling Association (ACA). It was in the mid-1990s that the AMCD and the Association for Counselor Education and Supervision (ACES) created the "Multicultural Counseling Competencies and Standards" (Sue et al., 1992) for purposes of inclusion in counselor education programs. The AMCD's standards provide a format for counselors and counselor education programs to incorporate multicultural training into professional practice and the curriculum of graduate counseling programs.

Counseling theory, practice, and training have been significantly influenced by the changing social and cultural demographics in the 21st century. Current projections for the U.S. population indicate a continued steady increase in the nation's continuing social and cultural diversity. For example, by the year 2050, 29% will be Latinx American, 13% African American, and 9% Asian American (Lee, 2019). Non-Hispanic Whites, who make up 67% of the population, are projected to be 47% in 2050 (Passel & Cohen, 2008). Racial and cultural demographics are changing in a more complex manner. According to the 2010 Census, citizens identifying themselves as multiracial increased by 32% from 2000 (Jones & Bullock, 2012). Although not included in the Census, 4% of U.S. adults identify themselves as being lesbian, gay, bisexual, or transgender (Gates, 2017).

The very definition of culture in counseling has likewise expanded; for purposes of this chapter, *culture* is broadly defined and includes race, ethnicity, nationality, gender, sexual orientation, socioeconomic class, age, disability, and other factors that may not be readily apparent (Pedersen, 1994). If administered a free association (FA) technique with the key word as "culture," most people's first response likely would be to say "race." (I have experimented with such an FA technique in my assessment course and roughly 90% of initial answers are "race" or "skin color.") This bias in one direction has historically been reflected in educational, social, governmental, and even in professional organizations. For example, as previously noted, the AMCD was chartered as the Association of Non-White Concerns in Personnel and Guidance. Most counseling students in 21st-century graduate programs are more facile in recognizing the broad spectrum of culture, though many retain culturally encapsulated opinions (Hayes et al., 2010; Lee, 2019). Given the dynamic, global nature of the 21st century and the likelihood of interacting with a very multicultural world, cultural competence is a necessity counselors deny or ignore at the peril of their career.

Despite the profession's best efforts, however, discrimination remains very active, as even many well-intentioned counselors may have internalized issues of bias and practice discrimination without any awareness on their part (D'Andrea, 2000; Kiselica, 1999; McIntosh, 1998). White, mainstream counselors are often reluctant to admit to harboring biased attitudes regarding race (D'Andrea, 2000; Lee, 2019; Sue & Sue, 2012). Ridley (2005) offered several examples of unintentional racism as manifested by counselors:

- avoiding the issue of cultural differences by claiming to be "color blind"
- being too color conscious, thus attributing all problems to a client's cultural background
- failing to recognize one's own issues of bias
- facilitating codependent relationships with ethnic clients out of a need to be needed
- misunderstanding a client's defensive reactions to the counselor's stereotypical thinking
- misunderstanding a client's culturally learned patterns of communication or behavior

Lee (2019) suggests that culturally responsive counseling should be based on three premises: First, diversity is real and should not be ignored; second, differences are just that—differences—and not necessarily deficiencies or indicators of pathology; and third, counselors working with diverse clients must avoid stereotypes and monolithic thinking. A multicultural perspective asserts that diverse clients may hold values and beliefs that are different from those of the counselor. Multicultural counselor education seeks to establish a foundation for cultural pluralism in counselor training, counseling practice, and also in the manner counselors conceptualize multiculturalism. In this chapter, I provide an overview of some of the issues related to becoming a culturally competent counselor.

Finally, the 2014 *ACA Code of Ethics* stresses the commitment of counselors to advocate on behalf of their clients. Effective advocacy involves confronting the social issues that adversely impact clients' mental, physical, sexual, emotional, financial, and cultural health. Standard A.7.a addresses the counselor's obligation to "advocate at [the] individual, group, institutional, and societal levels to address potential barriers and obstacles that inhibit access and/or the growth and development of clients" (ACA, 2014). Thus, given the broad nature of culture and the fact that professional ethics now require inclusion of cultural considerations in all counseling situations, all counseling students must include cultural considerations with each client they counsel.

The attention to multiculturalism in the *ACA Code of Ethics* emphasizes that multicultural competence is fundamental to ethical counseling practice. The *Code* states in the *Preamble* that counselors are committed to "honoring diversity and embracing a multicultural approach in support of the worth, dignity, potential, and uniqueness of people within their social and cultural contexts" (ACA, 2014, Preamble). Furthermore, standards related to diversity and multicultural competence are embedded throughout the *Code*. Beyond that, as the United States is becoming more culturally diverse and given that counseling is a global profession, meaning U.S.-trained counselors may likely work overseas, cultural diversity is a critical requirement for a counselor's development and competence. Therefore, any counselor or counselor in training must make a serious commitment to respecting diversity and developing multicultural competence. Regarding student counselors in training, a common question is, "How can I develop multicultural competence?" The following section begins a discussion of multiculturalism.

SELF-AWARENESS: THE FIRST STEP

The beginning place for developing cultural competence is to acknowledge how your own cultural identity impacts your beliefs, values, and attitudes regarding people in society. For example, you might ask yourself, "What is my culture?" This question may be more complicated than it appears. It involves not only your race but also your nationality, region, religion, political views, gender, socioeconomic status, sexual identity, and even more. All these variations on culture play a large role in our daily actions and meditations (Herlihy & Painter, 2019; Sue & Sue, 2012), not to mention our interactions with clients. Counselors would be well advised to understand how their view of culture impacts counseling individuals, groups, couples, or families (Association for Specialists in Group Work, 1998; Sue & Sue, 2012). As counselors must first acknowledge their own biases, the worksheet in Exhibit 2.1 provides a list of numerous cultures.

Now, consider the case of Stacy in Case Study 2.1.

30 • THE COUNSELING PRACTICUM AND INTERNSHIP MANUAL

Exhibit 2.1 Developing Cultural Competence: Personal Biases Worksheet

Read and fill in each blank line with the first thought that comes to your mind. Then discuss with a partner in dyads or triads.

Jew:

_____

Muslim:

_____

African American:

_____

Latinx:

_____

Asian:

_____

Undocumented alien:

_____

Person on welfare:

_____

Poor person:

_____

Gay or lesbian person:

_____

Transgendered person:

_____

Evangelical Christian:

_____

Disabled person:

_____

Unmarried parents:

_____

MAGA Republican:

_____

Janitor at your college:

_____

White person:

_____

MAGA, Make America Great Again.

Case Study 2.1 The Case of Stacy: Recognizing Personal Cultural Bias

Stacy, a White female counselor in a college counseling center, is counseling Jin-Lin, a first-generation, freshman Chinese American student. Jin-Lin is majoring in computer engineering, although he confesses he would prefer to become a high school math teacher. He maintains, however, that his parents would disapprove of him changing his major, as they view engineering as offering greater prestige and a higher salary, thereby providing the family with greater social standing and more financial support. Stacy's approach is to explore with Jin-Lin what he wants, as opposed to what his family thinks. She asks Jin-Lin if he could confront his parents and explain his own career aspirations, as this way, his parents would have to accept his aspirations over those of his family. Jin-Lin seems visibly surprised at Stacy's suggestion.

1. How effective do you think Stacy's approach will be? Why?
2. What would Stacy need to know about Jin-Lin's family and culture to be helpful?

Consideration: In Stacy's case, it might help her to understand that many Asian people are uncomfortable with confrontation, especially when involving family, and culturally, family wishes may often be valued over individual desires. Stacy's apparent approach of *treating the client as she would anyone else* would be a serious cultural error. Her approach may prove a significant stumbling block to further counseling with Jin-Lin. Stacy would be better off helping Jin-Lin explore his feelings related to his family's expectations with the understanding that collectivist cultures may not value individualism as Western cultures likely would. She might further enlist Jin-Lin's assistance in ways deeper communication might work with his parents.

MULTICULTURAL COMPETENCIES

Pedersen et al. (2002) and Arredondo et al. (1996) have outlined multicultural competencies for multicultural self-awareness:

- ability to recognize direct and indirect communication styles
- sensitivity to nonverbal cues
- ability to recognize cultural and linguistic differences
- interest in cultures other than your own
- sensitivity to the stereotypes and myths of other cultures
- ability to describe elements of your own culture
- ability to recognize relationships between and among cultural groups
- acknowledgment of your own racist attitudes

The final suggestion on this list is the one likely to cause the most discomfort among students and faculty in counselor education programs. Sue (1996) and Arredondo et al. (1996) have discussed how racist attitudes and practices are deeply embedded in the dominant culture. Some students and faculty are likely to argue that faulty assumptions may not necessarily be a reflection of racist attitudes. In the example of Stacy and Jin-Lin in Case Study 2.1, Stacy was very well intentioned regarding her approach and likely meant no disrespect. Her assumption that *all* clients do what is best for themselves, however, is well grounded in Western, individualist thinking. Because she is counseling an Asian client, Stacy would have been wise to ask Jin-Lin what he saw as his options. A counselor's failure to dialogue with their client around culturally sensitive issues is likely to be interpreted as cultural arrogance or cultural ignorance. In the case of Stacy and Jin-Lin, Stacy would be well advised to reflect on the differences in values between a Western, individualist culture and an Eastern, collectivist one. A note of caution must be mentioned here: Do not assume that simply because you are counseling, say, an Asian client such as Jin-Lin, that the said client holds a traditional, cultural worldview. Many people of collectivist Asian, Latinx, Middle Eastern, and so forth clients may well have ideas that run counter to traditional Euro-Western individualist values. Counselors would be prudent to keep an open mind regarding culture and solicit the client's input when questions arise. Remember, your cultural values may not be the same as the client's. Furthermore, the client may also have different values than the culture in which they were raised. So, go light on assumptions and check your impressions with your client. Clients will occasionally make surprising statements regarding their culture or cultures (e.g., increasing numbers identifying as multi ethnic).

Clearly, it is worthwhile to remember that clients are individuals; they may not necessarily share or even agree with the values commonly associated with their culture, religion, ethnicity, and other commonly cited cultural preferences. Therefore, assisting clients to examine their own wishes and goals versus those of society and their own culture is a critical aspect of the counseling process. In such instances, however, counselors must take care to provide the client the courtesy of inquiring how their options might be influenced by cultural norms. Counselors must also prepare clients to anticipate and address the consequences of going against cultural, family, religious, and other norms. During this process, mainstream counselors must be mindful to refrain from subtly (or *not* so subtly) trying to coerce the client into adopting Western values. Doing so is unethical, fundamentally disrespectful, ethnocentric, and plain poor therapy.

In addition to developing cultural competence, counselors must educate themselves when counseling culturally different clients. Ways of developing cultural awareness involve reading and studying various cultures. Naturally, it would be impossible for a counselor of any culture to be an expert on all other cultures. What is reasonable is for counselors to be open to learning basic information on cultures they encounter in counseling. Counselors can use a genogram to assist clients in exploring their cultural and migratory history (Alessandria, 2002). Instruments such as the Multicultural Counseling Inventory (MCI; Sodowsky et al., 1994) can also be used by counselors to assess their own cultural competence and awareness. Consider the case of Steve in Case Study 2.2.

The following list outlines cultural competencies that are recommended for counselors (Arredondo et al., 1996; Pedersen et al., 2002):

- knowledge about the histories of cultures other than your own
- understanding of the implications and ongoing problems of racism, oppression, and stereotyping and their impact on diverse clients

- knowledge of the language and slang of other cultures and of the effect of your own communication style on diverse clients
- knowledge of resources available for teaching and learning in other cultures
- knowledge of aspects of traditional counseling approaches that may be inappropriate for counseling clients from diverse cultures
- understanding of how your own culture is perceived by members of other cultures
- knowledge of institutional barriers that impede access to counseling services for many clients from diverse cultures
- professional expertise that is relevant to people in other cultures
- repertoire of information that people in other cultures will find useful

I would also add to the important list mentioned earlier the need to counsel from the perspective of cultural humility. A cultural humility approach involves all the aforementioned as well as cultivating an empathetic understanding for those culturally different clients, patients, and students we serve.

Case Study 2.2 The Case of Steve: Cultural Assumptions Leading to Culturally Inappropriate Questions

Steve, a Caucasian school counseling student, is interning in a large, public, inner-city high school. Steve is conducting a group information session on college preparation. The 10-person group is composed mostly of female African American and Latinx students. The discussion gravitates to the advantages and disadvantages of attending private versus public colleges. Steve notices that Juanita, a very good student, has remained silent. Juanita is wearing a cardinal red St. Anne's Catholic School sweatshirt. Hoping to draw her into the discussion, Steve asks her, "Juanita, wouldn't you feel more comfortable at a Catholic college instead of a public state university?"

1. How appropriate or inappropriate was the question Steve posed to Juanita?
2. What are some other strategies Steve could have used to invite Juanita into the conversation?
3. If you had been in Steve's situation, what approach might you have used to encourage Juanita's participation?

In the case of Steve, we see, once again, a counselor who might have been motivated by good intentions, yet he may be practicing in a culturally inappropriate manner. Despite her sweatshirt, we do not know for sure if she would be more comfortable at a Catholic institution, nor can we infer Juanita being of a particular religious tradition or any, as students wear shirts of all types. Now, it could well be that Juanita is Catholic and that she *might* prefer a Catholic college, but Steve does not know this to be the case; moreover, she is attending a public high school, not a Catholic one. No question, Steve must be careful in the future to refrain from such assumptions.

There are many ways counselors can increase their multicultural competence. There are numerous texts, journals (e.g., *Journal of Counseling and Development, Journal of Multicultural Counseling,* and *Professional School Counseling Journal*), books, podcasts, courses, and workshops. Lee (2001, 2019), Sue and Sue (2012), and others have opined that it is of critical importance for most counselors to experience the isolation that members of minority groups have historically experienced. They suggest working in a diverse setting, attending diverse religious and cultural events, and attending social functions for international students. One of the most important resources for your continued development is your clients. Working with people from diverse backgrounds illustrates the importance of culture, spirituality, and customs. My own experience working overseas in South Africa and remote indigenous Australia has cemented the need for culturally responsive counseling, counselor education, and training. When working with clients and students from diverse, non-Western cultures, cultural competence is a necessity, not a luxury, nor anything to be dismissed as wonkiness.

Regarding mainstream counselors experiencing cultural isolation first hand, experiences such as studying abroad, volunteering in emerging countries, and interning in inner-city settings are worthwhile endeavors. Perhaps in the near future, graduate counseling students will complete overseas internships in Asia, the Middle East, Central and South America, and so on. Such experiences could result in paradigm changes for counseling students and open new doors to the global counseling profession. While international internships for counseling students has not happened to any significant extent, my expectation is that international counseling internships will become a reality at some point in the future.

DEVELOPING CULTURALLY APPROPRIATE SKILLS

Another goal of multicultural education and practice is developing culturally appropriate skills and intervention strategies for counseling diverse clients (Sue, 1996). Becoming culturally skilled as a counselor requires that you go beyond your basic training in counseling techniques (Sue, 1996). Culturally skilled counselors recognize the need to serve as advocates, consultants, and liaisons to community-based organizations representing culturally different people (Lee, 2001). Furthermore, many of the traditional approaches to counseling focus on the needs of the individual, which may not be appropriate in counseling clients dealing with social oppression and discrimination (Remley & Herlihy, 2020). To be an effective counselor, you must develop an array of helping skills that account for not only the individual client but also the broader society in which your clients reside (see Case Study 2.3).

Advocates for multicultural counseling have challenged the profession to embrace a sense of social activism (Lee, 2006, 2019). This involves confronting the discrimination that negatively impacts many segments of society. The *ACA Code of Ethics* (ACA, 2014) addresses this; it states that "counselors advocate at individual, group, institutional, and societal levels to address potential barriers and obstacles that inhibit access and/or the growth and development of clients" (Section A.7.a). Such obstacles to development include racism, sexism, homophobia, discrimination against the mentally ill, religious oppression, and so forth.

Case Study 2.3 The Case of Harriet: Considering a Client's Multiple Issues and Possible Resources

Harriet, a 35-year-old African American woman, approaches a community mental health center seeking counseling services. During her intake with Robin, Harriet reports symptoms of depression, including loss of appetite, feeling sad, and a general feeling of hopelessness. Harriet denies any recent personal losses but states, "I've had lots of losses. My father in prison, my brother was killed in gang warfare, my boyfriend abandoned me, and I'm struggling to feed and house my kids." Harriet also states she is working a minimum-wage job, though she says she wants to get her General Educational Development (GED) certificate and attend the local community college but has not had the energy to study. Robin suggests a psychiatric screening with the psychiatrist, in the belief that medication is the most effective method to help Harriet address her depressed mood.

What do you think of Robin's approach? How helpful is her suggestion regarding medication?

1. What type of strategy might be most helpful for Harriet?
2. What issues and barriers should Robin anticipate when helping Harriet?

Robin might have been more effective had she taken a wider angle view of the multiple issues impacting Harriet. Instead of focusing solely on medication, she could have explored the resources and social supports available in Harriet's community. Robin's failure to engage Harriet on these possibilities represents an example of a well-intentioned counselor missing the forest for the trees. Furthermore, should Harriet need medication, counseling to address negative thoughts that tend to accompany depression might also prove helpful in lifting Harriet's depression. For many African Americans, faith-based communities are an important source of emotional, spiritual, and even financial support, and addressing cultural and social supports would evidence cultural competence and likely treatment that is more efficacious.

The following are skills and objectives suggested by Arredondo et al. (1996), Lee (2019), and Pedersen et al. (2002):

- skill at accessing appropriate service agencies and resources in the client's community
- repertoire of strategies for helping clients cope with culture shock and acculturative stress that may arise from immigration experiences
- ability to anticipate consequences of events in other cultures
- fluency in the languages of other cultures
- comfort in functioning in other cultures
- skill at finding common ground with members of other cultures while retaining your own racial or ethnic identity
- skill in helping clients to effectively intervene with institutional barriers and in using community resources when appropriate
- active involvement in activities aimed at reducing prejudice and enhancing cross-cultural counseling knowledge in the community

ETHICS AND MULTICULTURAL COUNSELING

AMCD's Multicultural Counseling Competencies offer guidelines for counselors' consideration in their efforts toward multicultural competent counseling. The critical issue in multicultural competence is for individual counselors to put these guidelines into practice (Sue & Sue, 2012). Standards regarding nondiscrimination and honoring diversity feature prominently throughout the *ACA Code of Ethics* (ACA, 2014) in numerous sections addressing the counseling relationship, assessment, professional responsibility, counselor education and supervision, and research. Multicultural competence requires counselors to keep in mind that the ethical reasoning of counselors is embedded within the counselor's worldview, which is shaped by sociocultural conditioning of which we are often unaware (Helms & Cook, 1999; Remley & Herlihy, 2020).

The *ACA Code of Ethics* (ACA, 2014, Section C.5) states: "Counselors do not condone or engage in discrimination against prospective or current clients, students, employees, supervisees, or research participants based on age, culture, disability, ethnicity, race, religion/spirituality, gender, gender identity, sexual orientation, marital/partnership status, language preference, socioeconomic status, immigration status, or any basis proscribed by law" (see Case Study 2.4). Many counseling professionals take the *ACA Code of Ethics* a step further, emphasizing that counseling professionals must take a social justice advocate role to prevent and fight against societal discrimination and prejudice (Lee et al., 2018; Saltzman & D'Andrea, 2001). For example, a counselor may advocate for physically disabled clients to have access to school buildings, for a lesbian woman to have a say in the medical care of her long-term partner, for an elderly client battling age discrimination, or for the right of a woman to choose to terminate pregnancy or keep her baby (see Case Study 2.5). Counselors are encouraged to lobby elected officials to remove barriers of discrimination against individuals and groups. Given the current political polarization affecting the aforementioned examples, advocacy and even political activism are obligatory. Clearly, counselors must be acutely aware of emerging legal changes, especially when they collide with professional ethics (Wheeler & Bertram, 2019).

Case Study 2.4 The Case of Paul: A Clash Between Religious Beliefs and Ethical Obligations

Paul is a gay African American minister of a Christian congregation in a southern state that actively maintains that being gay is a sin. Although Paul does not agree with the stance his church takes, he is nevertheless very committed to his religious faith. For the past year, Paul has been dating a man he met at a church conference. They have been very careful to keep their relationship a secret, but as the relationship grows, they wish to make it permanent. However, both partners are struggling with the knowledge that continuing the relationship would mean having to leave their church. Confused about how to proceed, Paul comes to see James, a counselor at a Christian counseling center. James, an

(continued)

Case Study 2.4 The Case of Paul: A Clash Between Religious Beliefs and Ethical Obligations (*continued*)

evangelical Christian, believes homosexuality is morally wrong and uses the Bible to justify his belief. However, during counseling, he is touched by Paul's honesty and humanness and feels torn between his religious convictions and his ethical obligation as a counselor. Feeling very conflicted, James seeks advice from his clinical supervisor.

1. What are the issues James must address in providing counseling to Paul?
2. What ethical issues are involved in this scenario?
3. If you were James's supervisor and he came to you for advice, how would you counsel him to proceed?
4. How might a counselor balance ethical practice and their own moral/religious code when the two seem in conflict? Would such balance even be possible?
5. Would James be guilty of unethical practice if he refused to counsel Paul because of his religious beliefs? Why or why not?

Case Study 2.5 The Case of David and Hussein: Shades of Oppression

David is a Jewish counselor educator at a public university in the Northeastern United States. During David's presentation on preventing discrimination at the ACA conference, Hussein, a young Palestinian professor of counselor education, stands and accuses David of hypocrisy because of David's well-known support for the State of Israel. David tries to regain control of the presentation, but the crowd becomes verbally engaged and is deeply divided over the issue. David's supporters maintain that Hussein's criticism is based on anti-Semitism; his opponents claim David is supporting an apartheid society. Many in the audience are confused regarding what to do because they see both David and Hussein as representatives of oppressed cultures and do not wish to oppose or alienate either. Regardless, the conflict is evident to all in attendance.

1. If you were in the session, how might you respond? What would be helpful in this complex, challenging situation?
2. If you were a leader in ACA, how would you proceed in this case? What would be your follow-up response?
3. What are the difficult issues involved in this conflict between David and Hussein?
4. How might the *ACA Code of Ethics* inform whatever action is taken?
5. What would be your learning "take aways" regarding this unfortunate conflict?

In this case, we see professional counselors representing two cultures, both of which have faced severe discrimination. Advocacy, in such cases, may well

(continued)

Case Study 2.5 The Case of David and Hussein: Shades of Oppression (*continued*)

lie in encouraging and facilitating dialogue among such disparate points of view, even if unilateral agreement is not realistic. Counselor educators and professional counseling organizations are clearly in a position to facilitate such difficult conversations. While a dialogue between David and Hussein might or might not facilitate lasting change, failure to dialogue on issues of conflict is simply abdicating professional responsibility. Clearly, in many cases, the issues are complex and clear answers may be difficult to discern, if not impossible in certain situations. The essential factor here likely lies not in agreement, as that may not be realistic in such a scenario, but in establishing difficult dialogues. Clearly, such conversation is very challenging for UN experts to say nothing of counselors and counselor educators. Still, complex issues require an earnest response. If we cannot facilitate difficult conversations in graduate counseling programs, where then can they occur? To borrow from Hillel and many others who have repeated the phrase, "If not now, when, if not us, then who?"

For student counselors working in practicum and internship placements, this could also mean confronting racist, sexist, and homophobic jokes and culturally offensive language. A simple method of supporting culturally sensitive counseling involves an intense self-examination regarding one's own language, attitudes, and behavior (see Case Study 2.6). Student counselors can also join the AMCD and read materials related to multicultural competence (e.g., *Journal of Multicultural Counseling* and texts such as *Multicultural Issues in Counseling: New Approaches to Diversity* [Lee, 2019] and *Multicultural Counseling Competencies*, 5th ed. [Sue et al., 1992]).

Case Study 2.6 The Case of Ali: Recognizing Cultural Conflicts and Applying Cultural Competence

Ali recently completed his doctorate in counselor education in a Council for Accreditation of Counseling and Related Educational Programs (CACREP)-accredited counselor education program on the West Coast. He also holds a master's in clinical mental health counseling and is a licensed professional counselor. He returns to his home country in the Middle East where cultural norms vary considerably from those in the United States. Ali has accepted a job running a counseling clinic and providing individual, family, and group counseling. He begins counseling Ahmed, an engineer who has recently returned home after 5 years working in Sydney, Australia. Ahmed confesses in an early session that he is gay. During his formative upbringing, he managed to suppress his sexual orientation due both to religious and strict legal repression. As being gay is

(continued)

Case Study 2.6 The Case of Ali: Recognizing Cultural Conflicts and Applying Cultural Competence (*continued*)

punishable by death in their country, Ali well understands Ahmed's delicate dilemma. Ahmed recounts it was only in Sydney where he explored his sexuality, eventually forming a partnership with a man. Now back home, his parents expect him to marry soon and have children. Further complicating matters, their country has made LGBTQ a capital offense. "I don't know what to do," a distraught Ahmed confides to Ali. "Can you help me?"

1. If you were Ali, how might you counsel Ahmed?
2. What are the conflicts involved in this scenario?
3. What might cultural competence look like in this scenario?
4. What is in the client's best interest here?
5. What do you think is most realistic in this situation?

FINAL THOUGHTS

The *ACA Code of Ethics* (ACA, 2014) also prohibits counselors from discriminating against groups that do not fall under the current federal nondiscrimination code. On June 26, 2015, the U.S. Supreme Court ruled that states cannot ban same-sex marriage. Gay and lesbian couples now have the same legal rights and benefits as heterosexual couples (CNN, 2015). Also, many cities and municipalities have enacted nondiscrimination laws designed to protect such vulnerable groups. Two high-profile nondiscrimination court cases involving counselor education training programs, *Ward v. Wilbanks* (2010; *Ward v. Polite*, 2012) and *Keeton v. Anderson-Wiley* (2011/2012), illustrate changing U.S. cultural norms and a backlash against such change. While the counseling profession can claim victory on the merits of both cases (Wheeler & Bertram, 2019), ongoing legislative efforts in southern states attempt to roll back pluralistic efforts (Human Rights, 2022). The *ACA Code of Ethics* also opens the door to further in-depth discussions regarding what is and what is not unethical behavior when the topic revolves around diversity.

Another complication regarding multiculturalism and discrimination involves the relatively recent expansion of the counseling profession into non-Western societies. In many societies, current cultural practice would be at odds with ACA's nondiscrimination clause, particularly regarding the role of women, LGBTQ populations, and religion, to name a few "hot button" topics. There are some societies that provide no equal rights to women and no legal protection from domestic abuse and where, most egregiously, being gay or lesbian and practicing a religion other than the official government-sanctioned one are each punishable by death (Hodges, 2009).

There are no easy answers to multicultural and societal conflicts such as the ones just mentioned. The counseling profession, at least the *Western* counseling profession, has posited itself as a pluralistic one and advocates for the rights of disadvantaged groups (e.g., women, gays and lesbians and the poor). But it is fair to state that many non-Western societies would not agree with the ACA regarding much of the ACA's nondiscrimination statement. A critical question is "How will ACA and its affiliate organizations (e.g., American Mental Health Counselors Organization [AMHCA], American School Counselor Association [ASCA], and ACES) remain consistent with their egalitarian policies without, ironically enough, seeming culturally insensitive to many non-Western cultures?" This disconnect between organizational pluralism and cultural variation will likely become a serious issue in the future as the counseling profession becomes more commonplace in Middle Eastern, African, and Asian societies. The ACA and other progressive mental health organizations have been reluctant to address these more complex international, cultural issues (e.g., discrimination versus cultural context). What may appear simple, for example, in the United States may not be so in, say, Saudi Arabia. Complex social-cultural-religious conflict represents a significant challenge for the emerging global counseling profession. How effectively the ACA, ASCA, AMHCA, ACES, and other organizations address such conflict and variation will likely go a long way in determining professional international success.

Counseling in a diverse world carries many challenges and rewards. A multicultural counseling perspective encourages counselors to become aware of their own biases, values, and assumptions by increasing their awareness of other cultural groups. A multicultural framework also involves developing culturally appropriate intervention strategies to address the particular needs of clients with regard to ethnicity, culture, spirituality, gender, disability, sexual orientation, and socioeconomic standing, to name a few. Because of the wide variation in global cultures, no one can reasonably claim to be an expert. Therefore, it is highly recommended for counselors to continue their education well beyond the classroom through workshops, networking, and reading texts on multicultural counseling.

CONCLUSION

Multiculturalism is the counseling profession's number one issue. With rapidly changing U.S. demographics and a growing international counseling presence, there is little question that addressing counseling from a multicultural perspective will be a critical issue for all counselors. Perhaps all of us, most especially those of us with little cross-cultural experience, could benefit from a dose of cultural humility. Cultural humility likely is essential for sound, ethical, effective practice, particularly when working with diverse populations (Hook et al., 2017). My best recommendation is something I learned from my spiritual training, and that is "Be not afraid." While we tend to fear what is different, when we engage on a person-to-person level as counselor to client, there is a better chance for a therapeutic encounter (Rogers, 1951). So, work to transcend fear of "the other," and chances are better therapy will be the result.

LESSONS LEARNED

I had noticed him looking at me or, more accurately, seeming to study me from the back of the room. His face bore a look of skepticism, and his arms crossed tightly across his chest put the exclamation point on the nonverbal message he appeared to be sending. I was spending a month in Australia's Northern Territory, providing trauma-informed education to remote schoolteachers in various far-flung public and parochial schools across the Northern Territory's vast and desolate geography. This indigenous community was a very remote setting in Central Australia. Central Australia, moreover, has a *lot* of remoteness. I was to spend most of the week in this particular location before flying back to Darwin via Alice Springs Friday afternoon.

DNA research suggests Aboriginal Australians are the world's oldest culture (Klein, 2016). For thousands of years, they roamed the continent hunting and gathering, raising families, creating rock art, developing musical instruments, and generally living in harmony with their environment. British arrival and colonialization of Australia, or the great southern land, meant the loss of their land, culture, and customs and their people being killed, forced into subservient roles, and forced to adopt to the oppressor's culture (Jalata, 2013). Having spent significant time in remote Australia, I was acutely aware of European people's oppressive history. Aboriginal Australians were not citizens under Australia's terra nullius policy until the Australia High Court decision in 1977 (Jalata, 2013). A consequence of colonialism has left many Aboriginal Australians rootless, disconnected from their traditional customs that served them well for perhaps 60,000 years. Aboriginal trauma, addiction, and suicide rates are some of the highest in the world (Koff, 2022). With all this depressing and distressing information in mind, the puzzling aspect was that there were not more people giving off their hostility vibe. Given this was my first day, having arrived just that morning, I considered this week might be a very long one.

Interestingly, I did not see him again until a couple of days later. I shall refer to him as *Keith*. I had been delivering trauma-informed care trainings, offering individual coaching sessions for teachers and administrators, and speaking to classes since practically stepping out of the utility vehicle (*ute* in Australia) and had just sat down for a coffee break when the assistant principal informed me someone desired to speak with me. In walked the hostile-looking man from two days earlier. He nodded and sat down, giving me a similar look as before. Finally, after an extended silence, he spoke. He introduced himself, starting with his culture (or *mob*, as is said in Aboriginal country) and his family and their dreaming (origin and land). Waiting until he was finished, I followed suit. Then another extended pause, and he inquired, "Why are you here?" Each time I venture into indigenous peoples' country, I acknowledge their country by name and pay respects to their cultural leaders, past, present, and emerging, something I had done upon arrival. Going through this he continued to look skeptical. "Look," he began, "we see so many whitefellas (term for all European people, male or female) passing through our land, offering all kinds of promises they don't intend to keep. What makes you any different?" From his viewpoint, I was simply another in a long line of majority people treading on his land and potentially violating his cultural ways. While feeling on the spot, his raw honesty was refreshing. I explained my role and that I would respect his cultural ways. This last sentence brought out his most significant concern. "But mate, how does all your whitefella methods help us?" I sat back and took a long moment myself.

I explained that having visited many cultural lands during my many visits to Australia, I have seen the damage inflicted by colonialization. I acknowledged that trauma healing, such as counseling, was only part of my role. I went on to articulate the need for cultural expressions such as art, dancing, celebrations, and sports like AFL (Australian Football League, popular among Aboriginal people), as well as meditation, singing, and living strong in culture (living traditional ways and refraining from alcohol and drugs). Interestingly, in fact shockingly, he nodded in agreement, the first time he had expressed any positive gesture toward me. He then spoke of not knowing what to make of me. He had not liked me from my initial talk, viewing me as a typical naive whitefella and sounding all too positive due to being ill informed on his people's history since colonization. "I just don't get you," he said. "I get the pols (politicians) who pass through and expect nothing good from them. But I can't figure you out."

I acknowledged my shortcomings, being a visitor from far away, while expressing having spent extended time in cultural lands working alongside the traditional custodians of the land (Aboriginal people). I further articulated my background in trauma and addiction recovery and my firm belief that addiction was essentially self-medicated trauma, and given the genocide inflicted, Aboriginal people were self-medicating generations of trauma. I sat back and waited for him to reply. He kept me waiting for what had to be a full minute, an eternity in Western culture. He shook his head and explained several of his people working at the school had spoken kindly of me, something that puzzled and concerned him. "You seem like a decent whitefella," he said, "but your people have been terrible to mine. You say the right things, but our history is those are the most dangerous people to us." There it was, *"the how can I possible trust you" talk*. Feeling somehow liberated in the face of his veracity, I acknowledged the terrible history and had no good answer for him. "No question, it's hard to trust, much like back in the U.S." Somehow, this seemed to be the correct answer. "Okay, mind if I attend your PD (professional development training) tomorrow?" I answered that I would be honored. He nodded, rose, and left the room.

The following morning, I was to present on trauma treatment and care to community leaders. From memory, some two dozen men and women filed into the staff room. After a brief introduction from the principal, I began by acknowledging their culture and paying respects to their leaders. Then, I briefly explained my background, role, and goals for the PD. The training was 90 minutes long and, as I do, it involved much participation from the audience. As most of the attendees had met me, participation was high. Keith sat on the back row again but seemed more curious and less visibly hostile than my initial training. Nearing the conclusion of the PD, he finally raised his hand to speak. "How can we get someone like you to stay here full time? You have good information but you're leaving tomorrow. We need someone to provide counseling full time. How do we get that?" I examined the audience; most looked on me with curiosity. Keith's questions seemed less a challenge than a plea for ideas. Once again, I acknowledged my shortcomings and suggested we speak after my PD.

Over coffee in the staff room, we spoke about how his people might get a full-time counselor. I acknowledged my shortcomings in this area and inquired about his working through political channels. After all, one counselor would be small change compared to the sums of money the territorial and commonwealth governments were spending in remote Australia. "But we get the same answers, mate," Keith replied. I encouraged him to join any cultural organization and lobby the government for qualified mental health professionals, as there was a dire shortage. In fact, my colleague Cheryl, a remote school counselor, served eight remote schools in an area larger than New York State. She and her boss had had no luck in persuading the politicians in Darwin to fund more remote school counselors. I could see Keith looking very discouraged, and admittedly, I was quite discouraged myself. Weary, we each sat in silence for a long period before he spoke again.

"You know, my mob have finally made gains of late. Maybe this (e.g., more counselors) is one of my next projects." I wished him well and offered to help in any way, such as meeting politicians while in country and writing letter when back in New York. He smiled and patted my shoulder. "You know, mate, those pols are the same the world over." He stood, we shook hands, and he walked off. One more time, I was left wondering if I were doing any good at all. At that point, I found myself wishing I could come to work in remote Australian country and support Keith's efforts to hire counselors to, as he would say, "Help us help ourselves." Instead, I was headed out the following day for a 5- to 6-hour drive to the next very remote school, one with the highest suicide rate in Australia. Despite the area having one of the world's highest trauma rates and suicide rates, there were insufficient funds to support basic services like addictions and trauma counseling. I considered my own country and the privilege my ethnicity and education had bought. I sat inert for several minutes, considering the overwhelming odds Keith and his people faced. Then, I finished my coffee, washed mine and Keith's cups, and headed to my room to pack for the long drive the following morning to another school.

RECOMMENDED RESOURCES

Website

Difficult Dialogues National Resource Center (www.difficultdialogues.org): The DDNRC was formed to support the integration of teaching and learning about difficult dialogues into university missions across the United States and the world. The Case of David and Hussein in Case Study 2.5 illustrates such a difficult conversation. There are numerous challenging conversations regarding race, religion, LGBTQ, and politics, to cite just a few.

Print

Barret, B., & Logan, C. (2007). *Counseling gay men and lesbians: A practice primer*. Wadsworth.
Cashwell, C. S., & Young, J. S. (2005). *Integrating spirituality and religion into counseling: A guide to competent practice*. American Counseling Association.
Dworkin, S. H., & Popo, M. (2012). *Casebook for counseling lesbian, gay, bisexual, and transgender persons and their families*. American Counseling Association.
Fukuyama, M. A., & Sevig, T. D. (1999). *Integrating spirituality into multicultural counseling*. Sage.
Harley, D. A., & Dillard, J. M. (Eds.). (2005). *Contemporary mental health issues among African Americans*. American Counseling Association.
Henriksen, R. C., Jr., & Paladino, D. A. (2009). *Counseling multiple heritage individuals, couples, and families*. American Counseling Association.
Lee, C. C. (2019). *Multicultural issues in counseling: New approaches to diversity* (5th ed.). American Counseling Association.
Pedersen, P. B., Draguns, J. G., Lonner, W. J., & Trimble, J. E. (2008). *Counseling across cultures* (6th ed.). Sage.
Perez, R., Debord, K. A., & Bieschke, K. J. (2009). *A handbook of counseling and psychotherapy with lesbian, gay, and bisexual clients*. American Psychological Association.
Roysircar, G., Sandhu, D. S., & Bibbins, V. E. (Eds.). (2003). *Multicultural competencies: A guidebook of practices*. American Counseling Association.
Sue, D. W., & Sue, D. (2002). *Counseling the culturally diverse: Theory and practice* (4th ed.). Wiley.
Vernon, A., & Clemente, R. (2005). *Assessment and intervention with children and adolescents: Developing multicultural approaches*. American Counseling Association.

A robust set of instructor resources designed to supplement this text is located at http://connect.springerpub.com/content/book/978-0-8261-6607-4. Qualifying instructors may request access by emailing textbook@springerpub.com.

REFERENCES

Alessandria, K. P. (2002). Acknowledging white ethnic groups in multicultural counseling. *The Family Journal, 10*, 57–60. https://doi.org/10.1177/1066480702101009

American Counseling Association. (2014). *2014 ACA code of ethics.* https://www.counseling.org/docs/default-source/default-document-library/2014-code-of-ethics-finaladdress.pdf

Arredondo, P., Toporek, M. S., Brown, S. P., Jones, J., Locke, D. C., Sanchez, J., & Stadler, H. (1996). Operationalization of the multicultural counseling competencies. *Journal of Multicultural Counseling and Development, 24*(1), 42–78. https://doi.org/10.1002/j.2161-1912.1996.tb00288.x

Association for Specialists in Group Work. (1998). *Principles for diversity-competent group workers.* https://asgw.org/wp-content/uploads/2021/07/ASGW-Guiding-Principles-May-2021.pdf

CNN. (2015). *Map: Same-sex marriage in the United States.* http://www.cnn.com/interactive/us/map-same-sex-marriage

D'Andrea, M. (2000). Postmodernism, constructivism, and multiculturalism: Three forces reshaping and expanding our thoughts and counseling. *Journal of Mental Health Counseling, 22*, 1–16.

Gates, G. J. (2017, January 11). *In U.S., more adults identifying as LGBT.* https://news.gallup.com/poll/201731/lgbt-identification-rises.aspx

Hayes, D. G., Prosek, E. A., & McLeod, A. L. (2010). A mixed-methodological analysis of the role of culture in the clinical decision-making process. *Journal of Counseling & Development, 88*, 112–119. https://doi.org/10.1002/j.1556-6678.2010.tb00158.x

Helms, J. E., & Cook, D. A. (1999). *Using race and culture in counseling and psychotherapy: Theory and process.* Allyn & Bacon.

Herlihy, B. J., & Painter, E. (2019). Ethical issues in multicultural counseling. In C. C. Lee (Ed.), *Multicultural issues in counseling* (5th ed., pp. 259–272). American Counseling Association.

Hodges, S. (2009, March). Counseling in the twenty-first century: Challenges and opportunities. *Counseling Today, 51*(9), 44–47.

Hook, J. N., Davis, D., Owen, J., & DeBlaere, C. (2017). *Cultural humility: Encouraging diverse identities in therapy.* American Psychological Association.

Hook, J. N., Farrell, J., Davis, D., DeBlaere, C., Van Tongren, D., & Utsey, S. (2016). Cultural humility and racial Microaggressions in counseling. *Journal of Counseling Psychology, 63*(3), 269–277. https://doi.org/10.1037/Cou0000114

Human Rights. (2022, June 30). *Human rights campaign on DeSantis's "Don't Say Gay or Trans" law going into effect, targeting LGBTQ+ youth and turning back the clock on equality.* Human Rights Staff. https://www.hrc.org/press-releases/human-rights-campaign-on-desantiss-dont-say-gay-or-trans-law-going-into-effect-targeting-lgbtq-youth-and-turning-back-the-clock-on-equality

Jalata, A. (2013). The impacts of English colonial terrorism and genocide on indigenous Australians. *SageJournals, 3*(3). https://doi.org/10.1177/2158244013499143

Jones, N. A., & Bullock, J. (2012). *The two or more races population: 2010.* U.S. Census Bureau. https://www2.census.gov/library/publications/cen2010/briefs/c2010br-13.pdf

Keeton v. Anderson-Wiley, 733 F. Supp. 2d 1368 (S.D. Ga. 2010), *aff'd*, 664 F.3d 865 (11th Cir. 2011), appeal dismissed, No. 110-099 (S.D. Ga. June 22, 2012).

Kiselica, M. S. (1999). Confronting my own ethnocentrism and racism: A process of pain and growth. *Journal of Counseling & Development, 77*, 14–17. https://doi.org/10.1002/j.1556-6676.1999.tb02405.x

Klein, K. (2016, August 23). *DNA study finds aboriginal Australians world's oldest civilization.* History Channel. www.history.com

Koff, J. (2022, May 16). *Aboriginal suicide rates.* Creative Spirits. https://www.creativespirits.info

Lee, C. C. (2001). Culturally responsive school counselors and programs: Addressing the needs of all students. *Professional School Counseling, 4*, 257–261.

Lee, C. C. (Ed.). (2006). *Counseling for social justice.* American Counseling Association.

Lee, C. C. (Ed.). (2019). *Multicultural issues in counseling: New approaches to diversity* (5th ed.). American Counseling Association.

Lee, C. C., Baldwin, R., Marmara, S. M., & Quesenberry, L. (2018). Counselors as agents of social justice. In C. C. Lee (Ed.), *Counseling for social justice* (3rd ed., pp. 3–20). : American Counseling Association.

McIntosh, P. (1998). White privilege, color, and crime: A personal account. In C. R. Mann & M. S. Zatz (Eds.), *Images of color, images of crime* (pp. 207–216). Roxbury.

Passel, J. S., & Cohen, D. (2008). *U.S. population projections: 2005–2050.* Pew Research Center.

Pedersen, P. B. (1994). *A handbook for developing multicultural awareness* (2nd ed.). American Counseling Association.

Pedersen, P. B., Draguns, J. G., Lonner, W. J., & Trimble, J. E. (Eds.). (2002). *Counseling across cultures* (5th ed.). Sage.

Remley, T. P., Jr., & Herlihy, B. (2020). *Ethical, legal and professional issues in counseling* (6th ed.). Pearson.

Ridley, C. R. (2005). *Overcoming unintentional racism in counseling and therapy: A practitioner's guide to intentional intervention* (2nd ed.). Sage.

Rogers, C. R. (1951). *Client-centered therapy*. Houghton Mifflin.

Saltzman, M., & D'Andrea, M. (2001). Assessing the impact of a prejudice prevention project. *Journal of Counseling & Development, 79*, 341–346. https://doi.org/10.1002/j.1556-6676.2001.tb01979.x

Sodowsky, G. R., Taffe, R. C., Gutkin, T. B., & Wise, S. (1994). Development of the Multicultural Counseling Inventory (MCI): A self-report measure of multicultural competencies. *Journal of Counseling Psychology, 41*, 137–148. https://doi.org/10.1037/0022-0167.41.2.137

Sue, D. W. (1996). Ethical issues in multicultural counseling. In B. Herlihy & G. Corey (Eds.), *ACA ethical standards casebook* (5th ed., pp. 193–197). American Counseling Association.

Sue, D. W., Arrendondo, P., & McDavis, R. J. (1992). Multicultural counseling competencies. *Journal of Multicultural Counseling, 20*, 64–88.

Sue, D. W., & Sue, D. (2012). *Counseling the culturally different: Theory and practice*. John Wiley & Sons.

Ward v. Polite, 667 F.3d 727 (6th Cir. 2012).

Ward v. Wilbanks, Case No. 09-CV-11237 (E.D. Mich. July 26, 2010).

Wehrly, B. (1991). Preparing multicultural counselors. *Counseling and Human Development, 24*(3), 1–24.

Wheeler, A. M., & Bertram, B. (2019). *The counselor and the law: A guide to legal and ethical practice*. American Counseling Association.

Wrenn, G. (1962). *The counselor in a changing world*. American Personnel and Guidance Association.

CHAPTER 3

Selecting and Applying for a Practicum/Internship

INTRODUCTION

The practicum and internship placements represent the backbone of any graduate counseling program (and in related training programs, e.g., in social work, marriage and family therapy, and psychology). Depending on the type of program; the particular institution you attend; and your state, territory, or country of residence, you will spend anywhere from 400 to 1,200 clock hours on your practicum and internship experience. The Council for Accreditation of Counseling and Related Educational Programs (CACREP, 2024) sets the standards for most counseling programs in the United States. In many countries, the counseling profession is self-governed, and professional counseling organizations provide credentialing and accreditation. For many counseling students, practicum and internship offer the first opportunity to work with clinical populations. Practicum and internship are challenging in a far different manner than standard classes, as counseling students now grapple with real people having genuine struggles. It is common knowledge that good field site supervisors on practicum and internship are very helpful in guiding students through the maze of client issues, whereas "poor" supervisors may exacerbate a practicum/internship student's learning trajectory. The practicum/internship site is vitally important, as is the field site supervisor. Likely, most counseling programs do their best to place a student in the appropriate school or agency. Still, placement is a very inexact science and poor "fits" occur. It is further accurate to mention poor supervisors do exist in the field. In this chapter, I discuss all aspects of selecting the appropriate practicum/internship site.

SELECTING A PRACTICUM/INTERNSHIP

Procedures for choosing a practicum and internship setting will vary depending on the counseling program. For example, in some programs, a placement coordinator or another faculty may actually select all the clinical placements and then assign the students to particular settings. In some cases, the program has an agreement with a particular agency or agencies, schools, and so forth. Some students will chafe at this approach due to lack of input, whereas others will be relieved the site is chosen for them. Although this method is regressive in nature, it does lessen the burden for the students.

A more common method of selection involves students and placement coordinator/faculty working jointly on practicum and internship selection. In many cases, the student meets with their faculty advisor and discusses the types of placements that might match up with the student's interests and aptitude. The important considerations are for students and faculty advisors to meet and discuss the student's interests regarding practicum and internship, along with what is realistic. Some counseling program placements are limited due to geography (rural usually), local competition (competing area counseling, social work, and psychology programs), theoretical orientation (e.g., pastoral counseling program will target specific placements, as will programs in addictions counseling), student transportation (whether the student have a vehicle or reliable access to mass transit), and so on. Fortunate counseling programs are those with a full-time placement coordinator to assist in student placement, monitor placement quality, conduct regular or semi-regular site visits, and devote time to developing new placement sites that full-time teaching faculty cannot provide due to multiple responsibilities.

One of the first tasks for you as a student seeking a practicum is to meet with your faculty advisor or field placement coordinator to discuss your interests. Begin thinking and researching the types of placements (or field settings) that you are interested in well ahead of deadlines. This means that if you must have a placement by mid-August, make sure you seek out your faculty advisor or practicum–internship coordinator in the late fall or early spring term of that academic year. Be aware of the differences in counseling different age groups, varying issues (such as addictions), public versus private schools, and sectarian issues (e.g., a strong pro-choice student may be a poor fit for, say, a Catholic agency). If you are enrolled in a school counseling program and looking for a placement, be aware that elementary school placement responsibilities are significantly different from those in high schools. Counseling students who are interested in mental health, rehabilitation, or other community-based programs will have several variables to consider: inpatient or outpatient psychiatric setting, addictions (outpatient or residential), college or counseling center, community college counseling center, correctional setting, and so forth. Your advisor can point you in the direction of possible placements that are within your area of interest. Your advisor should also be able to inform you whether or not your practicum aspirations are realistic. For example, some placements will not accept master's-level students, whereas others may insist on taking only social work interns, and some placements may require the student to intern for 2 full years, which may not be in the student's best interest if they wish to change placements after 1 year. This may be disappointing, but you need to know this information before investing too much time in the search process.

Now, because of the huge increase in the number of graduate counseling programs since I matriculated into a master's counseling program nearly 4 decades ago, necessity dictates my covering an unpopular though realistic issue regarding practicum and internship placement. Clearly, there are counseling programs that place the onus of securing a practicum and internship squarely on the shoulders of the student, with minimal or no help from faculty. This unfortunate—perhaps unethical—situation largely is a vestige of underfunded, understaffed programs. There also has been a proliferation of master's-level counseling programs over the past decade, some marginally funded, entirely online, overenrolled, and providing little guidance or support to students regarding practicum and internship placement. Unfortunately, as institutions increasingly target programs as "revenue" streams, overcrowded understaffed programs are likely to increase. In my opinion, this is a serious ethical and practical concern both for the profession and for students interested in graduate counseling programs. Sadly, the students are always the primary victims in such cash-focused scenarios.

At the very least, I recommend that after meeting with your advisor, you brainstorm some six to eight possible placements that are within your areas of interest. Then, get busy with a web search. Many local agencies, schools, and other institutions will have websites that you can research for more information. The following sections in this chapter show particular issues to target as you do your research for a placement. Having run community and university counseling programs, I can tell you that students who have done their homework on a given placement are far more likely to be selected. Students who provide an "I don't know why I want to do my practicum/internship here" type of response will not get a placement at said agency, as this suggests a lack of maturity and that the student did not do due diligence. So, know whom the school or agency serves and be able to answer pertinent questions regarding why you would be a good fit for that particular placement. This will be doubly true when you are applying and interviewing for jobs after you complete your graduate studies. So, know whatever is possible regarding the agency, school, hospital, or university center. Have a handful of pertinent questions to ask the interviewer even if you already know the answers.

As you gather information about various placement settings, you would be wise to keep track of the relevant details about each potential placement (e.g., your level of interest on a 1 to 10 scale, with 10 as the highest), along with your impressions about their suitability for you. Suitability has to do with interest and type of placement (e.g., middle or high school, inpatient or outpatient, and addictions or mental health). The school or agency will be asking itself if it trusts you to represent it, and you should ask the same regarding that placement. Exhibit 3.1 offers a practicum/internship site information form that you can use to keep track of each site that you evaluate.

Students should also be aware that it takes a great deal of effort on the part of the faculty to establish relationships with schools, hospitals, clinics, and college counseling centers. Because of the work involved, many counseling programs have longstanding agreements with particular schools and agencies. Such agreements ensure that the counseling program will have enough placements and the agencies will have practicum and internship students to help with their workload. Thus, the decision to seek a practicum with a given school or agency should not be taken lightly because one bad performance by a student could jeopardize an entire placement. (I have witnessed this personally!) It is also worth mentioning that practicum and internships provide a school or agency with a trial period, and occasionally, provided the student counselor has performed well and that there is an opening, a job offer from said placement is a possibility. Again, possible employment depends on the school or agency's policies, budget, and guidelines. Furthermore, your relationship with your field site

50 • THE COUNSELING PRACTICUM AND INTERNSHIP MANUAL

Exhibit 3.1 Counseling Practicum/Internship Site Information Form

Date of contract: _____/_____/_____

Agency/School/College site: _____

Address:

_____

_____

_____

_____

_____

Phone: (_____) - _____ Website:

_____

Contact name:

_____

Contact's job title:

_____

Contact's phone number: (   )_____-_____ ext.

_____

Contact's email:

_____

Write a brief description of the site, population it serves, whether inpatient or outpatient, and anything that seems pertinent.

_____

_____

_____

_____

_____

_____

(continued)

Exhibit 3.1 Counseling Practicum/Internship Site Information Form (*continued*)

Student's versus site's schedule: How well does your schedule match that of the site (e.g., Do you need weekend and evening hours for practicum/internship)?

Based on my contact with this site (phone conversation, email, interview, etc.), does the site seem:

Very interested in me doing a practicum/internship with them.

Moderately interested in me doing a practicum/internship with them.

Not interested in me doing a practicum/internship with them.

Based on my understanding of this placement, I would rate my interest in this site as:

Uninterested   Low Average   Above Average   High

I would rate my fit (e.g., values, type of population served, and view of staff and supervisor) for this site as:

Poor   Average   Good   Excellent

Next step: Do you have a formal interview set up with this site? Yes/No

If you have an interview set up, consider the following checklist:

Do you have an up-to-date résumé?

Do you have a cover letter highlighting your skills and experience?

Do you have directions to the site?

Have you visited its website to learn about the agency and the clients it counsels?

If you know someone who has interned at the site, have you spoken to them regarding their experience?

Do you have any concerns about this site? If so, how serious are they?

Have you spoken with your faculty advisor about this site?

Have you done any mock interviewing in order to prepare for a potential interview? (*Note:* Not all practicum/internships will require a formal interview, although many will. Treat a practicum/internship interview as serious as a job interview. It is good practice for the future. See Case Study 3.1.)

This form is to assist you in gathering information regarding potential practicum and internship placements. Copy this form and use it as a worksheet when searching for a placement. Use one sheet per placement.

Case Study 3.1 The Case of Siobhan

Siobhan is a first-year graduate student in an Australian counseling program. She is hoping to secure a placement in an in patient hospital. She applies and is called in for an interview with her first choice for a practicum and internship. She interviews with Dr. Wells, training director of the in patient behavioral medicine unit. The interview is going very well and Siobhan is feeling very confident. Dr. Wells gives her a tour of the unit, introducing her to relevant staff. Before she leaves, Dr. Wells says, "Oh, you would be able to work through university holidays? We're always short-staffed during those times. Our other graduate interns do this." Siobhan is torn: she wants to say yes, but her program requires students to be free of class and internship responsibilities. However, the placement seems perfect for her and the career she desires. She considers not telling her university field site coordinator of this conflict.

What would be in Siobhan's best interest in this scenario?

supervisor at the school or agency will be critical to future employment. Faculty recommendations certainly are very important, but a practicum or internship supervisor can specifically address a former student's performance in a workplace-type environment (e.g., "Does Sally get along with colleagues? Is she an ethical practitioner? How does she handle difficult clients/students?" "Can she maintain adequate self-care and be a long-term answer?"). Having written recommendations for more than 30 years and received calls from potential employers, the previous questions come up in virtually every call. No school or agency professional has ever asked, "What grade did Sally make in class X or Y?" Grades are important, but professional dispositions are far more so, particularly in terminal master's degree programs training professionals for school-or agency-type work. For students seeking doctoral-level education, grades and, even more significantly, research potential will be more critical.

Clinical Populations

A key question to consider is what type of clients you are interested in counseling. For students in school counseling programs, the issue is more basic. You will complete your practicum in an elementary, middle, or high school. Granted, there are variations on the theme, such as private schools, schools serving specialized students (e.g., schools for the visually impaired and the deaf and school in hospitals), and those educating "at-risk" or exceptional learners. Although all these settings involve counseling school-based populations, various responsibilities may vary considerably. Additionally, a school counseling intern's role will also depend on the supervising school counselor and the philosophy of the school principal. For example, some principals restrict counselors to academic counseling, whereas others believe school counselors should also provide personal counseling and even crisis intervention. Some schools provide ample group counseling, whereas others will offer very little. Naturally, there is much variation in school counseling placements.

Students studying mental health counseling, rehabilitation, marriage and family counseling, and the like will choose between inpatient and outpatient clinics, between addictions and mental health, or between a hospital and residential addictions treatment center, working with children, adolescents, adults, couples, families, and so forth. Like their school counseling colleagues, there may be a wide variation regarding duties. Some addiction agencies may provide the intern with only group counseling and other agencies with only individual counseling experience. Inpatient sites generally will be much different from outpatient mental health or addiction placements. My own experience is that outpatient placements *usually* provide more in-depth counseling. This may be because most inpatient client stays are brief, and thus counseling may be group support and brief check-in sessions, while outpatient treatment is the more traditional 1-hour session for eight to 12 sessions. Still, both inpatient and outpatient placements serve as valuable training grounds for future professional counselors.

Again, all students should carefully consider the population they are interested in counseling and discuss their interests with their advisor. Now, despite whatever you may have heard, completing a practicum and internship in, say, an addictions clinic does not mean you will be required to work in addictions for the rest of your professional career. A practicum and internship spent counseling in a high school does not mean you will never get a job counseling in a middle school. Fortunately, skills and interventions acquired in counseling programs can be tailored to various ages and populations. But there is one exception: If you are enrolled in a marriage and family counseling or therapy program, you will, of necessity, be required to counsel couples and families (Gladding, 2009), so some restrictions will apply.

Naturally, your interests may not be clearly defined, particularly if you are a younger graduate student. Do not overly stress regarding your potential placement because there is plenty of flexibility in the counseling field. It is not uncommon for counselors to begin their careers in a specialty area (e.g., addictions) and then move on to another very different area (e.g., mental health counseling). Some lateral moves within the profession will require more education or training (e.g., moving from an agency setting to a school setting or from being a mental health counselor to art therapist), whereas others will effect no change other than a focus on a different population (counseling children to counseling adults).

Here are some questions regarding client population for consideration in selecting a practicum/internship:

- What clinical populations would I like to counsel? I am interested in counseling these populations because _____.
- Would I prefer inpatient or outpatient settings? Why?
- What are the advantages or disadvantages to a practicum/internship in an elementary school? A middle school? A high school?
- Does the philosophy of the site match my personal values? This is particularly an issue with some private schools and agencies. What populations does the clinic's nondiscrimination statement include and exclude? Some agencies are pro-choice, whereas others are staunchly antiabortion. Some placements discriminate against gay and lesbian people—in direct violation of many (e.g., American Counseling Association [ACA], American School Counselor Association [ASCA], and American

Mental Health Counselors Organization [AMHCA]) codes of ethics. (Speak with your advisor regarding this issue.)

- Would I like the challenge of a special population such as a prison, jail, or state psychiatric hospital? Why would a correctional setting be a good fit as a practicum/internship?
- How diverse are the students and/or clients that the school, college, or agency serves?
- What training opportunities are available at this placement? Many placements provide additional training opportunities through workshops or in-service trainings (e.g., dialectical behavior therapy [DBT] groups, specialized training with sex offenders, and other mandated populations).

Some of these questions address *multicultural competencies* as espoused by Sue et al. (1992) and later adopted by the Association for Multicultural Counseling and Development (AMCD; Arredondo et al., 1996). The definition of *multicultural* is now more broadly defined to include issues of disability, socioeconomic status, religion, sexual orientation, and culture, as well as race or ethnicity. Some of the beliefs, knowledge, and skills of culturally skilled counselors are the following:

> Culturally skilled counselors understand their own cultural heritage. They recognize the limits of their multicultural competency and expertise. They understand how their own cultural heritage may contribute to their biases and how racism may affect their personality and work. They are constantly seeking to understand themselves as racial and cultural beings and are actively seeking a nonracist identity. They seek consultative help, are familiar with relevant research, and are actively involved with clients outside the counseling setting. They can send and receive verbal and nonverbal communications accurately and appropriately. (Arredondo et al., 1996, pp. 59–60)

Many counseling programs, particularly those accredited by the CACREP, address the various multicultural competencies through their curriculum, training, portfolio requirements, and diverse practicum and internship placements (Remley & Herlihy, 2020). An important factor in your development is to begin to consider multicultural issues when you counsel clients. No one needs to be a cultural anthropologist to be culturally competent. Rather, when you do work with the culturally different, read up on the culture of the client, and if you are unsure about something, ask your client for clarification. Most clients will appreciate that you were respectful enough to ask about their culture. Furthermore, given the literally thousands of cultures (and subcultures) in the world, no one can be an expert in all. The important consideration is to be respectful and acquire new information. Chapter 2, "Multicultural Issues, Complexities, and Considerations," provides a more detailed discussion of multicultural issues.

Level of Responsibility

It is also important to remember that as you progress from practicum through internship, you are likely given more responsibility with each successive placement. Your clinical supervisor's first priority is to ensure the emotional well-being and safety of the clients they serve. As you increase in skill and confidence levels, your supervisor is likely to give you more autonomy. My own experience is that practicum often is a student's most challenging placement because usually it is the first. Most graduate counseling students have not done anything quite like counseling work, and there may be an initial culture shock, particularly in inner-city or specialized schools (those serving special-needs students) and inpatient psychiatric placements. Practicum supervisors are more likely to restrict student responsibilities until they observe the student successfully managing them. Naturally, supervisors will vary considerably regarding what activities they allow the practicum student to perform. Most practicum supervisors will likely bring the practicum student along slowly, utilizing observation and then co-counseling with an experienced clinician. A few, however, may believe in immediate immersion, in which case the practicum student begins immediate counseling. Fortunately, most supervisors, ever mindful of liability, will be of the former as opposed to the latter school.

Another factor to consider is that, on your placement, you may work alongside doctoral interns from counselor education, counseling psychology, clinical psychology, social work, and other programs. Doctoral students will naturally be given more responsibility and autonomy than master's-level students. This may be frustrating for graduate students in master's degree programs, but master's-level students should bear in mind that this is not a personal criticism but rather reflects a higher level of training. Master's-level counseling students who matriculate on to doctoral programs in counselor education, counseling psychology, and the like will likely appreciate the greater degree of latitude at that point.

Your Site Supervisor

Your site supervisor will play a key role in your practicum/internship experience. In addition to clinical issues, site supervisors also serve as mentors and role models. CACREP requires the following for on-site supervisors (CACREP, 2024):

- a minimum of a master's degree in counseling or a related profession with appropriate certifications and/or licenses;
- a minimum of 2 years of pertinent professional experience in the program area in which the student is enrolled;
- knowledge of the program's expectations, requirements, and evaluation procedures for students; and
- relevant training in counseling supervision.

Ideally, your on-site practicum supervisor will be a professional credentialed in counseling. It is much easier for, say, a licensed counselor to mentor a graduate student in counseling than a graduate student in a social work program. Likewise, a student in a school counseling program is best suited to have a licensed or state-certified school counselor providing supervision than a school psychologist. Because of the proliferation of the various mental health professionals, however, social workers or psychologists often supervise graduate counseling students and professional counselors in the workplace. Although these related mental health professionals may do a very good job of supervising, it is unlikely that they will be as informed about issues specific to the counseling profession or be advocates for counseling organizations (such as the ACA), as they would for their own professional organizations (e.g., the American Psychological Association [APA] and the National Association of Social Workers [NASW]). Finally, all the mental health professions have their own codes of ethics. Fortunately, these ethical codes are more similar than different (Herlihy & Corey, 2015; Remley & Herlihy, 2020). However, if your on-site clinical supervisor is a social worker or psychologist, they likely will not be familiar with the ACA's ethical code. This means your faculty advisor or practicum/internship classroom instructor becomes even more important to you. You are legally responsible for practicing within your profession's code of ethics, and thus, it is imperative for you to read and understand it (Remley & Herlihy, 2020; Wheeler & Bertram, 2019).

While you are investigating a practicum site, here are some questions to ask regarding your site supervisor:

- In which mental health profession is your practicum/internship supervisor credentialed (e.g., counseling, psychology, or social work)?
- What is your practicum supervisor's primary code of ethics?
- What credentials does your practicum/internship supervisor hold (e.g., licensed professional counselor [or another counselor license], licensed clinical social worker, state-licensed or state-certified school counselor, licensed psychologist, registered psychotherapist, registered psychologist, or registered counselor)?

Although the various organizations may be initially confusing to you, the practicum provides an opportunity to begin to understand the larger scope of the mental health profession. Furthermore, you will spend your professional career working alongside psychologists, social workers, marriage and family counselors/therapists, and other mental health professionals. Establishing a respectful, working relationship across disciplines is necessary for counselors and anyone else in the broader mental health profession. On your practicum and internship, as well as during your future professional career, you will work in multidiscipline teams with many different mental health professionals, and this provides an opportunity to work collegially across disciplines. Cross-disciplinary collaboration likely provides the best possible opportunity to deconstruct the various silos that have long plagued the mental health profession.

An important consideration for all counseling students to be aware of involves the varying licensure standards regarding supervision during the practicum/internship. Many states simply specify that a mental health professional licensed in a core discipline (e.g., counseling, social work, or psychology) must supervise the graduate counseling student. Others, such as the state of Massachusetts, require the student to be supervised by a licensed mental health professional with 5 years of counseling experience. Because my university sits on an international border, I teach and supervise counseling students residing and practicing in Canada and New York. In our counseling program, we make all students aware of such variations (we have students from other countries as well). Therefore, ask your faculty advisor about any licensure requirements in your state. Even better yet, check out your state's licensure requirements online (a complete list of state licensure boards and websites is provided in Appendix B). ACA publishes a manual with licensure requirements from all 50 states and three territories, which is a worthwhile resource (www.counseling .org/docs/licensure/72903_excerpt_for_web.pdf).

If asked about their theoretical orientation, many counseling supervisors would likely state that they have an integrated or eclectic approach (Corey, 2017; Ivey & Ivey, 2007). Others may strongly identify with particular therapeutic approaches, such as solution-focused therapy (SFT), narrative therapy, DBT, cognitive behavioral therapy (CBT), Gestalt therapy, and so forth (Corey, 2017; Gladding, 2009). In many cases, the theoretical orientation of your supervisor may not radically change your experience as a supervisee. For example, a supervisor trained in CBT may not be significantly different from one operating from SFT or reality therapy. A supervisor whose theoretical orientation is psychodynamic or one who uses eye movement desensitization and reprocessing (EMDR) likely will use a far different approach. This is not a criticism of any particular approach but recognition of the reality that some approaches will require a different style of supervision due to the nature of the material involved. Regardless of the supervisor's theoretical orientation, supervision is critical to the practicum or internship student's development as a counselor.

The theoretical orientation of your supervisor notwithstanding, I strongly suggest that you "study up" on your supervisor's approach. For example, if your supervisor informs you that they use CBT in counseling, you will want to read up on it. It would also be advisable to ask your supervisor to recommend books, journal articles, and recordings on CBT. The supervisor's particular approach to counseling will strongly correlate to their supervision approach. It is likely wise to ask a potential supervisor what supervision theoretical approach they use when interviewing for a practicum or internship. You might ask your field site supervisor what are their philosophy and approach to supervision. (Theoretical approaches to counseling supervision are discussed in Chapter 7, "Models of Supervision: Classroom and Site Supervision.")

If the field site and university supervisor emphasizes one particular approach, it carries the advantage of narrowing the scope of practice for a practicum/internship student and gives the student the opportunity to develop a clear theoretical orientation. A disadvantage is that you may not learn enough about other viable therapeutic approaches. Furthermore, it is important to be aware of the research, which suggests that using any particular theoretical approach is far less important, in terms of overall effectiveness, than therapeutic attachment (Duncan et al., 2010; Wampold, 2001). More interestingly, some research suggests theoretical orientation may account for only a small portion of therapeutic success (Duncan et al., 2010), although many researchers will dispute this (Corey, 2017).

Accreditations and Affiliations of the Site

Practicum/internship placements are naturally going to have wide variation depending on the type of placement. A high school setting differs from a community mental health clinic, a psychiatric ward in a hospital, an inpatient addictions treatment center, a correctional setting, or a university counseling center. Part of your continuing education in the broader mental health field lies in understanding the variations among the numerous settings, the professionals that staff them, and the various accreditations such placements hold. Many counseling programs will separate school practicum/internship students from mental health, addictions, or rehabilitation placements for the weekly or biweekly classroom part, although some counseling programs mix practicum and internship classes for convenience and to better assist students in understanding the nuances of the counseling profession (e.g., school vs. mental health counseling vs. rehabilitation counseling). Counseling is carried out in all these types of placements, but naturally, student interns' responsibilities in a school counseling office will be distinct from a residential psychiatric center (few school counselors will use the *Diagnostic and Statistical Manual of Mental Disorders-text rev.* [5th ed.; *DSM-5-TR*; American Psychiatric Association, 2022], for example). Adaptability to the particular placement, required functions, and, certainly, treatment populations is crucial for success.

In Chapter 1, "Introduction to the Counseling Profession and the Practicum/Internship Experience," we have discussed the importance of accreditation for graduate educational programs in counseling. Similarly, many practicum sites will hold national certifications. National agencies that accredit clinical placements include the International Accreditation of Counseling Services (IACS), The Joint Commission (TJC, formerly the Joint Commission on Accreditation of Healthcare Organizations or JCAHO), and the Commission on Accreditation of Rehabilitation Facilities (CARF). These national accreditations are separate and distinct from educational, programmatic accreditations such as the CACREP, APA, NASW, Commission on Accreditation for Marriage and Family Therapy Education (COAMFTE), Association for Clinical Pastoral Education (ACPE), and so on. This text focuses on CACREP accreditation, given that the target audience is graduate counseling students (although non-CACREP programs and even undergraduate psychology and social work classes have used this book for field placement).

Field settings that have earned a national certification in their respective fields (e.g., CARF for rehabilitation counseling and ACPE for pastoral counseling centers) will likely have a stronger reputation in the mental health field and may provide a more enriching practicum or internship experience than unaccredited facilities. Placements in unaccredited agencies and college counseling centers, however, must not be viewed with disdain. Accreditation, although a probable indicator of quality, does not guarantee a successful placement, although it does signify that the setting has met the standard in the field. Accreditation, furthermore, does not ensure supervision will be better than in unaccredited treatment facilities, although, again, it likely implies higher quality.

If you are looking at a practicum placement and you notice that it is, for example, CARF accredited, then it would be wise to go to the CARF website and read up on the agency. The same would apply to any other listed accreditation, whether IACS, COAMFTE, or ACPE. When interviewing for a practicum or internship placement, you need to demonstrate your knowledge of that setting's accreditation, its mission, and how accreditation impacts patient or client care. You will also need to understand how the accreditation affects the services the agency delivers. It is also a good idea to ask the interviewer how accreditation has improved their agency. Going on an interview and being unaware of an agency's accreditation or being unaware of the ramifications of the accreditation will hurt your chances for placement. So, know the agency you are interviewing with and be able to address why you would be a good intern there.

The following are websites of common agencies:

- CARF: www.carf.org
- IACS: www.iacsinc.org
- TJC: www.jointcommission.org
- ACPE: www.acpe.edu
- COAMFTE: www.coamfte.org

These are the most common accreditations counseling practicum and internship students likely will encounter. Again, be aware of how these respective accreditations may influence your practicum and internship responsibilities. Your field site coordinator or faculty advisor is a good resource when you have questions, as is your field site supervisor.

Professional Practices and Resources

In addition to understanding the type of setting of your practicum (e.g., school, rehabilitation, or inpatient/outpatient addictions), you will need to be aware of professional and developmental issues within the setting. For starters, you want to ask about the orientation process your placement offers to new practicum and internship students. Some agencies and schools have formalized training, requiring a student to spend several days learning the agency, its operation, and rules and regulations. Others, particularly smaller agencies or schools, will have a very brief, informal training that may last but an hour. You are advised to ask whether the school or agency has a policies and procedures manual. If so, ask if you can borrow a copy. Speak with your field site supervisor if you have concerns or questions. In all settings, you will want to know the organization's guidelines, which hopefully will be contained in a formal document (printed or online) and made available to you. Your supervisor may ask you about CACREP, your professional code of ethics (e.g., ACA, ASCA, or American Rehabilitation Counseling Association [ARCA]), and related information. A free exchange among the student, counseling program representative, and field site supervisor is a healthy approach, as naturally, questions are going to come up, particularly if the school or agency has not previously taken interns from the student's program.

THE INFORMATIONAL INTERVIEW

After you have selected a few placements, contact them to see about arranging informational interviews. I would counsel students seeking a practicum to contact the appropriate person at the desired sites directly using the phone or email. Do not simply send out résumés and cover letters without first contacting the site directly. First, the site may not have a placement for you, in which case your résumés and cover letter will be ignored (likely recycled!). Second, most clinical supervisors, or their designee

60 • THE COUNSELING PRACTICUM AND INTERNSHIP MANUAL

(such as the personnel department), prefer to be contacted directly by phone or email, even though they are busy people. Your faculty advisor and/or the practicum/internship site coordinator will likely have many contacts themselves, and soliciting their opinion is a prudent practice. Your professor or practicum and internship coordinator may even be able to streamline the application process for you.

Many schools and agencies will have established guidelines that require the student to apply prior to an interview. Others, however, have very informal procedures and will be happy to arrange an immediate informational interview. Be sure to check with your selected site to see if an informational interview is a possibility. Some potential placements have a formalized application process requiring completing an application (often online) and attaching a résumé and cover letter, along with three letters of recommendation or references to contact. On this latter point, make sure a reference can give you a robust recommendation; otherwise, words of faint praise may torpedo your plans. Do not simply assume a reference will provide you a strong positive recommendation. Remember this when the time comes to apply for jobs after graduation as well.

Whether the interview is informational or more formal, you need to practice answering questions that your interviewer is likely to ask. I suggest you work with your advisor and/or the campus career center. You may also check texts such as *What Color Is Your Parachute?* (Bolles, 2015) or one I coauthored with Amy Reese Connelly, *A Job Search Manual for Counselors and Counselor Educators: How to Navigate and Promote Your Counseling Career* (Hodges & Connelly, 2010). You will need to be prepared to answer questions related to the setting of your interest. For example, if you are interviewing with a representative from an inpatient psychiatric center, be aware of what types of issues it treats, patient/client/student ages, number and training of staff, or whether it operates from a particular therapeutic orientation (e.g., CBT, EMDR, or rational emotive behavior therapy [REBT]) because these issues likely will come up in the interview. The more informed you appear regarding the agency or school you are interviewing with, the better your chances of a placement. When job search time comes, understanding the terrain becomes exponentially more important.

You should always prepare five to eight questions to ask the interviewer. Even if you are very well informed regarding the school or agency, ask questions anyway. You may discover more in-depth information, and questions suggest you have done your homework on the potential placement. Answering "I don't have any questions" suggests a lack of research, arrogance, or, perhaps, disinterest in the school or agency. "The Formal Interview" section later in this chapter offers a sample of interview questions. As with every opportunity, be as fully prepared as possible. Richard N. Bolles, author of the iconic *What Color Is Your Parachute?* was fond of saying that it is not the person who knows the most about the job who is most likely to be hired. It is the person who best knows how to get the job who is most likely to be hired (Bolles, 2015).

APPLYING FOR THE PRACTICUM/INTERNSHIP

Once again, some college counseling centers and agencies will have a formal application process that requires that you fill out an application packet, whereas others have an informal process where you are instructed simply to show up on a certain day and time for an interview. One large university where I have placed students has a very extensive application process, including a résumé or curriculum vitae (CV), cover letter, letters of recommendation, and a formal interview with several members of the counseling staff. Formality tends to be more common with doctoral students, although master's degree students will want to be prepared for all contingencies. Here are some tips to remember:

- Is there a formal application for the practicum/internship? If so, make sure you are aware of all the application requirements.
- If there is an application form, photocopy it and draft your answers in ink, then go back and type the answers in if you have access to a typewriter. In some cases, the site may send you an electronic copy, in which case you can save the document and then type and edit freely on your computer. The e-copy of a job application form is rapidly making typed applications obsolete.
- Make sure all words are spelled correctly. As the cliché goes, you do not get a second chance to make a first impression. Most egregiously, if you are applying for a practicum or internship in a school setting, misspelled words and poor grammar will weaken your application.
- Know the due date for the application. You might be a strong candidate, but a late application makes a statement about your lack of organization and follow-through. In many cases, an application arriving after the deadline will simply be recycled.
- If you do not understand something on the application, contact the site and ask for clarification. This illustrates initiative and provides another contact with the potential placement.
- Ask your faculty advisor or practicum/internship coordinator to read over your application prior to submitting it. They may have suggestions on how to improve your application.
- Does the application process require letters of support from faculty members or others? If so, give your reference ample notice before the deadline. Ample notice would be 10 to 14 days. Do not drop the reference request on them 3 days before the deadline.

Your Résumé or Curriculum Vitae

When planning to apply for a practicum or internship, I suggest you operate as if you are applying for a professional counseling job at a school, agency, or university counseling center. This involves having an updated and effective résumé or CV. A résumé generally is a one- or two-page summary of your skills, experience, and education; a CV is longer and more detailed. For master's-level counselors and counselor education students, a one- to two-page résumé is standard. For doctoral students in counselor education, use the CV model. Having made the previous statements on résumés and CVs, given the virtual world we all live in, the rules for résumés and CVs seem to be evolving. During my master's program in counseling, going beyond a one-page résumé was viewed as the cardinal transgression. Times have changed considerably as the print CV or résumé is giving way to the electronic version. Recently, I have even noticed three-page virtual résumés with employers seemingly unbothered with the length. Still, play it conservatively and stay within two pages for your résumé.

Because this book targets practicum and internship, I will not offer detailed information about how to write an effective résumé, CV, or cover letter. However, Exhibit 3.2 shows a sample of a cover letter used in applying for a practicum position, and Exhibit 3.3 shows a sample of a résumé typical for the internship-level student. In addition, some basic information and further career resources can be found in Chapter 12, "Termination in Counseling: How to Say Goodbye," and in Bolles's iconic *What Color Is Your Parachute?* (2015) and Hodges and Connelly's *A Job Search Manual for Counselors and Counselor Educators: How to Navigate and Promote Your Counseling Career* (2010).

Exhibit 3.2 Sample Counseling Practicum Application Cover Letter

March 17, 2023

Ms. Alice Ajanja, MS, LMHC, NCC

Director of Pathways Clinic

Ivy, NY 14221

Dear Ms. Ajanja:

Thank you for taking the time to speak with me on the phone regarding a practicum at Pathway Clinic. I look forward to our interview this Thursday at 1:00 p.m. I feel very positive regarding the potential of serving my practicum and internship at your clinic during the following year. I understand your agency serves many immigrant children, adolescents, and adults. As an immigrant myself, I understand the particular challenges that presents.

In addition to completing the first year of my 3-year clinical mental health counseling (CMHC) program at Old Main College, for 2 years, I also have served as a Big Sister through the YWCA–YMCA's Big Brother–Big Sister program. Since fall 2015, I have volunteered for the evening crisis line through Sunflower House and was given a letter of recommendation by my supervisor (enclosed).

I enjoy challenging opportunities serving high-needs populations, as I believe timely intervention is especially important in clients developing sound mental and emotional health. I would welcome the opportunity to learn from your supervision in the next academic year.

Respectfully,

Elisa Botha

Elisa Botha

Graduate Student in Clinical Mental Health Counseling

Old State College

Ivy, NY 14221

Encl.

Exhibit 3.3 Sample Counseling Internship Résumé

Leslie Hawkins

3333 Cataract Avenue

Niagara Falls, NY 14305

(716) 861-4441

Lhawkins@gmail.com

SUMMARY OF QUALIFICATIONS

Compassionate, conscientious helping professional with 3 years of classroom experience (serving what type of students? Mainstream? Special education?)
Candidate for a master's degree in school counseling
Completed three semesters of supervised field experience working with teachers and at-risk students
Currently working on the fourth semester of experience with school counselors and at-risk students
Familiar with the needs of emotionally disturbed and learning-disabled students

EDUCATION

Niagara University, Lewiston, New York

Master of Science in School Counseling, expected May 2023

State University of New York at Oswego, Oswego, NY

Bachelor of Arts in Special Education, August 2020

Minor: Psychology

Completed 25 semester hours in adolescent education
Made the dean's list for three semesters

RELATED EXPERIENCE

1/14/22- 5/12/22 **Mill Middle School**, Williamsville, NY

        School Counseling Intern

Observed individual and group counseling sessions with sixth-grade students
Observed an IEP meeting with the Committee on Special Education
Gained an understanding of the placement protocol for students with IEPs and other accommodation needs

9/2/22–present **89th Street Elementary School**, Niagara Falls, NY

        School Counseling Intern

Observed individual and group counseling sessions with students in grades pre-kindergarten through sixth

Fall 2017–2019 **SUNY Oswego Pride Alliance Executive Board**, Fredonia, NY

        Public Relations Director

(continued)

64 • THE COUNSELING PRACTICUM AND INTERNSHIP MANUAL

Exhibit 3.3 Sample Counseling Internship Résumé (*continued*)

Assisted in organization and promotion of events for the Pride Alliance, a student group geared toward the LGBT students and their allies on campus

Participated in weekly meetings with other members of the Executive Board to discuss and plan topics for general body meetings and events throughout the semester

Helped facilitate and lead weekly general body meetings that consisted of, on average, about 50 people

Created posters, online event announcements, and programs for every event that was sponsored or co-sponsored by the Pride Alliance

Mentored various LGBT students on campus, both during and outside weekly office hours

Was co-captain of the Pride Alliance "Relay For Life" team during the on-campus fundraiser in the spring of 2012

Collaborated with other multicultural groups on campus when facilitating and creating co-sponsored events

Spring 2018   **Dunkirk Middle School**, Dunkirk, NY

   Volunteer Tutor

Worked two-on-one with a sixth-grade, at-risk student twice a week
Prepared a weekly lesson plan
Kept track of student's progress with pre- and post test assessments

January 2019   **Gaskill Middle School**, Niagara Falls, NY

   Student Observer

Observed seventh- and eighth-grade classrooms, including some inclusive classes
Assisted seventh-grade students in writing and illustrating children's books
Assisted eighth-grade students with group reading and discussion of selected novels
Worked one-on-one with eighth-grade students at a first-grade reading level on reading a selected book

January 2019   **Niagara Falls High School**, Niagara Falls, NY

   Student Observer

Observed 11th-grade Regents and Advanced Placement classes
Graded practice Regents Exams and vocabulary quizzes

January 2020   **Niagara Falls City School District**, Niagara Falls, NY

   Student Observer

Helped teachers hand out and collect assignments
Aided students in their in-class reading and writing tasks

Summer 2017   **Niagara Falls City Recreational Department**, Niagara Falls, NY

   Daytime Recreational Aide

Supervised children at a local playground for 5 hours a day, Monday to Friday
Served lunches that were provided by the city

(continued)

Exhibit 3.3 Sample Counseling Internship Résumé (*continued*)

9/17–12/17	**St. Teresa's Parish**, Niagara Falls, NY
	Volunteer Sunday School Teacher

Taught a lesson once a week to a class of about 10 to 15 elementary-aged students

OTHER EMPLOYMENT

5/20–present	**Supermarket Liquors & Wines**, Niagara Falls, NY
	Cashier/Customer Service/Stock
Spring 2019	**SUNY Oswego**, Oswego, NY
	Night Desk Attendant
6/19–9/18	**Niagara Falls State Park**, Niagara Falls, NY
	Cashier and Tour Guide

ACTIVITIES

Take Back the Night Walk, Fall 2018
SUNY Oswego Pride Alliance, Fall 2018–Spring 2020
Intramural Broomball, Fall 2019–
Oswego Gospel Choir, Spring 2020–Fall 2020
The Vagina Monologues, Fall 2019

Note: Always include a short list of hobbies as it provides a more complete picture of you and may help create a connection through shared interests or highlight something interesting.

The Formal Interview

As previously mentioned, interviewing for a practicum or internship varies considerably. Some potential placement sites will request an interview with a clinical director and a select staff. In other cases, a single counselor or social worker will conduct the interview. Regardless of the possible variations, you will want to be thoroughly prepared and take a few copies of your résumé or CV to the interview.

The following are some key questions to anticipate and be able to satisfactorily answer during the interview:

- Why are you interested in applying for a practicum/internship at this agency or school?
- How might our school/agency/hospital fit with your long-term professional goals?
- What specific skills and abilities make you suited for this placement?
- What are your personal and professional strengths?
- What key weaknesses would you like to target for improvement?
- What questions do you have for me/us?

- What counseling theory do you primarily work from?
- Why should we accept you as a graduate intern?

See Chapter 12, "Termination in Counseling: How to Say Goodbye," for more interview questions and suggested answers, as well as certain inappropriate questions that should not be asked on an interview.

Here are some questions for you to ask the interviewer or interviewing committee during the interview:

- Who would be my primary supervisor? What are their training and credentials in counseling and supervision?
- Is the agency accredited? If so, by what accrediting organization?
- What types of counseling-related responsibilities would I be carrying out (e.g., individual, group, couples, or family counseling; psychoeducational groups; intakes; and assessments)?
- What theoretical orientation do staff counselors use (e.g., cognitive behavioral, solution focused, or Gestalt)?
- Will there be opportunities for additional training?
- When can I expect to hear a decision regarding a placement?

Actors, musicians, athletes, and politicians prepare well in advance of their big event, and you should do the same in preparing for an interview. Get with a friend, fellow student, or better yet, a career counselor at your institution and practice answering questions such as those mentioned previously. You might also have a friend or the career counselor videotape your mock interview and then provide critique. You do not need to be perfect, but interviewers will be impressed by prompt candidates, thorough answers, well-groomed applicants, good posture, and appropriate eye contact. Interviewers will be unimpressed by poor grooming, showing up late, interviewees who seem uninformed as to the school or agency function, and who answer "No, I have no questions" when asked. So, prepare for the interview so that you will *be prepared* for the interview.

When you have completed the interview process, always follow up with a thank-you letter. Interviewers will appreciate this simple gesture. Thank-you letters also illustrate that you know how to lay the foundation for future positive relations. Should you be accepted by this practicum/internship site, such follow-through will be important in interagency relations. Given we live in the 21st century, thank-you email messages will work just fine and are more immediate.

THE PRACTICUM/INTERNSHIP CONTRACT

Prior to beginning the practicum or internship, the student, the practicum/internship coordinator, and the on-site supervisor should sign a contract agreeing to the basic counseling and related responsibilities the student will be performing. Such contracts may be called a learning contract, a practicum and internship contract, and so forth. Regardless, the agreement should explicitly delineate responsibilities of the student, faculty, on-site supervisor, counseling program, and clinical setting. Contracts are critical for the student, agency/school, and counseling program to understand specific realms of responsibility. The contract also specifies whom the faculty should contact in the event issues arise during the placement. All parties—student, field site supervisor, and faculty or practicum/internship coordinator—should keep a copy of the contract.

At institutions where I have worked, the faculty develop the practicum/internship contract, and then the college or university's legal counsel review it to ensure legal issues are covered. Some agencies will also have their own contract and require the student, faculty, and on-site supervisor to sign. It is critical that supervisors and students develop a mutual understanding regarding the knowledge, skills, and dispositions that the placement and graduate counseling require. For example, CACREP-accredited counseling programs have specific responsibilities for practicum and internship regarding clock hours, direct contact hours, and supervision. The duties, obligations, organizational guidelines, and so forth should be made clear prior to the beginning of the placement.

Naturally, no contract can cover all eventualities, but contractual language should be clear and easily understood by all parties. The contract should address the following:

- Weekly supervision by the on-site supervisor and the faculty advisor. The CACREP standards require 1 hour of supervision per week, carried out in an individual or group format.
- The clock hours and direct contact hours the student is required to complete each semester.
- The type of clinical duties the student will be assigned. Examples may include individual, group, couples, and family counseling; addictions assessments; academic advising; whether the student will conduct testing and assessment and what types; intakes; and so forth.
- The name of the on-site supervisor, faculty representative, and the student intern.
- How supervisor–student conflicts are to be addressed.
- The right to terminate on behalf of both the counselor education program and the organization if either party feels the relationship is not working. This termination agreement protects the student, program, and placement.
- Duration of the internship. Some contracts specify that the placement will last for the duration of the student's practicum/internship (anywhere from 600 to 1,000 clock hours depending on the program), although others spell out an expectation of one academic year.

Documents for practicum and internship are offered in Appendix C.

FINAL ISSUES TO CONSIDER

Exhibit 3.4 offers a checklist of issues to consider and tasks to complete as you begin your search for a practicum/internship placement. In addition, here are a few final points to bear in mind:

- Have you purchased student liability insurance? The ACA and the AMHCA now include student liability insurance in the cost of student membership, so purchasing

68 • THE COUNSELING PRACTICUM AND INTERNSHIP MANUAL

a student membership in the ACA or the AMHCA is recommended as opposed to simply purchasing student liability coverage. Some counseling programs will require students to maintain membership in the ACA, AMHCA, ASCA, or another professional affiliate. In my own opinion, requiring a student membership is a worthwhile requirement that includes professional development as well as ethical and legal issues. (The ACA has an ethics email and phone number students can use: 1-800-347-6647 [×314] or ethics@counseling.org.)

- Have all parties—student, field site supervisor, and faculty/placement coordinator—agreed that the student is a good fit for the placement and the placement a good fit for the student?

- Have all parties agreed to and signed the practicum and internship contract? Can all parties live up to the specifications in the contract? Does the supervisor hold the appropriate training and experience (e.g., licensed or certified); can the field site supervisor give the required 1 hour of weekly supervision? (This can be an issue!) Be specific and cover all areas of concern.

- All parties should meet to finalize the agreed-upon supervision, beginning and ending dates of the practicum/internship, and how to work out potential student counselor–supervisor conflicts. Then, the student, supervisor, and program representative should sign the contract and make copies for all.

- Students would be wise to read up on the school's or agency's policies and procedures manual. (If it lacks a manual, this is a red flag!) This ensures you understand the "rules" of the placement and provides insights into the agency or school culture.

Exhibit 3.4 Counseling Practicum and Internship Search Checklist

Get a working résumé (if you lack one): Examine your work background for skills, experiences, and interests related to the type of placement you desire. Make sure your résumé is accurate, up to date, and targets the particular area (e.g., school, agency, college counseling center, or correctional facility).

Examining your résumé, what types of experiences do you have that would assist you in doing counseling work? (e.g., Have you been a BA/BS chemical-dependency counselor, case manager, or special education teacher or aide; staffed a collegiate living group as either a resident director [RD] or a resident advisor [RA]; and worked as a camp counselor?) Related experience usually helps when looking for a practicum as it implies you understand the demands of human services work.

Coursework: Be prepared to explain specific courses and additional training you have had that could bolster the case for the school or agency to select you. Have you been trained in diagnosis, treatment planning, assessment, or couples and family counseling? Have you had additional training in creative arts therapy (e.g., dance therapy, art therapy, and music therapy), trauma counseling, mediation, and so forth?

Interests and orientation: What type of setting do you prefer? Inpatient? Outpatient? Elementary, middle, or high school? Would you want a setting

(continued)

Exhibit 3.4 Counseling Practicum and Internship Search Checklist (*continued*)

that provides familiar work or one that offers something new? (For example, if you have been a middle school teacher, would you want to be placed in a middle school counseling office, or would you prefer a different setting?)

Scheduling: Because most graduate students in counseling programs also work, and perhaps have families and numerous other demands, what type of placement would best fit your schedule? For example, if you work day shifts during the week, you may need a placement that offers evening and weekend work. Be realistic regarding time commitments, travel to your placement, academic requirements, and such.

Types of clients: What types of clients are you interested in working with? Examples include age, cultural background, special populations, and so forth. If you are unsure about what types of clients you would like to counsel, you may wish to speak with your academic advisor to clarify your interests.

Ongoing training opportunities: When examining potential placements, does the school, agency, or university counseling center offer in-service training? If so, what types (some placements will provide training on various topics such as DBT, mediation, and play therapy? Some placements will offer training free of charge or at a discount to practicum and internship students.

Theoretical orientation: Do any of the placements you are considering operate on one theoretical approach (e.g., CBT, EMDR, psychodynamic, or a particular spiritual approach)? Consider this issue carefully, as some agencies may not fit well with your values. Is there a potential conflict regarding theoretical approach, spirituality, or something else?

The supervisor: Have you met with or are you familiar with the supervisor? Checking with your faculty advisor and students who have been supervised at a particular school, agency, or college counseling center is a good idea. Also, what type of qualities would you want a supervisor to possess? What type of supervisor would you work best with?

Do you have concerns regarding the placement (or placements) you are considering? Any issues of safety, supervision style, professional fit, and so forth (e.g., does counseling in a prison, psychiatric hospital, or other residential setting with higher risk clients intimidate you?).

Career issues: What are your career goals (e.g., I want to run an addictions treatment clinic)? How well does the placement you are considering fit with your career goal(s)? What types of placements would be most beneficial to your future career plans? (Be aware that your plans may change.)

Additional considerations: What other issues or concerns do you have regarding practicum and internship?

Make sure you have thoroughly examined your résumé and cover letter for typos regarding spelling, correct dates, educational and work history, and so forth. DO NOT LIE ON YOUR RÉSUMÉ OR CV! Present yourself in an appealing, professional, and accurate manner.

This checklist is designed to assist you in planning for the types of field placements that will best fit your background, interests, and orientation.

I also recommend you keep your faculty and placement coordinator updated on the status of your search for a practicum or internship. Your program should be assisting you in this process, but regular updates from you to your placement coordinator are essential. No one wants to be searching for a placement at the last minute prior to the term.

CONCLUSION

Hopefully, what you have read so far has helped you choose and achieve your desired practicum/internship placement. The clinical practicum and internship experience is the backbone of all graduate counseling programs. Most likely, this field experience in a professional clinical setting will be the most significant portion of your graduate training experience. You will naturally encounter clients grappling with a variety of mental health issues and disorders. You will also need to be well versed in your professional code of ethics as this code will be your guide throughout your placements and as a future professional counselor. Chapter 4, "Ethical and Legal Issues," provides a brief overview of common legal and ethical issues you may encounter.

LESSONS LEARNED

"So, you see I really want the placement at Best Clinic (false name). I'm just not interested in interning with an addiction setting," she added with emphasis, shifting about in her seat and crossing her arms as if the very thought was unpleasant. I countered that most students did not get their first choice and that being open to an alternate placement was simply good judgment. "But I want my first choice," she said. The student, a young graduate student of 22 years of age, had matriculated to our CMHC program via our 4+2 program, whereby undergraduate psychology majors with strong grades could enter the 4+2 program and take the first year of our CMHC program as seniors. Kathy (pseudonym) was an excellent student academically, popular socially, and the type of student professors enjoy having in class. She not only was current on the assigned readings, but she also came to class ready to analyze them. She eagerly participated during class discussion and had the respect of her peers as well. Her flexibility on her impending placement, however, was her area of concern. I tried to prepare her for potential disappointment, but she remained steadfast in her desire.

Sometime later, she presented to my office sporting a downcast look. "I didn't get the placement at Best Clinic," she offered, plopping down into the chair. I must confess to harboring a bit of schadenfreude on the matter. Kathy had the unbridled confidence many young, highly intelligent, motivated students possess. I was of the mind that this disappointment might prove good for her. Still, she was upset about this, which to her seemed like an unforeseen setback. Her desired placement has interviewed numerous graduate CMHC and social work students, taking an unusual length of time to advise applicants of their field placement offer or rejection. Kathy had been so certain about success that she had not bothered to apply to another practicum site. Complicating matters, it was the tern of term and she had no placement. Speaking with our placement coordinator, she bluntly informed that addiction settings were the only option.

Having worked as a substance abuse counselor, while simultaneously serving as a mental health counselor, I well understood why many mental health professionals, as well as graduate students, avoid counseling people with addictions: relapse rates are high, those with addiction typically use other drugs as well, trauma is ubiquitous, legal charges are common, and then counselors must administer those unpleasant urinalysis (UA) screenings. The UAs require the counselor to observe the client urinate into a plastic cup. Then, while gloved, the counselor fills out the name and date of test, while feeling the warmth from the client's urine. Due to a lack of male counselors, I had administered many UAs in my career. Having worked a yearlong, undergraduate internship in a public clinic as a senior psychology student, Kathy wanted no part of addiction work. During an uncomfortable hour-long advising session, she fought valiantly against the prospect of serving in an addictions clinic for a full academic year. Feeling frustrated, as well as weary, as Kathy was a real force, I played the only trump card I had: "Look, you either take this placement in addictions or you will wait a full year to go on placement." Delaying placement would add an extra year to her master's degree. Realizing futility at last, she capitulated and agreed to the placement. Leaving my office, she walked like a condemned sailor shuffling toward the end of the plank.

When fall term rolled around, Kathy was in my practicum class. In our 15-week semester, she must have spent 14 weeks of it complaining about the clients ("Smelly"), administration ("Lazy"), the facility ("Dirty"), and her onsite colleagues ("Too busy to help"). However, when it came to her counseling work, she was very game receiving strong evaluations from her supervisor. She did admit to liking her supervisor, an older woman and longtime addictions counselor. Still, Kathy gave all indications of being the type of student who counted the weeks until the end of the academic year, when, emancipated from her indentured servitude, she could celebrate freedom. For my part, I counseled her to cultivate a better attitude and open mind, as she would need a reference from her current supervisor. Kathy nodded, and despite remaining unhappy in her field placement, she weekly put on her best face and trudged into the clinic.

Having been a clinical supervisor for over 30 years and a counselor educator for near 25 years, I have formed some opinions regarding counselor interns and professional counselors. Some counselor adapt quickly to their setting and treatment population, while others struggle mightily. Those in the latter category often change settings or drop from the profession. Kathy, clearly a gifted student and intern, certainly struggled yet somehow managed to channel that anxiety into her clinical work. Despite a persistent despite to change placements, she managed to bracket off her feelings and be present for the clients. Her supervisor offered that Kathy was the best intern she had supervised in many years. Kathy was grateful, but going into the end of the year holiday, she steadfastly maintained the desire to change placement for her final year.

When spring term commenced after the break, the change in Kathy's demeanor was noticeable. She no longer began her sentences with, "Well, you know I don't like addictions counseling, but . . ." Instead, her commentary shifted to a sense of pride that she seemed to be reaching some clients. The psychiatrist, noticing Kathy's keen intelligence and resilience, requested Kathy accompany him on jail visits. Kathy was very proud of this and soon thereafter voiced that her supervisor had spoken with her about continuing the placement into her final year of the program. Kathy, who formerly would have shrugged off the offer (not around her supervisor!), agreed to consider it.

While maintaining she still planned to switch placements, I could tell she was seriously considering the offer. Around mid term, she announced to the practicum class that she would spend her final year at the addiction clinic. In fact, the clinic had offered her a job as an assistant counselor and then hired her as a counselor after graduation! The young graduate student who we practically had to browbeat into her lone placement option, one she accepted under vigorous protest, had now performed the academic version of a backflip and was entering the addictions profession! After the better part of an academic year, she now spoke with pride about embracing the many challenges her placement, new job, required. I have witnessed variations of the attitude turnabout Kathy embodied but rarely with such enthusiasm.

The term marched on until mid-May, ending with graduation of third-year CMHC students, while first- and second-year students moved forward and newly admitted graduate students enthusiastically and nervously anticipated the fall term start in three months. Now hired on staff, Kathy continued as an assistant counselor, assisting professional counselors and related staff, sending me the occasional email that the work was hard, often frustrating, but generally satisfying.

The following fall, she took my internship II course, scarcely resembling the formerly habitually dissatisfied practicum student. Her peers kindly chided her transformation, with Kathy laughing it off as "karma." The following spring, she graduated and entered the ranks as a full-time addictions counselor. Today, she runs an addictions clinic, this woman who had formerly been so adamant about avoiding addictions work. I write this as a preface in reminding anyone reading this text that one simply cannot foresee with certainty the outcome of any particular experience. No doubt, we all have our wants and preferences, occasionally grasping in desperation lest we see our desires slipping away. I think of that Buddhist idea of "keep that don't know self" during such times. Kathy learned the type of lesson forged only through the crucible of a hard-earned experience. Certainly, not all students like Kathy come through the other side with such aplomb.

 A robust set of instructor resources designed to supplement this text is located at http://connect.springerpub.com/content/book/978-0-8261-6607-4. Qualifying instructors may request access by emailing textbook@springerpub.com.

REFERENCES

American Psychiatric Association. (2022). *Diagnostic and statistical manual of mental disorders* (5th ed.). American Psychiatric Publishing.

Arredondo, P., Toporek, M. S., Brown, S. P., Jones, J., Locke, D. C., Sanchez, J., & Stadler, H. (1996). Operationalization of the multicultural counseling competencies. *Journal of Multicultural Counseling and Development, 24*(1), 42–78. https://doi.org/10.1002/j.2161-1912.1996.tb00288.x

Bolles, R. N. (2015). *What color is your parachute? 2016: A practical manual for job-hunters and career-changers*. Ten Speed Press.

Corey, G. (2017). *Theory and practice of counseling and psychotherapy* (10th ed.). Brooks/Cole, Cengage.

Council for Accreditation of Counseling and Related Educational Programs. (2024). *2024 CACREP standards: Section 3: Professional practice*. https://www.cacrep.org/section-3-professional-practice/

Duncan, B., Miller, S. D., Wamplod, B., & Hubble, M. (Eds.). (2010). *The heart and soul of change: Delivering what works in therapy* (2nd ed.). American Psychological Association.

Gladding, S. T. (2009). *Counseling: A comprehensive profession* (6th ed.). Merrill/Prentice Hall.

Herlihy, B., & Corey, G. (Eds.). (2015). *ACA ethical standards casebook* (7th ed.). American Counseling Association.

Hodges, S., & Connelly, A. R. (2010). *A job search manual for counselors and counselor educators: How to navigate and promote your counseling career*. American Counseling Association.

Ivey, A. I., & Ivey, M. B. (2007). *Intentional interviewing and counseling* (6th ed.). Thomson Brooks/Cole.

Remley, T. P., Jr., & Herlihy, B. (2020). *Ethical, legal and professional issues in counseling* (6th ed.). Pearson.

Sue, D. W., Arredondo, P., & McDavis, R. J. (1992). Multicultural counseling competencies and standards: A call to the profession. *Journal of Multicultural Counseling & Development, 20,* 64–88. https://doi.org/10.1002/j.2161-1912.1992.tb00563.x

Wampold, B. E. (2001). *The great psychotherapy debate: Models, methods, and findings*. Lawrence Erlbaum.

Wheeler, A. M., & Bertram, B. (2019). *The counselor and the law: A guide to legal and ethical practice* (8th ed.). American Counseling Association.

CHAPTER 4

Ethical and Legal Issues

INTRODUCTION

Ethical codes have been a part of the medical and healthcare professions for some 3,000 years. Hippocrates, a Greek physician, established the first professional ethical code. His *Hippocratic Oath* is taken by medical school graduates even in the 21st century (Remley & Herlihy, 2020). To protect the public and provide clarity for professionals, professions such as law, psychiatry, social work, and certainly counseling have established ethical codes.

For U.S. counseling students, reading and understanding the 2014 edition of the *ACA Code of Ethics* (American Counseling Association [ACA], 2014) is a vital requirement, as student and professional counselors are ethically and legally bound to follow their ethical code (Remley & Herlihy, 2020; Wheeler & Bertram, 2019). The basic core of the *ACA Code of Ethics* involves a concept known as *beneficence*, or acting in the best interest of the client (Wheeler & Bertram, 2019). Functioning in the client's best interests includes protecting confidentiality, practicing within your scope of competence, avoiding harm, avoiding conflicts of interest regarding your clients, and refraining from sexual and business relationships with clients, to mention a few. Professional counselors face these types of thorny ethical issues and many others on a regular basis. Counselors practicing in various specialty areas must also be familiar with the ethics of their particular specialty (e.g., American School Counselor Association, American Rehabilitation Counseling Association, American Mental Health Counselors Association [AMHCA]). This text focuses primarily on the *ACA Code of Ethics* as it represents the counseling profession's flagship organization. Counseling students in other countries must follow their profession's ethical code.

Beyond the ethical code, counselors must also comply with existing federal and state laws. In fact, an important component of ethical practice is an awareness of state, territory, and federal laws with regard to professional practice (Wheeler & Bertram, 2019). Like ethical codes, state, territorial, and federal laws are in a constant state of flux, influenced by legislative action, court decisions, politics, and societal changes. The landmark *Tarasoff v. The Regents of the University of California Berkeley* (1976) case and the Health Insurance Portability and Accountability Act (HIPAA, 1976) federal legislative action, both of which are discussed in this chapter, illustrate important examples of how legal and legislative decisions influence the counseling profession. Counselors who do not follow state, territorial, and federal laws face prosecution in criminal courts. Furthermore, civil litigation against a counselor may result when the said counselor has breached ethical guidelines such as fraudulent advertising, sexual intimacy with clients, and counselor incompetence. It is no exaggeration to say practicing within ethical and legal parameters is as important in counseling work as is a counselor's clinical skill.

COMPETENT ETHICAL PRACTICE FOR COUNSELORS

The mere reading of ethical standards is not the last word in ethical practice, but rather, it is a commencement. Students in counselor education programs, as well as professional counselors, need ongoing training and consultation regarding competent ethical and legal practice, as ethics, laws, and technological advances impact the profession. The most basic ethical requirement is that counselors "practice only within the boundaries of their competence" (ACA, 2014, Section C.2.a). But, how precisely can a counselor exactly determine their parameter of competence? It is difficult to answer this question because counseling is a very broad profession involving inpatient, outpatient, addictions, college and university counseling, rehabilitation counseling, school counseling, relationship counseling, and so on, and many of these specialty areas are vastly different in the scope of responsibility. However, just as an attorney could never be competent in every area of law (no matter what those large billboard ads might suggest!), counselors could never be competent to offer services in all therapeutic areas and counseling disciplines (Barnett & Johnson, 2015). A counselor who is skilled in treating individuals may not be adequately trained and competent in counseling families. Counselors who are very adept in counseling adult clients with severe mental disorders may not be competent in counseling elementary school children. The critical issue for all counselors, regardless of area, is to have adequate education, training, experience, supervision, proper licensure and/or certification, ongoing continuing education, and so forth. Naturally, no license, certification, registration, or degree can guarantee competence, but valid credentials (advanced degree, license, registration, and certification) suggest competence. All counselors must understand that striving for competence is a lifelong endeavor involving ongoing training, supervision, consultation, and self-reflection (Corey et al., 2015; Remley & Herlihy, 2020).

Competence is a serious legal and ethical issue because society expects professionals to be competent and asserts this standard through state-licensing boards, professional ethical codes, and the legal system (Wheeler & Bertram, 2019). Counselor competence is the second most frequently reported area of ethical complaint after sexual misconduct (Corey et al., 2015; Neukrug et al., 2001). Therefore, students reading this text must begin carefully considering this critical issue of counselor competence, as it will be the primary consideration in the remainder of your counseling career. Interestingly, competence is not defined in the *ACA Code of Ethics* and there is no precise standard certifying counselor competence. However, the *ACA Code of Ethics* (ACA, 2014) recommends consultation (Standard C.2.e.) and peer supervision (Standard C.2.d.) as means to evaluate one's ongoing effectiveness as a counselor. Continuous self-monitoring, self-assessment, and self-reflection also assist with developing and maintaining competence

(Johnson et al., 2012). Continued professional education throughout one's professional lifetime is an ethical necessity and is required by most state and territorial licensure boards. Competence in ethical practice is therefore a continuous project that constantly in a state of becoming due to ethical revisions, legal rulings, and technology and is never a finished project. Consequently, all counselors must be lifelong learners in order to maintain competence and keep current with a dynamic profession.

HEALTH INSURANCE PORTABILITY AND ACCOUNTABILITY ACT

One of the most far-reaching and influential congressional legislative actions with regard to the health and mental health field is HIPAA. Congress passed this sweeping legislation in 1996 to ensure people would be able to maintain insurance coverage when changing jobs and in response to concerns of privacy regarding the electronic transfer of records (Remley & Herlihy, 2020; Wheeler & Bertram, 2019). Counselors' and other mental health professionals' billing insurance must comply with HIPAA (1996) standards. HIPAA established a variety of standards to ensure privacy when storing and transmitting patient data. The law came about of concern that transmission of healthcare information via the internet and additional electronic means could lead to widespread problems in the protection of patient and client privacy. HIPAA also applies to healthcare information sent by traditional paper means.

Given that inpatient and outpatient agency practicum and internship sites in the United States will be subject to HIPAA regulations, it is very important that counseling students understand it. Naturally, your faculty and field site supervisors will likely provide both training and oversight regarding HIPAA and other federal policies influencing professional practice. Still, it is a good professional practice to be proactive and read the HIPAA requirements. You may visit the HIPAA website (https://aspe.hhs.gov). In addition, professional counseling organizations, such as the ACA, AMHCA, and others, periodically offer training in HIPAA compliance. The monthly periodical *Counseling Today* frequently offers information on maintaining HIPAA compliance.

INFORMED CONSENT

Informed consent means that clients must know and understand basic issues about the process of counseling: their legal rights, counselor responsibilities, fees charged, counselor training, counselor's theoretical approach to counseling, client access to records, confidentiality, and how to register formal complaints, among other concerns. The counseling relationship involves personal disclosure and is built on the foundation of trust, which provides a context for ongoing therapy (Pope & Vasquez, 2011). With rare exception, clients are not experts in the mental health arena and, of necessity, rely on their counselors to provide them with the information necessary to become active participants in therapy and make informed choices (Handelsman, 2001; Herlihy & Corey, 2015). Informed consent basically stipulates the rules of counseling for both the counselor and the client(s) and must be articulated before counseling services commence. Failure to adequately inform clients of their rights and counselor's responsibilities is substandard ethical practice and potentially puts the counselor and the school or agency in legal jeopardy (Wheeler & Bertram, 2019).

During informed consent, counselors must provide the client with information pertinent to the counseling relationship. As stated earlier, this includes fees, counselor training, and such but also outlines the client's rights and responsibilities, including provisions for mandated clients, the client's right to terminate counseling, expectations (e.g., the client and counselor are both punctual and fees are paid on time), emergency plans for counselor vacation and after-hours coverage, and so forth. Written documentation of these issues is critical, given possible liability issues (Wheeler & Bertram, 2019). In fact, HIPAA (1996) requires written documentation of informed consent (Madden, 1998). Counselors in the field should provide clients with a document outlining informed consent with a place for clients to sign and date, indicating they have read and understood the document. Client's understanding of informed consent is impacted by numerous factors such as age, education, mandated versus voluntary status, intellectual impairment, and cultural differences, to mention a few. It also is important to remain open to an alternative means of dispensing informed consent such as an interpreter or translator (Wheeler & Bertram, 2019). The critical issue is for counselors to do everything within reason to ensure clients have understood informed consent. After reviewing informed consent with clients, prudent counselors should ask clients if they have questions. My own experience is clients often do what many of us do at our doctor's office when presented forms: skip reading and sign with aplomb! As much as is reasonable, ensure clients understand what they are signing by asking them, "Do you understand?" and "What questions might you have about informed consent?" Furthermore, encourage them to ask questions anytime they are unclear about their rights.

It is worth noting that informed consent in couples, family, and group counseling is more complex than in individual therapy. Most important for the client to understand is that confidentiality cannot be guaranteed when there is more than one client in the session (Remley & Herlihy, 2020; Wheeler & Bertram, 2019). Counselors in group, family, or couples counseling must carefully explain the nature of counseling and how and why confidentiality is critical to the therapeutic process. As confidentiality cannot be guaranteed in group, family, or couples counseling, counselors must also work with groups, couples, and families to determine how a breach of confidentiality might be addressed.

The *ACA Code of Ethics* (ACA, 2014, Section A.2.b) outlines the information to be discussed with the client when obtaining informed consent:

- the purpose, goals, techniques, procedures, limitations, potential risks, and benefits of counseling services

- the counselor's qualifications, including relevant degrees held, licenses and certifications, areas of specialization, and relevant experience

- arrangements for continuation of services should the counselor become unable to continue counseling

- the implications of the *Diagnostic and Statistical Manual of Mental Disorders,* Fifth Edition, Text Revision (*DSM-5-TR;* American Psychiatric Association, 2022) diagnosis, use of assessments, and reports.

- fees and billing information (generally not applicable in schools and most college or university counseling centers)
- confidentiality and its limits
- the client's right to inspect their record and to participate in counseling treatment
- the client's right to refuse any recommended services or modality change and be advised of the consequences of refusal especially with regard to legally mandated clients

In addition to the issues suggested by the *ACA Code of Ethics*, numerous counseling professionals have recommended that additional information be included such as

- a description of the counselor's theoretical orientation (written in clear language the client can understand) or a brief statement regarding the counselor's philosophical approach to counseling (Corey et al., 2015);
- information regarding the logistics of counseling, such as length and frequency of sessions, procedures for making and canceling appointments, policies regarding phone contact between sessions, and how to contact the counselor in the event of an emergency;
- information regarding insurance reimbursement, including the fact that any diagnosis assigned will likely become part of the client's permanent health record and the risks inherent with this (Welfel, 2012);
- information alternatives to counseling, such as 12-step programs, peer support groups, self-help books, medication information, and other supportive services;
- when applicable, a statement regarding video or audio taping, along with a statement that the client's case may be discussed with the clinical supervisor or a consultant (Corey et al., 2015); and
- the client's recourse if dissatisfied with counseling services, including names and contact information for supervisors and addresses and phone numbers of licensing boards and professional organizations (Remley & Herlihy, 2020; Welfel, 2012).

Exhibit 4.1 offers a sample informed consent form that a client might sign.

Exhibit 4.1 Informed Consent Form for Counseling Clients

Jane Doe, MS, LMHC, NCC

1719 Freud Lane

Therapy, NY 10017

jane.doe@aol.com

Phone: (123) 456-7890

(continued)

80 • THE COUNSELING PRACTICUM AND INTERNSHIP MANUAL

Exhibit 4.1 Informed Consent Form for Counseling Clients (*continued*)

My Qualifications

My practice includes counseling with children, adolescents, and couples. I am also a New York State certified mediator. I hold a master's degree in mental health counseling and I am a licensed mental health counselor (LMHC) and a national certified counselor (NCC). I have postgraduate training in cognitive behavioral therapy from the Beck Institute in Philadelphia. My postgraduate experience includes 15 years as a community mental health counselor and I hold memberships in the ACA and the AMHCA.

The clinic's fees are set by your insurance carrier, so you want to consult your carrier for any questions. For uninsured clients, we offer a sliding fee scale with minimum fees set equal to the lowest billable insurance carrier ($60.00 per session). Most insurance carriers will allow eight to 10 sessions.

The General Course of Counseling

I appreciate that you have come to our clinic and I want to be thorough and specific in helping you achieve the goals you have set. My job is to provide assessment and counseling and work conjointly with you to set treatment goals. It is true that in counseling, success depends on the client actively wanting to change. Counseling is not an exact science, and at times, the counselor, in consultation with you, may need to revise the goals of treatment. Some assessment will be carried out at the intake time and other assessments may be added later for further clarification. Unless otherwise stated, all counseling sessions are 50 minutes long.

If you have been mandated for treatment to this agency, you will be required to sign a *Release of Information Form*, so this counselor and the agency can provide necessary information to the agency, parole officer, court, or other officials that mandated your treatment.

Anytime you have questions regarding your treatment, please feel free to ask.

Recordkeeping and Confidentiality

Ethically and legally, I am required to keep records of all our contacts. Legally, you have the right to see all information generated between us. You must provide explicit permission for information to be revealed, unless the law specifies otherwise (see exceptions to confidentiality). Thus, with your written consent, I will provide information to anyone with a legitimate need. You are also entitled to a copy of any records generated in this office. This clinic keeps records for 10 years past the last date of contact. Then, because of space and privacy concerns, records are destroyed in compliance with state law and professional ethics.

Exceptions to Confidentiality

The following are general legal/ethical exceptions to confidentiality (check with your state, territory, or province as there is variation):

(continued)

Exhibit 4.1 Informed Consent Form for Counseling Clients (*continued*)

- when child abuse/neglect is suspected
- when elder abuse is suspected
- in the case of imminent danger to self or others
- in the event of a clear and specified threat to a third party
- if a life-threatening contagious disease threatens a third party (e.g., AIDS and HIV)
- when a client provides written permission (i.e., Release of Information Form)
- if a judge mandates a release of information
- if a client sues a counselor or makes false charges against a counselor

Client as Consumer

As a client in counseling, you are encouraged to participate actively and fully in your own treatment. Many counselors will assign homework activities, reading, and so forth. You are encouraged to follow-through with as many homework assignments as possible. In addition, keep your counselor apprised when you cannot complete out-of-session assignments so that the two of you can make a new plan. Also, if you feel you do not fully understand something, ask your counselor for clarification. Clients who take an active approach to their treatment are likely to make more therapeutic progress than those who are passive.

Your Rights as a Client

Although you are encouraged to discuss the issues with your counselor first, if for any reason you believe your rights have been violated, you have a right to file a grievance.

For Ethical Issues

American Counseling Association (ACA)
5999 Stevenson Ave.
Alexandria, VA 22304
1-800-347-6647 (×314)

New York State Board for Mental Health Counselors
State Education Department
Office of the Professions
89 Washington Ave.
Albany, NY 12234-1000
www.op.nysed.gov

I have read and understand all information presented here in the informed consent document.

_____

Name   Date

CONFIDENTIALITY AND PRIVILEGED COMMUNICATION

The effectiveness of the counselor–client relationship is constructed upon trust. Confidentiality is the cornerstone of counseling and arguably the most important ethical concept in the delivery of counseling services. Without confidentiality, clients would be far less likely to disclose personal or sensitive information, and many would refrain from seeking counseling services entirely (Herlihy & Corey, 2015; Miller & Thelan, 1986; Remley & Herlihy, 2020; Wheeler & Bertram, 2019). Within the mental health profession, confidentiality is essential to the counseling relationship. Clients need to know that their counselors will respect their privacy, whereas counselors know that the foundation of an effective counseling relationship is built on trust. Clients involved in a deeply personal relationship like counseling have the right to expect that what they divulge in sessions is kept private (Corey et al., 2015; Herlihy & Corey, 2015; Wheeler & Bertram, 2019). Naturally, concerns regarding a counselor's ability to protect the right of confidentiality frequently emerge. However, complaints against counselors for breach of confidentiality are actually quite rare. Various studies have shown that less than 5% of complaints to ethics boards involve a breach of confidentiality (Garcia et al., 1995; Pope & Vasquez, 1998, 2011).

On the other hand, in one study, 62% of psychologists surveyed reported that they had unintentionally violated their clients' confidentiality (Pope et al., 1988). Some of the unintentional violations of confidentiality are listed here:

- *Sending confidential information through the internet:* Web-based counseling presents serious challenges to privacy due to hacking concerns.

- *Violations through email exchanges:* Counselors and clients should always assume email is not a confidential method of information delivery and should refrain from disclosing names, personal information, and other data in email.

- *Violations via text message:* Before texting a client, ensure this is a secure and acceptable means of transmitting messages. Text message should be brief and coded so that only the counselor and client understand them.

- *Violations over the telephone:* Telephone transmission of information may not be secure, particularly transmission using mobile phones.

- *Violations via fax:* Client information frequently is faxed from one organization to another; given how busy most offices are, confidential information can easily be passed on.

- *Confidential information left on answering machines:* Counselors in private practice should use an answering service and refrain from leaving any details on an answering machine.

- *Discussing cases in insecure locations:* Remley and Herlihy (2020) relate a story of two counselors discussing a client in a crowded elevator, only to discover that the client was standing behind them!

- *Completing confidential documentation in public places:* Once while sitting in a coffee shop, I noticed the woman at the table next to me was writing her case notes and seemed untroubled by the look of astonishment on my face. Make sure you take the same precautions in documentation as you take when counseling and do it behind closed doors.

Clearly, there are many ways counselors can unintentionally violate a client's confidentiality. Graduate students in counseling programs must be very diligent in maintaining client privacy. Although it is natural for students to want to debrief with one another, bear in mind your ethical obligations are the same as those of professional counselors (ACA, 2014, Section F.8.a). Your communications must not reveal any sensitive information that would allow third parties to readily identify clients. Case notes, assessments, and recordings of sessions must be stored in secure locations with access limited to faculty and on-site clinical supervisors. Remember, confidentiality is an ethical duty to maintain a client's privacy, itself a legal requirement (Wheeler & Bertram, 2019). A counselor may be sued for failure to protect a client's privacy unless the counselor is breaching confidentiality in a manner recognized by law (e.g., written authorization by the client, serious threat and foreseeable harm against self or others, or release of information required by minor abuse or as otherwise compelled by the law; Wheeler & Bertram, 2019).

Privileged Communication

The legal concept of *privileged communication* refers to any conversation that takes place within a protected relationship, such as that between an attorney and a client (Wheeler & Bertram, 2019). The law often protects against forced disclosure of such conversations, although there are exceptions. In most states, counselor–client communications are protected from disclosure similar to that of physician–patient or attorney–client communications. More importantly, the privilege applies when the counselor is called as a witness in an administrative hearing or courtroom (Wheeler & Bertram, 2019). Counselors should understand, however, that the privilege usually belongs to the client (the holder of the privilege) and not the counselor, although the counselor is charged with the responsibility of protecting the privilege (Wheeler & Bertram, 2019).

The application of privileged communication to the mental health field arose in the groundbreaking legal case *Jaffee v. Redmond et al.* (1996), which was the first U.S. Supreme Court case to uphold the concept of a psychotherapist–patient privilege in federal court. In the *Jaffee* case, a policewoman sought counseling from a licensed social worker after she fatally shot a suspect during a stabbing incident. The family of the decedent sued the police officer, police department, and the city, alleging the use of deadly force was in violation of the suspect's civil rights. In legal proceedings, the plaintiffs learned that the police officer had been in counseling and sought to compel the social worker to testify at the trial and turn over case notes and records on her counseling sessions with the officer. The case made went through the appellate process, eventually winding up at the U.S. Supreme Court. The Supreme Court ruled the social worker could not be compelled to reveal the private records of her sessions with the police officer. The case was the first to uphold the concept of psychotherapist–patient privilege that applied to psychiatrists, psychologists, social workers, counselors, and other mental health professionals.

Counselors should be aware, however, that the *Jaffee* decision applied to federal courts and that not all states expressively grant counselor–client privilege in state court proceedings. Counselors who are subpoenaed should always seek the advice of their supervisor and/or that of their legal counsel. Counselors should never simply comply with a subpoena, as doing so may constitute a violation of confidentiality and privacy

(Remley & Herlihy, 2020; Wheeler & Bertram, 2019). Now, a counselor cannot simply ignore a subpoena either, as that could result in legal charges against the counselor. Rather, counselors must contact their attorney and facilitate legal counsel working with the judge to address the subpoena. The judge may quash the entire subpoena or rule limited, specified information be released. Again, for those counseling students studying outside the United States, seek guidance from your faculty for guidance on limitations to privileged communication and confidentiality.

Exceptions to Confidentiality

Confidentiality is not an absolute or static concept, as courts and legislative actions are constantly reshaping its parameters (Wheeler & Bertram, 2019). Federal guidelines such as HIPAA also proscribe permissible exceptions to confidentiality. As was stated previously, clients should be made aware at the beginning of the counseling relationship of the legal limits of confidentiality (Wheeler & Bertram, 2019). It is important to discuss the occasions in which confidentiality may be breached because clients may not be aware that confidentiality is not absolute. Counseling students may fear that enumerating the limits of confidentiality could inhibit a client's disclosure, although this does not appear to be a realistic concern (Baird & Rupert, 1987).

There are several general and common exceptions to confidentiality (Remley & Herlihy, 2020; Wheeler & Bertram, 2019):

- in cases of suspected abuse or neglect (child abuse, elder abuse, and vulnerable populations)
- when the client is a danger to self
- when the client is a danger to others
- clients planning future crimes
- legal proceedings when counseling records may be subpoenaed (this would include a former client suing a former counselor, in which case the client could not assert privileged communication)
- when a client has signed a release of information
- when the client is a minor, confidentiality would go to the parent or guardian.
- clients with serious communicable diseases (e.g., HIV and AIDS)

Note: Counseling students studying and practicing outside the United States should seek advice from their faculty and professional counseling associations. Laws can vary considerably across borders.

Suspected Abuse

In most states, mandated reporting of suspected abuse laws has been enacted to cover teachers, healthcare workers, and mental health professionals (Remley & Herlihy, 2020). This law generally applies in cases of suspected child abuse or neglect, although in some states, it applies to other vulnerable populations such as the elderly or the disabled (Wheeler & Bertram, 2019). Under mandated reporting statutes, if a child tells a counselor that they are being physically or sexually abused (bruises or other injuries indicative of abuse or if the counselor has other reasons to believe a child is being physically, sexually, or emotionally abused), the counselor is required to notify the appropriate authorities (typically a department for child welfare or children's services). Counselors employing *good faith* reporting of suspected child abuse receive protection from litigation (Wheeler & Bertram, 2019).

After a report is made, a caseworker will be assigned to investigate. If the caseworker determines probable cause for abuse or neglect, they will refer the case to local law enforcement authorities. If, after an investigation, the authorities determine that abuse is occurring, the next step may be legal action for criminal prosecution of the abuser(s) or civil action to determine the best placement for the child's welfare. In many cases, the child will be removed from the home for a period (and in some cases, permanently). Child abuse and neglect are discussed further in Chapter 9, "Crisis Intervention in Practicum/Internship."

Suspected Child Abuse: A Reality Check

Students in counseling programs should be aware of the delicate issues involving child abuse and neglect. Children removed from the home for suspected parental abuse or neglect are also at risk for neglect and abuse from an overburdened foster care situation. Furthermore, in most cases, my experience is that the child often is returned to their abusive or neglectful home. There are not enough foster care placements available (and many are not viable ones), and residential care options (e.g., orphanages, senior care centers, and residential treatment facilities) are expensive in the long term, with society reluctant to pay additional taxes to support long-term residential placements. Reporting suspected child abuse, while required, is no panacea and no guarantee that the system will be able to protect the child. Complicating the foster care issue, children often prefer to remain with their abusive or neglectful family. Reasons for this are it is their family and they know and understand their current abusers/neglectors and do not know or understand new ones (e.g., the devil you know versus the one you do not).

Danger to Self and Others

Probably the most common situation in which a counselor will be required to breach confidentiality arises when a client makes direct and specific threats of suicide or of harm to a third party. The legal and ethical issues that arise in these situations are discussed in the landmark *Tarasoff* case (*Tarasoff v. The Regents of the University of California Berkeley*, 1976). The case began when a psychologist at the university counseling center received a viable threat from a student client. Prosenjit Podder informed his psychologist that he intended to kill his former girlfriend (Tatiana Tarasoff) when she returned from overseas. The psychologist reported the student's threat to the university police, who briefly detained him for questioning but then released him when he promised to have no contact with Tarasoff when she returned to the United States. The psychologist also reported his concerns to his supervisor, a psychiatrist who deemed no further action be taken as Podder did not meet state civil commitment criteria. Tragically, when Ms. Tarasoff returned to campus, Mr. Podder murdered her. The Tarasoff family sued the psychologist, psychiatrist, university counseling center, campus police, and the university's Board of Regents, claiming no one from U.C. Berkeley notified them of the danger. The Supreme Court decided that specific responsibilities and obligations arise on the therapist's part from the special counselor–client relationship and that this relationship may create additional responsibility on the part of the counselor. Specifically, the Supreme Court ruled:

> Once a therapist does in fact determine, or under applicable professional standards reasonably should have determined, that a patient poses a serious danger of violence to others, he bears a duty to exercise reasonable care to protect the foreseeable victim of that danger. (*Tarasoff v. Regents of University of California*, 1974, p. 345)

Thus, the *Tarasoff* court decision creates a duty to warn and protect identifiable third parties of serious and foreseeable danger (Wheeler & Bertram, 2019). For counselors, this landmark decision is akin to the legal profession's Miranda decision (i.e., the right to remain silent), as therapists in all except two states must adhere to its specifications.

Not all threats of violence may be serious ones; however, if a client makes an explicit threat regarding violence and has a plan to achieve it, then the *Tarasoff* case would definitely apply. If a client discloses thoughts, feelings, or intentions that place the client or an identifiable third party at risk, you must document the threat and the appropriate action taken, as well as notify the proper authorities. Competent documentation is essential in crisis situations, as they may ultimately involve the legal system. Should a case proceed to court for an involuntary commitment to a psychiatric or correctional facility, the case record will be carefully scrutinized by lawyers, the judge, and other professionals. You want to demonstrate in writing that you were thorough in your counseling, assessment, and decision-making and that you did everything possible to ensure the client's safety. (Working with potentially violent or suicidal clients is discussed in more detail in Chapter 9, "Crisis Intervention in Practicum/Internship.") A good maxim to remember is "If it ain't written down, it didn't happen the way you say." Effective prose backing sound decision-making may be what saves your professional reputation, if not staving off litigation. Poor documentation, conversely, may be harmful to your reputation and your client's treatment. Interestingly, counseling programs the world over likely put much emphasis on sound clinical and ethical training. My experience is far less emphasis goes into writing effective case notes, despite such possibly being as important as efficacious therapy, particularly as case notes verify treatment practice and plans.

Some state courts have issued legal decisions that limit or contradict the *Tarasoff* ruling. In Florida's *Boynton v. Burglass* (1991), counselors may breach confidentiality to prevent imminent harm, but they are *not* legally mandated to do so (Wheeler & Bertram, 2019). The case originally pertained to a psychiatrist but the *Boynton* judge clarified that the ruling applied to *all* psychotherapists. Therefore, in Florida, counselors may breach confidentiality to prevent clear and imminent harm to someone, but there is no mandatory duty as exists under the landmark *Tarasoff* decision. Florida law grants immunity for counselors breaching confidentiality in good faith (e.g., danger to self or others and with written permission). Counselors in Florida, however, should be mindful of new case law that may further define the scope of duty to warn and protect (Wheeler & Bertram, 2019).

Texas also declined to adopt the *Tarasoff* ruling. In 1999, the Texas Supreme Court held in the *Thapar v. Zezulka* case that counselors have no common law duty to warn readily identifiable third parties of a threat against them. By statute, Texas counselors are permitted to make disclosures to law enforcement or medical personnel in situations where there is an identifiable risk of imminent injury. However, there is no specific grant of immunity built into the Texas statute, which could create a decision-making challenge for the counselor (Wheeler & Bertram, 2019). The bottom line, of course, is for counselors to know and operate within the laws of their respective state or territory and seek clarification from supervisors or legal counsel when they are unsure of legal ramifications.

Clients Planning Future Crimes

Most legal cases impose liability on a counselor for failure to warn and protect a third party only when there is resulting personal injury (Wheeler & Bertram, 2019). However, the Vermont Supreme Court ruled that the *Tarasoff* duty could also apply in a property damage case. In *Peck v. Counseling Services of Addison County, Inc.* (1985), a client informed his counselor he planned to burn down his father's barn. But, under exploration of the issue, he then promised the counselor he would not commit the arson. However, the client did in fact burn down the barn, whereupon the client's father sued for damages. The Vermont Supreme Court ruled arson could pose a grave risk to human life and animal life and that property damage was a compelling reason to breach confidentiality and ruled for the plaintiff and against the counselor and her agency. Thus, in some states, *Tarasoff* carries an expanded duty to warn and protect for counselors.

If a client discloses that they are planning to commit future crimes, the law requires counselors to disclose this information in 17 states when the client is under investigation by law enforcement officials (Glosoff et al., 2000; Wheeler & Bertram, 2019). These states are Alaska, Arizona, Idaho, Illinois, Indiana, Kansas, Louisiana, Massachusetts, Montana, New Mexico, Oklahoma, Oregon, South Carolina, South Dakota, Tennessee, and Washington, as well as the District of Columbia (as of 2023). Types of criminal activity included in this exception are the distribution of controlled substances, selling stolen goods, and fraudulent schemes (Welfel, 2012). Counselors confronted by such circumstances should confer with their supervisor and legal representative to ensure compliance with the law and their professional ethics. Counselors working in Canada likewise have a Tarasoff duty to warn and protect (Sheppard, n.d.).

Legal Proceedings

Typical legal proceedings in which counselors may encounter forced disclosure involve cases of suspected child abuse, child custody, and civil litigation against counselors (Remley & Herlihy, 2020). In such cases, the counselor may be subpoenaed by an attorney to provide information from counseling sessions with a client. In the event you receive a subpoena to appear at a legal proceeding but no mention is made of records, do not take records with you unless instructed to do so by your attorney (Remley & Herlihy, 2020). When a subpoena is issued to you by a lawyer, your first step is to consult your supervisor. Your supervisor (or you if you are the supervisor) should consult with the attorney to determine whether the subpoena is valid and whether you should respond (Remley & Herlihy , 2020; Wheeler & Bertram, 2019). An attorney will review the subpoena and advise you what steps need to be taken. For example, the attorney could ask the lawyer who issued the subpoena to withdraw it, file a motion with the court to quash the subpoena, or advise you to comply with the subpoena. The critical point here is *do not attempt to deal with a subpoena without legal advice from an attorney.*

When a former client brings a case against a former counselor, the client's records no longer fall under the protection of "privileged" as discussed previously (Wheeler & Bertram, 2019). In such cases, counseling records are considered evidence necessary to establish the legal facts of the case. If a client decides to file an ethical complaint against a counselor or sue a counselor for any reason, the client must waive the right to confidentiality. This provides the counselor the opportunity to defend themselves against the client's claims.

In any case of forced disclosure, counselors must seek legal advice from competent counsel. Schools, agencies, hospitals, and other institutions all retain attorneys who will be able to deal appropriately with the subpoena. If you receive a subpoena (which is unlikely but *could* happen), report it immediately to your supervisor. Given the possibility that counseling records could be subpoenaed, however, it behooves counselors to be judicious in what they write in the records. Should any counselor or graduate counseling student be subpoenaed, their written records (e.g., case notes) are likely what will be called into question. Chapter 6, "Clinical Writing and Documentation in Counseling Records," discusses ways to take effective and comprehensive case notes.

Client Release of Information

This exception is based on the client's right to release information. The *ACA Code of Ethics* states, "Unless exceptions to confidentiality exist, counselors obtain written information from clients to disclose or transfer records to legitimate third parties. Steps are taken to ensure that receivers of counseling records are sensitive to their confidential nature" (ACA, 2014, Section B.6.g). Many clients in counseling will waive this right, especially when insurance reimbursement is concerned. Still, counselors must be certain to educate clients regarding written release of records and document such actions. (*Note:* Documentation, particularly in counseling services, clearly is the "devil in the details.")

A release from confidentiality does not give a counselor approval to release client information to anyone but rather to specified third parties who would have a legitimate need to know said contents. Additionally, the counselor must establish whether that third party will be able to respect the client's sensitive information. If the counselor has any hesitation about the wisdom of releasing the client's information to a particular person, the counselor should discuss their concerns with the client so that the client can make an informed decision. Remember, a client under distress may not be making sound judgments, and counselors must consider this accordingly.

Minor Clients or Legally Incompetent Clients

Issues of confidentiality and privileged communication become much more complicated when minor clients or incompetent adults are involved. Minors and legally incompetent adults cannot enter into legal contracts. Thus, their parents or guardians essentially make legal decisions for them (in loco parentis). Counselors must balance the rights of minor clients and incompetent adults with their parents' or guardians' need to know regarding the specifics of counseling sessions (Remley & Herlihy, 2020). At the same time, however, counselors have ethical obligations to such clients themselves (ACA, 2014, Section B.5.a). These issues can be particularly problematic in school settings, where the counselor also has the added responsibility of working within the framework of school district policies and their own school's principal.

There are also significant legal variations across states and territories. For example, the definition of *minor* varies; in many states, adulthood begins at 18 years of age, but in some, it is 19 or 21 years (Wheeler & Bertram, 2019). Furthermore, some states provide that 16-year-olds can withhold certain information from their parents, such as the use of birth control. The variations among state laws certainly make for challenging and confusing situations for counselors. Because of the complexities involved, Gustafson and McNamara (1987) recommended that therapists should create a written protocol that explicitly states the conditions of and limits to confidentiality in counseling minor clients. This protocol would be reviewed with each minor client involved, signed, and kept in the record. Providing a written record reduces the potential for confusion and protects the counselor, school, agency, or other party that may be involved should legal issues arise.

It is also worth mentioning that legal issues involving minors usually also involve their parents or legal guardians. Parents and guardians should also be aware of the parameters of confidentiality with regard to their children's therapy. Interestingly, while minor children cannot enter into contracts, school counselors evidently do not need parental or guardian permission to counsel school children (Remley & Herlihy, 2020). For example, parents may inform the school counselor or principal that they do not want their daughter seeing the counselor. But if the principal and counselor have good reason to believe the child needs counseling, they could proceed with counseling. Although counseling against parental wishes might seem insensitive, there may be compelling reasons for doing so. For example, I can recall one case where a father did not want his daughter receiving counseling. The school principal and counselor went against the father's wishes, citing the minor daughter's depressed and withdrawn behavior. During a session with the school counselor, the daughter disclosed that her father had been sexually abusing her.

Clients With Serious Communicable Diseases

Counseling clients with serious communicable illnesses raises several ethical and legal issues. Significant concerns for counselors involve confidentiality of client disclosures, the risk of discrimination against clients if their health status is not protected, and the welfare of third parties at risk for infection because of contact with the client (Welfel, 2012).

Mandated disclosure regarding communicable diseases is one of the more recent ethical and legal issues the mental health profession has faced and perhaps the most controversial because legal scholars continue to debate the merits of disclosure in this arena (Anderson & Barret, 2001; Harding et al., 1993; Wheeler & Bertram, 2019). The *ACA Code of Ethics* outlines guidelines for counselors regarding disclosure in cases of communicable diseases:

> When clients disclose that they have a disease commonly known to be both communicable and life threatening, counselors may be justified in disclosing information to identifiable third parties, if the parties are known to be at serious and foreseeable risk of contracting the disease. Prior to making a disclosure, counselors assess the intent of clients to inform the third parties about their disease or to engage in any behaviors that may be harmful to an identifiable third party. Counselors adhere to relevant state laws concerning disclosure about disease status. (ACA, 2014, Section B.2.c)

A gray area in most state laws covering communicable diseases refers to mandated disclosure by physicians and other healthcare providers and is often vague on the responsibilities of mental health professionals (Welfel, 2012). Furthermore, state laws on mandated disclosure of serious communicable illnesses vary widely. Most states allow or demand disclosure in cases of serious communicable illnesses, although some states mandate privacy for the client. In states that mandate privacy, a counselor could potentially be sued for disclosure to third parties (Welfel, 2012). Given such complexities and varying laws regarding disclosure in this arena, counselors must seek legal advice about the regulations that govern mandated disclosure and privacy.

Given the nature of serious, communicable diseases, the counselor might contact the local public health agency should the client refuse to identify their partner's name and contact information. The counselor might refer the client to a physician, but the client can always refuse to take the referral. A counselor might encourage the client call their partner during session and make the disclosure while under therapeutic support. Another variation is for the counselor to suggest the client bring the partner to the following session. Given the ongoing COVID-19 pandemic, serious and communicable diseases are a constant reality to address.

An added note regarding potentially contagious, life-threatening diseases is that the *ACA Code of Ethics* has made a significant change from the 2005 edition. Previously, the ethical code read: "Prior to making a disclosure, counselors confirm that there is such a diagnosis . . ." (ACA, 2005, Section B.2.b). When my colleagues and I on the 2014 Ethics Revision Task Force reviewed and revised the Code, we realized the impossibility of confirming such a diagnosis. For example, it is unlikely a physician would disclose such to a third party absent a legal mandate to do so, given HIPAA regulations. Second, the client may refuse to disclose the name of their physician. The language in the 2014 revision seems to me (naturally) a more functional one.

Counseling Terminally Ill Clients

Counselors working with terminally ill clients, whether in hospice or other agencies, may face several ethical, legal, moral, and spiritual issues. Terminally ill clients whose pain and suffering are intense may wish to examine the option of euthanasia during counseling sessions. The topic of "rational" suicide (Humphrey, 1996) raises many complex issues: Are counselors under the same obligation to prevent terminally ill clients from committing suicide as they would other suicides (see Case Study 4.1)? Does a terminal diagnosis actually change the counselor's duty to warn and protect? Does a client have a right to die? Are clients who wish to hasten their own death considered rational, or should they be considered mentally ill? The 2005 edition of the *ACA Code of Ethics* discussed the matter at length:

Counselor Competence, Choice, and Referral. Recognizing the personal, moral, and competence issues related to end-of-life decisions, counselors may choose to work or not work with terminally ill clients who wish to explore their end-of-life options. Counselors provide appropriate referral information to ensure that clients receive the necessary help.

Confidentiality. Counselors who provide services to terminally ill individuals who are considering their own deaths have the option of breaking or not breaking confidentiality depending on the specific circumstances of the situation and after seeking consultation or supervision (ACA, 2005, Section A.9).

Case Study 4.1 The Case of Harriet: The Counselor's Role Regarding Terminally Ill Patients and Suicide

Harriet is a 70-year-old former advertising executive who has lived a full and active life. An all-conference cross-country runner in college, she completed numerous marathons, half-marathons, and other athletic events. She was married and raised three children and has eight grandchildren. Harriet, a widow, was diagnosed with inoperable liver cancer and was given 6 months to live. She seeks counseling services from Malcolm to help her address end-of-life issues. After a couple of sessions, Harriet states that she will discontinue debilitating radiation and chemotherapy treatments; she goes on to say that if the pain becomes too unbearable, she will take her life. Malcolm wishes to continue counseling Harriet but decides he must break confidentiality should Harriet disclose a suicide plan.

1. What do you think about Malcolm's decision? Do you agree? Disagree? Why?
2. Are Malcolm's actions defendable on ethical, legal, and/or moral grounds?
3. In your opinion, what is in Harriet's best interests?
4. If Malcolm approached you for consultation regarding Harriet, how might you advise him?

The most recent revision of the *ACA Code of Ethics* (ACA, 2014), however, removed the previous section on end-of-life counseling due to the fact that the language could put the counselor in violation of state laws (i.e., "option of breaking or not breaking confidentiality"). The changes from the 2005 ethical standards to the 2014 ones illustrate the need for counselors to stay current in their profession and be aware of revisions to the *ACA Code of Ethics*, as such codes are living and not static documents. The next revision of the *ACA Code of Ethics* likely would occur roughly 10 to 12 years after the 2014 version, although court decisions could also affect the code before that time.

Counselors who work with terminally ill clients should now be familiar with these ethical statements but likewise aware of the changing landscape in one's state or territory of practice. Naturally, when working with end-of-life issues and decisions, counselors may find it necessary to consult a legal professional for guidance, given thorny legal issues involved.

Recommendations for Practicum/Internship

Here are some recommendations to consider if you are faced with an issue of confidentiality during your practicum/internship:

- Know your school's or agency's policies on breaching confidentiality. Keep a copy of the written policy at your disposal.
- Anytime you see the need to break confidentiality, consult with your site supervisor as soon as possible.
- Consult your ethical code for guidance (e.g., ACA, CCPA, PACFA, or BACP).
- Keep your faculty practicum/internship instructor or advisor apprised regarding crisis situations.
- Make sure that you have properly documented a clear rationale for breaching confidentiality in the case notes. You never know when a file may be subpoenaed or a judge mandates court disclosure. A general guideline is "If it's not written in a file, it didn't happen."
- In the event you are subpoenaed, do not immediately comply with the order; this could mean you have violated confidentiality. Go immediately to your supervisor, who will notify the school or agency attorney. Let the legal professionals fight the legal battles.

TECHNOLOGY AND CLIENT RECORDS

Many counseling agencies, schools, treatment centers, and private practitioners now maintain client records, schedules, and financial information on computer software. New technology, however, brings about new risks. Hackers may compromise the system and have access to sensitive client information; thus, security is paramount. Records must also be backed up in the event that data are lost. There are numerous software programs on the market specifically designed for counseling professionals' use. These programs can assist counselors in the creation and management of client records, including scheduling, billing, treatment planning, progress notes, reports to outside professionals (e.g., judges, child welfare, parole, and probation), and client termination summaries, to cite a few. There are numerous software packages for counseling and case management. With the advent of the super technology era, it is likely that all records will be kept by virtual means, which requires no warehousing. Keeping virtual documents, however, does leave the door open to hackers. Thus, no foolproof safekeeping practice exists.

Counselors must also maintain records for the minimum period set forth by federal or state law. Some states mandate 7 years, whereas others require 10 years (Wheeler & Bertram, 2019). Counselors may also wish to keep client records for years after treatment has ended because former clients have been known to request copies of case notes or counselors may need client records to protect themselves against litigation (Wheeler & Bertram, 2019). If there is no set minimum period for retention of records, a general practice is to keep records for a minimum of 7 years (Remley & Herlihy, 2020; Wheeler & Bertram, 2019). As a professional counselor, should your school or agency have a particularly sensitive record that you believe is wise to retain for a period longer than required, it would be prudent to have legal counsel advise you on the matter.

Counseling agencies, schools, and other mental health treatment or rehabilitation centers would be wise to adopt an official record retention policy. Records should be kept and transmitted in accordance with HIPAA requirements, professional ethics, and federal and state laws. The record retention policy should specify how records will be stored, where they will be stored (the location must be secure), and how and when they will be destroyed (Wheeler & Bertram, 2019).

BOUNDARY ISSUES: DUAL RELATIONSHIPS IN COUNSELING

Boundary issues in counseling typically involve *dual* or *multiple relationships*. According to Herlihy and Corey (2015), dual or multiple relationships occur when counselors take on roles outside the therapeutic encounter. Multiple relationships can involve combining the role of counselor with that of minister, teacher, colleague, committee member, friend, relative, and so forth. In certain settings, multiple relationships are not only expected but they may also be required. For example, school counselors often interact with students beyond the school counseling office. Pastoral counselors will be expected to have multiple relationships if they counsel as part of their ecclesiastical duties. Counselors working on small college/university campuses likely will encounter clients and former clients outside the counseling center. Counselors in residential treatment settings (e.g., correctional, addictions, and psychiatric) are required to treat patients in counseling sessions (individual or group) but also interact with them at lunch, on the grounds, and so forth. Certainly, counselors practicing in rural or remote areas will have no option but to have multiple relationships with clients. As a counselor who has practiced in rural and occasionally in very remote areas (e.g., rural U.S. Mountain West, Outback Australia, and rural South Africa), such settings require strong, though flexible, boundaries. The critical factor in multiple relationships is to ensure client privacy in areas where privacy is difficult to achieve. The *ACA Code of Ethics* (ACA, 2014) has explicitly outlined guidance for managing counselor–client boundaries in Section A.6. Counseling students should carefully review this section of the ethical code, as it appears boundary violations (or *perceived* boundary violations) are the primary reason for ethics complaints against counselors (Herlihy & Corey, 2015; Remley & Herlihy, 2020). Most multiple relationships likely are not ethical violations, but counselors must take care to ensure the client's rights are not compromised when relationships extend beyond the session. Naturally, some multiple relationships are ethical violations as noted in the following paragraph.

A sexual relationship between a counselor and a client represents a dual relationship whereby the counselor has committed an egregious ethical (and in some cases and certain states, a legal) violation. Sexual relations between counselors and clients are explicitly forbidden under the *ACA Code of Ethics*. For other dual relationships, however, the issue is less clear. The most recent revision of the *ACA Code of Ethics* recognizes that dual relationships are not necessarily unethical. Under Section A.5 ("Roles and Relationships with Clients"), the standard states:

> Sexual and/or romantic counselor–client interactions or relationships with current clients, their romantic partners, or their family members

are prohibited. This prohibition applies to both in-person and electronic interactions or relationships. (ACA, 2014, Section A.5.a)

Sexual relationships with former clients, their romantic partners, or their family members also are prohibited for a period of 5 years following the last professional contact (Section A.5.c). This prohibition applies to both in-person, teletherapy, or through any other medium. In fact, the code specifies there would need to be 5 years of no personal or professional contact with the former client and counselor. Should the counselor pursue a romantic/sexual relationship with a former client after the required 5-year no-contact period, the said counselor must do in-depth work to ensure such a relationship would not be harmful to the former client. Given the intense focus on prohibiting sexual intimacies between counselors and clients, it might surprise many to learn one of the most common malpractice allegations and litigations against mental health professionals is sexual misconduct (Pope & Vasquez, 2011; Remley & Herlihy, 2020). From my viewpoint of nearly 40 years in the counseling field, it seems such relationships would be fraught with numerous potential hazards to the former client. Thus, my recommendation is counselors should *never* enter into romantic/sexual relationships with former clients. As a point of comparison, the National Association of Social Workers ethical code prohibits sexual relationships with former clients entirely, regardless of the time lapse since the last professional contact (Remley & Herlihy, 2020).

The 2014 code also prohibits other multiple relationships with clients. Prohibitions include not soliciting client testimonials (Section C.3.b), promoting counselor products (Section C.3.f), and engaging in bartering with clients unless the counselor can document such is not harmful to the client (Section A.10.e). Anytime a counselor has a concern regarding whether the dual or multiple relationship is an ethical one, the counselor should take steps to clarify the relationship. The clarification process could involve reviewing relevant sections of the ethical code, consulting with a colleague, and doing intense self-reflection involving exploring motivations for a dual/multiple relationship. Basically, should you be prosecuted or investigated by the licensing board, the ACA, or another relevant body, you will be asked to defend your actions. So, make sure your actions are in the best interests of the client, document that, and be able to articulate a clear and succinct defense should the need arise.

While the *ACA Code of Ethics* no longer prohibits all nonprofessional relationships per se, ethical codes are about the best interests of the client. Determining what is in the client's best interests, however, is not always easy or straightforward. The critical factor in dual/multiple relationships is for the counselor to refrain from involvement in counselor–client relationships that could compromise the therapeutic encounter or be potentially harmful to the client. Herlihy and Corey (2015) identified four characteristics of dual relationships that make them problematic.

First, potential dual relationships can be *difficult to recognize*. They can evolve in subtle ways. For example, a counselor may accept an invitation from a client to go out for coffee. This may lead to more social encounters until the relationship has progressed into a sexual one.

A second characteristic of dual relationships is that their *potential for harm ranges along a wide continuum*—from extremely harmful to benign or even beneficial.

But because the onus of responsibility is on the counselor and not on the client, counselors must discern through consultation whether the potential benefit of crossing boundaries with a client outweighs the risks and harm (see Case Study 4.2).

Case Study 4.2 Navigating Dual Relationships With Clients and Former Clients

THE CASE OF ALICE

Alice, age 28, seeks counseling from Steve, an LMHC in an employee assistance program her employer contracts with. Alice's goal is to resolve issues of sexual abuse from her father that she endured when she was a teenager. After 3 months of counseling, Steve initiates a sexual relationship with Alice. He rationalizes his behavior by convincing himself that she is benefiting from a healthy sexual relationship with a positive adult concerned about her sexual well-being. Alice, on the other hand, feels somewhat confused. She feels in love with Steve but wonders about the nature of their relationship and whether Steve has done this before. She is also aware that Steve is in violation of his professional ethics, if not of the state law. She wants to discuss her concerns with Steve but also does not want to lose him either as a romantic partner or a counselor. Needing advice, Alice comes to your counseling office. She states that above all, she does not want you to breach confidentiality by reporting on Steve. How would you advise Alice? What is your ethical responsibility? Can you respect her wishes you not breach her confidentiality?

THE CASE OF HECTOR

Hector has been coming to see Tomasina, his counselor, for nearly 6 months. Through counseling, Hector has gained the self-confidence to complete his college degree. Hector requests Tomasina attend his graduation and graduation party because he credits counseling with Tomasina for making it possible for him to achieve this goal. After reviewing the *ACA Code of Ethics*, giving the matter some thought, and consulting with a colleague, Tomasina agrees to attend Hector's graduation.

1. What are the differences between Steve's and Tomasina's motivations regarding entering a dual relationship with their respective clients?
2. What, if any, potential harm could result from Tomasina's attending Hector's graduation and graduation party?
3. What potential harm could come from Steve's affair with Alice?
4. What potential harm—if any—could come to you, the counselor Alice seeks out for advice?
5. If you were a counseling supervisor, how would you have advised Tomasina?
6. What are the ethical issues a counselor must consider regarding dual/multiple relationships with clients and former clients?

The examples illustrate the extremes of dual relationships and counseling. Steve's motivations are suspect and a clear violation of ethics regardless of whether or not the relationship is mutually desired. Even if the client pursues the sexual relationship and wants it to continue, the counselor has committed a serious ethical and, in many states, legal violation. Tomasina's decision to attend graduation and the graduation party has a low probability of harming the client. The *ACA Code of Ethics* specifically states that an example of a potentially beneficial interaction is "attending a client's formal ceremony (e.g., wedding/commitment ceremony or graduation)" (ACA, 2014, Section A.6.b). Still, show due diligence by consulting the *ACA Code of Ethics*, consulting with a supervisor or colleague, and discussing any potential risks with your client. Finally, document all this in the case notes, in the unlikely event something unforeseen occurs and your judgment is called into question.

96 • THE COUNSELING PRACTICUM AND INTERNSHIP MANUAL

A third characteristic is, with the exception of sexual dual relationships, that there is very little consensus among mental health professionals regarding the propriety of dual relationships (Herlihy & Corey, 2015). Some, such as Lazarus and Zur (2002), have taken the position that it can be very beneficial for a counselor to engage in dual relationships with some clients. Others have taken an opposing stance. Kitchner (1992) suggests that the power differential between the counselor and the client makes it impossible for them to have a truly healthy relationship. It is also possible that counselors can knowingly or unknowingly exploit a client when dual roles are in play. Cottone (2005) has urged counselors to think in terms of detriment or harm to clients with regard to multiple relationships. His point is that the counselor is always in the position of authority. Thus, counselors must carefully consider potential harm to clients in multiple relationships.

Unfortunately, there is a paucity of research regarding the impact of dual roles and the effectiveness of counseling (Pope & Vasquez, 2011; Remley & Herlihy, 2020). There also is no clear consensus among counseling professionals on this issue, and in many cases, the surrounding culture may have as much impact as anything else. For example, while providing service work in remote Australia, I encountered an addictions counselor who treated indigenous Australians. He stated that, while practicing in an urban setting in Melbourne, he saw clients exclusively at the office. However, when he relocated to the Northern Territory's remote, indigenous Central Australia, the local tribe expected him to participate in kangaroo hunts and certain cultural ceremonies. He explained nonparticipation would risk his relationships with the indigenous community, and thus, he often participated, though admittedly his participation made his practice complicated. The recommendation here is that at this point in your student counseling career, limit dual/multiple relationships as much as possible.

The fourth characteristic that makes boundary issues so complex is that *some dual relationships are unavoidable* (as in the preceding Australian Outback case). For example, counselors practicing in rural, isolated communities may find it impossible to avoid dual roles with clients (see Case Study 4.3). Having spent 25 years as a counselor practicing in rural and remote communities, I would frequently discover a current or former client working on my car at the dealership, ringing up my grocery bill at the supermarket, or serving with me on a community agency. In some rural communities, there may be only one counselor for a 100-mile area, making referrals nearly impossible. As previously mentioned for school counselors, dual relationships are simply a fact of the school environment. Counselors in the military also face many of the same challenges (Johnson et al., 2005) as do members of particular subcultures (Lazarus & Zur, 2002). People's political affiliations, ethnic identities, religious values, and so forth can often lead to dual relationships as clients often seek counselors with similar values (Johnson et al., 2005).

Case Study 4.3 The Case of Ginger and Kimber: Counseling in a Remote Community

Kimber has been a client of Ginger's for several weeks. They both live in a small and remote community of 2,000 people in the remote western United States, nearly 70 miles from the nearest town. Kimber's husband and Ginger's partner serve on the advisory board for a local charitable organization. The husband and

(continued)

> ### Case Study 4.3 The Case of Ginger and Kimber: Counseling in a Remote Community (*continued*)
>
> partner develop a friendship and want to begin a social relationship that includes all four parties. Ginger's partner, Alice, suggests getting together with Kimber and Jim (Kimber's spouse) "Would be fun!"
>
> 1. How should Ginger respond when her partner suggests this social contact?
> 2. Do you think Kimber should inform her husband that Ginger is her counselor and that she would not be comfortable in such a social relationship?
> 3. What potential risks are posed for Ginger and Kimber should a social relationship develop?
> 4. Does the fact that they live in such an isolated community change the issue? If yes, how so?
> 5. If you were Ginger's supervisor, how would you advise her? (Remember, the onus in multiple relationships is on the counselor, not on the client.)
> 6. What does the *ACA Code of Ethics* suggest?

SEXUAL INTIMACY WITH CLIENTS

The most destructive and egregious form of dual relationships with clients is that involving sexual intimacy. The prohibition regarding sexual relationships is designed to protect clients from sexual and emotional exploitation. The ethical codes of all major helping professions specifically prohibit sexual relationships with clients (Wheeler & Bertram, 2019). Ignoring this ethical standard has led to client abuse and has been the downfall of otherwise capable counselors (Herlihy & Corey, 2015; Remley & Herlihy, 2020). Lamb and Catanzaro (1998) found that 8% of clinicians surveyed admitted to sexual violations with clients. It is likely that this statistic is low because of underreporting among various therapists surveyed. This statistic seems even more egregious when considering all the educational efforts, numerous ethical codes (e.g., ACA, APA, NASW, AAPC, AAMFT, BACP, and IAC), lawsuits, press coverage, and so on, for mental health professionals caught breaching this inviolable ethical standard. Likely, mental health professionals who violate the standard believe they will not be caught.

In addition to ethical standards, many states have laws against counselor–client sexual relationships (Wheeler & Bertram, 2019). This makes a counselor–client sexual relationship not only an ethical matter but also a criminal one. Moreover, it is important to note that sexual relationships are considered a crime even if the client is a willing participant and of legal age (Wheeler & Bertram, 2019). Should you have a sexual relationship with a client, the least you will lose if discovered is your job. You could lose your license, certification, spouse/partner, and livelihood; be sued; and in some states, even go to prison. Be aware!

Along with criminal laws, all states have laws that carry civil suits and damages for sexual intimacies with clients (Wheeler & Bertram, 2019). The *ACA Code of Ethics* expands this prohibition to include "[s]exual or romantic counselor–client interactions or relationships with former clients, their romantic partners, or their family members . . . for a period of 5 years following the last professional contact" (ACA, 2014, Section A.5.c). The language also expands on the ethical responsibilities of a counselor who might wish to become involved in a romantic relationship after 5 years by cautioning that the counselor must demonstrate forethought and document (in written form) whether the interactions or relationship can be viewed as exploitative in some way and whether there is still potential for harm to the former client. Again, the onus is always on the counselor to demonstrate they have *done no harm* to the client. Again, this writer's recommendation is that counselors *never* enter a sexual relationship with former clients, even after the 5-year no-contact period is exceeded.

Maintaining Professional Boundaries

Clearly, counselors involved in sexual impropriety with the clients they serve risk doing long-term and severe emotional damage to the clients. This is to say nothing of the professional damage to the counselor; their colleagues, employer, and family; and the profession in general. Simply put, counselors should not have sex with their clients, period.

Corey et al. (2015) emphasize several points that are specifically relevant for students in graduate programs. It is common and human to experience an attraction to clients. Therefore, the matter of counselor–client attraction must be recognized, processed, and dealt with. A fundamental aspect of such training recognizes the distinction between attraction and acting on that attraction. Students must feel it is safe to discuss feelings of attraction with their professors and clinical supervisors without the fear of being judged or criticized. If need be, graduate students should seek out professional counseling to help them clarify and separate personal and professional issues related to attraction.

Unfortunately, previous research suggests that despite ethical training and education, students who disclosed client attraction to their supervisor did not develop an appropriate understanding of the ethical boundaries regarding that attraction (Housman & Stake, 1999). A small percentage (7%) even thought that sex with a client might be ethical and therapeutic. On the other hand, 47% thought that any sexual feelings for clients were unacceptable. The former group could run into serious ethical and legal problems, whereas the latter may have difficulty because they may be unable to address feelings of attraction due to believing such feelings are morally or ethically wrong.

Recognizing that attraction is natural is the most realistic approach to take. There are some warning signs for counselors to pay attention to when they feel an attraction for a client:

- giving the client extra time beyond the session
- dressing up on the days you see that particular client
- revealing inappropriate personal information to the client, such as your relationship status, type of person you are attracted to, and so forth
- daydreaming about romantic escapades with the client
- agreeing to meet with the client outside the treatment center, school, and so forth
- encouraging the client to call you after hours even if it is not an emergency
- initiating physical contact with the client
- offering or accepting gifts from the client
- considering how to manage the 5-year no-contact clause in the *ACA Code of Ethics.*

Counselors finding themselves experiencing attraction to a client have an ethical responsibility to acknowledge and address it appropriately. Useful strategies might include consulting with a colleague, seeking supervisor, self-examining one's motives, and self-monitoring to assess whether your needs are being unmet by appropriate relationships. If necessary, seek counseling to further address your concerns.

Other Boundary Issues of Concern

Besides sexual relationships with clients, counselors should be cautious and judicious about entering into other dual relationships. Bartering with a client for goods and services is not prohibited by the *ACA Code of Ethics*, although a counselor should be very cautious about the practice. A common form of bartering involves the exchange of services. For example, a client might be a self-employed contractor having difficulty paying for counseling. He may offer renovation work in return for counseling services. This agreement raises many questions: Is it a fair exchange of services? Also, what if the counselor is unhappy with the renovation work? Conversely, what if the client is unhappy with the counseling? What happens if the client decides to leave counseling but has not finished the renovation work? What happens if the client sues the counselor (or vice versa)? Clearly such counselor–client relationships are fraught with concerns. *Advice:* Refrain from such dual/multiple relationships when the potential risks seem to outweigh the client rewards.

The *ACA Code of Ethics* offers guidelines for counselors to help them determine whether a potential bartering arrangement might be acceptable. The code states that counselors may participate in bartering only if three criteria are met: The relationship is not exploitive or harmful and does not place the counselor in an unfair advantage, "if the client requests it, and if such arrangements are an accepted practice among professionals in the community" (ACA, 2014, Section A.10.e). Still, the counselor must tread very lightly regarding bartering and avoid it in most circumstances.

Social relationships have been discussed previously. Essentially, counselors should limit social relationships to special occasions (e.g., funerals or weddings) as much as possible. When counselors blend the roles of the counselor and friend, they create a conflict of interest that compromises the objectivity needed for good professional judgment (Pope & Vasquez, 2011). Counselors will meet clients in outside social contexts without prior planning on either's part. Therefore, counselors should discuss with their clients how they might be affected by encountering the counselor outside the office and how such chance encounters should best be handled.

At times, clients will offer gifts to their counselors. As a counselor who has had their fair share of gifts offered (though nothing fancy or expensive), I can attest to the discomfort a counselor feels in choosing to maintain clear boundaries and a desire to not hurt the client's feelings (which could jeopardize therapy). One agency I worked in had a written policy prohibiting staff from accepting any gifts from clients. This policy was written into the informed consent form clients signed at the onset of counseling. Naturally, even if advised of such prohibitions, some clients will forget or will try to present a gift anyway. Whether to accept or not to accept a gift may also depend on its monetary value. Few counselors would accept a costly work of art from a client, although most would likely accept a crayon drawing from a child. Evidently, many mental health professionals would express the monetary value of the gift was the critical aspect. Borys (1988) discovered that 84% thought that it is ethically permissible to accept a gift worth less than $10, but only 18% thought that it is ethical to accept a gift worth $50 or more. The *ACA Code of Ethics* makes this statement:

Counselors understand the challenges of accepting gifts from clients and recognize that in some cultures, small gifts are a token of respect and gratitude. When determining whether [or not] to accept a gift from clients, counselors take into account the therapeutic relationship, the monetary value of the gift, the client's motivation for giving the gift, and the counselor's motivation for wanting to accept or decline the gift. (ACA, 2014, Section A.10.f)

As per Section A.10.f of the *ACA Code of Ethics*, it may also be prudent to consider the client's motivation. A client may be offering a gift as a small token of sincere gratitude. This would be considerably different from a client offering a gift as a means of manipulation. Remley and Herlihy (2020) recount an example of the client who was an excellent baker; the counselor accepted the first two baked offerings. When the client came with the third treat, the counselor used the situation as a means of exploring the client's motivation. Counselor–client exploration regarding motives behind gifts, while delicate, could also be the pathway to a deeper and more honest therapeutic relationship.

Counselors should also be aware of cultural considerations (see Case Study 4.4). Giving and accepting gifts is a common practice in many cultures as a means of showing gratitude and respect (ACA, 2014, Section A.10.f; Sue & Sue, 2012). Counselors need to ensure as much as possible that their own discomfort at being presented with a gift does not overshadow their sensitivity to what the gift means to the client (Remley & Herlihy, 2020; Sue & Sue, 2012). When counselors do choose to accept a gift, they should notify their supervisor. It might also be a good idea to document the gift in the case notes, its relative monetary value, and why the counselor accepted it.

Case Study 4.4 The Case of Jim: Cultural Expectations as a Tribal Reservation Counselor

Jim is an addictions counselor working on a tribal reservation in the American Southwest. As a member of the tribe, Jim is acutely aware of the delicate boundary between cultural expectations and professional ethics. Because he works in a traditional healing community, he is occasionally expected to visit clients in their homes, have meals with the client's family, and participate in spiritual purification ceremonies with them.

1. What types of ethical and boundary difficulties would you expect Jim to face in this scenario?
2. How does Jim's culture change his professional situation?
3. How might Jim manage both ethical responsibilities and cultural expectations? Or, what would be realistic regarding the balance between maintaining ethical boundaries and cultural norms?

There are many counselors in a similar situation to Jim. An interesting aside to note is that I have noticed that legal discussions regarding situations such as Jim's tend to be quite different from those regarding mainstream, dominant, White culture. It would be interesting to hear from Jim's tribal legal counsel regarding any ethical and legal risks of Jim's situation. Jim would be wise to seek such legal advice and to document accordingly.

LIABILITY INSURANCE

For counselors practicing in the United States and well beyond, professional liability insurance is an absolute necessity. Although graduate counseling students on practicums and internships are far less likely to be sued than professional counselors, they are not immune to litigation (Wheeler & Bertram, 2019). Counseling students in Council for Accreditation of Counseling and Related Educational Programs (CACREP)-accredited programs are required to carry student liability insurance, and many non-CACREP programs now require coverage as well. Fortunately, students who purchase a membership with the ACA or the AMHCA receive student liability insurance as part of their membership. Students may also purchase student liability insurance through many independent carriers.

For a client plaintiff to prevail in a malpractice lawsuit against a counselor, the plaintiff must prove the following elements (Prosser et al., 1988):

- The counselor had a duty to warn the client to use reasonable care regarding providing counseling services.
- The counselor failed to conform to the required duty of care.
- The client was injured.
- There was a reasonably close casual connection between the conduct of the counselor and the resulting injury (known as *proximate cause*).
- The client suffered an actual loss or was damaged.

Malpractice is the legal term pertaining to civil litigation against counselors and related mental health professionals. As in the preceding list, malpractice is based on negligence, or failure to foresee an injury the professional should otherwise foresee. Malpractice is state regulated and typically applies only when the professional is state licensed or certified (Wheeler & Bertram, 2019). Malpractice is commonly found in the following types of cases (Wheeler & Bertram, 2019, p. 65):

- The procedure used by the counselor was not within the realm of accepted professional practice.
- The technique used was one the counselor was not properly trained to use (lack of professional competence).
- The counselor failed to follow standard counseling procedures, resulting in harm to the client.
- The counselor failed to warn and/or protect others from a violent client.
- Informed consent to treatment was not obtained.
- The counselor failed to explain the possible consequences of the treatment.

Thus, significant factors in protecting yourself against malpractice are to read and understand your professional ethics, practice within them, seek supervision and consultation when necessary, continually upgrade your professional skills, and consult with an attorney should the need arise.

The good news regarding litigation against counselors and other mental health professionals is that proving all of these elements of malpractice is difficult (Remley & Herlihy, 2020). Roughly 20% of cases filed against mental health professionals result in a judgment against the therapist (Conte & Karasu, 1990). Still, even an unsuccessful lawsuit could potentially end a counselor's practice (Remley & Herlihy, 2020), and being sued is stressful, expensive, and time consuming (Remley & Herlihy, 2020). Once again, the best way to deal with lawsuits is to lessen the risk of litigation by practicing within the boundaries laid out in the *ACA Code of Ethics*, be meticulous in writing case notes, limit dual relationships as much as possible, refrain from romantic relationships with clients, receive ongoing supervision, and continue upgrading your education through your professional life. These simple recommendations are no guarantee against being sued, but they lower a counselor's window of vulnerability to lawsuits.

CONCLUSION

Ethical and legal issues tend to be perceived as significant concerns among graduate counseling students and for good reason (Remley & Herlihy, 2020). Fortunately, understanding and reviewing the *ACA Code of Ethics* (ACA, 2014) can provide a good deal of guidance and spare the student a lot of anxiety. Good communication with the field site supervisor and the on-campus faculty supervisor teaching practicum and internship classes can also help resolve misunderstandings and provide clarity for interns. Finally, as a graduate student, the standard of care is far greater for professional supervisors than graduate students (Remley & Herlihy, 2020; Wheeler & Bertram, 2019). The following chapter on clinical issues in the practicum and internship will provide some clarity as well.

LESSONS LEARNED

"There's something I need to discuss with you," she said, eyeing me directly. I nodded, waiting for whatever issue this middle-aged woman was about to disclose. *Anna* (pseudonym) was an intelligent, educated, single Caucasian female with no children who, until recently, had lived with her elderly mother. I was volunteering my counseling services at an agency that offered low-cost and free mental health services to the homeless, chronically mentally ill, and anyone else who walked through the door. It was my summer break from doctoral studies and I was working on campus part-time while spending one afternoon and evening at the agency. Sometimes, I co-facilitated group counseling; at other times, I provided individual therapy; and occasionally, I washed dishes, mopped floors, and vacuumed rugs, as the agency ran on a lean budget, with staff, volunteers, and even clients cleaning the aged building.

Anna was an unusual client for the agency. She was not a recovering addict, homeless, or grappling with a chronic mental illness, and she did not have PTSD, as virtually all other clients of mine. She presented composed and clear minded, absent any anxiety, depression, or psychosis, that I expected she came to discuss a loved one. Once she unpacked her story, however, I understood why she was seeking counseling. She related her elderly mother had recently died. Anna had recently retired from some professional career (I cannot recall what) and mostly simply "puttered about her house," as she described it. As her reason for seeking therapy, she had written on the intake form, "Existential reasons," the only time I can ever recall a client writing such. Thus, she commenced her unusual story.

She recounted being an only child, never marrying, and having a distant relationship with both her parents, who were deceased. She offered never having found much purpose or joy in her life. "Frankly, everything has been rather bland." As she continued in an even tone of voice and good eye contact, I wondered if she was minimizing depression or had a long-term case of dysthymia. Seemingly prescient, she stated, "No, I have never been depressed." She mentioned going to see a psychiatrist who prescribed an anti depressant and referred her to the local mental health authority. Neither the medication nor a handful of counseling sessions seemed to provide any improvement.

Finally, she ceased speaking. "So, how would you see me being helpful?" I inquired. She nodded and said, "As I have arrived at a decision, you are going to help me put my house in order." I then expected she would disclose a recent terminal diagnosis. However, her appearance—trim, fit, and of a healthy complexion—suggested excellent health. "Well, after watching both my parents wither and die, I will euthanize myself long before that happens to me. What I need from you is to help me process my life and prepare me for death." "So, has your doctor given you a terminal diagnosis?" I inquired. "Not at all. In fact she says I'm in perfect health." I leaned back in my squeaky, second hand office chair feeling puzzled. "Let me understand this. You are healthy but expecting to die soon?" "Yes," she nodded, "I plan to exit this life on my own terms." Realizing she was disclosing suicide with a plan, I inquired about timelines and the method. "I'm really not sure and that's part of my coming in." She also admitted she had not formulated a specific timeline or means for her own demise. There was one thing she was clear on: "I will be ending my life in the near future and on my own terms." I inquired as to whether she had explored additional options besides euthanasia and then the session became more revealing.

She recounted always feeling life was more a "chore" (her word) and that the only outlets she enjoyed were her walking and reading. "My daily walks and books have kept me going all my life." She held an advanced degree and regularly read two to three books a week. She had taken early retirement to care for her mother, who had died just over a year earlier, and as she no longer had home care responsibilities, she realized now was the time to sort through her life. Nearing the end of the hour, with her assuring me she was not actively suicidal and felt stable, we made an appointment for 3 days later and she left.

After the session, I consulted with another volunteering counselor and she was as puzzled as I was. "So, she's not depressed, not hopeless, is not self-medicating, and had no timeline nor identified means of suicide, correct?" I nodded and she threw up her hands. Then we called the director who was at home, and she was unable to shed any light on the matter either but offered she would call the attorney for advice. After the call ended, I reviewed my clinical write-up, filed the notes, and readied to leave. My colleague then poked her head in the door and asked, "Hey, in your opinion, what's in this client's best interest?" Realizing I had addressed the imminent life issues and legal requirements, I had neglected to address this question, despite her written statement of "existential concerns."

Three days later, she returned and I started with the question my colleague had asked. Anna sat back, momentarily quiet and in contemplation. "From my perspective, my best interest is dying with a sound mind, at home, without needing a nursing home like my dad or constant care like my mother." I probed into her intentions with my observation that she looked very healthy and that she might be able to enjoy her walks and books for a few more decades (she was somewhere in her fifties). While agreeing she was fit and healthy, she stated feeling a general sense of having lived well and on her own terms and felt ready to end her life in the near future. Feeling stuck, I inquired that she had mentioned "Putting her house in order." This captured her attention.

Anna described her parents as being well intentioned, but they are people with no real passion for life and with whom she had always felt distant. As she had no siblings or children and was not interested in travel, life seemed rather pointless to her. Recalling she was an avid reader, I asked if she had read Viktor Frankl's work on meaning in life. She was unfamiliar with Frankl, and thus, I assigned her to read *Man's Search for Meaning* and described the text. She seemed interested, and as the library was literally across the street, she planned to stop there after session. "I'll read it and report back in the next session," she added, with a look of agreement on her face.

Before I left, the director came to my office and informed me that, in the attorney's opinion, I had covered legal bases. She encouraged me to keep Anna in session, hoping she would find some purpose for living. She also approved of me having assigned Frankl's book as homework. I promised to keep her apprised of Anna's progress or decompensation.

During the next session, Anna returned looking well groomed and carrying Frankl's iconic book. She mentioned she had finished the book in one evening and was quite impressed with the author's resilience, while confessing she could not imagine how he could have his entire family murdered and find any semblance of hope in the aftermath. We unpacked the construct of hope the entire session. While she remained thankful for the assignment, she maintained the same attitude of feeling her life would reach its expiration in the near future, although she continued to be vague about timelines and other important specifics. I inquired again whether she felt hopeless. She was adamant about feeling hopeful, stating that while her life had not been the same as others', she had had a good career, excellent health, and considered herself fortunate. She did make a request, however, something I viewed as a positive sign. "Can we read another counseling type book?" she asked. Pleased, I assigned Carl Rogers's *On Becoming a Person,* thinking that Rogers's human potential focus might prove inspiring. Frankly, I was beginning to feel desperate for *any* inspiration.

I awaited the following session, eagerly hoping something in Rogers's popular book might change Anna's outlook. Once again, she arrived for the session looking healthy and in her usual agreeable mood. She stated preferring Rogers's over Frankl's book but found his views on psychotherapy puzzling. "It's difficult to believe someone so versed in psychology could imagine the patient and the therapist as equals," she offered. Rogers's text, however, did provide her impetus for deeper inquiry. She inquired whether Rogers's necessary and sufficient conditions for change were enough to facilitate client growth. I replied that CBT founder Aaron Beck opined that Rogers's conditions were necessary but not sufficient for client change. She then leaned forward in her chair. "So then, what do you see as being most important regarding positive therapeutic change?" I explained the *Stages of Change* that I had recently been reading about (Prochaska & DiClemente, 1986). I explained that in significant change, the client's motivation to change was the most significant factor. She looked thoughtful while considering this. She then asked how that related to the horrors Frankl endured. I replied that, much like Nietzsche's famous quote, it is a matter of the person with a *why* being able to endure almost *any* how. The important factor was finding one's why. "So, what's your why?" I asked, casting a line. "My why is my desire to end life on my own terms," she answered promptly.

We scheduled another appointment. My homework assignment for next session was for Anna to write a two-page essay on what brings meaning and purpose to her life. Anna diligently wrote the assignment down in her planner, seeming pleased at the topic.

She arrived early to the next session and sat reading a novel while I was finishing up in a staff meeting with the director. She smiled, appearing pleased to see me as usual. She sat down in my office and withdrew her essay, which she had neatly printed off on her home printer. She read her essay with a pleasant voice, the prose flowing out musically, and I imagined her grammar being perfect. She stated that her *why* emanated from her independence, namely, never marrying, having no children, a career that provided challenge and a good income, and her long hikes and many books she had read. Nowhere in her essay did she mention close friends, her parents, or extended family and no significant personal connections. Yet, this woman was not depressed, anxious, or hopeless and gave every indication of being satisfied with life, save her insistence at ending it at some undetermined times in the not too distant future. I was completely out of ideas and my colleagues and supervisor were as inert as I was. I had noticed she appeared to enjoy the homework assignments. This time, she offered a suggestion. "How about me interviewing my book club members on what they find meaningful in their lives?" I thought this was a great idea and heartily agreed. She smiled and left the office.

The following session would be our final. She again arrived early while I was in session with another client. She carried a folder, and inside were notes she had typed up from her interviews with members of her book club. The club was composed of several women in her age group. All the members, except her, had children and, in some cases, grandchildren. I am vague on specifics, but based on their answers, the women's sense of meaning and purpose seemingly came from their children and extended families. Anna reported feeling odd in listening to the women speak of raising children and caring for grandchildren, something foreign to her. After she finished overviewing her interviews, she stated, "I realize that I have never fit into society's bell-shaped curve." I asked how she felt about being an outlier. She smiled wistfully and recounted the story of how, in high school, she did not date and had no close friends. While being an excellent student and an honor society member, she remained invisible to peers, something that continued into her collegiate and graduate school years. "My life has taught me that I am not in the mainstream," she stated. "That's okay with me." There was a palatable silence as we both digested her words.

Unsure of what else to do, I returned to what had brought her to seek counseling and asked if counseling had helped in *getting her house in order*. She considered the matter for a few long seconds. "Our sessions have helped provide me clarity that I am on the right path for me." Feeling that my therapeutic efforts had been a failure, I offered,

"What might have made our time together more effective?" She thought again and shook her head. "I'm pretty satisfied with our sessions. But, my sense is you want me to change my outlook. Yet, I see no problem with my goal." Unable to think of anything else, I thanked her for her honesty and diligent work, while she noted appreciating time well spent. She exited therapy seemingly very satisfied with the outcome. I, on the other hand, felt the sense of having failed Anna in some critical way. After all, this intelligent, capable, likable, and healthy person, with potentially decades to live, planned to kill herself in a few years.

Unsettled, I consulted with the director who listened patiently and empathically but explained that as she had no specific suicide plan, no timeline, and no stated means, we had no legal foundation to hospitalize her. Even if we could get an involuntary commitment to a psychiatric hospital—which we could not—that would do little good. "You just have to accept you cannot force someone to change their mind."

Later I consulted with another volunteer counselor, one much more experienced that myself. She counseled that while understandable, I had placed my needs about that of the client. I articulated the ethical, legal, and moral angles regarding client suicide, her clear mind notwithstanding. My colleague shook her head and suggested perhaps I had done as well as one could have with the client. However, I felt very unsatisfied and unsettled with my apparent therapeutic nonsuccess. *Really, what was in Anna's best interests?* Her primary passion appeared to be reading and discussing books, but I could find nothing beyond that to offer her.

The lessons I have learned from the session with Anna are somewhat muddled. Clearly, Anna did not share my need for her to abandon her desire to euthanize herself. With the ethical and legal concerns addressed, albeit not to my satisfaction, a moral question remained, that is, does a client in therapy have the right to expedite their own demise? The right to die remains an unsettled issue in U.S. society, with less than 10 states and territories having made it legal (and even then, within parameters). Anna clearly was not mentally ill or distressed in any way, mentally or physically. She simply planned to die when ready. She was ready to commit euthanasia in the near future and was quite at peace with the thought, yet I was very uncomfortable with her mind-set. I wanted her to find reasons for living as long as she could, especially as she appeared very healthy, active, and absent any discernable mental disorder. Essentially, that Anna should discover inherent meaning and purpose in order to discover a passion for living and abandon any thoughts of future euthanasia was what I wanted for her, but it was not what she was invested in. Thus, my needs were driving therapy, not hers.

Perhaps the lesson learned herein is that we as counselors may have very limited influence with clients. Anna was very satisfied with our counseling sessions and left therapy seemingly in a good emotional space, while maintaining her eventual, although unspecified, plan of euthanasia. I, however, have continued to harbor a belief of having failed her. It would be most curious to learn what readers of this text make of Anna's situation and what they believe was in her best interest.

SPRINGER PUBLISHING CONNECT™ A robust set of instructor resources designed to supplement this text is located at **http://connect.springerpub.com/content/book/978-0-8261-6607-4.** Qualifying instructors may request access by emailing **textbook@springerpub.com.**

REFERENCES

American Counseling Association. (2005). *ACA code of ethics.* https://www.counseling.org/docs/default-source/library-archives/archived-code-of-ethics/codeethics05.pdf

American Counseling Association. (2014). *ACA code of ethics.* https://www.counseling.org/resources/aca-code-of-ethics.pdf

American Psychiatric Association. (2022). *Diagnostic and statistical manual of mental disorders* (5th ed.). American Psychiatric Publishing.

Anderson, J. R., & Barret, R. L. (Eds.). (2001). *Ethics in HIV-related psychotherapy: Clinical decision making in complex cases.* American Psychological Association.

Baird, K. A., & Rupert, P. A. (1987). Clinical management of confidentiality: A survey of psychologists in seven states. *Professional Psychology: Research and Practice, 18,* 347–352. https://doi.org/10.1037/0735-7028.18.4.347

Barnett, J. E., & Johnson, W. B. (2015). *Ethics desk reference for counselors* (2nd ed.). American Counseling Association.

Borys, D. S. (1988). *Dual relationships between therapist and client: A national survey of clinicians' attitudes and practices* [Unpublished doctoral dissertation]. University of California.

Boynton v. Burglass, 590 So. 2d 446 (Fla. Dist. Ct. App. 1991).

Conte, H. R., & Karasu, T. B. (1990). Malpractice in psychotherapy: An overview. *American Journal of Psychotherapy, 44,* 232–246. https://doi.org/10.1176/appi.psychotherapy.1990.44.2.232

Corey, G., Corey, M. S., Corey, C., & Callanan, P. (2015). *Issues and ethics in the helping professions* (9th ed.). Brooks/Cole-Cengage.

Cottone, R. (2005). Detrimental therapist-client relationships—Beyond thinking of "dual" or "multiple" roles: Reflections on the 2001 AAMFT Code of Ethics. *American Journal of Family Therapy, 33,* 1–17. https://doi.org/10.1080/01926180590889284

Garcia, J., Salo, M., & Hamilton, W. M. (1995). Report of the ACA Ethics Committee: 1994–1995. *Journal of Counseling & Development, 72,* 221–224. https://doi.org/10.1002/j.1556-6676.1995.tb01854.x

Glosoff, H. L., Herlihy, B., & Spence, E. B. (2000). Privileged communication in the counselor–client relationship. *Journal of Counseling & Development, 78*(4), 454–462. https://doi.org/10.1002/j.1556-6676.2000tb01929.x

Gustafson, K. E., & McNamara, J. R. (1987). Confidentiality with minor clients: Issues and guidelines for therapists. *Professional Psychology: Research and Practice, 18,* 503–508. https://doi.org/10.1037/0735-7028.18.5.503

Handelsman, M. M. (2001). Accurate and effective informed consent. In E. R. Welfel & R. E. Ingersoll (Eds.), *The mental health desk reference* (pp. 453–458). Wiley.

Harding, A., Gray, L., & Neal, M. (1993). Confidentiality limits with clients who have HIV: A review of ethical and legal guidelines and professional policies. *Journal of Counseling & Development, 71*(3), 297–305. https://doi.org/10.1002/j.1556-6676.1993.tb02216.x

Health Insurance Portability and Accountability Act (1996), Pub. L. No. 104-191, 110 Stat. 1936 (1996).

Herlihy, B., & Corey, G. (2015). *ACA ethical standards casebook* (7th ed.). American Counseling Association.

Housman, L. M., & Stake, J. E. (1999). The current state of sexual ethics training in clinical psychology: Issues of quantity, quality, and effectiveness. *Professional Psychology: Research and Practice, 30*(3), 302–311. https://doi.org/10.1037/0735-7028.30.3.302

Humphrey, D. (1996). *Final exit: The practicalities of self-deliverance and assisted suicide for the dying* (2nd ed.). Dell Trade Paperback.

Jaffee v. Redmond et al. 1996, WL 314841 (U.S. June 13, 1996).

Johnson, W. B., Barnett, J. E., Elman, N. S., Forrest, L., & Kaslow, N. J. (2012). The competent community: Toward a vital reformulation of professional ethics. *American Psychologist, 67*(7), 557–569. https://doi.org/10.1037/a0027206

Johnson, W. B., Ralph, J., & Johnson, S. J. (2005). Managing multiple roles in embedded environments: The case of aircraft carrier psychology. *Professional Psychology: Research and Practice, 36,* 73–81. https://doi.org/10.1037/0735-7028.36.1.73

Kitchner, K. S. (1992). Posttherapy relationships: Ever or never? In B. Herlihy & G. Corey (Eds.), *Dual relationships in counseling* (pp. 145–148). American Counseling Association.

Lamb, D., & Catanzaro, S. (1998). Sexual and nonsexual boundary violations involving psychologists, clients, supervisees, and students: Implications for professional practice. *Professional Psychology: Research and Practice, 29*(5), 498–503. https://doi.org/10.1037/0735-7028.29.5.498

Lazarus, A. A., & Zur, O. (Eds.). (2002). *Dual relationships and psychotherapy.* Springer Publishing Company.

Madden, R. G. (1998). *Legal issues in social work, counseling, and mental health*. Sage.

Miller, D. J., & Thelan, M. H. (1986). Knowledge and beliefs about confidentiality in psychotherapy. *Professional Psychology: Research and Practice, 17*, 15–19. https://doi.org/10.1037/0735-7028.17.1.15

Neukrug, E., Milliken, T., & Walden, S. (2001). Ethical complaints made against credentialed counselors: An updated survey of state licensing boards. *Counselor Education and Supervision, 41*, 57–70. https://doi.org/10.1002/j.1556-6978.2001.tb01268.x

Peck v. Counseling Services of Addison County, Inc., 499 A.2d 422 (Vt. 1985).

Pope, K. S., Tabachnick, B. G., & Keith-Spiegel, P. (1988). Good and poor practices in psychotherapy: National survey of beliefs of psychologists. *Professional Psychology: Research and Practice, 19*, 547–552. https://doi.org/10.1037//0735-7028.19.5.547

Pope, K. S., & Vasquez, M. J. T. (1998). *Ethics in psychotherapy and counseling: A practical guide for psychologists* (2nd ed.). Jossey-Bass.

Pope, K. S., & Vasquez, M. J. T. (2011). *Ethics in psychotherapy and counseling: A practical guide for psychologists* (4th ed.). Wiley.

Prochaska, J. O., & DiClemente, C. C. (1986). Towards a comprehensive model of change. In W. R. Miller & N. Heather (Eds.), *Treating addictive behaviors: Process of change* (pp. 3–27). Plenum Press.

Prosser, W. L., Wade, J. W., & Schwartz, V. E. (1988). *Cases and materials on torts* (8th ed.). The Foundation Press.

U.S. Department of Health and Human Services. (nd). Health Insurance Portability and Accountability Act of 1996. https://aspe.hhs.gov

Remley, T. P., Jr., & Herlihy, B. (2020). *Ethical, legal and professional issues in counseling* (6th ed.). Pearson.

Sheppard, G. (n.d.). *Notebook on ethics, legal issues, and standards for counsellors*. Canadian Counseling & Psychotherapy Association (CCPA). https://www.ccpa-accp.ca

Sue, D. W., & Sue, D. (2012). *Counseling the culturally different: Theory and practice* (6th ed.). Wiley.

Tarasoff v. Regents of University of California, 529P.2d 553, 118 Cal. Rptr. 129 (1974), vacated, 17 Cal. 3d 425, 551 P.2d 334, 131 Cal. Rptr.14 (1976).

Welfel, E. R. (2012). *Ethics in counseling and psychotherapy: Standards, research, and emerging issues* (5th ed.). Brooks/Cole-Cengage.

Wheeler, A. M., & Bertram, B. (2019). *The counselor and the law: A guide to legal and ethical practice* (8th ed.). American Counseling Association.

CHAPTER 5

Clinical Issues in Practicum and Internship

INTRODUCTION

In this chapter, I offer a brief overview of common clinical issues you may encounter at the practicum/internship site, along with suggestions and examples to assist you in counseling and assessment. Students beginning the initial placement may find the experience difficult at first because they are actually encountering real people with real issues instead of theoretical scenarios in a textbook or on an educational recording. Compounding the issue is the amount of information and data that accompanies counseling. The method, the information gathered, and how records are managed and stored vary depending on the type of placement (e.g., P-12 school, hospital, and in-patient drug treatment). Perhaps the most important concept for graduate counseling students to keep in mind when they are providing counseling is that the quality of the therapeutic relationship is likely more important than the particular technique or theoretical approach. Empirical research has validated this concept (Duncan et al., 2010). So, practicum and internship students, if you remember nothing else, in counseling, it is more about the relationship than anything else. While counseling programs will emphasize theoretical approach (e.g., cognitive behavioral therapy [CBT], Adlerian, and Gestalt) and technique (e.g., reframing, reflection of content, and empty chair), likely the most critical factor is developing therapeutic presence, as such likely facilitates the establishment of the therapeutic alliance (Duncan et al., 2010).

Although no one chapter or text could possibly cover all potential clinical issues and skills you need to address them, this chapter outlines some of the basic skills to be aware of, including building the therapeutic alliance, handling intake and basic assessments, understanding counseling techniques, and other basics. Chapter 6, "Clinical Writing and Documentation in Counseling Records," reviews clinical writing skills that you will need to document your counseling and intake sessions.

TELETHERAPY

With the advent of the COVID-19 era, the world has changed considerably. One of the most significant changes in the therapeutic community has the increased popularity of teletherapy. Prior to the pandemic, few of my students were conducting teletherapy. However, once the pandemic hit hard in early 2020, agencies, hospitals, and schools began utilizing distance communication technology such as Zoom and other related vehicles. As the pandemic has become endemic, teletherapy has rapidly replaced traditional in-person counseling, particularly in mental health agencies and private practices. While it is difficult to predict what the counseling world will look like in 10 years given the lightning speed of technology, it is likely teletherapy will evolve, becoming more popular than in-person counseling (Sampaio et al., 2021). Given such, all counseling programs and professional ethical codes the world over must adapt to this reality.

BUILDING THE THERAPEUTIC ALLIANCE

The most critical factor in establishing the counseling relationship is creating an attachment with the client or clients (Beck & Weishaar, 2008; Duncan et al., 2010; Rogers, 1951). Creating this alliance involves a process of establishing trust, respect, openness, and the willingness to take emotional risks (Beck, 2011; Ellis, 2001). Once an alliance is established, the client can begin to disclose to the counselor the reasons they have sought out counseling. The initial interview is your first and best opportunity to begin establishing such an alliance. Ivey et al. (2010) suggest a structured model for the initial interview:

- building rapport and structuring a process that has as its purpose the building of a working relationship with the client;
- gathering information, defining the problem, and identifying client assets to determine why the client has sought out counseling and how they view the issue;
- determining outcomes, which enables the counselor to plan therapy based on what the client is seeking, the client's viewpoint, and what life would be like without the existing problems;
- exploring alternatives and confronting incongruities, which is a critical task for the counselor to assist the client in resolving their problems; and
- generalization and transfer of learning, which are the processes whereby changes in the client's thoughts, feelings, and behaviors are carried out in their everyday life.

Weinrach (1989) advocated that counselors address issues most frequently raised by clients when beginning therapy. This may include some of the following questions:

- How often can I expect to have an appointment?
- How might I reach you in an emergency?
- What happens if I forget an appointment?
- How confidential are counseling sessions?
- What do I do in an emergency?
- When is it time to end treatment?
- What are my financial responsibilities?
- How often do I obtain reimbursement from insurance?

Beginning counselors should be aware that the counseling process might be new as well as intimidating to clients beginning therapy. Because clients come to counseling feeling burdened, overwhelmed, depressed, anxious, frustrated, and even hostile, they may not be well attuned to the therapeutic process. Therefore, you must, of necessity, be thorough in the intake and informed consent process and solicit from your clients whether or not they understand their rights and responsibilities. Furthermore, encourage them to seek clarification whenever they have questions or are confused about a therapeutic matter. Questions like those just mentioned can help clarify the counseling relationship and address the client's basic concerns. Remember also that while clients voice understanding, such articulation does not mean they actually *do* understand their rights, the process, confidentiality and its limits, and so forth. Be prepared to repeat informed consent particulars and inquire whether your clients/ students understand their rights.

It is also worth noting that not all clients enter the counseling relationship voluntarily. *Mandated clients* (those who are required to enter counseling by a spouse, boss, correctional facility, probation officer, judge, principal, dean of students, etc.) are a reality in all clinical settings, and mandated clients are likely to show less investment in the counseling process (Cox & Klinger, 2011; Hodges, 2016). Regardless of whether the client has come voluntarily or is mandated, the process of initiating therapy begins with acknowledging the issues listed previously. Mandated clients usually prove more challenging and are less compliant, at least initially (Duncan et al., 2010).

INITIAL INTAKE FORM

The intake form is a common information-gathering form preceding the clinical interview and counseling. Many counseling settings will use some variation of this form to gather basic information about a new client. Intake sheets typically include name, address, family history, previous counseling and psychiatric treatment, medications, and other information. The intake is usually common in mental health settings, although many schools use a similar form (sometimes called a developmental history form; Sommers-Flanagan & Sommers-Flanagan, 1999).

Exhibit 5.1 offers an example of an intake form.

112 • THE COUNSELING PRACTICUM AND INTERNSHIP MANUAL

Exhibit 5.1 Initial Intake Form for Counseling/Psychiatric Patients

Name: _____ Date: _____/_____/_____

Address: _____ City: _____ State: _____

Zip code: _____ Phone: _____ (H) _____ (W/C)

Identifying Information

Age: _____ Date of birth: _____ /_____ /_____ Place: _____

Sex: Female _____ Male _____ Height: _____ Ft. _____ In.   Weight: _____ Lbs.

Occupation: _____

Marital status: M _____   S _____   D _____   Sep. _____   Other: _____

Spouse's/Partner's name: _____ Age: _____

Occupation: _____ Employer: _____

Name(s)/Ages of children (if applicable):

_____

_____

_____

_____

Referral source: _____

Address of referral source: _____

Treatment History

Are you currently taking medication?   Yes: _____   No: _____

If yes, name of medication(s): _____

Provider of medication(s): _____

Have you received previous psychiatric/psychological treatment?

Yes: _____   No: _____

If yes, name the provider: _____

Dates of counseling/psychiatric treatment:

_____

_____

(continued)

Exhibit 5.1 Initial Intake Form for Counseling/Psychiatric Patients (*continued*)

Has any close relative ever had psychiatric treatment or been committed to a psychiatric hospital?

Yes: _____   No: _____

If yes, please explain:

_____

_____

_____

What factor(s) led you to seek counseling services?

_____

_____

_____

Symptoms: _____

_____

Treatment outlook: If you were to feel better, what would be different?

_____

_____

What personal strengths do you possess that can help with your treatment?

_____

_____

Family History

Mother's name: _____   Living: _____ Deceased: _____

Father's name: _____   Living: _____ Deceased: _____

Brother(s)/Sister(s):

Name: _____ Age: _____ Living: _____ Deceased: _____

Name: _____ Age: _____ Living: _____ Deceased: _____

Name: _____ Age: _____ Living: _____ Deceased: _____

(*continued*)

Exhibit 5.1 Initial Intake Form for Counseling/Psychiatric Patients (*continued*)

Educational History

High school: _____

    Location: _____

    Dates attended: _____ Degree: _____

College/University: _____

    Location: _____

    Dates attended: _____ Degree: _____

Technical school: _____

    Location: _____

    Dates attended: _____ Degree: _____

Graduate/Professional: _____

    Location: _____

    Dates attended: _____ Degree: _____

INITIAL ASSESSMENT

The types of assessment you conduct with clients will vary greatly depending on your field placement setting and client population. An educational placement, such as a middle school, will require considerably different data than a residential psychiatric center. The following considerations influence the assessment process (Hayes, 2017):

- *Who* is making the assessment? Is it a counselor, psychologist, or psychiatrist?
- *Where* is the assessment taking place? Is it in a high school counseling office, correctional setting, or psychiatric center?
- *When* is the assessment occurring? Is it during the junior year, in anticipation for college or technical school, or prior to starting graduate school?
- *Why* is the assessment being undertaken? Has the client been referred for counseling and assessment because of concerns about their mood? Is the client mandated?
- *How* is the assessment conducted? Is it done by computer, pen and paper, or orally?

In mental health settings, some variation of the Mental Status Examination (MSE) is utilized during the intake process (Seligman, 2004). School counselors, however, are unlikely to use the MSE, although they may use some type of developmental questionnaire. The MSE is designed to provide the counselor with baseline information

5: CLINICAL ISSUES IN PRACTICUM AND INTERNSHIP • 115

regarding the client's appearance, affect, cognitive functioning, orientation, judgment, short- and long-term memory, insight, and more (Polanski & Hinkle, 2000).

Although not a standardized psychological instrument, mental health professionals use the MSE for the purposes of assessment, diagnoses, and treatment of mental disorders. Typically conducted during the initial intake interview, the MSE can provide counselors with helpful categorized information for formalizing objective and subjective client data. Although numerous formats of the MSE exist, the two versions provided here offer examples of the MSE. Exhibit 5.2 shows a brief version of the MSE, and Exhibit 5.3 offers an MSE for older children, adolescents, and adults. The intake process, including the MSE, is an opportunity to build the therapeutic alliance.

Exhibit 5.2 Mental Status Examination (Brief Version)

Now, I am going to ask you a series of questions to test your concentration and memory. Answer to the best of your ability. Okay, any questions before we begin?

Orientation to Time:

What year is this? (1 point)

What season is this? (1 point)

What is the month and date? (1 point)

What day of the week is it? (1 point)

(Maximum of 4 points)

Orientation to Place:

What is the name of this institution/school/agency? (1 point)

What floor are we on? (1 point)

What city and state are we in? (1 point)

What county is this? (1 point)

(Maximum of 4 points)

Immediate Recall:

I am going to say three objects. After I say them, I want you to repeat them. They are "ball," "flag," and "tree." Now, say them. Remember them because I will ask you to repeat them later. (Interviewer: 1 point for each; maximum of 3 points)

Attention:

(Choose from either of the following items but not both.)

Serial 7s: Subtract 7 from 100 and continue until I tell you to stop. (Interviewer: Continue until subject makes an error. 1 point for each correct answer; up to a maximum score of 5 points)

Spell the word "world" backwards. (1 point for each correct letter; maximum of 5 points)

Delayed Recall:

What are the three words I asked you to remember? (1 point for each; maximum of 3 points)

(continued)

116 • THE COUNSELING PRACTICUM AND INTERNSHIP MANUAL

Exhibit 5.2 Mental Status Examination (Brief Version) (*continued*)

Naming:

Show subject a pen and wristwatch and ask to name them. (1 point for each; maximum of 2 points)

Repetition:

Repeat the following sentence exactly as I say it. "No ifs, ands, or buts." (1 point for each word; maximum of 3 points)

Stage Command:

"Now, I want to see how well you can follow instructions. I'm going to give you a piece of paper. Take it in your right hand, use both hands to fold it in half, and then put it on the floor." (1 point for each command; maximum of 3 points)

Reading:

Write a headline on a separate page, then ask the subject to read it out loud and do what it says. (1 point; Note: You may write anything. The point is to see if the client understands.)

Copying:

Draw a geometric figure such as a triangle or a square, then ask the subject to copy the figure. (1 point)

Writing:

On the same sheet of paper, ask the subject to write a complete sentence. (1 point)

Scoring Procedures:

Total (Maximum Score) = 30

Note:

Scores of 23–30 indicate expected or *normal functioning*. Scores lower than 23 suggest the presence of *cognitive impairment*.

> 23–30 = *no cognitive impairment*
>
> 18–23 = *mild cognitive impairment*
>
> 0–17 = *significant cognitive impairment*

MSE scores may be invalid if the subject has less than a ninth-grade education, is intoxicated, or is under the influence of other drugs.

An MSE is a common subjective form of assessment that typically accompanies a clinical intake. This MSE is a common example of a brief or short version. Short versions are often used in clinical settings to regularly assess change in a client.

Sources: Adapted from Folstein, M. F., Folstein, S. E., & McHugh, P. R. (1975). "Mini-mental state": A practical method for grading the cognitive state of patients for the clinician. *Journal of Psychiatric Research, 12*(3), 189–198. https://doi.org/10.1016/0022-3956(75)90026-6; Polanski, P. J., & Hinkle, J. S. (2000). The mental status examination: Its use by professional counselors. *Journal of Counseling & Development, 78*, 357–364. https://doi.org/10.1002/j.1556-6676.2000.tb01918.x.

Exhibit 5.3 Mental Status Examination for Older Children, Adolescents, and Adults

The areas to be covered for the written MSE report:

Prior to beginning, explain:

Who are you (e.g., certified school counselor or licensed professional counselor)?
What setting are you in (e.g., school, hospital, clinic, or prison)?
Why is the MSE taking place (e.g., teacher request, standard procedure, or client mandated by court or parole and probation)?
Informed consent. (Confidentiality and its limits, training or education, fees [if applicable], and the rights and responsibilities of the person being assessed)
Always ask the person being assessed, "Do you have any questions?"

When interviewing a client, always remain calm and in control. Exaggerated verbal and nonverbal responses may invalidate the interview.

A. Heading

Name:

Age:

Date of birth:

Gender:

Interview site:

Date of interview and report:

Person making the referral:

Reason for referral:

B. Appearance and Behavior

How did the client present themselves?
How did the interviewee look? (Note grooming, height, weight, facial appearance, special adornments, jewelry.)
How did the interviewee act during the interview? (Note any bizarre gestures, postures, repetitive movements, poor eye contact, slow movements, excessive movements, etc.)
Was the interviewee's behavior appropriate for their age, education, and vocational status?
How did the interviewee relate to the interviewer (e.g., whether they were wary, friendly, manipulative, approval seeking, hostile, or superficial)?

C. Speech and Communication

How was the general flow of the interviewee's speech (e.g., whether it was rapid, controlled, hesitant, slow, or pressured)?

(continued)

Exhibit 5.3 Mental Status Examination for Older Children, Adolescents, and Adults (continued)

Does the interviewee have speech impediments?

How was the general tone and content of the interviewee's speech? (Note, for example, over- or underproductivity of speech, flight of ideas, paucity of ideas, loose associations, rambling, tangentially connected ideas, neologisms, bizarre use of words, and incoherence.)

What was the relationship between verbal and nonverbal communication?

Was there a relationship between tone and content of the communications?

How interested was the interviewee in communicating?

D. Thought Content

What did the interviewee discuss? (Note, for example, content that they brought up spontaneously.)

What were the problem areas?

Were there any recurring themes?

Were there any signs of psychopathology, such as obsessions, delusions, hallucinations, phobias, or compulsions?

E. Sensory and Motor Functioning

How intact were the interviewee's senses—hearing, sight, touch, and smell?

How adequate was the interviewee's gross motor coordination?

How adequate was the interviewee's fine motor coordination?

Were there signs of motor difficulties such as exaggerated movements or repetitive movements (e.g., tics, twitches, tremors, bizarre postures, slow movements, or rituals)?

F. Cognitive Functioning

What was the general mood of the interviewee (e.g., whether they were sad, elated, anxious, tense, suspicious, or irritable)?

Did the interviewee's mood fluctuate or change during the interview?

How did the interviewee react to the interview (e.g., whether they were cold, friendly, cooperative, suspicious, or cautious)?

Was the interviewee's affect appropriate for the speech and content of the communications?

What did the interviewee say about their mood and feelings?

Was the self-report congruent with the interviewee's behavior during the interview?

G. Insight and Judgment

What is the interviewee's belief about why they were coming to the interview?

Is the belief appropriate and realistic?

Is the interviewee aware of their problem and the concerns of others?

(continued)

Exhibit 5.3 Mental Status Examination for Older Children, Adolescents, and Adults (*continued*)

Does the interviewee have ideas about what caused the problem?
Does the interviewee have any idea about how the problem could be alleviated?
How good is the interviewee's judgment in carrying out everyday activities?
How does the interviewee solve problems of living (e.g., impulsively, independently, responsibly, or through trial and error)?
Does the interviewee make appropriate use of advice or assistance?
How much does the interviewee desire help for their problems?

H. Questions to Ask the Interviewee

(*Note:* This section targets older children, adolescents, and adults. For preschool and K–2, many of these questions may be inappropriate.)

Key: Questions 1–4 and 8–10 test general orientation to time, place, and person, respectively; 11–16 test recent memory; 17–20 test remote memory; 21–23 test immediate memory; 24–25 test insight and judgment; and 26–28 test oral reading and spelling skills.

What is today's date?
What day is it?
What month is it?
What year is it?
Where are you?
What is the name of this city?
What is the name of this clinic (or school, university counseling center, etc.)?
What is your name?
How old are you?
What do you do?
Who is the president of the United States?
Who was the president before him?
Who is the governor of this state?
How did you get to this clinic (or school counseling center)?
What is your father's name?
What is your mother's name?
When is your birthday?
Where were you born?
Did you finish elementary school (if appropriate)?
When did you finish high school (if appropriate)?
Repeat these numbers back after me: 6-9-5, 4-3-8-1, 2-9-8-5-7.
Say these numbers backwards: 8-3-7, 9-4-6-1, 7-3-2-5-8.
Say these words after me: ball, flag, tree.
What does this saying mean: "A stitch in time saves nine"?

(*continued*)

> ### Exhibit 5.3 Mental Status Examination for Older Children, Adolescents, and Adults (*continued*)
>
> What does this saying mean: "Too many cooks spoil the broth"?
> Read back the three words I gave to you earlier. (ball, flag, tree)
> Write the words given previously. (ball, flag, tree)
> Spell these words: spoon, cover, attitude, procedure.
>
> #### I. Conclusion
>
> At the conclusion of the MSE report, write your name and credentials:
> Longer versions of the MSE are more typically used when a client is beginning counseling. The format presented in this exhibit represents one example of an MSE. The Mini MSE (MMSE) is much briefer (usually half the questions) and likely as valid and reliable as the longer MSE. Some agencies will use the MMSE in place of the MSE as a time-saver.

COUNSELING TECHNIQUES

Most counseling programs offer graduate training from various theoretical approaches (Gladding, 2009; Remley & Herlihy, 2020). In your program, you may study theoretical approaches such as psychodynamic, client-centered, rational emotive behavior, cognitive behavioral, solution-focused, narrative, and existential therapies, just to name a few. Because they explore so many counseling theories, students often put together an integrative approach, meshing techniques from this list of various theories. The proliferation of approaches and techniques can definitely be confusing for students regarding what particular theoretical set of techniques to use with which particular client.

The reality is that interviewing, like counseling, is a trial-and-error and retrial process between the counselor and client. There is no one-size-fits-all approach that faculty and clinical supervisors can give to students. Student counselors in a practicum/internship may simply need to try different theoretical approach techniques. The more you use various techniques, the more you can learn and build on your existing skill set. Here are some basic counseling techniques and interventions you will likely use in practicum and internship:

- Open-ended questioning: "What brought you in for counseling today?"
- Reflection of feeling: "How did you feel when . . .?"
- Paraphrasing: "So, it sounds like you were upset at. . . ."
- Summarizing: "It sounds like you believe that you are beginning to feel a sense of confidence regarding recovering from your divorce. You are reaching out to friends,

attending a weekly support group, even contemplating dating again. That sound about right?"

- Scaling question: "On a scale of 1 to 10, with 1 meaning you feel *very depressed* and 10 meaning you feel *great*, where would you put yourself today?"

- Gestalt empty chair technique: "Okay, let's say your father was sitting in that empty chair beside you. What would you want to say to him regarding his verbal abuse?" Also, the empty chair technique can be conducted using a psychodrama approach, where the client will sit in the empty chair and play the role of the absent person (e.g., father, mother, or spouse). Clients may also play themselves.

- Reframing: "You mentioned, 'I always fail.' However, earlier, I heard you say you just completed a college degree. It seems to me it might be more accurate to say, 'I have my failures, but I'm also successful.'"

- Homework: "Okay, here is what I'd like you to do between now and next week's session. You have talked about a desire to make friends. Therefore, I'd like you to speak with three new people in the next week. Then, we'll discuss how that goes in next week's session."

- Artwork (with younger clients): "Okay, Ellen, I have some paper and crayons. I'd like you to draw your family on this large sheet."

- Role-play: This is similar to the empty chair technique discussed previously. Clients, especially couples and families, are primed for role-plays. Individual counseling also should involve role-plays from time to time. Role-plays are used for issues involving confrontation, asking for a date, assertiveness with a roommate, setting limits with a parent, and so forth. Remember, clients are more likely to take healthy risks if they practice ahead of time.

- Miracle question: "Alright, say when you woke the next day the issue(s) that brought you to counseling were resolved. What would then be different about your life? What would others notice was different about you? How would this miracle change your life?"

- Self-reflection: "Now, you have mentioned continuing to have very angry thoughts about your former spouse that upset you. Now, in the future, when those thoughts recur, here is what I'd like you to do. The technique is called reframing, where you will replace negative thoughts with healthier, more realistic ones. So, you'll replace those thoughts with: 'It's unfortunate our marriage did not work out. But now I have the chance to have a healthy relationship.'"

- Self-talk: Reframing is part of addressing our self-talk. We tend to believe the things we tell ourselves. So, we want our self-talk to be reasonable, accurate (not inflated), and rational. Also, it is helpful to use reality testing by asking ourselves: "What's the evidence that I'm a loser? What's the evidence I never do anything right?" Overly critical self-talk is usually inaccurate and leaves us anxious and depressed. More rational self-talk helps us manage anxiety and depression (Ellis, 2001). "Instead of saying 'I'm a loser' whenever you have a disappointment, I'd like your self-talk to be: 'Okay, that was disappointing, but I'll improve and eventually be successful.'"

The preceding is only a brief list of several techniques that students likely will use on their practicum and internship. Do not become too overwhelmed by techniques because they take time to learn. Also, keep in mind that theoretical approach and technique may not be the most important aspect of counseling success and likely will be secondary to the theoretical alliance. As per the preceding list, you will get to practice what you preach to clients. Most people preach better than they practice, so be patient with yourself. As a cognitive counselor, I encourage you to carefully monitor and revise your self-talk from defeatist to realistic and proactive. We tend to believe what we tell ourselves, and so be vigilant (Ellis, 2001).

When you use techniques and interventions, give the client time to answer before moving on to the next intervention. Remember, pause time is cultural, and while some cultures may take but a second to respond, non-Western cultures (and indigenous U.S. cultures) may take 3 to 4 seconds (Lee, 2019; Sue & Sue, 2013). Present yourself as calm and engaged, suggesting to the client(s) that they are your only point(s) of focus. Clients will likely be encouraged that you are attending to them so intently. In fact, it is unlikely that anyone else will attend to clients the way that their counselors do. After all, counseling, unlike friendship, is a one-sided relationship and is all about the client(s). It is also very important to be genuine when you are counseling clients. Although there is no exact formula on authenticity, it starts with understanding your own beliefs, attitudes, and values and remaining nonjudgmental when the client's beliefs, attitudes, and values are different from yours. This sounds easy, but clients with radically different political, sexual, spiritual, educational, and/or cultural backgrounds may challenge you in ways you have not considered. It also is important to remind readers that a values-based referral is not ethical practice. In fact, the only ethical reason for referral is incompetence (Standard A.11.b). So, review your code of ethics (e.g., ACA, ASCA, and AMHCA).

One of the most critical aspects of the practicum experience is learning to trust your own instincts (Gladding, 2009). Some counselor educators might call this process learning to listen to your "inner voice." A former supervisor of mine was fond of saying, "When you have extended spent time counseling, you develop an inner counselor as your guide. Education, experience, self-reflection, and intuition help develop this inner counselor. Learn to heed this voice." To become a successful counselor, each student in training must learn to recognize their own voice and to put the suggestions of that inner voice into action. Listening to our inner voice is likely another path to becoming the genuine practitioner, which Carl Rogers (1942, 1951) wrote about decades ago. In addition, understand that the inner voice will not be perfect regarding what technique or intervention to use with a client because counseling is an inexact science requiring you to utilize many different skills. Still, awareness of your own inner counselor voice is likely the most reliable path to take in the counseling experience, particularly when nothing else seems to be working.

THE CLINICAL RECORD

Keeping accurate client records is vital to effective counseling and ethical practice. Remley and Herlihy (2020) suggest client records contain the following information:

- Intake information: This category includes personal demographic data about the client, such as name, address and phone number, date of birth, gender, ethnicity, education, marital status, and previous psychiatric and counseling history.

- Assessment/testing information: Assessment provides specific information the counselor might otherwise not have on areas such as current drug use, depression, suicidal ideation, hopefulness, and so forth.

- Psychological and/or educational or career assessment: The Beck Depression Inventory-II (BDI-II), Beck Anxiety Inventory (BAI), Minnesota Multiphasic Personality Inventory-2/A (MMPI-2/MMPI-A), Strong Interest Inventory, Myers-Briggs Type Indicator (MBTI), SAT/ACT, and so on.

- Psychosocial family assessment: Assesses the client's current level of functioning in their family and/or their community. Prior to the Fifth Edition, the *Diagnostic and Statistical Manual of Mental Disorders, Fifth Edition, Text Revision (DSM-5-TR)* system asked for a Global Assessment of Functioning or a Children's Global Assessment Scale (GAF/CGAS). While the *DSM-5-TR* (American Psychiatric Association, 2022) eliminated—unfortunately—the multiaxial system and GAF/CGAS, counselors should consider scaling-type questions based on client functioning. Higher scores on a 1 to 10 or 1 to 100 scale suggest greater autonomy and higher functioning.

- Vocational and educational situation: How stable is the client's employment status? What is their level of education or desired education?

- Drug and alcohol assessment: Assesses past and current use of chemical substances through interviewing and testing with the Alcohol Use Disorders Identification Test (AUDIT), Michigan Alcohol Screening Test (MAST), Substance Abuse Subtle Screening Inventory-4 (SASSI-4), and other assessments related to drug and alcohol addiction and abuse.

- Health assessment: Assessment of recent health issues, surgeries, procedures, and current use of medications.

- Treatment plan: The treatment plan identifies and sets the parameters for counseling, including statement of the problem, treatment goals, and steps to reach the goals.

- Case notes: Documentation of progress, clinical impressions, evaluation of each session, and homework assigned to the client (see Chapter 6, "Clinical Writing and Documentation in Counseling Records," for more information on how to write effective case notes).

- Termination record: A summarization of treatment, success, lack of success, and so forth (see Chapter 12, "Termination in Counseling: How to Say Goodbye," for more information on client termination).

- I would add to this list to keep any pertinent information provided by outside professionals (e.g., family physician, parole and probation, and child protection), as collateral information may be essential as well as good legal and ethical practice (American Counseling Association, 2014; Wheeler & Bertram, 2019).

CLOSING THE SESSION

Standard counseling sessions are typically 50 minutes (there may be some variation for group, couples, and family counseling and counseling in P–12 schools). Counselors, especially new ones, should try to begin and end sessions on time because this illustrates to clients the importance of set beginnings and endings. Counselors who allow sessions to begin late and extend beyond the parameters are modeling poor boundaries to the client. Such "loose" behavior on the part of the counselor may ultimately be unhealthy for the client in jobs, relationships, and in other social encounters. Of course, this statement is culture specific. Western cultures tend to value more rigid timelines, whereas some Eastern and indigenous cultures have more flexibility regarding time (Lee, 2006, 2019; Sue & Sue, 2013). Still, counselors must be cognizant of timely schedules because clients and colleagues will likely expect you to be prompt and lack of timeliness may create a backlog. (*Note:* In my own experience, physician appointments seldom have been on time. Counseling appointments have very different expectations.)

Many beginning counselors do have difficulty closing sessions with clients who insist on pushing the session beyond its limits. There is the old adage of the client who says nothing of note for 49 minutes, then drops a bombshell when their hand is on the office doorknob (e.g., "I'm pregnant," "My home is being foreclosed," "I've just flunked out of college," and my favorite, "Uh, see. . . I'm kind of having an affair"). I have experienced many such *doorknob* statements myself. If a client truly is in crisis—that is, a danger to themselves or others—then do not let the client leave (see Chapter 9, "Crisis Intervention in Practicum/Internship," for more information on clients in crisis). In the absence of such a risk, it is important that you stay as close to the set parameters as possible. Addressing session timeliness during informed consent is strongly encouraged. Regardless, you will need to reassert closings with some clients and this may take some degree of practice. Closing sessions in a timely manner has been a challenge for many people I have trained and supervised (including myself).

Benjamin (1987) emphasizes two important concerns in closing a counseling session. First, both the counselor and the client should be aware that the session is ending. This means the counselor has covered time limits in the intake session. Counselors would also be wise to make some statement during closing time like, "Okay. It looks like our time is about up. . . ." Second, disclosing new material should be gently discouraged during the closing. If the client "drops" something on you at the very end of the session, you might say, "That's an excellent starting point for next time" (if the disclosure is not a crisis). Use a kind though firm tone of voice during closing, and rise from your seat as this indicates an ending.

When it comes to ending sessions, be brief and simple. Remind the client of time limits by saying, "We have just 5 minutes left." This can help the client refocus and serves to keep the session on track. You might also say something like, "Time is almost up. Could you summarize what you learned today?" Gladding (2009) emphasizes that it is helpful to have the client summarize what happened in the session. This emphasizes the client's responsibility by forcing the client to reflect back on the salient points and recap them. This is also a tacit way of illustrating that the counselor values what the client sees as the important points of the session. The counselor certainly can provide the summarization, but it prevents the client from achieving momentum. Some counselors use nonverbal gestures such as standing up or pointing to their watch. There are many ways to end the session. The best guideline is to be clear, low key (so as not to hurt the client's feelings), and firm. Then, the final aspect of session termination is setting an appointment for the next session.

FINAL SUGGESTIONS

Here are some suggestions for your transition to the practicum/internship experience:

- Remember, in the beginning, everyone was a rookie. Give yourself time to make the transition. When you feel stressed and overwhelmed, check in with your supervisor. Also, get to know your fellow practicum/internship students. You can be good supports for one another. In fact, some graduate students have even begun practicum/internship support groups.

- As you begin practicum, be aware that you will be critiqued. The important aspect here is to be open to critical feedback. Even with the most benign and constructive type of feedback, it is natural to experience some degree of defensiveness. Be open to the feedback from your on-site clinical supervisor and your faculty practicum supervisor. But, do not be afraid to ask clarifying questions (see Chapter 7, "Models of Supervision: Classroom and Site Supervision," for more information on critique and feedback).

- Take initiative. Clinical supervisors are generally impressed with practicum and internship students who read and ask questions regarding agency, hospital, school, or university counseling center policies. If there are written policies and procedure manuals at your site (and there should be!), read the manual and ask your supervisor any question you might have about school/agency/hospital policies.

- Make a point of showing up on time for all your shifts. Interestingly, in all my years as a counselor educator, one of the most common complaints is tardy practicum/internship students. Be on time! If you know you may be late, call your placement ASAP.

- Complete all responsibilities in a timely manner. Make sure all case notes are completed and filed after each session (or certainly before you leave the practicum site).

- Make sure you practice regular self-care. Counselors cannot begin to help people in need unless they are emotionally healthy themselves. Make time for stress-reducing activities that you enjoy, such as physical fitness (e.g., jogging, cycling, swimming, power walking, yoga, and aerobics), and centering activities such as meditation, prayer (for those so inclined), reading, and so forth. Incidentally, self-care is part of your ethical code (American Counseling Association, 2014) and possibly one of the ethical tenets given least attention. My own experience is self-care is the most violated of all the ethical standards. Do not join this all-too-lengthy list of over stressed and soon-to-burn-out counselors.

- Understand that counseling actual people can be a complex endeavor. Give yourself time to adjust as counseling is unlike any experience you have previously had. While the counselor–client (or counselor–student) relationship may be friendly, it is not a friendship. Friendships are about both parties, while counseling is entirely about the client. A healthy counselor–client relationship would be a very unhealthy friendship.

CONCLUSION

Finally, I tell all my students not to fear making mistakes. In fact, I instruct them they *should* make mistakes because making mistakes indicates they are stretching their skill set. One of the worst mistakes student counselors can make is being inert due to "fear of saying something wrong." "Good" clinical supervisors are not going to chastise a student counselor for a basic semantic mistake. Fortunately, it is unlikely you will tell the client something that will be permanently damaging. You will commit occasional errors of commission and omission because every counselor, no matter how talented and experienced, does. If you believe you have offended the client, honesty is the best policy (e.g., "I apologize. I may have offended you by that question/comment. Let me try and rephrase. . . ."). Very few clients will expect perfection from their counselor (and should a client expect perfection, that would be an issue for the two of you to explore!). The critical factor is that you are able to learn from your mistakes. Be proactive and solicit advice from your on-site supervisor and university supervisor. Some call embracing and learning from mistakes "failing forward."

Finally, one of the best skills you can begin to hone is the power of self-talk and self-reflection (Beck & Butler, 2005; Ellis, 1999). As you proceed through your practicum and internship experience, notice how your self-talk evolves. Ideally, your self-talk should become more proactive (e.g., "I'm making real improvement as a counselor" type) and less negative or uncertain (e.g., "I can't possibly help anyone"). Granted, some graduate students will not be appropriate for counseling work, but that is different than having negative or, as Ellis (1999) would say, irrational self-talk. Even if you honestly believe you are not a good fit for the counseling profession, I would encourage you to adopt proactive self-talk such as: "It's unfortunate that I am not a good fit for counseling work but I will find another career and can still be helpful to others in my own way." Essentially, while not everyone can be a counselor, everyone *can* be a helper in some fashion. Some of the most helpful I have encountered in my life have been teachers, coaches, ministers, custodians, and others. Monitor your self-talk through self-reflection and revise it to be more optimistic and realistic. You will feel better and function better as a counselor, and your personal life likely will be more rewarding.

LESSONS LEARNED

"I feel like such an idiot!" exclaimed a young female graduate student, tears streaming down her face as she wiped her eyes with a tissue. Kelly (pseudonym) had always been a very gifted student, making strong grades and generating regular praise from teachers, professors, and peers. She had performed predictably strong in two subject courses she had previously taken with me but was struggling to create the therapeutic alliance and facilitate an effective session. Kelly was not unique among her cohort in making the transition from practicing mock sessions with peers to addressing real issues with actual clients. What was different was Kelly had such lofty expectations based upon a lifetime of academic success. Struggle seemed novel to her, and as such, she was seriously doubting her ability. For my part, her struggles seemed typical, and her practicum supervisor felt confident Kelly would improve, given her intelligence, effort, and willingness to accept constructive feedback. Kelly, however, was being very self-critical, something especially common to high-quality students I have taught and supervised.

She was in my practicum course along with five other students. Her placement was a small mental health clinic in the Greater Toronto Area, Canada. Her field site supervisor had selected Kelly in a competitive process. That factor likely placed even more stress for her as she offered feeling she was "letting everyone down." Neither her field site supervisor, peers, nor I could dissuade her that such struggles were natural and expected. My counsel to her was that the practicum experience (100 clock hours, of which 40 direct client contact hours were required) was a time to learn the placement, establish a relationship with the staff, and develop basic skills in co-counseling clients. Kelly had been assisting staff in co-facilitating groups and assisting in co-counseling with her supervisor and other therapists. The bi weekly reports showed that Kelly was doing acceptable work. Kelly, however, viewed any evaluation less that exceptional as "failure" (her word).

I further explained the practicum experience was meant to prepare students for Internship I, which required 300 clock hours, with 120 in direct client contact. Our Clinical Mental Health Counseling program required 1,000 clock hours and a minimum of 400 direct client contact hours over 2 academic years. The four-semester field placement experience thus was the backbone of the program. I counseled Kelly that actual counseling experience required a new set of skills, differing significantly from a regular subject course. She understood this on a rational level, but as counseling professionals well understand, many beliefs are *not* rational, even in a stellar student like Kelly.

Late in the term, Kelly's field site supervisor asked her to lead a group session. Kelly had been making steady progress, albeit with the occasional stumble. Her confidence had increased as the term progressed, and her supervisor gave her strong evaluations. She appeared poised to take a step up in her development. Her supervisor would naturally be present to take the reins should something unforeseen develop. In counseling work, the unforeseen is going to occur periodically. Kelly evidently did a good job starting the session with check-ins and then seamlessly transitioned into the session. As it was an anxiety management group, the members were to report on successes and setbacks, with the focus being on using CBT homework to manage their fears. The session was proceeding without incident as members reported on the vagaries of their successes and challenges since the previous week's session. All went well until Kelly invited a quiet member to share her story. Evidently, this young woman had just experienced a relationship breakup that was quite traumatic. Just as she commenced speaking, she burst into tears. Crying was common, and this was not what caused Kelly difficulty but rather the response of some group members. One member immediately jumped in expressing to the client experiencing the breakup, "You don't have to talk about it if it makes you sad." Another countered, "Stop trying to rescue people. That's invalidating!" The two members then began bickering, each trading verbal barbs, until the disagreement escalated into threats, resulting into group members taking sides and throwing the group into chaos. Kelly attempted to regain control but was unable to quell the ensuing mob-like atmosphere. Fortunately, after letting the conflict proceed to allow Kelly to address, the supervisor stepped in, reminding the group of the rules, appropriate feedback, and that future threats would result in members being removed from the group. A seasoned counselor and supervisor veteran with a strong voice, group members respected her and quieted.

The supervisor then righted the group, having them discuss what had happened and how to avoid future counter-therapeutic behavior. According to the supervisor, the melee actually turned into the classic teachable moment. Kelly, however, viewed the experience as an abject failure on her part. "I should have been able to manage it myself," she informed the class during a check-in period. Her classmates all provided encouraging feedback, most volunteering they also would have struggled to regain therapeutic order. She admitted her supervisor had been encouraging, explaining to Kelly that such times can be challenging for even experienced clinicians to manage and thus the reason for an accomplished veteran as co-facilitator. Kelly, however, was hearing none of their counsel, deflecting with self-defeating *shoulds* and *oughts*. Finally, I asked, "If you had been the supervisor and a practicum student your supervisee, how might you counsel that student?" Despite being a gifted person intellectually, she was nevertheless deficient in self-compassion. She knew the situation was beyond her experience and skill level but insisted on unrealistic standards. Her peers and I encouraged her to practice self-understanding and treat herself with the compassion she would offer another, although I knew our words had not had their desired effect.

After speaking with her field site supervisor again, who assured me she would continue to encourage Kelly to be more self-compassionate, I contemplated alternate strategies on my end. Taking an aged counseling workbook off my office shelf, I perused the dog-eared pages, finding a section on writing about healing from trauma. Tailoring the exercise to Kelly's situation, I drafted several self-reflective questions such as the following: What positive traits did you use during this challenging experience? How did you show determination? How did you show courage? How did you evidence resilience? What does this difficult experience suggest regarding your ability to continue developing as a counselor in training? Printing the questions off, I scheduled a meeting with Kelly for later in the week.

She arrived to my office seeming upbeat. This was, however, to be her *putting on a brave face* look. She admitted the group experience had been difficult for her, continuing to default to her negative self-statements. Explaining the value of constructive self-talk, I handed her the reflective questions, explaining that her assignment was to answer the questions. Furthermore, if her answers continued to be full of unrealistic self-blame, I would be making comments and requiring rewrites. She took the pages, inquiring, "What is the purpose for this exercise?" "For you to begin to habituate more self-affirmation." She nodded and asked, "Is this a 'fake it till you make it' exercise?" "No," I reframed, "it's a practice until you gain confidence and believe what you tell yourself." She left seeming unsure of the effect.

The following week, she arrived before practicum class. To my astonishment, she handed over a hefty collection of the self-reflective questions. Realizing her tendency toward self-criticism, she had copied the pages many times over and rewritten answers to the questions. Her answers began with her usual "I should have . . ." voice but then transitioned into something akin to "Now that I have had this experience, I feel more able to manage a difficult situation," type answers. "I get what you and my on-site supervisor have telling me, but the writing helped it to sink in." I encouraged her to remember this approach and use it with patients in clinical practice. She smiled, adding, "I need to keep using it on me. I'm still a work in progress."

No question, all counselors, counselor educators, supervisors in the field, hardened veterans, and counseling students are a work in progress (Rogers, 1951). I have learned and relearned this professional lesson numerous times over nearly 40 years.

Whenever my hubris emerges, patients, clients, and students the world over have appropriately humbled me. Before my life has run its course, there will be more such learning experiences. So, lean in to constructive feedback, embrace your less-than-perfect self, acknowledge your strengths and challenges, learn from all these, and keep moving forward.

 A robust set of instructor resources designed to supplement this text is located at http://connect.springerpub.com/content/book/978-0-8261-6607-4. Qualifying instructors may request access by emailing textbook@springerpub.com.

REFERENCES

American Counseling Association. (2014). *ACA code of ethics*. https://www.counseling.org/resources/aca-code-of-ethics.pdf
American Psychiatric Association. (2022). *Diagnostic and statistical manual of mental disorders* (5th ed., text revision). American Psychiatric Publishing.
Beck, A. T., & Weishaar, M. (2008). Cognitive therapy. In R. J. Corsini & D. Wedding (Eds.), *Current psychotherapies* (8th ed., pp. 263–294). Thomson Brooks/Cole.
Beck, J. S. (2011). *Cognitive behavior therapy: Basics and beyond* (2nd ed.). Guilford Press.
Beck, J. S., & Butler, A. C. (2005). Treating psychotherapists with cognitive therapy. In J. D. Geller, J. C. Norcross, & D. E. Orlinsky (Eds.), *The psychotherapist's own psychotherapy: Patient and clinician perspectives* (pp. 254–264). Oxford University Press.
Benjamin, A. (1987). *The helping interview*. Houghton Mifflin.
Cox, W. M., & Klinger, E. (Eds.). (2011). *The handbook of motivational counseling: Concepts, approaches, & assessment* (2nd ed.). Wiley.
Duncan, B., Miller, S. D., Wampold, B., & Hubble, M. (2010). *The heart and soul of change: Delivering what works in therapy* (2nd ed.). American Psychological Association.
Ellis, A. (1999). *How to make yourself happy and remarkably less disturbable*. Impact.
Ellis, A. (2001). *Overcoming destructive beliefs, feelings, and behaviors*. Prometheus Books.
Folstein, M. F., Folstein, S. E., & McHugh, P. R. (1975). "Mini-mental state": A practical method for grading the cognitive state of patients for the clinician. *Journal of Psychiatric Research, 12*(3), 189–198. https://doi.org/10.1016/0022-3956(75)90026-6
Gladding, S. T. (2009). *Counseling: A comprehensive profession* (6th ed.). Merrill/Prentice Hall.
Hayes, D. G. (2017). *Assessment in counseling: A guide to the use of psychological assessments procedures* (6th ed.). American Counseling Association.
Hodges, S. (2016). *The counseling practicum and internship manual: A resource for graduate counseling students* (2nd ed.). Springer Publishing Company.
Ivey, A. E., Ivey, M. B., & Zalaquett, C. P. (2010). *Intentional interviewing and counseling: Facilitating development in a multicultural society* (7th ed.). Cengage Learning.
Lee, C. C. (Ed.). (2006). *Counseling for social justice*. American Counseling Association.
Lee, C. C. (Ed.). (2019). *Multicultural issues in counseling: New approaches to diversity* (5th ed.). American Counseling Association.
Polanski, P. J., & Hinkle, J. S. (2000). The mental status examination: Its use by professional counselors. *Journal of Counseling & Development, 78*, 357–364. https://doi.org/10.1002/j.1556-6676.2000.tb01918.x
Remley, T. P., Jr., & Herlihy, B. (2020). *Ethical, legal and professional issues in counseling* (6th ed.). Pearson.
Rogers, C. R. (1942). *Counseling and psychotherapy*. Houghton Mifflin.
Rogers, C. R. (1951). *Client centered therapy*. Houghton Mifflin.
Sampaio, M., Haro, N. V. M., De Sousa, B., Melo, V. W., & Hoffman, H. G. (2021). Therapists make the switch to telepsychology to safely continue treating their patients during the COVID-19 pandemic. Virtual reality telepsychology may be next. *Frontiers in Virtual Reality, 1*, 576421. https://doi.org/10.3389/frvir.2020.576421
Seligman, L. A. (2004). *Diagnosis and treatment planning in counseling* (3rd ed.). Kluwer.
Sommers-Flanagan, R., & Sommers-Flanagan, J. (1999). *Clinical interviewing* (2nd ed.). Wiley.
Sue, D. W., & Sue, D. (2013). *Counseling the culturally diverse* (6th ed.). Wiley.

Weinrach, S. G. (1989). Guidelines for clients of private practitioners: Committing the structure to print. *Journal of Counseling & Development, 67,* 299–300. https://doi.org/10.1002/j.1556-6676.1989.tb02607.x

Wheeler, A. M., & Bertram, B. (2019). *The counselor and the law: A guide to legal and ethical practice* (8th ed.). American Counseling Association.Exhibit 5.2 Mental Status Examination (Brief Version)

CHAPTER 6

Clinical Writing and Documentation in Counseling Records

INTRODUCTION

Writing clear and descriptive clinical case notes is very different from most other types of writing. By now, you have likely had lots of experience writing American Psychological Association (APA)-style research papers in your counseling classes. You may also have written poetry, short stories, journal articles, and maybe even website blogs. In these cases, the objective is to entertain, persuade, or inform. Unlike these aforementioned types of writing, your objective in writing case notes is merely to create an accurate and informative record of treatment and client progress (or lack thereof). Although it is likely that training in counseling skills receives the most attention in graduate programs, clarity in clinical writing may be even more important (Mitchell, 2008; Remley & Herlihy, 2020; Wheeler & Bertram, 2019), especially if a client's file is subpoenaed and the counselor is required to testify and defend their case notes in a courtroom. This chapter provides an overview on writing clear, concise, and effective case notes. "Counselors have an explicitly stated legal and ethical duty to create and maintain client records on every client" (Wheeler & Bertram, 2019, p. 153). Failure to maintain adequate records could also form the basis of malpractice, as it breaches the standard of care expected from a mental health professional (Wheeler & Bertram, 2019). Counseling students should remember that like all other counseling training, developing good, clear, and concise clinical writing skills takes time and comes through experience. Your practicum and internship placements likely are good beginning points for developing effective clinical writing skills. Having made such a statement, it is also noteworthy to admit that many counselors and supervisors are not good clinical writers.

Remember, when writing case notes, you are not writing for a wide audience—in fact, in most cases, you actually hope your case notes never see the light of day! You must be aware, however, that your notes are not simply for yourself but serve as treatment history for future clinicians, human service professionals, law enforcement personnel, the client, and, shudder, even the courts. An ineffective clinical writer who makes numerous grammatical errors or leaves out pertinent information will lose their professional credibility at minimum and, at maximum, could be on the short end of a lawsuit. Should the unlikely and unfortunate event of a lawsuit against you happen, you want the written case record to support your therapy. Without adequate documentation of adherence to the *ACA Code of Ethics* (American Counseling Association [ACA], 2014), as well as failure to document competent treatment, a counselor's legal and ethical vulnerability is increased (Mitchell, 2008; Remley & Herlihy, 2020; Wheeler & Bertram, 2019).

Unfortunately, many graduate counseling programs seem to put little emphasis on training students in writing clinical case notes (Cottone & Tarvydas, 2003). This is of great concern when one considers that what is (and is not) recorded in case notes can be the difference between legal culpability and sound legal standing (Wheeler & Bertram, 2019). Many professions, such as medicine, train students with the expectation that their notes will be read by various professionals and that they must always be prepared to defend whatever is in the record (Remley & Herlihy, 2020). The *ACA Code of Ethics* requires counselors to maintain counseling records and, furthermore, to provide adequate documentation (ACA, 2014). Adequate documentation is not explicitly defined, though it often includes case notes, a treatment plan, *Diagnostic and Statistical Manual of Mental Disorders, Fifth Edition, Text Revision* (5th ed.; *DSM-5-TR*; APA, 2022) diagnoses, any testing, and documentation from previous clinical and other providers (e.g., psychiatric records, previous counseling, and law enforcement).

Case notes are one of the most important records for counselors, as they are records counselors generate themselves. Writing effective case notes typically is a function of practice and experience. Most writers are made, not born (and my experience is that this includes all types of writing—clinical, fiction, poetry, magazine, etc.). As a college professor and a writer myself, I can verify that writing does not come easy to most people. (It certainly has not come easy to me!) Most of us struggle to transform our thoughts into coherent sentences and paragraphs that address what needs addressing. The best teacher for writing case notes is some combination of instruction, reading an experienced clinician's case notes, perusing appropriate reference texts on writing case notes, suggestions from clinical supervisors and/or colleagues, and plenty of practice in writing your own. During your practicum or internship, ask for tips from veteran counselors regarding effective case notes. Notice how they have learned to write, what they put in their notes, and, just as important, what they leave out. The specific style and content will vary from one counselor to another, and differences will exist regarding the types of clients counseled or evaluated. However, the professionalism of skilled colleagues will likely be consistent. Case note writing is an area where your on-site field supervisor, or another seasoned counselor, should be your coach. Your field supervisor may analyze your case notes and provide pointers on length, content, and quality. Students in school counseling placements likely will have far less documentation than those in agencies, hospitals, and correctional facilities. Nevertheless, because good professional writing is essential across many areas of the counseling field, school counseling students would be wise to develop their case note writing as well, as they have also been compelled to testify in courts of law.

CLIENT RECORDS AND THE STANDARD OF CARE

In the distant past, it was common practice that mental health professionals intentionally refrained from keeping client records (Wheeler & Bertram, 2019). This unfortunate, foolish, and now unethical practice is, necessarily and thankfully, passé. In this electronic era, the legal and ethical standards regarding information, storage, and transmission of client records have become a critical focus in the mental health field. Counselors have an explicitly stated legal and ethical duty to create and maintain client records on every client (ACA, 2014; Wheeler & Bertram, 2019). Failure to maintain adequate client records could form the basis of a claim of professional malpractice because it breaches the standard of care expected of a practicing mental health professional (Wheeler & Bertram, 2019). As previously mentioned, the *ACA Code of Ethics* is explicit regarding a counselor's duty to record adequate records: "Counselors create, safeguard, and maintain documentation necessary for rendering professional services" (ACA, 2014, Standard A.1.b). Well-documented client counseling records are possibly the most effective tool counselors have for establishing client treatment protocols, ensuring an ongoing standard of care, and supporting competent care. The "well-documented" aspect is the most critical part of case records. Well documented does not mean drafting lengthy case notes but rather ones that address pertinent issues with brevity.

Ethical and legal standards affect all counselors. Regardless of the setting you ultimately work in, whether school, hospital, correctional facility, or university counseling center, you will need to become competent and skilled in writing clear case notes, not merely because you may be compelled to testify in a court of law or an ethics hearing or defend your case notes to your workplace supervisor. Aspirational ethics require a counselor to strive to exceed basic ethical parameters. Thus, should you find yourself in these unfortunate and sometimes traumatic experiences and your case notes become the focus of examination, you will be in a stronger position. On this matter, I can speak from experience. As a director of a county clinic early in my career, I was compelled to go to court regularly. In every case, the attorneys focused most of their attention on the written records, either my own or that of one of the clinicians I supervised. Essentially, I learned the hard way that I (and others) had to be prepared to defend anything we recorded in case notes. After all, although a client or counselor's memory will fade with time, written records remain. Furthermore, should an important detail be omitted from client records, such inattention could be costly as well.

Standard of Care: Clinical Management

Clear, concise case notes and well-maintained clinical records clearly assist in the clinical case history and provide a rationale for past and current treatment. Because the nature of counseling implies continuous growth and change, case notes should reflect how the client is progressing in their treatment. Case records provide documentation of quality care, including what has worked, what has not worked, and why. Case records also ensure some degree of protection from legal liability by demonstrating and documenting the strategic planning on the part of the counselor and treatment team. Case notes also establish that the counselor conducted themselves as competent professionals (e.g., was ethical and within legal parameters). After all, written

134 • THE COUNSELING PRACTICUM AND INTERNSHIP MANUAL

records are the only concrete proof the counselor has regarding client treatment and therapeutic progress. As it is often said in the mental health field, "If it ain't written down, it doesn't exist." So, ensure recording of critical areas of treatment . As a counselor, you will deal with three conflicting principles (Mitchell, 2008, p. 17):

- the client's right of confidentiality versus the counselor's obligation to protect society;
- the client's right to receive service in the least restrictive setting versus the counselor's obligation to provide close supervision, continuous monitoring, and a safe environment; and
- the client's right to die versus the counselor's obligation to save lives (this one is particularly contentious; see the next heading regarding documenting end-of-life issues).

One of the more distressing issues that can arise in counseling is when a client discloses the intent to harm themselves or other parties. When clients disclose thoughts, feelings, or intentions that place themselves or an identifiable third party at risk, the counselor must document the threat and the appropriate action taken, as well as notify the proper authorities. Competent documentation is essential in crisis situations, as they are likely to involve the legal system. Should a case proceed to a court for an involuntary commitment to a psychiatric center, correctional facility, referral to child protection caseworkers, or to court officials, the case record will be carefully scrutinized.

DOCUMENTING COMPLICATED END-OF-LIFE ISSUES

Having written the previous paragraph emphasizing the very real need to protect clients (and others), the finer nuances of self-harm call out for additional elaboration. Clearly, all competent counselors would quickly intervene in cases of foreseeable harm regarding a child, an adolescent, or an adult. Nevertheless, for seniors in counseling, particularly those with terminal illnesses, the issue of protecting the client versus client autonomy likely is murkier for many counselors. The ethical dilemma of a client's right to die has long been debated in Western society, and as of this writing (2023), 10 states—Oregon, Colorado, Washington, Montana, California, Hawaii, Vermont, New Jersey, Maine, and New Jersey—as well as Washington DC, have enacted physician-assisted suicide. While right-to-die issues and situations are far more common in the medical profession, counselors and other mental health professionals may also grapple with this thorny issue.

The issue confronting counselors is how to respond when a terminally ill client discloses the intention to end their life. Under typical circumstances, the counselor would have an ethical (and legal) duty to take action to prevent the client from carrying out a suicidal intent. Said action likely would involve breaching confidentiality to prevent the client from attempting suicide. With elderly, terminally ill clients, many counselors may have conflicting emotions. Beyond the counselor's feelings, legal issues may include the following: (a) who is the client (the terminally ill patient or the family members); (b) who has legal competence to determine what course of action is in the best interest of the patient (the terminally ill patient or a health-care guardian); (c) the strongly held views by everyone involved concerning the proper (moral, ethical, and legal) course of action; (d) state laws that may be more or less prescriptive in terms of the duties and responsibilities of health and mental health professionals; and (e) the values of the counselor who is providing services (Wheeler & Bertram, 2019, pp. 208–209). The *ACA Code of Ethics* (ACA, 2014) provides some guidance at least with regard to professional ethics:

> Counselors who provide services to terminally ill individuals who are considering hastening their own deaths have the option to maintain confidentially, depending on applicable laws and the specific circumstances of the situation and after seeking consultation or supervision from appropriate professional and legal parties. (Standard B.2.b)

As a member of the ACA Ethics Revision Task Force that revised and developed the 2014 edition of the *ACA Code of Ethics*, we struggled to revise the end-of-life section of the 2005 edition as members of the task force had competing ethical and moral positions—as is natural on sensitive issues. Any counselor counseling a terminally ill client who professes an intention to hasten their death likely will tread a precarious legal and ethical precipice. Beyond professional ethics and legal issues, moral and religious issues and the right to self-determination may weigh as heavily as any other considerations. The classic ethical question of "What is in the client's best interest?" may be challenging to satisfactorily answer in assisted suicide. For example, should a terminally ill client be compelled to receive expensive, unwanted, painful, and ultimately unhelpful treatment against their wishes? Would death actually be in the client's best interest, particularly when considering death is a natural part of life? Should adult clients of rational mind be allowed the ultimate option, that being the right to choose when and how to die? Who exactly, if anyone, should be empowered to terminate a human life? These weighty questions naturally provoke much debate across spiritual, moral, ethical, and certainly political lines. Due to the confluence of issues, concerns, and legalities, obtaining competent legal advice and sober consultation with an experienced colleague is crucial.

The more pragmatic issue for readers of this text is how and what to document in such a situation. My best advice, although perhaps not very helpful, is to seek out consultation from a seasoned, trusted colleague and to obtain legal advice. While few counselors have faced end-of-life euthanasia, *some* have, and in the future, more are certain to confront this issue. Regardless of personal beliefs, the *ACA Code of Ethics* mandates that counselors refrain from imposing their values, attitudes, and beliefs on clients (ACA, 2014, Standard A.4.b), while refraining from value-based referrals (ACA, 2014, Standard A.11.b). Thus, a counselor confronted with a terminally ill client voicing euthanasia in a state or territory without an assisted death law is in a perilous situation. The *ACA Code of Ethics* attempts to provide some flexibility to counselors faced with terminally ill clients (ACA, 2014, Standard B.2.b).

The legal, ethical, and moral implications regarding assisted death can become quite complex. Speaking from the experience of drafting an ethical guide in the face of shifting public opinion and dominant legal complexities, assisted death is a legal and ethical "briar patch" potentially facing any counselor. Get good legal advice; consult with a trusted colleague, certainly your supervisor; and document judiciously, reflecting on the advice you received as well as your own good sense.

Quality documentation also facilitates continuity of care from one counselor to another counselor or related professional (Wheeler & Bertram, 2019). Whether the transfer is temporary (e.g., the counselor is on vacation or out of the office) or permanent, the case record provides continuity of care. In such cases, well-written, up-to-date case notes are a means of communicating important information to a new clinician or court official. No doubt, clear, concise, and effective case notes are "in the client's best interest." As counselors, make sure you have made a reasonable effort to provide adequate documentation so that the next counselor or professional can understand treatment history and provide continued quality of care.

Standard of Care: Legal Implications

Clearly, this text has been quite emphatic regarding the legal implications of counseling, as litigation casts a very long shadow over the mental health profession. Counseling records sometimes become legal documents in court cases—such as when clients are involved in custody battles, malpractice litigation, workers' compensation, probation hearings, charges of abuse, involuntary commitments to psychiatric hospitals, and so forth. The standard of practice regarding records and the documentation of counseling services continues to evolve, often through legal changes. The full impact of congressional acts such as the Health Insurance Portability and Accountability Act (HIPAA) have yet to be tested in court (Wheeler & Bertram, 2019), but counselors should assume the highest standard. *Tarasoff v. The Regents of the University of California* case (1976), *Jaffee v. Redmond et al.* (1996), and *Thapar v. Zezulka* (1999) have all impacted the counseling profession in significant ways (e.g., established the duty to warn in *Tarasoff*; psychotherapist [including counselor] privilege in federal court in *Jaffee*; and in *Thapar*, a judge ruled Texas counselors have no duty to warn nor do they have immunity should they do so). Case notes should reflect that the counselor made the client aware of their rights through informed consent (see Chapter 4, "Ethical and Legal Issues"). Clients must clearly understand the limits of confidentiality and that a counselor will need to break confidentiality under certain required circumstances (e.g., danger to self or others, legally mandated court testimony, and suspected child abuse). Fortunately, few cases will evolve into a judicial hearing, but the counselor must prepare each case record with the understanding that the case could proceed to court. Also, always remember that with a legally mandated client, a court official (or parole or probation officer/committee) likely will be reviewing the file, and your case notes, reports, and assessment findings could make a significant difference in a client's life.

So, assume the client record you are creating will wind up scrutinized in a courtroom or another formal and serious forum. This foundation will assist you in carefully creating a well-documented file that will accurately reflect the client's progress. Because client records can become public records (as in court proceedings), counselors should not include identifying information about third parties (such as family members, alleged extramarital lovers, or illegal acts), unless that information has a direct bearing on the client's treatment.

Clearly, client records do not always reflect a favorable impression on the client and may be detrimental in a legal hearing. For example, if counseling a convicted sex offender who has been noncompliant with treatment, your written record must reflect that noncompliance. In some cases, you may actually find a client likable and want to inflate said client's compliance and progress in counseling. Clearly, however, such inaccuracy could be construed either as malpractice, falsifying a legal document, or both, which could jeopardize a counselor's career (Mitchell, 2008; Remley & Herlihy, 2020; Wheeler & Bertram, 2019). Essentially, your ethical integrity and potential legal standing to practice as a professional lie as much in your documentation acumen as with your clinical skills. The wrong lesson to learn from this chapter is that documentation and case notes are an impossible chore. Frankly, the simpler you make your case notes, the better off you—and your clients—will likely be. Be thorough, but be concise as possible. Furthermore, work to ensure that the case file is complete and that additional documentation (e.g., treatment plan, assessment, and records from other providers) is present.

Standard of Care: Health Insurance Portability and Accountability Act Compliance

As discussed in Chapter 4, "Ethical and Legal Issues," counselors who practice in public and private settings who bill insurance companies fall under the HIPAA of 1996. The major intent of the HIPAA was to address electronic transmission of client care information through media such as the internet. Lawmakers have constructed statutes to ensure further HIPAA compliance, especially with regard to client privacy (Wheeler & Bertram, 2019). Some counselors, such as school counselors and counselors working in college and university counseling centers, may be exempt from the HIPAA, although many of the latter may attempt to operate in compliance with the HIPAA regardless of a given desire to meet a higher standard of care.

HIPAA primarily affects the counselor with regard to electronic transmission of mental health records (e.g., progress notes, treatment plan, and assessment). Privacy refers to the right of a person to be left alone and to control their personal information (Wheeler & Bertram, 2019). The term *privacy* is often used interchangeably with the term *confidentiality*, though *confidentiality* typically refers to a professional's (i.e., counselor) ethical duty, whereas *privacy* is the client's legal right to protect their personal information from third parties. The HIPAA Privacy Rule (2013), established by federal action, provides a greater sense of patient privacy previously lacking due to variations in state laws. This amendment to HIPAA arose because of concerns that transmission of healthcare information through the internet and other electronic means could lead to gaps in protection of patient confidentiality. The HIPAA Privacy Rule applies to both paper and electronic transmissions of protected health information (PHI) by covered entities. Covered entities are health and mental health professionals who transmit any PHI such as healthcare claims, health plan enrollment, and coordination of benefits (Wheeler & Bertram, 2019). These would include communication between counselors, billing insurance, and sending such information through electronic or paper means. Incidentally, counselors must also be aware of state law if their state of residence *exceeds* HIPAA standards of client/patient protection of privacy.

Counselors must keep abreast of HIPAA changes that may affect their obligations to clients. The HIPAA Privacy Rule of 2013 also specifically permits clients to receive copies of their records in electronic form and/or have the records sent in electronic form to third parties, provided health records get transmitted through electronic means (Wheeler & Bertram, 2019). While it is difficult to predict specific changes to currently existing federal privacy law, given the global virtual world we inhabit, future regulation regarding privacy is certain to occur on a periodic basis.

CASE NOTES

Given the time, effort, and referencing in this text regarding legal issues, it should be clear that understanding legalities, as well as professional ethics, is paramount for counselors. While the prose in this text is heavy on legal rulings, court cases, and congressional acts, there is much uncertainty in select areas of mental healthcare. Counseling records include two broad sections of information identified by HIPAA as PHI. PHI examples include (a) client demographic information (e.g., name, date of birth, address, telephone number, and email address) and (b) diagnosis, prognosis, treatment plan, progress to date, dates of service (beginning and end of client sessions), participants in session, and financial data (charges, payments, and balance; Wheeler & Bertram, 2019). This type of PHI is confidential but, under appropriate circumstances, is accessible to third-party providers such as insurance companies.

An added level of protection granted to case notes maintained in a separate physical or electronic location makes this practice appealing. This means that disclosure of case notes requires a separately executed client authorization if the case notes are maintained in a separate file (Remley & Herlihy, 2020). Naturally, counselors can easily integrate case notes within a single file and such is common practice. In such practices, case notes would fall under the general guidelines governing disclosure (see Chapter 4, "Ethical and Legal Issues"). While many counselors would argue the need to maintain *psychotherapy* case notes separately, given what appears to be added protection against subpoenas, one may wish to proceed with caution. Two files require an extra location—either electronic or physical—to file confidential case records. This means an added complication and one extra step with every record. My own experience through decades in mental health and higher education is things all too often get misplaced. Thus, many counselors prefer to have just one case record. There are risks in either situation of one versus two case note locations. My own counsel is that whatever is written, whether it be one or two records, must be clear, concise, and understandable to non mental health professionals. Remember, juvenile justice workers, child protection caseworkers, and lawyers may review them. In the past, I have had my records subpoenaed and been compelled to defend them in court, which has taught me well on this matter. So, be very clear in record keeping, and make sure the case record supports your treatment. If the case record you wrote does not support the treatment you provided, you could be in legal jeopardy (Wheeler & Bertram, 2019). So, make sure to craft your case notes carefully and in congruence with treatment provided.

Although HIPAA provides a definition of psychotherapy notes, important questions remain unanswered. For example, would standard **S**ubjective, **O**bjective, **A**ssessment, and **P**lan notes (SOAP notes, discussed later in this chapter) fall under *psychotherapy notes*? In my experience, many agencies assume they are. What about the couples, family, or group counselor who considers the couple, family, or group as the client? How would HIPAA impact such practices? Alternatively, what about the counselor who has ethical concerns regarding the legitimacy of *DSM* diagnoses, based on past, present cultural, and gender discrimination (Schwartz & Feisthamel, 2009) and refuses to use the system? These and other relevant questions regarding HIPAA remain unanswered (Wheeler & Bertram, 2019). Given past history (e.g., *Tarasoff, Jaffee,* and *Boynton*), the courts may eventually be called upon to decide such issues.

Standard of Care: Risk Management Strategy

The final reason for keeping records is very simple. Well-documented case files provide effective defense for counselors responding to lawsuits or ethical complaints (Remley & Herlihy, 2020; Wheeler & Bertram, 2019). Should questions arise regarding the counselor's actions or in legal and ethical hearings, well-documented records provide protection. If you are accused of incompetence, malfeasance, and violating legal or ethical parameters and your treatment actions were not adequately noted in the record, you have little defense. Clear case notes, assessments, treatment plan, and so forth are essential documents that provide a rationale for treatment. Colleagues and clinical supervisors in the same agency, school, and hospital also typically read case files, and this collateral support strengthens the counselor's case. A question counseling students likely have at this point is "What constitutes adequate documentation?" This is an excellent question. Unfortunately, "adequate documentation" is not explicitly defined. Nevertheless, there are some clearly understood parameters of *adequate* documentation:

- client identification information (e.g., name, age, gender)
- previous treatment (e.g., medical, mental health, educational—whatever is pertinent and available)
- informed consent document: states client's rights and responsibilities including parameters of confidentiality and so on
- financial arrangements (e.g., insurance, private pay, and employee assistance program)
- clinical assessment and/or *DSM-5-TR* diagnosis
- release of information (if pertinent)
- collateral information (e.g., test results; letters regarding client educational, psychological, and/or vocational history; reports; information regarding the client obtained from other sources; past clinical records; communications from third parties)
- treatment plan
- case notes
- academic standing, grades, and so on (P–12 school settings)
- anything else pertaining to the treatment of the client (Adapted from Wheeler & Bertram, 2019)

Wheeler and Bertram (2019) refer to high-risk cases, such as those involving potentially suicidal clients, clients who express homicidal intent, HIV-positive clients with multiple sexual partners, and cases of suspected abuse. From a risk management standpoint, they recommend documentation with the following steps:

- *At-risk situation*: Document what the client did or said that suggested they were considering engaging in or were actively engaging in a high-risk activity. Be clear and specific. For example, "Client stated she had a plan for suicide by swallowing pills after session today." Alternatively, if more subtle, "Client said he was really getting 'tired of his ex-wife's obnoxious new boyfriend and planned to take him out.'" Then explain that you clarified with the client what "take him out" meant.

140 • THE COUNSELING PRACTICUM AND INTERNSHIP MANUAL

- *Assessment*: Based on your clinical experience and knowledge of the client, document the severity level of this threat. Clearly explain how you determined the severity level. Did you use a standard assessment such as the Columbia-Suicide Severity Rating Scale (C-SSRS); Beck Depression Inventory-II (BDI-II); Adapted SAD PERSONS Scale; Danger Assessment instrument; specific intake questions; review of past client history; scaling questions (1 to 10, with 1 being low and 10 high); and so on? Standard assessments with a research base behind them always are an advantage (e.g., BDI-II, Minnesota Multiphasic Personality Inventory-2 [MMPI-2], and Drug Attitude Inventory [DAI]). There is nothing necessarily wrong with using subjective assessments in counseling (e.g., scaling questions), as they are common and helpful. However, as they lack a strong research base and are subject to wide reliability and validity concerns, a prudent counselor would pair them with an objective test. Subjective tests lacking research support may also be more open to question in a courtroom.

- *Options*: List the options you consider as appropriate responses based on your assessment. Listing options demonstrates that you were thinking broadly and that you considered a range of alternatives before reaching a decision.

- *Rule out*: Briefly describe what options you ruled out and why each was determined to be inappropriate. These descriptions clarify your clinical decision-making and make the case that you acted appropriately.

- *Consultation and/or supervision*: If there is time, obtain and document any colleague's consultation or supervision you received to evaluate and clarify a course of action.

- *Actions taken*: Describe the options you chose, including what you said and did. This helps clarify how you implemented the options you determined to be appropriate.

- *Follow-up*: Document what happened, what you did, and how things progressed until there was resolution. (Adapted from Wheeler & Bertram, 2019)

My experience has taught me the wisdom of one additional step: *Consult your supervisor*. Anytime that you encounter a high-risk case, consult with your supervisor as soon as possible, document that you consulted them, and note any suggestions. From experience as a clinical supervisor, the worst nightmare is to be caught unaware because a counselor did not apprise them of a high-risk situation. Because supervisors are held to a higher standard than line counselors and other therapists, they inherit greater liability. The legal principle known as *respondeat superior* (Latin for "let the master answer") holds that supervisors with authority over supervisees are accountable for a supervisee's negligence (Christie et al., 1997). So, consult your supervisor immediately in any potential high-risk situations. Failure to apprise your boss regarding a high-risk, potentially litigious situation is very poor job security!

As a counselor-in-training, you must understand that no amount of protection is absolute. However, should you maintain an up-to-date case file; document clear case notes, treatment plans, and so forth; and follow the suggestions in the previous discussion of high-risk cases, you will have the odds on your side. But, regardless of how thorough you are regarding case notes, adequate documentation, and consultation with your supervisor, the risk remains, albeit, very small. Furthermore, as a student you *likely* fall under your university's liability; however, this issue seems unclear, as graduate students generally are not considered university employees. Thus, carrying student liability insurance is necessary. As previously noted, most counseling

RECOMMENDATIONS FOR RECORDKEEPING

As discussed in Chapter 4, "Ethical and Legal Issues," agencies and settings differ in terms of how they take, maintain, and store records. Many are moving to electronic-based notes systems. Whether your school or agency uses paper or electronic records, Mitchell (2008) offers the following advice regarding record keeping:

programs likely require students to purchase liability insurance. Student membership in the ACA, American Mental Health Counselors Association (AMHCA), American School Counselor Association (ASCA), Canadian Counselling and Psychotherapy Association, and other professional counseling organizations carries student liability insurance along with the membership.

RECOMMENDATIONS FOR RECORDKEEPING

As discussed in Chapter 4, "Ethical and Legal Issues," agencies and settings differ in terms of how they take, maintain, and store records. Many are moving to electronic-based notes systems. Whether your school or agency uses paper or electronic records, Mitchell (2008) offers the following advice regarding record keeping:

- Service providers need timely, accurate, and comprehensive information. Lack of information can impede quality of care because the decision-making process is placed at risk.
- An organization must comply with its own written policy related to record keeping and confidentiality. In the event of litigation or allegations of unethical conduct, "failure to comply" can be used against the service provider.
- One way to avoid misuse of information is to have trained employees who are committed to protecting the privacy of each client. (p. 45)

Mitchell (2008) also offers eight assumptions counselors should make regarding electronic records:

- The counseling record will be subpoenaed and the court must understand what went on in counseling.
- The counselor may or may not be with the agency when it happens. Someone else will have to read and understand what the counselor wrote.
- Legislation that opens a record to the client exists now or will be passed. In fact, the *ACA Code of Ethics* already provides the client with reasonable access to records.
- The counselor's notes will not be accurate if they take days or weeks to write a note, so they should be written as soon as possible. (Practicum and internship students will not be retained if such delays occur!)
- The note will be the best possible reflection of the counselor's professional abilities.
- Client contact is not considered a professional service until the counselor's entry is in the record.
- The notes may be used by an official board of inquiry (e.g., licensure board and ethics panel).
- The service documentation and personnel file may be requested by a board of inquiry (essentially, a board of professional counselors charged with reviewing ethics complaints) in the event of allegations of unethical conduct. The *ACA Code of Ethics* also requires that counselors cooperate with investigations. (p. 46)

Counselors never know when a client's file will be inspected. Therefore, always write case notes and organize the client's file on the assumption that whatever is written will be read and evaluated at some point in the future. You must defend what you have included in the record, especially with regard to clinical treatment. Keeping this possibility in mind should not overly inhibit you but should help you keep close to the facts. It is important to remember the following:

- Your clients have a legal right to review their record.
- Your clients have a right to demand that you provide copies of case notes to their physician, other mental health professionals, and attorneys.
- Your clients have a right to subpoena your case notes. If they sue you, they lose their right to privacy, as the counselor has a right to protect themselves in a lawsuit.
- Third parties can also subpoena case notes when involved in legal cases involving the client, even over the client or counselor's objections. You will need your attorney to address subpoenas. Do not simply send documents the subpoena requests, as you may then be guilty of violating the client's privacy.
- The legal representatives of deceased clients, in most states, have a right to inspect the deceased client's case notes. However, deceased clients maintain confidentiality and a right to privacy absent legal rulings. Should a family member who is not the deceased client's legal representative request to view their loved one's file, you likely will need to refuse. (Check with your attorney as state laws may vary.)
- In cases of litigation, case notes and other confidential documents may become public. Thus, prepare your clients for the possibility. When counseling mandated clients, apprise them that a third party may request copies of pertinent documents or information regarding treatment.
- Make sure you have been very thorough regarding the client's rights during informed consent.
- Once again, you may be compelled to testify regarding why you wrote what you wrote in the case notes. Essentially, once you write something in a case file, you are responsible for defending what you wrote.

GENERAL RECOMMENDATIONS FOR WRITING CASE NOTES

There are three key points to keep in mind with regard to case notes. One, case notes provide a track record of the client's treatment, progress, or lack of progress. Two, case notes provide clear documentation of decisions and actions the counselor has made during treatment. Three, case notes provide a rationale and defense for the counselor should an ethical or legal issue arise. Case notes also provide evidence the counselor is following best practices—in other words, what any clinically sound, ethical counselor would do in similar circumstances.

Objective Versus Subjective Information

One important element is the ability to distinguish objective information (who said what or what you directly witnessed during a session) from subjective impressions (conclusions you developed while counseling the client). Quite often, because of the large volume of clients you counsel, and with the passage of time, you may confuse the objective with the subjective. It is important to separate what you observed or documented from what you *believe*. (I know from experience lawyers will hammer away on this issue!) Objective documentation is what you will be held accountable for in a court case should you be unfortunate enough to be the object of such. For example, do not write, "The client seems to be a drug addict," especially if you have no direct evidence of addiction. The client may not be an addict, and recording of such libelous information could significantly harm the client and be grounds for a lawsuit against you (Wheeler & Bertram, 2019). On the other hand, if the client is being treated for chemical dependency, noting that fact that "the client appears to have been abusing substances based upon own admission, drug screenings, and his answers on the SASSI-4 (Substance Abuse Subtle Screening Inventory-4)" would be accurate record keeping. Just remember, objective information is what the client has said and done and is verifiable. For example, "The client has been court mandated for addictions evaluation and counseling after being cited for driving under the influence (DUI)" or whatever is accurate.

Keep Comments Concise

Because a client may be verbose, keep client quotations to a minimum, with only the most significant included; otherwise, counselor accuracy may be called into question (Cameron & Turtle-Song, 2002). Hart et al. (1985) suggest an individual can accurately recall only vestigial bits of verbatim information. (*Note:* My experience is many counselors overstate their memory of counseling sessions.) This suggests that after a 50-minute counseling session, a counselor's ability to recall specific information with any accuracy is questionable (unless of course the session was recorded). So, keep quotations to a minimum; note only key words or a brief phrase. Key words or phrases might include plans for suicide, homicide, comments suggesting a dramatic change in life circumstances, a major change in the client's well-being, employment, marital status, and so forth. Quotations document inappropriate or abusive language toward the counselor or others. Comments suggesting client denial need documenting. For example, a father accused of abusing his son with a whip might say, "I only use a whip when necessary!" Because the child's physical and emotional health may be at stake, recording his comments and, likely, tone of voice is important. The counselor might note, "When confronted regarding belt marks on his son's legs, the father stated in a loud, defensive tone, 'I only use a whip when necessary!'"

Note Behavioral Changes

It is also important to document statements that suggest the client may be confused regarding time, place, and person or is experiencing an abrupt change in their mental status. For example, if the client is disoriented and confused as to who they are or the circumstances regarding being in counseling, the counselor should record this. To assess the client's mental status, administering a Mental State Examination or a Mini-Mental State Examination is appropriate (see Chapter 5, "Clinical Issues in Practicum and Internship").

Recording a client's change in attitude, either positive or negative, is relevant because it serves as evidence for counseling effectiveness or ineffectiveness. A statement such as "Counseling has helped me get sober and put my life back together," might be written, "Client reports 'counseling has been very effective regarding sobriety.'" This information is especially important if the client was mandated and initially oppositional. The goal is not to provide a verbatim account of what the client said but to reflect current areas of client concern and to support or validate the counselor's interpretations and interventions. Essentially, *successful* counseling means achieving treatment goals. This particular area also suggests for mandated clients that the counselor needs a concrete understanding of what the mandating party considers successful. For example, what specific behavioral changes does the client need to evidence? Naturally, if addiction is the primary issue, sobriety is key. Counselors will further need to assist mandating parties in what is realistic in therapy. A school principal or probation officer saying "She needs to change her behavior" is too vague. Specifically, *what* behavior needs to change? *How* much change is required? *What* would successful therapy look like? Referring administrators, magistrates, and parents often seem vague on specific changes. As a counselor-in-training, you need to gather specifics to measure client success or nonsuccess. Furthermore, clients are more likely to meet specific target behaviors. Remember, keep concepts simple and focus on a measurable change.

Be Judicious and Supportive

Because insurance officials, court officials, other mental health professionals, and so forth may read case notes, the counselor should be judicious about the type of information included in the case record. Political, religious, and racial views should not be included in the case notes unless they directly relate to the focus of treatment (Eggland, 1988). The counselor should not repeat inflammatory statements that are critical of other mental health providers because such comments could antagonize clinicians and compromise client care. Instead of using the actual names of the client's object of animus, the counselor might substitute with terms such as "other staff" or "another mental health professional" and so on. It is of further importance to remember that the names a client mentions during counseling sessions should not be included in the record unless those persons have a direct relationship to the client's treatment. So, before including a name, ask yourself, "How is this person's name related to the client's treatment?" Always remember, you are not necessarily getting the *truth* from a client but rather their perception of the truth (sometimes even less!). Beyond legalities, fairness to named persons not present to defend themselves would seem sound ethical practice.

Another guideline to follow is to be constructive in how you word case notes (Baird, 2005). Remember again, your clients have a right to inspect the file and you do not want to record anything that might incite additional animus, assign blame, or be personally demeaning. You do want to record an accurate synopsis of the client's treatment, including successes, issues still in progress, relapses, and so forth, but you must be professional and ethical in the manner in which you record these important clinical details. Professional case notes will lessen the probability the client (or another official) will be offended. So, to borrow from Shakespeare, record the truth but do so in a manner that does not appear inflammatory or personally demeaning.

Keep It Brief

Brevity is the operative word when writing case notes. Counselors should express essential ideas but keep notations brief because of space and time constraints. Instead of writing, "the client says," use shorthand terms such as "reports," "states," "describes," "indicates," "complains of," and so forth (Cameron & Turtle-Song, 2002). Instead of writing, "Today the client says, 'I'm having lots of conflicts with coworkers since the last counseling session where we met and talked about jackasses I work with!'" the counselor might write, "Client reports increased conflict at work since last session." Furthermore, because it is obvious that the counselor is the scribe, it is not necessary for the counselor to refer to themselves. Be concise but thorough in record keeping.

Students often ask me, "How long should it take me to write case notes?" My suggestion is a 10-minute time frame because this is about the maximum time you can expect between sessions (often, you may have less, of course). Naturally, there are times when you are unable to record case notes until the end of the day. As was previously noted regarding difficulty recalling specific events in a particular counseling session, my recommendation is for counselors to keep notes during the session. These brief summaries of critical points can be a real asset in reminding the counselor of the particulars of the session. During days when I had back-to-back sessions for 6 to 7 hours a day, taking brief in-session notes was invaluable to writing accurate case notes, as I could not possibly remember all pertinent points and, without in-session notes, likely would have confused particular issues with clients. Then, once I wrote the case note, I shredded handwritten in-session notes. I would also inform clients about the purpose behind in-session notes to demystify the process. I always informed my clients that they could view my in-session notes anytime. Very few clients ever took me up on my offer. Again, do not write anything inflammatory or use actual names, and shred in-session notes after completing case notes.

Farther along on the topic of writing in-session notes, I have met a few therapists of the opinion that writing in-session notes was detrimental to therapy. I have found no research to support this opinion; furthermore, most counselors cannot recall much of the session. Such notes have been essential to me. Naturally, some counselors feel different regarding writing in-session notes and their practice may vary. Your own field site supervisor may have a different practice and that may work for them, though it would not function well for me. School counselors may write far fewer case notes, and the structure, expectation, and approach to therapy are typically different in a school versus an agency or hospital. Still, school counselors will need to document academic and behavioral information.

THE SUBJECTIVE, OBJECTIVE, ASSESSMENT, AND PLAN FORMAT

There are several different formats used for writing case notes (e.g., SOAP, DAP [data, assessment, and plan], and narrative recording). These various formats provide a continuity and consistency to a generally subjective exercise on the part of the counselor. Because of its popularity among mental health professionals, I recommend the SOAP format. Exhibit 6.1 shows a sample SOAP write-up form, which uses *DSM* categories.

Subjective

This section should provide a narrative of the client's feelings, concerns, problems expressed, goals, thoughts expressed, the intensity of problems expressed, and the

146 • THE COUNSELING PRACTICUM AND INTERNSHIP MANUAL

Exhibit 6.1 *DSM-5-TR* and SOAP Client Case Note Format

Page 1 of 2

Name(s) and age(s) of client(s): _____

_____

_____

Date: _____/_____/_____ Code(s): _____ Session #: _____

Presenting Problem: _____

_____

_____

_____

_____

Medications: _____

Cite Criteria for Primary Diagnosis:

_____

_____

_____

_____

_____

DSM-5-TR Preliminary Diagnostic Impressions (For educational and training purposes only. Not intended as a final diagnosis):

Prescriptive. Not intended as a final diagnosis.

Subjective (S): _____

_____

_____

_____

_____

_____

_____

_____

_____

(continued)

6: CLINICAL WRITING AND DOCUMENTATION IN COUNSELING RECORDS • 147

Exhibit 6.1 *DSM-5-TR* and SOAP Client Case Note Format (*continued*)

Page 2 of 2

Objective (O): _____

_____

_____

_____

_____

_____

_____

_____

Assessment (A): _____

_____

_____

_____

_____

_____

_____

_____

Plan (P): _____

_____

_____

_____

_____

_____

_____

Codes: psy. = psychiatric referral; ac = acute; cr = chronic; R/x = meds; Tx = treatment; pr = parental access restricted; wc = ward of court; npr = no previous records.

Counselor's Signature: _____

DSM-5-TR, Diagnostic and Statistical Manual of Mental Disorders, 5th ed., text revision; SOAP, subject, object, assessment, plan.

problems' impact on significant relationships. Relevant comments provided by close family members, court officers, and other officials are noted. The client's perception of the issues should be clear to an outside reader of the record. Counselors should be thorough although brief in their summarizations.

Example of a subjective (S) entry: "I feel very guilty about how my alcoholism has impacted my relationship with my kids." This would be a subjective statement as you may not believe the client or have a realistic way to verify the statement. Using third-person writing style also is acceptable. For example, "Client states 'feeling guilty' regarding inability to manage addiction."

Objective

The objective section is composed of what can be "seen, heard, smelled, counted, or measured" (Cameron & Turtle-Song, 2002, p. 288). Generally, there are two types of objective information: outside documented reports and the counselor's own observations of the client's behavior during the session. The latter, the counselor's observations, are composed of any psychological, interpersonal, or physical findings relevant to treatment. Objective information could consist of the client's appearance; verbal and nonverbal behavior; affect; voice tone; body posture; and compliance with treatment, oppositional nature, and client strengths. This section may also refer to the client's mental status and competence to continue treatment. Supportive outside written reports, such as psychological or psychiatric reports, assessments, medical records, prison records, school records, and so forth, would be included in the objective section. Remember to note any client changes or discrepancies and when they occur (e.g., client becomes irritated in discussing a topic or blushes when a certain name is mentioned).

The counselor's choice of language in this section should reflect accuracy in content. Avoid terms that seem less precise such as "appeared," "seemed," "possibly," and so forth, as they appear less certain. Naturally, because counseling is not an exact science, some degree of latitude is expected. Terms such as "evidenced by" is a descriptive term that implies direct observation. For example, let us say the client arrived 15 minutes late for session, was unkempt, and had difficulty maintaining their focus in session. This behavior is inconsistent with previous sessions where the client was on time and engaged with the process. When writing this in the case notes, the counselor might say, "Appeared depressed as evidenced by tardiness, less involvement in the counseling process, and poorly groomed."

When writing the objective section of the report, the counselor should refrain from using pejorative language ("slob"), stating opinion not supported by facts ("lazy"), and personal judgments ("He is a loser"). Refrain from terms that have a negative connotation and are subject to speculation such as "dysfunctional," "rude," "obnoxious," "normal," "abnormal," and the like. For example, a counselor should not write, "Client arrived stoned to the session and proceeded to be uncooperative and unprofessional." The counselor might instead record, "Client presented smelling of pot, struggled to maintain focus throughout session, and had difficulty sitting upright in the chair."

Example of an objective (O) entry: "The client's clothes were wrinkled and soiled, and he was giving off a malodorous smell."

Assessment

The assessment section is a summarization of the counselor's clinical impressions regarding the client's problem or problems (Cameron & Turtle-Song, 2002). The assessment section serves to synthesize and analyze the information expressed in the subjective and objective sections. The assessment section includes psychiatric diagnoses based on the *DSM-5-TR* (APA, 2022). Although there is much controversy regarding use of the *DSM* and certain diagnoses in particular, *DSM* diagnoses are considered a standard part of treatment (Remley & Herlihy, 2020; Wheeler & Bertram, 2019) and required for financial reimbursement. Diagnoses are simply a reality of professional practice. Ginter and Glauser's (2001) opinion is that the assessment section of the SOAP format includes clinical impressions. Sometimes clinical impressions will be recorded in the form of "rule out" or "rule in" when the counselor is not entirely confident in assigning a diagnosis. Clinical impressions can assist other clinicians in reaching a final diagnosis because they provide guidance on previous assessment. When reporting clinical impressions in the SOAP notes, counselors should clearly identify them as such. Counselors should also identify the evidence for the prospective diagnosis because this documents the clinical process the counselor followed and that the counselor operated within standard procedures (see Box 6.1).

The assessment portion of the SOAP format is the section most likely to be reviewed by outside reviewers such as counselors, psychologists, social workers, court officers, child welfare caseworkers, and such (Cameron & Turtle-Song, 2002). Consequently, counselors should take pains to ensure the subjective and objective sections support the assessment section, as these portions lay the foundation for a diagnosis or diagnostic impressions. When considering a diagnosis, the counselor should ask the following questions: "Are there sufficient data to support a particular client diagnosis?" (Cameron & Turtle-Song, 2002) and "Am I prepared to defend my diagnosis to colleagues, supervisors, and legal magistrates?" I have had to defend my diagnoses before all the aforementioned officials and said experienced taught me to be prepared.

Box 6.1 Clinical Impressions Relating to Case Notes and Diagnoses

Appropriate use of clinical impressions is vital both for writing good case notes and for effective counseling practice. Consider the following example: A counselor working in an outpatient mental health clinic is conducting an intake and assessment for a 6-year-old boy referred by his school counselor for possible attention deficit hyperactivity disorder (ADHD). The school counselor's report describes the child as having difficulty maintaining his focus for even brief time periods (i.e., 5 minutes), is constantly out of his seat, frequently interrupts his teacher and peers, and has a tendency to self-injury caused by constantly hurrying (e.g., running into chairs and tables and tripping). When taking the child's history, the mother disclosed she often consumed alcohol throughout her pregnancy. Although there is not enough evidence for a diagnosis of fetal alcohol syndrome, the counselor's clinical impression is to "rule out fetal alcohol syndrome" and to refer the child for a neurological evaluation. The neurologist can examine the counselor's report as they consider a diagnosis.

The counselor must be prepared to defend any diagnosis they render to parents, colleagues, supervisors, probation officers, and child welfare officials and, if necessary, in a courtroom. Naturally considering the full ramifications of a diagnosis can be intimidating, although declining to provide a diagnosis based on the fear of the consequences is also unappealing and possibly unethical. The best advice for counselors is to make the most informed decision possible and to be able to demonstrate the steps you took to arrive at your diagnosis. Consulting with your supervisor or a trusted colleague is a good idea when you are unsure of selecting a particular diagnosis. It may well be that diagnosis is the "tar baby" of mental healthcare, given the volume of debate and disagreement regarding the *DSM* system, and that some researchers have questioned the utility and validity of the *DSM* (Duncan et al., 2010; Wampold, 2001). Regardless, using the *DSM* classification is typically required for third-party reimbursement, and many mental health professionals, as well as medical, educational, correctional, and judicial professionals, expect a diagnosis. Unless the counselor works in a P–12 school, most university counseling centers, or in a private practice that does not bill insurance, you likely will have to render a *DSM* diagnosis.

Example of an assessment (A) entry: "Client's addiction was assessed using the SASST-4 (Substance Abuse Subtle Screening Test-4) and with a urine analysis (UA) test. SASSI-4 results suggest client was defensive regarding drug use and UA was positive for methamphetamines."

Plan

The final section of the SOAP format is the treatment plan. The subjective, objective, and assessment sections serve as the foundation for the plan, and any plan should include short-term and long-term goals. This section generally consists of two parts: the action plan and the treatment prognosis. The information to be noted in this section includes the date of the next appointment (or, if it is the final session, to note that this is the final session and include aftercare), interventions used during the session, treatment progress, and homework assigned (if any).

The counselor should note client progress, or lack thereof, in the plan section because this will have a direct bearing on further treatment. Typically, progress assessments are described in terms such as "good," "fair," "excellent," "guarded," or "poor," accompanied by an explanation supporting the progress assessment. The plan section of the SOAP format completes the case notes section.

Example of a plan (P) entry: "Client has been mandated for 12 sessions of addiction counseling. Client will have random UAs to test for treatment compliance, with weekly individual and group counseling sessions to reduce anxiety. The goal is to reduce anxiety scores on the Beck Anxiety Inventory by 50% in 12 weeks. Client was offered weekly secular or narcotics anonymous (NA) meetings and chose NA. Will monitor with NA facilitator."

Table 6.1 summarizes each SOAP section and the type of information that should be recorded. Case Study 6.1 and Case Study 6.2 provide examples of SOAP case notes.

Regarding the case of Latisha in Case Study 6.2, some students reading the text may have questions regarding Maria Jose's handling of Latisha's religious concerns. In previous eras, counselors often were reluctant to address spiritual issues given that

6: CLINICAL WRITING AND DOCUMENTATION IN COUNSELING RECORDS • 151

TABLE 6.1 SOAP CASE NOTES EXAMPLES

Section	Definition	Example
Subjective (S)	What the client tells you, what pertinent others tell you about the client, how the client experiences the world	Client's feelings, concerns, and problems; comments by clinicians and pertinent others; client's orientation to time, place, and person; client's verbalized attitudes toward helping
Objective (O)	Factual information, what the counselor personally witnessed, what was measured through testing or assessment, documentation from other parties	The client's appearance, affect, behavior, test results, and so forth; materials from other agencies to be noted and attached
Assessment (A)	Summarizes the counselor's clinical thinking regarding the patient's diagnosis	Include clinical diagnosis and impressions; may include *DSM* diagnosis (or possible diagnoses)
Plan (P)	Describes the parameters of treatment; consists of an action plan and prognosis	Action plan: include interventions used, treatment progress, and direction; include date of next appointment. Prognosis: include the anticipated gains from the intervention

Source: Adapted from Cameron, S., & Turtle-Song, I. (2002). Learning to write case notes using the SOAP format. *Journal of Counseling & Development, 80*, 286–292. https://doi .org/10.1002/j.1556-6678.2002.tb00193.x

Case Study 6.1 The Case of Pierre: SOAP Write-Up for Agitated, Court-Mandated Client

Pierre is a 28-year-old, Caucasian male, court-mandated client. He was arrested following a domestic dispute involving his female partner. Pierre presents for the first session agitated and oppositional to treatment. He discloses to his counselor, Steve, "I didn't do anything wrong... everybody uses a little force... I was just manning up!" Throughout most of the initial session, Pierre remains defiant. He outlines his struggles in the relationship, explaining how he works 60 hours per week to support his partner and two kids and never misses work. He says with much animus, "My damn girlfriend can do anything she wants, but I'm the one that gets arrested!" He demands that the counselor write the judge a letter explaining that he has no problems. Later in the session, Pierre says that

(continued)

152 • THE COUNSELING PRACTICUM AND INTERNSHIP MANUAL

Case Study 6.1 The Case of Pierre: SOAP Write-Up for Agitated, Court-Mandated Client (*continued*)

he grew up in a physically and verbally abusive home. At age 17, he ran away to live with his maternal grandparents, who seemed to provide the only stability in his life. At age 20, he was twice arrested for driving while intoxicated and once for a fight at a party. He reports that he feels more aggressive when he has been drinking. Pierre admits to consuming "a couple of drinks a night... no big deal, you know." He also reports that when he gets angry, he feels like exploding and sometimes becomes violent, punching walls, kicking the trash can, throwing chairs, and occasionally hitting his partner. He also admits that he has "been physical" with his kids on at least two occasions but maintains that he gets physical only "when they need to be controlled." Before the session ends, he opines, "This counseling is sissy stuff. How the hell are you going to help me with the judge, huh?" Then, he angrily slams the door and storms from the office.

SOAP WRITE-UP FOR PIERRE

S: Client admitted previous use of violence "when they [family] need to be controlled." He reports experience of domestic violence in family of origin. He reports running away from home at age 17 to live with grandparents to escape family violence.

O: Recently, client was arrested for domestic assault on his female partner and court mandated to counseling. Today was client's initial session and he was guarded throughout. At session's conclusion, he became agitated when informed he would need to attend treatment for 16 weeks, angrily stating, "Counseling is sissy stuff!" and "How are you going to help me with the judge?" before slamming the door and storming from the office.

A: *DSM-5-TR* Diagnosis: Physical Abuse of Adult [V61.1]. Clinical impressions: Rule out Abuse of Children [V.61.21]. Rule out Alcohol Use Disorder 303.90 (F10.20) Severe

P: Rescheduled for following week (6/12/19) at 3 p.m. Prognosis is guarded because of lack of insight into behavior and mandated client apparently because of a lack of motivation for behavioral change. Will assess potential for future violence using the Domestic Violence Screening Assessment (DMSA). Will refer to 16-week batterers' intervention group in addition to continuing individual cognitive behavioral counseling. Will refer to Addiction Counseling Unit for alcohol evaluation. Next session plan is to introduce recognizing and stopping anger before it explodes.

6-5-20XX
Steve Washington, LMHC, NCC
Counselor, Jackson County Mental Health

DSM-5 -TR, *Diagnostic and Statistical Manual of Mental Disorders*, Fifth Edition, Text Revision; SOAP, subject, object, assessment, plan.

6: CLINICAL WRITING AND DOCUMENTATION IN COUNSELING RECORDS • 153

Case Study 6.2 The Case of Latisha: SOAP Write-Up for Depressed Client

Latisha is a 32-year-old, single, admittedly isolated African American female who seeks counseling services at Rainbow Counseling Services. She has been assigned to Maria Jose, a Latina counselor who recently completed her master's in counseling. Latisha appears very shy and reticent, making infrequent eye contact. Her clothes are wrinkled, her hair uncombed, and she evidences a slight body odor. Maria Jose administers the BDI-II, and Latisha scores 33 (very high), which indicates she is not suicidal and is hopeful. Maria Jose explains her BDI-II score, inquiring regarding her hopefulness and lack of suicidality. Latisha answers, "I get depressed sometimes but wouldn't take my life. I give everything over to God as he is my rock and my support and keeps me afloat... he isn't finished with me yet." Latisha further asks Maria Jose, "Are you a Christian? I would like a Christian counselor." Maria Jose briefly explains her ethical responsibility to be open and fair to clients regardless of spiritual orientation and adds, "You may pray in session if you need and I will be silent and respectful." Latisha appears pleased with Maria Jose's request and becomes more animated. At the session's end, she makes a follow-up appointment. "You really helped me today!" she says before leaving.

SOAP WRITE-UP FOR LATISHA

S: Client reports feeling depressed and concurrently that her religious faith in God assists her in coping. Client maintains she has much to live for and that "God isn't finished with me yet."

O: Client appeared lethargic though compliant in session. She was poorly groomed with a slight malodorous smell and made infrequent eye contact. She did maintain her focus on the session and answered each question on the intake and BDI-II.

A: Client's score of 33 on the BDI-II is very high though she denies suicidality and states she feels hopeful about the future, expressing much confidence in her religious faith. Client appears motivated for treatment and seemed energized after my agreement that she can pray in session while I am silent.

P: Scheduled the next session for 6/12/20XX at 3 p.m. Will readminister the BDI-II at session's end to check progress. Plan to reduce her depression by 50% in eight sessions. Plan to assist client in making two friends for social support and encouraging her to attend regular religious services in her faith as she has identified this as a support.

BDI-II, *Beck Depression Inventory*, Second Edition; SOAP, subject, object, assessment, plan.

counseling typically was a secular service. More recently, the profession has realized spirituality/religion may be a viable means of emotional support for clients (Cashwell & Watts, 2010; Cashwell & Young, 2011). The critical issue regarding spirituality in session likely involved boundaries and roles. Maria Jose demonstrates her respect for Latisha's values by agreeing to her request to pray in session but maintains her boundary by stating she will be a nonparticipating, silent observer. If this session were taking place in a pastoral counseling center, church, synagogue, mosque, and so on, the role, expectation, and boundary likely would be different. It is worth pointing out, however, that religious leaders who also are professional counselors and members of the ACA must also follow the *ACA Code of Ethics*. As a former pastoral counselor, professionals in such settings must be very clear during informed consent regarding professional roles and boundaries.

Final Thoughts on SOAP Format

Case notes and client files are legal documents and must be legible (preferably typed), accurate, and concise (Mitchell, 2008; Sommers-Flanagan & Sommers-Flanagan, 1999; Wheeler & Bertram, 2019). A good general guideline to follow is to write your notes immediately after the session because your memory is freshest at that point. In addition, review case notes prior to the next session to facilitate continuity from the previous session to the current one. Furthermore, you may have to transfer the client to another counselor or official; in that case, readable, legible, and coherent case notes will enhance treatment effectiveness and reduce liability. Refrain from technical jargon because it is not descriptive and can be misunderstood should another professional read the file.

For consistency purposes, record all client contacts, including phone messages, emails (although use of emails should be discouraged because of security concerns), letters, and other forms of communication, using the SOAP format. When an error occurs, never erase or use correction fluid (the latter if typed). Note the error by either crossing out the error in pen or writing "error" and then record your initials. Should your agency utilize electronic records, use that system to add to the record, noting you are making an addition and cite reasons for the addendum. Some agencies even have correction sheet reports for such contingencies, with the counselor explaining the error and signing the document. The counselor should identify the mistake and correction for the record.

Document all professional client-related contacts. For example, note any pertinent client information provided from a case manager, parole officer, physician, school counselor, and so forth in the record. At the conclusion of the SOAP format, the counselor should date and sign their legal name and include job title and credentials. The counselor should also sign their name immediately below the last line of the *plan* section of the SOAP notes.

CONCLUSION

My own experience in more than 30 years working in mental health clinics and as a counselor educator training future professionals is that clear, concise clinical case note writing is an acquired skill. My further experience is that most students struggle with learning to write effective clinical notes. Even veteran counselors can, at times, find themselves challenged to be concise while at the same time addressing all pertinent treatment issues and concerns. So, if you are a graduate student, master's or doctoral level, and feel you are struggling, rest assured you are scarcely alone in your struggle. I would recommend you seek out your site supervisor for suggestions, as well as your program faculty. The good news is through your placement experience, you are very likely to improve on clinical writing.

LESSONS LEARNED

I was immediately shocked and very concerned by Bob's (pseudonym) clinical writing sample. Bob was a new counselor at the clinic where I served as clinical director. He was in a second career (I cannot recall his previous one), and while very affable and skilled in session, his writing skills were rudimentary, to put it kindly. One of the other counselors on staff who had been co-facilitating an anxiety treatment group had flagged me on the matter. "I don't mean to tattle," she began, "and he's good at counseling, but his clinical writing is grammatically poor and clinically unsound." Naturally, many clinicians write quick therapeutic notes, often using common abbreviations. As such, some degree of sentence fragmentation is accepted. However, much more concerning was Bob's use of pejorative language. Pulling several of his client files, I saw the concern his colleague had appraised me on. Thus, I scheduled a meeting with Bob.

I remember him as a late thirtyish, Caucasian male who sported a perpetual good-natured manner. He impressed me as someone who always managed to find the ray of sunshine in whatever dark clouds were gathering, except in his case notes, which were loaded with language like "client seems foolish," "dense," "lazy," and many other pejorative adjectives we do not use as clinicians. As hard as it was to recruit counselors and other staff to our rural location, an uneasy feeling that perhaps I might need to fire him emerged. We had been short-staffed for a few months and nobody looked forward to resuming that deficit. However, having sat uncomfortably in the witness chair during court hearings with an attorney grilling me on my writing and that of supervisees, I knew well the importance of fact-based clarity in a written record.

Bob arrived at my office after an early morning session. Well groomed, wearing his usual amicable face, he offered a kind, heartfelt good morning and sat down before me. As kind and friendly as he was, I dreaded our conversation. Of course, apparent kindness can sometimes be a façade people use to manipulate others. My gut feeling regarding Bob, however, was that his written rhetoric was more benign, albeit no less inappropriate. I explained to Bob that we needed to cover his clinical writing due to questions I had. He nodded soberly but displayed no evident anxiety. Pulling as file from stack (this was in the twentieth-century era of physical files), I pointed to some of his written work and explained the importance of using non inflammatory language as an ethical responsibility and in fairness to the client and as other officials may wind up reading the file. He seemed to ponder the message yet looked puzzled. I inquired if he understood my meaning. He confessed writing had never been his strongest subject in school, his previous career, nor now, it appeared. "So, is there a workbook I might use as a means of improvement?" he inquired. At that time, there were few published resources on writing effective clinical notes. I loaned him a handbook, but most of the focus of the book was on longer psychological evaluations, not basic counseling notes. As he had a full day of sessions, I bade him goodbye, making a point to follow up and review his notes later than afternoon.

Late that afternoon before closing, I reviewed his clinical case notes. No question, Bob was a completely incompetent writer: misspelled words, vague notes that were difficult to understand, and inappropriate language ("He's a bad patient as his attendance is inconsistent"), and his penmanship was even worse than my own (quite a statement!). Frankly, I wondered how I could keep Bob on staff given his written deficits. However, his actual counseling work was very good. "He's very skilled with clients and never seems to get rattled," offered a fellow counselor. Despite my frustrations with Bob's prose, he was a good counselor and quite popular with the staff. Thus, I resolved to find some way to help him write clear, effective, and brief case notes. Clearly, for ethical, legal, and practical reasons, I could not write his notes for him.

The answer came in a conversation with a contract counselor, Sally (pseudonym), an experienced counselor with her own private practice. One afternoon, she stopped by the clinic to hand out flyers for a workshop she was giving at a local hotel. Noticing I looked stressed, she inquired how things were going. I explained my dilemma with Bob (withholding his name). She listened patiently and then offered help. She explained her two-day workshop would include clinical writing. Sally, who previously had worked at the clinic years earlier, was well regarded by long time staff for her many skills. Evidently, clinical writing was one of them. Inquiring as to the cost of the workshop, I decided the cost would be well worth it. Later, I spoke with Bob and he had a good attitude about needing to improve his writing. No doubt, Bob realized that absent improvement in the written area, he would not be keeping his job.

The workshop was the following week. Sally provided samples of effective and ineffective clinical writing samples. She also had each participant complete a mock write-up of a counseling session, requiring all participants to turn in the writing sample to her. Then, on the lunch break, she reviewed them, providing written feedback. Then, she required the participants to rewrite their notes following her instructions. At the conclusion of her training, she called me. Sally informed me that Bob had been an active participant but struggled with the writing component. She recommended a book she had purchased many years ago while in graduate school. The text was short, just over 100 pages, and was out of print. Loaning Bob her dog-eared copy with her own handwritten notes in the margins, he commenced reading the book. I instructed Bob to make appointments with me twice per week for the next three weeks.

Each session with Bob was a full hour long. I had him write case notes on fictional session, requiring him to rewrite each entry until he improved to the set rubric. Carrying the aged, crinkled book borrowed from Sally, he industriously thumbed back and forth through the yellowed pages for reference and then meticulously drafted sample note before sliding them to me. The workshop, Sally's book, and two weeks of steady practice with me had improved his clinical writing skills. Truth being required, he was not about to win any clinical writing contests were he to find and enter one. He remained grammatically challenged, leading me to suggest he purchase a copy of Strunk and White's uber popular and enduring *The Elements of Style* (2022). I then assigned him an additional week of case note review and practice with me. As was his MO, he complied with a good attitude.

We completed our final week of case note style coaching and writing. While enjoying the time editing and reviewing Bob's case note prose, I had many additional duties to attend to as clinical director. I complimented Bob for his positive attitude and improvement. The kindly man nodded his head in appreciation and then articulated his intention to continue improving his writing skills. He admitted his college and graduate school professors had taken it easy on him. I encouraged he make use of the Strunk and White book and to review it regularly. Dutiful as always, he kept the book on his desk, ready for his perusal. I continued to spot-check his files, something I informed him I would do. He continued to make marginal improvement, leaving me and his colleagues feeling better, especially as we would not need to fire him and necessitate being short handed while scouring the area for a new counselor.

There is a plethora of lessons in any period of difficulty in life, be those trials personal, occupational, or academic. My several decades and numerous roles in the mental health field have taught me a legion. Some have been very painful, grief inducing, and occasionally leaving me feeling betrayed and lonely. The experience with Bob and his writing was a lighter one, although an important lesson nevertheless. That is, somehow busy as I might become, the smallest detail is capable of causing disaster. While case notes, for example, get far less emphasis than counseling skill and effectiveness, the notes provide an ongoing case history and are the theological equivalent of the devil being in said details. Thus, the little things in our lives and practice often need the most attention. For any intrepid student reading this section, my advice is that you take your clinical writing very seriously. Should you fail to do so, you may very well sit uncomfortably in a courtroom witness chair grilled by a merciless attorney intent on exposing your shortcomings in a very public venue. Be prepared!

RECOMMENDED RESOURCES

Jongsma, A. E., Jr., & Berghius, D. J. (2006). *The adult psychotherapy progress notes planner* (3rd ed.). Wiley.
Jongsma, A. E., Jr., & Peterson, M. L. (2014). *The child psychotherapy progress notes planner* (5th ed.). Wiley.
McInnis, W. P., & Bughius, D. J. (2006). *The child psychotherapy progress notes planner*. Wiley.
Patterson, T., & McClanahan, T. M. (1999). *The couple and family clinical documentation sourcebook: A comprehensive collection of mental health practice forms, handouts, and records*. Wiley.
Wiger, D. E. (2005). *The clinical documentation sourcebook: The complete paperwork resource for your mental health practice* (3rd ed.). Wiley.
Strunk, W., Jr., & White, E. B. (2022). *The elements of style* (4th ed.). Independently published.
Zuckerman, E. L. (2000). *Clinician's thesaurus: The guidebook for writing psychological reports* (5th ed.). Guilford Press.

A robust set of instructor resources designed to supplement this text is located at http://connect.springerpub.com/content/book/978-0-8261-6607-4. Qualifying instructors may request access by emailing textbook@springerpub.com.

REFERENCES

American Counseling Association. (2014). *ACA code of ethics*. https://www.counseling.org/resources/aca-code-of-ethics.pdf
American Psychiatric Association. (2022). *Diagnostic and statistical manual of mental disorders* (5th ed., text revision). American Psychiatric Publishing.
Baird, B. N. (2005). *The internship, practicum, and field placement handbook: A guide for the helping professions* (4th ed.). Pearson/Prentice Hall.
Cameron, S., & Turtle-Song, I. (2002). Learning to write case notes using the SOAP format. *Journal of Counseling & Development, 80,* 286–292. https://doi.org/10.1002/j.1556-6678.2002.tb00193.x
Cashwell, C. S., & Watts, J. S. (2010). The new ASERVIC competencies for addressing spiritual and religious issues in counseling. *Journal of Counseling & Development, 55*(1), 2–5. https://doi.org/10.1002/j.2161-007X.2010.tb00018.x

Cashwell, C. S., & Young, J. S. (2011). *Integrating spirituality and religion into counseling: A guide to competent practice*. American Counseling Association.

Christie, G. C., Meeks, J. E., Pryor, E. S., & Sanders, J. (1997). *Cases and materials on the law of torts* (3rd ed.). West.

Cottone, R. R., & Tarvydas, V. M. (2003). *Ethical and professional issues in counseling* (2nd ed.). Merrill/Prentice Hall.

Duncan, B., Miller, S. D., Wamplod, B., & Hubble, M. (2010). *The heart and soul of change: Delivering what works in therapy* (2nd ed.). American Psychological Association.

Eggland, E. T. (1988). Charting: How and why to document your care daily and fully. *Nursing, 18*(11), 76–84. https://doi.org/10.1097/00152193-198811000-00030

Ginter, E. J., & Glauser, A. (2001). Effective use of the *DSM* from a developmental/wellness perspective. In E. R. Welfel & R. E. Ingersoll (Eds.), *The mental health desk reference* (pp. 69–77). Wiley.

Hart, J., Jr., Berndt, R. S., & Caramazza, A. (1985). Category-specific naming deficit following cerebral infarction. *Nature, 316*, 439–440. https://doi.org/10.1038/316439a0

Health Insurance Portability and Accountability Act of 1996 (HIPAA), Pub. L No. 104-191, 110 Stat. 1936 (1996). See also HIPAA Privacy Rule, 45, C.F.R. 160.101-312, 164.106, 164.500-534 (2013).

Jaffee v. Redmond et al. 1996 WL 314841 (U.S. June 13, 1996).

Mitchell, R. W. (2008). *Documentation in counseling records: An overview of ethical, legal, and clinical issues* (3rd ed.). American Counseling Association.

Remley, T. P., Jr., & Herlihy, B. (2020). *Ethical, legal and professional issues in counseling* (6th ed.). Pearson.

Schwartz, R. C., & Feisthamel, K. P. (2009). Disproportionate diagnosis of mental disorders among African American versus European American clients: Implications for counseling, theory, research, and practice. *Journal of Counseling & Development, 87*, 295–301. https://doi.org/10.1002/j.1556-6678.2009.tb00110.x

Sommers-Flanagan, R. S., & Sommers-Flanagan, J. S. (1999). *Clinical interviewing* (2nd ed.). Wiley.

Strunk, W., Jr., & White, E. B. (2022). *The elements of style* (4th ed.). Independently published.

Tarasoff v. Regents of University of California, 529 P.2d 553, 118 Cal. Rptr. 129 (1974), vacated, 17 Cal. 3d 425, 551 P.2d 334, 131 Cal. Rptr. 14 (1976).

Thapar v. Zezulka, 994 S. W. 2nd 635 (Tex. 1999).

Wampold, B. E. (2001). *The great psychotherapy debate: Models, methods, and findings*. Lawrence Erlbaum.

Wheeler, A. M., & Bertram, B. (2019). *The counselor and the law: A guide to legal and ethical practice* (8th ed.). American Counseling Association.

CHAPTER 7

Models of Supervision: Classroom and Site Supervision

INTRODUCTION

The practicum/internship experience involves not only the on-site clinical experience but also structured supervision, individual and group, at the clinical placement and in the classroom setting. As mentioned in Chapter 1, "Introduction to the Counseling Profession and the Practicum/Internship Experience," graduate counseling students in Council for Accreditation of Counseling and Related Educational Programs (CACREP)-accredited program (practicum and internship) standards require an average of 1 hour per week of supervision with a faculty member and an on-site supervisor and, for practicum, an additional average of 1.5 hours per week of classroom group supervision. In this chapter, I provide guidance to help you and your fellow students make the most of your supervision experience, both in the classroom setting and with your on-site supervisor. Before getting into the specifics of counselor supervision, I want to give a general word regarding supervision in graduate-level counselor training programs. Remember, while counselors are specifically trained in supervision models (particularly at the doctoral level), not all on-site supervisors have received such training. Furthermore, on-site supervisors will vary in their supervision skill, just as clinicians vary in their counseling ability. Some excellent counselors may be mediocre supervisors. There are mediocre counselors, likewise, who are very good clinical supervisors.

Perhaps the most important thing to understand is that you can learn from a poor supervisor just as you can from a skilled one. Naturally, the learning experience is more fulfilling with a skilled supervisor. Remember also, you are learning the knowledge, skills, and dispositions of supervision, and one day you will likely be a supervisor.

Bernard and Goodyear (2014) have defined *clinical supervision* as an intervention provided by a senior or experienced member of a profession to a junior or aspiring member of that same profession. Supervision has been described as an attachment process involving the development of a bond or working alliance that gradually loosens as the conclusion of supervision nears (Nelson et al., 2016). Clinical supervision involves a myriad of roles including mentor, coach, teacher, consultant, and evaluator, to list a few. Supervisors are responsible for the welfare of the supervisee, as well as that of their supervisee's clients (Remley & Herlihy, 2020). As employees of schools, agencies, and hospitals, supervisors have an obligation to their school or agency to ensure compliance with state and federal laws, policies and procedures adhered to, and quality services provided by the school or agency.

Consultation is like supervision and involves at least three parties in counseling: the consultant, consultee, and consultee's client or client system (Remley & Herlihy, 2020). The difference between supervision and consultation is that supervision generally is a more formal process involving evaluating the supervisee. Consultation, moreover, typically involves two clinicians of relatively equal rank or experience, and often, there is no formal evaluative process. All counselors will be involved both in supervisions relationships (as supervisor and supervisee) and consultation (whether the party seeking consultative services or the respondent). Consultation is very common among mental health professionals in schools and agencies (Remley & Herlihy, 2020). Dougherty's (2014) definition of consultation is widely cited and accepted. He describes consultation as follows:

> An indirect process in which a human services professional assists a consultee with a work-related (or caretaking-related) problem with a client system, with the goal of helping both the consultee and the client system in some specified way. (p. 8)

PRACTICUM/INTERNSHIP CLASS

Practicum and internship classes are very different from other courses you will take, such as counseling theories, assessment, and research methods. Practicum and internship classes are experientially based and seldom involve examinations, memorizing material, writing APA-style term papers, and so on. Typically, students discuss pertinent aspects of their placement, site supervisor, challenges, aspects they enjoy, what they are learning, issues on the site, and so forth. The practicum class will discuss (and perhaps view recordings of) confidential counseling sessions or at least mock counseling sessions, with clinical feedback. Thus, as a graduate student, you must treat the experience as if it were a supervision meeting. Like a supervision meeting in an agency or school, a large part of the practicum or internship classroom experience will involve presenting clinical cases and then receiving critiques from your peers and the professor. Although the practicum class can initially be anxiety provoking, it may eventually develop into a very rewarding and enriching experience. A sample course syllabus is provided in Exhibit 7.1.

Exhibit 7.1 Sample Counseling Practicum/Internship Class Syllabus

Public State University Spring 20XX
Graduate Mental Health Counseling Program
Department of Educational Leadership and Counseling

(continued)

Exhibit 7.1 Sample Counseling Practicum/Internship Class Syllabus (*continued*)

Professor: Haoua Doe, PhD, LMHC, ACS	Phone: (123) 456-7890 (office)
Office: 328 D Academic Complex	(123) 456-7780 (home)

Email: professor@counseling.edu
Office Hours: M 1:00–3:00 p.m.
          W 2:00–4:00 p.m.
          Th. 1:00–3:00 p.m.
          Or by appointment

Course Number and Title

EDU 679: Mental Health Practicum
Wednesday 4:20–7:05 p.m.
Office # 112

Catalog Description

This course is designed to provide graduate counseling students with an introduction to professional issues in mental health practice (e.g., counseling, critiquing peers, consultation, professional issues, and ethics and in preparation for the subsequent counseling internships (EDU 685, EDU 686, and EDU 678). Students will be placed in a counseling setting for a minimum of 100 clock hours and will have weekly group seminars. This course also incorporates the ethical standards of the American Counseling Association (ACA; www.counseling.org) and those of the American Mental Health Counselors Association (AMHCA; www.amhca.org). Canadian students may wish to consult the Canadian Counseling and Psychotherapy Association (CCA; www.ccpa-accp.ca/). Students are also expected to gain relative skills, especially in the realm of consultation with other mental health professionals. Practicum and internship classes are based upon CACREP standards (www.cacrep.org).

Textbook

Hodges, S. (2024). *The counseling practicum and internship manual: A resource for graduate counseling students in a dynamic, global era* (4th ed.). Springer Publishing Company.

Educational Philosophy

The constructivist framework of the graduate Mental Health Counseling program forms the basis for all courses. EDU 679 (Mental Health Counseling Practicum) serves as a foundational class for mental health counselors, including professional roles and identity, a focus on the American Counseling Association's (ACA's) *Code of Ethics and Standards of Practice*. The University Mental Health Counseling program also follows the requirements of the Council for Accreditation of

(continued)

162 • THE COUNSELING PRACTICUM AND INTERNSHIP MANUAL

Exhibit 7.1 Sample Counseling Practicum/Internship Class Syllabus (*continued*)

Counseling and Related Educational Programs (CACREP). The eight CACREP core areas are listed as follows:

Professional Identity: *Addressed in EDU 679*
Social and Cultural Diversity: *Addressed in EDU 679*
Human Growth and Development: *Addressed in EDU 679*
Career Development: *Not addressed in EDU 679*
Helping Relationships: *Addressed in EDU 679*
Group Work: May be addressed for the individual student depending on the practicum site
Assessment: *Addressed in EDU 679*
Research and Program Evaluation: *Not addressed in EDU 679*

Course Objectives and Requirements

Demonstrate skills in individual/group/relationship counseling using appropriate theoretical and practical perspectives.

Demonstrate knowledge of professional ethical standards as defined by the ACA and the American Mental Health Counselors Association (AMHCA). Apply knowledge of ethical and legal perspectives to relevant counseling situations.

Recognize and respond appropriately to professional limitations.

Become familiar with community resources and know when and where to refer clients.

Learn the value of providing and receiving professional consultation regarding counseling individuals, couples, families, and groups.

Learn to give and receive feedback in the seminar format.

Follow established professional and ethical guidelines regarding counseling multicultural and diverse client populations.

Weekly attendance in seminar. *More than two absences will result in an unsatisfactory (U) grade. An unsatisfactory grade requires the student to wait until the following year to repeat EDU 679.*

Read assigned chapters in text and be ready to discuss in the seminar format.

A score of 70% or higher on the final ethics examination is also required before a student may progress to EDU 685. The final is based on ethical and legal issues through readings in the text and in-class discussion.

Students must also receive a satisfactory evaluation in their practicum placement to move to Internship I (EDU 685).

Video of a taped 30-minute session with a classroom partner or a client in a professional setting. Students may counsel from a person-centered, cognitive behavioral, solution-focused, integrative, and so on framework. In addition, each

(continued)

Exhibit 7.1 Sample Counseling Practicum/Internship Class Syllabus (*continued*)

video will be preceded using the SOAP/*DSM-5* and intake form in your *Mental Health Counseling (MHC) Handbook.* In practicum, the mock video sessions will not be graded. Next semester, in Internship I (EDU 685), mock sessions will be graded.

Learn the nuances of consultation with counselors, other mental health professionals, human services agencies, and law enforcement.

All students must provide proof of student liability insurance prior to beginning practicum. Additionally, students must maintain student liability insurance throughout internship.

Methods of Instruction

Weekly sessions will be organized using a seminar approach. It is expected that students will have read and are prepared to discuss previously assigned material (i.e., text). Students will be expected to communicate their experiences in the practicum setting to other students and faculty. Feedback from others in the practicum will enhance students' perceptions and facilitate learning new approaches to counseling. Students will also present a videotape of a role-played counseling session to others in the practicum for feedback on the use of counseling skills. The professor will use the session rating form on page 27 of the *MHC Handbook.*

Outline of Course

CLASS MEETING DATE	ACTIVITIES
Week 1	Introduction to practicum. Schedule videotape presentations. Textbook information.
Week 2	Read Chapters 1, 2, and 3. Video: *Ethical and Legal Issues.*
Week 3	Read Chapter 4: "Client Welfare."
Week 4	View professional video and critique.
Week 5	Student videotape presentation. Read Chapters 5 and 6: "Confidentiality," and "Records and Subpoenas."
Week 6	Student videotape presentation. Read Chapter 7: "Competence and Malpractice."
Week 7	Student videotape presentation. Read Chapter 8: "Boundary Issues."

(continued)

164 • THE COUNSELING PRACTICUM AND INTERNSHIP MANUAL

> ## Exhibit 7.1 Sample Counseling Practicum/Internship Class Syllabus (*continued*)

Week 8	Student videotape presentation. Read Chapters 9 and 10: "Families" and "Groups."
Week 9	Student videotape presentation. Read Chapter 11: "Evaluation, Testing, and Diagnosis."
Week 10	Student videotape presentation. Read Chapter 12: "Private Practice."
Week 11	Student videotape presentation. Read Chapter 13: "Technology and Health Care."
Week 12	Student videotape presentation. Read Chapter 15: "Supervision and Consultation."
Week 13	View/critique professional counseling videotape. Read Chapter 17: "Resolving Ethical and Legal Issues."
Week 14	Last class. Ethics examination.

Grading

The final grade (*S, U,* or *I*) will be determined by class attendance (no more than two absences); a passing score on the ethics examination (70 and above is passing); satisfactory performance on videotapes; and feedback from the students, on-site supervisor evaluation, and the university professor. Satisfactory performance in all the aforementioned areas will result in a grade of satisfactory (*S*). A deficient mark in any of the previously mentioned areas will result in a grade of unsatisfactory (*U*). A *U* grade would result in the student retaking EDU 679 the following year.

Checklist

Satisfactory evaluation by site supervisor and evaluation of supervisor (turn in by final class, December 3).

Passing the ethics examination (grade of 70 or higher).

No more than two classroom absences.

Satisfactory performance on videotape—not graded, but demonstrating a basic ability to create a therapeutic environment.

Must turn in practicum timesheet (see pp. 35–36 in *MHC Handbook*). Turn in by final class.

(continued)

Exhibit 7.1 Sample Counseling Practicum/Internship Class Syllabus (*continued*)

Bibliography

American Counseling Association. (2014). *2014 ACA code of ethics.* https://www.counseling.org/resources/aca-code-of-ethics.pdf

Herlihy, B., & Corey, G. (2020). *ACA ethical standards casebook* (8th ed.). American Counseling Association.

Wheeler, A. M., & Bertram, B. (2019). *The counselor and the law: A guide to legal and ethical education* (8th ed.). American Counseling Association.

When possible, practicum and internship students make recordings of actual counseling sessions. Video recordings are preferable because they allow students to observe nonverbal components of the session, as well as give everyone in the class a concrete picture of how the counselor-in-training conducted the session. Unfortunately, during the past several years, placements (at least in my area) seem to be more restrictive regarding allowing practicum and internship students to record sessions. Many programs must work around such a restriction by having student's record mock sessions with a supervisor. This restriction regarding prohibiting on-site recordings is very unfortunate, given counselors-in-training are an important part of this country's mental health treatment. In fact, judging by the Bureau of Labor Statistics (BLS), counselors, particularly mental health counselors, addictions counselors, and others, are among the fastest growing mental health professions (BLS, 2019). Such curtailment likely is due to liability concerns on the part of schools and agencies.

There are several procedures to follow when recording client sessions. The *ACA Code of Ethics* (American Counseling Association [ACA], 2014, Section B.6.c) states that clients must be informed of session recordings and must give their consent to the process prior to recording the session. Although no legal or ethical requirement stipulates that permission be given in writing, standard practice generally includes written forms of consent. Programs, students, and counselors would be wise to follow such practice (Remley & Herlihy, 2020). Exhibit 7.2 shows a sample permission-to-record form.

Exhibit 7.2 Client Permission to Record Counseling Session for Supervision Purposes

I/We, _____, hereby grant permission for our counselor to videotape/audiotape (circle appropriate recording choice) our counseling session on the following date(s):_____

I/We understand that the purpose of this recording is for the clinical supervision of my/our counselor's work. I/We provide for the following people to view the recording:

(continued)

Exhibit 7.2 Client Permission to Record Counseling Session for Supervision Purposes (*continued*)

_____ (Supervisor)

_____ (Practicum/Internship Group)

The above named persons will also hold the information on the recording confidential.

The recording will be erased after the supervisor has reviewed it.

_____   _____

Client Signature   Date

_____   _____

Client Signature   Date

_____   _____

Client Signature   Date

Parental/Guardian Permission to Record Session Form

The graduate counseling program at Northern State University conducts a practicum and internship course for the purpose of training future professional counselors. The practicum/internship class is an advanced course requirement of all degree candidates in Northern State University's graduate counseling program. Graduate students in the counseling program are required to record counseling sessions as part of their professional training and development and to be of more assistance to the clients they counsel. The counseling sessions conducted with your child will be reviewed by the student counselor's faculty supervisor (or, in some cases, the supervisor at this site) and a small group of graduate students in the practicum/internship. The faculty supervisor, on-site supervisor, and graduate counseling students are all held to confidentiality and the contents of this recording will not be revealed beyond the course. Once the recording has been played, it will be erased. By signing this form, you give permission for your child to be recorded.

Thank you for your cooperation in this important matter.

Parent's/Guardian's Name _____

Student Counselor's Signature _____

Date: _____ / _____ / _____

Students must also understand that information stored on a DVD, flash drive, or any other device must be kept in a secure setting and then erased after it has been reviewed by the clinical supervisor and/or the practicum/internship class (Wheeler & Bertram, 2019). *Note:* Be careful not to leave sensitive recorded material in unsecure locations. Unless your agency (and you) has an encrypted site, you may put yourself and your clients at risk. As more and more clinicians utilize technology for counseling and additional clinical services, secure software becomes even more critical. Having made this statement, however, I am flummoxed when counselors, counselor educators, and counseling supervisors bemoan the lack of security in advanced technology yet think nothing of disclosing sensitive information to a colleague through the telephone, a medium scarcely secure! Regardless, take reasonable precautions to secure recordings and counseling through the medium of technology. What are reasonable precautions? Well, if you were the client, patient, or student, would you be satisfied with the level of care taken with your current due diligence regarding storage privacy?

You should review your recording prior to the in-class presentation. For counseling students in agencies, generally, programs require students to complete an intake form with a Mental State Examination or Mini-Mental State Examination, diagnostic form, and SOAP (**S**ubjective, **O**bjective, **A**ssessment, and **P**lan) or DAP (**D**ata, **A**ssessment, and **P**lan or another format) case note format regarding the session (see Chapter 5, "Clinical Issues in Practicum and Internship," and Chapter 6, "Clinical Writing and Documentation in Counseling Records," for examples of some of these forms), plus a *Diagnostic and Statistical Manual of Mental Disorders, Third Edition Text Revision* (DSM-5-TR; American Psychiatric Association [APA], 2022) diagnosis (if at an agency) and sample treatment plan. These materials will provide you with a format for tying the case together and give the class an organized context of the client's presenting issues, ongoing struggles, counselor observations, and prognosis for treatment. Counseling students in school settings generally will complete more developmental and less "clinical" forms. School counseling forms might include a school-based intake form, possibly with an orientation-times-five questionnaire (e.g., "Who are you?" "Where are you?" "Who is your father/mother?" "Why are we talking?" "What day is it?"), grade point average, career/vocational issues, supports, family, and so forth.

MODELS OF SUPERVISION AND CRITIQUE

There are numerous models of counselor education and supervision (Benshoff, 1993; Borders, 1991; Remley & Herlihy, 2020). In counselor education programs, supervision serves the dual purposes of monitoring counselors'-in-training performance and monitoring the well-being of clients receiving services from graduate counseling students (*ACA*, 2014, Standard F.1.a). Professional research in counselor supervision recognizes that there are two types of supervision—administrative and clinical (Borders & Leddick, 1987; Remley & Herlihy, 2020). Administrative supervision focuses on administrators providing supervision to counselors and other employees in an agency, a school, a hospital, and so forth. Clinical supervision, on the other hand, is the process where mental health professionals review the clinical work of counselors or counselors-in-training with the goal of facilitating counselor effectiveness. In this text as well as in counselor education programs, the focus will be on clinical as opposed to administrative supervision. Naturally, counseling students will receive on-site supervision from a licensed counselor, social worker, psychologist, certified school counselor, and so on. Counseling students also receive weekly supervision and training from a faculty member so that supervision and training can be comprehensive.

Borders (1991) advocated an instructional model involving goal setting, reading, and discussion of journal articles, case presentations, and review and critique of counseling sessions by peers and faculty. In this approach, students specify questions they would like to address and the types of feedback they are seeking. Then, each student presents a recording critiqued by the professor and students in the class. (In this approach, all members of the class critique the student presenting the case.) Naturally, different students will have different reactions: one student may focus on the nonverbal behavior of the client, whereas another will attend to the content. Some will focus more on specific techniques used and others will be more concerned with whether the counselor paid enough attention to the affective domain. Students might approach the presentation from various orientations: humanistic, cognitive behavioral, or client centered, for example.

During the critique, the supervisor monitors the discussion to clarify the student's comments and to ensure that the feedback is constructive. The student being critiqued may ask clarifying questions to enhance their understanding of the intention of the comments and to seek clarification. The supervisor also sets the stage by explaining the approach and appropriate feedback style, as well as modeling how to receive feedback. Another variation is the structured group supervision model (SGSM) developed by Wilbur et al. (1991). The SGSM uses five phases:

1. The request for assistance statement: In this phase, students may seek support for personal growth, technical skills, and better understanding of the therapeutic process.

2. The questioning period and identification of focus: Students take turns questioning the student presenter.

3. The feedback statements: In this phase, group members may offer feedback related to the session with the intent of assisting the student counselor's continued development. Wilbur et al. (1991) suggest that during this phase, the student remains silent and focuses entirely on receiving the feedback. Wilbur et al. also point out that the "silence" reduces the possibility of a defensive response. Group members are instructed to offer critique in the form of statements such as "If this were my client . . ." or "What I might do . . . ."

4. A pause period: Perhaps the most innovative aspect of the SGSM is the pause phase. Following the feedback, there is a period of 10 to 15 minutes (5–10 minutes may be a more realistic time frame) during which the supervisee is encouraged to reflect on the critique while the class takes a short break.

5. An optional discussion period: After the break, the group reassembles and the supervisee responds to the feedback. These reflections may involve comments on feedback, insights gained from the critique, how the comments were helpful, and what they might do differently in the next counseling session.

Other practicum supervisors may be more informal and use a less structured approach to assessment. Many will use a round-robin format where each peer in the

7: MODELS OF SUPERVISION: CLASSROOM AND SITE SUPERVISION • 169

class critiques the student counselor. The student being critiqued is not held to silence as in the SGSM and may ask clarifying questions. The faculty supervisor is generally the last to provide feedback, minimizing unduly influencing the student critique.

With any feedback approach used, the instructor would be prudent to explain the nature of feedback at the onset of the semester and then model appropriate styles of critique (e.g., commenting on the counseling approach and effectiveness versus making a personal criticism). The instructor should also avoid interrupting the feedback to empower students providing feedback. The goal of feedback is twofold: to provide an opportunity for the student counselor to stretch their counseling skills and to enhance students' development in providing critique.

WRITTEN FEEDBACK

After the class discussion, a session rating scale or critique form may be used by students and/or the faculty supervisor to rate the student counselor's effectiveness.

Naturally, the critique form cannot address all areas of the therapeutic encounter but provides a brief analysis of the relative effectiveness of the student counselor. Exhibit 7.3 shows a sample session rating form. Many schools and agencies serving as practicum and internship settings will have their own critique form.

Exhibit 7.3 Student Counseling Session Rating Form

Date: _____ / _____ / _____

Student:_____ Evaluator:_____

Audiotape:_____ DVD/Videotape:_____ In-class role-play: _____

Brief summary of session content: _____

_____

_____

_____

Specific Criteria	Rating (1 = *Least*; 5 = *Best*)
Opening: Was informed consent thorough and professional? Was confidentiality covered?	1 2 3 4 5

(continued)

170 • THE COUNSELING PRACTICUM AND INTERNSHIP MANUAL

Exhibit 7.3 Student Counseling Session Rating Form (*continued*)

Specific Criteria	Rating (1 = *Least*; 5 = *Best*)
Rapport: Did the counselor establish a good therapeutic alliance (e.g., voice tone, appropriate eye contact, paraphrasing, and summarizing)?	1 2 3 4 5
Attending skill: Did the counselor use minimal encouragers and refrain from unnecessary interruptions? Additionally, was the counselor skilled in using therapeutic silence?	1 2 3 4 5
Open-ended questioning: Did the counselor make appropriate use of open-ended questions?	1 2 3 4 5
Affective domain: Did the counselor demonstrate appropriate empathy?	1 2 3 4 5
Challenging/confrontation: Did the counselor confront the client (if the situation warranted it)?	1 2 3 4 5
Solution skills: Did the counselor offer appropriate solution-seeking input (through techniques such as the empty chair, miracle question, and role-plays)?	1 2 3 4 5
Cultural issues: Did the counselor appear to understand and respect cultural issues?	1 2 3 4 5
Goal setting: Did the counselor set effective goals for a follow-up session?	1 2 3 4 5
Closing: Was closing well orchestrated? Or, was it too abrupt?	1 2 3 4 5

On the following 1-to-10 scale, how effective was the student counselor in facilitating the counseling session? (1 = *least effective*, 10 = *most effective*) Circle the appropriate number:

1   2   3   4   5   6   7   8   9   10

(*continued*)

Exhibit 7.3 Student Counseling Session Rating Form (*continued*)

What the student did best during this session was

_____

_____

_____

Regarding this session, what the student most needs to improve on is

_____

_____

_____

Constructive comments for the student counselor's continued development:

_____

_____

_____

_____

Signature of Evaluator

OFFERING FEEDBACK TO PEERS

As part of practicum/internship (and throughout your counseling career), you will be involved in analyzing counselor effectiveness and offering suggestions for improvement. Until now, you may not have had much opportunity to hone your feedback skills and will likely need coaching from your instructor and on-site supervisor. Student critiques often run a continuum from overly critical to too vague to overly positive. Overly negative feedback can impinge on a student counselor's confidence, whereas uncritical positive comments provide little educational value. An instructor must strive to create an environment where honest and critical comments are given and received. This latter point requires a deft touch on the part of the supervisor and an open perspective on the part of the student. Supervisors will need to provide constructive feedback while realizing even positive comments may elicit an undesired reaction from a student. It is worth expressing, therefore, that supervision also is a work in progress on the part of the supervisor. Students, remember you are developing future supervision skills.

Kadushin (1985) offered guidelines for supervisors to follow when providing critique on students' work. These guidelines stress the importance of giving feedback that is specific, timely, focused on concrete behaviors, descriptive rather than judgmental, focused on the behaviors of the student rather than their personal characteristics, phrased in the form of tentative statements rather than authoritative conclusions, focused on positive issues, and, finally, selective rather than a laundry list. Consider the following example:

> *Unhelpful feedback:* "Hector, I think you need to engage the client more." (Too vague. How could Hector "engage" the client? Be specific.)

> *Helpful feedback:* "Hector, I think a specific way you could engage the client in the session might be to ask more open-ended questions such as 'How could you begin to create healthy friendships?' or 'What could you do right now to establish a functional relationship with your father?'" (The feedback in this example was targeted and specific.)

Students in a practicum or internship also receive weekly clinical supervision at their placement from an experienced, licensed, or properly credentialed supervisor. These supervision meetings are to target specific issues related to the student counselor's performance at the agency or school. The supervisor's critique will generally focus on the following questions:

- Is the student counselor able to establish the therapeutic relationship?
- Is the student counselor able to set realistic goals with the client?
- What struggles does the student counselor appear to be having?
- How well does the student counselor facilitate therapeutic change during sessions?
- Does the student counselor understand their professional ethics? Can they use them effectively in session?
- Is the student counselor able to receive constructive feedback and incorporate it into improving their counseling skills?

Supervisory Style

There are various supervisory methods to use with practicum/internship students. The type of supervision provided will mostly depend on the theoretical orientation of the on-site clinical supervisor. Although the effectiveness of supervision on counselor development has been widely studied, no evidence supports one methodology as being superior to another (Granello & Granello, 2007). Interestingly, only once in my entire counseling career has anyone ever asked me, "What is your theoretical supervision style?" I was asked this question at an interview for a faculty position in counselor education, not in a treatment facility. However, when you become a counselor/clinical supervisor, be prepared to articulate a supervision style and be wary, while not judgmental, of supervisors who cannot do so. In fact, my belief is some field site supervisors would be stumped at such a question. Your field supervisor has developed their own supervision style after several years of experience, both being supervised and providing supervision. Likely, supervisors are influenced most by the persons who supervised them during their graduate school training or an influential supervisor when they were newly minted counselors or other therapists.

Examples of Clinical Supervision Styles

BERNARD'S DISCRIMINATION MODEL

One of the most commonly employed and researched supervision models is the discrimination model, originally published by Bernard (Bernard & Goodyear, 2014). The discrimination model is composed of three separate foci for supervision (i.e., intervention, conceptualization, and consultant) and three possible supervision roles (i.e., teacher, counselor, and consultant). The supervisor could respond in one of nine ways (three roles × three foci; Bernard & Goodyear, 2014). For instance, the supervisor may take on the role of teacher while focusing on a specific intervention used by the supervisee in the client session or the role of counselor while focusing on the supervisee's conceptualization of the work. Because the response is always specific to the supervisee's needs, it changes within and across sessions.

The supervisor first evaluates the supervisee's ability within the focus area and then selects the appropriate role from which to respond. Bernard and Goodyear (2014) caution supervisors not to respond from the same focus or role out of personal preference, comfort, or habit but instead to ensure the focus and role meet the most salient needs of the supervisee in that moment. Supervisors utilizing the discrimination model must be very organized and mindful regarding the supervisory relationship and be clear as to what role they are "playing" out with the supervisee.

PSYCHODYNAMIC APPROACH TO SUPERVISION

Psychodynamic supervision is based upon Freud's model of transference and countertransference (Frawley-O'Dea & Sarnat, 2001). Frawley-O'Dea and Sarnat (2001) further classify psychodynamic supervision into three categories: patient centered, supervisee centered, and supervisory matrix centered.

Patient centered, based on Freud's model, focuses the supervision session on the patient's issues and behaviors. The supervisor assumes a didactic role with the goal of assisting the supervisee to understand and treat the patient. The supervisor is a dispassionate expert and, thus, an authority figure. As long as the supervisee agrees with the supervisor, little conflict is inherent (Smith, 2009). Given that the psychodynamic supervisor is posited as an authority figure, some supervisees may have difficulty voicing disagreement, particularly if they are struggling with confidence—something common with beginning counselors. Likely, most counseling students are not under supervision from a psychodynamic supervisor (though such may well supervise some practicum and internship students, especially in large urban areas).

Supervisee-centered supervision, which focuses on the content and process of the supervisee's experience, became popular in the 1950s (Bernard & Goodyear, 2014).

The supervisor's uninvolved, authority role remains the same, but as attention is transferred to the supervisee's experience as a counselor, the approach becomes more experiential than didactic (Bernard & Goodyear, 2014); as the supervisor remains the distant authority figure, the supervisee remains in the position of the "inferior." Proponents of psychodynamic-based supervision would point out that all supervisors would be the authority figure, regardless of the supervision model utilized. While this point is true (or should be), the model may lend itself to scrutiny more than a process-oriented conversation.

The supervisory-matrix-centered approach differs in that in addition to focusing on the client, it also addresses the supervisor–supervisee relationship. No longer is the supervisor an austere, uninvolved expert. The relationship is relational, with the supervisor an active participant in establishing a two-way conversation with the supervisee (Frawley-O'Dea & Sarnat, 2001). The relationship also involves an examination of *parallel process*, defined as the "supervisee's interaction with the supervisor that parallels the client's behavior with the supervisee as the therapist" (Haynes et al., 2003).

FEMINIST MODEL OF SUPERVISION

Feminist theory asserts that an individual's experiences are reflective of society's dominant values, attitudes, and opinions (Brown & Brodsky, 1992). Feminist counselors view the client's experience within the context of a patriarchal society. Thus, the view of anxiety, depression, bipolar disorder, and so forth is through the lens of a patriarchal society and not via *DSM-5* language (Brown & Brodsky, 1992). Many feminist counselors are ardently opposed to the *DSM* as a tool of a patriarchal society and may eschew using the medical model (Haynes et al., 2003).

Feminist supervisors, then, may counsel the supervisee to acknowledge power differentials in the client–counselor relationship and encourage the supervisee to understand the role of privilege. Given that the supervisor holds a position of power over the supervisee, the relationship may form grounds for more collaborative discussions, at least to the extent possible. Feminist supervisors may also focus on empowerment of the supervisee and, in turn, facilitate the counselor's work to empower clients, many of whom may live along the margins of society as disempowered individuals, couples, and families. Feminist models of supervision have become more popular in recent years (Haynes et al., 2003).

INTEGRATED DEVELOPMENTAL MODEL

The integrated developmental model (IDM) of supervision, developed by Stoltenberg (1981), updated by Stoltenberg and Delworth (1987), and later by Stoltenberg et al. (1998), is a popular and well-researched supervision model (Smith, 2009). The IDM describes three levels of counselor development (Falender & Shafranske, 2004):

Level 1: Supervisees are generally entry-level students who are high in motivation but also high in anxiety and fearful of evaluation.

Level 2: Supervisees are at mid-level and experience fluctuating confidence and motivation, often linking their own mood to success with clients.

Level 3: Supervisees are essentially secure, stable in motivation, have accurate empathy tempered by objectivity, and use therapeutic self in intervention.

The IDM emphasizes the need for the supervisor to select skills and interventions appropriate to the level of the supervisee. When supervising a Level 1 supervisee, the supervisor would want to balance the supervisee's anxiety and dependence by a display of support and direction. If supervising a Level 3 supervisee, the supervisor would emphasize autonomy and engage in a more constructivist discussion. The critical factor in the IDM is matching feedback with the supervisee's appropriate level; otherwise, the supervisee may feel either overwhelmed or restricted. A supervisor who refuses to engage in more parallel conversation with a Level 3 supervisee is likely to encounter a high degree of frustration and resistance. Likewise, a supervisor who expects autonomous behavior from a Level 1 supervisee likely will increase the supervisee's anxiety.

The IDM has become popular as a supervision model, offering many advantages, especially in breaking down information into shorter, working stages of development. Students may understand short, simple stages of development more readily, and such may ease their anxiety regarding supervision. The IDM, however, does have weaknesses as it focuses predominantly on the development of graduate students in training and pays little attention to post-degree supervision (Smith, 2009). Furthermore, the IDM presents few suggestions for specific supervision models that are applicable at each specific supervisee level (Haynes et al., 2003). An alternative development model developed by Rønnestad and Skovholt (1993, 2003) addresses the IDM's initial weaknesses by providing a framework to describe counselor development.

RØNNESTAD AND SKOVHOLT'S SUPERVISION MODEL

Rønnestad and Skovholt's model is based on a longitudinal, qualitative study conducted by interviewing 100 counselors/therapists, ranging in experience from graduate students to professional counselors/therapists with a mean of 25 years of counseling experience (Rønnestad & Skovholt, 1993). Rønnestad and Skovholt analyzed data and developed a stage model, a theme model, and a professional model of development and stagnation (Rønnestad & Skovholt, 2003). The first three phases (i.e., the lay helper phase, the beginning student phase, and the advanced student phase) essentially correspond with the levels of the IDM (Smith, 2009). The remaining phases (i.e., the novice professional phase, the experienced professional phase, and the senior professional phase) are self-explanatory in terms of the relative occurrence of the phase in relation to the counselor's career.

In addition to the phase model, Rønnestad and Skovholt's (2003) research enumerated 14 themes of counselor development. They are as follows:

- Professional development involves an increasing higher-order integration of the professional self and the personal self.
- The focus of functioning shifts dramatically over time from internal to external to internal.
- Continuous reflection is a prerequisite for optimal learning and development at all levels of experience.
- An intense commitment to learn propels the developmental process.
- The cognitive map changes: Beginning practitioners rely on external expertise, whereas seasoned practitioners rely on internal expertise.

176 • THE COUNSELING PRACTICUM AND INTERNSHIP MANUAL

- Professional development is a long, slow, continuous process that can also be erratic.
- Professional development is a life long process.
- Many beginning practitioners experience much anxiety in their professional work. Over time, anxiety is reduced through experience.
- Clients serve as a major source of influence and serve as primary teachers.
- Personal life influences professional functioning and development throughout the professional life span.
- Interpersonal sources of influence propel professional development more than "impersonal" sources of influence.
- New members of the field view professional elders and graduate training with strong affective reactions.
- Extensive experience with suffering contributes to heightened recognition, acceptance, and appreciation of human variability.
- For the practitioner, there is a realignment from self as hero to client as hero. (Adapted from Rønnestad & Skovholt, 2003)

Rønnestad and Skovholt (2003) conclude that counselor development is a complex process requiring continuous self-reflection. They also conclude that, much like the counselor–client therapeutic alignment's robust influence on treatment outcomes, their results suggest a "close and reciprocal relationship between how counselors/ therapists handle challenges and difficulties in the client relationship and experiences of professional growth or stagnation" (p. 40).

COGNITIVE BEHAVIORAL SUPERVISION

Just as cognitive behavioral therapy (CBT) has become a very popular approach to counseling, cognitive behavioral supervision is likewise common (Beck et al., 1993; Haynes et al., 2003). Cognitive behavioral supervision makes use of tangible thoughts and behaviors, particularly that of the supervisee's professional identity and their reaction to the client (Haynes et al., 2003). Cognitive behavioral techniques used in supervision include setting an agenda for supervision sessions, bridging from previous sessions, assigning homework to the supervisee, and capsule summaries by the supervisor (Beck et al., 1993). The supervisor–supervisee relationship is akin to that of teacher–student, and though it is collaborative, it is also directive, with the supervisor leading. A large part of cognitive supervision, like therapy, involves a scientific inquiry model of posing questions like "What's the evidence for ____?"

PERSON-CENTERED SUPERVISION

Carl Rogers developed person-centered therapy with the belief the client has the capacity to resolve life problems without interpretation and direction from the counselor (Corey, 2017). Similarly, person-centered supervision assumes that the supervisee has the resources to develop effectively as a counselor. The supervisor, then, is not an *expert* in the person-centered model but rather an experienced consultant, coach, and collaborator. The supervisor's role is to establish an environment whereby the supervisee can be open to the supervision experience in order to develop fully as a clinician

(Lambers, 2000). Like Rogers's necessary and sufficient conditions (e.g., genuineness, empathy, and unconditional positive regard; 1951) in therapy, the same concepts are applied to clinical supervision.

SOLUTION-FOCUSED SUPERVISION

de Shazer (1985) developed solution-focused brief therapy as a therapeutic approach in the 1980s. As the name suggests, the approach focuses on being brief and focusing on solutions as opposed to a focus on problems. Therapeutic attention is devoted to building on the client's idea of a future goal and discovering the inner resources needed in order to achieve this goal (De Shazer, 1985).

Solution-focused supervision lends itself well to clinical supervision, as well as in counseling, as its interventions are easily transferrable to clinical supervision encounters. Constructivist questions such as those in the following list might be utilized in supervision:

- "So, how were you able to help the client improve their mood?"
- "How were you able to gain confidence this past semester?"
- "What have you learned about yourself during your practicum/internship/job?"
- "What would you cite as your clinical strengths?"
- "What's different when you feel you are being helpful to clients?"

When addressing the supervisee's strengths, resources, and skills, the supervisor adopts the persona of the curious inquirer. For example, asking how the supervisee managed a particular situation despite challenges enables the supervisor to acknowledge their ability to identify skills utilized in order to identify the particular solution.

One of the solution-focused staples is the miracle question. Regarding a focus on specific goals, the supervisor asks:

"If you went to sleep tonight and a miracle occurred related to your confidence as a counselor (or any issues of concern) where you were more confident, how would your work as a counselor be different? What would you notice? What would I notice?"

The miracle question provides the format for the supervisee to drop anxiety and speculate on future success (Kim Berg & Szabo, 2005).

Subsequent supervision sessions focus on solutions rather than problems. Soliciting "What has improved?" at the onset of a supervision session, as opposed to "How are things?" encourages the supervisee to focus on their clinical growth. At the conclusion of the supervisory session, the supervisor summarizes the supervisee's strengths, skills, and improvement. The solution-focused supervisor provides feedback based upon the supervisee's choice of language. Thus, the importance of active listening coupled with constructivist-type responses is highly emphasized. I offer the following suggestions regarding solution-focused supervision:

- Utilize active listening to what the supervisee is saying (e.g., "I hear you saying you are concerned about this client's ongoing depression.").
- Use constructivist-type responses to assist the supervisee in identifying strengths, skills, and inner resources (e.g., "If you could bring that client into the supervision session right now, what might you say to him or her now?").

- Use encouragement by actively demonstrating interest and encouraging a more collegial supervisory relationship, though not an equal one (e.g., "You are making a good effort with this recovery group. Now, here's something to think of for the next session . . .").
- Cite and name specific supervisee strengths, skills, and resources (e.g., "You have made a lot of progress in confronting relapse.").
- Use scaling questions to assist the supervisee in measuring clinical growth (e.g., "On a scale of 1 to 10, with 10 high, how would you rate your counseling skill at this point?").

The goal of a solution-focused supervisory approach to clinical supervision is to enhance the supervisee's experience and lessen their degree of anxiety, thus enhancing the likelihood the supervisee will develop more confidence and competence. As the solution-focused supervision approach is more collegial, supervisees may report feeling less anxiety during supervision sessions. It is also likely, however, that some supervisees may find an "overfocus" on strengths limiting and may at times prefer explicit criticism. Research on the solution-focused supervision model is not as extensive as more established models, and more research in this area of the clinical supervision literature is needed (Corey, 2017).

SYSTEMS APPROACH TO SUPERVISION

In the systems approach to supervision, the crux of the supervision relationship targets mutual involvement of both parties (Holloway, 1995). Holloway describes seven dimensions of supervision: (a) central supervisory relationship, (b) functions of supervision, (c) tasks of supervision, (d) the client, (e) trainee, (f) supervisor, and (g) the institution. The functions and tasks of supervision are at the foreground of interaction, while the latter four dimensions represent unique contextual factors that, according to Holloway, are covert influences in the supervisory process. Supervision for any particular issue reflects some combination of these seven dimensions (Smith, 2009). Thus, a systems approach to supervision covers multiple levels related to the various intersecting "systems" in which the supervisee and client exist. Examples of systems may be schools, businesses, correctional institutions, religious institutions, cultures, families, and so forth.

Supervision Styles

You may discover that your field site supervisor may have a radically different style than the one supervising your classmate. Some on-site supervisors are quite formal and require a student to tape an entire session. Others will listen to a brief segment of a tape or none at all. Some supervisors will ask students to work on a particular skill, such as delivering confrontation or using a particular intervention. Supervisors vary greatly across the continuum of styles, opinions, theoretical approaches to counseling, and in how they deliver feedback (i.e., constructivist versus overtly negative in feedback).

It is clear that in the supervisor–student relationship, the power differential rests with the on-site supervisor. Thus, students must become facile in negotiating a delicate balance of appearing open to critique and at the same time developing appropriate assertiveness. Openness to critique would involve listening to feedback that may be critical. The assertiveness aspect of the student's role would be to ask for clarification if they were unclear about the message. Consider this example:

> **Supervisor:** I need you to work on the treatment plan more, okay?
>
> **Practicum student:** I would like to do that. What specifically could I do to improve my performance in this area?

If you do not know what your supervisor is suggesting, or if they seem vague (such as in the given situation), seek clarity by asking questions. Good supervisors will appreciate your initiative. Granted, there are poor supervisors out there and some of you will have the misfortune of working under them. Having a poor supervisor, however, also provides you the opportunity to learn to deal effectively with such professionals, as you will encounter them in your career. When you do get a supervisor who seems to be a poor communicator, is overly critical, sloppy, or seems burned out, you need to find a "safe" area to debrief this. Safe areas could include other practicum or internship students and fellow graduate students in your counseling program.

If you believe your supervisor is incompetent or unethical (as opposed to merely ineffective), your first step would be to talk with your faculty advisor or the coordinator of practicum/internship placement (Chapter 4, "Ethical and Legal Issues," addresses ethical issues). Your advisor would then need to dialogue with your on-site supervisor or the director of the setting in which you have been placed. In many cases, establishing a healthier supervisor–supervisee relationship is possible. Otherwise, a new supervisor will be assigned to you. It is also possible that you will need a new placement, although that should be a last resort. It has also been my experience that in most cases (although not all), addressing conflicts with your supervisor paves the way for a more trusting and respectful relationship.

Site Supervisor as Mentor

You need to develop a strong rapport with your on-site supervisor, as they will not only be writing an evaluation of your performance but will also serve as the natural contact for clinical advice. The following statement is one you need to remember when faced with ethical, legal, moral, or other dilemmas that occur at your placement site: When in doubt, always contact your supervisor at the soonest possible time. This will save both you and your supervisor much anxiety. Having been a supervisor in clinics and universities for many years, I can reinforce that supervisors do not like surprises. Keep your supervisor informed, and that will help make your practicum–internship experience more rewarding (and less stressful!). Furthermore, when applying for employment post-graduation, on-site supervisors can be strong references. Remember, the on-site practicum–internship supervisor can elaborate on-the-job strengths. Therefore, you want your on-site supervisor to view you in a favorable light.

Not all questions or concerns are ethical ones. In fact, it is likely most of your questions will turn out to be operational in nature. Operational concerns relate to the ways the placement site carries out treatment, its rules, chain of command, and professional orientation of its staff (e.g., psychologist, counselor, social worker); whether the setting holds one of the various accreditations (e.g., The Joint Commission,

180 • THE COUNSELING PRACTICUM AND INTERNSHIP MANUAL

American Association of Pastoral Counselors [AAPC], International Accreditation of Counseling Services [IACS], and Commission on Accreditation of Rehabilitation Facilities [CARF]); and so forth. In my more than 20 years of experience with practicum and internship placements, most student concerns and conflicts fell into this latter category. Besides paying careful attention to whatever orientation your site provides, you will want to develop your own checklist of questions to ask your on-site supervisor:

- What types of training and professional development are provided to practicum/internship students (many practicum/internship sites will train or send students to training in various techniques, treatment models, etc.)?
- What types of resources are available to practicum/internship students (e.g., computers, access to a library, research opportunities)?
- How are client or patient records kept (e.g., online or written and locked in a secure)?
- What are the policies regarding taping client sessions? (Some organizations record all client sessions and require clients to sign a waiver as part of consent to treatment.)
- What are the emergency procedures in the event of a crisis (e.g., hostage situation; an assault at the setting; death of a client, patient, or staff member; suicide attempt)?
- Although you are a counselor-in-training, your supervisor (or most staff) may be a psychologist or social worker. Which code of ethics will you need to know and operate under?
- Has your placement informed you of how to address an allegation of sexual harassment, child abuse or endangerment, communicable disease, or any mandated reporting issue?

These questions represent a beginning point; as you proceed through your practicum and internship, you will likely come up with many more questions. Keep your smartphone or a notebook handy, so when you have questions and concerns, you can write them down. It is also worth mentioning that no policy manual, no matter how voluminous and comprehensive, can possibly address all contingencies. So, be smart and proactive by keeping notes and asking pertinent questions. Your supervisor will likely be impressed at your initiative. If they are not, you may wish to consider whether the setting is the right one for you. While there are no guarantees, preparation, being proactive, and accepting feedback in a mature manner will likely help you strengthen the relationship with your on-site supervisor.

CONCLUSION

No doubt, being a clinical supervisor is not an exact science. Clinical supervisors will vary in their skill and facility in providing helpful supervision to graduate interns, as well as to professional staff. One of the most difficult issues counselor educators deal with is the unequal level of quality supervision their interns receive on placement, especially in the initial practicum. A guideline I have found helpful is to remind students that supervisors will vary in styles and approaches. Furthermore, one can learn from a marginal supervisor as well as from a good one. No question, learning from a good supervisor is far better, as behavioral dispositions and modeling are powerful.

As a counselor educator and professional counselor for a few decades, I have experienced the continuum of poor to excellent supervision. The reality is many counselors will have similar experiences to me as well. My advice is to learn as much as you can from whomever supervises you. Further, learn also from superiors who may be line staff, as with their professional dispositions, communication ability, and experience, they can serve as a wealth of information in your development as a counselor.

LESSONS LEARNED

The young graduate student sat before me, her leg dancing as she waited my critique on her video. I was in my final year in the doctoral program and was serving as a graduate assistant in an internship course. I have served in such a role in the counselor education program and helped teach a similar course in the separate psychology department. I had come to see myself having a facility in clinical oversight, having worked several years as a counselor and been a graduate teaching assistant for several years. Generally, my relationships with students was good and the evaluations reinforced my belief in self-efficacy. However, Sarah (pseudonym) was sorely testing my belief.

My family lineage includes a few generations of teachers. My grandfather, who helped raise me, was a one-room schoolteacher in rural Arkansas. He liked nothing better than imparting his lecturing prowess to my four siblings and me during our formative years. Although skilled in oration, his listening acumen needed work. No doubt, I had listening deficits, especially when I first began supervising in the classroom and the field. Most of the undergraduate and graduate students, however, appeared to find my supervision style acceptable. That is until one particular day when Sarah and I were meeting. I could not have imagined how a prosaic time with a jittery student would prove a pivotal moment in my evolution as a clinical supervisor.

Sarah listened to my feedback much in the same manner a dental patient might endure a particularly unpleasant root canal procedure. She looked miserable, moved anxiously in her chair, and gazed at me with watery eyes. I recall wondering if she was ill. Winding up my feedback, which although included corrective instruction, was scarcely scathing in nature. Sarah, however, seemed traumatized. Finally, I inquired if she understood what I was saying. "Yes," she articulated, on the verge of tears, "You think I am a terrible counselor." Flabbergasted, I sat back in my chair, having articulated nothing of the kind for her to draw such a conclusion. No doubt, she had improvement to make, but she was doing acceptable work. However, she clearly tended to skew to the negative extreme. I had taught and supervised overly self-critical students, but Sarah would have won the prize in self-talk flagellation! I attempted to help her understand that I viewed her doing acceptable work, that her ethics were good, and that she likely would become a good counselor. "You just don't understand," she replied, "If I'm not doing excellent work, it's terrible." With apologies to Albert Ellis, my best REBT intervention fell flat with Sarah. She was either doing exceptional work or she "sucked!" as she put it. Her bipolar thought process regarding developing counseling skills placed considerable pressure on her, resulting in anxious thoughts and behaviors. However, no intervention on my behalf had any noticeable effect in assisting Sarah to moderate her problematic thoughts.

As with all ethical, prudent counselors who do not know what to do, I sought out my supervisor, a professor in the program. Unfortunately, she admitted struggling with Sarah as well, leaving to consider holding her from moving to the second internship experience. My supervisor explained Sarah had struggled through practicum and was exhibiting the same anxious-type behaviors in internship, regardless of the individual attention she and I had put into her. Now, holding counseling students back from progressing in field placement is scarcely a novel practice. However, I was hoping that as Sarah's skill level was good, noted by her field site supervisor, we would be able to help her reduce her anxiety, proceed through field experience, and graduate on time. Part of me wondered if I was failing Sarah in some way. As a relatively new supervisor, I was struggling to bracket off my feelings from the supervisory relationship. "Remember, this is a professional, not personal, relationship," instructed our counselor supervision professor. I had to wonder if he was speaking chiefly to me when he uttered that sentence.

The faculty has recommended that Sarah seek counseling services to address her anxiety regarding receiving feedback. She volunteered that she had been working with a counselor at counseling services but that it had been of minimal help. Given that we had passed the midpoint of term, it was becoming increasingly unlikely that she would pass her internship experience. I considered the bracketing off comment from my professor. "What makes this student's success so important to you?" Kris (pseudonym), a fellow doctoral student, asked. Kris's was an excellent question and I lacked a satisfactory answer. Thus, I sought out the counsel of another doctoral student, Jane (pseudonym), who had many years supervising in the field. She listened patiently without interrupting until I finished. "Look, you are a counselor educator and supervisor-in-training. There is no a magic supervision wand. We do the best we can to help counselors-in-training and new counselors in the field develop. From my standpoint, you are overly involved in her success. Remember, it is not awful or terrible if she has to repeat the course and graduate a year later. In fact, that might be for the best."

I left the conversation with Kris, feeling simultaneously liberated and ashamed. I had lost much objectivity and become personally involved in Sarah's progression. Now, such is common, especially among new clinical supervisors. Jane's words were instructive, reminding me that I was falling into the trap of *awfulizing* a student's lack of progress. However, the most impactful part of Jane's counsel was her use of the term *magic wand*. I recalled reading that the solution-focused therapy cofounder (along with spouse Insoo Kim-Berg) published an innovative book titled *Words Were Originally Magic* (1994). de Shazer wrote of the use of words, metaphors, and creative questions in therapy. I loved the miracle question and considered that perhaps using some of de Shazer's language might be worth a try in supervision with Sarah.

A few days later, I met with Sarah for our weekly individual supervision session. She arrived edgy as usual and sat in the chair as if it were her execution. Putting my personal investment aside, I was direct, explaining that my efforts did not appear to be helping her move beyond her significant anxiety. I further elaborated that while her skill level was acceptable, her inability to take constructive feedback was a significant concern. She stayed rigid, with her eyes cast down, and I was expecting tears. After a long moment, she spoke, admitting she did not know what to do either, having worked on the matter for the better part of the term in counseling. I gently broached that perhaps repeating the course would help and that she reframe that not as failure but as building more confidence. She shook her head but said nothing. Suddenly, a thought popped into my head, courtesy of reading de Shazer's book (1994). "If you awoke tomorrow and this fear of criticism were no longer an issue, how might your graduate school experience be different?" For the first time since we had begun supervision, Sarah sat back in her chair with her head upright. She smiled and replied, "I expect I would feel confident, unafraid of criticism, and my anxiety would be low. I would be happier."

We sat in silence for a long moment, both of us soaking up her answer. "Sarah, that's where you need to get to, even if it takes repeating the course and delaying graduation. Managing feedback is that important for your development as a counselor." Naturally, she did not receive my words with enthusiasm, but for the first time, she did not sink into despair. She simply nodded.

Sarah's experience involved the proverbial good-news/bad-news scenario. The bad news was she failed the internship due to her inability to manage feedback. The good news was she continued working on her anxiety in therapy. The following year, after much personal growth (and work!), her anxiety was lessened and she passed the internship, eventually graduating with her master's degree. No, her experience was not ideal, but in counseling and supervision work, ideal exists in people's minds. Regarding de Shazer and Kim-Berg's book, words and phrases can be powerful, transforming, and yes, debilitating and self-defeating, as in Sarah's case. While words may not be *magic* per se, the story we tell ourselves certainly can cast a spell on our behavior and well-being. Ellis, Beck, de Shazer, and Kim-Berg all knew that well. Sarah also learned the power of words and reframing in defeat and eventual success. For my part, I learned my limitations as a supervisor; that failure may not be *failing*, of the necessity of bracketing off my personal involvement; and that clinical supervision is very demanding work.

 A robust set of instructor resources designed to supplement this text is located at http://connect.springerpub.com/content/book/978-0-8261-6607-4. Qualifying instructors may request access by emailing textbook@springerpub.com.

REFERENCES

American Counseling Association. (2014). *ACA code of ethics*. https://www.counseling.org/resources/aca-code-of-ethics.pdf

American Psychiatric Association. (2022). *Diagnostic and statistical manual of mental disorders* (5th ed.). American Psychiatric Association.

Beck, A. T., Wright, F. D., Newman, C. F., & Liese, B. S. (1993). *Cognitive therapy of substance abuse*. Guilford Press.

Benshoff, J. M. (1993). Peer supervision in counselor training. *Clinical Supervisor, 11*, 89–102. https://doi.org/10.1300/J001v11n02_08

Bernard, J. M., & Goodyear, R. K. (2014). *Fundamentals of clinical supervision* (5th ed.). Allyn & Bacon.

Borders, L. D. (1991). A systematic approach to peer group supervision. *Journal of Counseling & Development, 69*, 248–252. https://doi.org/10.1002/j.1556-6676.1991.tb01497.x

Borders, L. D., & Leddick, G. R. (1987). *Handbook of counseling supervision*. American Counseling Association.

Brown, L. S., & Brodsky, A. M. (1992). The future of feminist therapy. *Psychotherapy, 29*, 51–57. https://doi.org/10.1037/0033-3204.29.1.51

Bureau of Labor Statistics. (2019, April 12). *Community and social service occupations*. https://www.bls.gov/ooh/community-and-social-service/home.htm

Corey, G. (2017). *Theory and practice of counseling and psychotherapy* (10th ed.). Thomson Brooks/Cole.

de Shazer, S. (1994). *Words were originally magic*. W.W. Norton.

de Shazer, S. (1985). *The keys to solutions in brief therapy*. W. W. Norton.Dougherty, A. M. (2014). *Psychological consultation and collaboration in school and community settings* (6th ed.). Cengage Brooks/Cole.

Falender, C. A., & Shafranske, E. P. (2004). *Clinical supervision: A competency-based approach*. American Psychological Association.

Frawley-O'Dea, M. G., & Sarnat, J. E. (2001). *The supervisory relationship: A contemporary psychodynamic approach*. Guilford Press.

Granello, D. H., & Granello, P. F. (2007). *Suicide: An essential guide for helping professionals and educators*. Pearson/Allyn & Bacon.

Haynes, R., Corey, G., & Moulton, P. (2003). *Clinical supervision in the helping professions: A practical guide*. Brooks/Cole.

Holloway, E. (1995). *Clinical supervision: A systems approach*. Sage.

Kadushin, A. (1985). *Supervision in social work* (2nd ed.). Columbia University Press.

Kim Berg, I., & Szabo, P. (2005). *Brief coaching for lasting solutions*. W. W. Norton.

Lambers, E. (2000). Supervision in person-centered therapy: Facilitating congruence. In E. Mearns & B. Thorne (Eds.), *Person-centered therapy today: New frontiers in theory and practice* (pp. 196–211). Sage.

Nelson, K. W., Oliver, M., Reeve, J., & McNichols, C. (2016). Gatekeeping and supervisory intervention: Complex ethical processes. In T. P. Remley, Jr., & B. Herlihy (Eds.), *Ethical, legal, and professional issues in counseling* (6th ed.). Merrill.

Remley, T. P., Jr., & Herlihy, B. (2020). *Ethical, legal and professional issues in counseling* (6th ed.). Pearson.

Rogers, C. R. (1951). *Client-centered therapy*. Houghton Mifflin.

Rønnestad, M. H., & Skovholt, T. M. (1993). Supervision of beginning and advanced graduate students of counseling and psychotherapy. *Journal of Counseling and Development, 71*, 396–405. https://doi.org/10.1002/j.1556-6676.1993.tb02655.x

Rønnestad, M. H., & Skovholt, T. M. (2003). The journey of the counselor and therapist: Research findings and perspectives on professional development. *Journal of Career Development, 30*, 5–44. https://doi.org/10.1177/089484530303000102

Smith, K. L. (2009). *A brief summary of supervision models*. Department of Counselor Education, Marquette University.

Stoltenberg, C. D. (1981). Approaching supervision from a developmental perspective: The counselor complexity model. *Journal of Counseling Psychology, 28*, 59–65. https://doi.org/10.1037/0022-0167.28.1.59

Stoltenberg, C. D., & Delworth, U. (1987). *Supervising counselors and therapists*. Jossey-Bass.

Stoltenberg, C. D., McNeill, B., & Delworth, U. (1998). *IDM supervision: An integrated developmental model for supervising counselors and therapists*. Jossey-Bass.

Wheeler, A. M., & Bertram, B. (2019). *The counselor and the law: A guide to legal and ethical practice* (8th ed.). American Counseling Association.

Wilbur, M. P., Roberts-Wilbur, J., Morris, J. R., Betz, R. L., & Hart, G. M. (1991). Structured group supervision: Theory into practice. *Journal for Specialists in Group Work, 16*, 91–100. https://doi.org/10.1080/01933929108415593

CHAPTER 8

Counselor Self-Care: Managing Stressful Demands During Practicum/Internship

INTRODUCTION

Among the various mental health disciplines, the counseling profession is unique in that it was conceived from a strength-oriented wellness approach (Gladding, 2009; Myers et al., 2000; Witmer & Granello, 2005). Such an approach promotes a healthy and balanced life not only for clients but also for counselors themselves. The intention of this chapter is to assist you in creating and maintaining a healthier, more balanced life as you proceed through the demands of practicum and internship. As future counselors, it is essential that you maintain a healthy lifestyle during your professional years (and well beyond, of course) in order to best serve your clients, to say nothing of your own well-being. Healthier counselors will likely be better counselors and enjoy more productive years in the profession. Self-care is part of the *ACA Code of Ethics* (American Counseling Association [ACA], 2014) as a buffer against impairment (Standard C.2.g), as is monitoring our effectiveness (Standard C.2.d). From my own anecdotal observation over the years, having witnessed many counselors' poor and marginal self-care, it is likely that substandard self-care is the most violated standard in the *ACA Code of Ethics*. So, as counselors assisting others in developing healthier lifestyles, it is essential we practice what we teach. Be mindful that clients and others outside the profession watch professionals such as counselors to assess whether we are good role models. I can recall a saying from childhood: "Your behavior speaks so loudly I cannot hear what you are saying."

As graduate students in a counseling program, you will also meet counselors, psychologists, social workers, and other mental health professionals who *do not* practice what they teach regarding self-care. Unfortunately, there are far too many counselors and related mental health professionals who struggle with addictions, codependence, anger management issues, and dangerously inflated egos and whose behavior you will not want to emulate. You are not expected to have perfect dispositions, never get upset, or have a total lack of conflicts. You are expected to learn to manage the challenges of your practicum and internship (and, more significantly, the demands of your life!). As a young graduate student, I had much difficulty in managing the stress involved in working, meeting academic demands, and managing a challenging practicum and internship setting. I hope this chapter provides some insights into recognizing stressors that accompany counseling a struggling population of clients. Furthermore, it is worth mentioning that for some students, their supervisors and fellow graduate students may provide more stress than the population they counsel! Workplace conflicts and poor supervisors, not lack of professional knowledge, are the primary reason people leave their jobs (Bolles, 2015).

DEVELOPING AND MAINTAINING A HEALTHY AND MINDFUL LIFESTYLE

There are many different pathways, plans, theories, approaches, books, journal articles, and other resources devoted to living a healthy and fulfilling life. The fact that so many authors, counselors, theologians, personal trainers, coaches, and such attempt to provide counseling, coaching, and information to manage stress and teach mindfulness, a balanced diet, exercise routine, and so forth is indicative of just how stressful daily life has become in this postmodern age. As graduate students on a practicum or internship, you are no stranger to the challenges of external demands. The practicum or internship experience placed atop family responsibilities, a job, academic work, and financial demands can create great stress in your life (Remley & Herlihy, 2020). The irony of life as a graduate student in counseling is that while you are working to assist your clients to live healthier, more fulfilling lives, the demands of graduate school and practicum/internship, combined with work and home front demands, can potentially derail your own sense of harmony and balance. Somehow, you must learn to effectively address this contradiction and develop healthy coping mechanisms. While every professional likely preaches better than they practice, developing healthy routines is essential for good physical, mental, and emotional health.

In this chapter devoted to managing stress on the practicum and internship, I have created several exercises for the purposes of self-reflection. Self-reflection is a critical task not only for counselors but also for anyone in any occupation or walk of life and is a process of examining oneself during times of difficulty or success. The ability to step back from an experience, however successful or disappointing, can be a key skill for personal success as a counselor. I entitle this first section of the chapter "Developing and Maintaining a Healthy and Mindful Lifestyle." It is important for me to acknowledge that I have likely not created anything new in addressing the issues of healthy lifestyle or "wellness," as it is often referred to in the counseling field (Myers et al., 2000). Also included are assessments on quality of life, burnout, and mindfulness. Regardless of how we decide to refer to managing stress, living a balanced life, and mindful living, we usually address the same common themes of how to live a fulfilling, meaningful, and healthy life. I also offer a list of additional resources at the end of this chapter for counseling students to consider.

One of the first topics to address is that of stress. Stress is simply an everyday fact of life for everyone. Stress is an external change to which we are required to adjust our lives. Generally, we think of stress as being negative, such as death of a loved one, unemployment, divorce, and other such challenges. But positive changes in our lives can also bring about stress as well. For example, getting married or partnered, moving across the country for a new job, buying a home, traveling overseas, making your first conference presentation, and, of course, entering graduate school are all exciting experiences, but they can also bring about new stressors that complicate our lives. Stress is not all bad of course, as we need some degree of stress in order to meet the demands in life. One researcher has established that a manageable level of stress actually seems good for physical and emotional health (McGonigal, 2019). The key herein is *manageable* stress.

We can experience stress from three different sources: the environment, somatic ways, and our thoughts (Davis et al., 2008). Environmental stressors might be conflicts in the workplace, harsh weather, pollution, overcrowding, impoverishment, and living in unsafe areas. Environmental stressors are the ones we commonly see played up in the media, such as the 2009 catastrophic oil leak off the coast of Louisiana; slums in major cities; and the trauma brought about by natural disasters such as that of Hurricane Katrina in New Orleans, Hurricane Sandy in 2012, the tsunami in Sri Lanka, and the earthquake in Haiti a few years ago. Environmental concerns clearly illustrate the connection between harmony with the environment and a less stressful life or the exact opposite. Other common origins of environmental stress involve difficulties with your spouse/partner, roommates, and colleagues at the office, academic demands, and so forth.

The second source of stress is somatic, or how your body interprets stress. High-paced work settings, poor diet, sleep disturbances, and addiction all stress the body. Our fight–flight–freeze response, inherited from primitive ancestors who dealt daily with life-and-death issues, remains presently active. These genetic traits were passed on to the subsequent generations to assist people in their adaptation to environmental demands. Consequently, we all have, as part of our physiological system, the innate tendency to prepare the body to face the stressor or to flee from it. An adaptive example of *fighting* might be the coworker who requests to speak with the party with whom they are having conflicts. Unhealthy fighting is when the same coworker screams obscenities at the other party. Adaptive *fleeing* is when someone takes a temporary break from the stressful event (say, an argument with their spouse) and then returns and asks to speak with the party with whom they are having the conflict. Unhealthy fleeing is when the hurt person says, "They don't bother me," when in fact the other person's nasty comments or disrespectful actions do in fact bother them. Denial is a type of unhealthy fleeing. The critical factor here is healthy fighting and fleeing. The freeze response may occur when the fearful party cannot think of another response and stays put in the face of, say, verbal abuse.

The third source of stress derives from our thoughts. How you interpret or label stressful events will, in great measure, determine how well you resolve stress (Ellis, 2001). One of the ways our assumptions can add to stress is when we mistakenly interpret messages. For example, interpreting your supervisor's grimace to mean they are upset with you will likely create stress. But verifying this assumption might clear up the misunderstanding. In the event your boss is upset with you but has not voiced displeasure, addressing the issue is a pathway of moving through the stress. Remember that your supervisor's facial expressions, for example, may or may not have anything

THE COUNSELING PRACTICUM AND INTERNSHIP MANUAL

to do with you. So, do not overly interpret messages, but certainly investigate them. Posing the question "What's the evidence for my assumption?" is both good therapy and good personal practice to habituate.

Effects of Stress

Stress is difficult to define in a precise manner because it is a highly subjective phenomenon that differs for each of us. Experiences that are stressful for some are pleasurable for others. For example, some people actually look forward to swimming with sharks (namely, my spouse—but reef and nurse sharks, not great whites!), whereas others (myself) are terrified at the prospect. We respond to stress in different ways: some people eat less when stressed, while others overeat; some turn pale, whereas others blush and some use healthy coping skills such as exercise and talking with friends, and others self-medicate with alcohol and other drugs. Here are some common signs of stress:

- frequent headaches
- disturbed sleep
- trembling of limbs
- neck ache, back pain, or muscle spasms
- dizziness
- sweating
- frequent colds
- stomach pain
- constipation or diarrhea
- hyperventilation
- frequent urination
- decreased sexual desire
- excessive worry or anxiety
- increased anger or frustration
- decreased or increased appetite
- depression or mood swings
- difficulty concentrating
- feeling overwhelmed
- feelings of worthlessness
- suicidal thoughts
- social withdrawal
- excessive defensiveness
- reduced work efficiency
- constant fatigue

Tips for Managing Stress

Because stress is a reality in daily life, you cannot eliminate it. You can, however, manage the stress that comes into your life. The following are several tips for managing stress.

Tip #1: Recognize Stress and Deal With It Accordingly

- Learn to say "no." This may take some practice. Know your limits and stay within them. For many of us, this takes practice, as it can be difficult in reality.
- Limit time with people you find stressful. Conversely, maximize your time with people you find affirming and supportive.
- Take a break from stressors. If traffic causes you unmanageable stress, take a different route or use alternative forms of transportation if possible (e.g., carpool, mass transit, or cycling). If the evening news stresses you, take occasional breaks from reading the paper, online news, or watching TV.
- Refrain from overly discussing upsetting topics (there is a time and place for such discussions, of course, just not too often). If discussing politics, religion, sex, or even sports causes you too much conflict, perhaps refrain from discussing them, at least with select people. If people try and engage you in arguments over these topics, simply inform them, "I don't discuss these topics."
- Prioritize your schedule. Make "to do" lists in order of importance. If there are unnecessary tasks, move them to the bottom of the list or eliminate them.

Tip #2: Be Proactive

- Find constructive ways to express your feelings instead of suppressing them. Practice expressing your feelings with a trustworthy friend and solicit feedback from that friend. This way, you will be more prepared to do so on your practicum/internship.
- Learn to be assertive. There is more on assertiveness later in the chapter.
- Manage time effectively. Poor time management skills will lead to additional stress. Prioritize your workload and this will help reduce your stress level.
- Be willing to compromise in conflicts. Do not make all the compromises, but make the ones you can.

Tip #3: Reframing Problems

Reframing is a basic counseling technique. Here are some examples of how you might use reframing:

- Reframe personal conflicts as "growth opportunities" and seek to resolve them.

190 • THE COUNSELING PRACTICUM AND INTERNSHIP MANUAL

- Be realistic and let go of perfectionism. You are going to make mistakes on your practicum/internship. Make them and learn from them. Ask your supervisor for advice. Join the "recovering perfectionist" (RP) movement!

- Step back from a stress situation and ask, "How big an issue will this be in 6 months or a year?"

- On a regular basis, take time to reflect on the successes and blessings in your life. Challenging periods in life have a way of obliterating personal successes. So, take stock of your successes.

Tip #4: Accept What You Cannot Change and Change What You Can

- *You cannot control other people.* So, focus on how you react to their behavior and strategize more effective ways to deal with challenging people. A potentially more effective approach is focusing more on your goal as opposed to people's behavior. Remember that you cannot control another person's behavior, but you can manage your own.

- *Get support.* Discussing concerns with close friends can be very helpful. For one thing, you realize you are not alone; also, sharing a concern may provide an outside perspective you might find useful.

- *Forgiveness.* No one is perfect and, with rare exception, other people are not out to make our lives miserable. Learning to forgive perceived slights can free you from negative energy. If you have trouble with forgiving others, counseling may be a viable option for you. Forgiveness often is more for the forgiver than the perceived transgressor.

- *Self-reflection.* What do I need to change about myself? You might ask a few trusted friends to help you with this. Do they see areas you could improve on? How could you improve on these areas? What would self-improvement look like?

Assessing and Preventing Compassion Fatigue and Burnout

Compassionate fatigue and burnout are serious risks for counselors and counselors in training. Compassion fatigue (CF) represents frustration, feeling low energy, negative thoughts, workplace and home conflicts, and most symptoms of burnout (Stamm, 2005). Burnout is a longer term and more serious problem. Burnout may be described as a state of physical, mental, and emotional exhaustion brought about by long-term stress (Carter, 2013). Potential warning signs of burnout might include the following (Carter, 2013):

- *Chronic fatigue:* It is a sense of never feeling rested during the workday or weekends.

- *Insomnia:* Stress impacts sleep quality. You may experience difficulty falling or staying asleep.

- *Impaired concentration:* Feeling overwhelmed compromises your ability to remember basic details you typically recall with little difficulty.

- *Physical symptoms:* These may include shortness of breath, chest pain, gastrointestinal problems, dizziness, and headache. Naturally, all these should be assessed by a medical professional.

- *Increased illness:* Because your immune system is compromised, you may become more susceptible to colds and the flu.
- *Loss of appetite:* Food may no longer be appealing.
- *Anxiety:* Your anxiety may increase as you move from CF to burnout. Panic attacks are a possibility.
- *Depression:* You likely will feel sad initially, increasing in severity to ongoing depression. If sadness persists longer than a few days, seek professional help.
- *Anger:* As stress increases, momentary irritability may turn into angry outbursts.

The Professional Quality-of-Life Scale

The Professional Quality-of-Life Scale (ProQOL; Stamm, 2005) is the current version of the former CF Test (Figley, 1995). Stamm (2005) modified the ProQOL to strengthen its psychometric properties and due to a preference for the more positive name of professional quality of life. Essentially, he wanted the instrument to have more of a healthy assessment and instructional focus and utility. Stamm's redevelopment research was based on more than 1,000 participants and statistically modified to include stronger subscale items (Stamm, 2005). The ProQOL now consists of three subscales: Compassion Satisfaction, Burnout, and Secondary Traumatic Stress (STS). The Compassion Satisfaction scale refers to the enjoyment we derive from providing counseling work (and related work) and a high score is a hopeful sign. The Burnout scale assesses CF and is associated with feelings of hopelessness, dreading work, and a lack of empathy for people we serve. The STS scale evaluates whether counseling survivors of trauma is causing severe stress and a trauma-like response in the counselor providing services. Potential symptoms may include fear, difficulty sleeping, dread of certain clients, and increased anxiety (Stamm, 2009–2012). The ProQOL offers counseling professionals a means of assessing quality of life, as well as potential risk for burnout. Burnout risk is assessed as low, average, or high. The same scoring differentiation and cutoff scores are also used for the Compassion Satisfaction and STS scales. My recommendation is for counseling students and counseling professionals to take the ProQOL periodically to assess stress and coping levels. The ProQOL is reprinted with the author's permission in Exhibit 8.1.

A Healthy Assets Ledger

To build on your wellness practice, consider the following reflective questions. These questions are for you to use for purposes of self-exploration regarding personal, professional, and spiritual growth. Your answers are best utilized as a means of assessing emotional–spiritual–occupational–social balance in your life.

Reflective Questions to Consider

- How well developed and balanced are the personal, occupational, social, and spiritual (if appropriate) dimensions of your life?

- Who do you say you are? Also, how does who you say you are compare to how others appear to view you? Or, how great is the distance between who you really are and who you want to be? Be realistic, but be honest about this "divide."
- How does this self-view correlate with how significant people in your life view you? (You may wish to discuss this with relevant people in your life.)
- What is your most fulfilling time of the week? Why? If you feel a lack of fulfillment during your week, how could you create more meaning in your life?
- How would you describe this stage of your life?
- What issues and/or challenges are creating difficulty for you?
- How could you begin to lessen or better manage these challenges?
- What are your key strengths?
- What skills, hobbies, interests, and talents do you possess?
- What areas of your life would you like to explore? (*Note:* This could apply to personal relationships, travel, continuing education, career, or anything you deem important.)
- In what ways are you dependent on others?
- In what ways are you self-reliant?
- What conflicts are inhibiting your personal growth and professional effectiveness?
- How could you take steps to resolve these conflicts?

Exhibit 8.1 Professional Quality-of-Life Scale

Professional Quality-of-Life Scale (ProQOL)
Compassion Satisfaction and Fatigue
(ProQOL) Version 5 (2009)

When you [help] people you have direct contact with their lives. As you may have found, your compassion for those you [help] can affect you in positive and negative ways. Below are some questions about your experiences, both positive and negative, as a [helper]. Consider each of the following questions about you and your current work situation. Select the number that honestly reflects how frequently you experienced these things in the <u>last 30 days.</u>

1 = Never	2 = Rarely	3 = Sometimes	4 = Often	5 = Very Often

1. I am happy.
2. I am preoccupied with more than one person I [help].
3. I get satisfaction from being able to [help] people.
4. I feel connected to others.
5. I jump or am startled by unexpected sounds.
6. I feel invigorated after working with those I [help].
7. I find it difficult to separate my personal life from my life as a [helper].

(continued)

Exhibit 8.1 Professional Quality-of-Life Scale (*continued*)

8. I am not as productive at work because I am losing sleep over traumatic experiences of a person I *[help]*.
9. I think that I might have been affected by the traumatic stress of those I *[help]*.
10. I feel trapped by my job as a *[helper]*.
11. Because of my *[helping]*, I have felt "on edge" about various things.
12. I like my work as a *[helper]*.
13. I feel depressed because of the traumatic experiences of the people I *[help]*.
14. I feel as though I am experiencing the trauma of someone I have *[helped]*.
15. I have beliefs that sustain me.
16. I am pleased with how I am able to keep up with *[helping]* techniques and protocols.
17. I am the person I always wanted to be.
18. My work makes me feel satisfied.
19. I feel worn out because of my work as a *[helper]*.
20. I have happy thoughts and feelings about those I *[help]* and how I could help them.
21. I feel overwhelmed because my case *[work]* load seems endless.
22. I believe I can make a difference through my work.
23. I avoid certain activities or situations because they remind me of frightening experiences of the people I *[help]*.
24. I am proud of what I can do to *[help]*.
25. As a result of my *[helping]*, I have intrusive, frightening thoughts.
26. I feel "bogged down" by the system.
27. I have thoughts that I am a "success" as a *[helper]*.
28. I can't recall important parts of my work with trauma victims.
29. I am a very caring person.
30. I am happy that I chose to do this work.

What is my score and what does it mean?
In this section, you will score your test and then you can compare your score to the interpretation below.

Scoring
Be certain you responded to all items.
Go to items 1, 4, 15, 17, and 29 and reverse your score. For example, if you scored the item 1, write a 5 beside it. We ask you to reverse these scores because we have learned that the test works better if you reverse these scores.

You Wrote	Change to
1	5
2	4
3	3
4	2
5	1

To find your score on **Compassion Satisfaction**, add your scores on questions 3, 6, 12, 16, 18, 20, 22, 24, 27, and 30.

(continued)

Exhibit 8.1 Professional Quality-of-Life Scale (*continued*)

The Sum of My Compassion Satisfaction Question	So My Score Equals	My Level of Compassion
22 or less	43 or less	Low
Between 23 and 41	Around 50	Average
42 or more	57 or more	High

To find your score on **Burnout**, add your scores on questions 1, 4, 8, 10, 15, 17, 19, 21, 26, and 29. Find your score in the table below.

The Sum of My Burnout Questions	So My Score Equals	My Level of Compassion
22 or less	43 or less	Low
Between 23 and 41	Around 50	Average
42 or more	57 or more	High

To find your score on **Secondary Traumatic Stress**, add your scores on questions 2, 5, 7, 9, 11, 13, 14, 23, 25, and 28. Find your score in the table below.

The Sum of My Secondary Traumatic Stress Questions	So My Score Equals	My Level of Compassion
22 or less	43 or less	Low
Between 23 and 41	Around 50	Average
42 or more	57 or more	High

Your scores on the ProQOL: Professional Quality of Life Screening

Based on your responses, your personal scores are below. If you have any concerns, you should discuss them with a physical or mental healthcare professional.

Compassion Satisfaction _____

Compassion satisfaction is about the pleasure you derive from being able to do your work well. For example, you may feel like it is a pleasure to help others through your work. You may feel positively about your colleagues or your ability to contribute to the work setting or even the greater good of society. Higher scores on this scale represent a greater satisfaction related to your ability to be an effective caregiver in your job.

The average score is 50 (SD 10; alpha scale reliability 0.88). About 25% of people score higher than 57 and about 25% of people score below 43. If you are in the higher range, you probably derive a good deal of professional satisfaction from your position. If your scores are below 40, you may either find problems with

(continued)

Exhibit 8.1 Professional Quality-of-Life Scale (*continued*)

your job or there may be some other reason, for example, you might derive your satisfaction from activities other than your job.

Burnout _____

Most people have an intuitive idea of what burnout is. From the research perspective, burnout is one of the elements of compassion fatigue. It is associated with feelings of hopelessness and difficulties in dealing with work or in doing your job effectively. These negative feelings usually have a gradual onset. They can reflect the feeling that your efforts make no difference, or they can be associated with a very high workload or a nonsupportive work environment. Higher scores on this scale mean that you are at higher risk for burnout.

The average score on the burnout scale is 50 (SD 10; alpha scale reliability 0.75). About 25% of people score above 57 and about 25% of people score below 43. If your score is below 18, this probably reflects positive feelings about your ability to be effective in your work. If you score above 57, you may wish to think about what at work makes you feel like you are not effective in your position. Your score may reflect your mood; perhaps you were having a "bad day" or are in need of some time off. If the high score persists or if it is reflective of other worries, it may be a cause of concern.

Secondary Traumatic Stress _____

The second component of Compassion Fatigue (CF) is secondary traumatic stress (STS). It is about your work-related, secondary exposure to extremely or traumatically stressful events. Developing problems due to exposure to others' trauma is somewhat rare but does happen to many people who care for those who have experienced extremely or traumatically stressful events. For example, you may repeatedly hear stories about the traumatic things that happen to other people, commonly called vicarious traumatization. You may see or provide treatment to people who have experienced horrific events. If your work puts you directly in the path of danger, due to your work as a soldier or civilian working in military medicine personnel, this is not secondary exposure; your exposure is primary. However, if you are exposed to others' traumatic events as a result of your work, such as providing care to casualties or for those in a military medical rehabilitation facility, this is secondary exposure. The symptoms of STS are usually rapid in onset and associated with a particular event. They may include being afraid, having difficulty sleeping, having images of the upsetting event pop into your mind, or avoiding things that remind you of the event.

The average score on the burnout scale is 50 (SD 10; alpha scale reliability 0.81). About 25% of people score above 57 and about 25% of people score below 43. If your score is above 57, you may want to take some time to think about what at work may be frightening to you or if there is some other reason for the elevated score. While higher scores do not mean that you do have a problem, they are an indication that you may want to examine how you feel about your work and your work environment. You may wish to discuss this with your supervisor, a colleague, or a healthcare professional.

Source: From Stamm, B. H. (2012). *Professional quality of life: Compassion satisfaction and fatigue version 5 (ProQOL).* https://www.proqol.org/uploads/ProQOL_5_English_Self-Score_3-2012.pdf

Regarding Major Successes and Failures in Your Life

- When you consider your major successes, what has worked well and why? What did your major successes teach you?

- Regarding your failures, what seemed to go wrong and why? What did your failures teach you? Remember, self-compassion practice is asking growth-oriented questions as what failure and disappointment has taught you.

- What could you do differently next time either to build on success or to ensure you did not fail in the next opportunity? This is a critical question to consider. Sometimes the answer is "Nothing." At other times, the answer may be very enlightening and helpful for the future.

Exhibit 8.2 represents a self-monitoring system using scaling questions. This assessment technique provides a sense of where you are in the respective domains. The self-rating questions provide a constructive method of assessing current self-care. This approach is not intended as a substitute to replace good personal, professional, and spiritual growth but to serve and support wellness in these areas.

Exhibit 8.2 Dimensions of a Healthy Lifestyle: Self-Monitoring System

Spirituality/Religious Life and/or Life Meaning and Purpose
My spiritual/religious practice provides a sense of purpose and helps me address major life challenges.
(*Note:* An alternate phrasing for nonspiritual/nonreligious people might be: "My sense of life meaning/purpose provides fulfillment and helps me address the challenges in my life.")

$$1 \quad 2 \quad 3 \quad 4 \quad 5 \quad 6 \quad 7 \quad 8 \quad 9 \quad 10$$

(1 = *No help at all*; 10 = *Strongly helps*)
If your score was less than 5, how could you improve your situation?

Mindfulness in Life
I live in the present moment and fully accept myself nonjudgmentally. I use meditation (or prayer) and daily gratitudes and personal affirmations.

$$1 \quad 2 \quad 3 \quad 4 \quad 5 \quad 6 \quad 7 \quad 8 \quad 9 \quad 10$$

(1 = *No mindfulness practice*: 10 = *A strong mindfulness practice*)
If your score was low, how might you incorporate regular mindful practices into your life?

(continued)

Exhibit 8.2 Dimensions of a Healthy Lifestyle: Self-Monitoring System (*continued*)

Personal Vision
"I have a clear vision in my personal, spiritual, and professional life."

1 2 3 4 5 6 7 8 9 10

(1 = *No vision*; 10 = *I have a clear vision*)
If you do not have a clear personal, spiritual, or professional vision, how could you develop one? Visioning is a key component to success in all these areas.

Self-Worth
"I feel worthwhile as a human being and have a strong sense of self-acceptance. Although I am not perfect, I feel generally good about myself."

1 2 3 4 5 6 7 8 9 10

(1 = *I am worthless*; 10 = *My self-worth is very strong*)
If you are experiencing low self-esteem, how could you begin to feel better about yourself? What actions could you take to begin to feel more self-confident?

Goal Setting
"I feel self-confident about setting and meeting goals and demands in my life."

1 2 3 4 5 6 7 8 9 10

(1 = *I lack confidence in my ability to meet demands and the goals I set*; 10 = *I feel very confident in setting, planning, and meeting goals and demands*)
If you lack clear goals in your life, how could you begin to create some clear goals?

Rational Thinking
"I believe I perceive my life and life situations in a rational manner. I seldom engage in overly negative thinking."

1 2 3 4 5 6 7 8 9 10

(1 = *I frequently engage in irrational thinking*; 10 = *I am very rational in my beliefs*)
If you have rated yourself as frequently engaging in irrational beliefs (e.g., "I am a loser," "I am worthless," or "No one could ever love me"), how could you begin to think in a more rational manner? (Or, if you are unsure as to whether your beliefs are rational, you might consider asking someone you trust for feedback.)

Emotional Understanding and Regulation
"I am in touch with my emotions and am able to express the full range of emotions appropriate to the situation. I also am not governed by my emotions."

1 2 3 4 5 6 7 8 9 10

(*continued*)

198 • THE COUNSELING PRACTICUM AND INTERNSHIP MANUAL

Exhibit 8.2 Dimensions of a Healthy Lifestyle: Self-Monitoring System (*continued*)

(1 = *I am not able to regulate my emotions and often express emotions inappropriate to the situation;* 10 = *I am able to regulate my emotions and experience emotions appropriate to the situation*)

If you find you are not experiencing an appropriate range of emotions or you find you are too often ruled by your emotions, how could you begin to change this? Remember, you will have "negative" emotions, so the task is to regulate them appropriately.

Resilience

"I am a resilient person, and I am able to analyze, synthesize, and make a plan to deal with challenges and projects that come my way."

1   2   3   4   5   6   7   8   9   10

(1 = *I do not feel resilient;* 10 = *I am very confident in my resiliency*)

If you do not feel resilient (or you are not as resilient as you would like) or do not have the ability to resolve difficulties in your life, what could you do to begin to develop more resilience? (*Note:* If you feel stuck on strategizing with this component, perhaps begin by making a list of ways you feel resilient. Or ask someone who knows you well to list ways they see you as being resilient.)

Sense of Humor

"I possess a healthy, appropriate sense of humor that helps me deal with the stresses of life."

1   2   3   4   5   6   7   8   9   10

(1 = *I have no sense of humor;* 10 = *I have a healthy sense of humor*)

If you do not feel your sense of humor is either strongly developed, appropriate, or provides an effective release of stress, what could you change to improve the situation?

Fitness or Recreation

"I have a regular weekly fitness/recreational routine that helps me stay physically and emotionally fit."

1   2   3   4   5   6   7   8   9   10

(1 = *I have no activity routine;* 10 = *I have an active physical/recreational routine*)

If you do not have a regular weekly fitness routine, what could you do to change this? (Remember, you do not need to become a marathoner, competitive cyclist, swimmer, or dancer. It is simply about developing a regular routine of 20 minutes a day, at least 3 days a week.)

(continued)

Exhibit 8.2 Dimensions of a Healthy Lifestyle: Self-Monitoring System (*continued*)

Healthy Diet
"I regularly eat a balanced diet, including healthy vegetables and fruits."
(*Note:* Healthy is not meant to imply you *never* eat unhealthy foods because that is not realistic. In fact, sometimes it is good for the psyche to eat ice cream, cookies, and so forth. Just do not do it too often. Rather, it is about eating unhealthy food in moderation.)

1   2   3   4   5   6   7   8   9   10

(1 = *My diet is unbalanced and unhealthy*; 10 = *My diet is balanced and healthy*)
If your diet is unhealthy (e.g., eating high-fat food, "junk" food, and fast food too often), how could you begin to eat a healthier diet? (For in-depth help, you may wish to consult a dietician.)

Healthy, Mindful Living
"I maintain a healthy, mindful lifestyle by not abusing alcohol or other drugs, by wearing a seat belt, by having regular medical exams, and by refraining from high-risk activities (e.g., casual sex, binge drinking, binge eating, and restricting food)."

1   2   3   4   5   6   7   8   9   10

(1 = *I do not live a healthy, mindful life*; 10 = *I maintain a healthy, mindful lifestyle*)
If you find you are not living a healthy, mindful life, what steps could you take to change this?

Managing Stress and Anxiety
"Through my diet, workout routine, mindfulness practice, and social connections, I have the ability to manage stress and anxiety. When I find I am unable to manage the stress and anxiety in my life, I check in with close friends and family or, if the need arises, I see a counselor."

1   2   3   4   5   6   7   8   9   10

(1 = *I am regularly unable to manage the stress and anxiety in my life*; 10 = *I am able to manage the stress and anxiety in my life*)
If you find you regularly have difficulty managing the stress and anxiety in your life, how could you begin to manage that stress and anxiety better?

Sense of Self
"I feel that my self-identity is strong and well developed."

1   2   3   4   5   6   7   8   9   10

(1 = *My sense of self is incongruent with who I am because I try too hard to be who others want me to be*; 10 = *My sense of self is very congruent with who I am*)

(*continued*)

200 • THE COUNSELING PRACTICUM AND INTERNSHIP MANUAL

Exhibit 8.2 Dimensions of a Healthy Lifestyle: Self-Monitoring System (*continued*)

Some people struggle with their own identity for various reasons, such as enmeshment with family, codependence with a loved one, low self-esteem, and so forth. If you find you are struggling with an inability to develop your own identity, what are some options for exploration (options that would reduce your struggle or help you resolve your personal identity struggles)?

Connection to Family or Culture
"I feel a strong connection to my family or culture."

1   2   3   4   5   6   7   8   9   10

(1 = *I feel no connection to my family or culture*; 10 = *I feel a strong and healthy connection to my family and culture*)
In the event you feel no connection to your family or culture, what would you say accounts for this? Also, how could you begin to make stronger connections to your family and culture?

Career/Vocational Development
"I feel a sense of satisfaction in the career I am pursuing" (e.g., mental health counselor, school counselor, or rehabilitation counselor).

1   2   3   4   5   6   7   8   9   10

(1 = *No satisfaction*; 10 = *Maximum satisfaction*)
If your chosen career does not provide personal challenge and satisfaction for you, what steps could you take to create more fulfillment and satisfaction? (Or, if you are unemployed, how could your job search become more fulfilling? Or how could this period of unemployment be more productive?)

Hobbies
"My hobbies help me relax and provide a sense of enjoyment."

1   2   3   4   5   6   7   8   9   10

(1 = *I have no hobbies or they provide no sense of enjoyment or relaxation*; 10 = *My hobbies are a pure joy*)
If you lack hobbies or outside interests from work, how could you create some fulfilling pursuits?

Social Life
"I have healthy, fulfilling relationships that provide me a sense of emotional connection and help make life more rewarding."

1   2   3   4   5   6   7   8   9   10

(continued)

Exhibit 8.2 Dimensions of a Healthy Lifestyle: Self-Monitoring System (*continued*)

(1 = *I have no significant relationships, they are shallow, or they provide little in the way of emotional connection*; 10 = *I have healthy and fulfilling relationships and they are an important part of my life*)
If you lack significant personal connections or your relationships do not provide you a sense of emotional connection, how could you begin to address this? (Or how could you begin to create fulfilling relationships?)

Intimacy
"Intimacy, or love, is a central part of my life, and my relationship with my spouse/partner provides the grounding, intimacy, and close connection I need." (*Note:* Intimacy could involve sexual intimacy or even a close, nonsexual relationship.)

1   2   3   4   5   6   7   8   9   10

(1 = *Intimacy is largely absent from my life*; 10 = *Intimacy is a large part of my life and provides me with great satisfaction*)
If intimacy seems absent from your life or seems unhealthy or unfulfilling, what do you need to do to change this situation?

Questions Regarding Self-Care
Regarding these dimensions, which appear to be the strongest? Which appear to be the weakest? How could you improve your strengths and build upon your weak areas? What action could you take to improve your self-care? What supports do you need to create a healthier lifestyle? If you are unsure how to create a healthy self-care lifestyle, who could you ask for help (e.g., your doctor, counselor, a nutritionist, your spiritual leader, family member, friend)?

Additional Considerations for Managing Stress

Setting Limits With Others

- Do you have difficulty saying "no" to other people? If you do, how could you begin to say "no" when you know doing so is necessary? What makes setting limits difficult for you? Is it guilt? Fear? Something else? How could you begin to practice setting limits with others? For example, saying "no" when you mean no?

- What healthy risks can you undertake to enhance your personal and professional growth?

- When you think about the type of people who cause you stress, what is it that they do that is stressful for you? Okay, now that you have identified what is stressful about their behavior, how could you manage your stress level around them?

Developing Connections

- Would you want to make friends with someone like yourself? Why or why not? If "no," what might you wish to change?
- If you feel isolated, how could you begin to develop meaningful relationships?
- If you are in a marriage or partnership and you are not feeling fulfilled, how could you begin to create a greater sense of fulfillment in that relationship?
- If you are not in a relationship and would like to be, how could you begin to create such a relationship? (Or, what qualities would you like in a partner?)
- Recall a difficult period in your life. How did you navigate your way through this time?
- How do you go about creating meaning in your life?
- Make a list of at least five skills you already possess that you can use to keep yourself well and fit.

Work and Career

- Are you pursuing the career you truly belong in? Why or why not?
- Why did you choose to pursue counseling as a career? How happy are you thus far?
- What is your dream job or dream career? (Describe in some detail: title, location, etc.)
- How can you begin to create your dream job? What steps are necessary?
- Setting goals is important for success. What are your major goals for the next 5 years?
- In what ways have you changed since entering your graduate counseling program?

Mentoring

- Who are some people who have inspired you? *Note:* They need not necessarily be people you have met. For example, many have been inspired by the likes of Martin Luther King, Jr.; Mahatma Gandhi; Mother Teresa; Dalai Lama; Stephen Hawking; and so forth, even though they have never met these people.
- Name five people and state/record how they have inspired you.
- Who are some people who share your hobbies and interests?
- Cite some organizations you are actively involved in.
- List some people who share your spiritual beliefs (or who share your personal values).

The Importance of Meaning and Purpose in Life

Meaning in life is a concept of central importance to the human condition and has been studied across numerous disciplines (Schulenberg et al., 2011; Wong, 2012a, 2012b). Meaning in life has been a focal point of interest to theologians and philosophers for centuries, and more recently, the issue has become influential in the rapidly growing positive psychology movement (Schulenberg et al., 2011; Seligman, 2002; Sharma et al., 2017; Wong, 2012a). Meaning in life is positively correlated with happiness, well-being, resilience, coping skills, hope, self-esteem, and empowerment and inversely correlated with depression, post traumatic stress disorder (PTSD), addiction, anxiety, and suicidality (Duffy & Boque-Bogden, 2010; Seligman, 2002; Wong, 2012a). People who perceive their lives as having meaning are more likely to be happier, healthier, less depressed, and less anxious. "The presence of meaning is an excellent marker of the good life" (Peterson & Park, 2012, p. 292).

While life meaning seems an important issue, the term is amorphous and often misunderstood (Heintzelman & King, 2014). A perusal of the bestseller list, not to mention numerous workshops offered, suggests that the public is intensely interested in developing increased life meaning. While targeted as a necessity to emotional health, life meaning may be increasingly rare in a secularized society (Frankl, 1997; Wong, 2012a, 2012b). Thus, there is a dynamic tension between the hypothesis regarding the importance of meaning in life and research, suggesting many people lack appropriate life meaning. Given the dynamic nature of a fast-paced, Western world and the well-documented angst regarding 21st-century college and graduate students' mental health needs (Much & Swanson, 2010), meaning and purpose in life likely are critical necessities for emotional balance and well-being.

The Meaning in Life Questionnaire (MLQ) is a 10-item test assessing two dimensions of meaning in life on a 7-point scale from *absolutely true* to *absolutely untrue* (Steger et al., 2006). The "Presence of Meaning" subscale measures how the level of meaning in respondents' lives and the "Search for Meaning" subscale assesses respondents' level of motivation to find or deepen life meaning. The MLQ has demonstrated validity and reliability in research on clinical and nonclinical populations (Schulenberg et al., 2011).

CONFLICT MANAGEMENT SKILLS

A big part of health and wellness involves managing conflict (Weinhold & Weinhold, 2009). As a future counselor, you will have many opportunities to help clients and fellow students identify, address, and manage conflict. Conflict between people is actually a very natural occurrence; yet, many people find conflict to be traumatic and stressful. Conflict need not necessarily be traumatic, however, and if well managed and addressed, it may provide the foundation for personal growth. The critical factor regarding conflict is that we acknowledge it and then strategize on how to resolve it.

The first step in managing conflict is to admit that it exists. Because counseling can be demanding and stressful work, it is likely that you will have ample opportunities to work on developing competence in dealing with conflict. I have listed common assumptions about conflict and then a reframed response to these assumptions.

Assumption 1: "All conflict is bad and should be avoided."

Reframed response: Conflict is not necessarily "bad." Acknowledging and addressing conflict can be liberating and improve self-confidence.

Assumption 2: "Conflict is awful and terrible."

Reframed response: Conflict is neither "awful" nor "terrible," although refusing to admit or address it can result in poor health. The trick is learning to manage conflict. This requires revising your self-talk, monitoring your blood pressure, and good emotional regulation (i.e., do not speak out of anger).

Assumption 3: "I simply can't deal with conflict."

Reframed response: Dealing with conflict is sometimes unpleasant for me. However, the more experienced I become at addressing conflicts, the more confident and effective I become at resolving them.

Assumption 4: "When I have conflicts they always 'blow up' into something unmanageable, so it's just better to ignore them."

Reframed response: Sometimes my attempts at conflict resolution go awry and tempers can escalate. However, in many, if not most cases, I am able to navigate conflict without causing further injury. Remember: good emotional regulation, revised self-talk, and monitoring blood pressure.

Now, a critical factor beyond admitting the existence of conflicts is how we go about resolving them. Fortunately, people can improve their conflict resolution skills with practice. As a counselor operating from a cognitive framework, I believe conflict resolution is grounded in childhood experiences of observing and participating in family conflicts. Our parents or guardians consciously or unconsciously modeled styles of conflict resolution, which we internalized and then repeated in our conflicts with siblings and peers. Some families are more functional at addressing conflicts; children raised in more functional homes will have an early advantage at conflict resolution. Children raised in less functional, dysfunctional, abusive, or neglectful homes will likely have more struggles in resolving conflicts, as past conflicts may have been denied or blown up into destructive aggression. Cultural background naturally also relates to how people manage stress and conflict (Lee, 2019). Thus, when navigating conflict, be aware that people navigate conflict very differently.

Conflict Resolution Styles

- *The Denier:* "Conflict? What conflict?" "Everything's just perfect."
- *The Minimizer:* "It's not anything to worry about." "No big deal."
- *The Overly Responsible Type:* "It's all my fault."
- *The Avoider:* "It's better to avoid conflict regardless of the cost."
- *The Aggressor:* "You have to get in people's faces! That's how you resolve conflicts."
- *The Mindful Type:* "Okay, there is a conflict. What steps can I take to resolve it?"

Examine the types and think about which type best fits how you generally behave when faced with conflicts. No one will always choose only one type, but decide which of the conflict resolution styles most frequently describes you. Now, think about which of these styles you would prefer.

The following questions are aimed to focus your awareness on your current conflict resolution style and how you would like to modify it:

- Which of the mentioned conflict resolution style types would usually describe the manner in which I deal with conflicts?
- What do I fear about conflicts? (Or, what is the worst thing that could happen regarding conflicts?)
- What types of conflict situations do I find most challenging?
- Who were my role models in learning how to address conflicts?
- What are my strengths in resolving conflicts?
- How effective is my style of conflict resolution?
- In what situations does my approach to resolving conflicts work?
- In what situations does my approach to resolving conflicts seem ineffective?
- What would I want to change about my style of conflict resolution?
- How could I begin to change my approach to conflict resolution?
- What is one small change I can make that will help me address conflicts more effectively?
- My biggest challenge in improving my conflict resolution skills is . . . .
- Think of someone who seems effective in resolving conflicts. What conflict resolution skills do they possess?
- What, in my professional training and background, assists me in resolving conflicts?
- What types of conflict resolution work do I see myself performing in the future?
- What types of conflict resolution roles would be inconsistent with my future practice as a counselor?
- How would being skilled in conflict resolution assist me in becoming an effective counselor?

Box 8.1 presents conflict scenarios designed to help you think about your own approach to conflict management.

THE COUNSELING STUDENT AS CLIENT

Counseling work can certainly be very stressful, as clients bring in difficulties of their own and there may be job conflicts with coworkers. As a graduate student in a counseling program, you have the added complication of coursework, along with seeing clients, balancing a home life, and numerous additional demands. Many counseling programs now mandate a few counseling sessions for their students. Counselors who have had the experience of being clients themselves have a more complete understanding of the therapeutic process (Norcross et al., 1988). Putting yourself in the vulnerable position as a client also provides you the opportunity of experiencing the "other side" of the therapeutic experience and likely can help you develop more empathy for clients and their struggles.

Box 8.1 Conflict Resolution Practice for the Counseling Practicum/Internship

CONFLICT SCENARIO ONE

You have just commenced your practicum. You get along very well with most of the staff and fellow graduate practicum students. However, after a few weeks, you discover that another practicum student seems to be constantly belittling you (e.g., "You haven't learned much about counseling, have you?" and "Your approach to counseling is all wrong."). You decide not to address the issue, hoping it will just resolve itself. Then, one of the other graduate students informs you the student in question is bad-mouthing you to the others.

How might you resolve this apparent conflict? What actions would be most constructive? What would healthy resolution look like? Now, if possible, role-play the scenario out with a classmate or friend. The more you practice resolving conflicts, the more skilled you will become at resolving them. You cannot force the other person to act professionally and respectfully, but you can behave both ways.

CONFLICT SCENARIO TWO

You have completed practicum and are beginning internship at your placement. Your new supervisor seems very harsh with his criticism and is somewhat sarcastic during supervision sessions, making comments such as "This is subpar work!" and "I can't believe your last supervisor saw your work as worthy of passing practicum." Your supervisor also discloses that he really did not want to supervise you but was forced to do so by the director of clinical services. Intimidated and discouraged, you soon discover yourself avoiding him whenever you can; as weekly supervision arrives, your stomach is upset and you feel very anxious. You realize this is an unhealthy situation and you would like to switch supervisors, but you worry the answer will be "no" and that your supervisor may hold your actions against you. What steps might you make to deal with this conflict? Who might be supports for you in this challenging situation?

Suggestion: List your conflict resolution strengths on a sheet of paper or on an electronic device. Then, rank order these strengths. A further suggestion is soliciting a well-known, trusted person to see if they agree with your list. What areas might you need to improve upon? Specifically, how might you improve you conflict resolution strengths. You might also practice mock conflict resolution with a friend or classmate. Then, discuss how well the mock session went, with a focus on improvement. Then, continue practicing after considering the feedback from a mock conflict session.

I can state from experience that many counselors and other mental health professionals sometimes are reluctant to seek counseling services for themselves, out of their fear or arrogance or simply being unaware of the extent of their personal issues. Self-care is a critical component of effective function for counselors and an issue addressed in the *ACA Code of Ethics* (2014, Standard C.2.g). As a future professional counselor, graduate school is the optimal time to begin addressing your own mental health to ensure whatever personal concerns you have do not impact your counseling work. This is not to say you must be perfect to be a counselor; every counselor, no matter how successful and well adjusted, has some personal "baggage." Most importantly, understand your issues and work to improve on them. After all, such is the nature of counseling work.

If you decide that entering personal counseling would be a good idea, you should be aware that many counselors, psychologists, social workers, and other mental health professionals have already reached similar conclusions. Mahoney (1997) reported that 87% of mental health professionals surveyed admitted they had entered personal counseling at some point in their careers. Personal counseling was rated by mental health professionals as second to practical experience as the most important influence in their professional lives. A study of 500 counselors and psychologists revealed that 93% rated the experience from mildly positive to very positive (Baird et al., 1992). Other notable counseling professionals such as Sam Gladding (2009) have posited personal counseling as a critical growth experience for counselor development. In fact, in the event that it has been a lengthy period of time since a counselor was a client, it is likely a good idea to seek counseling services as a mental health "checkup" and to better empathize with the clients being served.

Pope and Tabachnick (1994) conducted a study of more than 800 psychologists, in which 84% admitted to having been in personal therapy. The most often cited reasons for mental health professionals to seek counseling were (in descending order) depression; divorce or relationship difficulty; struggles with self-esteem; anxiety or career, work, or study concerns; family of origin issues; loss; and stress (Pope & Tabachnick, 1994). Among those surveyed, 85% described the therapeutic experience as very or exceptionally helpful. What these and other studies suggest is that personal counseling can be very important for our own emotional health and personal growth. Furthermore, personal counseling helps counselors and other therapists remain healthy, and in doing so, they likely are more effective at providing counseling. Furthermore, many counseling professionals have chosen to become helping professionals because of positive, life-transforming experiences through their own personal counseling (perhaps even readers of this text).

In addition to counseling, support groups can serve an important role for counselors and certainly for graduate students. I am not aware of counseling programs that require student participation in support groups, but it is a worthwhile concept, particularly given the stressful nature of graduate study, practicum and internship demands, and because the Council for Accreditation of Counseling and Related Educational Programs (CACREP, 2016) standards essentially mandate training reflective counseling professionals. In my own graduate counseling program, we were required to participate in an intensive growth experience for 3 days. I was both a participant as a master's degree student and later a group facilitator as a doctoral student. My experience in both groups was educational and very informative regarding the power of the group experience on individuals. However, my belief is that an ongoing support group would be more impactful regarding students' personal growth and development.

FINAL SUGGESTIONS FOR SELF-CARE

Kenneth Blanchard, famous for the best-selling book *The One Minute Manager*, co-wrote a follow-up book titled *The One Minute Manager Gets Fit* in 1986. He was motivated to write this book after realizing that he was so consumed with chasing success that he forgot the most important thing: to keep his life in balance (Blanchard et al., 1986). He ate junk food and failed to work out; consequently, his weight ballooned, and his blood pressure rose to dangerously high levels (Blanchard et al., 1986). In the book, he listed the following as a means of assessing fitness level:

- I love my job (most of the time).
- I use safety precautions like wearing a seat belt in moving vehicles.
- I am within 5 pounds of my ideal weight.
- I know three methods to reduce stress that do not include the use of drugs or alcohol.
- I do not smoke.
- I sleep 6 to 8 hours each night and wake up refreshed.
- I engage in regular physical activity at least three times per week (including sustained physical exertion for 20 to 30 minutes, e.g., walking briskly, running, swimming, biking, and strength and flexibility activities).
- I have seven or fewer alcoholic drinks a week.
- I know my blood pressure.
- I follow sensible eating habits (e.g., eat breakfast every day; limit salt, sugar, and fats like butter, eggs, whole milk, breakfast meats, cheese, and red meat; and eat adequate fiber and few snacks).
- I have a good social support system.
- I maintain a positive mental attitude. (p. 36)

The list contains many common-sense items, yet it is clear that many people, including some graduate students and professional counselors, struggle with many of them. Regular medical checkups on an annual basis are also highly recommended. Graduate students who lack health insurance should check with their student health service, as medical care is usually subsidized by student fees and is significantly less expensive than off-campus providers. Furthermore, as previously noted, good self-care is an ethical construct (Standard C.2.g); graduate counseling students would be wise to begin working on self-care development. Professionals at college and university counseling centers, student health centers, and clergy are in a good position to assist with this. Social support systems are critical for well-being as well. Students feeling isolated would be wise to check with a counselor or another of these aforementioned professionals. Support groups can be helpful as can getting involved in a club or organization in an interest area (e.g., running club, meditation group, and hiking club).

Assessing Your Stress

Stress is a major component of health-related issues and conditions related to anxiety, depression, and a number of somatic problems (Burns, 1993). The Perceived Stress Scale-4 (PSS-4; Cohen et al., 1983) is a brief test to assess your stress level.

Self-Care: Your Owner's Manual on Well-Being

Self-care plans can provide a buffer against compassionate fatigue or burnout (Stamm, 2005). A sample self-care plan is provided in Exhibit 8.3 for the reader's consideration.

Exhibit 8.3 A Sample Self-Care Plan for Counselors and Counselors in Training

Secondary trauma, compassion fatigue, and burnout are serious concerns for any counselor or counselor in training. These may be avoided, however, provided a counselor has a good self-care plan. For a viable self-care plan, I recommend a minimum of seven dimensions: physical, emotional, cognitive, social, financial, spiritual care, and creative self-care. Naturally, there will be many variations to self-care plans, even within the seven dimensions I have recommended. The following is one example of how to construct a self-care plan.

Author's note: An active self-care plan is very helpful in managing stress counselors and counselors in the training phase. A self-care plan, though helpful, is no guarantee against compassionate fatigue or burnout.

Physical Self-Care Dimension
This includes activities you do regularly to care for your body in healthy ways. Healthy examples may include regular exercise (e.g., jogging, yoga, and weight training), a balanced diet, abstinence from tobacco and alcohol (or moderate consumption), regular sleep, and annual physicals. In the space provided, identify three activities you regularly engage in (or plan to engage in) to take care of your physical self:

_____

_____

Emotional Self-Care Dimension
This includes healthy activities you engage in to care for your emotional self. Examples may include daily or weekly journaling, counseling (if necessary), joining a support group, practicing healthy self-talk and positive affirmations, and so on. In the space provided, list three activities you currently do or plan to engage in to care for your emotional self:

_____

_____

Cognitive Self-Care Dimension
Cognitive self-care includes activities you undertake to engage your mind in a creative task. Cognitive self-care activities might include reading for pleasure, playing scrabble, completing crossword puzzles, continuing education for your career (or future career), taking classes for enjoyment, learning a new skill, and

---

(continued)

Exhibit 8.3 A Sample Self-Care Plan for Counselors and Counselors in Training (*continued*)

so on. In the space provided, list three cognitive self-care examples you regularly engage in (or will engage in):

_____

_____

Social Self-Care Dimension

As humans are social creatures, it is important to maintain healthy relationships. Examples could include socializing with friends, family, and colleagues; joining clubs and organizations; going to plats or movies with a spouse/partner/friend; and so on. In the space provided, identify three social self-care activities you currently engage in (or will engage in) to care for your social self:

_____

_____

Financial Self-Care Dimension

Financial self-care includes how you spend and save money and make responsible financial decisions. (*I realize this can be challenging as a graduate student on a fixed budget.*) Examples include balancing your checking account; maintaining a healthy savings account; speaking with a financial planner regarding investments or future investments; attending a financial planning class; or purchasing some of your clothes at Goodwill, the Salvation Army, and so on. In the space provided, identify three activities that you currently do or are planning to do for financial self-care:

_____

_____

Spiritual and Mindfulness Self-Care Dimension

Most people are spiritual beings in some manner. This may include membership in a faith community (e.g., church, mosque, or temple), 12-step community, regular individual or group meditation, mindfulness practice, and so on. *Author's note:* A person may have no spiritual inclination but likely finds ways to incorporate meaning and purpose into their life. If you are not spiritually inclined, consider how meaning and purpose manifest in your life. In the space provided, identify three spiritual/meaning activities you regularly engage in (or plan to engage in):

_____

_____

(*continued*)

Exhibit 8.3 A Sample Self-Care Plan for Counselors and Counselors in Training (*continued*)

Creative Self-Care Dimension
Everyone is a creative person. Creativity does not require world-class talent and fame but simple ways whereby you regularly engage in such pursuits. Creative expressions may include singing solo or in a choir; playing a musical instrument; writing poetry, prose, or music; creating any work of art; performing in community theater; and so on. In the space provided, cite three creative activities you regularly engage in (or will engage in):

_____

_____

CONCLUSION

The practicum and internship experience is intense and can be a very demanding and, occasionally, stressful time for a graduate student. The good news is that survival rates are very high and it is likely that you will manage stressful times quite well. You should expect occasional times, however, when you feel overwhelmed or "stressed out." These times, though unpleasant, also provide some of the greatest opportunities. You will get to practice the same stress management techniques and skills you have been teaching your clients. This is where self-reflection, reframing, meditation, prayer, exercise, friendships, and so forth are so valuable and rewarding. Be aware of your stress and anxiety levels, and monitor them closely so that you remain physically and emotionally healthy. A burned-out counselor—one who tries to be everything to everyone—fails to set limits, lacks assertiveness, eats a poor diet, and has no significant friendships and is likely to be of limited value to their clients. So, understand yourself and your emotional and physical limitations and work to stay within them. Use assessments such as the ones in this chapter to assess stress levels, a healthy lifestyle, meaning in life, and others to develop a self-care plan that is realistic and works for you.

LESSONS LEARNED

I was experiencing stress from all sides of my life. While ensconced in doctoral studies (meaning, *struggling*), I was working as a graduate teaching assistant in the psychology department, serving as a resident director of a co-operative university living group, and working two nights a week as a contract counselor for a local mental health agency. During a frightful February, these various roles came together in a nexus of stress and personal trial. The fall term had been generally uneventful, notwithstanding the usual stressful life of a graduate student. The co-op living group was small and my contract counseling work was only one evening a week. Thus, I found myself lured into a false sense of security and competence, in my business and haste, forgetting that university life is particularly dynamic, with change often coming suddenly and without warning. Change did come suddenly and absent warning, toppling my life as casually as a strong wind would an empty can.

The difficulty began after lunch, with a resident of the co-op unit approaching me in crisis. After listening to him briefly, he acknowledged being suicidal and even had thought of a specific suicide plan. I walked him over to the counseling center and left him in the capable hands of the staff. Figuring to check in with him when he returned to the housing unit, I was off to class and thereafter running a counseling lab. That afternoon, a student from my lab asked to speak with me after class. She related that her longtime boyfriend had just broken up with her and she was in crisis. She denied suicidal thoughts but stated she could barely rise from bed. I listened to her and suggested counseling services. She agreed, and for the second time that day, I walked a student to the counseling center. Once again, figuring to check on her after the following class, I hurried home for a quick dinner, as this was the night I was counseling at the agency.

That evening, I saw two clients. While neither were suicidal, one had just lost his job and his means of paying for child support. Further complicating matters, he was being evicted from his apartment in two weeks with no back up housing, that is, he would once again become homeless. "What am I going to do? I will lose visitation with my kids and be living on the street again!" Having worked with this client for several sessions, he was chronically on the edge of relapse, and while he denied it, my sense was he was using and thus the reason for his job loss and upcoming eviction. His life seemed to be chronically falling apart, making my intervention very stressful. I was one in a long line of therapists in his life, none of us having much success.

Arriving home completely spent, hoping for a quiet night, the suicidal student's roommate was literally waiting at my door. The suicidal student, while in crisis, evidently did not meet criteria for hospitalization. The roommate, while empathetic regarding his roommate's emotional plight, was emotionally exhausted. As a graduate student in a demanding science program, he simply could not continue living with a roommate habitually in crisis and requested a room change. After discussing the realities of a room change, such as no room immediately available, I promised to address the situation the following morning. Nowhere near satisfied, the student left my cramped apartment.

Feeling stressed, I turned on evening jazz music and began walking in figure eights in my matchbox-size living space. As I ambled about the room, jazz music mere white noise, my options appeared unappealing. I enjoyed teaching and needed the graduate assistant pay, meager as it was. Although my residence director job paid even less, the job eliminated rent pay, while at the same time creating a lot of stress. Dropping the evening counseling work would be the easiest course of action, but I enjoyed the work and wanted all the counseling experience I could acquire prior to going on the job market. It seemed there would be no easy resolution to my complex situation. After extended pacing and meditating while moving, fatigue set in, and turning off the music, I went to bed.

With no class or work the following morning, I took a long run through a path south of campus. The wooded pathway, misty air, and physical exertion were all a good antidote to my stressed life. Arriving home, I ate a snack and began arranging to move the worn out-roommate only to discover such a move could take weeks. I checked in with his roommate who had been in crisis, and found that he was slightly improved and had a session at counseling services that afternoon. Naturally, I had to set firm limits, as he wanted me as his "home counselor." Extricating myself from his room with difficulty, I crossed campus and made an impulsive decision: Why not make an appointment at counseling services myself? Interestingly, while an experienced counselor and having interned at a university counseling center, the thought of seeking counseling myself came late to me. I had been in counseling previously of course, but it had been some period of time. Returning to counseling was to be a very wise decision.

My counselor was a gentle, middle-aged male with over 30 years of experience in the field. Spending three to four sessions together, he gently probed and helped me prioritize my own well-being, something I had been sorely neglecting of late. Instead of dropping my counseling work, he suggested I broach the idea of me cutting back hours as opposed to ceasing altogether. He suggested I consider this a first step approach to try for a few weeks. If even one day a week was too much with the teaching and supervising the university co-operative living group, then I could drop the therapeutic work altogether.

Walking back across campus, I found myself feeling lighter with the impending reduction in my work life. Ironically, for many years, I had been delivering psycho-educational trainings on managing stress and well-being, while compromising my own emotional health with an exhausting schedule. I further reflected having known many colleagues who, like myself, maintained burnout schedules at their own peril. As I mentioned earlier in this chapter, marginal self-care is the most violated of all professional counseling ethics. Having had my awakening, I would like to write that my self-care focus became paramount, and nevermore did I risk my emotional and physical well-being. However, like a moth to the flame, it was not even a year before finding myself weighed down by saying *yes* to too many people and projects. Like an addict on a binge, I relapsed into over commitment (e.g., full-time doctoral studies, teaching, counseling, and serving on an agency board), until a frayed psyche steered me back into counseling.

I recall an old debate from my addictions counseling experience. A senior colleague, sober for many years, informed me that he had been the worst type of addict, using multiple substances and, even more concerning, enticing others into sharing his addictions. He eventually achieved sobriety, albeit after family estrangement, ruining a promising career, and permanently compromising his health. He confessed, "Whether I am a good example of turning my life around or a poor one for having wreaked so much carnage on myself and others depends on point of view." Admittedly, I have never fallen to the depths of my former colleague, but my role modeling on self-care is very open to debate. Too often my M.O. has been a *do-as-I-say* approach, pushing me close to the burnout line. Ignoring self-care by an overly busy life coupled with ignoring a social life is a sure recipe for burnout. I recall a story psychiatrist Dr. Gabor Mate told, where he was kicked out of his own retreat due to the fact he was so obviously burned out! The lesson learned herein is counselors and therapists can get away with poor self-care (including agencies that make us ill), until we cannot. *Counselors beware!*

RECOMMENDED RESOURCES

Resources for Meaning in Life

Frankl, V. E. (1969). *The will to meaning*. Beacon Press.
Hodges, S. (2023). *Creating a meaningful life: A practical guide for counselors, therapists, and other helping professionals*. Routledge.

Resources for Managing Stress

Brinkman, R., & Kirschner, R. (2002). *Dealing with people you can't stand: How to bring out the best in people at their worst*. McGraw-Hill.
Greenberger, D., & Padesky, C. A. (1995). *Mind over mood: A cognitive therapy treatment manual for clients*. Guilford Press.
Myers, J. E., & Sweeney, T. J. (Eds.) (2005). *Counseling for wellness: Theory, research, and practice*. American Counseling Association.
Williams, M. B., & Poijula, S. (2000). *The PTSD workbook: Simple effective techniques for overcoming traumatic stress symptoms*. New Harbinger.

Resources for Conflict Resolution

The following books are good resources for ideas, self-reflection, and skill building regarding conflict resolution:

Barsky, A. E. (2017). *Conflict resolution for the helping professions* (3rd ed.). Oxford University Press.
Fisher, R., & Ury, W. (1981). *Getting to yes: Negotiating agreement without giving in*. Penguin Books.

A robust set of instructor resources designed to supplement this text is located at http://connect.springerpub.com/content/book/978-0-8261-6607-4. Qualifying instructors may request access by emailing **textbook@springerpub.com.**

REFERENCES

American Counseling Association. (2014). *ACA code of ethics*. https://www.counseling.org/resources/aca-code-of-ethics.pdf
American Institute of Stress. (n.d.). *50 common signs and symptoms of stress*. https://www.stress.org/stress-effects#effects
Baird, B. N., Carey, A., & Giakovmis, H. (1992). *Personal experience in psychotherapy: Differences in therapists' cognitions* [Paper presentation]. Western Psychological Association, Portland, OR.
Blanchard, K., Edington, D. W., & Blanchard, M. (1986). *The one minute manager gets fit*. Quill.
Bolles, R. N. (2015). *What color is your parachute? A practical manual for job-hunters and career-changers*. Ten Speed Press.
Burns, D. D. (1993). *Ten days to self-esteem*. Harper.
Carter, S. B. (2013, November 26). The tell-tale signs of burnout. . . do you have them? *Psychology Today*. https://www.psychologytoday.com/us/blog/high-octane-women/201311/the-tell-tale-signs-burnout-do-you-have-them
Cohen, S., Kamarck, T., & Mermelstein, R. (1983). A global measure of perceived stress. *Journal of Health and Social Behavior, 24*(4), 385–396. https://doi.org/10.2307/2136404
Council for Accreditation of Counseling and Related Educational Programs. (2016). *2016 CACREP standards*. https://www.cacrep.org/for-programs/2016-cacrep-standards

Davis, M., Eshelman, E. R., & McKay, M. (2008). *The relaxation and stress management workbook* (6th ed.). New Harbinger.

Duffy, R. D., & Raque-Bogdan, T. L. (2010). The motivation to serve others: Exploring relations to career development. *Journal of Career Assessment, 18*, 250–265. https://doi.org/10.1177/1069072710364791

Ellis, A. (2001). *Overcoming destructive beliefs, feelings, and behaviors*. Prometheus Books.

Figley, C. R. (1995). *Compassion fatigue: Coping with secondary traumatic stress disorder in those who treat the traumatized*. Brunner Mazel.

Frankl, V. E. (1997). *Man's search for ultimate meaning*. Plume.

Gladding, S. T. (2009). *Counseling: A comprehensive profession* (6th ed.). Merrill/Prentice Hall.

Heintzelman, S. I., & King, L. A. (2014). Life is pretty meaningful. *American Psychologist, 69*, 561–574. https://doi.org/10.1037/a0035049

Lee, C. (2019). *Multicultural issues in counseling*. American Counseling Association.

Mahoney, M. J. (1997). Psychotherapists' personal problems and self-care patterns. *Professional psychology: Research and practice, 28*, 14–16. https://doi.org/10.1037//0735-7028.28.1.14

McGonigal, K. (2019). *The joy of movement: How exercise helps us find happiness, hope, connection, and Courage*. Penguin.

Much, K., & Swanson, A. L. (2010). The debate about increasing college student psychopathology: Are college students really getting sicker? *Journal of College Student Development, 24*(2), 86–97. https://doi.org/10.1080/87568220903558570

Myers, J. E., Sweeney, T. J., & Witmer, J. M. (2000). The Wheel of Wellness counseling for wellness: A holistic model for treatment planning. *Journal of Counseling & Development, 78*(3), 251–266. https://doi.org/10.1002/j.1556-6676.2000.tb01906.x

Norcross, J. C., Strausser, D. J., & Faltus, F. J. (1988). The therapist's therapist. *American Journal of Psychotherapy, 42*, 53–66. https://doi.org/10.1176/appi.psychotherapy.1988.42.1.53

Peterson, C., & Park, N. (2012). Character strengths and the life of meaning. In P. T. Wong's (Ed.), *The human quest for meaning: Theories, research, and applications* (2nd ed., pp. 277–295). Routledge.

Pope, K. S., & Tabachnick, B. G. (1994). Therapists as patients: A national survey of psychologists' experiences, problems, and beliefs. *Professional Psychology: Research and Practice, 25*, 247–258. https://doi.org/10.1037/0735-7028.25.3.247

Remley, T. P., Jr., & Herlihy, B. (2020). *Ethical, legal and professional issues in counseling* (6th ed.). Pearson.

Schulenberg, S. E., Strack, K. M., & Buchanan, E. M. (2011). The meaning in life questionnaire: Psychometric properties with individuals with severe mental illnesses in an inpatient setting. *Journal of Clinical Psychology, 67*, 1210–1219. https://doi.org/10.1002/jclp.20841

Seligman, M. E. P. (2002). *Authentic happiness: Using the new positive psychology to realize your potential for lasting fulfillment*. Free Press.

Sharma, V., Martin, D. B., Koenig, H. K., Feder, A., Iacoviello, B. M., Southwick, S. M., & Pietzak, D. H. (2017). Religion, spirituality, and mental health of U.S. military veterans: Results from the national health and resilience in veterans study. *Journal of Affective Disorders, 217*(9), 197–204. https://doi.org/10.1016/jad.2017.03.071

Stamm, B. H. (2005). *The ProQOL manual*. Sidran Press.

Stamm, B. H. (2012). *Professional Quality of Life: Compassion Satisfaction and Fatigue Version 5 (ProQOL)*. https://socialwork.buffalo.edu/content/dam/socialwork/home/self-care-kit/compassion-satisfaction-and-fatigue-stamm-2009.pdf

Steger, M. F., Frazier, P., Oishi, S., & Kaler, M. (2006). The meaning in life questionnaire: Assessing the presence of and search for meaning in life. *Journal of Counseling Psychology, 53*(1), 80–93. https://doi.org/10.1037/0022-0167.53.1.80

Weinhold, B. K., & Weinhold, J. B. (2009). *Conflict resolution: The partnership way* (2nd ed.). Love Publishing.

Witmer, J. M., & Granello, P. F. (2005). Wellness in counselor education and supervision. In J. E. Myers & T. J. Sweeney (Eds.), *Counseling for wellness: Theory, research, and practice*. American Counseling Association.

Wong, P. T. P. (2012a). Introduction: A roadmap for meaningful research applications. In P. T. P. Wong (Ed.), *The human quest for meaning: Theories, research, and applications* (2nd ed., pp. xxix–xlvi). Taylor & Francis.

Wong, P. T. P. (2012b). The meaning mindset: Measurement and implications. *International Journal of Existential Psychology & Psychotherapy, 4*, 1–3.

CHAPTER 9

Crisis Intervention in Practicum/Internship

INTRODUCTION

No area of professional counseling practice creates as much stress and anxiety as crisis situations. For purposes of this chapter, *crisis* is defined as situations in which a client poses a danger to self or others (Wheeler & Bertram, 2019). This includes clients who may be potentially suicidal, those who threaten to harm a third party (e.g., homicidal ideation or to commit serious physical injury), and cases of child abuse and neglect. Due to the nature of client crisis, there are ethical and legal ramifications for counselors to consider and to follow. Essentially, the guideline is "What decisions would a reasonable professional make in crisis situations?" (Wheeler & Bertram, 2019). *Reasonable* clinical decision are not defined, although conducting a thorough suicide potential assessment, following ethical guidelines and applicable laws, would be the beginning. Consulting with your supervisor and, if necessary, notifying pertinent outside officials (e.g., the police, hospital, parent or guardian) likely would fall under the reasonable heading. The final responsible act is to accurately document your actions in the case record. Should a crisis become a legal matter, your documentation becomes of utmost importance regarding protecting you (and the school, clinic, hospital, etc.) from liability. Thus, your documentation in a crisis likely is as important as conducting yourself in a thorough, reasonable, and professional manner.

Most practicum and internship settings, whether in schools, agencies, residential treatment centers, hospitals, and so forth, likely will try to screen potential crisis clients away from practicum and internship students due to the complexity and potentially litigious nature of a crisis. Because no screening system is perfect, however, counseling programs must prepare students for the possibility that they will encounter crisis clients on practicum. In fact, many supposed "non crisis" clients assigned to the practicum or internship student may, because of stressful circumstances, escalate into a crisis. No doubt, a client may disclose being in crisis due to the intern having built a healthy, trustworthy relationship with the client. This chapter provides an overview of crisis situations and ways interns can begin addressing them. The most important

WHAT DEFINES A CRISIS?

The definition of a crisis can vary considerably, whether the discussion involves personal; interpersonal; or all-campus, all-hospital, and so on. In light of risks counselors potentially face in P–12 schools, addiction treatment, in patient psychiatric settings, Veterans Affairs (VA) medical centers, and so forth, *crisis* is simply defined as a valid threat to self and others. This threat may apply to serious injury to self, others, or property destruction. Some crises will be far more serious than others, though all crises must be taken seriously by counselors and other professionals (Zdziarski et al., 2007). Suicide and homicide are not the only threats that present ethical, legal, and clinical challenges to counselors. The International Society for the Study of Self-Injury (n.d.) defines *nonsuicidal self-inj*ury as "the deliberate, self-inflicted damage of body tissue without suicidal intent and for purposes not socially or culturally sanctioned" (para. 1). Counselors working with adolescents and even adults are aware of self-injurious behaviors such as cutting, burning, piercing, and other non suicidal self-injurious behaviors. These self-abusive practices, while usually not intended as serious self-injuries, can nevertheless be cause for concern (Whitlock, 2009).

Counselors working in schools, universities, large hospitals, and correctional settings may well feel more concern from colleagues, given the past 20 years' history of mass shooting sprees in school and work settings. Colleagues, working in such settings may well experience concern from non clinical colleagues, and fears likely may be heightened with threats regarding violence toward self or others. Fortunately, most threats are just that, *threats*. However, given the proliferation of semiautomatic weapons, all threats are serious ones, as one never really knows when a threat will become a tragedy.

THE DUTY TO WARN

Before we discuss crisis situations, it is necessary to review confidentiality and its exceptions, which are discussed in detail in Chapter 4, "Ethical and Legal Issues." Confidentiality is not absolute, and federal and state laws mandate several exceptions where confidentiality must be broken (state and territorial laws vary, so you must know the laws of your jurisdiction). These situations typically include the following:

- potential suicide
- credible threats made against third parties (e.g., homicide, property destruction, and theft)
- abuse (children, the elderly, or other vulnerable persons)
- court-mandated disclosure by a judge
- when the client signs a release of information

As discussed in Chapter 4, "Ethical and Legal Issues," the landmark court case involving confidentiality is *Tarasoff v. The Regents of the University of California* (1976). In the *Tarasoff* case, an ex-boyfriend named Prosenjit Podder informed a psychologist at the University of California, Berkeley, that he intended to kill his ex-girlfriend, Tatiana Tarasoff, when she returned from overseas. Neither the campus police nor the counseling center notified Ms. Tarasoff, and Podder murdered Ms. Tarasoff when she returned to the United States. The Tarasoff family sued the University of California, citing negligence, but they lost in state court. Upon appeal to the California State Supreme Court, however, the decision was reversed, and the plaintiff was awarded damages. The California State Supreme Court specifically stated:

> [O]nce a therapist does in fact determine, or under applicable professional standards reasonably should have determined, that a patient poses a serious danger of violence to others, he bears a duty to exercise reasonable care to protect the foreseeable victim of that danger. (*Tarasoff*, 1976, p. 345)

> Thus, the *Tarasoff* decision established a therapist's duty to warn and protect. This decision has radically changed the nature of the counseling relationship in a manner that has created more responsibility for the counselor. The duty to warn exception is sometimes referred to as the mental health profession's "Miranda" rule (Remley & Herlihy, 2020). When clients disclose a viable threat to themselves or another party, the counselor must breach confidentiality and notify appropriate parties (e.g., the police and potential victims if feasible) of serious and foreseeable risk to the individual or others. Failure to adequately address a crisis or to warn appropriate parties could result in legal and ethical sanctions, and suspension of a counselor's license or certification. (Remley & Herlihy, 2020; Wheeler & Bertram, 2019)

Now, having read the preceding paragraph, students should be aware of two state's notable exceptions to the *Tarasoff* decision. Texas is one of two states where a judge has explicitly ruled *Tarasoff* does not apply. In 1999, the Texas Supreme Court declared that mental health professionals have no common law or duty to warn readily identified third parties of a patient's threats against them (*Thapar v. Zezulka*, 1999). By Texas state statute, however, counselors are permitted to make certain disclosures to law enforcement or medical personnel in situations where there is an imminent risk of physical injury to a third party (Wheeler & Bertram, 2019). Of more concern, however, there is no specific grant of immunity built into the statute, which could create a difficult decision-making challenge for the therapist (Tex. Health & Safety Code 611.004, 2017). The larger concern for counselors practicing in Texas is adherence to a state law that runs counter to the lessons of *Tarasoff*, professional ethics, and moral concerns. It will be interesting to see if the *Thapar* decision is reversed in coming years or if other states and territories follow Texas. (My belief is the former appears more likely than the latter.)

In 1991, a Florida appeals court declined to apply the *Tarasoff* decision, ruling that imposing a duty upon therapists to warn third parties would undermine client–patient confidentiality and trust. The Florida court also opined that imposing a duty to warn would be the equivalent of a therapist using a crystal ball to foresee potential violence (*Boynton v. Burglass*, 1991). Unlike Texas, however, Florida has a statute permitting therapists to warn third parties without risk of litigation, but reporting is not mandatory according to case law (*Boynton v. Burglass*, 1991; Fla. Stat. 491.0147, 2018). Thus, counselors working in Florida may breach confidentiality in the case of clear and foreseeable danger to a person and do so with less anxiety than in Texas, although no *Tarasoff* duty exists as of this publication.

In the aftermath of numerous high-profile shooting tragedies in recent years (e.g., Sandy Hook Elementary, Virginia Tech University, Northern Illinois University, Columbine High School, *and far too many others*), mandated disclosure (i.e., *Tarasoff* type) likely will be more, not less, emphasized. Nevertheless, Texas and Florida remain outliers regarding the *Tarasoff* duty to warn and protect third parties. Counselors who proceed to work in these two states will need to consult closely with supervisors and legal counsel in order to remain vigilant regarding ethics, legalities, and good judgment. While the following statement has become a cliché in this text, counselors-in-training must always seek out their supervisor when faced with a crisis situation or what they perceive as a potential crisis.

Students using this text in other countries must be aware of the laws of the region and country they study and work within them. Having taught on an international border for over 20 years, and having taught, trained, and consulted overseas, I have illustrated that laws can vary considerably across borders. Your faculty and field site supervisors are key mentors to say nothing of the particular ethical code your national counseling profession follows (e.g., British Association for Counseling and Psychotherapy [BACP], Canadian Counseling and Psychotherapy Association [CCPA], Psychotherapy and Counseling Federation of Australia [PACFA], American Counselin Association [ACA]). Regardless of culture or nationality, all counselors must be prepared to address serious and foreseeable harm to the client or other persons.

SUICIDAL CLIENTS

Suicide usually is the most common concern with regard to crisis (though crisis certainly is broader than suicide). Suicide is the second leading cause of death among college students and is a serious risk among high school students and the elderly (Granello & Granello, 2007). There are several commonly held myths regarding suicide. Sadly, you may even hear mental health professionals repeating them. Common suicide myths include the following (Sommers-Flanagan & Sommers-Flanagan, 1999):

- Discussing suicide will cause the client to attempt it.
- Clients who talk of suicide will not attempt suicide.
- Suicides increase around Christmas and New Year's Eve.
- Only insane people attempt suicide.
- When a suicidal patient's mood improves, it is a sign the danger is over.
- Suicide is more prevalent among poorer classes of people.
- Suicide generally happens without warning.

Many counselors fear they might say the wrong thing and precipitate a suicide attempt. Fortunately, there is virtually nothing you could say to induce suicide (Captain, 2006; Granello & Granello, 2007; Sommers-Flanagan & Sommers-Flanagan, 1999).

In my experience counseling crisis clients, I have found that these individuals seemed visibly relieved when I inquired about the possibility of suicide. This likely was because the weighty secret the clients had been carrying was no longer a secret and because they acted to get help, meaning they were now actively seeking assistance. Most clients who are contemplating suicide are actually relieved to discuss the topic and generally are appreciative that someone has asked (assuming of course that the topic is discussed in a caring, non judgmental way). It is also important to ask the client whether they have a plan (ask for details) and the likelihood to carry out that plan. The client's responses will give you a sense of their intent (Capuzzi & Gross, 2008). Fortunately, most clients never proceed to the planning stage of suicide. Unfortunately of course, some do make plans, make attempts, and succeed.

Students occasionally disclose a fear the client will get mad if queried about suicide. In my opinion and clinical experience of nearly 30 years, if the client does become angry at the question, it is likely a positive sign, as it may indicate that the client has not given up hope. I am far more anxious counseling potentially suicidal clients who appear calm. Such rationality and composure may indicate that the client has made a decision to commit suicide and is at peace with the idea of their own self-inflicted death (Capuzzi & Gross, 2008; Granello & Granello, 2007). So, counselors must be able to, of necessity, ask clients if they are suicidal (or homicidal), both to assuage legal and ethical concerns and to reassure the client. An essential question in the mind of the client in crisis likely is "Can this counselor help guide me through my crisis period into safety?" You want that crisis client to believe you can help them, and therefore, displaying a calm, confident demeanor and a caring voice tone will go a long way in easing that client's fears. So, act confident even if, on the inside, you are feeling tense. Remember, you have your field site supervisor, other senior clinicians, and your faculty for support and assistance.

Ethical and Legal Mandates Regarding Suicide

The *ACA Code of Ethics* (American Counseling Association [ACA], 2014) clearly addresses the issues of suicide and client welfare:

> The general requirement that counselors keep information confidential does not apply when disclosure is required to protect clients or identified others from serious and foreseeable harm or when legal requirements demand that confidential information must be revealed. Counselors consult with other professionals when in doubt as to the validity of an exception. (Section B.2.a)

State laws also mandate that counselors and other professionals (e.g., psychologists, nurses, and physicians) also breach confidentiality when the issue of self-harm arises (Remley & Herlihy, 2020). As a counselor, you must also be prepared to take appropriate measures to prevent suicide. Appropriate measures would generally include a thorough risk assessment, consulting with your supervisor, notifying the appropriate parties, documenting the actions you took in the case record, and scheduling the client for an immediate follow-up session. In many cases, the client may be temporarily hospitalized, depending on a variety of factors such as a suicide plan, insurance, and hospital availability. Remember, as a graduate intern, you are not the

Talking With a Suicidal Client

Here are some suggestions for discussing the issue of suicide with a client:

- Remain calm. Do not panic or show any signs of discomfort. You want the client to believe you are composed in the face of their crisis.
- If you are concerned that a client might be suicidal, specifically ask, "I'm wondering if you might be considering suicide?" In my experience, most clients seem relieved that their weighty secret has been lifted.
- Do not try to argue with the client about their plan or give them minimizing advice (e.g., "It'll get better," "It's really not that big a deal," "What will your family think?").
- It is critical that the suicidal client feel "heard" and not judged. Listen empathically, and let the client know you accept them, thus validating their struggles. It is also worth remembering that suicidal clients feel very isolated. You are very possibly the first person to whom the client has disclosed their intent for self-harm, and your empathic presence may go a long way in helping to resolve the immediate crisis.
- Most crisis clients have thought of suicide but have not made a plan. If this is the case with your client, get the client rescheduled at the soonest possible time (the next day, if possible). Provide the client with a 24-hour crisis number or the national suicide hotline number (call 988; text SMS: 988) so they know help is readily available. Naturally, you may need to facilitate a brief hospitalization.
- Remember, when the client discloses thoughts or even a suicide plan, that client is saying "Help me" to the counselor. If you can get the client to admit to suicidal thoughts or intent, you have a very good chance to stop a suicide attempt.

How to Assess Suicidal Risk

Because suicide assessment is not an exact science, counselors would be wise to apply a broad approach to treating suicidal clients. McGlothen et al. (2005) suggest that professionals consider five aspects for all potentially suicidal clients:

- *Plan.* The verbalization of a plan of how the client would attempt suicide suggests lethality. The more detailed and specific the plan, the greater the potential lethality.
- *Intent.* The stated intent to follow-through on a suicide plan also suggests higher lethality.
- *Means.* The means by which the client plans to accomplish a suicide attempt can be revealing. The more deadly the means (e.g., gun), the greater the lethality. Women make three times the attempts, but men "succeed" at suicide at approximately four times the rate of women (American Foundation for Suicide Prevention, 2013). The

difference is that men use more lethal means (e.g., a gun). So, does the client have access to a gun or rifle?

- *Prior attempts.* Previous suicide attempts also suggest the client has previously seen suicide as a viable option. This suggests higher lethality. Typically, clients must work up to making a suicidal attempt, and previous attempts indicate the client is beginning to see suicide as a viable option.
- *Substance abuse.* A history of substance abuse—especially alcohol—increases lethality because substance abusers often display less management of crisis situations. It is a good idea, therefore, to use a standard alcohol and drug assessment such as the Alcohol Use Disorders Identification Test (AUDIT); Substance Abuse Subtle Screening Inventory-4 (SASSI-4); Michigan Alcohol Screening Test (MAST); and so on.

McGlothen et al. (2005) also suggest the following general guidelines in gauging lethality:

- *Low lethality.* Suicidal ideation (thoughts of suicide) is present but intent is denied, and the client does not have a concrete plan and has never attempted suicide in the past.
- *Moderate lethality.* More than one general risk factor for suicide is present, suicidal ideation and intent are present but a clear plan is denied, and the client is motivated to improve their psychological state.
- *High lethality.* Several general risk factors for suicide are present, the client has verbalized suicidal ideation and intent, and they have communicated a well-thought-out plan with immediate access to resources needed to complete the plan.
- *Very high lethality.* The client verbalizes suicidal ideation and intent, and they have communicated a well-thought-out plan with immediate access to resources needed to complete the plan, demonstrate cognitive rigidity and hopelessness for the future, deny any available suicide support, and have attempted suicide in the past.

Essential Factors of Suicide Risk Assessment

- Assessment of each person is unique.
- Assessment is complex and challenging.
- Assessment is an ongoing process.
- Assessment uses multiple perspectives.
- Assessment tries to uncover foreseeable risk.
- Assessment relies on clinical judgment.
- Assessment is treatment.
- Assessment errs on the side of caution.
- Assessment takes all threats, warning signs, and risk factors seriously.
- Assessment asks the tough questions.

224 • THE COUNSELING PRACTICUM AND INTERNSHIP MANUAL

- Assessment tries to uncover the underlying message.
- Assessment is done in a cultural context.
- Assessment is collaborative.
- Assessment is documented. (Granello & Granello, 2007, p. 184)

Assessing suicide in adolescents may be particularly difficult because of the fact that this population is still developing coping mechanisms, understanding that crisis is a temporary situation, and tend to be more impulsive. In 1996, Juhnke adapted the SAD PERSONS (Sex, Age, Depression, Previous attempt, Ethanol/alcohol abuse, Rational thinking loss, Social supports lacking, Organized plan, No spouse, and Sickness) checklist for use with adolescents and called it the Adapted SAD PERSONS checklist (see Exhibit 9.1). The adapted scale can be used to assess suicidal risk factors and provide general intervention recommendations for school counselors and counselors working with youth.

Exhibit 9.1 Adapted SAD PERSONS Scale (A-SAD)

S—Sex (males = 10 points; females = 0 points)

A—Age (older adolescents are at higher risk and receive more points)

D—Depression or affective disorder (the more serious the disorder, the more points)

P—Previous attempts (score recent attempts and more lethal attempts higher)

E—Ethanol/drug abuse (score drug or alcohol use or abuse higher)

R—Rational thinking loss (score evidence of rational thinking loss higher)

S—Social supports lacking (score lack of close friendships or social supports higher)

O—Organized plan (score specificity and lethality higher)

N—Negligent parenting (score neglect, abuse, family stress, and suicidal modeling higher)

S—School performance (score aggressive behaviors, vandalism, or deterioration of academic performance higher)

SCORING GUIDELINE

Assign points (0–10) to match severity for each risk factor. Total scores can range from 0 to 100.

Scores of 0 to 29: Students should be encouraged to participate in counseling services and be given information about crisis services.

Scores of 30 to 49: Students should be strongly encouraged to receive counseling and close follow-up services. School counselors should contact parents or guardians and make a thorough suicide assessment.

(continued)

Exhibit 9.1 Adapted SAD PERSONS Scale (A-SAD) (*continued*)

Scores of 50 to 69: Students in this range should be strongly considered for an evaluation for hospitalization.

Scores of 70 and above: Scores in this range suggest both environmental turmoil and severe emotional distress. Scores at this extreme end of the continuum warrant immediate hospitalization. Child protective services should be contacted in cases where family turmoil does not allow adequate assurance of care.

Caution: Suicide risk assessment is a complex process and cannot identify all persons who will attempt suicide. The Adapted SAD PERSONS Scale should not be used as the sole or primary assessment to determine, measure, consider, or estimate suicide risk or suggest interventions. The scale and its generally suggested actions should be used as merely one component of a structured, multicomponent, and thorough suicide assessment process facilitated by a suicide assessment, threat, or safety committee minimally composed of multiple clinicians, clinical supervisors, legal counselor, and a client or student ombudsman or advocate.

Source: Reprinted with permission from Juhnke, G. (1996). The Adapted SAD PERSONS: A suicide assessment scale designed for use with children. *Elementary School Guidance & Counseling, 30,* 252–258. https://www.jstor.org/stable/42871225

The adapted version does not assign specific points for most of the items; rather, the counselor assigns 0 to 10 points for each item based on the severity of risk.

There are other assessments for suicidality and depression (which is a significant risk factor for suicide). The Columbia-Suicide Severity Rating Scale (C-SSRS), which assesses suicidal ideation and suicidal behavior (Posner et al., 2011), has become popular in risk assessment. Perhaps the most widely used instrument for assessing depression is the Beck Depression Inventory-II (BDI-II; Beck et al., 1996). The BDI-II is often considered as the preferred instrument because of the large amount of research validating its effectiveness (Beck et al., 1996). It is a 21-item self-report that assesses levels of depression and predicts the likelihood of suicide in adolescents and adults. It is completed by the client and usually takes less than 10 minutes. According to Beck et al. (1996), BDI-II scores ranging from 0 to 13 represent *minimal depression*; total scores from 14 to 19 suggest *mild depression*; total scores from 20 to 28 represent *moderate depression*; and total scores from 29 to 63 suggest *severe depression*. More significantly, the BDI-II has two key items strongly correlated with suicide. One item asks about suicide potential and another, hopelessness. Interestingly, it seems the latter item on hopelessness is a better predictor of suicide than the question on suicide itself (Beck et al., 1996). Given the power of the construct of hope and that of hopelessness, Frankl (1969) seems to have succinctly made the hope–life and meaning–life affirming connection decades previously (logotherapy essentially is a therapy of meaning; Frankl, 1969). Assessing hope in potentially suicidal clients is a "must" for all counselors. This may involve encouraging the client to cultivate friendships, seek ongoing counseling, consider medication (at least temporarily), join a support group, incorporate a fitness routine and healthy diet, seek appropriate opportunities through work or schooling, reduce use of alcohol and drugs, and many other things.

For more information about this instrument, go to www.psychcorp.pearsonas-sessments.com and search for "Beck Depression Inventory-II."

Additional Risk Factors

Most people who attempt suicide have a diagnosable mental disorder (Granello & Granello, 2007), such as major depression or bipolar disorder. Here are some additional risk factors that may increase the risk for suicidality:

- Substance abuse
- Posttraumatic stress disorder (PTSD)
- An eating disorder
- A particular diagnosis (e.g., borderline personality disorder, histrionic personality disorder)
- Mental illness such as schizophrenia
- A history of previous suicide attempts
- Gender: Males are three to five times more likely to commit suicide than females (Granello & Granello, 2007).
- Age: Elderly Caucasian males have the highest suicide rate. In addition, suicide is the second leading cause of death among college students and is rising among high school-age adolescents (Sommers-Flanagan & Sommers-Flanagan, 1999).
- A recent and major precipitating event (e.g., death of a loved one, divorce or breakup, loss of job, major disappointment, academic difficulty, loss of home)
- For children and adolescents, peer taunting and shunning have been associated with several high-profile suicide cases in recent years (Moore, 2010).
- Access to firearms or other lethal means

Steps to Take When a Client Is Contemplating Suicide

The most effective means of preventing suicide is to recognize the warning signs and respond to them. As mental health professionals, counselors are expected to read and interpret the signs of suicide and to intervene appropriately. Counselors should heed the following suggestions:

1. Take all suicide threats seriously. This is the first and most significant guideline of suicide and homicide prevention.
2. Of all suicidal individuals, 75% give some type of warning sign (American Foundation for Suicide Prevention, 2013). Examples of warning signs might be vague threats (e.g., "I might not be around much longer"), giving away treasured

possessions, risky behavior (e.g., driving very fast, illicit drug or alcohol abuse, and risky sexual behavior), nonlethal self-injurious behaviors (e.g., cutting, burning, numerous injuries), withdrawal from social activities, pessimism, sleep problems, increased alcohol use, a plan for suicide, and so on.

3. When you do encounter a potentially suicidal client, do not simply advise them not to commit suicide, as such advice is unlikely to work. Instead, ask the client to postpone an attempt of suicide. When you get an agreement to delay suicide, this provides an opening for considering additional possibilities other than self-harm.

4. Remember, when a client discloses an intention of suicide, what they are saying to you is "Help me!" A client telling you is an advantage in building a relationship and stopping a potential suicide. So, be calm and work on the relationship.

5. Fortunately, most clients who bring up suicidal thoughts or intent never make a plan for suicide. Of those who make a plan, few follow-through on the plan. (But again, treat each gesture seriously.)

6. Get the suicidal client to commit to ongoing counseling. In addition, get the client a referral for a medication screening, as they may need antidepressant medication, at least temporarily. If the client refuses, be sure to document your suggestions for legal and ethical reasons.

7. Never leave the suicidal client alone. If you need to consult with a colleague or supervisor regarding a suicide prevention plan, get a colleague or secretary to stay with the client while you consult. Furthermore, never leave sharp instruments (e.g., scissors, sharp letter opener, dinner knife) available for clients to use.

8. Always consult with your immediate supervisor about the situation. Moreover, document the situation, how you assessed the client, the consultation, and the plan you made. Does the client need to be hospitalized? If the client needs hospitalization, the police or other authorized personnel should provide transportation. Suicidal clients will probably need to be screened for medication by a psychiatrist or other healthcare professional. Does the client live alone? Does the client have the means to attempt suicide? If so, get the means away from them. (See Case Study 9.1 for an example of the supervisor consultation process.)

9. Have the client sign a safety contract. Some research suggests that safety contracts may not be a good idea. Experts seem to be divided on this issue. Many include safety contracts because no current research indicates contracts increase liability (Wheeler & Bertram, 2019). My own belief is that signing one's name is a concrete act of commitment to health and safety.

10. Remember, it is not your role to prevent suicide but rather to provide the best treatment plan to interrupt any suicide plan (Remley & Herlihy, 2020; Wheeler & Bertram, 2019). Basically, your job as a counselor is to provide the client with the best chance for recovery.

11. After the crisis has passed, review the case with your colleagues and supervisor to learn from the experience.

12. Finally, isolated people are more likely to attempt suicide. Teaching clients how to make healthy friendships goes a long way in reducing the risk of suicide. Perhaps all treatment plans for suicide prevention should include increasing social contacts.

228 • THE COUNSELING PRACTICUM AND INTERNSHIP MANUAL

Case Study 9.1 The Case of Juan: Assessing Suicide Risk and Determining Immediate Steps

Jai-Lin is a newly graduated counselor who has just been hired as an addictions counselor at a large agency serving voluntary and mandated clients. Many of her clients have histories of violence and have been incarcerated. Lately, she has been counselor to Juan, a 35-year-old ex-con whom she is counseling for addictions. During the fifth session, Juan discloses he has been depressed of late. Jai-Lin inquires for more specifics. Juan states his partner has moved out and he has just lost his job and has relapsed on cocaine and alcohol. He fears his probation officer may recommend his probation be revoked, which would send him back to prison. Jai-Lin asks whether he is considering suicide. Juan says yes and that while he legally cannot possess a handgun, he knows where he can get one. Jai-Lin inquires whether he has a plan for suicide and Juan answers, "Not right now." Jai-Lin is unsure whether Juan is at risk and whether she must inform Juan's probation officer.

Jai-Lin takes Juan into the waiting room while she confers with her supervisor. The supervisor suggests Juan be recommended for overnight hospitalization. The supervisor makes the decision not to inform Juan's probation officer at this point as he has not violated the conditions of his parole. Jai-Lin takes Juan back into her office and informs him she will proceed with hospitalization, at least on an overnight basis.

- Did Jai-Lin make sound clinical and ethical decisions regarding Juan's treatment?
- Did Jai-Lin's supervisor make the correct call in not informing Juan's probation officer? Explain why "yes" or "no."
- What would you have done in this situation if you had been Jai-Lin?
- Had you been Jai-Lin's supervisor, would you do anything different that the supervisor in this scenario?

Assessing Suicidal Risk in Schools

Although it could be argued that assessing suicide risk is the same regardless of the setting, middle and high schools pose unique challenges because of the educational and social nature of children and adolescents. Capuzzi (2009) has proposed 15 steps in assessing suicide risk in schools:

1. Remember the meaning of the term *crisis management*. This initial step refers to the need to assess a crisis and manage the situation until the risk has passed. Rapid decisions must be made by counselors and other school officials to prevent suicide.

2. Be calm and supportive. Remember that a suicidal adolescent likely feels hopeless. The demeanor and attitude of the counselor or intervener is crucial.

3. Be nonjudgmental. Statements such as "This is no big deal, it'll pass" are minimizing statements that ignore the seriousness of the student's issue and may precipitate the adolescent to slip further into depression.

4. Encourage self-disclosure. The act of talking about painful issues is the first step in getting needed help. If the adolescent feels they can be honest, the assessment will be more accurate.

5. Acknowledge the reality of suicide as a choice, but do not "normalize" suicide as a choice. For example, you might say, "It is not unusual for adolescents to feel upset with relationships or other disappointments. Suicidal thoughts may sometimes come up in such situations, but there are other choices, such as what you are doing now—talking about the issues."

6. Actively listen and positively reinforce. Make appropriate eye contact, encourage the student to continue talking, be soft in your tone of voice, and so on. Allowing the adolescent to be heard conveys respect.

7. Do not attempt in-depth counseling. You want to establish the relationship and get the student assessed as quickly as possible. When the crisis has passed and the student is more stable, in-depth exploration and goal setting can begin.

8. Contact another professional. A second school counselor, psychologist, or social worker may be able to catch issues you might miss. No matter what plan you establish, document all that was done.

9. Ask questions to explore lethality. The following questions may help determine the risk:

   - What has happened to make life so difficult?
   - Are you thinking of suicide?
   - How long have you been thinking of suicide?
   - Do you have a suicide plan?
   - Do you know someone who has committed suicide?
   - How much do you want to live?
   - How much do you want to die?
   - What do you think death is like?
   - Have you attempted suicide in the past?
   - How long ago was the previous attempt (or most recent attempt)?
   - Have you been feeling depressed?
   - Is there anyone to stop you? (Significant relationships can make a difference.)
   - On a scale of 1 to 10, with 10 being high and 1 being low, what is the number that best predicts the possibility you will attempt suicide?
   - Do you use alcohol or drugs?
   - Have you experienced significant losses during the past year or earlier losses you have never discussed?
   - Have you been concerned, in any way, with your sexuality?
   - When you think about yourself and the future, what do you visualize?

10. Make crisis management decisions. Develop a crisis intervention plan for the suicidal adolescent to be followed until the crisis is over and long-term counseling is initiated.

11. Notify parents or legal guardians. Parents or legal guardians must be notified in crisis situations. Naturally, students may be very nervous about bringing their parents into the situation, but this must be done both for legal and clinical reasons. When the crisis has passed, the parents or guardians should be part of treatment planning. Family counseling may be in order.

12. Consider hospitalization. All suicidal adolescents should be screened for hospitalization, though many will not be hospitalized. In some cases, short-term hospitalization may be required.

13. Write contracts. Though suicide contracts are not foolproof, professionals may use contracts as a concrete method of getting the adolescent to commit to long-term safety. Contracts should include the following:

- agreement for safety
- the adolescent's agreement to obtain enough food and sleep
- the adolescent's agreement to discard items that could be used in a suicide attempt (e.g., guns, weapons, medications)
- a specified time span for which the contract is in force
- the number of an after-hours crisis line so the adolescent has 24-hour access to help
- phone numbers of people to contact if the feeling of crisis escalates
- healthy ways the adolescent will structure their time (e.g., walks, talks, movies)

14. Organize suicide watches. If hospitalization is not readily available due to insurance issues or remote location, family and friends may take shifts staying with the adolescent until the crisis passes.

15. Refuse to allow the youth to return to school without an assessment by a mental health counselor, psychologist, psychiatrist, social worker, or other qualified mental health professional. Some fear that the assessment may alienate an adolescent, but it establishes that treatment is ongoing and that the school took the crisis seriously. (pp. 40–47)

All P–12 schools (and colleges also), hospitals, clinics, and agencies should have a written crisis management plan to deal with crisis situations such as suicide (see Case Study 9.2). The plan should identify key personnel (e.g., counselors, psychologists, social workers, nurses, physicians, principal, police). The treatment team at the school should regularly review the plan so that everyone knows their role. The plan should identify who is responsible for ensuring that crisis management is carried out. Just as schools have conducted drills for natural disasters such as tornadoes and hurricanes, they should practice their crisis management plan in simulated crisis situations. This provides school personnel the opportunity to refine and improve their potential response in the face of an actual crisis. With so many high-profile school suicides and school shooter tragedies in the past 20 years (e.g., Sandy Hook, Columbine High School, Jonesboro High School, and Paducah High School and also higher education, with tragedies at Northern Illinois University, University of Alabama Huntsville, and Virginia Tech), school, university, and hospitals and agency personnel must have a disaster management plan. Counselors and other trained school personnel must be facile in recognizing and checking out the warning signs for suicide and homicide and intervening before such plans are actualized. Because counselors will not be able to cover all possible eventualities, some suicides and, tragically, some homicides will occur, so colleges, schools, and community leaders must have a plan for managing crises.

Case Study 9.2 The Case of Jewel: Following a School Crisis Management Plan

Rachel is a school counselor at Riverdale High School, a school in a run-down section of the inner city. She is in her third year and has the respect of her colleagues and the students. One day, Jewel, a 17-year-old senior who has beaten many odds to become an honors student, comes into her office crying. Jewel tells Rachel her boyfriend has just broken up with her. She is very distraught and states, "I see my life crumbling!" She had planned to join her boyfriend, currently a freshman at a university 3 hours away, next fall. "He promised he'd never leave me," she says through tears. Complicating matters, Jewel was taken from her mother, a single parent, due to her mother's addiction, and she is currently living in foster care. She has never met her father and is not close to any other family. "Life isn't worth living!" Jewel sobs.

Rachel asks Jewel if she has thought of suicide, and Jewel admits she has. Rachel inquires how Jewel might harm herself, and Jewel opines she will swallow a bottle of aspirin and that she is considering doing this after school. Rachel explains to Jewel that she must confer with her supervisor and has Jewel wait with the secretary. Her supervisor explains the school policy of notifying the parent or guardian. The supervisor calls the foster mother while Rachel confers with Jewel back in the office. The foster mother comes to the campus and meets with Rachel and Jewel, and Jewel discloses she will not attempt suicide and mainly is angry at her boyfriend and wants to "strike back at that asshole!" Jewel's foster mother is insistent on taking Jewel to their pastor for spiritual guidance as opposed to a counselor. Rachel is concerned and expresses to the foster mother that Jewel could benefit from extended mental health counseling and a psychiatric evaluation. Jewel's foster mother becomes angry and exclaims, "We don't go to godless counselors. We pray!" Then, she leaves the school, taking Jewel with her.

- How well did Rachel and her supervisor handle the situation?
- If you were the supervisor, what would you have done?
- Regarding Jewel's well-being, what might be the next step?

After-Crisis Counseling

Fortunately, few clients will attempt suicide (Granello & Granello, 2007; Sommers-Flanagan & Sommers-Flanagan, 1999). Because clients who have previously contemplated or attempted suicide are vulnerable to further attempts (Sommers-Flanagan, 2007), you will need to lay therapeutic groundwork to help them work through difficult times without becoming suicidal again. A significant part of after-crisis counseling involves assisting clients in developing resilience (Beck et al., 1996; Parr et al., 1998). Purpose in life, strongly correlated with hopefulness and resilience, also appears to be an important construct for counselors to nurture in their clients and students (Hodges et al., 2014; Steger et al., 2006). Thus, what might help create a stronger sense of meaning and purpose for the client in crisis? My own anecdotal experience as a counselor suggests building healthier social connections will be a part of a client's well-being.

Developing and cultivating relationships and, thus, hope are not easy or simple matters, particularly for a client who feels beaten down by life's sometimes harsh experiences. Marketing hope to a client is scarcely as simple as getting a physician to prescribe antidepressant or antianxiety medication (Glasser, 2004). Nevertheless, I have outlined some questions to help you challenge clients' negative beliefs. Regardless, while medication may reduce depression and anxiety, it does nothing to promote skill development. Developing skills to combat depression and anxiety is an important tool for clients to develop. The following self-reflection exercises are structured to assist clients (or counselors) to see beyond their present difficulty and to entertain the belief that the difficult period is temporary and will pass. Suicidal clients tend to believe crisis periods are ongoing and will not improve, thus reinforcing a sense of hopelessness (Beck et al., 1999).

- What have you learned during this difficult period that will help you deal with stress, disappointment, or future trauma?

- In your opinion, what do you believe you most need to work through a difficult time?

- If a good friend of yours were to have attempted suicide or have contemplated suicide, what belief(s) would you want to see this friend change?

- What are your strengths? Cite three core strengths you possess. If you cannot come up with three, then ask close friends, trusted family members, coaches, ministers, teachers, or coworkers you respect.

- On a scale of 1 to 10, with 1 meaning *you have no hope in your life* and 10 meaning *you have a great sense of hope and meaning*, what score would you give yourself? If your score is, say, 1, what do you need to do to raise it to a 2 (if a 2, to raise it to a 3, and so forth)?

- Examine the various people in your life: family, friends, fellow students, coworkers, and members of a club or organization you are involved in. Now, find three people you admire in your various contacts. When you are ready, ask how they developed a sense of life's meaning and hope.

- How could you begin to develop self-confidence and hope in your own life? What steps could you begin to take? (*Note:* If you cannot think of specific steps, then ask close family, friends, or your counselor what steps they would like to see you take.)

- Having recently been through a crisis period in your life, what advice do you have for counselors, psychologists, the clergy, teachers, parents, and anyone else regarding how to be helpful to people in crisis? What could or should have been done that would have helped you?

- Consider the following questions for self-exploration: Who am I? Who do I want to be? How can I begin to become the person I desire to be? What strengths can you use to help you get there?

- Where does your sense of life's meaning or purpose come from? How could you strengthen your sense of life's meaning or purpose?

- On a scale of 1 to 10, how committed are you to making the changes that will promote your personal resilience and become the person you desire?

- Draw a picture of your present mood and circumstances. How does your picture look? Are the colors bright with hope or dark with despair? Now, draw a picture of how you would like your life to look. Compare the two pictures and ask yourself, "How can I begin to create my life to look more like the second drawing?"

- Imagine when you wake up tomorrow the issues and concerns that have burdened you have disappeared. What would be different about your life?

Clients in crisis or even in post-crisis recovery will need more than the aforementioned self-reflections. Counselors will need to teach clients to set limits with others, hold themselves accountable for their destructive behavior, and encourage and challenge them to change their self-talk, behavior, and so forth. Some clients will need medication, a healthier diet, friendships, meaningful work, and so forth. In short, it takes many things to prevent and develop resilience against suicide. Counseling students also would be wise to work with their supervisor to brainstorm additional suicide prevention strategies.

ASSESSING DANGER TO OTHERS

Like assessing suicide, predicting potential risk to third parties is not an exact science (Granello & Granello, 2007; Sommers-Flanagan & Sommers-Flanagan, 1999). There are numerous methods of prediction, which involve a multimodal approach. This section of the chapter gives an overview of practical tips for assessing difficult client situations you may encounter while on practicum and internship. As always, using the instincts you have honed through your counseling program, following the *ACA Code of Ethics*, consulting with your practicum or internship supervisor, and reading pertinent articles in relevant professional journals are all standard practices to follow.

The particular issues and challenges of your client and the circumstances with which they are struggling often dictate the types of interventions you will utilize. The guiding mantra in difficult cases, however, involves crafting a strong therapeutic alliance, as this is one of the most critical aspects of treatment (Duncan et al., 2009). The therapeutic alliance provides a sound relationship with the client that can make a positive difference during times of crisis. Although there have been many research studies on counseling over the past century, the following are some general guidelines that likely apply to all counseling situations:

- establishing a safe, secure space for counseling
- establishing the therapeutic alliance with the client

234 • THE COUNSELING PRACTICUM AND INTERNSHIP MANUAL

- helping the client to construct meaning in their life
- working with the client to instill hope in their life
- identifying the client's support systems: personal (optimistic attitude), familial, cultural, spiritual (if appropriate), and vocational
- assisting the client in developing a more balanced lifestyle (e.g., Myers et al. [2000] wheel of wellness)
- teaching more realistic, positive self-talk
- role-playing important issues in the session
- giving homework on the pertinent issues covered in counseling (e.g., assigning the client to make three new social contacts each week)
- promoting behavioral change

Assessing the Potential for Violence

Assessing a client's potential for violence should come in the intake portion of the interview. The intake interview should consist of assessment, client history, review of case records (e.g., medical records, psychiatric records, previous counseling records, incarceration), and the client interview. A few structured assessments are available for counselors to use in determining the risk level for violence. One of the more popular threat assessment instruments is the Structured Assessment of Violence Risk in Youth (SAVRY) that has 24 at-risk factors (e.g., history, social or contextual, individual), as well as an additional six protective factor items (Borum et al., 2002). Also, the Suicide Assessment Checklist (SAC; Rogers et al., 2002) and the SAD PERSONS Scale (Patterson et al., 1983) target adult clients. Acts of violence occur with more frequency than many in the profession appear to think. Some research suggests that around 20% of emergency department patients are violent and that 40% of psychiatrists are assaulted at least once in their careers (Tardiff, cited in Shea, 1998). It is also fair to say that certain client populations pose more risk than others. Residential psychiatric care, correctional facilities, and mandated counseling with domestic batterers are all examples of counseling situations that carry a greater potential for violence.

The following is a sample of questions counselors can use to determine the potential for violence:

- First and most importantly, does the client have a history of violence (e.g., bullying, cruelty to animals, domestic violence, or workplace violence)?
- Does the client make references to violence and see violence as a means to meet their needs?
- Does the client tend to get physically or verbally aggressive when abusing substances such as alcohol or other drugs?
- Does the client have a prevalence of violent ideation? Such clients may idealize violence and are likely more prone to commit acts of violence.

- Does the client have a history of mental illness? Although mental illness alone is not a predictor of violence, mental illness plus substance abuse can be a significant factor (Sudders, 2010).
- Does the client have a history of being the victim of violence? Clients who have been the victims are more likely to be perpetrators of violence.
- Does the client have a history of using physical and verbal violence to control people?
- Does the client have a documented history of cruelty to animals or bullying?
- Has the client made threats of violence to third parties?
- Does the client have access to weapons?
- Does the client belong to a social group that advocates and encourages violence?
- The highest level of threat appears to be characterized by the following:
  - It involves direct, plausible, and specific threats.
  - It poses imminent and serious danger to self and others.
  - Client implies specific steps have been taken toward violence (e.g., stalking and acquisition of a weapon; National Association of School Psychologists, n.d.).
  - Client has a documented history of violent acts.
  - Client is male (Federal Bureau of Investigation, n.d.).

While this research concerns school violence, the indicators are generalizable to community mental health situations.

Managing Risky Clients and Situations

You need to carefully monitor the case until the danger has passed. Monitoring activities should include follow-up with the police; the intended victim; the client; and other pertinent agencies such as parole, probation, child protection, and so forth.

The following are risk management suggestions for your agency or school:

- *Risk management tool kit:* Create a file or binder in which you keep all copies of relevant risk management materials, which include the following:
  - Ethical codes
    - Relevant code(s) of ethics: ACA, American School Counselor Association (ASCA), American Mental Health Counselors Association (AMHCA), CCPA, Singapore Association for Counseling, and others.
    - Ethical decision-making model (Corey et al., 2007)
  - Laws or statutes
    - Counselor licensure statute and rules: Know whether your state has a duty to warn based on a communicable threat. Does the law provide immunity for good faith acts?
    - Mandated reporting laws for vulnerable populations (e.g., minors, elderly, and adults with major disabilities)

- Civil/involuntary commitment to a psychiatric center (mental health and/or substance abuse)
- Health Insurance Portability and Accountability Act (HIPAA)
○ Subpoena checklist if a former client or anyone else subpoenas you regarding a legal matter
  - Consult an attorney (an agency, school, hospital, and others will have an attorney on retainer). State law and HIPAA may apply, depending upon the circumstances. Remember that state law may outweigh HIPAA if it is more protective of the client's privacy rights. If your attorney agrees, go on to Steps 2, 3, and 4.
  - Ascertain whether the client, after consulting their attorney, will provide you with written authorization to release information or to testify. If you maintain psychotherapy notes as defined by HIPAA, you must have a specific authorization form in order to release these notes. (If your state has specific protection for personal notes, you might not be required to release them, even with client authorization.)
  - If the opposing attorney declines to provide you with signed authorization from the client, request that the client's attorney then file a motion to quash the subpoena or a motion for a protective order.
  - If the preceding steps do not produce either your client's informed authorization or a court order, send a written notice to the attorney who issued the subpoena or had the court clerk issue it. This notice should be customized to the particular facts.
  - If you are subpoenaed to court or a deposition and the time is inconvenient or you will not be available, have your attorney contact the attorney who issued the subpoena. Assuming you have appropriately handled the privilege issue, it is often possible for the attorney to schedule you at a set date and time or put you "on call" in case you are not needed. Under instructions from your attorney, send a letter to the attorney who initiated the subpoena with language stating that in order to testify or release records or other protected health information, you must receive one of the following: (a) written, informed authorization from the client to release the information requested or (b) a court order to release the information or testify, as commanded by the subpoena. Remember, you are a HIPAA-covered entity and must follow HIPAA guidelines.
○ Attorney: List of local attorneys who have expertise in mental health and health law. Also, annually review these documents to ensure current familiarity, and update when/as appropriate. (Your school or agency likely has an attorney who represents them.)
- *Colleague consultation:* Two heads are better than one. Obtain colleague consultation when confronted with difficult counseling situations. To that end, identify colleagues for whom you have professional regard, and establish in advance the need of a reciprocal consultation relationship.

- Informed consent: Develop an informed consent process (written document, verbal explanation, and commitment to reviewing consent as circumstances change); be sure the process clearly defines confidentiality, privilege, and privacy guidelines, as well as limits and exceptions to confidentiality, privilege, and privacy, and make sure these are consistent with state laws and professional ethics.

- Institutional policies: Know the internal policies that regulate the practice of counseling in your school or agency. Adhere to these policies. If there are policies that are at odds with legal or ethical requirements, bring these to the attention of appropriate officers within the institution.

- Termination and abandonment: Avoid terminating a client who is in crisis. Otherwise, termination should be accomplished, when appropriate, after giving adequate notice and referrals. As "adequate" is not specifically defined, make sure you have documented the client's progress (or lack thereof), timeline for preparing the client for termination, and a clear rationale for why the client is being terminated or referred. The rationale should include consulting with your supervisor or a senior colleague.

- Document all clinical decision-making and the rationale behind each decision. In the school setting, policies on documentation and record keeping may differ from rules for private practice counselors.

- Obtain prior medical and behavioral history: Has the client acted out violently in the past? What were the circumstances? Was it premeditated? Does the client frequently make impulsive decisions? Is substance abuse an issue? Is the client delusional? Is there reason to believe the client is only discussing a fantasy, not a real threat?

- Manage co-occurring relationships: Co-occurring relationships (dual roles) must be effectively managed to prevent harm to clients. This is true regardless of whether the co-occurring relationship is a regular part of your job responsibilities (for example, school counselors who counsel students and also have other relationships) or evolve from unforeseeable circumstances or is an intentional or conscious choice. Be mindful of your state licensure board's position on boundary issues, as well as updated guidance in the *ACA Code of Ethics* (ACA, 2014) on roles and relationships with clients, supervisees, and others.

- Practice within your scope of competence: Recognize and respect the limitations of your competence; expand competence by securing the appropriate education, training, or supervision.

- Supervision: Supervisors and supervisees are at risk if supervision is not properly administered. Supervisors and supervisees should be mindful in the selection process to ensure a good fit (e.g., theoretical approach, supervision style, and availability of supervisor), clearly define the mutual expectations of both supervisor and supervisee monitor to ensure fulfillment of the expectations. If required, engage in regular supervision as defined by statute or policy.

- Professional liability insurance: Obtain and maintain professional liability insurance, preferably coverage that will provide attorney representation if a complaint is brought against you by the state licensure board, as well as attorney fees and settlement/damages resulting from a civil lawsuit.

238 • THE COUNSELING PRACTICUM AND INTERNSHIP MANUAL

- Inquire about the client's access to weapons, homicidal ideation, and current plans.
- Consider all appropriate responses and the consequences of each (e.g., warning the potential victim(s), calling the police, involving a psychiatrist, and hospitalizing the client). If clinically appropriate, involve the client in your decision-making. Do not reveal confidential information that is not necessary to protect potential victim(s). (Wheeler & Bertram, 2019, pp. 151–152)

Following such guidelines cannot guarantee a client will refrain from harming themselves or others or totally absolve a counselor from all liability should harm occur to the client or others. Regardless, following such a list certainly can help establish that the counselor is acting within the standard of care expected of professional counselors.

Tips for Managing Emotions and Behavior When Addressing a Suicide or Potential Suicide

The following list on self-regulation with crisis clients is based on my more than 2 decades of providing counseling, assessment, and crisis intervention. Naturally, this is not a comprehensive list, but these are some tips that have worked for me and others I have supervised:

- Remain calm when counseling or assessing a client in crisis. Remember, your demeanor can be a steadying influence on the client. Even if you do not feel calm, give the outward appearance thereof.
- Reassure the client that coming in to talk about the crisis was a positive step toward recovery.
- Remember to breathe in slow, deep breaths. This is a mindfulness-based technique. Slowed respiration inhibits racing thoughts (Lalande et al., 2016).
- Remember that hope (optimism) likely is the most important construct in suicide prevention (Beck et al., 1996). This is important both for the counselor and client.
- As per item 4 in this list, monitor and revise your self-talk to be optimistic, such as "My counseling interventions will be helpful for this client."
- Remember, you have an experienced supervisor for help and support.

A Few Additions to the Preceding Lists

As a longtime counselor and former director of counseling clinics, I would also make a few additions to the preceding lists:

- Maintain professional memberships for the duration of your professional life (e.g., ACA, ASCA, and AMHCA).
- Read professional articles that address suicide screening, risk factors, and prevention (e.g., in publications such as the *Journal of Counseling and Development, Professional School Counseling*, and the *Journal of Mental Health Counseling*).

- Attend regular relevant professional trainings on managing clients in crisis, either at a national, state, or local conference or through health providers.

- Be aware of any legal issues that complicate crisis situations, for example, the *Thapar v. Zezulka* (1999) decision in Texas, whereby counselors are prohibited from breaching confidentiality in a crisis situation.

CHILD ABUSE AND NEGLECT

As discussed in Chapter 4, "Ethical and Legal Issues," counselors are mandated reporters of suspected child abuse and neglect. The Child Welfare Information Gateway (2016) defines *physical abuse* and *neglect* as follows:

> *Physical Abuse:* Physical abuse is generally defined as "any nonaccidental physical injury to the child" and can include striking, kicking, burning, or biting the child, or any action that results in a physical impairment of the child. In approximately 38 States and American Samoa, Guam, the Northern Mariana Islands, Puerto Rico, and the Virgin Islands, the definition of abuse also includes acts or circumstances that threaten the child with harm or create a substantial risk of harm to the child's health or welfare. In seven States, the crime of human trafficking, including labor trafficking, involuntary servitude, or trafficking of minors, is included in the definition of child abuse.
>
> *Neglect:* Neglect is frequently defined as the failure of a parent or other person with responsibility for the child to provide needed food, clothing, shelter, medical care, or supervision to the degree that the child's health, safety, and well-being are threatened with harm. Approximately 25 states, the District of Columbia, American Samoa, Puerto Rico, and the Virgin Islands include failure to educate the child as required by law in their definition of neglect. Ten States and American Samoa specifically define medical neglect as failing to provide any special medical treatment or mental health care needed by the child. In addition, four States define medical neglect as the withholding of medical treatment or nutrition from disabled infants with life-threatening conditions. (p. 2)

Signs of potential physical abuse include the following:

- sudden changes in behavior or school performance
- appears very wary, as if anticipating danger or disruption
- seems overly compliant or overly responsible
- has unexplained bruises, burns, black eyes, and so forth
- seems frightened of their parents and uncomfortable when time to go home
- appears initially frightened at the approach of an adult
- reports injury by a parent or another caregiver

Signs of potential sexual abuse include the following:

- reports sexual abuse by parent or caregiver
- suddenly begins sexually acting out
- runs away or discloses they are considering running away
- displays unusual sexual knowledge or behavior
- complains of pains in the vaginal or anal area
- becomes pregnant or contracts a venereal disease

Signs of potential emotional abuse include the following:

- seems overly fearful at speaking up in class or in peer groups
- appears to isolate themselves when on the playground or during recess
- appears depressed and seems unattached to parents or family
- may display either overly compliant or acting-out behavior regarding disagreements with peers or authority figures

Some common signs of potential neglect may include:

- frequent absence from school
- often has no money for lunch or no lunch packed from home
- frequently has medical concerns such as ear infections, dental problems that go untreated, or is underweight
- often looks poorly groomed, disheveled, or dirty
- abuses alcohol or drugs
- discloses they are responsible for own care, despite being a minor

Reporting Child Abuse or Neglect

Counselors, like physicians, nurses, teachers, and other health and mental health professionals, are mandated reporters and must report cases where they believe child abuse or neglect is occurring (Remley & Herlihy, 2020). Counselors and other professionals must be trained in recognizing child abuse and neglect before being licensed to practice or prior to accepting educational and treatment jobs (Remley & Herlihy, 2020). Confidentiality must be breached in cases where the counselor believes there is reasonable cause to suspect abuse or neglect. All states and U.S. territories have "hold harmless" provisions that prevent mandated reporters from litigation when they report in good faith. Good faith means a professional (e.g., counselor, nurse, school psychologist, teacher, or physician) reports child abuse or neglect based on reasonable cause (e.g., the child has marks or unusual bruising, reports being excessively disciplined [whipped with a stick], parent has abandoned the child, or excessive absences with no parental support). Reporting from a lack of good faith standpoint would involve a professional filing a false report against a parent or guardian simply out of anger. A false report could result in suspension of a certification and licensure to potential incarceration.

Cases of abuse and neglect must be reported even when the minor does not want a report made against their parents or guardians (Remley & Herlihy, 2020). There may be numerous reasons why a child or adolescent would not want abuse or neglect reported, including the potential breakup of the family, fear of retribution by an abusive adult, fear of being removed from the home to the unknown (i.e., foster care), stigmatization by peers, and judgment that they snitched on family members. Counselors need to inform and prepare the child for all eventualities when they prepare to report suspected abuse or neglect. Extended counseling services are clearly in order, especially regarding victimization and displacement.

Beginning counselors should be aware of the "double-edged sword" regarding reporting child abuse and neglect. In some communities, child protection agencies may be perceived more as the villain than the alleged perpetrator because of a history of removing children from the home for perceived unfair reasons. Counselors may even find themselves under pressure from some authorities not to report some instances of abuse. Regardless of what administrators may see as "bad PR," counselors are mandated reporters and must report legitimate concerns regarding child welfare (ACA, 2014; Remley & Herlihy, 2020; Wheeler & Bertram, 2019). Furthermore, the child sexual abuse scandal that rocked Pennsylvania State University and sent shock waves through the country illustrates what can happen when administrators put reputation above the law.

CONCLUSION

Assessing and managing crisis situations are likely to be the most challenging part of your practicum and internship experience. Probably the most important thing to remember is that you do not have to go through the experience of crisis intervention alone. It is crucial that you involve your supervisor as soon as possible and discuss with your faculty advisor. Regardless of whether these issues are suicide prevention, counseling victims of trauma, or dealing with a child endangerment case, chances are very good that you will be helpful in providing resolution that will bring a reduction in stress level for the client.

LESSONS LEARNED

"So, you see, my life just is crashing around me…and I'm empty," said my thirty-something client, her dry eyes long past the watering stage. I shall refer to her as Sylvia (pseudonym). Sylvia was a recently divorced woman sharing custody with her ex-spouse. Evidently, her ex-spouse had reconnected with a former lover and commenced an affair that resulted in him leaving the marriage, leaving Sylvia devastated. Depressed and feeling hopeless, she has disclosed to a close friend about having a suicide plan. Naturally alarmed, the friend had driven her to the clinic, whereupon she was brought to my office.

Sylvia was a well-educated woman who earned a good salary as a financial manager. She had met her spouse several years earlier while at a regional conference. They dated for a couple years and then married. Soon thereafter, a daughter arrived. Sylvia reported that her spouse became distant about a year after their daughter was born. "He just wasn't present anymore," she stated. She reported trying to engage him in conversation regarding the change, but he insisted nothing was wrong. Finally, she suggested marriage counseling and was happy he agreed. During the first session, however, he disclosed he had been having an affair with a former partner and now wanted a divorce. "I don't love you anymore," he had explained. Devastated, Sylvia reported "sleepwalking" through the next few weeks and, thereafter, becoming depressed and finally planning suicide.

Sylvia's situation was nothing new to me, having heard many such clients disclose a divorce or a similar ending having precipitated a crisis. What made her memorable is a bit difficult to explain. She informed me she had always been a positive-oriented person. Typically, she was the one friends told their troubles to during difficult times. During her undergraduate years, she has minored in psychology and served as a resident advisor (RA) in a university residence hall. She had sought out training in peer helping and reported others appeared to find her a "good listener." She had even served on the board of a Big Brothers Big Sisters mentoring program, something she referred to as previously fulfilling. Currently in the throes of crisis, however, she reported nothing was fulfilling. "I just want to die," she said.

A long experience with crisis clients has taught me not to confront crisis clients directly with reasons for living or dying. Rather, my approach is to be present and establish a relationship before anything else. Naturally, establishing safety comes quickly on the heels of the therapeutic alliance. Having established she had an active plan, I facilitated overnight hospitalization. As her daughter was with Sylvia's ex-spouse, there was not a current child endangerment situation. She agreed to hospitalization and the authorities transported her to the hospital. Thinking she might remain there for a couple of days, I was surprised when she returned to the clinic the following afternoon. (As she had been a voluntary patient, she could leave the hospital anytime.) She requested me, and we commenced counseling.

Having been strongly influenced by Viktor Frankl's philosophy of meaning in life, my approach was to find a way for the client to regain that sense of purpose. Every client I have counseled, from grade-schoolers to the elder, has informed me that their life had become less meaningful, albeit few use the term *meaning*, but couch it in terms of sadness, depression, addiction, acting out in various ways, and even suicidal thoughts and behavior. On a related note, Nietzsche wrote of those with a *why* able to endure almost any *how*. Basically, counseling, especially with suicidal clients, is about helping them identify a *how*. While still very hurt, Sylvia seemed a little more energetic than the previous day. Likely, this was due to actively seeking help. So, I asked her, "What would be your reasons for staying alive?" I recall her eyes widened at my question, and she hesitated and finally mentioned seeing her daughter grow up.

While we unpacked her relationship with her daughter, my sense was she remained labile. I asked what she would need in order to keep living. She took a long pause and finally replied, "I don't know." Using my whiteboard, I had her list reasons for living and for dying. The living list was far longer (her daughter, family, friends, seeing grandkids, etc.), but I remained unconvinced. She denied an active suicide plan and said that had passed, thus why the hospital discharged her. Nearing the end of session, I asked where her life's sense of purpose had previously come from. She replied it had come from feeling she had a clear purpose of raising her daughter, having a happy marriage, and being successful in her career. Acknowledging her marital state, I inquired how she viewed her parenting and career. She stated she felt she had been a good parent and was very successful in her career. Clearly, these two realms of her life were not enough, at least at present. I suggested we examine her marriage and its beginning and ending, as my experience has been that grief is healthy and that divorce is a type of grief.

She had informed me that drawing was a hobby and that she had been talented at it from a young age, winning several awards even through college years. I assigned her to draw two pictures: one displaying her life currently and a second depicting where she would like to be in 6 months. She appeared reluctant but, with encouragement, agreed to the drawings. I further suggested she bring in the drawings so we could discuss them. The following session, her affect appeared slightly improved. She brought in the drawings, and while her skill was not the purpose for the exercise, she clearly was talented, having drawn excellent representations of her, close family and friends, nature, and others. I requested she explain them to me. She took me through the first drawing, which evidenced dark images: her likeness appearing withdrawn; her ex-spouse with his back turned and walking away; and her daughter in the corner looking concerned, with toys, books, and other belongings strewn about the floor. In the second drawing, far more light was evident, and drawings of her daughter, parents, and a couple of friends looking happy were evident. Her home space looked clear and well organized, and there was a drawing of her playing happily with her daughter. I asked her to explain these two drawings. Her explanation mirrored my own thoughts. Being bright, she offered, "So, this is about me recreating my life to look more like drawing number two." I agreed and suggested, "So, perhaps your, purpose is working to transition from drawing one to drawing two." She gave a wistful smile.

We would spend a dozen sessions together, with Sylvia completing weekly drawings of her improvement, ranging from incremental to finally a graduation drawing of her and her daughter holding hands and stepping out into a beautiful sunny day. I inquired what had been most important in her grief transition. She replied immediately that it was her weekly drawings. "They gave me a focus and outlet to work with my grief and anger." She went on to say drawing was her grounding. "So, your drawing is your why," I replied. She nodded. "Yes, I now know my why. It keeps me happier, makes me a better parent, and helps me address life challenges." She offered me her final drawing, but I suggested she keep it and perhaps give it to her daughter one day. She exited therapy not fixed, not totally healed, and not without more healing but as someone who was steady on her own metaphorical balance and who had a clear sense of meaning and purpose.

The lesson Sylvia's case reinforced in me is that counseling is, to a great extent, about helping clients and patients discover their why. As Nietzsche wrote, the why comes before any how, meaning that focusing on helping the client discover, cultivate, or reengage with meaning and purpose (the whys) is essential for therapeutic success. For clients like Sylvia, finding their why likely is the difference between life and death. So, future counselors, find your why. Then, go and help your clients, patients, students, and others find theirs.

RECOMMENDED RESOURCES FOR SUICIDE PREVENTION

Capuzzi, D. (2006). *Suicide across the lifespan: Implications for counselors.* American Counseling Association.
Granello, D. H., & Juhnke, G. A. (2010). *Case studies in suicide: Experiences of mental health professionals.* Merrill.
McGlothin, J. M. (2009). *Developing clinical skills in suicide assessment.* American Counseling Association.
Westefeld, J. S. (2009). *Suicide assessment and prevention* [DVD]. Microtraining Associates.

ORGANIZATIONS FOR THE PREVENTION OF SUICIDE

Because suicide prevention tends to be the most common type of crisis situations counselors encounter, here is a short list of organizations that provide education for counselors and others:

American Association of Suicidology (www.suicidology.org) provides information to counselors, schools, colleges, and so forth.
American Foundation for Suicide Prevention (www.afsp.org) provides research and information to professionals and nonprofessionals.
International Association for Suicide Prevention (www.iasp.info) provides information for a broad forum of academics, practitioners, and suicide survivors.
Jed Foundation (www.jedfoundation.org) supports mental health and suicide prevention of college and university students.
National Organization for People of Color Against Suicide (www.nopcas.com) provides support to persons of color to assist in suicide prevention.
Suicide and Mental Health Association International (www.suicideandmentalhealthassociationinternational.org) is dedicated to preventing suicide and related mental health issues.
Youth Suicide School-Based Prevention Guide (theguide.fmhi.usf.edu) provides accurate and user-friendly information.

SUICIDE HOTLINES

Note: Remember, the new national suicide prevention hotline is 988 (text, SMS, 988). Most communities also have a regular crisis line, and all counselors should know this number and make it available to clients. In addition, here are other resources:

Eldercare Locator, a public service of the U.S. Administration on Aging. Call for potential elder abuse situations that are dangerous, threatening, or serious. (**1-800-677-1116**). (Monday to Friday, 9:00 a.m. to 8:00 p.m. Eastern time)
GLBT National Help Center: 1-888-843-4564. (Monday through Friday 1:00 p.m. to 9:00 p.m. Pacific time, Monday through Friday 4:00 p.m. to midnight, Eastern time; Saturday 9:00 a.m. to 2:00 p.m. Pacific time, noon to 5:00 p.m., Eastern time)
National Sexual Assault Online Hotline: 1-800-656-HOPE (4673) (24 hours a day, 7 days a week)
National Suicide Prevention Lifeline: 1-800-273-8255 (24 hours a day, 7 days a week, in English and Spanish)
TEEN LINE: 1-800-852-8336. (The line is open nightly from 6:00 p.m. to 10:00 p.m. Pacific time.)
Veterans Crisis Line: 1-800-273-8255 (press 1) (24 hours a day, 7 days a week, 365 days a year). Confidential services or text to 838255

A robust set of instructor resources designed to supplement this text is located at http://connect.springerpub.com/content/book/978-0-8261-6607-4. Qualifying instructors may request access by emailing **textbook@springerpub.com**.

REFERENCES

American Counseling Association. (2014). *ACA code of ethics*. https://www.counseling.org/resources/aca-code-of-ethics.pdf

American Foundation for Suicide Prevention. (2013). *Preventing suicide*. https://afsp.org

Beck, A. T., Brown, G. K., Steer, R. A., Dahlsgaard, K., & Grisham, J. R. (1999). Suicide ideation at its worst point: A predictor of eventual suicide in psychiatric outpatients. *Suicide & Life-Threatening Behavior, 29*, 1–9. https://doi.org/10.1111/j.1943-278X.1999.tb00758.x

Beck, A. T., Steer, R. A., & Brown, G. K. (1996). *Manual for Beck Depression Inventory-II*. The Psychological Corporation.

Borum, R., Bartel, P. A., & Forth, A. (2002). *SAVRY: Structured assessment of violence risk in youth*. Psychological Assessment Resources.

Boynton v. Burglass, 590 So.2d 446 (Fla. Dist. Ct. App. 1991).

Captain, C. (2006). Is your patient a suicide risk? *Nursing, 36*(8), 43–47. https://doi.org/10.1097/00152193-200608000-00039

Capuzzi, D. (2009). *Suicide prevention in the schools: Guidelines for middle and high school settings* (2nd ed.). American Counseling Association.

Capuzzi, D., & Gross, D. R. (2008). *Youth at risk: A prevention resource for counselors, teachers, and parents* (5th ed.). American Counseling Association.

Child Welfare Information Gateway. (2016). *Definitions of child abuse and neglect*. U.S. Department of Health and Human Services, Children's Bureau. https://www.childwelfare.gov/pubPDFs/define.pdf

Corey, G., Corey, M. S., & Callanan, P. (2007). *Issues and ethics in the helping professions* (7th ed.). Thomson Brooks/Cole.

Duncan, B., Miller, S. D., Wampold, B., & Hubble, M. (2009). *The heart and soul of change: Delivering what works in therapy* (2nd ed.). American Psychological Association.

Federal Bureau of Investigation. (n.d.). *The school shooter: A threat assessment perspective*. Critical Incident Response Group. National Center for the Analysis of Violent Crime.

Fla. Stat. 491.0147 (2018).

Frankl, V. (1969). *Psychotherapy and existentialism: Selected papers on logotherapy*. Simon & Schuster.

Glasser, W. H. (2004). *Warning: Psychiatry can be hazardous to your health*. American Counseling Association.

Granello, D. H., & Granello, P. F. (2007). *Suicide: An essential guide for helping professionals and educators*. New Pearson/Allyn & Bacon.

Hodges, S., Denig, S., & Crowe, A. (2014). Attitudes of college students towards purpose in life and self-esteem. *International Journal of Existential Psychology & Psychotherapy, 5*, 124–131.

International Society for the Study of Self-Injury. (n.d.). *What is nonsuicidal self-injury?* https://www.itriples.org/what-is-nssi

Juhnke, G. (1996). The Adapted SAD PERSONS: A suicide assessment scale designed for use with children. *Elementary School Guidance & Counseling, 30*, 252–258. https://www.jstor.org/stable/42871225

Lalande, L., King, R., Bambling, M., & Schweitzer, R. D. (2016). Guided respiration mindfulness therapy: Development and evaluation of a brief therapist training program. *Journal of Contemporary Psychotherapy, 46*(2), 107–116. https://doi.org/10.1007/s10879-015-9320-5

McGlothen, J. M., Rainey, S., & Kindsvatter, A. (2005). Suicidal clients and supervisees: A model for considering supervisor roles. *Counselor Education and Supervision, 45*, 135–146. https://doi.org/10.1002/j.1556-6978.2005.tb00136.x

Moore, K. (2010, February 3). Residents demand answers after S. Hadley bullying death. *The Boston Globe*, B3. http://archive.boston.com/news/education/k_12/articles/2010/02/03/residents_demand_answers_after_s_hadley_bullying_death/

Myers, J. E., Sweeney, T. J., & Witmer, J. M. (2000). The Wheel of Wellness counseling for wellness: A holistic model for treatment planning. *Journal of Counseling & Development, 78*(3), 251–266. https://doi.org/10.1002/j.1556-6676.2000.tb01906.x

National Association of School Psychologists. (n.d.). *Threat assessment: Predicting and preventing school violence*. https://www.nasponline.org/resources-and-publications/resources-and-podcasts/school-climate-safety-and-crisis/school-violence-resources/school-violence-prevention

Parr, G. D., Montgomery, M., & DeBell, C. (1998). Flow theory as a model for enhancing student resilience. *Professional School Counseling, 1*(5), 26–31. https://www.jstor.org/stable/pdf/42731866

Patterson, W. M., Dohn, H. H., Bird, J., & Patterson, G. A. (1983). Evaluation of suicidal patients: The SAD PERSONS scale. *Psychosomatics, 24*(4), 343–349. https://doi.org/10.1016/S0033-3182(83)73213-5

Posner, K., Brown, G. K., Stanley, B., Brent, D. A., Yeshiva, K. V., Oquendo, M. A., & Mann, J. J. (2011). The Columbia suicide severity rating scale: Initial validity and internal consistency findings from three multisite studies with adolescents and adults. *American Journal of Psychiatry, 168*(12), 1266–1277. https://doi.org/10.1176/appi.aip2011.10111704

Remley, T. P., Jr., & Herlihy, B. (2020). *Ethical, legal and professional issues in counseling* (6th ed.). Upper Pearson.

Rogers, J. R., Lewis, M. M., & Subich, L. M. (2002). Validity of the Suicide Assessment Checklist in an emergency crisis center. *Journal of Counseling and Development, 80*, 493–502. https://doi.org/10.1002/j.1556-6678.2002.tb00216.x

Shea, S. C. (1998). *Psychiatric interviewing: The art of understanding: A practical guide for psychiatrists, psychologists, counselors, social workers, nurses, and other mental health professionals* (2nd ed.). Saunders.

Sommers-Flanagan, J. (2007). The development and evolution of person-centered expressive art therapy: A conversation with Natalie Rogers. *Journal of Counseling and Development, 85*, 120–125. https://doi.org/10.1002/j.1556-6678.2007.tb00454.x

Sommers-Flanagan, R. S., & Sommers-Flanagan, J. S. (1999). *Clinical interviewing* (2nd ed.). Wiley.

Steger, M. F., Frazier, P., Oishi, S., & Kaler, M. (2006). The Meaning in Life Questionnaire: Assessing the presence of and search for meaning in life. *Journal of Counseling Psychology, 53*(1), 80–93. https://doi.org/10.1037/0022-0167.53.1.80

Sudders, M. (2010, January 27). Kerrigan family faced dilemma with their adult son. *The Boston Globe*, B6.

Tarasoff v. The Regents of the University of California, 13 Cal. 3d 177, 529 P.2d 533 (1976).

Tex. Health & Safety Code 611.004 (2017).

Thapar v. Zezulka, 994 S.W.2nd 635 (Tex. 1999).

Wheeler, A. M., & Bertram, B. (2019). *The counselor and the law: A guide to legal and ethical practice* (8th ed.). American Counseling Association.

Whitlock, J. (2009, December). The cutting edge: Non-suicidal self-injury in adolescence. *Research Facts and Findings*. ACT for Youth Center of Excellence. http://www.selfinjury.bctr.cornell.edu/publications/2009_1.pdf

Zdziarski, E. L. II, Dunkel, R. W., Rollo, J. M., & Associates. (2007). *Campus crisis management: A comprehensive guide to planning, prevention, response, and recovery*. Jossey-Bass.

CHAPTER 10

Ensuring Safety on Practicum and Internship

INTRODUCTION

Amid all the excitement of beginning practicum and internship, where many counseling students encounter their first actual clients, one must, of necessity, consider the nature of the counseling relationship. Many students are idealistic and likely attracted to the profession due to the helping nature of the field. Thus, it would be no stretch to say counseling students and professional counselors are idealistic with regard to philosophical orientation. While idealism clearly holds an important place in the counseling profession, it must, of necessity, be grounded in realism. Many clients, particularly those in mandated situations involving domestic violence, those who are incarcerated, students in overcrowded inner-city schools, and some mentally ill populations, are at greater risk for violence. Therefore, counseling programs must be prepared to discuss the safety of practicum and intern students on placement. Many schools and agencies do a very good job of creating safety plans for students, clients, and staff, though it is accurate to state some do not. This brief chapter covers some of the basics regarding safety on the practicum and internship. Naturally, no given placement, no matter how conscientious or well staffed, can absolutely guarantee an intern's safety. (Absolute safety in life is of course a myth.) While accurate statistics are challenging to find in the literature, the Centers for Disease Control and Prevention (CDC) cites the following statistics regarding workplace violence: 73% of women, 62% of workers aged 25 to 54, and 76% of healthcare employees all experienced workplace violence, with 22% missing 3 to 5 days of work and another 22% missing over a month recovering from workplace violence (CDC, 2020). Field experience likely will be a safe experience, but students need to be aware of safety plans and protocols while on practicum and internship.

The risks of encountering violence during your practicum/internship vary considerably depending on the nature of your setting and the population you counsel. A practicum in an elementary school, for example, is likely to be considerably less risky than interning in a maximum security prison or inpatient psychiatric facility. As we can regularly see in the media, schools and agency settings carry with them the potential risk for violence. Therefore, all students should be prepared to deal with violence and the aftermath of potential physical and psychological symptoms of violence. In illustrating this important issue, I will step back a few decades in time.

My first job after completing my master's degree was in a large residential psychiatric center that provided long-term treatment for children and adolescents between the ages of 8 and 19. As the unit I worked in was composed of children roughly aged 10 to 13, I felt secure regarding my physical safety. After all, I was considerably larger and physically stronger than the residents. In the first 5 months of employment, however, I was assaulted twice (though not seriously). A short time later, however, I was threatened by a large male with a broken bottle. This patient had a history of violence and the encounter definitely was traumatic. Thankfully, I had a good relationship with this patient and was able to assist him to de-escalate. Nothing in my graduate counseling program, however, had prepared me to deal with client violence directed toward me. After all, I was a counselor and counselors are "nice" people, so naturally no one would want to hurt us, right? Being threatened and physically attacked served as a "slap" of reality. Fortunately, most counselors will complete their practicum and internship experience without any danger to their physical and psychological safety. Still, the potential for violence toward the clinician must be accounted for in counselor education programs as well as when out on the job as a professional counselor.

Studies of violence against mental health professionals have yielded varying estimates on the potential that a counselor or other therapists will be assaulted (Baird, 2005). Work conducted by Tully et al. (1993) and Reeser and Wertkin (2001) are among the few in the field to have studied violence against mental health professionals. Thackery and Bobbit (1990) reported that, among the participants in a regional conference, 59% of clinical staff and 28% of non clinical staff indicated they had been attacked at least once. Pope and Vasquez (2016) reported almost one in five psychologists reported having been physically attacked by a client and more than 80% reported being fearful a client would assault them. Other potentially dangerous and intimidating behaviors have also been reported in the mental health profession. Romans et al. (1996) reported that, out of a sample of 178 counseling staff, roughly 6% reported being stalked and 10% had a supervisee who had been stalked. Some suggest that violence may be underreported in the field and that therapists are likely to face assault at some point in their careers (Tully et al., 1993; Whitman et al., 1976). A survey of more than 200 doctoral students in psychology found students rated their training in managing potentially violent clients as less than adequate (Gately & Stabb, 2005). Clearly, violence against counselors and other therapists would appear as an important area of research. Likewise, more suggestions on how counselors can remain safe during internship and during their professional years would seem of paramount importance.

These studies should not be taken to mean that most clients are dangerous. In fact, most clients do not pose a significant risk to assault, stalk, harass, or threaten counselors. The studies do suggest there is some inherent risk over a long career. It would also be worth mentioning that driving an automobile over the course of a lifetime is also somewhat risky, yet few people cease driving because of the risks involved. Still, the potential of assault is real and counseling programs must prepare students to deal with it. In this chapter, we explore various ways you might identify, defuse, or deal with violence during your practicum/internship.

Case Study 10.1 The Case of Ramona

Ramona is a graduate student who has just begun practicum at an urban clinic that provides mental health and addictions counseling and runs a day treatment program for chronically mentally ill adults. During her weekly practicum class at the university, while discussing the book chapter on safety and risk assessment, she realizes she does not know the agency's safety plan. Her professor encourages her to speak with her field site supervisor at the agency. The following day, Ramona asks her supervisor about the agency's safety plan but is rebuffed by her supervisor, who expresses, "Just hit the red button on the side of your phone. Someone will come to assist." Ramona is uncomfortable with her supervisor's cavalier attitude regarding her safety and that of others.

Should Ramona taker her supervisor's advice? Or, would you advise her to follow up on this matter? What further action might you suggest she take?

PREDICTORS OF CLIENT VIOLENCE

Kinney (1995) cites several risk factors as rough predictors to use in assessing the potential for a person to commit workplace violence. These, I think, are useful to keep in mind when dealing with clients in your practicum/internship setting:

- emotionally disturbed status
- extreme stress in personal life circumstances and/or job
- substance use or abuse
- frequent disputes with supervisors or authority figures
- routine violation of company/agency/school policy or rules
- sexual and other harassment/bullying of coworkers or peers
- threats of violence, either verbal or written (including electronic communication)
- preoccupation with weapons and violence
- an isolated person with a minimal support system (p. 25)

There are other factors you should keep in mind that may help you identify a potentially violent client:

A history of violent behavior: A fundamental tenet in the therapeutic world is that the best predictor of future behavior is previous behavior. If a client has a history of violence, it is wise to understand the circumstances that facilitated the client's violence (e.g., a history of violence toward women and bullying others). Other factors to recognize are the triggers of violence, such as stress, alcohol, drugs, confrontation, and so forth.

A history of victimization: Many perpetrators of violence are themselves victims of violence. Most victims of violence will not become violent themselves

(Granello & Granello, 2007). However, some victims learn that violence is a viable method of controlling others and resolving conflicts. Does the client have a history of sexual, verbal, or physical abuse? Some traumatized clients may be more prone to perceiving potential threats and striking out against those they consider a viable threat (Granello & Granello, 2007). No doubt, traumatized clients with posttraumatic stress disorder (PTSD) who are stuck in the fight, flight, or freeze response—especially those who fight—are more prone to lashing out with violence when triggered (van der Kolk, 2015).

Substance use and abuse: The use of alcohol and drugs plays a major role in precipitating violence (Beck et al., 1992). In most therapeutic settings, clients will not be under the influence of alcohol or drugs. However, counselors will frequently work with clients who, when under the influence of a chemical substance, become impaired in judgment; their internal controls break down, and they become aggressive.

Going off of psychopharmacologic medications against medical advice: The use of medications in mental health therapy has a long and controversial history. There is little doubt, however, that medication, if properly used, can aid in counseling work. A significant concern is clients who suddenly cease taking their medications. This is particularly problematic for clients taking antipsychotic drugs to help manage their delusions and hallucinations and potentially violent behavior. If you are counseling clients who have been prescribed antipsychotics, you need to monitor their behavior carefully. Have aggressive incidents suddenly increased? If so, a critical question to ask such a client is "Have you recently gone off your medications?" Chronically mentally ill clients who go off medication against medical advice will begin to decompensate, typically resulting in risk to themselves and potentially others.

Although psychoactive medications usually reduce the risk of violence, there is some evidence that certain medications may actually increase the propensity for violence (Baird, 2005). Haller and Deluty (1990) reported a significant relationship between antipsychotic medication and violent attacks on psychiatric staff. An important footnote here is that it seems the patients reacting with violence appear to be a minority.

Access to weapons: A big factor in assessing violence potential involves the client's access to weapons. In inpatient settings, the risk of handguns is minimized, although makeshift weapons (e.g., scissors, broken glass, and other sharp instruments) are a concern. Even when staff has carefully screened a patient or client for weapons, swinging fists and legs, headbutting, and the like can become a risk.

One colleague of mine was counseling an estranged husband who was upset with his wife's decision to file for divorce. The client admitted to the counselor that he had a plan to shoot his ex. After being informed by the counselor that the police would need to be notified to detain him and take charge of the weapon, the client seemed calm. He replied, "That's why I brought this in," and reached into his coat, took out a loaded handgun, and handed it over to the astonished counselor! Although this situation ended peacefully, it illustrates the potential risk inherent in counseling work. The potential for violence, though usually small, is always present. Any perusal of the media will reveal a regular, ongoing spate of mass violence, usually shooting sprees. Mass gun violence has become disturbingly common in society with no end in sight, given handguns and assault weapons ubiquity.

Stress: Stress is frequently the catalyst for behavioral regression (Beck et al., 1992), and clients under a good deal of pressure should be viewed with caution, particularly if they do have a history of violence.

Ability to regulate emotions and manage behavior: Clearly, some clients are able to regulate their emotions and manage their behavior and make healthier choices than others (Goldstein, 1999). Several factors impact a client's ability to regulate emotions and manage behavior. Mental disorders or neurological conditions, for example, may impair a client's judgment, especially under stress. Substance use or abuse will also impair a client's ability to manage their behavior. Clients with violent ideation who see violence as a means of justification (i.e., "might makes right") are less likely to regulate their emotions and more likely to use violence (Goldstein, 1999). Anecdotally, I have noticed school bullies and men who batter are particularly likely to fall into the category of those unlikely to regulate emotions and thus have difficulty managing behavior without violent means.

Medication noncompliance: Clients who have gone off medication, or who have been inconsistently medicated, may not be able to respond to reason from staff. Some mental illnesses (such as some types of schizophrenia) can manifest in intense paranoia, and any attempt to dialogue with clients in this state is likely to be counterproductive. Sadly, clients who cannot manage their behavior may need to be restrained by the staff. Needless to say, graduate students should not be involved with physically restraining clients unless the health and safety of themselves, staff, or other patients dictate such a response.

Prejudices regarding other cultural, ethnic, or religious groups of people: Clearly, some persons in society harbor extreme prejudice against those culturally different. The last several years have born witness to unarmed African Americans shot or killed in various ways by police, Asian people harassed and attacked, and immigrants targeted by hate speech. Be aware of a client's violent speech regarding particular groups of people (e.g., immigrants, women, Jews, and Muslims). Most hate talk is just that (bad enough!), but be aware it may be more than mere hate speech (itself a concern). Of course, any type of hate should be an issue in counseling. LGBTQ persons are particularly prone to targeted acts of violence in schools, colleges, and in the workplace, especially in the wake of anti-LGBTQ+ legislation (Santoro, 2022). Needless to say, hate rhetoric and discriminatory legislation have negatively impacted LGBTQ+ people's mental health (News, 2023).

Identifying Children or Adolescents at Risk for Violent Behavior

The following checklist of early warning signs can serve as a practical technique for counselors in schools and other settings to use when assessing the potential for violence among children or adolescents. Although this is not a comprehensive list, it provides basic information for violence prevention toward self and others:

- expresses self-destructive or homicidal ideation
- expresses feelings of hopelessness
- has a history of self-destructive behavior
- begins giving away formerly valued possessions
- appears withdrawn from peers
- engages in bullying peers or cruelty to animals
- has significant changes in mood
- has difficulty with impulse control or regulating emotions
- experiences difficulty sleeping and has significant changes in appetite
- has evidence of significant behavioral change
- has a history of trauma and tragedy
- engages in substance abuse
- has been a victim of child abuse
- has become involved in a gang
- has experienced a significant loss
- has been tormented or teased by others
- preoccupied with fighting or violence
- preoccupied with violent TV shows, movies, DVD games, and so forth
- has a history of antisocial behavior
- has a history of being violent (American Academy of Experts in Traumatic Stress, 2010)

DEALING WITH AGGRESSIVE BEHAVIORS

Workplace violence has become increasingly prevalent in American society. The National Institute for Occupational Safety and Health (NIOSH, 1996) estimated that over 2 million acts of violence occur in the workplace each year. Dealing with the possibility of client assault involves recognizing risks and learning how to de-escalate potentially dangerous situations before they become violent. Prevention is the best measure: When you accept a practicum or internship placement, it is wise to inquire about and become familiar with the safety plan. If the school, agency, or hospital does not have one, you should be concerned and speak with your site supervisor and advisor in the counseling program. Given gratuitous acts of violence over the past few decades (e.g., Columbine High School, Sandy Hook Elementary, and Virginia Tech

University, among numerous other shootings), all workplaces need a safety plan. If you have reason to believe a client is likely to harm you, a coworker, or anyone else, you must discuss the potential threat with your supervisor immediately. Do not try to deal with a potentially dangerous situation alone. The U.S. Secret Service and U.S. Department of Education's (2002) key finding was that there is no accurate profile of students who engage in targeted school violence, and it is likely that such is the case with adolescents and adults in treatment. Regardless, keep in mind a few basic factors:

- Unusual behavior (e.g., speaking to oneself and hallucinations) may be unsettling but usually does not necessarily indicate violent or dangerous behavior. (Keep in mind that non-mental health professionals will likely feel more threatened by "unusual" behavior and may want counselors and other mental health professionals to have such people committed. Remember: Unusual behavior is not necessarily a predictor of violent behavior, nor is it necessarily grounds for hospitalization.)

- Developing good relationships with clients may be a good way to lessen the risk of violence. In fact, the stronger your relationship is with a client/student/inmate, the more likely it is that you will be able to de-escalate a potentially violent situation. On this, I speak from experience.

- Be aware of a client's issues so that you may notice signs of aggression and intervene before violence occurs. Particularly pay attention to a client's articulation of violence, as that may be an issue to address.

- In residential placements, be aware of bullying and how it may precipitate violence among peers. When you witness bullying, immediate intervention is necessary.

- Be aware that developmental issues may determine the seriousness of potential violence. A 6-year-old who makes a vague threat to "get you!" obviously does not carry the same level of seriousness as a 35-year-old male prison inmate making a specific threat. Regardless, take all threats seriously and follow up on the threat through the established channels (e.g., agency and legal).

- However, notwithstanding the previous point, take all verbal threats seriously. Report them immediately to a supervisor or a colleague.

- Know the violence prevention plan and the response to violence plan at your practicum/internship.

- If your practicum or internship placement offers safety training, it is strongly suggested that you take it.

- Do not attempt to intervene alone. Although numerous strategies go into preventing and dealing appropriately with violence, a common first response is for staff to make a show of numbers; in some places that I have worked, the first response to any potentially violent situation was for all available staff to converge on the scene. Even very agitated patients may become compliant in the face of a large number of staff. Certainly, never approach a potentially violent client or patient on your own.

- Conduct yourself in a calm, confident manner with clients even when you do not feel that way. This statement is not anything against Rogers's (1980) core condition of genuineness, nor is it about arrogance. Rather, if you look and sound more confident, others will have more confidence in you and you are less likely to be a victim.

254 • THE COUNSELING PRACTICUM AND INTERNSHIP MANUAL

- Learn basic self-defense techniques: Size matters in physical altercations. Nevertheless, professional training in self-defense may provide a small window to slow down an assailant, providing the counselor an opportunity to flee for safety.

- Remove potential weapons from your office: Do not have anything that could be turned into a weapon, such as a letter opener, scissors, paperweight, or other heavy object. Scissors and letter openers should be locked in drawers if kept in an office.

DEFUSING VIOLENCE

People use violence for various reasons. For most, violence occurs when an individual perceives a threat and responds out of fear. Fortunately, most people are not violent when they are afraid. *The Gift of Fear: Survival Signals That Protect Us From Violence* (DeBecker, 1997) says people who use violence can be understood by considering their justifications, alternatives, consequences, and abilities. Someone using violence feels justified doing so, sees few alternatives, is willing to accept the consequences, and has the ability (e.g., physical and, mental) to unleash violence (DeBecker, 1997). Many violent people carry a history of violence, either as victim or perpetrator, and act out in violent ways because it may be their normal (Levers, 2022).

However, most people who get angry do not become violent (thankfully!). People who successfully manage their anger will see more viable, constructive options instead of violence. For example, preferable options other than violence might be:

- attempting to use reason to defuse a tense encounter
- suggesting a mediator to negotiate a settlement
- walking away from the encounter to "cool off"
- consulting with a colleague to debrief and generate options to resolve the conflict

When someone is angry and potentially violent, it is helpful to try to determine why they are angry. Using a calm tone, you might ask, "I can see you are upset. What has led to your being so upset?" You want to send the message that you acknowledge the individual's anger and wish to understand it. Approaching the client from the standpoint of reason and understanding is likely the best chance of defusing a potentially violent situation. If the client's hostility level decreases, you may be able to reason with them and create the beginning of their self-understanding.

Unfortunately, it should be acknowledged that remaining calm and centered is very difficult in the face of an overt threat when adrenaline is coursing through the autonomic nervous system. Remaining calm in the face of hostility and imminent violence takes a lot of practice. Law enforcement officials and first responders who regularly face threats undergo training to practice remaining calm under duress (Tunnecliffe, 2007). Violence de-escalation training is no guarantee against violent acts, but learning cognitive and behavioral strategies likely are a good idea for counselors (Levers, 2022).

If the client continues to be agitated, you might calmly state, "I see you are very upset. I want to understand why and be helpful." This is far more likely to be effective than raising your voice tone, invading the client's physical space, or loudly demanding that the client calm down. In fact, telling an upset person to calm down will likely sound insulting and could well have the opposite effect. Your body language and voice tone may do far more to defuse the situation than anything else, particularly when dealing with traumatized, substance-abusing clients in public mental health settings and schools.

Another factor in calming angry people is to establish a dialogue. Some patients and clients may be angry because they feel misunderstood and marginalized. My counseling experience working with the unemployed, underemployed, incarcerated, and people on probation has shown me how many people feel unimportant and disempowered. When people feel such marginalization, it is no surprise they respond by lashing out in anger.

Your most effective response with angry people is to acknowledge them and then to establish a dialogue. By engaging the frustrated, angry, and potentially violent client in a conversation, you build a stronger relationship and increase the chances of being able to defuse a potentially violent situation. The following is an example of a dialogue with an upset client.

Client:	I've had it with these fucking rules! This is bullshit! (Client is becoming more and more agitated; red in the face; nostrils flared; with rapid, shallow breathing; and looking physically aggressive.)
Counselor:	Steve, I can see you are upset. What is going on? (The counselor speaks softly but firmly and asks a reflective question to get Steve to think. The counselor's question also demonstrates respect, as opposed to simply being concerned about the rules.)
Client:	I'm tired of the counselors always picking on me . . . always assuming I'm using again! I'm not fucking using! (Steve is still very upset. Remember that success may not come quickly, but keep the upset person talking and see if their anger de-escalates.)
Counselor:	Okay, well, I'm happy to hear that you feel so strongly about working your program and staying sober.
Client:	I do! But just like prison, no one believes me!
Counselor:	Well, I know Sonya had given you some real positive feedback in our last group. You seemed pretty happy about that, right? (Remind client of positive experiences that may have been forgotten under duress.)
Client:	Yeah . . . (Calms down when he recalls the praise.) Yeah, she did . . . I guess I forgot.
Counselor:	Steve, I'd like you to feel I was trying to be helpful to you as well. What needs to happen so that you feel we are working together?
Client:	(He pauses, considering what the counselor has just said.) I don't exactly know for sure . . . maybe just what you are doing now . . . taking time with me.
Counselor:	Alright. Maybe this is a start.

In this example, Steve begins feeling very angry and implying everyone is against him. The counselor, mainly by listening and soliciting information, is able to de-escalate the situation before it erupts into violence. The counselor's question,

"What needs to happen so that you feel we are working together?" is an example of turning the tables on an angry client in a therapeutic manner. Steve, who has complained that no one understands him, is confronted with someone who wants to understand him. Steve then puts serious thought into the question, and at this point, therapy can begin to take place. A potentially dangerous situation has just been transformed into a therapeutic encounter. This is what therapy is all about. It goes without mentioning that not all such encounters would turn out as successfully. In some cases, the counselor would need to be able to calmly end the session and request the client return the following day (or as soon as possible). Should the client make a clear and serious threat against the counselor or a third party, then a duty to warn identifiable third parties exists as in *Tarasoff v. The Regents of the University of California* (1974). Defusing anger and subsequently preventing violence through remaining grounded and speaking softly though confidently is always the best safety plan for any counselor or other professionals.

Calming Angry Clients

Shea (1998) has outlined a number of basic warning signs to which clinicians should be attuned regarding the potential for client violence. While this is not a comprehensive list, he recommends the following:

- Be aware if the client's verbal disclosures become increasingly hostile or threatening.
- The client becomes agitated and paces in a threatening manner.
- The client makes angry, threatening, violent gestures, such as pounding the table, shaking their fist at you, or infers assaulting someone else.
- The client grasps their chair or the table very tightly, causing white knuckles.
- The client snarls or bares their teeth.
- The client has a history of violence. (Shea, 1998)

To calm aggravated clients and to reduce the possibility of violence, you may wish to consider the following guidelines. Naturally, many of the following are much easier said than done:

- Position yourself in front or to the side of the client but do not block the exit. Likewise, do not let the client block the exit as this may be your escape.
- Speak slowly and in a reassuring, conversational tone of voice.
- Explain your actions beforehand to avoid arousing the client's suspicions. Example: "I'm going to pick up the phone and call for someone to help us."
- Make appropriate eye contact, but do not glare or give off angry looks. Try and look as though you are concerned about a friend.
- Provide extra space between you and the client. Slowly scoot your chair back to indicate respect for space.
- Do not touch the client unless in the extreme situation where the client assaults you. Then, defend yourself as best you can and exit the room as soon as possible.

- Reassure the client there is a peaceful resolution to the situation. Encourage the client to verbalize his or her anger as opposed to acting on it.
- Do not argue with the belligerent or threatening client. Such is likely to exacerbate the situation. Be silent and display a calm body posture.
- Be aware of your school's/agency's/hospital's safety plan. Is there a "red" button or code word to alert colleagues and security? Do you know the best escape route from the building?
- Trust your intuition. If you believe you are in danger, explain to the client you need to leave. Notify another staff member as soon as possible. If the client has a knife or gun, ask calmly for the client to set it on your desk. If the client threatens you, try to calm him or her with soft language, then call for help or leave the office. (Do not leave a weapon with the client if you can avoid it.)

This list clearly provides no blanket of protection in the face of violent clients. All counseling practicum and intern students should address safety concerns with their field site supervisor and a member of the counseling faculty.

SELF-DEFENSE TRAINING

To my knowledge, few, if any, graduate counseling programs provide students any training or information on how to protect themselves if assaulted. In fact, my experience is that counselor educators typically do not think of this aspect. In this era of major acts of violence in school and business settings, graduate counseling programs must consider preparing students in personal safety. Schools and agencies must also, of necessity, set up safety plans to protect employees, clients, and graduate interns. Naturally, no agency, hospital, prison, or addictions treatment center can *guarantee* to protect you, and most schools and agencies are not set up to be high-security settings and likely should not be so. Therefore, it is important that you receive training in ways to protect yourself.

There are many different types of self-defense training that may be worth looking into. The reality, of course, is that a diminutive female counselor may have limited ability to protect herself against a large male client. Still, some degree of training is better than none at all. My recommendation would be to find a reputable self-defense class that offers training, with an emphasis on defensive techniques. This should also include physical training, which has many health and stress-relieving benefits beyond the safety aspect. Better physical conditioning and some knowledge of self-defense will likely increase your confidence, and that may be an asset if you are confronted by a hostile client. Again, helpful self-defense means creating the opportunity to surprise and temporarily disable or slow down an assailant who physically attacks, providing the counselor or intern the opportunity to flee from the assailant. Helpful self-defense is not about being the aggressor, as violent self-defense should be the last option, utilized only when all others fail.

Regardless of your physical size or level of training, your best asset is good common sense. Your first option is always to try to calm a potential assailant. In fact, a counselor's ability to reason with a hostile client or patient is likely far more important than physical conditioning. Many angry clients are actually frightened and thus the reason for their aggressive behavior. If you can help dispel their fear, you may avoid a potential assault and be in a better therapeutic position. Basically, you want to reason with the client and point out how avoiding a fight is to their benefit. Another possibility, at least in some situations, is to flee from the situation. If you cannot calm the client and you are backed into a corner and forced to defend yourself, then use whatever defense you can muster. Certainly, protect vital areas and call for help as loud as you can. Use your legs for kicking, as they can generate more force than your arms and leave you less exposed. If you can just momentarily slow down your attacker, you may be able to reach help. Remember that safety is often about improving the odds.

It goes without mentioning, of course, that preventing an assault is the best protection of all. Prevention also involves agency policies and procedures regarding staffing, training, a viable safety plan, and making sure clients understand that the repercussions for violent behavior will be serious. Some agencies even put in their informed consent that should the client make a specific threat, the police will be called. In the event of an assault, regardless of how serious, the agency should press legal charges to send the clear message of zero tolerance toward violent acts against staff. Interns would be wise to ask their field site supervisors about such policies related to safety plans, crisis training, and psychological debriefing.

WORKPLACE VIOLENCE PREVENTION PLAN

All schools, agencies, and so forth need plans to assess for violence, prevent violence, and deal with the aftermath of violence. A few basic steps for violence prevention are the following (Kinney, 1995, pp. 46–47):

- Identify vulnerabilities in the school, agency, or treatment facility. Does the facility have a means of assessing violence? Is there an emergency plan to deal with violence after it occurs?

- Naturally, violence prevention is the most important goal. Develop early intervention systems to identify and intervene before violence occurs (e.g., mediation programs, peer helping programs, and bullying prevention programs).

- Develop a threat protocol to assess for violence and a plan to deal with the aftermath of violence. Then, practice the plan routinely through emergency drills to ensure everyone knows their role in trauma management. In addition, when threats occur (e.g., whether verbal, written, or via text messages), always take them seriously and follow up with an investigation.

- Establish who in the school, college, or agency will be responsible for communication to the staff, families, media, and so forth. A clear communication plan reduces rumors and assists with timely information and sends the message that the facility has a plan.

- Develop feedback measures to assess how the violence prevention program is working. Use focus groups for detailed insight and survey the staff.

- Review past incidents of violence to see how successfully they were managed.

WHAT TO DO AFTER AN ASSAULT

If the worst has come to pass and you have been assaulted, you need immediate assistance. Notify staff, medical personnel, your supervisors, and law enforcement officials (if necessary). Get a medical checkup to ensure you are not injured. If you have been injured, be aware of who is responsible to pay the cost of treatment, whether it is the practicum/internship placement, yourself, your insurance, or your counseling program. This is often a gray area. It goes without saying you should have your own personal insurance. In my own experience as a former clinical director and current professor of counselor education, this is an overlooked area of practicum and internship. Fortunately, in all my years as a counselor educator, no students have been assaulted. But not all programs can make the same statement, and the potential for violence is always present, particularly with certain populations (e.g., domestic batterers, clients with a history of violence, and psychotic clients) and placements (e.g., correctional facilities, inpatient psychiatric centers, and counseling in homes).

Should an assault occur, you need to document what happened and why you responded the way you did. You also need to speak with your immediate supervisor as soon as possible because that person will likely need to file an incident report for the agency or for insurance purposes. Your supervisor likely will request that you file a written report of what happened, including what led up to the violence, your response, and how the matter ended. Given the emotion-laden nature of violence, you may need a few days to write the report, then a little time to ensure you have been accurate. This is not to imply you are fabricating. Hastily written traumatic experiwwences may lead to factual errors, and as the incident is likely to become a legal matter, you need to be as factual as possible.

After you have received medical care, made the report, and spoken with your supervisor, it is important to debrief the traumatic experience with a supportive colleague (Tunnecliffe, 2007). Debriefing, followed by long-term counseling, can assist you in making the transition back to feeling healthy. It should be stated, however, that in the aftermath of an assault, you are likely to experience a transition period before regaining your emotional equilibrium (van der Kolk, 2015; 1994). Feeling tense and frightened, having higher blood pressure, and experiencing flashbacks are all normal symptoms of recovery and are nothing to hide or be ashamed about. These are all symptoms of a normal and healthy response to trauma. Most victims of trauma have symptoms that will significantly remit in 30 days. So, give yourself time to let your body and your psyche heal. As a counselor who has been the victim of an assault, I can tell you that healing does take time and will involve at least some of the symptoms mentioned earlier. Fortunately, most survivors do not develop PTSD (Levers, 2022; Tunnecliffe, 2007; van der Kolk, 2015; 1994).

Another factor regarding healing involves the perpetrator who assaulted you. Residential treatment programs will have sanctions for assault and, depending on the severity of the assault, there may be legal charges. My recommendation is that students and professional counselors, psychologists, and other staff should press charges when assaulted. Pursuing legal action sends a clear message that assault is taken seriously and that sanctions will follow. Most treatment facilities will likely back you up if you decide to pursue legal action, although it is realistic to note that some may not (often because of concerns about negative publicity). Victims of violence who feel

260 • THE COUNSELING PRACTICUM AND INTERNSHIP MANUAL

Case Study 10.2 The Case of Juan

Theo is a licensed mental health counselor employed at an urban hospital located in a large city in the Northeastern United States. The hospital offers inpatient and outpatient psychiatric services, including individual and group counseling, medication management, and crisis services. Theo splits his time between counseling outpatients and working 2 days on the inpatient ward. During a shift on the inpatient floor, Julio, a 35-year-old Latinx male with a diagnosis of bipolar I disorder, becomes triggered when he gets into an argument with another resident over a pool game. Unable to regulate his emotions, Julio begins hitting his opponent with the pool stick. Theo sees what is happening and intervenes. He calls out to Julio, who turns his anger on Theo. Backed into a corner, facing an angry, out-of-control Julio, Theo quickly considers his options. Someone has sounded the code red alert but the hospital is under staffed and Theo knows he is on his own for several minutes.

1. What would be Theo's most prudent course of action?
2. Would violence against a patient even in self-defense be justified?
3. What ethical, legal, and practical concerns might come from Theo's encounter with Julio?

unsupported by their employers are likely to feel revictimized and may experience more significant trauma (Kinney, 1995).

Some type of restitution should be made between the perpetrator and the victim. Many schools and agencies have a written policy on this. Some communities have programs such as Victim–Offender Reconciliation Programs (VORP) that bring the victim and offender together (with the victim's approval) so that the offender can apologize and the victim can discuss how the violence has impacted them on a personal, medical, familial, and occupational level. Such programs can provide important closure for the victim, provided the offender is truly remorseful and the victim is ready to face the assailant.

CONCLUSION

Predicting violent behavior is at best difficult, with no profile evidencing strong reliability or validity with regard to predicting violence (Isaacs, n.d.; Zdziarski et al., 2007). Perhaps the best type of defense for counselors to employ is to understand the population they counsel and take appropriate precautions. Appropriate precautions would mean building appropriate relationships with clients, students, inmates, and so on so that they view you as helpful and not an authority figure. Be informed regarding the specific mental health and behavioral issues of the clients assigned to your care. Do your best to develop a caring relationship that incorporates techniques to calm angry clients. As previously mentioned, speaking calmly and somewhat quietly is a prudent behavior in the face of hostility. Body language is of critical importance as well. Despite the intensity of the moment, you must find a way to keep your posture as relaxed and nonaggressive as possible (again, easier said). Do not corner a client in an office. Always give them an escape route (and give yourself one as well). It is important to ask the aggrieved person, "How can I be helpful?" This may force the angry client to self-reflect, which might calm them somewhat. Never adopt a challenging attitude in the face of anger, as that is likely to be received as a challenge at best and as disrespect at worst. An angry client who feels disrespected is more likely to lash out physically. Remember to seek first to understand, as this likely is the best strategy in de-escalating a crisis.

As previously mentioned in this chapter, self-defense training is a very good idea for everyone, especially for counselors working in correctional facilities. It must be reemphasized, naturally, that physical defense should be the refuge of last resort. No matter the size or self-defense expertise of the counselor, physical self-defense is dangerous to both the aggressor and the defender. So, use force only as a last resort. If you can, exit from the situation and seek assistance. Or, call for assistance using a "red button" or code word. Know your agency's/school's/prison's safety plan. To repeat, you will likely be safe throughout your practicum and internship and the odds certainly are with you. But be prepared as there are no guarantees.

The Occupational Safety and Health Administration (OSHA, 2015) recently published guidelines for preventing workplace violence for healthcare and social service workers. OSHA's report offers numerous suggestions for assessing the potential for violence and addressing the aftermath of violence. Their global checklist includes the following:

- assessing risk factors for workplace violence
- inspecting work areas (e.g., for building security, potential hazards, and locked doors)
- inspecting exterior building areas
- inspecting parking areas
- security measures (e.g., physical barriers, CCTV monitors, alarm systems, and panic buttons)

OSHA makes the report available free of charge, and counselors may download the full report at www.osha.gov/Publications/osha3148.pdf.

So, good luck in your practicum and internship and stay safe.

LESSONS LEARNED

I do not recall how the unforgettable incident began, but I cannot ever forget the experience nor the terror involved. A recent graduate from a counseling program, I had been hired at a residential psychiatry facility serving children and adolescents. The patients, or "residents" as the staff referred to them, were minors who were either adjudicated via juvenile justice, transferred from the state psychiatric center, or privately placed by their families. As a staff counselor, my shift worked Tuesday through Saturday, with Saturday being a 16-hour shift (from 8:00 a.m. to midnight). The weekend routine was structured very different from weekdays, with regular off-site outings in addition to room chores and group therapy. Residents with viable home visits could leave for the weekend, provided they were at the adequate behavioral level.

262 • THE COUNSELING PRACTICUM AND INTERNSHIP MANUAL

Our level system ranged from Level 1 (lowest level and least privileges) to Level 4 (highest level with the most privileges). The designation of "risk" indicated that the resident had no privileges and was ineligible for outside excursions, including home visits.

One of the residents in care, whom I will refer to as Tom (pseudonym), was an older adolescent who had resided at the center for a few years. He was a tall, wiry-framed, athletic male diagnosed with paranoid schizophrenia. His situation was rather complicated. He was technically eligible for discharge to his family, given he had met his behavioral benchmarks (e.g., completing therapy, making academic progress toward graduation, and remaining between behavioral levels 3 and 4). Sadly, however, that very week, when he was expecting to be discharged into the care of his family, his mother dropped a bombshell at the family reunification meeting. Much to Tom's shock and dismay, as well as to the social worker conducting the meeting, his mother informed him that she would not be taking him home due to his past behavior of assaulting a sibling and because she felt unable to care for a mentally ill son. When the social worker explained that the funding for her son's treatment would expire and he had to be discharged, she replied, "I will dump him on CSD's doorstep" (CSD being Children's Services Division). Naturally, Tom was devastated at hearing his mother expressing she no longer wanted him at home and was terminating her relationship with him.

My own upbringing was somewhat sketchy with regard to my relationship with my own mother. During early childhood, my mother was institutionalized in a psychiatric hospital for over 5 years. When she returned to my grandparents home, where my four siblings and I were living, her bipolar disorder symptoms caused many complications. While she said many unpleasant things to us, never did she say anything as vile as "I don't want you home." Naturally, many of his friends leaving for long weekends on home visits only enhanced his sense of familial alienation and lit the fuse of a smoldering rage. Like my colleagues, I was acutely aware that Tom was in a dark place and needed much understanding and therapy. What I was unprepared for was just how volatile he had become, especially as we had always had a good relationship. In fact, he frequently sought me out for counsel.

The eventful Saturday shift began in a low-key fashion, starting with eating breakfast with the residents, followed by group therapy, and then an outing. Tom, however, requested not to participate in the outing and instead opted to spend time reading. We agreed, and as the center emptied out for various social and educational excursions, Tom remained behind with the remaining staff, of which I was one. I cannot recall what else I did that morning, though likely some variation of reviewing the previous day's case notes and contacting various colleagues regarding the residents in my section. All in all, the long double shift was proceeding quickly and smoothly. After lunch, I agreed to help Tom with kitchen cleanup. While my memory of all specifics has waned after 35 years, I retain a vivid recollection of his outburst. I remember Tom being very careless with the dishes during cleanup. I gently requested he be a little more careful when he suddenly and unexpectedly snapped and turned on me. Breaking a bottle of soda, he cornered me while jabbing the broken bottle end at me in a menacing fashion. Tom was a couple inches taller than me, and his long arms and quick hands made my situation dire. Despite being young and in excellent shape due to distance running and weight training, I was no match for Tom, especially due to the jagged soda bottle. Emotionally distraught and clearly triggered, he screamed obscenities while thrusting the ugly broken bottle end just inches from my face. Terrified, with adrenaline coursing through my veins, I seriously wondered if Tom was going to kill me.

Tom had gravitated toward me from the time I began at the center. Often, we spoke of music and working out (he was a runner as well), and he even inquired of me how to ask a woman for a date, as he had never dated. During past times, when upset, I was one of the staff he would request to speak with. I had witnessed him upset previously but had never seen Tom so enraged and out of control. During this tense, frightening experience, I realized my only chance at getting out of this situation without serious injury or worse was to calm him down—a very challenging task! Speaking calmly as possible (challenging in the face of a deadly weapon swung by a tall, athletic, enraged psychiatric patient!), I validated his pain and anger and asked if we could just sit and talk as we often did when he was upset. I explained, "I know you're really hurting, but give me a chance to help." Then, taking a risk, I held out my arms, hoping not to get slashed. "Please Tom," I pleaded calmly, as much for me as for him. Then, Tom began to slow his jabbing down. I nodded in encouragement, seeing a little light in this dark tunnel. After several long seconds, he dropped the broken bottle and looked ready to collapse. Then, sobbing, he came and embraced me. I held the formerly violent, now remorseful Tom until additional staff arrived to transport him to a locked facility just off the campus. Once he was escorted from the center, I fell apart and commenced crying as the reality of a very close call with severe injury or death hit me like a punch to the solar plexus. Traumatized, I cannot recall much thereafter, other than someone drove me home.

The following Wednesday, I met with the supervision team. They required me to go through how the *incident* (their words) came to occur. The interview turned into an interrogation, leaving me feeling blamed for Tom's explosive rage. That evening after the shift, my immediate supervisor took me out for a drink at a local pub. He was clearly concerned about me, although at no time did he inquire, *How are you doing?* In point of fact, no colleague asked about my well-being, offering hubristic anecdotes of their own close calls instead. No supervisor debriefed me and no superior or colleague suggested I seek counseling. Ironically, the only concern for my well-being was expressed in a letter by Tom, who had perpetrated the harrowing experience. My sense was that the management and the veteran staff viewed the job as inherently risky and their overriding message was that I should just pull myself together. Feeling further traumatized by my employer's invalidation, I gave notice shortly thereafter. Most revealing, the clinical director, who I had never found particularly empathetic, inquired why I was leaving. While not normally one who traffics in profanity, it required significant restraint not to reply, *Why the fuck do you think I'm quitting?* Somehow, I managed to work the standard 2 weeks before starting a new job at a different agency. To have to return each shift to a place where I could have been killed on the job was traumatic but definitely less so than the realization that no one, including counselors, social workers, or psychologists, harbored any concern for my well-being.

The lesson I learned during this harrowing experience at the onset of my career is that sometimes one has to fire a toxic, callous employer. The fact that a staff composed of mental health professionals expressed no empathy toward me after such a traumatic experience was alarming. While I would like to believe my experience was an outlier, 35 years in the mental health profession have illustrated otherwise. Many mental health centers are underfunded, understaffed, overwhelmed, and run with an eye toward best profit over best practice. The United States is the lone Western country without a government healthcare plan for all citizens. Consequently, we have the world's highest healthcare costs. While there is no perfect solution, our hands-off approach leaves too many working poor without healthcare coverage. The cost is passed on to hospitals and treatment agencies, leaving health and mental health coverage in a very precarious financial situation, resulting in too few staff to serve a large volume of patients. The most disturbing lesson, however, was the realization that the management and treatment staff viewed me as expendable. Had I been killed, I expect any lingering concern would have been more about tort liability than grief. If mental health professionals, however, are so cavalier regarding their staff's safety and emotional well-being, one shutters regarding the treatment of, say, coal mine workers. So, hire and keep the employers who treat you with respect and concern and *fire* the ones that treat you poorly. Firing a toxic employer could prevent PTSD, compassion fatigue and burnout and could possibly even save your life.

RECOMMENDED RESOURCES

Website

Bureau of Justice Statistics (U.S. Department of Justice) website providing statistics on workplace violence. (http://www.bjs.gov/index.cfm?ty=pbse&sid=56)

Print

Carr, J. L. (2005). *American College Health Association campus violence white paper*. American College Health Association. https://www.nccpsafety.org/assets/files/library/ACHA_Campus_Violence_White_Paper.pdf

Hart, T. C. (2003). Violent victimization of college students. *Bureau of Justice Statistics Special Report*. http://www.bjs.gov/content/pub/pdf/vvcs00.pdf

Namie, G., & Namie, R. (2000). *The bully at work: What you can do to stop the hurt and reclaim your dignity*. Sourcebooks.

VandenBos, G. R., & Bulatao, E. Q. (Eds.). (1996). *Violence on the job*. American Psychological Association.

A robust set of instructor resources designed to supplement this text is located at http://connect.springerpub.com/content/book/978-0-8261-6607-4. Qualifying instructors may request access by emailing textbook@springerpub.com.

REFERENCES

American Academy of Experts in Traumatic Stress. (2010). *Identifying students "at-risk" for violent behavior: A checklist of "early warning signs."* https://www.aaets.org/article108.htm

Baird, B. N. (2005). *The internship, practicum, and field placement handbook: A guide for the helping professions* (4th ed.). Pearson/Prentice Hall.

Beck, A. T., Wright, F. D., Newman, C. F., & Liese, B. S. (1992). *Cognitive therapy of substance abuse*. Guilford Press.

Centers for Disease Control. (2022). *Fast facts: Injury data*. https://www.cdc.gov/niosh/topics/violence/fastfacts.html

DeBecker, G. (1997). *The gift of fear: Survival signs that protect us from violence*. Little Brown.

Gately, L. A., & Stabb, S. D. (2005). Psychological students' training in the management of potentially violent clients. *Professional Psychology: Research and Practice, 36*(6), 681–687. https://doi.org/10.1037/0735-7028.36.6.681

Goldstein, A. P. (1999). *The prepare curriculum: Teaching prosocial competencies*. Research Press.

Granello, D. H., & Granello, P. F. (2007). *Suicide: An essential guide for helping professionals and educators*. Pearson/Allyn & Bacon.

Haller, R. M., & Deluty, R. H. (1990). Characteristics of psychiatric inpatients who assault staff severely. *Journal of Nervous and Mental Disease, 178*(8), 536–537. https://doi.org/10.1097/00005053-199008000-00012

Isaacs, A. R. (Ed.). (n.d.). *The school shooter: A threat assessment perspective*. Federal Bureau of Investigation.

Kinney, J. A. (1995). *Violence at work: How to make your company safer for employees and customers*. Prentice Hall.

Levers, L. L. (Ed.). (2022). *Trauma counseling: Theories and interventions, second edition*. Springer Publishing Company.

News, T. (2023, January 19). Anti-LGBTQ policies on LGBTQ youth. *The Trevor Project*. https://www.thetrevorproject.org/blog/new-poll-emphasizes-negative-impacts-of-anti-lgbtq-policies-on-lgbtq-youth/

Pope, K. S., & Vasquez, M. J. T. (2016). *Ethics in psychotherapy and counseling: A practical guide* (5th ed.). Wiley.

Reeser, L. C., & Wertkin, P. A. (2001). Safety training in a social work education: A national survey. *Journal of Teaching in Social Work, 21*, 95–114. https://doi.org/10.1300/J067v21n01_07

Rogers, C. R. (1980). *A way of being*. Houghton-Mifflin.

Romans, J. S. C., Hays, J. R., & White, T. K. (1996). Stalking and related behaviors experienced by counseling center staff members from current or former clients. *Professional Psychology: Research and Practice, 27*, 595–599. https://doi.org/10.1037/0735-7028.27.6.595

Santoro, H. (2022, December 12). How anti-LGBTQ+ rhetoric fuels violence. *Scientific American*. https://www.scientificamerican.com/article/how-anti-lgbtq-rhetoric-fuels-violence/

Shea, S. C. (1998). *Psychiatric interviewing: The art of understanding: A practical guide for psychiatrists, psychologists, counselors, social workers, nurses, and other mental health professionals* (2nd ed.). Saunders.

Thackery, M., & Bobbit, R. G. (1990). Patient aggression against clinical and nonclinical staff in a VA medical center. *Hospital and Community Psychiatry, 41*, 195–197. https://doi.org/10.1176/ps.41.2.195

Tully, C. T., Kropf, N. P., & Price, J. L. (1993). Is the field a hard hat area? A study of violence in field placements. *Journal of Social Work Education, 29*, 191–199. https://doi.org/10.1080/10437797.1993.10778814

Tunnecliffe, M. (2007). *A life in crisis: 27 lessons from acute trauma counseling work*. Bayside.

van der Kolk, B. (1994). The body keeps score. *Harvard Review of Psychiatry, 1*(5), 253–265. https://doi.org/10.3109/10673229409017088

van der Kolk, B. (2015). *The body keeps the score: Brain, mind, and body in the healing of trauma*. Penguin.

Whitman, R. M., Armao, B. B., & Dent, O. B. (1976). Assault on the therapist. *American Journal of Psychiatry, 133*, 424–429. https://doi.org/10.1176/ajp.133.4.426

Zdziarski, E. L. II., Dunkel, N. W., Rollo, J. M., & Associates. (2007). *Campus crisis management: A comprehensive guide to planning, prevention, response, and recovery*. Jossey-Bass.

CHAPTER 11

Addressing Trauma in Counseling: Interventions for Victims, Survivors, and Practicum and Internship Students

INTRODUCTION: ACKNOWLEDGING THE TYRANNOSAURUS REX IN THE THERAPEUTIC ENCOUNTER

Anyone following the media or social media or who has witnessed violence on a personal level can attest to the reality that trauma is a fact of life. From automobile accidents, military personnel in war zones, bullying behaviors in schools, to survivors of intimate partner violence, trauma is an all-too-common experience (Levers, 2022). Sadly, the world can be a brutal, unpredictable place, thus making children, adolescents, and adults vulnerable to long-lasting, often untreated trauma. The aftermath of trauma can manifest in numerous ways related to hyperarousal, cardiovascular troubles, somatic issues, gastrointestinal problems, sexual dysfunction, sleep irregularities, relationship conflicts, and numerous other concerns. Due to societal, cultural, and familial concerns, many people will carry unresolved trauma with them for an entire lifetime, never articulating the cruelty and violence inflicted upon them. There are numerous ways people experience and survive through traumatic events. This chapter aims at exploring some of these in a brief manner, while offering concrete interventions for treatment considerations. At the conclusion of the chapter, a list of suggested resources for further trauma education and treatment will be offered.

Traumatic events can bring about physical, psychological, and even existential wounds that may last a lifetime. For many people, the very thought of addressing the worst experiences in their lives can be very daunting. It is no wonder, therefore, that many trauma survivors are reluctant to seek professional counseling services and may instead self-medicate with alcohol and other drugs to dull the pain. Many brave survivors, however, do seek treatment. Due to the nature of trauma, the therapeutic process is inherently one of healing a shattered self. "In order to understand the whole person who has experienced trauma, clinicians need to grapple with the ubiquity and the ugliness of traumatic events as well as to engage with the complexity of trauma-associated responses" (Levers, 2022, p. 1). Trauma recovery is a complex process involving revising self-talk; managing and eventually extinguishing flashbacks and somatic concerns; and coming to view themselves on the healing journey from victims, to survivors, to thrivers. Many treatment considerations emerge: Was it a single trauma (i.e., an automobile accident) or ongoing (e.g., regular sexual violation by a family member)? Was it a natural disaster (e.g., earthquake) versus a terrorist attack (suicide bomber)? Does the survivor have a strong support system or are they isolated? Is there self-medication involved or sobriety? Essentially, many factors are considered when developing a trauma treatment plan. Given so much uncertainty in the world, with regard to family dynamics, school issues, sociocultural tensions, and global violence, promoting resilience must be a central part of any approach to trauma treatment. We want people to survive trauma, seek treatment, and then thrive in post-treatment. Thus, the term *thriver* identifies clients who have benefitted from treatment, healed, learned from the healing process, and no longer remain captive to their trauma.

As this book is for students in graduate counseling programs and on the journey to becoming healers, the focus will be on covering the basics of trauma treatment while offering concrete treatment suggestions. All graduate students and professional clinicians need ongoing training in trauma treatment and recovery. I intend to offer an integrated approach involving holistic care. No doubt, several preferred trauma treatments have emerged, such as acceptance and commitment therapy (ACT), eye movement desensitization and reprocessing (EMDR), dialectical behavior therapy (DBT), and mindfulness-based cognitive therapy (MBCT), among other efficacious approaches

TRAUMA DEFINED

First of all, the most basic question to entertain is *what is trauma*? *Trauma* is an "emotional response to a terrible event like an accident, rape or natural disaster," (American Psychological Association, n.d.). Trauma may describe the aftereffects of a car wreck, a sexual assault, armed robbery, or an unexpected death. Trauma can stem from a single episode (e.g., automobile accident) or be ongoing (e.g., childhood sexual abuse lasting years). Single-episode trauma (i.e., small t trauma) likely will be distinct from ongoing trauma, the latter of what is sometimes referred to as *complex trauma or big T trauma*. Complex trauma likely will be more ingrained and difficult to treat than single episode. How does one survive trauma? How does one learn to heal through the pain and eventually come to see themselves as a thriver? As humans, we seem to be programmed for predictability. We believe things will always be as they are, meaning relative health, a stable marriage or partnership that always works, a viable career that lasts until we are ready to retire, and healthy children who are above average. Then life happens, and someone we love is killed in an auto accident. Perhaps, we are unceremoniously fired from our job, our spouse abruptly leaves, or that wonderful person we just met and began dating sexually assaults us. These painful, traumatic events sadly occur to people every day. Previously, we may have believed in a just, peaceful world concept, only to have it violently shattered. Suddenly, you no longer feel you are captain of your fate and feel vulnerable to a callow world. You struggle to make sense of what happened and why. In trauma's aftermath, you feel you have lost much of the meaning of your life.

One of the first steps in addressing trauma is to recognize its impact. Trauma can impact cognitions, emotions, relationships, behaviors, attitudes, and dreams, among others (van der Kolk, 2015). Recognizing trauma's impact and moving forward to help, however, can be the start toward healing and discovering renewed purpose in life. Simply put, bad things certainly happen to good people on a regular basis, and everyone needs to make a plan for dealing with traumatic experiences (Chodron, 1997; Kushner, 1981). More significantly, counselors must, of necessity, develop expertise in trauma treatment given its prevalence in therapy (Monson & Friedman, 2006). There simply is no escaping the reality that many clients seeking treatment in schools, colleges, and university settings and in public and private community mental health treatment have been impacted by trauma (Webber & Mascari, 2018). Sadly put, trauma is ubiquitous in all societies.

ACUTE STRESS DISORDER AND POSTTRAUMATIC STRESS DISORDER

The difference between an acute stress disorder (ASD) and posttraumatic stress disorder (PTSD) is time. If ASD symptoms continue beyond 30 days, a diagnosis of PTSD is assigned (American Psychiatric Association [APA], 2013). The diagnostic criteria for ASD are as follows:

- Exposure to actual or threatened death, serious injury, or sexual violation in one (or more) of the following ways:
  - directly witnessing the traumatic event(s)
  - witnessing, in person, the event(s) as it occurred to others
  - learning that the event(s) occurred to a close family member or close friend
  - experiencing repeated or extreme exposure to aversive details of the traumatic event(s) (e.g., first responders collecting human remains or police officers repeatedly exposed to details of child abuse)

  Note: This does not apply to exposure through electronic media, television, movies, or pictures, unless this exposure is work related (APA, 2013).

POSTTRAUMATIC STRESS DISORDER

For PTSD, the *Diagnostic and Statistical Manual of Mental Disorders, Fifth Edition, Text Revision* (5th ed.; *DSM-5-TR*; APA, 2022) has included expanded categories beyond that in ASD. *DSM-5-TR* addresses exposure, symptomology, avoidance, negative mood, arousal, dissociative symptoms, age, and so on (APA, 2022). For a complete description of ASD and PTSD, review *DSM-5-TR* (APA, 2022). Risk and prognostic factors also are addressed in *DSM-5-TR*. Furthermore, there was a discussion of including what has come to be called *complex trauma* in *DSM-5-TR,* though such did not occur. Complex trauma is generally described as long-term trauma, such as in the case of repeated sexual violation, prisoner of war torture victims, battered women and/or partners in domestic violence situations, and the like (van der Kolk, 2003, 2015). Complex trauma is a term you will hear increasingly as you progress through your career in schools, agencies, treatment centers, hospitals, and so on. While *DSM* has yet to incorporate the term, such is likely in future editions. Clearly, there is a spectrum of severity for all disorders and/or life circumstances, and such is also true for trauma, based on episodes (single episode vs. ongoing), severity, client resilience, environmental support factors, and so on.

FACTORS OF TRAUMA

Numerous factors will help determine how clients will respond to a traumatic event. Age (younger persons often are more reactive than older), surprised (sudden death) versus preparation for a trauma (e.g., a hurricane or tornado), severity of injury (e.g., physically, emotionally, sexually), and the way the survivor views the trauma are a few of the components that impact the survivor. We can begin to consider three types of factors that influence the development of an ASD and PTSD. These are pre-event factors, event factors, and post-event factors (Williams & Poijula, 2016). Relatively 10% to 20% of trauma survivors will develop PTSD (Sidran Institute, n.d.). The good news, however, is that PTSD is treatable with favorable success rates (van der Kolk, 2015).

Case Study 11.1 The Case of Malcolm

Malcolm is a military veteran and licensed mental health counselor working in a VA Medical Center, many of whom are diagnosed with PTSD. He has begun treating Jaime, a combat veteran. Jaime has struggled with PTSD symptoms, (e.g., flashbacks and night terrors) and self-medicates with alcohol. He is dual-diagnosed with alcohol use disorder-moderate and is being treated for his substance abuse by another VA therapist. Jaime states that his difficulties in self-soothing increase his urge to self-medicate. Malcolm has been trained in trauma-sensitive therapies (EMDR and emotional freedom therapy [EFT]) and knows tapping or touching (from EFT) has demonstrated efficacy with self-soothing and reducing the compulsion to self-medicate. He explains EFT and tapping or touching pressure points, but Jaime, a self-admitted skeptic of all psychotherapies, seems unenthusiastic. Malcolm is very concerned about Jaime's continued misuse of alcohol and his anxiety, knowing the combination suggests Jaime is at high risk for a suicide attempt. Despite Jaime's insistence that he would never attempt suicide due to his strong Catholic faith, Malcolm is nevertheless concerned.

How might Malcolm address Jaime's reluctance to try an efficacious approach like EFT?

Pre-Event Factors

While there are numerous possible pre-event factors that can impact future trauma, the following are some common ones:

- previous exposure to trauma, such as childhood sexual abuse, emotional and physical abuse, or witnessing abuse (e.g., domestic violence)
- a history of anxiety or depression, particularly when untreated
- an unstable family history (e.g., psychiatric disorders, financial challenges, foster care situations)
- early onset of substance abuse
- absence of social support to assist in troubled times
- early loss of family, home, and close relations
- genetics: some people appear less resilient to trauma than others (Meichenbaum, 1994)

Event Factors

The following are some of the factors contributing to the development of PTSD. These may include

- proximity to the traumatic event (e.g., bomb exploded 100 yards away or witnessed father abusing mother);
- your self-talk regarding the event (what you tell yourself about the event and recovery; Ellis, 1994);
- age when experiencing/witnessing the trauma (younger persons are more vulnerable);
- being a victim of ongoing trauma (e.g., ongoing sexual abuse, war, chaotic home); and
- being a victim of multiple traumatic events.

Post-Event Factors

Post-event factors include those that exist after the traumatic event has concluded. They may include

- lack of strong emotional and social support;
- negative self-talk regarding one's ability to cope and persevere;
- either no accessing therapeutic help or lacking the resources to access help;
- inability to find meaning in the post-event suffering;
- developing an ASD after the event (after 30 days, continued trauma is diagnosed as PTSD); and

- experiencing physiological (increased blood pressure and heart rate, startle reaction) and avoidant (isolation from peers and loved ones) or numbing sensations (blunted affect, periodic dissociation).

The good news is that help for trauma sufferers is available, though more so in some communities than others. Self-talk, or what the survivor tells themselves after the trauma, seems to be a very important factor (Ellis, 1994), that is, does the survivor tell herself that "I am a survivor and will seek out help to overcome this trauma," or rather, "This was awful and terrible, and I will never feel good and safe again"? Self-talk is where I recommend all cognitive therapy for trauma survivors begins. Furthermore, self-talk, or cognitive reframing/restructuring, will need to be lifelong for optimal results (Ellis, 1994). Counselors should monitor client self-talk to gauge therapeutic effectiveness. Naturally, clients can quickly learn to monitor and revise their own self-talk for optimal effectiveness.

Additional important factors that may have positive implications for trauma recovery and resilience include an internal locus of control, or believing you have the resources to work through the difficulty. An internal locus of control is strongly related to self-efficacy, or the confidence you will indeed get better through your attitude and actions (e.g., counseling, exercise, positive thinking; Meichenbaum, 1994). Perhaps even more significant is the survivor developing a sense of life meaning regarding survival to traumatic events (Park & Folkman, 1997). Furthermore, survivors who are motivated to improve believe they can improve, and those who access healthy coping strategies (e.g., counseling, exercise, healthy diet) tend to have the highest success rates of recovery (Meichenbaum, 1994).

ASSESSING TRAUMA

There are a number of assessments you may use to assess trauma. These include the Trauma Symptom Inventory (TSI), PTSD Checklist (civilian and military), Trauma History Screen (THS), Social Readjustment Rating Scale (SRRS), and some of the common screeners counselors would use in clinical settings. You would also use a clinical interview to delve into a client's history to determine when the trauma occurred, length of time, severity, symptomology, and so on. Be prepared for traumatized clients to exhibit fragmented memories (van der Kolk, 2003, 2015). This is likely due to dissociation during trauma, something especially common in survivors of long-term abuse. Some clients may even report watching their trauma from above, as if an outside bystander (van der Kolk, 2003, 2015). Frankly, dissociation may, in reality, be the mind's way of protecting victims from further intensive abuse by shutting down the senses and psychologically distancing the sufferer.

Regarding dissociation and memory gaps, counselors must be diligent to ensure they do not "uncover" false memories into the client. Recovered memories are a significant controversy in the field and disagreement continues regarding their possibility. Regardless, Meichenbaum (1994) recommends consideration of several important points with regard to remembering a trauma:

- Remembering is a reconstructive process, not merely a retrieval of a record of past experience. Typically, we forget more than we remember.

11: ADDRESSING TRAUMA IN COUNSELING: INTERVENTIONS FOR VICTIMS, SURVIVORS • 273

- Your memories can be influenced and distorted over time. (Confabulation is where a survivor fills in memory gaps. This is a common occurrence.)
- Reconstructing a memory does not bring up everything in exact detail.
- Strong belief in inaccurate memories is possible (like confabulation).
- Clients do not have to recall everything about a traumatic event in exact detail. What is important is to be able to recall enough to process the event, accompanying cognitions, emotions, and body sensations.

Meichenbaum (1994), like Ellis (1994, 2000), adds that a survivor's belief regarding the trauma is a significant factor in their ability to recover from the trauma. Basically, a belief that one can heal from trauma provides motivation, that is, if you believe you can heal, you are more likely to seek treatment and work the plan. If you do not believe healing is possible, likely, one does not seek treatment or does but does not work their treatment plan. The set of questions in Exhibit 11.1 will help assess a survivor's beliefs regarding their trauma.

Healthy Self-Talk in Healing

Many survivors of trauma often blame themselves for becoming traumatized, despite the fact they are victims, often using judgmental terms such as shoulds, oughts, musts and other absolute terms, thus increasing the anxiety (Beck & Haigh, 2014; Ellis, 1994, 2000). The power of our internal dialogue can lead us from equilibrium to a panic attack. Fortunately, the converse also is true. Reframing is a staple of cognitive therapy involving catching, challenging, and changing (the 3 Cs of reframing) our self-talk, helping us talk ourselves down from the ledge of absolute panic and terror (Ellis, 2000). By targeting our negative automatic thoughts and challenging their validity, we can begin to calm ourselves and quiet our amygdala and tame that T-Rex stalking the periphery of consciousness.

Some examples of negative self-talk and cognitive methods to address them are cited below:

- *Catastrophizing or minimizing:* In catastrophizing, small errors are magnified (e.g., "I forgot my lunch. I am such an idiot!"). To reframe catastrophizing the statement, one might say, "I forgot my lunch. Hey, everyone does at some point. I'll buy lunch today." Alternately, in minimization, we undermine our actual accomplishments (e.g., "Yeah, I got an A on the exam, but it's because the test was easy."). To reframe a minimization, we might say, "Yes, I made an A on the exam. I worked hard and did very well!"
- *Overgeneralization:* An isolated event is seen as a regular occurrence (e.g., "She turned me down for a date. No one will ever want to partner with me."). A possible reframe might be "She wasn't interested in me. Okay, that's disappointing, but I will keep asking others, and someone will want to date and partner with me."
- *All-or-nothing thinking:* Experiences are either all good or all bad (e.g., "The salad was mediocre, so the dinner was terrible," ignoring an excellent main course). A reframe might be "Well, for the most part, the dinner was very good."

274 • THE COUNSELING PRACTICUM AND INTERNSHIP MANUAL

- *Mind reading:* The individual believes their interpretation of what someone is thinking must be accurate without investigating (e.g., "The boss was frowning when she passed me in the hallway. She's going to fire me!"). The reframe to this one might sound like this: "Perhaps the boss had something else on her mind, and the frown had nothing to do with me."
- *Fortune telling:* An unfortunate practice of anticipating negative outcomes, then behaving as if one's prediction has come true (e.g., anticipating a job interview, the applicant predicts they will never get the job, and then, in a self-fulfilling manner, performs badly on the interview). A possible reframe might look like this: "I have prepared for this interview, have the skill set, and will do well on this interview, possibly resulting in a job offer."

The above examples are but a few examples of cognitive behavioral therapy (CBT) and rational emotive behavior therapy (REBT), and while simple, they function quite effectively in helping clients stop a panic attack when triggered.

Creating Safe Spaces

In many cases, it is impossible to achieve safety without moving to a safe location. Victims of domestic violence (e.g., verbal, physical, and sexual) must get to shelters and other safe locations. The set of questions in Exhibit 11.2 will help assess a survivor's access to safe spaces. If you could create a safe space where you would feel secure and relaxed, where would that space be located? The safe space can be an actual location or an imaginary one in your mind. Focus on the surroundings of your safe space, the colors, pleasant smells, sounds, and tactile sensations. Then, allow your senses to take in the sounds, odors, and the feel of that space. While attending to the space, begin slowly breathing in through your nose (taking 3–4 seconds) and then slowly exhaling out your mouth (3–4 seconds). Visualize your safe space while breathing slowly via your noise and exhaling out your mouth for 5 to 10 minutes, feeling that warm, pleasant sensation moving throughout your body. Your safe space is only for you and those you trust. Others may enter only with your permission. This latter point speaks to the need for secure boundaries, as trauma survivors have had their boundaries violated, and secure, while flexible boundaries, are necessary for healing.

Subjective Units of Disturbance Scale

The Subjective Units of Disturbance Scale (SUDS) provides a personal, subjective method for the clients to assess their distress level at times when they may feel insecure or unsafe. Lower SUDS levels suggest a more relaxed mood, whereas higher scores indicate more personal distress. The SUDS scale has 11 points, from 0 to 10, ranging from completely relaxed to extreme distress (see Exhibit 11.3). Counselors should remind clients that SUDS scores will fluctuate depending on the situation, day, and their ability to manage triggers that activate distress.

Exhibit 11.1 Trauma Beliefs Inventory

Select the beliefs that most accurately represent your beliefs regarding your trauma-related experiences. The important matter is what you tell yourself regarding recovering from trauma. More optimistic beliefs suggest more positive treatment outcomes. More pessimistic answers suggest a need to seek treatment from a mental health professional.

1. I believe I am a victim, though with work and support, my mood will improve. Yes_ No_
2. I feel very hopeful regarding my future. Yes_ No_
3. I feel guilty for having been victimized. Yes_ No_
4. I have been self-medicating with alcohol and other substances to deal with my trauma-related anxiety. Yes_ No_
5. Because of my trauma experience(s), I am more self-critical. Yes_ No_
6. I am having difficulty sleeping (or have nightmares) due to my trauma. Yes_ No_
7. I have been having suicidal thoughts due to my trauma. Yes_ No_
8. Despite my traumatic experience(s), I believe I am a very resilient person able to heal from my experience(s). Yes_ No_
9. I have a strong support system that includes supportive family, friends, and a community (e.g., colleagues and spiritual community). Yes_ No_
10. I have a strong relationship with my own sense of spirituality, the higher power, God, and so on. Yes_ No_
11. I have been able to reclaim my personal autonomy and power from the trauma or abuser. Yes_ No_
12. I have formed a successful, intimate relationship. Yes_ No_
13. I am having success in setting healthy limits with people in my personal and professional life. Yes_ No_
14. I recognize that the traumatic event(s) were not my fault and understand that the trauma was not my fault. Yes_ No_
15. I am managing my anger in a healthy manner, and I am not feeling controlled by it. Yes_ No_
16. I have attended counseling (individual and/or group) to help heal from the trauma. Yes_ No_
17. I am generally able to get a good night's sleep. Yes_ No_
18. I believe I am a good person worthy of loving others and being loved. Yes_ No_
19. I recognize that what I most control is my attitude in any given situation. Yes_ No_
20. I am very hopeful about my personal and vocational future. Yes_ No_

Developing a Support System

As you continue working through your traumatic experiences and deal with the symptoms, it is important to create social and emotional support systems. Supportive family and friends are important, and support may be found through coworkers, support groups, faith-based institutions, 12-step recovery programs (e.g., Alcoholics Anonymous, Narcotics Anonymous, Adult Children of Alcoholics), or social organizations. You also need to have an emergency plan in the event you feel unsafe and need to access resources during times when your supports may be unavailable (e.g., holidays, late night or early morning hours). Exhibit 11.4 provides an outline of a support system.

Exhibit 11.2 Creating Safe Spaces

Answer the following questions as candidly as you can:

1. Do you have a safe place where you will not be abused? If so, where?

   _____

2. What makes this place safe and special to you?

   _____

   _____

3. What types of activities do you do in this safe place (e.g., yoga, meditation, journaling)?

   _____

   _____

4. Have you set aside a specific time or day of the week to visit this safe place? If yes, when?

   _____

5. If you were to rate your current personal safety, how would you rate your safety level?

   $$1 \quad 2 \quad 3 \quad 4 \quad 5 \quad 6 \quad 7 \quad 8 \quad 9 \quad 10$$

   (Safe)   (Unsafe)

   If you do not feel safe, what steps might you take to achieve safety?

6. Some trauma survivors maintain beliefs that continue to leave them feeling depressed, unsafe, and angry. These beliefs are expressed in ways such as "I believe I deserve to be punished," "I caused them to be abusive," "I am a bad person," or "I will never be free of abuse." Now, what can you do to

(continued)

11: ADDRESSING TRAUMA IN COUNSELING: INTERVENTIONS FOR VICTIMS, SURVIVORS • 277

Exhibit 11.2 Creating Safe Spaces (*continued*)

prevent any harmful actions or unhealthy self-talk (as previously noted) from hurting you further? _____

_____

7. As trauma survivors become healthier, their self-talk usually becomes healthier as well. Their self-talk may sound like these: "The abuse was not my fault," "My anger is a natural expression of the unfairness of the abuse," "I am very resilient and each day I get a little stronger," and "I am the most important person in my life and well worth healthy love." Now, in the following space, what is an example of your own healthy self-talk?

_____

_____

8. I am learning that being hopeful about my future is very important, regardless of what abusers have said. I am hopeful about

_____

_____

9. Make a list of your negative, unhealthy thoughts. Then, write three safe, healthy thoughts to contradict the negative, unsafe ones. Remember, each time unhealthy thoughts intrude upon your mind, contradict them with healthier ones.

10. Make a list of your personal, emotional assets. Then, list how each asset is helping you become a stronger, healthier person.

Exhibit 11.3 Subjective Units of Disturbance Scale

0   I am completely relaxed, with no distress.

1   I am very relaxed, whether working, studying, or socializing.

2   I am feeling no tension.

3   I experience a bit of tension and it is mildly distracting to my thoughts.

4   I am experiencing mild distress in my thoughts and in places in my body. Still, I am able to manage this distress.

5   My cognitive and bodily distress remain within a manageable range.

6   I am experiencing moderate distress in thoughts and in my body, though it remains manageable.

(continued)

Exhibit 11.3 Subjective Units of Disturbance Scale (*continued*)

7 My thoughts and body distress are unpleasant and causing me significant anxiety.

8 I am experiencing a high degree of distress with high levels of anxiety and bodily tension.

9 The distress is so high that it is impacting my cognitive and emotional functioning. My body tension is nearly unbearable.

10 I am in extreme distress and filled with panic, with tension throughout my body. I am having difficulty managing my negative thoughts and regulating my emotions.

At this point my SUDS score is _____

I chose this score because _____

_____

One thing I can do to lower my score 1-point is _____

SUDS, Subjective Units of Disturbance Scale.

Exhibit 11.4 Developing My Support System

The contact numbers I need to know are the following:

1. The local crisis line: _____

2. My spouse or partner: _____

3. My closest friend: _____

4. My counselor: _____

5. My physician: _____

6. A close family member: _____

7. The local hospital emergency department: _____

8. Another significant person (e.g., AA sponsor, neighbor, coworker, or another significant person): _____

9. My spiritual advisor: _____

(continued)

11: ADDRESSING TRAUMA IN COUNSELING: INTERVENTIONS FOR VICTIMS, SURVIVORS • 279

Exhibit 11.4 Developing My Support System (*continued*)

10. If none of these contacts are available and I need support, I can do one of the following activities to create personal safety until someone is available:

_____

_____

Acknowledging Positive Assets

Working through trauma successfully involves understanding positive assets. Use the questions in Exhibit 11.5 to help identify your strengths with regard to healing from trauma.

Exhibit 11.5 Acknowledging My Assets

1. As a survivor recovering from trauma, what do you see as your top three strengths?

   a.) _____ b.) _____ c.) _____

2. During your recovery, in what ways have you demonstrated resilience?

   _____

   _____

3. When you were struggling with the pain, anger, and anxiety, how did you find the will to keep working toward recovery?

   _____

4. How were you able to maintain your level of hope?

   _____

5. How were you able to maintain your sense of humor during your recovery?

   _____

6. Who were/are a few of your key supporters during your recovery?

   _____

   _____

(continued)

280 • THE COUNSELING PRACTICUM AND INTERNSHIP MANUAL

Exhibit 11.5 Acknowledging My Assets (*continued*)

7. What do you believe is the key to successful trauma recovery?

_____

_____

8. If another trauma survivor were to ask you for advice regarding recovery, what would you tell them?

_____

_____

9. What has your recovery taught you about your own resilience? _____

_____

10. Although no one would ever want to experience trauma for personal growth, many report they do indeed grow in response to experiencing trauma. In what ways have you grown as a result of your recovery? Growth can be emotional, physical, spiritual, educational, and so on.

_____

_____

_____

Journaling and Recovery

One of the methods many survivors employ to deal with their trauma is to write about what happened. Pennebaker and Campbell (2000) suggest that journaling about unpleasant and even traumatic experiences is beneficial for emotional health. Pennebaker and Campbell suggest you journal for 4 days each week. During those journaling days, write for 20 minutes each day. The only hard and solid rule is that you write continuously for the entire 20 minutes. If you start to feel you are running out of things to write, simply repeat what you have already written. Give yourself free reign during this time by turning off your internal editor and tuning out self-criticism regarding spelling, punctuation, and sentence structure. Just let your writing flow.

During your journaling, you likely will experience mixed emotions, from feeling liberated from your pain to feeling sad about what has happened (Pennebaker & Campbell, 2000). This range of emotions and cognitions is quite natural for someone who has experienced trauma. Remember, addressing your journal writing during counseling sessions may enhance the therapeutic encounter. Should you feel writing about your trauma, or at least aspects of your trauma, are too upsetting, then you may

11: ADDRESSING TRAUMA IN COUNSELING: INTERVENTIONS FOR VICTIMS, SURVIVORS • 281

wish to avoid addressing such in your journal. When you journal on your trauma, it is recommended to write the ways you are managing your trauma or having success in counseling to heal from trauma, and what we write can become ingrained in our beliefs (Pennebaker & Campbell, 2000). Use of scaling questions may prove helpful. For example, on a scale of 1 to 10, with 10 being very high and 1 very low, what is my anxiety level in writing about my trauma (or at least particular aspects of my trauma)?

Naturally, people keep personal journals to address all types of experiences such as family relationships and issues, romantic involvements, college and university experiences, new careers, retirement, for grief recovery, and so forth. Journaling can be a transforming experience in that it serves as an outlet for your effect and cognitions and provides concrete time for reflection and renewal. Specific instructions are detailed in Exhibit 11.6.

Exhibit 11.6 Steps to Journaling About Your Trauma

During this week, write about a traumatic experience in your journal. Each day, you will write for 20 minutes without stopping. When you complete the 20-minute cycle, consider what you have written. What do you learn from this journal entry? How will what you have written help you in the recovery process? (Remember, even slight help is an improvement.) If you wonder when the best time to journal is, usually it is the time that works best for you, be it early morning, midday, or evening.

Self-Reflecting on My Journal Experience

During your 4-day journaling cycle, what have you learned regarding your recovery, your strengths, values, hopes, and anything that seems important?

_____

_____

_____

_____

_____

_____

_____

Managing Flashbacks

A flashback is a memory of a past experience, either pleasant or unpleasant, that is occurring in present time. Flashbacks are actually quite common, though many people likely do not recognize them as such. For example, you may notice a particular smell that takes you back a couple of decades to a relative or friend's wedding, and suddenly, you are re-experiencing the past. The experience, triggered by a smell, is a flashback, though not one any counselors would concern themselves with. Matsakis, moreover, defines a *flashback* as a "sudden, vivid recollection of the traumatic event accompanied by a strong emotion" (1994, p. 33). A flashback can be brief or a recalled memory of a longer experience. Flashbacks more commonly refer to auditory or visual aspects of the traumatic experience but may also refer to somatic concerns (stomach or back pain), emotions (sudden, intense anger that seems an overreaction to a third party), and behaviors (a fight, flight, or freeze-type behavior when triggered). For trauma sufferers, a flashback puts them back in that traumatic event as if the trauma is reoccurring at that moment. Flashbacks may also be manifested in dreams, such as with night terrors experienced as actual events. Flashbacks may also appear as intrusive thoughts or as intense emotions (Meichenbaum, 1994; van der Kolk, 2015).

During a flashback, the trauma is reexperienced with great intensity, sometimes causing the sufferer to confuse present reality with the past experience. This may be the reason why trauma survivors have fragmented memories, as they lose track of real time due to flashbacks (Meichenbaum, 1994). Children and adolescents can also have flashbacks, often acting out the type of violence that was perpetrated upon them. Anyone who has worked with abused children would likely tell you they have witnessed this firsthand. Adults frequently act out their trauma as well, especially if self-medicating with alcohol or another substance (Meichenbaum, 1994).

Flashbacks may also be explicit memories of traumatic experiences or "bits and pieces" of the actual experience. Typically, a flashback includes some sensory and emotional part of the trauma. Due to perceived stress, cortisol is activated, and the endocrine system begins pumping epinephrine through the body, leading to hyperarousal and resulting in quick, shallow breathing; angry or frightening thoughts; and increased heart rate and blood pressure. Altogether, a flashback can be a very frightening experience for the trauma survivor. Fortunately, with practice and certainly counseling assistance, flashbacks may be managed, thus lessening their negative impact (Meichenbaum, 1994; Rothschild, 2010).

The use of cognitive reframing or monitoring and revising self-talk is a common part of cognitive therapy (Ellis, 2000). The following are some basic questions for trauma survivors to consider:

- What is this flashback trying to teach me?
- How might this unpleasant memory actually begin to help my recovery?
- When experiencing a flashback, what can I do to lessen the pain of the memory just a little?
- When these flashbacks are no longer a problem for me (or only a minor problem), how will my life be different? What will others notice that is different about me?

Counselors may also assist trauma survivors in revising their flashbacks by using the exercise in Exhibit 11.7.

Exhibit 11.7 Managing a Flashback

Consider a flashback that has been causing you discomfort.

1. Briefly describe the flashback and what you experienced. _____

    _____

2. How did the flashback sound, look, and feel? _____

    _____

3. When you have these flashbacks, has anything you have done worked, at least to a limited extent? If so, briefly describe. _____

    _____

4. Now, what could you do to begin to lessen the flashback's impact? For example, stop and call a friend, work to slow breathing, revise negative self-talk, take a walk, and so on.

    _____

    _____

5. How might you ground yourself to remain in the present when the flashbacks occur (e.g., clapping hands, stomping feet, taking notice of three objects in your immediate environment, three sounds you hear)?

    _____

    _____

Interrupting Flashbacks

The flashback interruption exercises in Exhibit 11.8 are adapted from Rothschild's (2010) *8 Keys to Safe Trauma Recovery: Take-Charge Strategies to Empower Your Healing*.

Nightmares and Trauma Dreams

Your clients may have recurring dreams where trauma is replayed or at least some aspect of the trauma is reexperienced. Some clients may have trouble sleeping and try and avoid bedtime altogether, thus reducing their health and well-being. Dreams, however, even unpleasant ones, may provide another window for treatment, thus lessening symptomology. The flashback-interrupting protocol in Exhibit 11.8 can be adapted to address trauma-based nightmares. You may use it with clients to help them prepare for nightmares or try the methods described in Exhibit 11.9. *Caution: People suffering from nightmares should be under the care of a counselor or other professionals trained in treating PTSD.*

284 • THE COUNSELING PRACTICUM AND INTERNSHIP MANUAL

The Dream Journal

Journaling appears to have good emotional and mental health benefits for those who regularly engage in journaling activity (Parker-Pope, 2015). Spoormaker (2008) advocates a cognitive procedure to reduce anxiety in the aftermath of nightmares. When the dream occurs, write it down (as much as you can recollect). Then, talk it through aloud and rewrite the ending as a strategy to manage the nightmare. Exhibit 11.10 provides more detailed instructions.

Exhibit 11.8 Flashback-Interrupting Protocol

1. The flashback I am writing about is _____

_____

2. Say to yourself (preferably out loud) the following sentences, filling in the blanks:

Right now I am feeling _____ (write in the name of the current emotion) and I am sensing _____ in my body (describe bodily sensations, at least three) because I am remembering _____ (name the trauma only, no specific details).

3. At the same time, I am looking around where I am now in _____ (current year), here at _____ (name the place where you are currently), and I can see _____ (describe what you see right now) is not happening anymore.

4. How did this flashback interruption work for you? _____

_____

5. How might this technique work even better? Any ideas? _____

_____

Exhibit 11.9 Managing Nightmares, So They Do Not Manage You

Addressing nightmares tends to be about grounding one's mind prior to bedtimes so that you have planted a strategy in your mind and can implement it upon waking (Hobson, 2009). The following is adapted from the work of Hobson (2009) and Spoormaker (2008). You will describe your anticipatory fear, which often is the most distressing part of nightmares. Then, you will address strategies to manage the nightmare during and after waking.

My most fearful aspect before going to bed is _____.

(continued)

Exhibit 11.9 Managing Nightmares, So They Do Not Manage You (*continued*)

I feel this fear in my body in _____, _____, and _____ (cite three locales or less if less).

During my nightmare, I will work on facing whatever is frightening. Be aware, you may need time to fully face fears in your dreams.

During the nightmare, I will tell myself, "This is only a dream, and this unpleasant dream is teaching me something I need to address."

Upon waking, you will name three objects you see, then rate your fear on a scale of 1 to 10, with 10 being high.

| 1 | 2 | 3 | 4 | 5 | 6 | 7 | 8 | 9 | 10 |

Low anxiety   Medium   High anxiety

Right now, my score is _____/10. Remember, you only need to lower your score by 1 point.

Now, use the following grounding exercises after rating yourself on the anxiety scale:

Look around your bedroom. Upon waking I see _____

_____

Because I am safe in my home, I know that _____ (name the trauma or nightmare) is not happening right now.

Next, sit up and put your feet firmly on the floor and feel the floor on your bare feet. Tell yourself, "I am here in my room, and the trauma is not occurring now." (Or, you may touch the wall, and feel the wall on your hands.)

Next, you will work to slow your breathing. Take in slow, deep breaths, imagining your feet on the floor (or hands on the wall), while silently repeating, "I am in my safe place." Breathe deeply, hold for 1 second, and then slowly exhale. Repeat for a couple of minutes or until you feel slightly more calm.

Now, rate your anxiety of the previous scale. Right now, my score is _____/10. How do your two scores compare? In the following space, describe what you can do to manage your anxiety during the day:

Strategy 1 _____

Strategy 2 _____

Strategy 3 _____

Always remember to monitor your self-talk and revise accordingly.

286 • THE COUNSELING PRACTICUM AND INTERNSHIP MANUAL

Exhibit 11.10 The Dream Journal

You will create a dream journal to address the nightmares you are having as a result of the trauma. Take a standard notebook or use your computer to detail any nightmares. Describe the bad dream in as much detail as possible, focusing on your senses (sights, sounds, smells, sensations on your skin, and tastes). The following lines are to give you an idea of length. Tailor the journal and write as much as necessary.

_____

_____

_____

_____

_____

Reviewing your nightmare, what are some ways you could change the nightmare's ending?

_____

_____

Even unpleasant experiences may help us manage our lives. How have your nightmares helped you to learn about your trauma recovery?

_____

_____

_____

As you continue to journal about your nightmares, consider also how journaling has helped you heal from your trauma.

SELF-MEDICATING TRAUMA

A significant issue for counselors who treat trauma is client self-medication with alcohol or other substances (Miller et al., 2011). Counselors treating trauma survivors would be wise to screen for alcohol and other drug abuse. Two quick and efficacious assessments available are the *CAGE* (**C**ut down use, **A**nnoyed when questions regarding substance use, **G**uilt at abuse, and needs an **E**ye-opener to start the day) questionnaire and the *Alcohol Use Disorders Identification Test* (AUDIT). The CAGE questionnaire can be quickly used in an intake interview as it is very brief. Clients are asked if they have ever felt the need to *cut* down their drinking, become *annoyed* when others ask about their consumption, felt *guilty* about their drinking, or needed an *eye-opener* to begin the day. Each item scores a 1 for "yes" responses and a score of 2 is considered clinically significant (Kitchens, 1994). Heck (1991) found that the effectiveness of the CAGE questionnaire in identifying problem drinkers could be significantly improved by asking clients about their social drinking habits, driving habits, and the age at which they began to drink. Problem drinkers seldom, if ever, select nonalcoholic beverages at social events; frequently drive when under the influence of alcohol; and started drinking at an early age, often during high school.

The AUDIT is a 10-item screening tool utilized to assess alcohol dependence and its consequences. The AUDIT was developed by the World Health Organization (WHO) over 2 decades through research across several countries. The AUDIT assesses three levels of alcohol consumption: hazardous or risky drinking (at risk for alcohol-related consequences), harmful drinking (presence of physical or mental consequences), and alcohol dependence (relying on alcohol as a coping mechanism). AUDIT items refer to recent alcohol use, alcohol dependence symptoms, and alcohol-related problems. AUDIT items are robust in distinguishing between low-risk and high-risk drinkers. Items 1 to 3 assess hazardous drinking, items 4 to 6 identify alcohol dependence symptoms, and items 7 to 10 screen for harmful drinking (Barbor et al., 2001).

The AUDIT can be completed as a self-report format or in a clinical interview. Items are ranked on a 5-point scale. Authors of the second edition AUDIT manual suggest a cut off score of 8 or higher for problem drinking. Scores of 0 to 7 warrant alcohol education; 8 to 15, advice on alcohol use; 16 to 19, advice and ongoing monitoring; and 20 to 40, referral to an addiction specialist for further evaluation and treatment (see Exhibit 11.11). The AUDIT has shown promise as an initial screener, with good reliability and validity, and is used for females and males (Barbor et al., 2001). The AUDIT also offers two shortened forms of the instrument: the AUDIT-3 and AUDIT-4, which contain three and four items, respectively. Gual et al. (2002) reported these abbreviated versions provided similar results as the original AUDIT.

Exhibit 11.11 The Alcohol Use Disorders Identification Test

Read the questions as written. Circle the answer that best describes your drinking habits.

1. **How often do you have a drink containing alcohol?**
   a. Never
   b. Monthly or less
   c. 2 to 4 times a month
   d. 2 to 3 times a week
   e. 4 or more times a week

2. **How many standard drinks containing alcohol do you have on a typical day when drinking?**
   a. 1 or 2
   b. 3 or 4

(continued)

Exhibit 11.11 The Alcohol Use Disorders Identification Test (*continued*)

   c. 5 or 6
   d. 7 to 9
   e. 10 or more

3. **How often do you have six or more drinks on one occasion?**
   a. Never
   b. Less than monthly
   c. Monthly
   d. Weekly
   e. Daily or almost daily

4. **During the past year, how often have you found that you were not able to stop drinking once you had started?**
   a. Never
   b. Less than monthly
   c. Monthly
   d. Weekly
   e. Daily or almost daily

5. **During the past year, how often have you failed to do what was normally expected of you because of drinking?**
   a. Never
   b. Less than monthly
   c. Monthly
   d. Weekly
   e. Daily or almost daily

6. **During the past year, how often have you needed a drink in the morning to get yourself going after a heavy drinking session?**
   a. Never
   b. Less than monthly
   c. Monthly
   d. Weekly
   e. Daily or almost daily

7. **During the past year, how often have you had a feeling of guilt or remorse after drinking?**
   a. Never
   b. Less than monthly
   c. Monthly
   d. Weekly
   e. Daily or almost daily

8. **During the past year, have you been unable to remember what happened the night before because you had been drinking?**
   a. Never
   b. Less than monthly
   c. Monthly
   d. Weekly
   e. Daily or almost daily

(*continued*)

> ## Exhibit 11.11 The Alcohol Use Disorders Identification Test (*continued*)
>
> 9. **Have you or someone else been injured as a result of your drinking?**
>   a. No
>   b. Yes, but not in the past year
>   c. Yes, during the past year
>
> 10. **Has a relative or friend, doctor, or other health worker been concerned about your drinking or suggested you cut down?**
>   a. No
>   b. Yes, but not during the past year
>   c. Yes, during the past year
>
> **SCORING THE AUDIT:**
>
> Scores for each question range from 0 to 4, with the first response for each question (e.g., never) scoring 0, the second (e.g., less than monthly) scoring 1, the third (e.g., monthly) scoring 2, the fourth (e.g., weekly) scoring 3, and the last response (e.g., daily or almost daily) scoring 4. For questions 9 and 10, which have only three responses, the scoring is 0 for the first (e.g., No), 2 for the second (e.g., Yes, but not in the past year), and 4 for the third (e.g., Yes, during the past year).
>
> A score of 8 or more is associated with harmful or hazardous drinking. A score of 13 or more in women and 15 or more in men is likely to indicate alcohol dependence.
>
> *Note:* The authors and the World Health Organization (WHO) have placed the AUDIT in the public domain. The test may be used without copyright. Clinicians must credit the authors and WHO as developers.
>
> *Source:* From Barbor, T. F., Higgins-Biddle, J. C., Saunders, J. B., & Monteiro, M. G. (2001). *The alcohol use disorders identification test: Guidelines for use in primary care* (2nd ed.). World Health Organization. https://apps.who.int/iris/bitstream/handle/10665/67205/WHO_MSD_MSB_01.6a.pdf

HEALING RITUALS FOR TRAUMA TREATMENT

There are several exercises that can be adapted for use with trauma survivors. Here, sample exercises are provided, such as the "empty chair" technique (Exhibit 11.12), "A Letter to My Traumatized Self" (Exhibit 11.13), and "Monitoring and Revising My Self-Talk to Be More Optimistic" (Exhibit 11.14).

Daily Gratitudes

Many people find daily gratitudes to be an important component of mindfulness-based therapy (Siegel, 2010). Exhibit 11.15 provides a template for listing five gratitudes. Gratitudes help ground us to the present moment and serve to help us navigate the often difficult journey in life. Some people hold daily gratitudes regarding their health, family, friends, career, and so on. The only guideline is that your list be yours and not someone else's. My suggestion is to find time each day to acknowledge your gratitudes.

THE COUNSELING PRACTICUM AND INTERNSHIP MANUAL

Exhibit 11.12 The Empty Chair Exercise for Trauma Survivors

INSTRUCTIONS:

1. Set up an extra chair facing the client.

2. Inform the client that the chair will be representing whatever they wished to project into it. That could be another person, themselves, part of their body, a behavior, and so on.

3. When the client has chosen who or what will go into the chair, invite them to begin by speaking whatever they need to say to whomever/whatever the empty chair represents (e.g., a person, a body part, or their trauma).

4. Role reversal should be encouraged at some point, that is, the client switches chairs and acts the part of the other person or object that was in the empty chair.

5. The exercise should go on as long as the client appears to be satisfied or at the counselor's discretion.

6. At the concluding portion of the exercise, the counselor may encourage, "Would you like to say one last thing?" Then, conclude the role-play portion.

7. The counselor can then help the client to deconstruct the experience by asking questions such as "What did you learn during the experience?" "How did you feel in your shoulders/stomach and back?" and so on (any part of the individual's body that they may have identified as an issue). How do you feel now that the role-play has concluded?

8. The counselor may then provide any feedback or offer insights regarding the role-play. Remember, focus on voice tone, body language, what the client said in either or both chairs (or was the client silent in one chair?), and so on.

EXHIBIT 11.13 A Letter to My Traumatized Self

INSTRUCTIONS:

1. Ask clients to draft a brief letter to their traumatized self. They should be encouraged to name their trauma (e.g., physical/emotional/sexual abuse, from combat, from an automobile accident). This letter can be written during the session or outside of the session. Likely, this letter would be written at a later stage of treatment.

2. Instruct the client to write a letter that speaks directly to the wounded part of themselves, for example, "You have hurt me for so long. But you have also taught me that I have to work to heal my pain. I have done that by coming for therapy, medication, getting sober, going to yoga. . . ." (or whatever has been done or is being done). Encourage the client to state the progress they have made during therapy.

(continued)

11: ADDRESSING TRAUMA IN COUNSELING: INTERVENTIONS FOR VICTIMS, SURVIVORS • 291

Exhibit 11.13 A Letter to My Traumatized Self (*continued*)

3. Ask the client if they would like to read the letter out loud during session.

4. Whether the client reads their letter aloud, help the client debrief what they have written. For example, you might ask, "What did you learn from writing (and reading, if applicable) your letter?" "How does this letter assist you in the healing process?"

5. Then, suggest the client imagine a time in the future, say 6 months or so from the present. At that present time, the client is no longer suffering traumatic effects. What will the client notice being different about their life? What might others close to the client (e.g., family, friends, and close colleagues) notice is different?

Exhibit 11.14 Monitoring and Revising My Self-Talk to Be More Optimistic

In the first part of this exercise, you will identify five persistent, negative thoughts. These likely are thoughts you find painful and disturbing. Perhaps they have plagued you for some time.

1. _____

2. _____

3. _____

4. _____

5. _____

Now, in the second part of this exercise, substitute positive, more realistic thoughts on the following lines:

1. _____

2. _____

3. _____

(*continued*)

292 • THE COUNSELING PRACTICUM AND INTERNSHIP MANUAL

Exhibit 11.14 Monitoring and Revising My Self-Talk to Be More Optimistic (*continued*)

4. _____

5. _____

In the final part of this exercise, you will begin to catch your negative thoughts and replace them with more positive, realistic ones as you previously did. Each day, commit to catching and changing five negative thoughts and replacing them with more positive ones. If you do so, it is likely you will feel better.

Exhibit 11.15 Daily Gratitudes

1. Today I am grateful for _____

2. Today I am grateful for _____

3. Today I am grateful for _____

4. Today I am grateful for _____

5. Today I am grateful for _____

Simple Breath Work/Meditation for De-Stressing

A simple method of relaxation is that of breath work, or meditation, depending on one's point of view. You can use meditation upon waking, before work, after lunch, before bedtime, or anytime that fits into your schedule. If you practice meditation regularly, you are likely to feel less stressed, more relaxed, sleep better, and feel more at ease (Kabit-Zinn, 2009). There are important general guidelines to observe when practicing meditation. Here are some examples:

- Find a time that works for you and practice daily, even if only for short intervals.
- Do not force yourself to think anything in particular. As some teach, meditation is about watching thoughts float past, as leaves on a stream.
- Practice in a safe place where you will not be interrupted.
- Some find a mantra—simply saying a phrase—helpful. For example, saying "Loving kindness" as one inhales and exhales is practiced by many. Another simple method is to count breaths: Breathing in is "one" and exhaling is "two." Silently repeat your mantra, as long as you meditate.

11: ADDRESSING TRAUMA IN COUNSELING: INTERVENTIONS FOR VICTIMS, SURVIVORS • 293

- When your mind wanders, and it will, just return your focus to the breath.
- A small percentage of trauma survivors may experience flashbacks. If so, cease meditation and continue working with a counselor.
- Using meditation in combination with yoga and exercise works very well and is recommended.

Case Study 11.2 The Case of Jen-Li

Jen-Li has just completed her doctorate in counselor education and holds a master's in clinical rehabilitation counseling and is a registered nurse (RN) and a licensed professional counselor and clinical supervisor working in an urban hospital. She oversees a staff of therapists and nurses serving in patient and outpatient clients. Moshe, a counselor she has been supervising, discusses a patient he has been supervising for trauma recovery. Moshe is trained in mindfulness-based cognitive therapy and EFT (tapping and touching body meridians). He reports the client has made progress but is sleeping poorly, thus feeling physically and emotionally weary. The problem is the night terrors the patient has 2 to 3 nights a week. Moshe asks, "What can I do to help this patient?"

If you were Jen-Li, what treatment strategies might you suggest to Moshe?

Body Work

Many trauma survivors carry trauma in their bodies and need focused body-centered work to re inhabit their own body (Van der Kolk, 2015). Trauma-sensitive yoga, tai chi, Qi gong, and Pilates are highly recommended for trauma survivors who need methods to self-soothe and reduce anxiety (Emerson, 2015; Van der Kolk, 2015). EFT involving tapping or touching meridians (pressure points) in the body has demonstrated efficacy in treating PTSD symptoms, anxiety, and depression (Sebastian & Nelms, 2017). Body work has become mainstream with practitioners in every sizable community. The recommendation here is to seek out teachers with trauma training. There are numerous resources on trauma-sensitive yoga as well. Body work such as yoga appears to have a proactive healing function.

CONCLUSION

Holistic trauma treatment involving the mind, body, and breath is very likely to become a dominant focus for graduate counseling programs and certainly for professional counselors working in the field. On a weekly basis, I receive flyers through email or the postal service, and trauma treatment is the most popular subject. Given the ubiquity of trauma in society, developing competence in counseling trauma survivors will be essential to a successful career. Fortunately, there are plenty of trainings, workshops, books, and journal articles for guidance. Many clinics have adopted one of the efficacious approaches to trauma treatment and provide in-house training and supervision. So, should you be feeling uneasy regarding your current skill level, remember you will receive much training and experience during your career. Further recommended is volunteering for any trauma trainings and certifications your future employer offers. No doubt, such training will be an asset in your counseling career.

Chapter Closing

After reading this chapter on trauma treatment, list five things you have learned.

1. _____.
2. _____.
3. _____.
4. _____.
5. _____.

LESSONS LEARNED

"I hear his footsteps most nights," said a 30-something male client as we began unpacking the trauma that had brought him to counseling. Pete (pseudonym) was well educated and held a professional job in the community. He had been referred to me to address his anxiety and use of alcohol. He presented at the clinic well groomed and seemed eager to get started. After the intake session, we commenced, and he disclosed being sexually abused by his stepfather over several years during adolescence. When he informed his mother, she did not believe him, compounding his sense of helplessness. He stated his mother's refusal to believe him left him feeling isolated and having no one for support. He disclosed developing intense anxiety around bedtime, given this was the time the assaults would occur. Evidently, his mother was a heavy sleeper and his stepfather would come to his room weekly and sodomize him. Realizing he was trapped, he considered suicide but decided to live, reminding himself that one day, he would be out of this hellish home. Then, his growth spurt began and he realized strength might be his vehicle out of hell. During high school, while playing football, he lifted weights steadily and became larger and stronger than his stepfather. Working up his courage, he confronted his stepfather, knocking him off his feet, warning there would be no further nightly visits, else he would deliver a severe beating to his abuser.

He found external validation through his athletic and academic achievements; however, these masked his trauma and deep sense of shame. "I am like a building that looks solid on the outside but, in reality, is crumbling internally," he said. He did seek counseling during college but dropped out of therapy when his counselor began to probe into his anxiety. His approach was to begin self-medicating with alcohol and extreme fitness. He became a triathlete, but while he performed well, earning many accolades, he admitted never feeling fulfilled. He had tried dating but even the slightest intimacy such as holding hands triggered him. "I meet women who are interested in me, but I never feel comfortable in developing any depth." He admitted to suicidal ideation but never having made a plan. He further explained, "I want to live and definitely want to feel healthy, but trauma is like a wolf stalking the periphery of my conscious." The only sexual experiences he had had were the abuse delivered by his stepfather. He had never established close friendships due to the need to shelter his status as a sexual abuse survivor. However, recently, he had developed a friendship with a female colleague and, after establishing trust, disclosed his abuse history to her. She encouraged him to seek treatment, and that was how he found his way to my office.

I had taken additional training in trauma treatment given the realization that most of my female clients had been sexually traumatized (meaning, roughly 70% of my caseload!). I had taken advanced trauma therapy in trauma-focused CBT. I explained to Pete my theoretical approach and that we would work in three phases: the first was safety and stabilization, meaning that he could say *stop!* anytime during treatment and we would stop the intervention; the second phase being working through the trauma, meaning the active phase of treatment; and the third phase being post traumatic growth, with a significant reduction, if not extinguishment, of symptoms. The final phase represented graduation from therapy and a celebration where we would acknowledge his successes.

I encouraged Pete to ask questions anytime and we commenced treatment. I worked with him on grounding to address his triggers. I explained five senses grounding such as five things he could see, four he could hear, three he could touch, two he could smell, and one he could taste and then had do a dry run using the five senses. Then, we worked on other grounding interventions such as clapping hands, stomping feet, four-square breathing, inhaling through the nose while counting 1,001 to 1,004 (seconds), and then exhaling 1,001 to 1,004 until breathing slows and he feels more relaxed. I then had him identify panicked thoughts when triggered. Evidently, there was not one specific negative self-statement but several, all being of the "I am unsafe" or "I am weak" variety. I explained cognitive reframing (the 3Cs: catch it, challenge it, and change it) and had him practicing reframing panicked self-statement with realistic ones, from "I am weak" to "I am a strong, capable person." I was careful to emphasize that these interventions would appear unnatural and might work less well initially, but with practice and confidence, he would begin to see a reduction in symptomology.

Then, I explained self-soothing, using tapping and touching from EFT. The intervention involved touching 11 meridians (pressure points) in the body. The approach worked to reduce chronic pain, numbness, and anxiety, utilizing the pressure points of acupuncture. I further explained the approach was 2,000 years old and had been validated in research for treating PTSD. Trained in a science field, he was skeptical. I encouraged him to give touching an honest effort, noting Chinese physicians had been using it for centuries and that my own spouse had found pain relief after a car accident and that the VA administration had approved it for PTSD treatment. Then, we did another dry run practice session utilizing touching.

Using a scaling question with 1 *low* and 10 *high*, I inquired about his current anxiety level. He replied it was a 6. I then showed him the 11 pressure points, using myself as a model and saying "I am healing" each time I touched a point. Then, I had Pete complete three rounds touching the 11 points while saying "I am healing." After completing the three rounds of 11 touches, I inquired about his anxiety score. Looking bewildered, he answered, "It's a 3." His anxiety had been cut by 50%! We then discussed my approach that would address mind, body, and breath. I explained that I would assess his progress using the SUDS and that our target would be to keep his average weekly SUDS score under 5. I assigned Pete to complete three rounds of touching once daily and as needed thereafter. The second assignment was to use the 3Cs thrice daily to address panicked cognitions.

Pete returned the following week looking more confident. His SUDS score averaged 5, suggesting incremental improvement, and he professed feeling more confident. He found reframing to be the most difficult task, but I encouraged him to continue, explaining CBT efficacy and that habituation was key. He reported that tapping seemed to provide the most help, while adding the five senses and basic grounding helped somewhat. When triggered, he had stomped his feet and noticed that helped reduce the anxiety. Given his improvement, I took this as an initial week of success. Pete was a reticent but motivated client, and after some four sessions, his mean anxiety score hovered between 4 and 5. He had begun dating his coworker, but they were taking intimacy slowly given his treatment. He did report feeling good about being in a romantic relationship for the first time in his life, while disclosing anxiety about looming sexual activity.

We continued treatment with the mind–body–breath work, both within and outside of sessions. His mean SUDS score continued to drop, reaching a 3. I inquired what else we might do to reduce his mean SUDS score by 1 point, and he answered it would take ending his nightmare. I asked him to tell me about the nightmares. He recounted classic-type dream scenarios of being pursued by something (likely his stepfather), with echoing footsteps. "It's like I'm running down a dark alleyway pursued by someone. I can hear the footsteps getting closer and I'm absolutely terrified!" Observing his affect during this time, he looked visibly agitated: rigid body posture, a grimace on his face, a lined forehead, and increased respiration. He reported his SUDS score was a 9 when recounting his night terrors and now was at 8. I suggested Pete do four-square breathing coupled with the mantra "I am safe." That completed, we went to his safe place, followed by the EFT 11 meridians intervention. After this battery of anxiety reduction interventions, his SUDS score dropped to a 3. No question, addressing night terrors was the next order of treatment.

I explained my approach would be to help him work up to turning to face his unknown pursuer in the dream. I also added the loud steps seemed to be significant and that we would address those also. I began by having Peter lie on the couch and pretend he was dreaming, reminding him to say the word "stop!" anytime the anxiety became too much (the 7–10 SUDS range). We began with him pretend sleeping, then moving into REM state where dreams occur. I requested he explain his nightmare aloud. He recounted walking down a dark alleyway. Soon, he found the pursuer was behind him and he began running, with the stalker chasing. "The footsteps are louder," he cried, and then he yelled, "Stop!" He opened his eyes, face looking moist. I congratulated him for getting so far in the dream reenactment and inquired about his SUDS scores before, during, and after the simulated dream. He scored the pre-dream 5, the dream 10, and the waking 7. He then began the EFT meridian exercise with the "I am safe mantra," reducing his SUDS scores to a 4 and then a 3.

I inquired if he would be willing to do a second dream simulation but, this time, with me accompanying him, explaining I would be offering encouraging comments while he was in the dream. I further explained I would ask him to turn and face the pursuer with the understanding I would be standing with him. I reminded him he could say *stop* anytime he needed, as he was in charge of the exercise. As he was entering the dream reenactment, I began to offer verbal encouragement such as "You are safe," and "I am with you," statements. As he was recounting being pursued, I suggested, "Let's turn and face your pursuer." "Stop!" he said but not as loud as last time. He looked less anxious as in the previous reenactment and reported 7 for his final SUDS score. I asked why he was less anxious and he replied, "You were with me." We then ran through another dream reenactment, and this time, he turned and faced the pursuer, whom he said was his stepfather. His final SUDS score was 6. We then did a fourth one, with his final SUDS score dropping to 5. I congratulated him of his successes and for his courage. He smiled, perhaps the first I had seen since we had begun treatment.

As our time was at an end, I encouraged Pete to turn and face his pursuer and to use the EFT meridian exercise, five senses grounding, and breathing exercises and to track his SUDS scores before bed, during the dream, and post-dream after the self-soothing interventions (e.g., EFT meridians, grounding, meditative breaths). He agreed and left the office. The next session, his affect was visibly improved. He reported working up to turning to face his pursuer and finally being able to do it! I praised him for his success and inquired what he attributed as the key to his success. He reported the mind–body–breaths approach, with the EFT touching and the practice during our last session. He offered the self-talk. He found that reframing was helpful prior to and after dreaming but that the meridians intervention worked best in reducing his anxiety. He added there was a surprise awaiting him when he turned around. When he turned to face what he expected to be his stepfather pursuing him in the dark alley, it turned out to be some kind person who was trying to catch up and provide assistance. While the nice pursuer was no one he could recall from actual life, he nevertheless realized the stalker was merely trying to get his attention. "You know, I suppose it was just my unconscious mind saying, 'Pay attention to me'" Pete stated.

Still wary of healing complex PTSD in less than 10 sessions, we spent another two sessions together practicing the dream reenactment. For the final session, I had him face an empty chair with his stepfather in the chair. He spoke to his abuser, explaining how the abuse and trauma had impacted him and also how his work in counseling was helping him heal. Finally, he said to his stepfather, "I forgive you, even though you never asked for forgiveness and even though you never showed remorse." He declined to have his stepfather speak to him expressing, "I no longer care what he thinks or says." I asked Pete to acknowledge the gains he had made, and he recounted coming to session being the most difficult part, closely followed by the initial dream reenactment and the actual night terror. He reported his lowest mean SUDS scores were in the 1 to 2 range. I praised his courage and work ethic again and asked if there was any other success I might be unaware of. He laughed, his face flushed a slight red, and replied, "Yes, but I will leave it to you to speculate on it."

I encouraged Pete to continue working using the mind–body–breaths and using SUDS scoring to assess continued care and recovery, explaining that even the most resilient people will become triggered at times. I emphasized that my door was always open should he feel the need to return for a refresher set of sessions. We then shook hands and he exited my office and my life.

The lesson learned and, more precisely, relearned is that trauma survivors need to feel a sense of control. My approach is to assure them they can stop anytime they feel too anxious (SUDS score of 7–10). A multimodal approach of breathing, revising self-talk, grounding, facing the fear, and practicing in session is very important in moving from victim to survivor to thriver.

RECOMMENDED RESOURCES

This is not an exhaustive list, but these are simply resources I have found helpful. I encourage you to seek the advice of others, such as professors, clinical supervisors, colleagues, and so on.

Curran, L. A. (2013). *101 trauma-informed interventions: Activities, exercises and assignments to move the client and therapy forward*. PESI Publishing & Media.
Linehan, M. M. (2014). *DBT skills training handouts and worksheets* (2nd ed.). Guilford Press.

A robust set of instructor resources designed to supplement this text is located at http://connect.springerpub.com/content/book/978-0-8261-6607-4. Qualifying instructors may request access by emailing textbook@springerpub.com.

REFERENCES

American Psychological Association. (n.d.). *Trauma*. https://www.apa.org/topics/trauma
American Psychiatric Association. (2022). *Diagnostic and statistical manual of mental disorders* (5th ed.). American Psychiatric Publishing.
Barbor, T. F., Higgins-Biddle, J. C., Saunders, J. B., & Monteiro, M. G. (2001). *The alcohol use disorders identification test: Guidelines for use in primary care* (2nd ed.). World Health Organization.
Beck, A. T., & Haigh, E. A. P. (2014). Advances in cognitive theory and therapy: The generic cognitive model. *Annual Review of Clinical Psychology, 10*, 1–24. https://doi.org/10.1146/annurev-clinpsy-032813-153734
Chodron, P. (1997). *When things fall apart: Heart advice for difficult times*. Shambala.
Ellis, A. E. (1994). *Reason and emotion in psychotherapy*. Birscj Lane.
Ellis, A. E. (2000). *How to control your anxiety before it controls you*. W. W. Norton.
Emerson, D. (2015). *Trauma-sensitive yoga: Bringing the body into treatment*. W. W. Norton.
Gual, A., Segura, L., Contel, M., Heather, N., & Colom, J. (2002). AUDIT-3 and AUDIT-4: Effectiveness of two short forms of the Alcohol Use Disorders Identification Test. *Alcoholism, 37*, 591–596. https://doi.org/10.1093/alcalc/37.6.591
Heck, E. J. (1991). Developing a screening questionnaire for problem drinking in college students. *Journal of American College Health, 39*, 227–234. https://doi.org/10.1080/07448481.1991.9936239
Hobson, A. (2009). The neurobiology of consciousness: Lucid dreaming wakes up. *International Journal of Dream Research, 2*, 41–44. https://doi.org/10.11588/ijodr.2009.2.403
Kabit-Zinn, J. (2009). *Wherever you go, there you are: Mindfulness meditation in everyday life*. Hatchet Books.
Kitchens, J. M. (1994). Does this patient have an alcohol problem? *Journal of the American Medical Association, 272*, 1782–1787. https://doi.org/10.1001/jama.272.22.1782
Kushner, H. (1981). *When bad things happen to good people*. Avon Books.
Levers, L. L. (Eds). (2022). *Trauma counseling: Theories and interventions, second edition*. Springer Publishing Company.
Matsakis, A. (1994). *Post-traumatic stress disorder: A clinician's guide*. New Harbinger.
Meichenbaum, D. (1994). *A clinical handbook/practical therapist manual: For assessing and treating adults with post-traumatic stress disorder*. Institute Press.

Miller, W. R., Forcehimes, A. A., & Zweben, A. (2011). *Treating addictions: A guide for professionals*. Guilford Press.

Monson, C. M., & Friedman, M. J. (2006). Back to the future of understanding trauma. In V. Follett & J. Ruzek (Eds.), *Cognitive-behavioral therapies for trauma* (2nd ed., pp. 1–13). Guilford Press.

Park, C. L., & Folkman, S. (1997). Meaning in the context of stress and coping. *General Review of Psychology, 1*, 115–144. https://doi.org/10.1037/1089-2680.1.2.115

Parker-Pope, T. (2015, January 19). Writing your way to happiness. *The New York Times*. https://well.blogs .nytimes.com/2015/01/19/writing-your-way-to-happiness

Pennebaker, J. W., & Campbell, R. S. (2000). The effects of writing about traumatic experience. *Clinical Quarterly, 9*(2), 19–21. https://web.archive.org/web/20050421202825/http://www.ncptsd.va.gov /publications/cq/v9/n2/V9N2.PDF

Rothschild, B. (2010). *8 keys to safe trauma recovery: Take-charge strategies to empower your healing*. W.W Norton.

Sebastian, B., & Nelms, J. (2017). The effectiveness of emotional freedom techniques in the treatment of post-traumatic stress disorder: A meta-analysis. *Explore (NY)*. https://doi.org/10.1016/j .explore.2016.10.001

Sidran Institute. (n.d.). *Post-traumatic stress disorder fact sheet*. Traumatic Stress Institute.

Siegel, D. J. (2010). *The mindful therapist: A clinician's guide to mindsight and neural integration*. W. W. Norton.

Spoormaker, V. I. (2008). A cognitive model of recurrent nightmares. *International Journal of Dream Research, 1*, 15–22. https://doi.org/10.11588/ijodr.2008.1.21

Van der Kolk, B. (2015). *The body keeps score: Brain, mind, and body in the healing of trauma*. Penguin.

van der Kolk, B. A. (2003). *Psychological trauma*. American Psychiatric Publishing.

Webber, J. M., & Mascari, J. B. (2018). Understanding disaster mental health. In J. M. Webber & J. B. Mascari (Eds.), *Disaster mental health counseling: A guide to preparing and responding* (4th ed., pp. 3–23). American Counseling Association.

Williams, M. B., & Poijula, S. (2016). *The PTSD workbook: Simple, effective techniques for overcoming traumatic stress symptoms* (3rd ed.). New Harbinger.

CHAPTER 12

Termination in Counseling: How to Say Goodbye

INTRODUCTION

Ethical termination of the counseling relationship should be planned, thoughtful, and prevent harm (Vasquez et al., 2008). Up until recently, the process of termination in counseling has largely been avoided in the literature (Gladding, 2009; Maholick & Turner, 1979). Research by Ward (1990) and Hill and Knox (2009) concluded that the reason for this deficit is twofold. First, termination is associated with loss, which is often an avoided topic in our society. Second, termination, unlike establishing the counseling relationship, is not always related to the skills that promote counseling. This chapter focuses on methods of termination and also illustrates some issues that impede termination both for the counselor and the client. It is worth mentioning that for some clients, the counseling relationship may represent the best relationship they have ever had. For clients whose primary positive human connection is during counseling, it is natural that they would seek to remain in counseling indefinitely. Counselors should discuss the issues regarding termination with the client well in advance of the final session. Such a conversation provides needed time to address the ending of a significant relationship. Remember, many clients may also have abandonment issues, and debriefing the soon-to-end counseling relationship is a critical necessity.

Gladding (2009) postulated that more emphasis has recently been placed on termination because of a greater societal acceptance of loss. Although much of Western society has traditionally been one of death-denying societies (Kübler-Ross, 1969), loss and grief are now popular topics in the counseling field, as numerous books, journal articles, and workshops target grief counseling. Terminations and endings are now associated with new beginnings and new adventures regarding the counseling relationship, and it is this latter point that is critical for successful client termination. It should also be acknowledged that a lack of termination training in counselor education programs results in incomplete education and could be a potential liability for counselors unskilled in ending counseling relationships. After all, endings are a significant part of the life process (Maholick & Turner, 1979), and to begin a new phase in life, a former experience must be completed (Perls, 1969; Rogers, 1961). Termination can also serve as a springboard for clients to move on to healthier, more growth-oriented behavior (Yalom & Leszcz, 2005).

Basically, termination is an important part of the counseling process for both the client and the counselor. Generally, counselors make the termination decisions (Gibson & Mitchell, 2008), typically based on successful completion of the treatment plan, but it is best if termination is mutually agreed upon by the counselor and the client. Prior to ending therapy, counselors assist clients in identifying the positive changes they have made and addressing potential future barriers to continued change (Murphy, 2015).

Endings in counseling also serve as important reminders of the life process. Relationships with family begin at birth, grow, develop throughout the life span, and terminate in death. Along the way, friendships end with relocation, marriages end in divorce, and collegial relations change as people accept new jobs and leave previous ones. Healthy adjustment to change depends on acknowledgment and mourning the end of relationships and transitioning to new ones (Humphrey, 2009; Perls, 1969). Proper termination of the counseling relationship conveys respect and may help prevent harm, both of which are important ethical considerations (Vasquez et al., 2008). Termination may, of course, be painful for the client, but it also presents the opportunity to create new and, often, more fulfilling relationships. It likely is worth mentioning that counseling is also a relationship that, by its very nature, should grow toward separation.

Termination has become a more common topic in recent years, especially with the emergence of time-limited approaches, such as narrative and solution-focused counseling (Gladding, 2009). These approaches begin with the assumption that each session may be the last and that, consequently, the counselor should be preparing the client for termination from the onset of therapy (Murphy, 2015; O'Hanlon, 1994). Acknowledging that time in counseling is limited could also help the client in becoming more proactive and doing less procrastinating. Understanding the limits of counseling may also spur the client to make more use of their time and change jobs, go back to finish college, end unhealthy relationships, and set new goals.

Successful counseling will result in attitudinal and behavioral changes in clients' lives. Such growth should naturally be a clear focus of counseling. Counselors also should encourage their clients to practice their new skills each week in their personal lives. Part of the therapeutic process also involves the counselor preparing the client for the ending of the counseling relationship. This also can involve a role-play. By role-playing termination, clients and counselors acknowledge and honor the relationship. As Gladding (1990) eruditely wrote, termination puts "insights into action" (p. 130).

Naturally, not all counseling relationships end as the counselor or client would like. Circumstances and issues may arise that facilitate the counselor terminating the counseling relationship against a client's wishes (Welfel, 2010). According to Standard A.11.c of the *ACA Code of Ethics* (American Counseling Association [ACA], 2014), counselors may terminate a counseling relationship in the following circumstances:

- when the client is no longer benefiting from or may be harmed through continued counseling;
- when in jeopardy of harm by the client or by another person with whom the client has a relationship; or
- when clients do not pay the fees as agreed upon.

When counselors are unable to be of assistance to clients, counselors must provide adequate notice and pretermination counseling and recommend other service providers when necessary. Also, counselors should do everything possible to ensure a smooth transition to a new counseling professional. If client insolvency is an issue, the counselor must provide a referral to a counselor or agency that offers a sliding fee scale (where allowed) or provides pro bono services. A referral to another provider will, of course, require the client to sign a release of information in order to share information and records with the new mental health professional.

It should be mentioned that clients often terminate the counseling relationship abruptly. Some research suggests that 30% to 60% of all counseling clients drop out of counseling before completing the treatment plan (Garfield, 1994). All professional counselors have experienced a client's discontinuation of services even when treatment was going well. Clients often drop out without notifying their counselor. The counselor's ethical obligation in such situations is to attempt to contact the client, suggesting a return to counseling to complete treatment or for a referral to another provider. Professional counselors will even experience court-mandated clients dropping from treatment even when noncompliance means a return to prison or jail! (I have witnessed this firsthand.) So, counselors must be prepared for clients to withdraw from counseling without notice, regardless of the circumstances or consequences. In such situations, counselors must attempt to contact the client and encourage completing treatment or taking a referral. Realistically, clients who drop out of counseling are often reluctant to return, as they have already made the decision to end therapy.

Finally, termination serves to reinforce that the client is ready to graduate from counseling as a healthier, more well-adjusted person (Rogers, 1961). Personally, as both a counselor and a former client, I much prefer the term "graduation" over termination because it implies goals have been met. Through the crucible of the counseling relationship, the client has grown and mastered many of the obstacles that originally brought them into counseling. The client's increased ability to manage the demands of life results in increased self-confidence and a healthier and more meaningful life (Yalom & Leszcz, 2005). The lack of appropriate termination would actually rob the client of a lot of potential growth! So, counselors and counseling students can utilize termination, or graduation, as an important growth step.

In this chapter, I discuss some issues regarding when and how to terminate counseling.

WHEN TO TERMINATE A COUNSELING RELATIONSHIP

Knowing when to terminate a counseling relationship is an inexact proposition. In the managed care system, typically, insurance companies determine the session parameters of counseling. Other factors that will influence termination are legally set limits (e.g., by a judge, probation officer, parent, or legal guardian) and whether the client is in a residential treatment setting. In my experience, clients often make the decision to end the relationship before the counselor. Still, it is important to dialogue with the client to ensure that they have thought through the process. If counseling ends too soon, clients may not be able to maintain the healthy behaviors they learned in therapy. Conversely, if termination is not addressed in a timely manner, counseling may drag on with no real focus, wasting time that could be used for needy clients (to say nothing of the cost). There are several issues to address when considering termination (Gladding, 2009, pp. 177–180):

- Have clients achieved behavioral, cognitive, or affective goals? When both clients and counselors have a clear idea about whether particular goals have been reached, the timing of termination is easier to figure out. The key is to establish a mutually agreed-on contract before counseling begins.
- Can clients concretely show they have made progress in what they wanted to accomplish? Specific progress may be the basis for making a decision about termination.
- Is the counseling relationship helpful? If either the client or the counselor senses that what is occurring in the counseling sessions is not helpful, termination may be appropriate.
- Has the context of the original counseling arrangement changed? In cases where there is a move or a prolonged illness, termination (as well as a referral) should be considered. Examine whether the client's initial problem or symptoms have been eliminated or significantly reduced.
- Does the client appear capable of coping with demands in their life?
- Is the client better able to relate to others and to give and receive love?
- Has the client progressed in their ability to be productive in career and life tasks?
- Can the client "play" and enjoy life?

I have also found it helpful to consider another factor: Is the counselor confident the client is ready for termination? This is nothing scientific, but experienced counselors often develop a sixth sense regarding a client's likelihood for success. Has the client been generally on time and seemed engaged in the sessions? If you gave homework, how consistent was the client's follow-through? What types of "slip ups" has the client had during treatment? Finally, how confident are you regarding the client's continued success? ("On a scale of 1–10, with 10 high, what is your confidence score?") These are just some of the questions to consider regarding termination. Wise counselors will attend to this "sense" and explore the client's own readiness for termination.

It is up to the counselor to explain termination clearly to the client at the earliest possible time. The initial intake is the ideal time to cover the topic, especially as essentials such as confidentially, fees, and related topics are covered during that session. This way, the client understands that at some point in the future, the counseling relationship will end. Termination should also be framed in terms of success. Here is an example:

Counselor: Now, at some point in the future, when you have met your goals for counseling, you will graduate from counseling. So, we want to keep that end point in mind.

As mentioned earlier, if the client has been mandated by a judge, probation officer, or another party, then termination will likely have more fixed parameters.

Counselor: Steve, the terms of your probation specify 12 sessions of anger management. Provided you have attended all sessions and have made progress, termination will occur at that point and I will write a report for your probation officer. Do you have any questions?

Here is another example:

Counselor: Jade, your health plan provides eight individual counseling sessions. Now, in the event we both feel you could use more, I can ask the HMO to authorize two additional sessions. Another option after eight sessions is to get you into a local support group.

These are all examples of the counselor explaining at the onset that the counseling relationship will end. This reduces the likelihood that the client will be surprised by termination.

DISCUSSING TERMINATION WITH THE CLIENT

Counselor: Shoshanna, I have seen you make a lot of progress over the past 9 weeks. Your depression, as evidenced by the Beck Depression Inventory-II, seems to have dropped significantly. You have also mentioned that you are managing your grief much better and that recently, you have been able to reach out and initiate social events with friends. These were the issues that brought you into counseling. So, I'm wondering how you feel about terminating from counseling in the next 2 weeks.

Client: You know, I'm kind of thinking the same thing. I do feel a lot better . . . still sad about my mother's death, but she did have a full life and she was old. I would like to have at least a couple of sessions to wrap up. Okay?

Counselor: Absolutely. Two more sessions sound very wise to me. We can also revisit the option of the grief support group during the next two sessions, as a support could be a good aftercare plan.

In many cases, termination may be a shared decision between the counselor and the client. For example, a client may say, "I believe I have made a lot of progress the past 3 months. I'm thinking one more session would be enough. What do you think?" Or the counselor may initiate the conversation by saying, "You appear to be in a very solid place. I'm thinking we could wrap up our relationship in two more sessions. What do you think about that?" In these examples, both the client's and the counselor's termination statements imply client growth and resolution of whatever issues brought the client into counseling. Both statements also involve verifying the message with the other party. I encourage counselors to include the client in any discussion of termination; including the client in significant discussions demonstrates your respect and trust in the client (Miller & Rollnick, 2002). The following is an example of a discussion of termination to a client:

Counselor: Shoshanna, I have seen you make a lot of progress over the past 9 weeks. Your depression, as evidenced by the Beck Depression Inventory-II, seems to have dropped significantly. You have also mentioned that you are managing your grief much better and that recently you have been able to reach out and initiate social events with friends. These were the issues that brought you into counseling. So, I'm wondering how you feel about terminating from counseling in the next 2 weeks.

306 • THE COUNSELING PRACTICUM AND INTERNSHIP MANUAL

Client: You know I'm kind of thinking the same thing. I do feel a lot better . . . still sad about my mother's death, but she did have a full life and she was old. I would like to have at least a couple of sessions to wrap up. Okay?

Counselor: Absolutely. Two more sessions sounds very wise to me. We can also revisit the option of the grief support group during the next two sessions as a support could be a good aftercare plan.

In the example, the counselor raises the topic of termination and frames it in such a fashion that client progress is noted in a concrete manner. The counselor also solicits the input of the client and thereby demonstrates trust and respect for the client's judgment. They agree on at least one more session, and the counselor mentions a support group in the event the client would like more emotional support.

Cormier and Hackney (2008) believe that when counseling relationships last more than 3 months, the final 3 to 4 weeks should be spent discussing the impact of termination. They suggest counselors inquire how their clients will cope without the counselor's support. Counselors may also address topics such as what has changed since the client has entered therapy, what the client has learned, and how the client's life will be different in the post-counseling phase. In my experience, it has been helpful to acknowledge the growth and hard work of the client, as most clients will appreciate having their personal work acknowledged by the counselor.

De Shazer and Berg (1988), proponents of solution-focused therapy, advocate using scaling questions to assess client growth. The following dialogue is an example of using scaling questions to discuss termination:

Counselor: Well, we are now at the end of counseling. On a scale of 1 to 10, with 10 being *high* and 1 being *low*, how helpful has counseling been for you?

Scaling questions provide some concrete idea of progress and allow the client to provide explicit feedback regarding what has and has not been helpful. Scaling questions focused on therapeutic effectiveness provide a forum for client and counselor discussion. Now, suppose the client answers in the following manner:

Client: On a scale of 1 to 10, with 10 high, today's session has been only a 2.

Counselor: Okay, what can we do next time to move it to a 3?

In this case, the counselor does not become defensive and argue with the client but rather accepts the client's verdict and reframes it to elicit what could be more helpful in the next session. Scaling questions could also be used at termination to help the counselor understand how they can be more helpful in the future.

Counselor: Okay, I ask this question to all clients about to graduate from counseling. On a scale of 1 to 10, with 1 being counseling was *not helpful* to 10 being counseling was *very helpful*, how would you rate your experience in counseling?

Client: I would rate it a 6.

Counselor: Well, it sounds like our time together was worthwhile. Now, what could we have done to make our rating a 7?

When using scaling questions, it is best to keep improvements small so as to make them appear more attainable (de Shazer & Berg, 1988). As much as possible, the counselor should make the termination session as positive as possible, and discussing outcomes and soliciting feedback from the client is the most direct way to achieve this.

THE TERMINATION PLAN

If you think a client may be ready for termination, there are several logistical issues to consider:

- Does the client have adequate resources outside the counseling relationship to sustain whatever gains were made in counseling? Resources might include supportive family, friends, colleagues, support groups, and so forth.
- Have you spent adequate time preparing the client for termination? Ideally, the counselor begins to prepare the client for eventual termination at the onset of therapy. Some professionals recommend an approach called *fading* (Dixon & Glover, 1984), which involves a gradual decrease in counseling, for example, going to 30-minute sessions or spacing sessions 2 weeks or more apart instead of meeting weekly. Another technique involves reminding the client about the remaining number of sessions: "Now, remember, we have three more sessions remaining." You do not want an abrupt termination or else you can undo successful therapeutic gains and potentially be liable for abandonment.
- Have you and the client agreed on an aftercare plan (if needed)? Has the client agreed to join a support group, if necessary?
- Have you documented in the case notes why you terminated the client?
- In cases of mandated counseling, has the client met the conditions set down by the court, probation officer, place of employment, disciplinary board, or other concerned institutions? Does the client need a letter stating they have met the conditions? If subpoenaed for a court hearing and you were mandated to testify, could you defend termination with the client? As legal hearings can be daunting, it is good to consider this regarding termination of therapeutic services. Remember, legal counsel will be probing to find the weak links in your treatment and clinical decision-making.

These issues will not apply equally to all clients, but they should be considered and discussed with the client before making a decision regarding termination. Counselors should also discuss termination issues with their supervisor.

CLIENT RESISTANCE TO TERMINATION

Counselors should be aware that some clients will resist termination. There are several reasons why a client might desire to remain in counseling even after the reasons that brought the client to counseling have been resolved. A client's resistance to termination is most common when the counseling relationship has been long term; involves a strong connection between the counselor and the client; or involves factors such as grief, fear of rejection, and previous abandonment (Cormier & Cormier, 1998; Welfel & Patterson, 2005).

Some clients have few close relationships and find counseling hard to give up. It is worth mentioning that healthy friendships involve both parties engaging in a two-way relationship. Counseling relationships, although friendly, are not true friendships because counseling is all about the client. Counseling is also a professional relationship, involving an ethical code, fees, time limits, and boundaries regarding time and social distance. It may be helpful for counselors to discuss the various differences between counseling relationships and friendships, should the client be reluctant to terminate.

Witness the following exchange of dialogue between the counselor and a client reluctant to terminate:

Counselor: Ellen, we have spent the last 6 months together. I have seen you make a lot of progress on your stated goal of managing your depression and establishing personal contacts, and recently, you were able to go back to work part time. I think it's time to talk about termination or, as I like to say, graduation.

Client: But I'm just not ready. Yeah, I am back at work, but I just went back a month ago and it's hard to get back in the swing of things. Also, I have made some progress making contacts but have yet to make a real friend. It's true that I do feel better—maybe a combination of new medication and such, but coming to see you weekly is something I look forward to and can't let go of.

Counselor: I appreciate that you have found our time together valuable. But, as I mentioned two sessions ago, we are running up to the end of your insurance benefits in 2 weeks. I can work with you two more sessions, then we refer you to a support group run by a colleague.

Client: I think a support group is okay . . . and I'm willing to begin, but I want to continue counseling with you.

Counselor: Well, we are up against a couple of issues. One, as your benefits expire, our agency requires we have a minimum charge of $60 per session. The more pressing issue is that you appear ready to graduate from counseling. You have met all your treatment goals and seem to be well on your way toward the life you wanted. Being a little nervous is understandable of course.

Client: I might be able to get the money through out-of-pocket pay. So, I can continue, right?

There is no simple way to terminate with a client who is not ready to hear about termination. The counselor in this dialogue might have inquired of the client for some idea of how she would know when she would be ready for termination. Another possibility is, if the counselor believes they have taken the client as far as they can, perhaps a referral to another counselor would be beneficial. In such cases, the counselor should discuss the situation with their supervisor, get support, and make a plan to address client resistance to termination.

A client's fear of termination is an issue to address directly. Here is an example:

Counselor: Erica, I want to follow up on the topic of termination. As I mentioned previously, we have two more sessions left. I know you have some concerns regarding termination.

Client: Yes. I'm not ready to let go of the support I'm getting here. I agree that I've made a lot of progress the past 4 months, but I want to keep our relationship. I don't think I can make it without you.

Counselor: I appreciate the hard work you have put into counseling, and both of us have noted the gains you have made, especially the past 2 months. Given how you felt when counseling began, I believe you are selling yourself short regarding your own progress and resilience.

Client: But I'm not ready to end our relationship. Finally, someone understands me. Losing our weekly time together is like losing the best friend I've had.

Counselor: The reality is that our time is coming to a close. My belief is that you are ready for the next step. I think it would be wise to explore your feelings and beliefs regarding termination today and the next couple of weeks. There are also some options regarding support groups for continued growth. I must also express that counseling is not the same as a friendship. Counseling is all about the client, and friendship is two ways. Remember, you are paying for a professional service. Counselors can provide a friendly service, but that is not the same as a friendship.

The client in this scenario is very reluctant to end counseling. This hesitancy is best addressed delicately but firmly. Clients reluctant to end counseling may be overly reliant on counseling. The counselor in this scenario could use some creativity. For example, the sessions could be staggered to bimonthly instead of every week, thus providing a little more transition time. However, extending the counseling relationship in such a manner might reinforce the client's neediness and be counter-therapeutic. The counselor would be wise to have the client explore her feelings regarding termination, including a list of her fears about termination as well as what she may gain by ending the counseling relationship. As previously mentioned, support groups are always an option, provided they exist.

It must be admitted, however, that some clients will be highly resistant to ending counseling. Several years ago, I encountered a woman who had been a client at an agency for more than 20 years. The agency, wisely, had recently decided that long-term clients (2 or more years, those whose insurance coverage had run out, and those who seemed more appropriate for case management) would be moved to the case management program for chronic patients, where they would participate in support groups, peer groups, and social activities and meet weekly with a caseworker, not a counselor. In most cases, this policy was working well. This particular client, however, demanded to speak to the clinical director (me). When I went to retrieve her file from the office, it was as thick as the *Diagnostic and Statistical Manual of Mental Disorders, Fifth Edition, Text Revision* (5th ed.; *DSM-5-TR*; American Psychiatric Association, 2022)! For this client, counseling likely was more about dependence than growth. Over her strenuous objections, she was referred to the case management program.

As a new counselor, you will notice that clients have many ways to resist termination, whether at the end of the session or the end of the counseling relationship. They may request additional counseling after their goals have clearly been met or sabotage what appears to be successful therapeutic progress because they want the counseling relationship to continue. Some clients may insist that their current counselor is the "only one" who has ever been helpful, thus using manipulation in an attempt to entice counselor guilt. With apologies to de Shazer who once held a mock funeral for client resistance (Corey, 2017), my experience is client resistance is alive and kicking! Part of your continued development as a counselor is learning to address client resistance in a helpful-oriented manner. Admittedly, such can be challenging with some clients.

COUNSELOR RESISTANCE TO TERMINATION

Although the ultimate goal in counseling is to help the client move toward independence from the counseling relationship, some counselors occasionally resist termination (Corey et al., 2007). Sometimes, counselors will encounter clients they feel a special bond with or, unfortunately, clients they become infatuated with. Counselors, especially beginning counselors, must take special care to ensure they are working in the best interest of the client whenever the issue of termination arises. Counselors who find themselves reluctant to terminate a client are encouraged to consult with a supervisor or trusted colleague to critique their motivations. Goodyear (1981) has cited reasons why counselors may have difficulty with termination:

- when termination signals the end of a significant relationship;
- when termination arouses the counselor's anxieties about the client's ability to function independently;
- when termination arouses guilt in the counselor about having not been more effective with the client;
- when the counselor's professional self-concept is threatened by the client abruptly and angrily leaving;
- when termination signals the end of a learning experience for the counselor (e.g., the counselor may have been relying on the client to learn more about the dynamics of a disorder or of a particular culture);
- when termination signals the end of a particularly exciting experience of living vicariously through the adventures of the client;
- when termination becomes a symbolic recapitulation of other (especially unresolved) farewells in the counselor's life; or
- when termination arouses conflicts regarding the counselor's own individuation (e.g., the counselor's own sense of self versus others).

In my observation, some counselors also form an unhealthy attachment based on an attraction to the client and are reluctant to see the relationship end (see Case Study 12.1). The ethical issues involved in dual relationships are covered in Chapter 3,

Case Study 12.1 The Case of Jordan and Yvonne: Reluctance to Terminate Due to Personal Feelings

Jordan has been counseling Yvonne for six sessions. Yvonne originally presented for counseling after a particularly painful ending to a romantic relationship. From the beginning, Jordan noticed he and Yvonne seemed to have a stronger than typical counselor–client attachment. Although he feels Yvonne is ready for termination, he is reluctant for their relationship to end because he enjoys spending time with her. He always looks forward to their session and thinks of her after the session has ended. Yvonne has also mentioned that she would like to be in a relationship with someone who "listens to me like you do and understands me like you." Jordan knows that ethically, he should refer her or terminate with her, given both their feelings. Yet, he is reluctant to terminate or refer her as he enjoys their time together.

1. If Jordan were to consult with you, how would you advise him?
2. What ethical issues and concerns would you want Jordan to consider regarding counseling Yvonne?
3. What if Jordan refuses to terminate her? What steps might you take then?

"Ethical and Legal Issues." Beyond ethical parameters, it must be mentioned that counseling is entirely about the client. Clients, particularly those with a history of unhealthy relationships, may mistake the counselor's professional concern with that of actual friendship. Counselors then must take special care to set and respect the boundary separating the professional from the personal. Termination for clients who believe they have a special relationship with the counselor may be particularly difficult. Such clients are likely to resist ending the relationship. When you do terminate from clients, be concise though sure to document the reasons for termination of counseling. If you are making a referral to another provider or support group, make sure you document such as well.

When counselors find they are having difficulty in ending a counseling relationship, it would be prudent for them to carefully assess the reasons for their reluctance (see Box 12.1). It is well worth mentioning that counselors certainly will have their own personal issues, inadequacies, and struggles. The problem develops when counselors have not adequately addressed these issues or struggles. Counselors with a history of abandonment may be particularly vulnerable to fears of termination (Guy, 1987).

In cases where termination has been difficult for whatever reason, Welfel and Patterson (2005, pp. 124–125) offer four suggestions for counselors:

1. "Be aware of the client's needs and desires and allow the client to express them." The client may wish to express gratitude. Counselors should accept such expressions of gratitude with a simple "Thank you." Do not minimize the value of the client's expression.

Box 12.1 Self-Reflections for Counselors Reluctant to Terminate With a Client

- List the reasons why you are reluctant to terminate with the client. Whose issues are the most significant, yours or the client's?
- Is this client in crisis, that is, a risk for suicide? Why or why not?
- Now, in examining these reasons, whose needs are being served by keeping the counseling relationship going?
- What would be in the best interests of the client? Also, what would be in your own best interests (e.g., ethically, legally, professionally, personally)?
- If a friend or colleague were in the position you are in, how would you advise that friend or colleague?
- What do you need to do to be ready to "let go" of this client and facilitate termination?
- What have you learned from this termination? How will that knowledge help you in future situations?

2. "Review the major events of the counseling experience and bring the review into the present." This suggestion provides the client the opportunity to review the progress they have made during counseling.
3. "Supportively acknowledge the changes the client has made." The counselor should let the client know they recognize the progress the client has achieved.
4. "Request follow-up contact." Counseling relationships eventually end, but the client needs to know the counselor is invested in the client's continued well-being. But use discretion here, as more "needy" clients may see this as an opening to extending the relationship. Put parameters on future contact, such as stating, "Give me a brief call . . ." (Gladding, 2009, p. 187).

REFERRALS AND FOLLOW-UP

Unfortunately, it goes without saying that counselors will not be able to help 100% of the clients who pass through their door. My experience is that beginning counselors frequently struggle when they encounter clients who make marginal progress. Counselors need to be realistic regarding making referrals when productivity ends. A referral involves arranging continued therapeutic assistance for clients when the current counseling relationship is not making satisfactory progress (Pietrofesa et al., 1984). There are numerous reasons referrals are made:

- The client has an issue the counselor does not know how to handle.
- The counselor is inexperienced in a particular area (e.g., substance abuse and couples' therapy).
- The counselor knows of a nearby expert who would be more helpful to the client.

- The counselor and client have incompatible personalities.
- The relationship between the counselor and the client is stuck in an initial phase of counseling. (Goldstein, 1971)

The client may resist a referral, perhaps feeling that such action implies a sense of failure on their part. Likewise, a client may feel rejected by the counselor. Thus, the counselor needs to make it clear that the reason for the referral to another professional is neither a failure nor a fault of either the client or the counselor. Perhaps, all potential gains within the current therapeutic relationship have been made and a referral is necessary in order for continued progress to be made. Counselors should also mention the professional to whom they are referring the client; get the client's signed release to contact that clinician; and then volunteer to make the referral for the client or, at the very least, encourage the client to make the call before the session's end. Ideally, the counselor would bring up the possibility of a referral during the informed-consent phase of the intake so that the client understands from the outset that a referral is a possibility.

When the counselor begins to believe that another counselor (or other professionals) would be more beneficial for the client, they should raise the issue for discussion with the client. Discussing the possibility of a referral provides the client a voice in the matter and also establishes a forum for the counselor and client to discuss the issue. Dialoguing on the pros and cons of referral may also take some pressure off both parties because addressing the topic of referral establishes that, perhaps, another counselor is more appropriate for the client's issue. Welfel and Patterson (2005) recommend a counselor spend at least one session with the client in preparation for the referral. Some clients may need several sessions before a referral can be made.

Following up with a client after counseling has ended has become more common in recent years (Okun & Kantrowitz, 2008). Following up with former clients also provides the counselor valuable client feedback regarding the effectiveness of counseling. It can also serve to reinforce that the counselor is still concerned about the client's progress even after counseling has ended. Contact may also pave the way for the client to return should they feel the necessity.

Follow-up can be conducted on either a short-term (3 to 6 months after counseling has ended) or long-term (more than 6 months after counseling has ended) basis. One of the difficulties, especially for more mobile clients, is that counselors may no longer have an accurate address for agency clients (it is easier to track school students). Many clients also are less invested in participating in follow-up activities when they are no longer seeking counseling services. In fact, the percentage of clients who respond to counselors' follow-up efforts is, in my experience, quite small. Naturally, for practicum and internship students, follow-up can be challenging, depending on whether the intern is leaving in 3 months or will be at the site another year. Regardless, post-counseling follow-up is challenging for counselors and the schools and agencies where they work for a variety of reasons (e.g., client relocation, other priorities, and working with another professional).

Follow-up with former clients can take many forms. In the counseling centers where I have worked, follow-up consisted of a simple evaluation form accompanied by a self-addressed stamped envelope. This provides the client the opportunity to evaluate the services provided. Having had some time and distance from counseling might also be beneficial for the evaluation process, as the client may have a clearer idea of how counseling has benefited them. In the immediate aftermath, gains that seemed so promising may look less so a few months later when the supportive structure of counseling has been removed. Conversely, clients may have a clearer understanding of the gains they have made through the counseling process. This method of sending the client an evaluation is a safe method of follow-up, although some may see it as impersonal.

A second method of follow-up is to invite the former client in for a session to discuss the progress they have made after counseling has concluded (Cormier & Cormier, 1998). This method is more personal and provides the counselor the most direct feedback. For counselors working in schools, bringing in former clients may not present a problem. However, the time and expense of scheduling former clients for a check-in session in many clinical settings can be prohibitive. Does the client need to pay? Is the follow-up session free? If the counselor works in an agency, college center, or another high-volume center with a waiting list, bringing in former clients for follow-up sessions is not feasible. It is also likely that the only clients who would show for a follow-up session are the ones who felt counseling was a real success.

Another common way for counselors to check on clients is to call them on the phone, through secure email or text (be careful regarding how this is done to assure client privacy), or to request the former client to call in after 3 to 6 months after counseling has concluded. This method provides easy access and is both time and cost efficient. This approach does involve some preparatory work, as the counselor should ask the client for permission to call before doing so. Again, email could also be used, although there are concerns about the privacy and security of such a method. Secure systems exist, though no system is totally secure (neither is the telephone secure either). Agencies and schools must take reasonable precautions in follow-up with clients and students.

Although follow-up can be time consuming, it can be very important to the counseling process. Follow-up provides the counselor a concrete method of evaluating the success of counseling. In my experience, most clients appreciate the opportunity to have a voice in the evaluative process. Counselors can also receive some helpful feedback regarding their own sense of effectiveness and what techniques worked best for the particular client. Counselors may also discover the client had a different idea of what was and was not helpful. Counselors must also be ready to receive critical feedback regarding themselves, their approach, and their effectiveness. The important thing for counselors (particularly beginning counselors) to remember is that the feedback and evaluation process provides valuable feedback into the effectiveness of their work. This piece of the counseling process may well be the most important of all.

ABANDONMENT

Counselors must be careful to avoid abandonment when terminating a client. Abandonment is a form of inappropriate termination and occurs when the client's treatment needs are not adequately addressed by the counselor when treatment ends or when the counselor simply drops the client from treatment (Vasquez et al., 2008). The *ACA Code of Ethics* (ACA, 2014, Standard A.11.a) and court decisions related to the medical profession (*Allison v. Patel*, 1993; *Manno v. McIntosh*, 1994) prohibit counselors from client abandonment. When the counseling relationship has been established, the counselor cannot arbitrarily discontinue services if said action puts the client at risk. Risk might be applied to clients in crisis (e.g., suicidal ideation, extreme vulnerability, or significant treatment goals not met). Counselors also "…must not abandon or neglect clients in counseling." Counselors assist in making appropriate arrangements for the continuation of treatment (ACA, 2014, Standard A.12.).

To prevent abandonment, counselors should provide reasonable notice prior to termination. In planned termination—that is, when a client has, say, a total of 12 sessions as per insurance coverage—the counselor could simply remind the client of the number of remaining sessions around session eight:

Counselor: So, Consuelo, we have three more sessions left after today.

Client: Alright. It's good to be reminded. Sometimes things slip up on people, you know?

Counselor: Absolutely. Now, during our last session in 3 weeks, we'll review treatment progress so you'll be ready to graduate from therapy.

The following week:

Counselor: Consuelo, we have two more sessions left after today.

In addition to termination, counselors must also provide clients reasonable notice or a substitute counselor when a planned absence occurs, such as a pregnancy, vacation, or other prolonged absence. Counselors must document their planning in the case record in the event the counselor's absence becomes an issue.

Hilliard (1998, in Remley & Herlihy, 2020), an attorney who represents mental health professionals sued by their clients, offers practical recommendations. Hilliard has recommended counselors never terminate a professional relationship over a client's objection when the client is angry or in a serious crisis situation. Providing additional time to address the client's anxiety or distress likely would help the client address unresolved issues and help make the transition from one counseling professional to another. As important, a judge or jury likely would not look favorably on a mental health professional's decision to abruptly end a relationship in the middle of a crisis (*Allison v. Patel*, 1993; *Manno v. McIntosh*, 1994; Wheeler & Bertram, 2019). If the client is in crisis, even if the client's insurance benefits have expired, the counselor should continue treatment until the crisis phase is over (Packman & Harris, 1998).

To protect mental health professionals from litigation for abandonment, Hilliard (1998) and Macbethet et al. (1994) have developed the following guidelines for mental health professionals to use when they are terminating clients who are resisting termination (in Remley & Herlihy, 2020, pp. 87–88):

- Honestly discuss with the client your intention to terminate and the specific reason for your decision.
- Give the client an opportunity to make changes that would be necessary to continue the relationship.
- Give written notice to the client that the relationship will be terminated.

- Offer the client one to three termination sessions.
- Give your client up to three referrals.
- Give your client places to contact in the event of emergencies.
- Place a summary of your interactions with the client around the termination issue in the client's file. Do not transfer that document to another individual or entity without an expressed written request from the client.
- Give the client plenty of time to find another mental health professional. If more time is requested, allow it.
- Transfer records to the new mental health professional.

CONCLUSION

Terminating with clients can be difficult for both the counselor and the client. It is natural for clients to want to "hang onto" a relationship that has been positive and growth oriented for them. After all, for some clients, the counseling relationship may have been their closest relationship. Nevertheless, termination is necessary for continued growth and development of the client. Counselors would do well to frame termination as "continued growth" and portray it as a type of "commencement." Such language suggests gains have been made and the client is ready for future challenges.

For counselors, especially graduate student counselors in training, learning to "let go" of clients they have worked with for extended periods can be very difficult, especially if the client has made significant progress. It is important for counselors to remember that the welfare of the client is of utmost importance. An important aspect of client welfare is acknowledging the completion of major treatment goals and the subsequent "graduation" from counseling. Counselors having difficulty with termination should seek out their supervisor for advice on the matter. It is also recommended that counselors engage in self-reflection and ask themselves, "What makes termination with this client so difficult?" The difficulty may arise from issues within the counselor that need addressing. If a counselor continues experiencing difficulty with termination, individual counseling is recommended in order for the counselor to examine personal issues regarding relationship endings. After all, counselors are human and may have abandonment issues in their own life that they need to further address.

Though many people would prefer not to think about it, endings are a natural part of the life process as people move away, divorce, take new jobs, marry, launch adult children to college, work, join the military, and so on, and of course, everyone eventually dies. That endings are as common as beginnings, however, scarcely makes them easy, and in fact, terminations often present challenges for everyone. As covered in this chapter, some clients will resist and perhaps even sabotage termination, as they may see they are losing a "friend" or a major support system. Thus, dialoguing with the client on termination is an important part of counseling treatment and presents a valuable opportunity. Work with your field site supervisor and university supervisor to manage such challenging situations because termination may present difficulties for you, the counseling student. The good news is that the more experience you gain with termination, the more competent you will become with such endings. It is also accurate to say that many clients will see termination as a positive sign of growth and will be looking forward to "graduating" from counseling. Some counselors and counseling sites will even hold "graduation" for clients. This practice is more common in 12-step programs (1 year of sobriety), residential programs, group treatment, and even some schools. At one residential psychiatric agency where I worked, the person completing treatment was honored with a cake, as well as testimony from counselors, parents, guardians, and peers regarding the client's growth and progress. Whatever the counselor does, acknowledging completion by honoring the client's accomplishment is a good practice regarding completion. Celebrating achievements, which certainly includes "graduating" from counseling, can be a healthy habit.

LESSONS LEARNED

"Can you take Sue (pseudonym) on as a client?" Jane (pseudonym), one of the counselors I was supervising, had previously counseled her several times during her long career in our rural, mountain west community. As director of clinical services, I served in an administrative capacity, overseeing all clinical programs while carrying a caseload of 7 to 10 clients per week. According to the counselor, Sue had a tendency toward dependency. "She's very nice, shows up on time, and is compliant. Unfortunately, she always finds creative ways to sabotage her treatment." Jane then went on to detail a long list of times Sue torpedoed her treatment in order to extend services, including feigned suicidal ideation. "I think she might work better with a male counselor," Jane opined with emphasis. This left me wondering if Jane and the treatment staff viewed me as their rescue boat, off-loading a pesky, persistent client who seemed to be using therapy in lieu of deeper friendships. After some back and forth negotiation, I agreed to take her on my caseload, especially as the treatment team was maxed out with clients.

When Sue arrived for her initial session with me (after the intake staff had assessed her), she appeared well groomed, upbeat, and excited to meet her new counselor. She was a middle-aged, heavy-set, Caucasian, never-married female with no children, although she had several close family members within an hour radius. She reported being active in her church and enjoyed volunteering at a senior center. The intake assessment (computerized structured clinical interview for *DSM*) seemed inconclusive regarding a diagnosis. Previous assessments and therapists suggested her concerns would be more a social-environmental *DSM-V* code-type diagnosis. As such would not be insurance reimbursable, that meant the client would be forced to pay out of pocket for services. Unlike most residents of our rural farming community, this posed no barrier for Sue as she came from a family of means. She was also well educated, holding an associate's degree in business from the local community college and a bachelor's degree from one of the state universities. Unsure what to make of her thick file (era prior to e-files), I did what I always did when in doubt: I asked the client how I might be helpful.

Sue smiled and explained that while she had had a good career—she had recently retired—and generally good family relationships, she had never felt very satisfied with her life. "I enjoy volunteer work, teach Sunday school at church, and see family weekly. But, something is always missing." I inquired what that something might be, and she shrugged. I noted she had a long history at the clinic and asked how helpful previous counseling had been. She replied that counseling had helped her maintain her generally positive mood but again stated "something is missing." I inquired what that something might be, but she shook her head. I asked if she had friendships outside her family, and she stated most in her social group and age had children or even grandchildren, leaving her disconnected from them.

"So, would you say the missing piece in your life is a close friendship?," I asked." "Yes, I think so," she replied in evident sincerity and without hesitation. Using counseling as a substitute for friends had been Jane's view of Sue. My spouse's culture has a colorful Yiddish statement of "tuchus oyfn tish" (pronounced TOOK-us OY-f'n tish) or literally "put your butt on the table," or *tell me the truth*. In that vein, I asked gently as possible, "I'm wondering if you are coming to counseling as a substitute for missing friendships." She answered, "That's what Jane and your colleagues think. I get why they think that." My read of Sue thus far was she was honest. Of course, Jane had mentioned Sue's tendency to sabotage termination in order to continue with ongoing counseling. In fact, Sue's treatment history went back nearly 20 years, something common in a previous era, primarily in psychodynamic therapy.

We spent the rest of the session with Sue talking about her growing up in a tight-knit, upper-middle-class family and feeling loved. She stated, however, feeling a distance from her parents and siblings. "I'm not sure why, but I have always been an outlier." She reported being on good terms with her family of origin. The biggest issue had been her spinsterhood, but everyone accepted her decision to remain single. "I like kids but prefer not to raise them." As the session was at the end, I assigned her homework of writing about how her life would be different when this vacuum in her life was filled (she liked to journal).

The following week, Sue returned well groomed and appearing happy, holding a folder in her hand. She brought along her completed homework assignment and volunteered to read aloud what she had written. She was a descriptive writer, evidencing good insight into the nature of her issue. She had written that whenever she established a strong friendship or set of friendships, she would find the meaning that her life had always lacked. Suddenly, it dawned on me that friendship, while a critical part of what was missing, might not be the only factor. I inquired what she meant by the term *meaning*. She paused and then spoke of being raised that meaning came from God and her family. While professing a continued belief in this, this steadfast belief had not "filled her cup," she stated. Thus, we began unpacking the term meaning.

I asked Sue how she defined meaning. She paused and then explained it was easier to cite examples. She mentioned her volunteering work with seniors as the time she felt happiest and most useful. "I had a good career with a fair amount of responsibility, but found little satisfaction in corporate work." After nearly 30 years, she had retired and reported not missing her career. I asked how often she volunteered at the senior center and she said 2 to 3 days a week. Given she gleaned such fulfillment from this, I asked if she would like to spend more time volunteering. She exclaimed, "Yes," but also stated a desire for increased self-understanding. "It's like I never made that internal journey to my core self that I read of others doing." This latter part intrigued me and I asked if she would explain her meaning. She then launched into a memory from her freshman year of college. She related a class discussion where the professor and her fellow students discussed psychoanalysis. While she disagreed with Freud's theory, she could relate to desiring a deeper understanding of herself as distinct from her family of origin. She recounted loving, albeit somewhat rigid, parents who viewed family, faith, and work as the essential components in life. While she agreed to an extent, she had since early college years harbored the sense that some critical component was absent from her life.

It began to dawn on me that perhaps my colleagues had misread Sue. Maybe it was not so much her utilizing counseling as a friendship substitute, but rather she was on a journey to fill a deeper void. I inquired about that missing component. She replied that she was unsure what it was, just that she was missing something. We continued to discuss the matter until the end of the session. For homework, I assigned her to journal on this missing element and then inquired what else she might find helpful. She smiled and replied, "Perhaps more study on philosophy. I wanted to major in philosophy during college but knew my parents would object. I offered that the matter seemed important and assigned her to read one chapter on a philosopher or philosophy of her choosing. Nodding as eager as any student I had taught, she agreed and strolled purposefully from the office.

Passing Jane in the hallway, the two exchanged greetings. Jane poked her head into my office and inquired about Sue's progress. "Quite well," I answered. A bewildered Jane simply stared at me and then shook her head. "Watch out for her velcro approach. She grabs hold and won't let go." I smiled and Jane walked off, shaking her head.

The following session, Sue had written several pages, some of her entries were based upon our session and others on her reading. She had commenced reading Paul Tillich, a theologian and philosopher, selecting Tillich's seminal opus, *The Courage to Be*. While I have taken several graduate philosophy courses and read Tillich, I certainly was no expert. I asked what she learned from reading Tillich. She then launched into reading aloud from her journal. No question, Sue was a far deeper thinker than my colleague Jane believed. Sue was also a very skilled writer, and her prose evidenced what appeared to be a solid grasp of Tillich's ontological question regarding God, being, and meaning. No doubt, she knew far more theology and philosophy than myself. After she had completed reading from her journal, she looked at me expectantly. I complimented her for her serious study on such a depth-oriented matter and asked, "What's the most important takeaway from your reading and writing?" After a working silence, she related that the most important takeaway was how much she enjoyed reading Tillich and then writing a reflection on his book. Then came her strongest aha: "I have spent my life living for my family. Through counseling, reading Tillich and my journal, I am finally on the journey to selfhood. That's my ground of being," she said, the latter a reference to Tillich's work. We spent the entire session discussing how she would start living her own life, while continuing to love her family. We spoke of healthy boundaries and the pressures she might face from her family. She seemed confident in setting limits with her father and siblings. Given her mention of existentialism, I suggested she might read Viktor Frankl and Rollo May's work, as both wrote of existential therapy in very different ways.

Sue continued her torrid pace with reading and writing reflections upon what she had learned in her personal journal, which she read to me weekly. During our sessions, she was always the most prepared client I could recall having worked with, and I looked forward to our session each week. I found myself wishing I could continue working with Sue indefinitely and wondered if she would find a way to sabotage termination. She had made progress to the extent that it became clear she no longer required my help, and moreover, she had passed me by! Given she had been a habitual client over many years, granted with discontinuing and then restarting therapy, my termination plan had not been as clear as was typical. My treatment plan included Sue finding more meaning in her life (weekly 1–10 scale scores). Her initial mean weekly score had begun around 4, but she now rated her mean score around 8 to 9. Staffing her case with a veteran at the clinic, my colleague's advice was to have a termination conversation with Sue during the next session. My colleague even asked, "You haven't discussed termination with her previously?" Chagrined at my oversight, I shook my head.

The following session, instead of commencing with her reading from her journal, I broached termination and stated that it seemed she was doing very well and that likely we were close to her graduating from therapy. She smiled and admitted she had begun thinking along the same lines. "I realize my past history here at the clinic suggests I'm a therapy junkie. But now, I have more purpose and direction in my life." I acknowledged that she certainly seemed to have found her calling and that she had made significant progress over several sessions. She then inquired if I would like to hear the latest edition of her journal. I eagerly agreed.

She had just finished reading *Man's Search for Meaning*, Frankl's most popular opus. She related to Frankl's concept of the existential vacuum, noting that her very life had been lived mostly devoid of personal meaning. After reading her insightful journal, she inquired if my approach with her was more logotherapy than CBT. I smiled and stated, "Perhaps so," although I had her catching and reframing self-statements such as "My life is meaningless," to "I am discovering meaning and purpose in my life." She had decided to begin taking philosophy courses at the local community college and planned to continue journaling on her personal growth. She stated feeling more alive than she could recall in her entire life. Nearing the end of the session, she informed me she believed this session would be our last. Surprised and pleased, although honestly, somewhat disappointed as I was enjoying our sessions, I nevertheless acknowledged her growth. She smiled, and holding up the latest philosophy text she was reading (I do not recall what book or philosopher), she exclaimed, "This is that missing piece!"

There have been occasions as a counselor and professor when it felt like I was in the right place in the universe. I had gone from Jane having to browbeat me into taking Sue onto my caseload. However, Jane's experience did not become my experience. Philosophically, perhaps Sue needed to struggle with Jane and others before becoming ready to focus on her own existential needs. I had done very little in reality other than provide Sue a safe, private space to discuss how to fill her void, and then write about her progress. I have had the occasional trouble in getting a client to agree to termination, and certainly, there are those who simply dropped out of counseling for various reasons. I cannot recall any former client more motivated than Sue once she discovered her niche. Post-therapy, I would occasionally see Sue at the coffee shop in our small rural town, discussing a book with a classmate or friend. She invariably would hold up a different philosophy book and smile. Perhaps Frankl was right, for certainly the driving force in Sue's life was the meaning she derived from reading, meditating upon, and writing reflections on various philosophical approaches. I had actually done little standard counseling, other than assist Sue in discovering her passion. Then again, that was all she required.

RECOMMENDED RESOURCES

The following reading recommendations do not represent a comprehensive list but are some works I have found thought provoking and enlightening. (*Note:* Please forgive me listing my own book. I do recommend it of course.)

Buber, M. (2010). *I and thou*. Martino Publishing.
Frankl, V. E. (1946). *Man's search for meaning*. Beacon Press.
Hahn, T. N. (2005). *Happiness: Essential mindfulness practices*. Parallex Press.
Hodges, S. (2023). *Creating a meaningful life: A practical guide for counselors, therapists, and other helping professionals*. Routledge.
Klinger, E. (1978). *Meaning and void: Inner experience and the incentives in people's lives*. University of Minnesota Press.
Yalom, I. D. (2019). *Becoming myself: A psychiatrist's memoir*. Basic Books.

A robust set of instructor resources designed to supplement this text is located at http://connect.springerpub.com/content/book/978-0-8261-6607-4. Qualifying instructors may request access by emailing textbook@springerpub.com.

REFERENCES

Allison v. Patel, 211 Ga. App. 376, 438 S.E. 2d 920 (1993).
American Counseling Association. (2014). *2014 ACA code of ethics*. https://www.counseling.org/resources/aca-code-of-ethics.pdf
American Psychiatric Association. (2022). *Diagnostic and statistical manual of mental disorders* (5th ed.). American Psychiatric Publishing.
Corey, G. (2017). *Theory and practice of counseling and psychotherapy* (10th ed.). Cengage.
Corey, G., Corey, M. S., & Callanan, P. (2007). *Issues and ethics in the helping professions* (7th ed.). Thomson Brooks/Cole.
Cormier, L. S., & Cormier, W. H. (1998). *Fundamental skills and cognitive behavioral interventions* (4th ed.). Brooks/Cole.
Cormier, L. S., & Hackney, H. (2008). *Counseling strategies and interventions* (7th ed.). Pearson/Allyn & Bacon.
de Shazer, S., & Berg, I. K. (1988). Doing therapy: A post-structural re-vision. *Journal of Marital and Family Therapy, 18*, 71–81. https://doi.org/10.1111/j.1752-0606.1992.tb00916.x
Dixon, D. N., & Glover, J. A. (1984). *Counseling: A problem-solving approach*. Wiley.
Garfield, S. L. (1994). Research on client variables in psychotherapy. In A. E. Bergin & S. L. Garfield (Eds.), *Handbook of psychotherapy and behavior change* (4th ed., pp. 190–228). Wiley.
Gibson, R. L., & Mitchell, M. H. (2008). *Introduction to counseling and guidance* (7th ed.). Merrill/Prentice Hall.
Gladding, S. T. (1990). Coming full cycle: Reentry after the group. *Journal for Specialists in Group Work, 15*, 130–131. https://doi.org/10.1080/01933929008411922
Gladding, S. T. (2009). *Counseling: A comprehensive profession* (6th ed.). Merrill/Prentice Hall.
Goldstein, A. P. (1971). *Psychotherapeutic attraction*. Pergamon Press.
Goodyear, R. K. (1981). Termination as a loss experience for the counselor. *Personnel and Guidance Journal, 59*, 347–350. https://doi.org/10.1002/j.2164-4918.1981.tb00565.x
Guy, J. D. (1987). *The personal life of the psychotherapist*. Wiley.
Hill, C. E., & Knox, S. (2009). Processing the therapeutic relationship. *Psychotherapy Research, 19*, 13–29. https://doi.org/10.1080/10503300802621206
Hilliard, J. (1998). Termination of treatment with troublesome patients. In L. E. Lifson & R. I. Simon (Eds.), *The mental health practitioner and the law* (pp. 216–221). Harvard University Press.
Humphrey, K. M. (2009). *Counseling strategies for loss and grief*. American Counseling Association.
Kübler-Ross, E. (1969). *On death and dying*. Macmillan.

Macbeth, J. E., Wheeler, A. M., Sither, J. W., & Onek, J. N. (1994). *Legal and risk management issues in the practice of psychiatry.* Psychiatrists' Purchasing Group.

Maholick, L. T., & Turner, D. W. (1979). Termination: The difficult farewell. *American Journal of Psychotherapy, 33,* 583–591. https://doi.org/10.1176/appi.psychotherapy.1979.33.4.583

Manno v. McIntosh, 519 NW2d 815 (Iowa App. 1994).

Miller, W. R., & Rollnick, S. (2002). *Motivational interviewing: Preparing people for change* (2nd ed.). Guilford Press.

Murphy, J. (2015). *Solution-focused counseling in schools* (3rd ed.). American Counseling Association.

O'Hanlon, W. H. (1994). The third wave: The promise of narrative. *Family Therapy Networker, 18*(6), 19–26, 28–29. https://www.hgi.org.uk/resources/delve-our-extensive-library/mental-health-services-nhs-cbt-psychotherapy/psychotherapys

Okun, B. F., & Kantrowitz, R. E. (2008). *Effective helping: Interviewing and counseling techniques* (7th ed.). Cengage Brooks/Cole.

Packman, W. L., & Harris, E. A. (1998). Legal issues and risk management in suicidal patients. In B. Bongar, A. I. Berman, R. W. Maris, M. M. Silverman, E. A. Harris, & W. L. Packman (Eds.), *Risk management with suicidal patients* (pp. 150–186). Guilford Press.

Perls, F. S. (1969). *Gestalt therapy verbatim.* Real People Press.

Pietrofesa, J. J., Hoffman, A., & Splete, H. H. (1984). *Counseling: An introduction* (2nd ed.). Houghton Mifflin.

Remley, T. P., Jr., & Herlihy, B. (2020). *Ethical, legal and professional issues in counseling* (6th ed.). Pearson.

Rogers, C. R. (1961). *On becoming a person.* Houghton Mifflin.

Vasquez, M. J. T., Bingham, R. P., & Barnett, J. E. (2008). Psychotherapy termination: Clinical and ethical responsibilities. *Journal of Clinical Psychology: In Sessions, 64,* 653–665. https://doi.org/10.1002/jclp.20478

Ward, D. E. (1990). Termination of individual counseling: Concepts and strategies. *Journal of Counseling & Development, 63,* 21–25. https://doi.org/10.1002/j.1556-6676.1984.tb02673.x

Welfel, E. R. (2010). *Ethics in counseling and psychotherapy: Standards, research, and emerging issues* (4th ed.). Brooks/Cole.

Welfel, E. R., & Patterson, L. E. (2005). *The counseling process: A multitheoretical integrated approach* (6th ed.). Thomson Brooks/Cole.

Wheeler, A. M., & Bertram, B. (2019). *The counselor and the law: A guide to legal and ethical practice* (8th ed.). American Counseling Association.

Yalom, I., & Leszcz, M. (2005). *The theory and practice of group psychotherapy* (5th ed.). Basic Books.

CHAPTER 13

Completing the Practicum/Internship and Preparing for the Future as a Professional Counselor

INTRODUCTION

This chapter is devoted to completing the practicum/internship sequence and preparing for your job search. The first part of the chapter addresses termination of the field supervisor–intern relationship. The latter section will be devoted to preparing for the job search, including preparing a résumé or curriculum vitae (CV), letters of reference, cover letters, interviewing, and issues of licensure and credentialing.

As you complete your final semester of field placement, it is important to keep in mind that you carry the reputation of your counseling program with you during internship. Counseling students who perform well on internships showcase their counseling program in a favorable light. Conversely, counseling students whose performance is subpar or who have ethical issues potentially harm their program's reputation. Because future practicum and internship placements depend on the willingness of the field placement site, it is important that you always be mindful of how you complete your final internship placement. Ideally, besides completing all internship requirements, you will express your gratitude to your field site supervisor and colleagues in the school, agency, hospital, and so forth, in addition to saying goodbyes to your clients.

TERMINATING THE FIELD SUPERVISOR–INTERN RELATIONSHIP

In the previous chapter, we reviewed termination with clients. A key question during that process clearly is "Has this client (or student) made adequate progress in counseling?" A similar question could be asked of graduate counseling interns prior to termination: "Has this intern made the type of progress we would expect a beginning counselor to have made?" Because interns are usually in the final stage of their graduate program, field supervisors are preparing them to be future counseling professionals (Remley & Herlihy, 2020). As completion of the final internship is a critical step in the education of future counselors, field supervisors and interns should ensure ample time is set aside for evaluation and discussion of the intern's development prior to the intern's completion of the final internship.

Most interns will experience some formal type of evaluation process (Remley & Herlihy, 2020; Williams, 1995). A sample evaluation form is shown in Exhibit 13.1. Such evaluation forms should be filled out and then forwarded, to the graduate counseling program. Before the form is sent on to the appropriate faculty member, the field supervisor and intern should meet to discuss the evaluation.

The most difficult part of the evaluation process lies in the giving and receiving of critical feedback (Herlihy & Corey, 2015). As a longtime counselor educator and supervisor, I have witnessed interns who receive 95% positive feedback and perhaps 5% critical feedback. Frequently, it is the 5% that the intern focuses on! Although it may be human nature to focus on the deficit, interns must learn to address both, keeping strengths and deficits in the proper perspective. Praise can help the intern develop confidence, and constructive criticism assists the intern in shoring up the areas of concern. Constructive criticism ideally provides the type of information interns can use for improvement. In point of fact, the criticism can be far more instructive than praise, albeit far less pleasing to the ears of the party being critiqued.

One method of soliciting constructive criticism is for the field supervisor to require the intern to write a self-evaluation, identifying their strengths as well as areas of concern (Baird, 2005; Capacchione, 2000; Hodges & Connelly, 2010). This exercise requires the intern to engage in intense self-reflection, which is required for future success as a counselor (Covey, 1996). Then, when the supervisor and intern meet, they can compare and contrast the two evaluations. My recommendation is for the field supervisor to go over the intern's self-evaluation prior to completing their own; this not only provides a window into the intern's thinking but also sets the stage to compare and contrast the intern's evaluation to the supervisor's evaluation. Furthermore, the supervisor is better prepared for potential conflicts during the evaluation supervisory meeting.

Many field site supervisors may simply ask the intern to write up a narrative of their strengths and areas of concern. Others may simply ask the intern to do this verbally. For posterity's sake, my recommendation is for the intern to write the self-evaluation because this provides more structure and organization to the intern's self-reflection process. A sample of a written self-evaluation is shown in Exhibit 13.2. Formalized self-reflection, particularly in writing, means the intern is required to put more energy, innovation, and investment into the evaluation process, meaning they likely will better understand their strengths and challenges. As a 30-year veteran of counseling, supervising, and teaching, I am frequently surprised how little insight some student counselors have regarding their strengths and challenges.

13: COMPLETING THE PRACTICUM/INTERNSHIP AND PREPARING FOR THE FUTURE • 325

Exhibit 13.1 Sample Counseling Internship Evaluation Form

Site Supervisor's Evaluation of Student Counselor's Performance
(Return to: Counseling Program, Niagara University, College of Education)

Note: This form should be completed at the conclusion of each practicum and internship. Clinical supervisors are encouraged to go over the results with their students.

Name of Student Counselor:

_____

Name of Clinical Supervisor:

_____

Directions: The supervisor will circle the number most closely approximating the student counselor's skill rating in each of the following areas.

GENERAL SUPERVISION RATING	POOR		SATISFACTORY		EXCELLENT	
Demonstrates a personal commitment to developing professional competencies	1	2	3	4	5	6
Possesses a good working attitude	1	2	3	4	5	6
Accepts and uses constructive criticism	1	2	3	4	5	6
Communicates well with peers and supervisors	1	2	3	4	5	6
Recognizes both strengths and limitations and works to improve clinical skills	1	2	3	4	5	6
Punctual with case notes and other documentation	1	2	3	4	5	6
Keeps appointments on time	1	2	3	4	5	6
Researches client information prior to session	1	2	3	4	5	6
Appears relaxed and confident in dealing with counseling and clinical issues	1	2	3	4	5	6
Presents a nonjudgmental attitude regarding clients and their issues	1	2	3	4	5	6

(continued)

Exhibit 13.1 Sample Counseling Internship Evaluation Form (*continued*)

GENERAL SUPERVISION RATING	POOR		SATISFACTORY		EXCELLENT	
Able to gain client trust	1	2	3	4	5	6
Facilitates client's exploration of personal issues	1	2	3	4	5	6
Professional and ethical	1	2	3	4	5	6
Able to deal with mandated or hostile clients	1	2	3	4	5	6
Recognizes and deals with client manipulation	1	2	3	4	5	6
Uses silence effectively in counseling	1	2	3	4	5	6
Uses self-disclosure appropriately	1	2	3	4	5	6
Aware of own biases and how they impact the therapeutic relationship	1	2	3	4	5	6
Skilled in using confrontation in session	1	2	3	4	5	6
Facilitates realistic goal setting with the client	1	2	3	4	5	6
Writes clear, appropriate treatment plans	1	2	3	4	5	6
Explains, administers, and interprets tests correctly	1	2	3	4	5	6
Terminates/refers clients at appropriate times	1	2	3	4	5	6
Able to use appropriate techniques and interventions properly	1	2	3	4	5	6
Makes sound clinical decisions in counseling	1	2	3	4	5	6

Additional Comments (use back if necessary):

_____

_____

_____

Clinical Supervisor _____	Date: _____
Student Counselor _____	Date: _____

Interns who have had a good working relationship with their supervisor will likely experience only mild anxiety heading into the formal evaluation meeting. In such cases where the intern has already completed a self-evaluation and has had the benefit of several months (or in some cases, years) of feedback from the supervisor, the fear factor regarding the final evaluation is likely quite low. Regardless of the field supervisor–intern relationship, I would encourage the student to prepare for the formal evaluation by considering the following suggestions:

- Remain composed and do not become defensive. Even if you disagree with the supervisor's evaluation, do not react with anger. It is sometimes very difficult to receive critical feedback, but doing so with respect and a cool head is good preparation for the future. After all, the final internship evaluation will not be the last time you receive critical evaluation. Remember, you do not have to agree with the feedback; you do need to remain present and respectful during the evaluation meeting.

- If you find yourself feeling overly anxious about the formal evaluation, find ways to combat the stress—a workout routine or talking with friends, family, a support group, through counseling, and so forth.

- Make a "worst case/best case" list of what you may hear in the evaluation meeting. After each item on the list, write out a respectful response (which may include saying nothing and listening). On the other hand, if a compliment is given, a simple "thank you" may be appropriate.

- If you feel the need, have a classmate, friend, family member, or counselor role-play being the supervisor giving you a formal evaluation. During this "mock evaluation," write down both strengths and weaknesses you believe the supervisor will point out. Then, have the mock supervisor mention these. Practice provides a greater likelihood you will manage the evaluation session with more professionalism and less distress.

- Let the supervisor control the meeting. This conveys respect and illustrates maturity on your part. Supervisors will likely resent an intern trying to take over the evaluation meeting.

- The supervisor may ask if you have questions or comments regarding the evaluation. This is your opportunity to clarify anything that seems unclear to you. Again, work to manage your emotions even if the evaluation is disappointing in some areas. If you have made it to the end of the placement with this particular school, agency, or university counseling center, the strengths likely outweigh the weaknesses.

- At the conclusion, regardless of how the meeting has gone, thank the supervisor for the opportunity to work at the setting. Remember, your counseling program needs practicum and internship placements, and a respectful departure will help maintain good relations between your program and the field organization.

328 • THE COUNSELING PRACTICUM AND INTERNSHIP MANUAL

Exhibit 13.2 Intern's Self-Evaluation of the Counseling Practicum/ Internship Performance

On the following issues, rate yourself based on the scale as follows:

1 = *Needs Improvement*; 2 = *Below Average*; 3 = *Average*; 4 = *Above Average*; 5 = *Excellent*; N/A = *Not Applicable*

Counseling skills:

    1   2   3   4   5

Writing clear, concise case notes:

    1   2   3   4   5

Competence and confidence in leading a group session:

    1   2   3   4   5   N/A

Competence and confidence in leading a psychoeducational presentation:

    1   2   3   4   5   N/A

Understanding and applying the ethical code (e.g., ACA, AMHCA, or ASCA):

    1   2   3   4   5

My professional dispositions on the placement (e.g., being on time, completing case notes in a timely manner, showing respect to the staff, dressing appropriately, and managing critical feedback):

    1   2   3   4   5

Taking initiative by reading relevant books, journal articles, viewing DVDs, and attending trainings and workshops (if offered):

    1   2   3   4   5   N/A

My own work ethic while on the practicum/internship:

    1   2   3   4   5

Readiness for the job market through my growth on the practicum/internship and having an updated résumé/CV, a cover letter, and practiced interviewing skills:

    1   2   3   4   5

Because of my experience on the practicum/internship, I have clear and measurable professional goals:

    1   2   3   4   5

(continued)

13: COMPLETING THE PRACTICUM/INTERNSHIP AND PREPARING FOR THE FUTURE • 329

Exhibit 13.2 Intern's Self-Evaluation of the Counseling Practicum/ Internship Performance (*continued*)

Overall, I would rate my progress during this placement as (note longer scale: 1 = Poor, 5 = Average; 10 = Excellent):

1   2   3   4   5   6   7   8   9   10

Narrative Section

In the space provided, please comment on additional areas of interest related to your development while on the practicum/internship. Use an additional sheet of paper if you need more space.

12. As a counselor, my greatest strength appears to be

_____

13. The area I most need to improve in is

_____

_____

Additional comments regarding my experience in practicum/internship:

_____

_____

_____

_____

_____

_____

_____

_____

_____

_____

_____   _____/_____/_____

Practicum/Internship Student's Signature   Date

ACA, American Counseling Association; AMHCA, American Mental Health Counselors Association; ASCA, American School Counselor Association.

330 • THE COUNSELING PRACTICUM AND INTERNSHIP MANUAL

In addition to the field supervisor's evaluation of the intern, some counseling programs have the interns complete a field supervisor evaluation form, even though such evaluations are not always shared with the field supervisor. A sample student evaluation of a field supervisor form is available in Exhibit 13.3.

If you are asked to evaluate your field supervisor, you need to be prepared to offer honest and constructive insights yet use discretion when delivering critical feedback, as of course you may need that supervisor's support for your job search. Council for Accreditation of Counseling and Related Educational Programs (CACREP)-accredited programs very likely will require the student to evaluate the fieldsite supervisor. Needless to say, the intern's evaluation of the supervisor should not be shared with the supervisor. First, it would be prudent to ask for a form, such as the one shown in Exhibit 13.3. A form provides you with a format to convey your opinions in a reasonable way. Reflect on the following considerations prior to evaluating your field supervisor:

- How strong is your relationship with the supervisor? If the relationship is strong, you will likely feel more confident in evaluating them.

- What is your level of trust in your supervisor? While the intern's evaluation of the supervisor should remain private, trust or lack thereof will impact the evaluation. Furthermore, if there is a lack of trust, why is that? The reasons can be licit or illicit.

- How important is this supervisor's recommendation for you? If this supervisor has been the only one you have had, the reference is critical. If this supervisor is one of two or three, then perhaps their reference is less weighty for you. (I am writing this one in the unfortunate event that intern evaluations of the supervisor are shared with that person.)

- Some interns actually want to share their evaluation with the supervisor. If so, they may wish to practice providing feedback. Having a friend, classmate, family member, counselor, and so on participate in such a role-play is recommended.

- An alternative to providing face-to-face feedback would be to write the supervisor a letter after you have completed all work at the site and grades have been turned in. It may be wise, however, to consider whether such a letter might jeopardize a future reference from the supervisor.

Exhibit 13.3 Student Counselor's Evaluation of On-Site Supervisor

Directions: Circle the number that best represents how you, the practicum/internship student, feel about the supervision received from your on-site (agency) supervisor. This information will not be shared with your on-site supervisor without your consent.

My Supervisor:	Poor		Fair		Good	
Gives appropriate time for individual and/or group supervision	1	2	3	4	5	6

(continued)

Exhibit 13.3 Student Counselor's Evaluation of On-Site Supervisor (*continued*)

Provides constructive feedback in supervision sessions	1	2	3	4	5	6
Recognizes and encourages further development of my clinical strengths and capabilities	1	2	3	4	5	6
Encourages and listens to my ideas and suggestions	1	2	3	4	5	6
Helps to define specific, concrete goals for me during the practicum or internship experience	1	2	3	4	5	6
Is available when I need consultation	1	2	3	4	5	6
Models ethical practice through their professional behavior	1	2	3	4	5	6
Makes the effort to remain current in the counseling field.	1	2	3	4	5	6
Maintains confidentiality within the clinical setting	1	2	3	4	5	6
Helps me formulate my own theoretical approach to counseling	1	2	3	4	5	6
Explains their criteria for evaluating student interns in clear terms	1	2	3	4	5	6
Applies these criteria fairly in evaluating my counseling performance	1	2	3	4	5	6
Demonstrates respect to clients, staff, and student interns	1	2	3	4	5	6
Encourages me to discuss concerns encountered in the practicum or internship setting	1	2	3	4	5	6
Through my work with this supervisor, I have learned new counseling techniques, interventions, or assessments.	1	2	3	4	5	6
The supervisor has helped make this practicum/internship a valuable experience.	1	2	3	4	5	6
Because of my experience with the supervisor and this agency, I would recommend this site to other students.	1	2	3	4	5	6

Additional Comments and/or Suggestions:

_____

_____

_____

Date:_____/_____/_____   Student:_____

332 • THE COUNSELING PRACTICUM AND INTERNSHIP MANUAL

Good supervisors will desire feedback on ways to enhance their supervision skills. Regardless of the outcome, a two-way evaluation in which both the supervisor and the intern provide feedback is the healthiest process when termination arrives.

The following self-reflection exercise is to help prepare you for the job search, potential interviews, and a future career as a counselor in an agency, school, or hospital. It is recommended that readers write down answers to each item and discuss with another student (Box 13.1).

Box 13.1 Self-Reflection Exercise for the Conclusion of the Internship

- Through your practicum and internship experience, you have gained a broader understanding of how to identify and address the educational, career, emotional, and mental health needs of the students and clients you have counseled. Another aspect of your field placement is how what you have learned fits into the needs of your chosen career. Examine and respond to the following questions.

- What specific skills and interests have you gained through your practicum and internship experience?

- The practicum and internship experience is a challenging one. During this process of counseling others, what have you learned about yourself?

- What lessons have you learned from working with different types of people (clients, supervisors, colleagues, and fellow students)?

- In what ways have you benefited from your practicum and internship experience?

- What specific skills, talents, and interests are you likely to use in your new counseling position?

- What type (or types) of counseling setting are you considering for your first job after graduate school?

- Regarding the previous question what specifically interests you about working with the settings you have listed?

- What advice would you give to a fellow graduate counseling student regarding choosing a practicum or internship?

- Considering your experiences on practicum/internship and in your graduate counseling program in general, what changes would you like to see (e.g., course or curricular changes, changes to the practicum/internship, changes in the counseling profession, or anything that seems relevant)?

- Regarding cultural considerations, how well did your practicum or internship prepare you? Regarding multiculturalism and your placement, what recommendations would you make to the faculty in your program?

- Regarding professional ethics, how would you rate the staff at your placement? Did they seem ethical in their professional work (e.g., counseling, clinical discussions, and supervision)?

- What was the most important thing you learned on your practicum or internship? Why?

PREPARING FOR THE JOB SEARCH

Because the practicum/internship is all about preparing to become a professional counselor, this book would not be complete without some basic orientation to prepare for the job search. Although this section of the text is a brief overview (there are many more comprehensive job search books and websites available), it will provide some basic information and point the way for further information that may be helpful in assisting you in landing that initial job.

A job search involves many facets: planning, résumé writing, mock interviewing, applying, interviewing, following up, dealing with rejection, entertaining an offer, accepting a job, negotiating salary, and relocating, to name a few. The remainder of the chapter focuses on the basics of this process. A more recent wrinkle, given wings through COVID, is interviewing via Zoom, Webex, or another audio–video platform. Unlike previous eras, job application is online.

THE VISIONING PROCESS: CREATING YOUR DREAM CAREER

Career professionals will tell you the first step to success is the ability to visualize a desired goal. Surprisingly, many clients I have counseled and students I have taught do not have a clear vision for their careers. The lack of a clear vision may set up a graduating counseling student for some degree of struggle. Richard Nelson Bolles, late author of *The New York Times* bestseller and iconic *What Color Is Your Parachute?* had a popular saying: "If you don't know where you're going, you'll likely end up somewhere else." Thus, the need for vision works regarding a career (and personal life as well). The second and more important task is to strategize on how to achieve the goal. One of the most popular methods for strategizing is creative visualization, or *visioning* for short (Capacchione, 2000). Successful people in every occupation tend to use some type of visioning process. Some notable visionaries are Nelson Mandela, Mohandas Gandhi, Martin Luther King, Jr., and Mother Teresa. Vision includes optimistic thinking, which is strongly correlated with success (Seligman, 1998). Visioning is a simple process requiring just a few basic pieces of information:

- **Personal history**. How did you arrive at your current station in life? What experiences led you to becoming a professional counselor or counselor educator? What valuable lessons have you learned along the way? What advice might you give to someone considering counseling or counselor education as a career?

- **Values.** What values are important to you? Psychologist Milton Rokeach (1979) conducted extensive research in the study of values. His findings suggest that the most successful people find work that is congruent with their personal values. For example, if your religion or spirituality is important to you, then perhaps you should find a spiritually affiliated school or agency. If working with inner-city youth is where your passion lies, a job in a wealthy suburban school may not be a good fit for you. So, what are your top five values? How might these values guide your job search and counseling career? Prediction: *Should a potential job hold significant values conflicts, that job likely is not a good fit for you regardless of salary.* Consider your values carefully. I can recall compromising my values to accept a job and dearly regretting it later!

- **Professional identity.** Sure, you know you want to be a professional school/rehabilitation/career/mental health/addictions counselor. However, professional labels such as "counselor" do not tell the entire story. For example, some mental health counselors may decide to retrain to become school counselors or vice versa. In addition, many experienced counselors may move into administrative roles, such as clinical director, and do more administrative work and less actual counseling. A few readers may even wish to earn a doctorate in counselor education and become a counselor educator! Would your long-term goals include moving into administration? Would those changes be healthy for you? Why or why not?

- **Goals.** What are your immediate, short-term, and long-term career goals? Are you interested in running a school counseling center? Being director of a college counseling center? Becoming dean of students at a large university? Moving overseas? Becoming president of the American Counseling Association (ACA), American School Counselor Association (ASCA), American Rehabilitation Counseling Association (ARCA), Canadian Counseling and Psychotherapy Association (CCPA), British Association for Counselling and Psychotherapy (BACP), and the like? Goals are fluid and subject to personal changes over time, but it is still a good idea to set goals and to revise them periodically as your interests and values change over time and through experience. Career goals, like those in a treatment plan, provide targets to measure success against. Furthermore, it is okay to not meet target goals. Sometimes, we discover that we might have been aiming at the wrong target! Still, set goals and assess goal achievement. Then, reevaluate what further action you may wish to take. That could be revising goals, dropping some, or creating new ones.

- **Action plan.** Everyone with a vision needs an action plan to achieve it. An action plan is a rough road map to success and should consist of concrete steps leading up to the vision (see Box 13.2). The visioning process should also involve estimated time frames to provide a sense of how you are proceeding toward your goal. Action plans also are flexible as circumstances will intervene. Life will happen, bringing unexpected, exciting, and disappointing news. Nevertheless, planning ahead anyway is your best option.

Even if you are not presently interested in becoming the ACA president, this example illustrates that setting a clear goal helps you strategize how to work to reach that goal. You should also be flexible with timelines and remember that you will have some failures along the way. Do not let failures get you too down as they offer the opportunity for self-reflection and reassessment. In fact, failures can provide the incentive and the wisdom for future success. Perhaps inventor Thomas Edison is the best example of this ethic. Edison's experiment failures far outnumbered his successes. Yet, he needed the failures to help pave the road to his success. So, be of the mindset of allowing your failures to teach you healthy lessons.

Thus, consider the following when creating a visioning plan:

- **Be conscious of the present.** Think long term as in the previous example. However, do not let long-term planning trip you up in the present. Doing well in your present is the first step to achieving your long-term goals.

- **Set a time frame.** Remember, long-term goals will take time and you will need to revise them when setbacks and life circumstances change (e.g., marriage, divorce, children, moves, promotions, and job loss). Disappointments will happen. I can recall numerous job rejections and feeling very discouraged. Then, I received some prudent counsel. I was encouraged to reframe each rejection as "One rejection closer to landing that first job." This simple act of reframing provided a greater sense of purpose and lessened my sense of failure. So, when you are not having the success you desire, reframe your thoughts accordingly. Positive, rational self-talk is a must.

- **Be flexible.** Your goals will change over time and that may be good. For example, you may start out with the long-term goal of running a university counseling center but decide over time that you are more interested in being a training director at a college counseling center. This would be an example of clarification, or simply learning that the original goal was not as congruent with your values and interests as previously thought. Remember, life is dynamic and all about change.

- **Review your action plan periodically.** You need to check on your progress regularly. If you are not being successful, why not? In addition, what does success actually mean to you? Have your interests and values changed?

- **Be mindful.** Mindfulness means being grounded in the center of your own being, nonjudgmentally, while connected to others. Make sure the goals you have set actually fit with your values. This may be the most difficult process you encounter in your career journey. You may need years of struggle, professional counseling, and some type of meaningful self-reflecting practice to maintain a mindful career.

- **Be aware that the profession is rapidly evolving.** Prior to COVID-19, teletherapy (or telemedicine) was scarcely on most counselor's radar. As a result of the pandemic, teletherapy is rapidly becoming as common as in-person counseling, especially given it may be as efficacious as in-person counseling (Richards & Vigano, 2013). The graduate students in my program have been using teletherapy extensively during field placement (in fact, counseling in person and using teletherapy). If you were to say, "I will not accept any job requiring me to use teletherapy," you likely will remain unemployed for some time, if not permanently. Technology will be an even larger part of your job in the future. For example, some experts believe artificial intelligence (AI) will be the most powerful force in the 21st century (Thrun, 2023). AI has profound implications for the profession, including crisis screening, clinical intakes, assessment, and even actual counseling.

Box 13.2 Sample Action Plan

- If your ultimate goal is to become president of the ACA, your action plan might look something like this:
- Become active in the state affiliate of the ACA (1–3 years).
- Transition into a state leadership role through the following steps (1–2 years):

(continued)

Box 13.2 Sample Action Plan (*continued*)

- Serving on the planning board for the state conference
- Serving on the editorial board of the state journal
- Running for president, vice president, or another office of the state organization
- Submitting manuscripts to the state journal and national ACA-affiliated journals
- Attend the annual ACA conference for networking opportunities.
- Volunteer, make presentations, and host receptions at ACA conferences to boost your profile with the organization (3–6 years).
- Get published in academic journals, national newsletters, and in venues such as *Counseling Today*. Sit on ACA subcommittees to further boost your profile and understand the organization (3–4 years).
- Run for secretary or vice president of the ACA (2 years).
- Finally, you run for president, using everything you have learned previously regarding visibility, a coherent platform, networking, and so forth. You win!

ACA, American Counseling Association.

Some techniques for career visioning are as follows:

- **Open-ended questions.** "What do I want in my career?" and "Now that I know what I want career-wise, how can I create it?"
- **Meditation.** Many people have a meditation practice that calms and centers them. Some people use meditation as part of the creative process.
- **Visualization.** When you picture yourself 5, 7, or 10 years down the line, what does that picture look like? What does your career involve? Where are you living? Who else is in the picture?
- **Focusing.** This assists in clarifying how to plan and prioritize the preceding visualization process. For example, what needs to happen before you can open your own private practice?
- **Career journaling.** For many people, journaling allows them the opportunity to document how their career is proceeding, what challenges, satisfactions, struggles, changes, failures, successes, and so on they face. Not everyone finds journaling helpful, but for those who enjoy it, journaling can be a type of self-discovery regarding career and personal insights.
- **Collage making.** Do not denigrate this potentially creative exercise. Collage making can be fun; it can also help you create a picture of your career dreams. Use a collage to explore your future dreams and goals. This provides a concrete example of what your desired future may resemble.

13: COMPLETING THE PRACTICUM/INTERNSHIP AND PREPARING FOR THE FUTURE • 337

- **Informational interviewing.** Choose two or three people whom you respect and who know you well. Ask them to address the following questions about you (Hodges & Connelly, 2010, p. 14):
  - What qualities do you possess that will help make you successful in your career?
  - What steps do you need to take to realize your career goal(s)?
  - What is your strongest quality?
  - What is your chief weakness?

THE CAREER CENTER

The career center on your campus can offer numerous services for the soon-to-be-graduated intern. One of the most valuable services is the letters of reference bank. With this, your field supervisor(s) and advisor can write letters of reference that can be stored at the center. Reference letters can be open or closed. Open references mean that the student has the right to inspect the letter. Closed letters cannot be read by students.

Students frequently ask me, "Should I have an open or closed file?" I always feel somewhat torn because I believe when we agree to serve as a reference, it should be an open process. However, I also know that some hiring committees view closed files as more authentic. So, make the best decision you can. You may feel more confident in closed files if you are confident about the people who are writing the letters. I have written reference letters both for open and for closed files and my letter would be the same for both. Once again, it also comes down to how much trust you have in the person writing the reference letter. Ideally, people would not write reference letters for students unless they honestly had faith in the students' counseling ability.

The career center counselors can also critique your résumé and cover letter (you might show them to your supervisor as well). It never hurts to have fresh eyes examine your materials for errors and accuracy and to make sure you present yourself in the strongest possible light to a potential employer. Remember, initial screenings of résumés and cover letters often are to screen out applicants. You want to be "screened in," so be aware that spelling errors, wrong dates, or simply misleading information will get your application relegated to the recycle bin.

PROFESSIONAL NETWORKING SITES

You should also consider using appropriate social networking sites such as LinkedIn. LinkedIn provides a method of building vocational connections. Refrain from using social sites such as Facebook as a professional networking vehicle. Facebook works fine for transmitting social and familial information, but many people post compromising photographs and information on such sites and that can derail a promising career before it begins. Professional sites such as LinkedIn are typically understood to be more appropriate sites for networking with other counseling professionals. LinkedIn offers an easy, quick method of linking with fellow counselors and even soliciting recommendations. It is likely that in this rapidly accelerating electronic world, sites such as LinkedIn represent future "career centers" or at least serve as an ancillary career center (though certainly not as good as an actual career counselor). Naturally, the ACA, American Mental Health Counselors Association (AMHCA), ASCA, and organizations such as the National Board for Certified Counselors (NBCC) have their own networking capabilities (another reason to have membership). Regarding networking, the questionnaire in Exhibit 13.4 provides some guidance.

REQUESTING REFERENCES

As you complete your final internship and prepare for the job search, you should be soliciting letters of recommendation from professors and field supervisors. Your letters of reference ideally should be written by counseling professionals, such as professors in your counselor education program, your faculty advisor, major professors, field site supervisors, and possibly supervisors or professionals in related fields who may be able to address pertinent areas related to counseling work. These references may be required to either write a formal letter on your behalf or merely be accessible for a verbal discussion about you with a potential employer. Although most counseling applications typically require three references, some may ask for five. So be prepared for the possibility of needing additional references. Again, you are wise to seek references from those with whom you have a good relationship, as they likely will write you the strongest reference. Your candidacy will be sunk by tepid praise from a reference who views you as mediocre, so be prudent!

Exhibit 13.4 A Networking Questionnaire

Networking at social and professional events can be very helpful to your career. Developing relationships is important as people in the profession of counseling are more likely to recommend you when they have a positive impression. The following informal assessment may serve as a general guide for your networking practice.

Instructions: Answer each question by circling the number that best represents your opinion. Higher scores suggest more comfort engaging in networking.

1 = Strongly Disagree   2 = Disagree   3 = Neutral

4 = Agree   5 = Strongly Agree

I enjoy attending professional social functions.	1 2 3 4 5
I tend to take the initiative in introducing myself to people I don't know.	1 2 3 4 5
On a scale of 1 to 10, with 1 being low and 10 high, my comfort in social situations is between 7 and 10.	1 2 3 4 5
I listen attentively, providing others the opportunity to speak without interruption.	1 2 3 4 5

(continued)

13: COMPLETING THE PRACTICUM/INTERNSHIP AND PREPARING FOR THE FUTURE • 339

Exhibit 13.4 A Networking Questionnaire (*continued*)

I ask questions related to topics of interest others have mentioned to me.	1 2 3 4 5
I carry business cards, offer them to colleagues, and collect them from others.	1 2 3 4 5
I make an effort to remember people's names and use them in future conversations.	1 2 3 4 5
If someone I meet suggests I call to discuss their school/agency/treatment center, I follow up on their suggestion in a timely manner.	1 2 3 4 5
If someone is not interested in talking with me, I move on to someone else without feeling rejected.	1 2 3 4 5
I am active on LinkedIn or another professional website.	1 2 3 4 5

Average score _____

If below 6, you may need to focus on addressing issues of social engagement and comfort.

On the 1 to 5 scale, with 1 = low and 5 = high, how satisfied am I with my networking score?

1   2   3   4   5   (circle your score)

If you are not satisfied with your networking score, you could improve your score by _____. (Answer verbally/write out.)

Prior to sending off your résumé or cover letter, you must *ask* each person on your list if they would be willing to serve as a reference. This may seem elementary, but you might be surprised how many times I have received a phone call from an employer asking about an applicant who never asked if I would serve as a reference. Such unexpected calls are always embarrassing and usually sink the counselor's candidacy. Failure to ask if a former supervisor or professor will serve as a reference sends the message you potentially do not respect your references well or that you were sloppy in your approach. Ask!

Consider the strength of the referral before asking anyone to serve as a reference. As one who has written scores of reference letters for the past two decades, my guideline is that I must be able to write a strong letter of reference or I will refuse to serve as a reference. Be aware that weak or nebulous references are worse than none at all. So, as soon as possible during your final semester, line up your references. As you do so, consider the following:

- Provide your referral sources with a résumé or CV. This helps them fill in the gaps about your vocational life. No matter how well I know a student, I always learn something additional from their résumé or CV.

340 • THE COUNSELING PRACTICUM AND INTERNSHIP MANUAL

- Do not ask your references to write a letter at the last moment. This shows poor planning on your part, and your reference may not be able to write the letter with short notice or might be annoyed at such a last-minute request. Ideally, give your references 2 weeks to write letters of reference.

- Make sure you keep your references informed as to how your job search is proceeding. I personally appreciate hearing how my students are progressing on the job search. When you land a job, let your references know—they will be happy to know their supervision and hard work have paid off.

- Most applications now suggest emailing letters of reference and may not require a mailed letter of reference. However, be ready just in case a school or agency does its business the 20th century way. Likely, all will be managed through electronic means.

DEVELOPING A RÉSUMÉ OR CURRICULUM VITAE

A résumé or CV provides a description of your educational and occupational life. The résumé or CV provides a sketch of you for a potential employer's perusal. This is no time to be overly modest; your résumé is your calling card and summary of your professional life. Be your best self. But be honest in whatever you write on your CV or résumé! Overly embellishing on a résumé or CV (e.g., lying) can cost you a job and maybe even a career.

The recommended reading list at the end of the chapter offers many comprehensive references to help you craft a résumé and conduct other aspects of your job search. I highly recommend you consult one or more of them. Here are some basic tips to get you started (Hodges & Connelly, 2010, p. 34):

- Your education and transferrable skills are of critical importance. Your experience, training, education, and skills serve as a bridge to desired employment. Make sure you design your résumé or CV in a manner that clearly highlights your training and skill areas. List all degrees, degrees in progress, certifications, work history, awards, and so forth.

- Make sure your résumé makes chronological sense. Begin with the most recent position and work your way back. In addition, I recommend that you list your graduate assistantship just as you would list a job—because in essence, it is *job-like*.

- Claim the highest skills ethically possible. For example, if you have co-facilitated counseling groups for 2 years, certainly list that. Do not, however, list that you developed and oversaw the group treatment model at your school or agency if this is untrue.

- Be able to elaborate on anything you list. For example, if you list that you are proficient in dialectical behavioral therapy (DBT), for example, you must be prepared to demonstrate you have mastered the basic concepts of this theoretical approach. Ability to document certification would also be very helpful.

- Include membership in relevant professional organizations. Membership demonstrates a stronger commitment to the profession. It also suggests you are more likely to keep informed of research and emerging trends in the counseling field. My personal opinion is that counseling graduates and professional counselors should hold membership in the ACA, their particular counseling specialty area (e.g., ASCA, AMHCA, ARCA), and their state counseling organization.

- Make your résumé or CV reader-friendly. When a search committee member first looks at your résumé or CV, they will give it a 30- to 45-second speed read

(Bolles, 2022). Make sure it is clearly organized. Use a common 12-point font (such as Times New Roman).

- Do a spelling and grammar check. Have a career counselor or someone else you trust read it for content and mechanics. Misspellings and poor grammar are likely to get your application eliminated from consideration.

- There is no one "right" résumé or CV format. Make sure your résumé makes sense, flows logically, is factually accurate, and fits with the counseling position for which you have applied. For example, if you are applying for an inner-city high school counselor position, make sure your application letter reflects the particular demographics of that school, as opposed to an elite private school.

- Cover your most recent years of work experience in the greatest detail, depending on your age and years in the field. Do not be discouraged if you are a recent graduate of a counseling program. At your age and experience level, you are not expected to have many years of professional experience. After all, everyone starts somewhere.

- Having held multiple jobs is no longer the problem as it was in previous generations. In this era, people are expected to have held three, four, or even more jobs (Bolles, 2022). In higher education, the general understanding is that you must "move out to move up," and that is likely to be reflected in your résumé or CV. However, when you enter into a professional counseling position, you will be expected to stay at that job for 4 to 5 years. Job hopping—leaving or trying to leave a job every 1 to 2 years— will hurt you in future job searches.

- Be factually correct. You are responsible for anything you list in your résumé or CV. If you are caught lying or embellishing, the least you will lose is a job. In some cases, you may forfeit your career. Be warned: Potential employers have little tolerance for the ethically challenged!

- Provide all contact information. List landline and cell phone numbers, email, and so forth.

In developing your résumé and cover letter, I encourage you to use language that describes your experience, skills, and interest in a concise, descriptive, and eloquent voice. The best way to illustrate your work in the cover letter and résumé is with action words that present your case in a lively manner. Here is a sampling of action words:

accomplished	directed	negotiated
achieved	drafted	organized
advised	edited	planned
assisted	established	presented
chaired	facilitated	presided
collaborated	implemented	reorganized
consulted	integrated	researched
counseled*	lectured	revised
developed	monitored	supervised

*Use of this word should occur only after completing a counseling practicum and internship!

WRITING A COVER LETTER

In writing the cover letter, you want to keep several elements in mind:

1. Open the letter with a respectful business-like address such as "Dear Director," "Dear Search Committee," or another title that conveys respect. Do not use informal titles even if you know the persons to whom you are writing. Remember, the cover letter indicates you understand professional protocol.

2. As with your résumé, type using a standard 12-point font (such as Times New Roman or another traditional style). If you are delivering hard copies—less common in this electronic era—have your résumé and cover letter printed on quality, heavy stock paper.

3. In the opening paragraph, explain why you are interested in the job and show that you understand the population the organization serves. For example, if you are applying for a position as a school counselor in an inner-city school or alternative school, briefly illustrate your knowledge of and experience with that student population.

4. Keep it brief: one to one and one-half pages. Employers are busy people and tend to cease reading if the cover letter is too lengthy. A too-lengthy cover letter may also read like an "I love me letter," and such is a turn off. Smart employers want team players.

5. Hit the highlights of your qualifications for the position: Cite your counseling experience (practicum/internship) and theoretical approach. (If the school or agency uses a particular approach, indicate your knowledge and experience with it if appropriate.) In addition, if you have special training in a particular approach (e.g., DBT, eye movement desensitization and reprocessing [EMDR], acceptance and commitment therapy [ACT], and mindfulness-based CBT [cognitive behavioral therapy]), indicate that as well.

6. If you have experience related to the counseling field, you certainly want to mention that. Related experience (such as working as a case manager, teaching assistant, resident advisor, and bachelor's-level addiction counselor) should also be mentioned. Such suggests you understand what is involved in professional work and are thus better prepared for the job.

7. If you have experience doing something interesting such as teaching overseas, being a Peace Corps or AmeriCorps volunteer, or anything that is outside the typical experience (whatever you deem that to be), list it. Such experience could make a difference.

8. In the final paragraph, wrap up by stating that you look forward to meeting to discuss your interest and fit for the job. Provide your phone number and email address.

Exhibit 13.5 Sample Counseling Position Résumé

Reggie Martinez, Master's Candidate, BA, AA

327 Springdale Ave.

Palouse Hills, WA 96332

(817) 555-0234 (c)

rmartinez@hotmail.com

PROFILE

Master's degree candidate seeking a challenging counseling position at a community mental health clinic.

SUMMARY OF QUALIFICATIONS

Five years of experience supervising college students in collegiate living groups, providing peer advising, crisis intervention, and educational programming.

Nearing completion of 700-hour practicum/internship in community counseling agency.

Trained in grief counseling during practicum/internship.

Developed an outreach program for Latinx youth.

Selected as the Graduate Student of the Year at Washington State University.

EDUCATION

Master's Degree Candidate (will graduate in June 2021) in Clinical Mental Health Counseling, Washington State University, Pullman, WA (CACREP-accredited program)

Bachelor of Arts (2016) in Cultural Anthropology at Western Washington University, Bellingham, WA (Minor: Psychology)

Associate of Arts (2015) in Psychology at Seattle Area Community College

RELATED WORK EXPERIENCE

Mental Health Counseling Practicum and Internship (2022–2024), The Rainbow Center, Moscow, ID.

Provided individual and group counseling to clients in Spanish and English

Co-facilitated support groups for parents of gay and lesbian children

Developed a grief support group for parents who have had children die

Presented psychoeducational workshops to schools, service organizations, and law enforcement officers

Served as crisis counselor for evening crisis call center

Assisted in rewriting the *Rainbow Staff Employee's Manual*

(continued)

THE COUNSELING PRACTICUM AND INTERNSHIP MANUAL

> **Exhibit 13.5 Sample Counseling Position Résumé (*continued*)**

Resident Director, Department of Housing and Residence Life, Washington State University, Pullman, WA (2019–2022)

Director of International Student residence hall, with students from 33 countries

Oversight of 150 undergraduate and graduate students and scholars-in-residence.

Supervisor for five residence advisors

Responsible for coordinating educational programming in residence hall

Mediated conflicts between residents in the residence hall

Provided crisis intervention and referred students to the university counseling center

Participated in Safe Haven training for gay, lesbian, and transgender students

Resident Advisor, Department of Residential Life, Western Washington University, Bellingham, WA (2014–2018)

Floor supervisor in coeducational collegiate residence hall (30 students)

Responsible for educational programming

Served as peer counselor for students

Referred students to the counseling center, health services, and the career center

Mediated disputes between students on the floor

President, Student Government Association, Seattle Area Community College, Seattle, WA (2013–2014)

President of student organization representing 25,000 community college students

Responsible for oversight of student fee budgeting, programming approval, and selecting committee chairs

Voting member of the Seattle Community College's Board of Trustees

Charged with lobbying for student needs, such as a new student union, recreation center, and campus residence halls

AWARDS

2020–2021, Graduate Student of the Year. Presented by the Association for Gay, Lesbian, and Transgender Student Association, Washington State University, Pullman, WA

2012–2013 Seattle Area Community College's Presidential Scholarship

PUBLICATIONS

Martinez, R. (2020). Barriers to providing counseling services to Latino clients: Some reflections from the trenches. *Journal of the Washington Counseling Association, 12,* 22–34.

Martinez, R. (2019). Experiences as a first generation Latino graduate student. *The Advocate, 10,* 3–5.

(continued)

13: COMPLETING THE PRACTICUM/INTERNSHIP AND PREPARING FOR THE FUTURE • 345

Exhibit 13.5 Sample Counseling Position Résumé (*continued*)

Martinez, R. (2016, October 15). Racism and homophobia: One Latino's struggle for acceptance. *Seattle Post, 57*, pp. A.1, 22.

ADDITIONAL TRAINING

Trained in Dialectical Behavioral Therapy (Rainbow Center, 2019–2020)

Washington State Certified Mediator

Solution-Focused Counseling, Pullman, WA, June 22–25, 2019

PROFESSIONAL MEMBERSHIPS

Chi Sigma Iota (Counseling Honorary)

American Counseling Association (ACA)

American Mental Health Counselors Association (AMHCA)

Washington State Mental Health Counselors Association (WSMHCA)

HOBBIES

Running, cycling, traveling, and writing poetry

REFERENCES

Sam Cogan, PhD, Associate Professor of Counseling, Counselor Education Program, College of Education, Washington State University, Pullman, WA, (509) 633-0134, email: scogan@wsu.edu.

Angela Hermes, MS, LMHC, The Rainbow Center, Moscow, ID, (509) 714-1027, email: hermesa@yahoo.com.

Harriet Wilson, EdD, Assistant Dean of Students/Coordinator of International Students, Washington State University, Pullman, WA, (509) 618-9090, email: hwilson@wsu.edu.

Exhibit 13.6 shows a sample cover letter.

Exhibit 13.6 Sample Counseling Position Cover Letter

March 13, 2023

1339 Easy Street

Vista View, AR 72301

(*continued*)

Exhibit 13.6 Sample Counseling Position Cover Letter (*continued*)

Personnel Department

Hickory Ridge School District

5555 Cardinal Lane

Hickory Ridge, AR 72709

Dear Personnel Officer:

Please consider me an applicant for the school counseling position at Hickory Ridge High School. I noticed the advertisement in a recent online edition of the *Northwest Arkansas Times*. Currently, I am a graduate student completing my studies and will graduate with my master's degree in school counseling this May at the University of Arkansas. In addition to coursework, I have completed 700 hours of practicum and internship at a local high school. I have also served as a teacher's aide in a public school for 5 years and have a good understanding of both academic and personal issues that impact a student's learning environment.

My practicum and internship were spent at Fayetteville Technical High School, where I assisted the school counseling staff with academic, career, and personal counseling. This past semester, I co-facilitated two counseling groups for students at risk for dropping out of school. I also led an after-school group targeted at gang prevention.

During my counselor education studies at the University of Arkansas, I was selected as a member of the honorary Chi Sigma Iota counseling fraternity and have even served as president. During this past year, I also worked part-time at the Beacon Light Center, where I provided personal, career, and academic counseling to at-risk adolescents.

My résumé and three letters of reference requested in the advertisement are being forwarded from the Career Center at the University of Arkansas. I would welcome the opportunity to discuss my interest in the school counseling position with you in the near future. If you have additional questions, please feel free to contact me at (123) 456-7890 or through email at noone@hotmail.com.

Respectfully yours,

Althea Jefferson

Althea Jefferson

THE JOB INTERVIEW

Some questions you will face in an interview will be generic, whereas others will be specific to a school, agency, or college counseling center. The sample questions in this section are not comprehensive but will hopefully give you a sense of the types of questions you should be prepared to answer. It may also be helpful to have a career counselor, classmate, spouse, or friend play the role of interviewer. As previously stated, practice is *highly* recommended.

There are a couple of important points to consider before interviewing. If you do not know the answer to a question, please say, "I don't know." This displays both honesty and a lack of pretension. As a veteran interviewer, I can usually spot someone trying to "manufacture" answers when they have no idea what they are speaking about. After all, you have just completed a master's program and are not expected to know everything. So, do not act as if you do know it all.

Second, you do not want to be too lengthy with your answers, as those interviewing you will lose interest. Bolles (2022) suggests the 50/50, 2-minute rule. The 2-minute maximum suggests that you keep your answers thorough but brief. The longer you talk, the less interested the interviewer (or search committee) will be in your answers. After all, if you are too wordy at the interview, you may be too talkative as a counselor. In addition, the longer you speak during an interview, the greater the likelihood you will disclose something you would rather not disclose (Hodges & Connelly, 2010). Be brief and thorough, and use discretion in your answers.

Here are some sample interview questions:

- **Why do you want this job?** This is a critical question. You want the search committee to believe this school, agency, or college counseling center is your primary interest and focus. Be able to tie your answer to the mission of the organization, something like "I enjoy the challenge of working in an addictions treatment agency and wish to make my career in this counseling field. Your agency treats addicts in recovery utilizing CBT and DBT for trauma and offers an extensive training program and continuing education for employees." Don't say, "I think your school is a good stepping stone for my career." This latter response suggests, "You're just a short step on my career path and I'm not committed to you."

- **Tell me about yourself.** This is your opportunity to take initiative in the interview. What interviewers want to hear is how you can tie your brief biography into why you are a good fit for the job. I would suggest that you weave your personal experience and strengths into a 60-second answer that sums up your "fit" for the position, for example, "I grew up in a family of teachers, with my mother a principal and my father a school counselor, and have maintained a high value on education. I volunteer with disadvantaged children every year in the Big Sister/Big Brother program. I believe my personal background and training as a school counselor have provided me valuable experience for working alongside teachers, counselors, and administrators such as those here at Levett Middle School."

- **What special training or skills do you offer?** This is where additional training or related skills and experience come in handy. For example, if you are a trained or certified mediator, mention that. Perhaps you have spent several years supervising collegiate residential living communities or advanced training in art therapy or adventure-based therapy; mention this and tie the experience into how much it has enhanced your counseling ability. Remember, administrators are always interested in getting multitalented employees.

- **What is your experience with this particular clinical population?** This is where your practicum/internship comes in handy, as does any related experience. Again, use your professional and related experiences to address the question. Weave in your practicum and internship experience, training, related experience volunteering with special populations, and so forth.

- **Could you describe your strengths and weaknesses?** Everyone has weaknesses, and you are no exception. An overused line I have heard *way* too many times in job interviews goes something like "I'm a perfectionist and very hard on myself." To me, this sounds contrived and scarcely original. So try to relate a weakness that can be turned around into a strength. For example, "Well, I am young and have just completed my graduate degree. But, I'm a quick learner, and in a couple of years, I will be older and more experienced. I'm also very willing to take coaching and feedback." The strength aspect of this question is much more honest and original. Cite your experience on practicum and internship, related work, and so forth.

- **If offered this position, how long could you see yourself working here?** In most cases, it is best not to give a specific time. Instead, you might answer something like "I would like to work here as long as I have fresh challenges and opportunities. And, I hope to be challenged and have opportunities here for several years to come." If they pin you down with demands for a year answer, something suggesting long-term is best, for example, "I would foresee myself working at this agency/school/hospital for 5 to 7 years." Of course, one never really knows!

- **What theoretical counseling approach do you work from?** This is often a tough question for recent graduates of master's degree counseling programs, as the program may not have provided one single approach. So, cite the approaches you have primarily used on practicum and internship and under what situations you used them. Also, let the committee know you are open to learning new skills, techniques, and approaches. As trauma treatment is an issue, have a working familiarity with ACT, DBT, EMDR, and so on.

- **What are your professional goals?** Wise interviewees will tie their answer to the job at hand. For example, if you are interviewing for a school counseling position, you might express that you would like to direct a high school counseling program. You might also mention a few marking points along the way (such as attaining licensure, national certification, and additional training). The dreaded "I have no goals" or "I don't believe in setting goals" is guaranteed to end your candidacy for the job as it suggests you see no need for continued professional growth. You might be surprised at the number of interviewees who profess to a dearth of professional goals! So, set goals and measure your progress regularly.

- **How do you handle conflict?** Be judicious with your answer, but be authentic. Inability to get along with coworkers is a huge reason people are fired or quit their jobs. A possible answer to this question might be something like this: "I work to calm myself, reviewing the main points of the disagreement. Then, I try to seek out the other party from the standpoint of trying to understand their point of view. If we then cannot come to agreement, perhaps asking a colleague or supervisor to mediate might be a good idea."

- **What if a parent, teacher, coach, and so forth demands to know what you and a student or client are working on in counseling?** For school counseling applicants, this is a question to see how well you remember your professional ethics (and legal issues like FERPA as well!). You might want to briefly allude to the relevant legal issues in your answer. Remember, laws vary from state to state. So, know the relevant laws for the state you plan to work in.

- **Regarding research, what is your specialty area?** If you are completing a doctorate in counselor education and supervision and applying for an academic position or a research position, you need to be able to articulate your research interests, experience, and publications. In addition, check out the department's website to see how your research interests match those of the faculty. It is also worthwhile to scope out whether the opening is a replacement position ("Why did the last person leave?") or a newly created position.

- **Have you ever been fired from a job?** If you were terminated for a cause, explain what that was. Emphasize how you have learned and grown from this experience. Remember, the world is full of successful people who were fired from previous jobs.

- **What did you like about our agency/school/treatment center that interested you enough to apply for the job?** This is a critical question. The interviewer(s) want(s) to hear your in-depth knowledge of the agency or school and its programs, missions, goals, client population, talented staff or faculty, and so forth. Be brief but thorough. Illustrate that you are knowledgeable about what they do. For sure, check out the website to learn as much as you can. If you know someone who works at the school/agency, ask them relevant questions.

- **What do you see as the pressing issues in the field for the next decade?** This question is designed to see how well you understand the profession and potential changes. Good answers also illustrate that you have kept up on professional reading of journals. The "pressing issues" are subjective, so be prepared to support any answers you give. For example, a potential answer might be, "I believe multiculturalism is the most important issue because of the large influx of immigrant and multicultural populations and the fact we live in a globally interconnected era."

- **How have you or how would you support multiculturalism?** Be prepared to address how you support multiculturalism and include specific examples. Concrete examples might include having served on the school district's diversity task force, having counseled multicultural populations, having studied and/or worked abroad, and so forth. Remember, everyone has some part in multiculturalism as multiculturalism includes race, culture, socioeconomics, gender, sexual orientation, geography, and so on.

- **What professional counseling organizations do you hold membership in?** If you are preparing for a job search and are not a member of a professional counseling organization, I would strongly suggest you join the pertinent ones (e.g., ACA, ASCA, or ARCA). The lack of a professional membership, especially in flagship organizations like the ACA, suggests you may not be committed to your profession and that you may not be current in your profession.

- **What salary would you expect to receive?** Never quote a specific figure. Answer with something like, "Somewhere in the advertised range" or "Something reflecting my training or experience." Never state a dollar amount until you receive a job offer! This is a mistake too many inexperienced job seekers—and even some experienced ones—make.

- **What do you know about the mission of this university, school, or agency?** This is a question that is becoming more commonly asked in interviews. Make sure you have read and understood the mission, which should be posted on the university/school/agency's website. In addition, be prepared to explain why your experience and background fits the mission of the organization. If you do not know the mission, search committees will interpret that to mean you were not prepared for the interview and do not understand the school or agency.

- **Why should we hire you?** All interviews are an attempt to address this overarching question. This question usually comes at the end of the interview and is the candidate's opportunity to state their special qualifications and fit for the job. You need to be brief and sound confident but not cocky. Here is one possible answer: "I believe myself to be the best candidate for the addiction counseling position because I have spent the past 2 years counseling in a residential addiction treatment center. I also have experience counseling trauma survivors and have completed DBT training. My plan is to make a career as an addictions counselor and one day to run a clinic such as this one. Hire me as a counselor and I'll make you very happy you did." Suggestion: Practice your answer with a friend or colleagues. Then ask if they would hire you based on your answer.

- **Do you have any questions for us?** Of course you do! This is your opportunity to take control of the interview and it comes at the tipping point. I cringe whenever I hear job candidates state, "No, I have no questions." Such an answer implies the candidate did not do their homework. You must always have questions to ask, even if you already know the answers to them. Chapter 3, "Selecting and Applying for a Practicum/Internship," offered suggested questions when choosing a practicum/internship placement; many of these questions would also be appropriate for a formal job interview. (Adapted from Hodges & Connelly, 2010, pp. 68–70)

Inappropriate Questions

Unfortunately, some interviewers will ask inappropriate questions during interviews. As a young counselor seeking a job, I was occasionally asked inappropriate questions at a job interview. Interviewers asking inappropriate questions may be unintentional (although ignorance is no excuse) or deliberate. Most public and private institutions, clinics, and hospitals sign an Equal Employment Opportunity Commission (EEOC) statement that pledges they will not discriminate based on race, age, creed, national origin, disability status, sexual orientation, veteran status, gender, and so on. Thus, questions concerning any of these issues should generally not be raised in an interview.

Examples of inappropriate questions might include the following:

- "Are you married?" or "Do you have children?"
- "What church do you attend?"
- "Mind if I ask you some personal questions?" (*Of course you would mind*—everyone minds! I was once asked this very question at an interview for a counseling position! Yes, I did mind! I was not offered the job, nor would I have accepted an offer.)

13: COMPLETING THE PRACTICUM/INTERNSHIP AND PREPARING FOR THE FUTURE • 351

- "What political party do you belong to?"
- "Do you have a *normal* sexual orientation?"
- "How many times a day do you pray?"
- "I don't see a ring on your finger. Are you dating anyone?"
- "Are you related to anyone who could help us politically?"

Be aware that if you are interviewing for a counseling job in another country (e.g., Australia, Canada, or Singapore), the laws will be different. A good suggestion is to do an online search for cultural, legal, and other significant issues you may encounter.

The professional way to respond to illegal or inappropriate questions is to be tactful and ask clarification-type questions. While it might be very understandable if you were to get angry and respond in a likewise manner, you are a professional, and professionals conduct themselves professionally even when the interview team or an administrator does not.

> **Example of illegal/inappropriate question:** "Are you married?"
>
> **Potential Answer:** "How does that question relate to the job?" or "Why is this important information to know?" You might use humor to defuse the situation: "Hmmm . . . I don't think the interview police allow that question." A more low-key and humorous approach does not suggest that illegal or inappropriate questions are any laughing matter, but rather they provide the interviewee an opportunity to send a message in a manner that does not inflame the situation.

Inappropriate or illegal questions should rightfully lead you to wonder about the day-to-day ethics of the workplace. Should you be asked illegal or inappropriate questions on an interview, you may wish to consider whether you want to work at a school or agency with such lax ethics and callous disregard for federal law. Once the interview is over, you may consider contacting the appropriate person (usually in human resources) and informing them of your experience. You also have the right to contact your state's Department of Labor and file a complaint. Naturally, as a vulnerable person on a job search, it is wise to consider the ramifications of reporting versus not reporting. Consider the potential risks versus the rewards. Just as important for you, ask yourself what type of school, agency, or academic department you want to work in. If the potential job site does not seem a good fit for your personal values, you will likely be unhappy working there. As a counselor who spent more than 20 years providing career counseling and career advising, I have heard many sad stories from employees whose values are not a good fit for their place of work. Accepting a job is a bit like a marriage; you can get out of it but the getting out is emotionally draining and very expensive.

DEALING WITH REJECTION

On the path to career success, you will experience some rejection. This section of the chapter offers concrete suggestions to manage your disappointment if you do not get a position that you wanted. Fortunately, such rejection is not personal (except in rare cases), will pass, and does not have to keep you from landing another viable job. Rejection is also universally experienced as everyone has been rejected for something they desired.

So, you have just suffered a setback in your job search. That dream job—the one you seemed perfect for—was offered to someone else. Perhaps you had a great interview where the search committee seemed to hang on your every word (or so you thought). You left the interview convinced you would soon be getting a call with a job offer. Then sometime later, with a brief and stilted phone call, your dreams burst into flames of disappointment. You hang up the phone, stunned and numb from the shock of rejection. You try to make sense of it, but your mind cannot seem to accommodate the unexpected setback. "How could they have selected someone else?" you wonder, replaying the interview in your mind, closely examining clues you may have missed.

This scenario has been experienced by just about every job seeker in history. The critical factor is to acknowledge that you will have failures because they are natural. For each job advertised, typically, only one person will be selected. This means, of course, that if 30 applicants apply for a mental health counseling opening, 29 will be disappointed. Thus, job rejection is not only a common shared experience, but there is almost no way around some degree of occupational rejection.

There are several reasonable reasons for job rejection (Hodges & Connelly, 2010, pp. 88–91).:

- A more qualified candidate was selected. Or, the interviewer or search committee *thought* the successful candidate was more qualified. Remember, the job search and hiring process is an inexact science at best—for both job seeker and hiring parties.

- The successful candidate seemed a better fit for the position. A candidate with less experience might be hired because they have a counseling specialty area other candidates lack (e.g., trauma counseling experience, play therapy experience, and mediation training) or simply seemed to connect better with the search committee.

- Fit has cultural and gender implications. For example, if all the current counseling staff at a school are, say, female, a male candidate may have a better chance at the job. No interviewing committee will admit to making such considerations, but believe me, as a 40-year veteran of search committees, they do consider such.

- The successful candidate was simply better prepared than the other finalists. Bolles (2022) makes the point that the most prepared applicant will likely be hired over a more qualified one. Preparation includes a well-crafted résumé or CV, succinct and error-free cover letters, and good interviews. A more qualified candidate could torpedo their candidacy by lack of preparation in these critical areas.

- A candidate's behavior was inappropriate during the interview. Inappropriate behavior could be having more than one drink at dinner with search committee members, a candidate making racist or sexist jokes, rudeness to committee members, or raising inappropriate topics during the interview. Remember, you are always "on the clock," even during breaks.

- A candidate displayed a lack of confidence at the interview. You might be the most qualified candidate, but if you do not present as such, someone else will get the job offer. Self-critical comments such as "It's nothing," "Anyone could have done it," or "My colleagues actually did most of the work," send the wrong message. Be confident, not cocky or self-absorbed, but confident. A candidate was dishonest. Were you caught in a lie on your résumé or CV? Did you overly embellish your credentials during the interview phase? Be honest; it will save you a lot of angst. (*Note:* I am rewriting this section as the saga with Congressman George Soros, who has lied about his education, employment history, family background, and almost all else, continues to evolve.) A candidate's appearance was unprofessional. Granted, the counseling profession is not as formal as that of, say, banking or finance. Nevertheless, play it conservative; women should wear dress slacks, skirt, or dress. Men should wear a tie or sport coat. Do not go overboard with cologne or perfume or jewelry.

- The search was a failed one. Sometimes, a committee will not hire because of a shallow applicant pool or a general dissatisfaction with the finalists. This happens, so work to not take it personally. As the saying goes, a person's (or persons') failure to see your value is not necessarily an accurate statement of your value.

- There was behind-the-scenes politicking. You can never really know what goes on behind closed doors. Politics certainly comes into play at times and a surprise candidate emerges as the top choice. Or the interview committee ranks the candidates 1 to 5 and the pertinent administrator selects the fourth- or fifth-ranked candidate. I have seen this happen more than once.

- A candidate posted inappropriate content on the internet. Social networking sites have created a medium for sharing information and meeting new people. They also contain and chronicle much outlandish behavior. Make sure your online persona matches what you wish to convey in your job search.

Transforming Your Disappointment

Fortunately, most applicants are resilient and understand there will be other job opportunities. The important point is to learn from disappointment and adapt that knowledge to new opportunities. When you get the disappointing phone call, email, or, as in past eras, the thin envelope, here are some suggestions for dealing with job rejection:

- Allow yourself some time to adjust to the situation. Do not push yourself to feel "okay." Talk the situation over with a trusted friend or colleague. Be honest with yourself about the disappointment and pain. Remember also, there will be other job opportunities.

- Stay physically active. Activity routines are a staple of health, especially during a job search. Physical activity works off anxiety and depression and promotes relaxation.

- When you have a little distance from the disappointment, reflect back on the experience. What went wrong? What seemed to go well? How could you improve for the next application or interview? This aspect of self-reflection is a critical task in the job search process.

- Get feedback from someone in the professional field. If you are seeking a school counseling position, ask a professional school counselor to look over your résumé or CV and for tips. Practice interviewing with a career counselor or a professional counselor and have them grade you.
- Identify two or three close friends/colleagues you can get support and a reality check from.
- If needed, go in for personal counseling to address your frustration and the stress generated by the lack of getting hired.
- Monitor and reframe your self-talk. Notice if you are telling yourself negative messages, such as "I'll never get hired" and "Nobody wants me." Reframe to more positive and realistic self-talk, such as "I'm having difficulty, but I'll keep applying and improving and someone will hire me," or "Someone will eventually give me an opportunity and I'll be ready." (Additional strategies for professional self-reflection may be found in Box 13.3.)

EVALUATING A JOB OFFER

Congratulations, you have a job offer! This is a big deal even if you are not interested in the job. When you receive an offer, it may be tempting to accept on the spot, especially during tough economic times. Be aware that if you accept the job unconditionally, you may be losing any leverage you might have in the negotiation process. Certainly, you want to express excitement and gratitude on receiving the offer and you may even feel the salary and benefits are very good. Still, as this is a big step, ask for a few days to think it over. Most employers, reasonable ones anyway, will respect this request.

Be thorough in your decision-making process because you do not want to hastily accept a job only to find there is something you missed in the process (e.g., moving expense reimbursement and annual raises). There are many issues to consider:

- What life changes would accepting this job entail?
- What expenses would I incur by accepting the job (e.g., moving expenses, selling or buying a home, uprooting children from school and friends, and moving away from family)?
- What would I be gaining by accepting this offer (other than a paycheck)?
- What would I be giving up by accepting this job (e.g., location, friends, and family)?
- Does the salary range seem equitable compared to other jobs of this type? Will it be enough to live on? In addition, what will my counter offer be?
- How excited am I about this offer? Would I want to work with the staff? Does this position offer good potential for professional growth? (These are what I call the gut comfort questions: How does my gut feel when I consider accepting the offer? I have learned to pay attention to my gut.)

Box 13.3 Professional Self-Reflection

- How would you describe your current job search?

- Ideally, where would you like to be in your professional life? Describe the job, geographic location, salary, and anything else that seems pertinent.

- How can you begin to create the professional life you described in the previous question? Cite anything that could help you accomplish your professional goals.

- If you were recently rejected for a job (or jobs) you wanted, what did you learn that could help you in future job searches?

- What supports do you have for this transitional time? Examples of support can be family members, friends, a spiritual community, fellow graduate students, support groups, and the like.

- What personal strengths do you have that will assist you in coping with this transition time? Examples of personal strengths are a positive outlook, good work ethic, fitness routine, and the like.

- Think of when you were faced with previous challenges. How have you coped with previous disappointments? How can previous experience assist you now?

- Think of someone who has successfully transitioned through job rejection and then found success. Ask them for tips on how you can do the same.

- Ask yourself, "What else can I do to become the strongest candidate possible?"

- When you are hired into a professional counseling position, how will your life be different? What joys and challenges might the new professional role present?

- What would potential employers find attractive about you? What criticisms might they have? What is your ratio of strength to criticisms?

- Networking is an essential component of a successful job search. What can you do to create an effective supportive network?

- When writing cover letters, creating résumés or CVs, interviewing, and so forth, what message would you like to convey? How can you create that desired message?

- If you were looking to hire a counselor or counselor educator, what qualities would you be looking for? Now, how well do you match up to those qualities? If you do not match up to the desired qualities, what do you need to do to meet them?

- If a potential employer were to say, "Tell me five reasons why I should hire you," how would you answer?

Source: Hodges, S., & Connelly, A. R. (2010). *A job search manual for counselors and counselor educators: How to navigate and promote your counseling career* (pp. 94–96). American Counseling Association.

If you are still unsure about accepting the job, a simple and common technique to try is a pro–con exercise. Using a pen, split a sheet of paper down the center. Label the left side "pro" and the right side "con." Then, list all the pros and cons you can think of. Naturally, you want the pro list to be longer than the con list. If the con list is longer or the lists are of about equal length, this should give you pause before accepting the offer. Let us examine such a list:

Pro	Con
It is a job.	It is an expensive area.
It includes good salary and benefits.	It requires an expensive move.
It is in a desirable area of the country.	It is far from friends and family.
It has good potential for promotion.	I might get other offers.
I would have likable colleagues.	
The area has job potential for my partner.	
I am excited about the job!	

In this case, the pros outnumber the cons, although there are significant cons in the list. Thus, this candidate has a difficult decision to make. There are some significant pros as well, and the most significant one may be item number 7— excitement about the job. Some readers may be in the enviable position of entertaining several offers at once, and the pro–con lists would be longer than a list for one offer. Regardless, the ultimate decision to accept or reject the offer can be a difficult one. Talking the matter over with friends, family, spouse, or partner and, if need be, a counselor can be helpful.

Here is another example of a counselor weighing an offer:

Pro	Con
It is a very good job.	It is a 500-mile move.
We love the location!	I will be leaving friends.
They will help my partner search for a job.	My partner will need to find a new job.
Excellent potential for promotion.	
I like the staff/faculty.	
The salary and benefits are very good.	
They will pay $3,000 for the move.	
We are close to family.	
I am very excited about the job!	

In this example, the pros seem to far outnumber the cons. It is likely that this counselor would have an easier time making a decision of whether to accept the position than the previous scenario. Another method of assessing whether or not to accept a job involves a decision tree. In the following example, continue down the list until you arrive at a "no" answer. A "no" answer would suggest that you seriously consider whether accepting this job is a wise decision.

Step 1: Do I really want this job? On a scale of 1 to 10, with 10 high, how excited am I about this job?

Step 2: Does this job fit my needs or my family's needs regarding professional challenge, financial security, benefits, stability, and lifestyle?

Step 3: If taking this job necessitates a move, would I or my family be willing to relocate?

Step 4: Would the relocation be worth the disruption in our lives (e.g., distance from family and friends, school change, spouse's or partner's job change)?

Step 5: Are the administration and staff (or faculty) at this position actually supportive of diversity? Might I be just a "check the box" hire?

Step 6: Do I feel committed to this job for 3 to 5 years?

Step 7: Does the job environment seem healthy (e.g., healthy collegial relations, small annual turnover rate, and supportive supervisor)?

Step 8: Can I say, "This is the type of job I'm really excited about"?

Step 9: Do the pros of accepting this job outweigh the cons?

If you answered "yes" to the question, "Do the pros significantly outweigh the cons? Yes or no?" this should provide you some insight. If you answered "no," that answer has the same guiding principle as "yes." Another critical question to consider is "Am I excited about the prospect of this job?" Well, *are you* (Hodges & Connelly, 2010, p. 81)?

If You Reject the Offer

Be professional. Thank whoever has offered you the position. If the person asks why you are turning down the offer, be as honest as you feel comfortable. For example, if the staff seemed rude, you might want to consider whether you would actually disclose that. If you are rejecting the offer because of salary, because you found a job that offers a better fit with your goals, or because you have found one in a preferred geographic location, that likely will not be as difficult to mention. Remember, the counseling profession can be very small, so do not burn any bridges.

If You Accept the Offer

This is the place all job seekers want to be; they have an offer and have decided to accept it. Now, your work is still not done. Anyone extending a job offer understands that a savvy candidate will attempt to negotiate the best possible terms. Many people, and this may especially be true of counselors fresh out of graduate school, may be uncomfortable with negotiation, especially during tough economic times. Determine what salary you and your family need, then practice negotiating with a career counselor or friend. Here are some things to keep in mind regarding negotiation:

- You may have been given a specific salary figure (likely). Your ability to move that figure upward will depend on what you have to offer (e.g., special training, related experience, publications), your apparent skill level, and how much the employer wants you.

- Beyond salary, what are the other negotiables? Is a costly move involved? Are you a dual-income family and losing one income with the move? Can the employer assist your spouse or partner in finding a job?

- How good are the benefits? What and *who* does the health plan include (e.g., domestic partners, stepchildren)? What about the retirement package? If you are young, do not discount this issue because it will become increasingly important over time. In fact, many Americans have inadequate pensions (Olen, 2014).

- How many vacation days do you receive per year? How many sick days?

- What type of annual salary increase or merit increase is offered? Will you have a probationary period? Does the job involve tenure, and, if so, what is the length of time before you can apply for tenure?

- What opportunity is there for advancement in this clinic/school/agency?

- Will the employer pay for you to receive additional training (e.g., attending conferences, workshops)?

- Regardless of what transpires, be courteous during the negotiation phase. Do not become rigid and make statements such as "This is my final offer!" Be flexible when necessary without giving in on everything. For example, you might be more flexible on salary, but hold the line on moving expenses.

- When you agree to a package, get the agreement in writing.

Your new employer will expect you to be enthusiastic when you begin. Be realistic and give yourself time to adjust to a new place, new colleagues, and new challenges. Remember that most people struggle in their jobs not because they lack the skill but because of conflicts with coworkers (Bolles, 2022). Therefore, extend yourself to your new colleagues by asking for their input, ideas, and critique. Be respectful when you disagree in staff meetings, and learn to listen to people you find difficult.

FINAL THOUGHTS ON CONCLUDING YOUR PRACTICUM/ INTERNSHIP, GRADUATION, AND BEGINNING YOUR CAREER

- Remember, your career as a professional counselor is just beginning. The first job you begin your career with is unlikely to be the one where you finish your career. So, if you do not get your first choice in a job when you graduate, remember you likely will have other jobs.

- Because you are new in the profession (e.g., recent graduate) and lack licensure (or certification for many school counselors), your initial job out of graduate school may not be one you stay with for the long term. However, remember that, although the initial job after graduation may not be ideal, it provides you the opportunity for professional growth and to receive supervision for licensure. State licensure, registration (license equivalent in other countries), and 3 to 5 years' experience give you professional mobility.

13: COMPLETING THE PRACTICUM/INTERNSHIP AND PREPARING FOR THE FUTURE • 359

- Although graduate school experiences vary, many graduate students experience their counseling programs as nurturing environments. Do not expect your first professional job to be like your graduate program. In fact, it may seem fast-paced and, at times, callous.

- Make sure to keep your résumé or CV current so that when more desirable positions become available, you are ready to apply. Advice: Try and stay in your first job a minimum of 3 years. This provides time to grow as a professional and suggests you are not just in and out the job door. Of course, life happens and one has to adjust.

- Take advantage of all trainings your school, agency, college, and so forth has to offer. As a professional counselor, you should be a lifelong learner. Certificate trainings in specific clinical, legal, or professional issues are great ways to upgrade and expand your skills. Take advantage of these.

- If the agency, school, or college counseling center has a preferred treatment approach (e.g., DBT, CBT, EMDR, or solution-focused therapy [SFT]), keep an open mind about it, even if you prefer a different theoretical approach. Working from a new theoretical modality also broadens your experience and enhances your clinical skills.

- Set some professional goals for yourself, such as to develop expertise in the treatment model you are learning (e.g., CBT and DBT), to develop harmonious relationships with the staff, to stay in the job for 2 years, to receive training in a new skill area, and so forth.

- Keep a folder of the applications you make for employment. Many students, especially doctoral students looking for an academic job, may make 20 to 30 applications. You want to keep the positions you apply for from merging together in your mind, and a file of all applications filed can assist with organization. In addition, some search committees work slower than others do. I once applied for a job and did not hear from the search committee until 6 months later.

- Anytime you apply for a counseling position, be sure to examine the website of the organization.

- Use appropriate social medial sites for career networking. LinkedIn is one of the preferred networking sites career professionals use. LinkedIn is relatively easy and simple to use and provides an efficient way to link with colleagues in your area, state, country, and abroad.

CONCLUSION

Congratulations! You are nearing the end of your graduate counseling program and preparing for the job search. The good news is the demand for counselors is high and that translates into very good job prospects. Having said this, make sure you prepare thoroughly for all interviews. Even if you are unsure you want the job, treat it as if you do as this is valuable practice; you also never really know what you will end up liking or disliking job-wise. I have experienced such a sea-change in my own career and many former students have informed me, "I thought I would hate this job and discovered the opposite." (The converse of this statement can be true as well.) So, be prepared for all interviews and follow suggestions in this chapter and other valuable

360 • THE COUNSELING PRACTICUM AND INTERNSHIP MANUAL

recommended resources. Finally, keep yourself updated on changes in the field and be aware of the role technology plays. As previously stated, monitor advances in AI as AI will plan an increasingly important role in counseling and the broader mental health field.

LESSONS LEARNED

"Would you mind if I asked you some personal questions?" asked a member of the interviewing committee, facial angles harsh. Now, of course anyone would and moreover *should* mind when asked such an invasive, inappropriate, and illegal question during an interview. A quick glance around the table told me nobody, including the executive director, was going to object to the offending party's question. Taking a breath, I explained my willingness to answer any question related to the job or my qualifications for the job. Unfortunately, that did not bring an end to the saga and the person repeated the question with even more emphasis. After a long pause, the buzzing of the fluorescent lights the only audible sound, I suggested I was not the right person for the job, then exited with as much dignity as possible. I was stunned, as this was a mental health facility! Yet, this unfortunate, perhaps shocking, experience would not be the last interview mishap in my long career.

A couple of years later, I was interviewing for a job at an agency. The job was a temporary counseling job that was to run for 6 months. The timeline was fine with me, as in reality I was only looking for summer employment given I would be back at my university graduate position in late September. I was called for an interview. Two staff members interviewed me. They asked the standard fare of questions which were easy to address and the duo appeared very happy with my answers. They asked me a few of the usual questions: "What are your key strengths?" "What is your theoretical approach to counseling?" and the like. I recall one of the interviewers seemed particularly pleased with me. "You are a very strong candidate," she offered, noting my varied experience of counseling, including inpatient as well as outpatient therapy, and that I had teaching experience. She explained running psychoeducational groups would be part of the job. "Great!" I added, and the duo nodded appropriately. "Actually, we would like you to consider a permanent job. You could work part-time while going to school. Are you interested?" I explained that yes, I would be interested and would find a way to balance school, graduate assistanceship, and this job. "Wonderful! We'll be in touch by tomorrow," one said with a broad smile. I left the room head high, floating on my hubris.

The following day, there was no call. Nor was there a call the day after or the one after that. Stunned, I called and spoke to the woman who had asked me to apply for the permanent job. Her voice tone was my answer. Stammering about, she explained their recommendation had been turned down. Unable to process the 360-degree turnabout, I asked what had happened. "Sorry, I'm not supposed to say anything. It's not you. That's all I can say." I thanked her for her time and hung up. Unable to process my emotions, I did what I always do when upset: I put on my running clothes and took a long jog. Fortunately, I was hired at a different agency just days later (with better pay!) and all was fortunately well again. However, my tribulations on the job search front would continue.

13: COMPLETING THE PRACTICUM/INTERNSHIP AND PREPARING FOR THE FUTURE • 361

After completing my doctorate, I ran a community mental health clinic and, after that, directed a university counseling service. Both of these experiences were positive ones with the types of challenges one would expect, namely, clients with significant mental health challenges, hiring and firing staff, and doing *budget yoga* to make dollars stretch. Counseling clients with addictions, PTSD, and mental disorders, while difficult, is a challenge counselors are trained to address. Then, there are those other stresses we are never quite adequately prepared for, at least initially.

After several years running clinical programs, providing counseling, and teaching as an adjunct, I began to apply for counselor education faculty positions. Some positions happened to be running their searches over the summer. During this time, my spouse and I each had the summer off and would drive around the country in our van, visiting family, friends, and national parks, accompanied by our friendly German Shepherd. During our travels, one of the counselor education programs interviewed me from the road. I was offered a second interview and we set the date. My spouse had work in San Francisco, and after dropping her off, I spent the better part of two days driving to the campus interview. The chair of the committee agreed to stable my dog in a kennel and then helped me get checked into the hotel. That night, I had dinner with the search committee. All were friendly, with one exception. This fellow taught in a related program in the department. Little was said but his body language suggested skepticism.

The following day, the morning portion of the interview involved me doing a teaching demonstration, which went well. The interview with the counselor education faculty also went well, as did that with the department chair and the dean of the College of Education. Then came my research presentation. The audience was small, composed of the search committee, counseling faculty, department head and a few students, and the skeptical member from the previous night's dinner. My topic is a research proposal I had developed to study meaning in life among clients in counseling. Then, the fireworks began. I could scarcely explain my proposal as the skeptical man kept interrupting my talk practically every minute. He seemed to object to everything I uttered: "Life was meaningless," he snapped when I referenced Viktor Frankl's theory, "CBT is simply behavior therapy and Skinner, not Beck and Ellis, should be credited," "Behavioral management is more effective than counseling," and the like. The search committee chair attempted to placate this unruly man, but he continued his rant. Audience members looked anxiously about, likely pondering a dash for the door, something I was considering myself. Finally, the red-faced department chair suggested that as time is almost up, perhaps we should adjourn. As I packed up my portfolio, the hostile man actually came forward and offered his hand, expressing, "Nothing personal." With nothing to lose, I declined his offer of a handshake. Humiliated, I walked in silence alongside the equally disturbed search committee chair.

I never heard an adequate explanation for the rude, totally unprofessional attack directed at me, although various excuses were offered: "He's not in our program," "He's everyone's problem," and "He's just a critical academic" (No kidding!). Not one person actually offered an apology. Disappointed, I crossed this program off my job list. However, they were not finished with me. They refused to reimburse me, claiming I selected an expensive hotel, and therefore, they would reimburse only 50% of my hotel expenses (despite the search committee having selected the hotel). They also said that they were not responsible for the kennel cost for my dog (despite having offered). and they attempted to get out of mileage reimbursement for what I incurred driving from the Bay area to their campus. After 6 months of jousting with them over unpaid expenses, I copied my receipts and sent them to the dean of the College of Education, explaining my side of what had occurred. Fortunately, I had saved copies of my receipts, otherwise I would have been out a good deal of money. Siding with me, the dean forced the department chair to fully reimburse my expenses. He also wrote me an apology, explaining he had investigated and determined there had been unprofessional conduct. I thanked him and, although still smarting from the experience, considered myself fortunate not to be moving into such a toxic workplace.

A few months later, arriving home from campus, a letter from a community college greeted me. Puzzled at what it might be about, I opened the envelope and commenced reading. The letter from some magistrate at the college explained that while they were impressed by my qualifications, I would not be granted an interview for a counseling position. Still smarting from my experience out west, I initially felt deflated. Sitting down to a cup of coffee, however, it dawned on me that I could not recall applying for the job. I reviewed the rejection letter and then perused my application folder. I had *not* applied for a job at the college! I was being rejected for a position I had not even applied for! The absurdity of the experience triggered a laughing fit that puzzled my spouse, who arrived as I commenced the frivolity. I shared the news with her and we shared a needed moment of levity. Ironically, this *pseudo* rejection buoyed my mood. Not long thereafter, I was hired as an assistant professor of counseling at Niagara University, where I would teach for 21 years.

Job searching, subsequent success, and *far* more rejection have taught me many valuable career and life lessons. Most especially, keep good records, otherwise I would have lost a good deal of money from the counseling program that refused to reimbursement me. Applicants should also keep in mind that until they have a solid offer from an official able to make the offer, *they do not have an offer*. In the case of the interviewer informing me I would be hired, I expect she was well intentioned. However, she was not empowered to offer me the job. So, until you have something in writing, *you do not have a viable offer*. Regarding the rejection of the position I had not applied for, keep records of the jobs you do apply for so you can laugh over any such absurdities.

Finally, as you are in a vulnerable position during the job search, have an active self-care plan. Seek support from your family and friends, spiritual life, or whatever is meaningful (e.g., meditation, daily gratitude acknowledgement, journaling), and keep physically active. Looking back on a long career in mental health and higher education, my self-care plan has seen me through many professional disappointments, heartbreaks, and unfulfilled promises. In fact, self-care likely is more important than anything you have been taught in your graduate program, as the regular practice of well-being likely is what keeps you vibrant in your career. When interviewing for my current job in Australia, I was asked what I considered most important in success. I replied that self-care, in all ways mentioned, was the most important element of success, as in absent well-being, there is no real success, and disillusionment, unproductivity, and likely burnout will invariably result. So, put your own mental, emotional, and physical health and well-being above your job. Leave any job that asks you to do otherwise, especially as counseling is designed so that we have happier, more fulfilling lives.

RECOMMENDED RESOURCE

Bolles, R. N. (2022). *What color is your parachute? A practical guide for job-hunters and career changers*. Ten Speed Press.

A robust set of instructor resources designed to supplement this text is located at http://connect.springerpub.com/content/book/978-0-8261-6607-4. Qualifying instructors may request access by emailing textbook@springerpub.com.

REFERENCES

Baird, B. N. (2005). *The internship, practicum, and field placement handbook: A guide for the helping professions* (4th ed.). Pearson/Prentice Hall.
Bolles, R. N. (2022). *What color is your parachute? A practical manual for job-hunters and career-changers*. Ten Speed Press.
Capacchione, L. (2000). *Visioning: Ten steps to designing the life of your dreams*. Tarcher/Putnam.
Covey, S. R. (1996). *The seven habits of highly effective people*. Simon & Schuster.
Herlihy, B., & Corey, G. (2015). *ACA ethical standards casebook* (7th ed.). American Counseling Association.
Hodges, S., & Connelly, A. R. (2010). *A job search manual for counselors and counselor educators: How to navigate and promote your counseling career*. American Counseling Association.
Olen, H. (2014, February/March). You call this retirement? Boomers still have work to do. *AARP The Magazine*. http://www.aarp.org/work/retirement-planning-little-savings-means-working.html
Remley, T. P. Jr., & Herlihy, B. (2020). *Ethical, legal and professional issues in counseling* (6th ed.). Pearson.
Richards, D., & Vigano, N. (2013). Online counseling: A narrative and critical review of the literature. *Journal of Clinical Psychology, 69*, 994–1011. https://doi.org/10.1002/jclp.21974
Rokeach, M. (1979). *Understanding human values: Individual and societal*. Simon & Schuster.
Seligman, M. E. P. (1998). *Learned optimism* (2nd ed.). Pocket Books.
Thrun, S. (2023, March 29). R. Schroeder's Where will generative AI lead? Inside Higher Ed. https://www.insidehighered.com/digital-learning/blogs/online-trending-now/where-will-generative-ai-lead
Williams, A. (1995). *Visual and active supervision: Roles, focus, technique*. W. W. Norton.

Appendix A: List of Professional Counseling Organizations

(*Note:* Be aware licensing and credentialing requirements are subject to periodic change.)

AMERICAN COUNSELING ASSOCIATION

The American Counseling Association (ACA) is the flagship organization for counselors and the world's largest organization representing the counseling profession. All counselors should hold a membership in the ACA. Membership in the ACA also includes a subscription to the *Journal of Counseling and Development*, the monthly magazine *Counseling Today*, and numerous other tools for professional development.

The ACA (www.counseling.org) also includes 19 affiliate divisions representing various counseling specialties and many different counseling interest groups:

- **American College Counseling Association**

  The American College Counseling Association (ACCA) is the primary professional organization for college, university, and community college counseling professionals. ACCA membership is also open to psychologists, social workers, and so forth.

  www.collegecounseling.org

- **American Rehabilitation Counseling Association**

  The American Rehabilitation Counseling Association (ARCA) represents the profession of rehabilitation, rehabilitation counseling faculty, and graduate students in rehabilitation counseling.

  www.arcaweb.org

- **Association for Adult Development and Aging**

  The Association for Adult Development and Aging (AADA) serves as the professional organization devoted to supporting counselors serving senior populations.

  www.aadaweb.org

- **Association for Assessment and Research in Counseling**

  The Association for Assessment and Research in Counseling (AARC) promotes the ethical and effective use of assessment (testing) in the counseling profession.

  www.theaaceonline.com

- **Association for Child and Adolescent Counseling**

  The Association for Child and Adolescent Counseling (ACAC) aims to focus on the training needs of counselors who work with children and adolescents while also providing professional support to those counselors, whether they are school counselors, play therapists, counselor educators, and so on.

  www.acachild.com

- **Association for Counselor Education and Supervision**

  The Association for Counselor Education and Supervision (ACES) is an umbrella organization for counselor educators in all counseling affiliates (e.g., clinical mental health counseling, school counseling, marriage and family counseling), as well as counseling supervisors out in the field. ACES membership is also open to counseling psychologists and members in related mental health professions.

  www.acesonline.net

- **Association for Creativity in Counseling**

  The Association for Creativity in Counseling (ACC) is a professional affiliate organization for creative arts counseling (e.g., art, music, dance, and drama therapy) as well as novel counseling approaches. The ACC also encourages creative expression in the manner of poetry, prose, musical performance, and so forth by individual counselors.

  www.creativecounselor.org

- **Association for Humanistic Counseling**

  The Association for Humanistic Counseling (AHC), formerly C-AHEAD, a founding association of the ACA in 1952, provides a forum for exchange of information about humanistic-oriented counseling practices and promotes changes that reflect the growing body of knowledge about humanistic principles applied to human development and potential.

  www.afhc.camp9.org

- **Association for Lesbian, Gay, Bisexual, and Transgender Issues in Counseling**

  The Association for Lesbian, Gay, Bisexual, and Transgender Issues in Counseling (ALGBTIC) educates counselors on concerns regarding the needs of lesbian, gay, bisexual, and transgender clients. The ALGBTIC also serves as an advocacy organization both within and beyond the counseling profession.

  www.algbtic.org

APPENDIX A: LIST OF PROFESSIONAL COUNSELING ORGANIZATIONS • 367

- **Association for Multicultural Counseling and Development**

  The Association for Multicultural Counseling and Development (AMCD) strives to improve the understanding of multicultural issues in counseling. Multicultural issues could be related to race, sexual orientation, class, disability, culture, religion or spirituality, and many other issues.

  www.multiculturalcounselingdevelopment.org

- **Association for Specialists in Group Work**

  The Association for Specialists in Group Work (ASGW) provides professional leadership and promotes research in the field of group counseling in schools, colleges/universities, correctional facilities, hospitals, and so forth.

  www.asgw.org

- **Association for Spiritual, Ethical, and Religious Values in Counseling**

  The Association for Spiritual, Ethical, and Religious Values in Counseling (ASERVIC) is devoted to exploring and addressing spiritual, religious, and ethical issues in counseling.

  www.aservic.org

- **Counselors for Social Justice**

  The Counselors for Social Justice (CSJ) is one of the newest ACA divisions and is committed to plurality on a broad array of social justice issues including an end to oppression and injustice impacting clients, students, families, communities, schools, workplaces, governments, and other social and institutional systems.

  www.counseling-csj.org

- **International Association of Addictions and Offender Counselors**

  The International Association of Addictions and Offender Counselors (IAAOC) advocates for the development of effective practice in substance abuse treatment, counseling juvenile offenders, and counselors working in correctional facilities.

  www.iaaoc.org

- **International Association of Marriage and Family Counselors**

  The International Association of Marriage and Family Counselors (IAMFC) is the ACA division devoted to studying and promoting the field of couples and family counseling.

  www.iamfconline.org

- **Military and Government Counseling Association (MGCA); formerly Association for Counselors and Educators in Government (ACEG)**

  The Military and Government Counseling Association (MGCA) is dedicated to exploring counseling issues and concerns in municipal, state, federal, and military settings.

  www.acegonline.org

Additional Professional Counseling Organizations

- **National Career Development Association**

  The National Career Development Association's (NCDA) mission is to promote career and vocational counseling and development.

  www.associationdatabase.com/aws/NCDA/pt/sp/Home_Page

- **National Employment Counseling Association**

  The National Employment Counseling Association's (NECA) charge is professional leadership and development for counselors working in employment settings.

  www.employmentcounseling.org

Additional Professional Counseling Organizations

- **American Mental Health Counselors Association**

  The American Mental Health Counselors Association (AMHCA) is the professional organization specifically representing clinical mental health counseling.

  www.amhca.org

- **American School Counselor Association**

  The American School Counselor Association (ASCA) is an independent counseling organization promoting the profession of school counseling.

  www.schoolcounselor.org

Additional Professional Associations (Independent of the American Counseling Association)

- **American Art Therapy Association**

  The American Art Therapy Association (AATA) is an organization of professionals dedicated to using art in a therapeutic, healing manner. The AATA provides standards of professional competence and promotes knowledge in the field of art therapy.

  www.arttherapy.org

- **American Association of State Counseling Boards**

  The American Association of State Counseling Boards (AASCB) promotes unification and reciprocity among U.S. state counseling licensure requirements.

  www.aascb.org

- **American Dance Therapy Association**

  The American Dance Therapy Association (ADTA), founded in 1986, is a professional organization dedicated to the profession of dance/movement therapy.

  www.adta.org

- **American Music Therapy Association**

  The American Music Therapy Association (AMTA) was unified in 1998 to support the development of the therapeutic use of music in counseling and therapy.

  www.musictherapy.org

- **American Society of Group Psychotherapy and Psychodrama**

  The American Society of Group Psychotherapy and Psychodrama (ASGPP) was founded in 1942 to support therapeutic uses of drama.

  www.asgpp.org

- **Association for Play Therapy**

  The Association for Play Therapy (APT) is a national professional society established in 1982 to foster contact among mental health professionals interested in exploring the therapeutic power of play to treat clients, particularly children.

  www.a4pt.org

INTERNATIONAL COUNSELING ORGANIZATIONS

Note: This is not a comprehensive list, but it features a sampling of international counseling organizations.

- Asociacion Argentina de Counselors (AAC)

  www.aacounselors.org.ar

- Australian Counseling Association (ACA)

  www.theaca.net.au

- British Association for Counseling and Psychotherapy (BACP)

  www.bacp.co.uk

- Canadian Counseling and Psychotherapy Association (CCPA)

  www.ccpa-accp.ca

- Counseling Association of Taiwan (CAT)

  www.counselingassociationoftaiwan.org

- European Association for Counseling (EAC)

  www.eac.eu.com

- Hong Kong Professional Counseling Association (HKPCA)

  www.hkpca.org.hk

- Indonesian Counseling Association (ICA)
  www.indo-counseling.org

- International Accreditation of Counseling Services (IACS)
  www.iacsinc.org

- International Association for Counseling (IAC)
  www.iac.irtac.org
  (The IAC has affiliate organizations in several countries.)

- Irish Association for Counseling and Psychotherapy (IACP)
  www.iacp.ie

- Korean Counseling Association (KCA)
  www.counselors.or.kr

- New Zealand Association of Counselors (NZAC)
  www.nzac.org.nz

- Psychotherapy and Counseling Federation of Australia (PACFA)
  www.pacfa.org.au

- Singapore Association for Counseling (SAC)
  www.sacsingapore.org

- The South African Association for Counselors (SAAC)
  www.counsellorassociation.co.za

Professional Accrediting Organizations for the Counseling Profession

- **Center for Credentialing and Education**

  The Center for Credentialing and Education (CCE), an affiliate of the National Board for Certified Counselors, Inc., provides credentialing to counselors and related professionals. The CCE offers several certifications including approved clinical supervisor (ACS), distance credentialed counselor (DCC), board certified coach (BCC), and several more.

  www.cce-global.org

- **Commission on Rehabilitation Counselor Certification**

  The Commission on Rehabilitation Counselor Certification (CRCC), like the NBCC, provides certification for individual rehabilitation counselors. Certification, unlike licensure, is usually a voluntary credential for counselors. Licensure, often a mandatory credential, is overseen by state licensure boards (see State Licensure Boards).

www.crccertification.com

- **Council for Accreditation of Counseling and Related Educational Programs (CACREP)**

  The CACREP, an ACA organizational affiliate, is the international accrediting organization for counseling programs. The CACREP accredits graduate counseling programs in colleges and universities. The types of graduate counseling programs accredited by the CACREP are doctoral programs in counselor education, as well as master's degree programs in clinical mental health counseling, marriage and family counseling, school counseling, student affairs and counseling, college counseling, and most recently, clinical rehabilitation counseling.

  www.cacrep.org

  email: cacrep@cacrep.org

- **National Board for Certified Counselors**

  The National Board for Certified Counselors (NBCC) serves as an independent credentialing organization for the counseling profession. Although U.S. states and territories are responsible for licensing counselors, the NBCC provides certification for specialty areas. Examples of NBCC specialty area certifications are the national certified counselor (NCC), national certified clinical mental health counselor (NCCMHC), national certified career counselor (NCCC), and approved clinical supervisor (ACS). The NBCC also offers certification examinations that most U.S. states and territories use for licensure examinations, such as the National Counselor Examination (NCE), Certified Clinical Mental Health Counselor Examination (CCMHCE), and more.

  www.nbcc.org

  email: nbcc@nbcc.org

ADDITIONAL WEBSITE OF INTEREST

- The U.S. Bureau of Labor Statistics

  The U.S. Bureau of Labor Statistics (BLS) compiles and publishes the online *Occupational Outlook Handbook* (OOH), a publication that offers growth projections for thousands of occupations. The OOH covers counseling and related occupations. The BLS OOH publication is very important for tracking growth in the counseling profession.

  www.bls.gov/ooh

Appendix B: State Licensure Boards and Requirements

Here is some basic information regarding licensure requirements by state as of 2018. For complete information, please visit the state licensing board website as credentialing requirements may change.

ALABAMA

Alabama Board of Examiners in Counseling

950 22nd St. North, Suite 765

Birmingham, AL 35203

(800) 822-3307

(205) 458-8716

(205) 458-8718 (fax)

Walter H. Cox, Ex. Officer: Walter.Cox@abec.alabama.gov

http://abec.alabama.gov

Title of License: Licensed Professional Counselor (LPC)

Associate Licensed Counselor (ALC)

Note: ALCs work under LPCs to attain hours for licensure.

Educational Requirements: Master's degree in counseling from a Council for Accreditation of Counseling and Related Educational Programs (CACREP; or its equivalent) defined as 48 semester hours or 72 quarter hours

Experiential Requirements: ALC is given when a master's degree is verified. No experiential requirements. LPC: 3,000 hours of supervised experience in professional counseling with board-approved supervision. An applicant may subtract 1,000 hours of the required professional experience for every 15 graduate semester hours (or 22.5 quarter hours) obtained beyond the master's degree from a regionally accredited college or university, provided that such hours are clearly related to the field of professional counseling. This formula can be used for up to 2,000 hours.

Exam Required: National Counselor Examination (NCE)

ALASKA

AK Division of Occupational Licensing
Board of Professional Counselors
P.O. Box 110806
Juneau, AK 99811-0806
(907) 465-2551
(907) 465-2974 (fax)
Eleanor.vinson@alaska.gov
www.commerce.alaska.gov/web/cbpl/ProfessionalLicensing/ProfessionalCounselors
.aspx
Title of License: LPC
Educational Requirements: Master's degree in counseling from a regionally or nationally accredited institution approved by the board and consisting of at least 60 graduate semester hours. The degree must include coursework in eight core areas. Related professional field includes psychology, marital and family therapy, social work, and applied behavioral science.
Experiential Requirements: 3,000 post-master's supervised hours, including 1,000 hours of direct client contact and 100 hours of face-to-face supervision over a 2-year period. The supervisor must be a licensed mental health professional.

The face-to-face supervision can be by telephone or electronic means due to remote distances. Supervision must be under an LPC or other licensed mental health professional approved by the board.
Exam Required: NCE

ARIZONA

AZ Board of Behavioral Health Examiners
3443 N. Central Avenue, Suite 1700
Phoenix, AZ 85012
(602) 542-1882
(602) 364-0890 (fax)
Counseling Contact:
Pamela Osborn
Pamela.Osborn@azbbhe.us
www.azbbhe.us
Title of License: LPC

> Licensed Associate Counselor (LAC): must practice only under direct supervision as prescribed by the board and shall not engage in independent practice

Educational Requirements: Master's degree in counseling or a related field from a CACREP- or CORE-accredited program or a program that includes a minimum of 60 semester hours and completion in 14 content areas. As of October 31, 2015: If a program is not accredited by CACREP or CORE, it must require 700 clinical supervision hours and a minimum of 24 semester hours in eight content areas.

Experiential Requirements: 2 years/3,200 hours of full-time post-master's supervised work experience in psychotherapy, including assessment, diagnosis, and treatment. 100 hours of clinical supervision and 1,600 hours of direct client contact are required. No more than 400 of the additional hours can be psychoeducational.

Applicant must receive a minimum of 10 hours of clinical supervision obtained during direct observation or a review of audiotapes/videotapes by the clinical supervisor while the applicant is providing treatment and evaluation services to a client.

Exam Required: NCE, National Clinical Mental Health Counselor Examination (NCMHCE), or Certified Rehabilitation Counseling Exam (CRCE)

ARKANSAS

AR Board of Examiners in Counseling

P. O. Box 989

Little Rock, AR 72201

(501) 683-5800

(501) 683-6349 (fax)

arboec@sbglobal.net

https://abec.statesolutions.us

Title of License: LPC

> Licensed Associate Counselor (LAC): an applicant with less than 3 years of post-master's level supervision experience, if all other requirements have been met

Educational Requirements: Master's degree or higher in counseling from a program that reflects the CACREP or CORE curriculum and consists of 60 semester hours from a regionally accredited institution

Experiential Requirements: 3 years/3,000 hours of post-master's supervised counseling experience (1 year = 1,000 hours). Fifty percent of the hours have to be client contact hours.

One year of experience may be gained for each 30 semester hours earned beyond master's degree (up to 2 years), provided the hours are clearly counseling in nature and acceptable to the board.

Supervision must be under an LPC approved by the board. Telephone supervision is allowed for less than 25% of the total amount.

Exam Required: NCE and an oral exam

CALIFORNIA

CA Board of Behavioral Sciences

1625 N. Market Boulevard

Suite S-200

Sacramento, CA 95834

(916) 574-7830

(916) 574-8625 (fax)

www.bbs.ca.gov

California Association for Licensed Professional Clinical Counselors

P.O. Box 280640

Northridge, CA 91328

www.calpcc.org

Title of License: Licensed Professional Clinical Counselor (LPCC)[1]

Professional Clinical Counselor Intern (PCCI): an unlicensed person who has completed the education requirements and is registered with the board to complete the supervision requirements to be licensed as an LPCC (has to renew annually for up to 5 years)

Educational Requirements: Master's degree or higher that is counseling or psychotherapy in content:

Enrolled before 8/1/12 and graduate before 12/31/18: minimum of 48 graduate semester hours.

Enrolled after 8/1/12 or graduate after 12/31/18: minimum of 60 graduate semester hours.

Additional Educational Requirements

- 15 contact hours in alcoholism and other chemical substance abuse, dependency
- 10 contact hours in human sexuality
- A two-semester unit or three-quarter unit survey course in psychopharmacology
- 15 contact hours in spousal or partner abuse assessment, detection, and intervention strategies[1]
- 7 contact hours in child abuse assessment and reporting
- 18 contact hours in California law and professional ethics for professional clinical counselors[1] (possible that graduate coursework will suffice)
- 10 contact hours in aging and long-term care[1]
- 15 contact hours in crisis or trauma counseling[1]

---

[1] There are stipulations regarding the types of hours that will be accepted. Please consult your state regulations.

Experiential Requirements: 3,000 hours of post-master's supervised counseling experience; 1,750 have to be direct client contact hours

Areas with guidance on:

- 500 hours maximum for group counseling
- 250 hours maximum for phone crisis counseling
- 150 hours minimum of clinical experience in a hospital or community mental health setting
- 1,250 hours combined total maximum:
  - direct supervisor contact
  - client-centered advocacy
  - 250 hours maximum in administering tests
  - 250 hours maximum in attending conferences

Exam Required: NCMHCE (as of January 1, 2014; taken after experiential requirements have been fulfilled) and the California jurisprudence exam (taken while acquiring supervision)

COLORADO

CO Division of Professions and Occupations

1560 Broadway, Suite 1350

Denver, CO 80202

(303) 894-7768

(303) 894-7764 (fax)

Karin.gleichauf@state.co.us

mentalhealth@dora.state.co.us

www.colorado.gov/pacific/dora/dpo

Title of License: LPC

> Licensed Professional Counselor Candidate (LPCC)[2]: an applicant who has completed the education requirements and is under a licensed supervisor; valid for 4 years (if not registered as an LPCC, must register as a registered psychotherapist in the Registered Psychotherapist Board Database)

Educational Requirements: Master's degree or higher in professional counseling from a CACREP-accredited program or equivalent program from a regionally accredited college/university consisting of 48 semester hours, completion of coursework in core areas, and a practicum and/or internship. *Note:* If enrolled after August 31, 2014, the program must consist of 60 graduate semester hours.

---

[2] There are stipulations regarding the types of hours that will be accepted. Please consult your state regulations.

Experiential Requirements: 2 years/2,000 hours of post-master's practice in applied psychotherapy under board-approved supervision. (Doctoral degree can be 1,000 in 12 months.) 100 hours of supervision is required, 70 of which must be face-to-face individual supervision.

The teaching of psychotherapy can count up to 600 hours and 30 hours of required supervision.

Note: Electronic supervision is allowed—initial 2-hour meeting must be in person, and every 6 months, an in-person meeting must be held and the electronic supervision must be audio and visual (as of July 20, 2012).

Exams Required: NCE and CO jurisprudence exam

CONNECTICUT

CT Department of Public Health

Professional Counselor Licensure

410 Capitol Ave., MS# 12APP

P. O. Box 340308

Hartford, CT 06134-0308

(860) 509-7603

(860) 509-8457 (fax)

oplc.dph@ct.gov

www.ct.gov/dph

Title of License: LPC

Educational Requirements: Master's degree or higher in counseling or a related mental health field from a regionally accredited institution of higher education consisting of at least 60 semester hours and completion of required coursework

Experiential Requirements: 3,000 hours of post-master's supervised experience in professional counseling

A minimum of 100 hours of direct supervision by an appropriately licensed individual is required.

Exam Required: NCE or NCMHCE

DELAWARE

DE Board of Mental Health and Chemical Dependency Professionals

Cannon Building

861 Silver lake Blvd.

Suite 203

Dover, DE 19904-2467

(302) 744-4500

(302) 739-2711 (fax)

www.dpr.delaware.gov

Title of License: Licensed Professional Counselor of Mental Health (LPCMH)

Licensed Associate Counselor of Mental Health (LACMH): an individual licensed for the purpose of gaining experience required for licensure as an LPCMH; must work under direct supervision of an LPCMH or other health professional approved by the board

Educational Requirements: Master's degree or higher in clinical mental health, including a minimum of 48 semester hours

Must also be certified by NBCC as a national certified counselor (NCC) or certified by another national mental health specialty certifying organization approved by the board.

Experiential Requirements: 2 years/3,200 hours full-time clinical professional counseling experience to be completed within a 4-year period

1,600 hours must be under professional direct supervision acceptable to the board (100 hours must be face-to-face supervision; live video conferencing is considered face to face but cannot exceed 50% of the supervision). 1,500 hours must be direct client contact hours (750 hours have to be individual).

30 graduate semester hours or more beyond master's degree may be substituted for 1 year/1,600 hours of required experience, provided that hours are clearly related to the field of counseling and acceptable to the board.

Note: If your degree was conferred after June 30, 2012, you will receive credit only for experience that you gained as a Delaware-licensed associate counselor of mental health.

Exam Required: NCE or NCMHCE

DISTRICT OF COLUMBIA

DC Board of Professional Counseling

Board of Professional Counseling

717 14th St. NW, Suite 600

Washington, DC 20005

(202) 724-4900

(877) 672-2174

(202) 727-8471 (fax)

hpla.doh.dc.gov/hpla

Title of License: LPC

Educational Requirements: 60 graduate semester hours including a master's degree in counseling or a related field from an accredited institution

Master's degree to include coursework in 10 core areas, including a counseling practicum or internship.

Experiential Requirements: 2 years/3,500 hours of post-master's supervised professional counseling experience

200 hours of supervision (100 hours must be immediate supervision under an LPC)

Exam Required: NCE

Note: Will accept NCMHCE or CRCE if already taken in another jurisdiction

FLORIDA

FL Board of Clinical Social Work, Marriage and Family Therapy, and Mental Health Counseling

4052 Bald Cypress Way, BIN C-08

Tallahassee, FL 32399-3258

(850) 245-4474

(850) 921-5389 (fax)

mqa_491@doh.state.fl.us

https://floridasmentalhealthprofessions.gov

Title of License: Licensed Mental Health Counselor (LMHC)

Provisional Mental Health Counselor: a person provisionally licensed to provide mental health counseling under supervision; valid for 24 months. Issued to licensure applicants who have completed their clinical experience requirement intending to provide services in Florida while satisfying coursework and/or exam requirements

Educational Requirements: Master's degree or higher from a CACREP-accredited mental health counseling program that includes 60 semester hours, a course in human sexuality, and a course in substance abuse;

OR

Master's degree or higher from a program related to the practice of mental health counseling from an accredited institution that includes 60 semester hours; 12 specific course content areas; and 1,000 hours of supervised practicum, internship, or field experience;

AND, for both options,

Completion of an 8-hour Laws and Rules course and a 2-hour Prevention of Medical Errors course from a board-approved provider and, within 6 months of licensure, have to complete the following from a board-approved provider:

• 3-hour course on HIV and AIDS

• 2-hour domestic violence course from a board-approved provider

Experiential Requirements: 2 years of supervised post-master's clinical experience in mental health counseling that consists of at least 1,500 hours providing psychotherapy face to face with clients and at least 100 face-to-face hours of supervision (50 of which can be group supervision)

Supervision must be under an LMHC or equivalent.

Exam Required: NCMHCE

GEORGIA

GA Composite Board of Professional Counselors, Social Workers, and Marriage and Family Therapists

237 Coliseum Dr.

Macon, GA 31217-3858

(478) 207-2440

(866) 888-7127 (fax)

https://sos.ga.gov/index.php/licensing/plb/43

Title of License: LPC

> Associate Licensed Professional Counselor (ALPC): an applicant who has met the educational requirements and has registered with the board an acceptable contract for obtaining post-master's experience under direct supervision; valid for 5 years

Educational Requirements: Master's degree or higher in a program that is primarily counseling in content or in applied psychology from an institution accredited by a regional body recognized by the Council on Higher Education Accreditation (CHEA)

Completion of specific coursework and a supervised practicum or internship consisting of at least 300 hours is required.

Experiential Requirements: 4 years/2,400 hours of supervised, post-master's directed experience in professional counseling in a work setting acceptable to the board, with a minimum of 120 clock hours of supervision (can count up to 1 year of experience from practicum/internship)

Note: On December 6, 2013, there was a proposal to increase the number of required hours to 3,000.

A minimum of 2 years of supervision must be provided by an LPC. Please consult your state regulations for requirements regarding clinical supervision for licensure.

Exam Required: NCE

GUAM

Guam Board of Allied Health Examiners

Rte. 10, Suite 9

Mangilao, Guam 96910

(671) 734-7295

(671) 734-2066 (Fax)

www.guamhplo.org

Title of License (Article 13)

Licensed Professional Counselor (LPC)

Education Requirements: A masters' or doctorate from an accredited school in the United States or territory

A minimum of 3,000 hours of documented client service, of post-graduate experience under supervision of an LPC, clinical psychologist, or psychiatrist OR

If an applicant cannot document 2 years of post-graduate supervised experience, they may submit proof of having worked under an internship program that provided the 2 years of post-graduate experience, approved by the board.

Licensed Mental Health Counselor

- a doctorate or masters' degree from an accredited school in the United States or territory
- passed the NCMHCE
- documented evidence of 1,000 hours of post-master's clinical work in diagnostic and treatment planning

HAWAII

HI Department of Commerce and Consumer Affairs—Professional and Vocational Licensing (PVL)

Mental Health Counselor Program

P. O. Box 3469

Honolulu, HI 96801

(808) 586-2697

counselor@dcca.hawaii.gov

www.hawaii.gov/dcca/areas/pvl/programs/mental

Title of License: LMHC

Educational Requirements: Master's degree or higher in counseling or an allied field related to the practice of mental health counseling, with a minimum of 48 semester hours (or 72 quarter hours) of coursework in core areas, from an accredited institution. Also, two academic terms of a supervised mental health practicum intern experience for graduate credit of at least 3 semester hours (or 5 quarter hours) per academic term in a mental health counseling setting, with at least 300 hours of supervised client contact under a licensed supervisor

July 5, 2007: Changes in Hawaii Revised Statutes Chapter 453D-7(c)(1) and (2) allow individuals who obtained a graduate degree before July 1, 2007, an alternate method to verify the practicum and postgraduate experience.

Experiential Requirements: 2 years/3,000 hours of post-master's supervised experience in the practice of mental health counseling, with 100 hours of face-to-face clinical supervision under a licensed supervisor

Experience shall be completed in no less than 2 years and in no more than 4 years.

Exam Required: NCE

Note: Will accept the NCMHCE or the Commission on Rehabilitation Counselor Certification (CRCC; if taken after 1/1/2000 and before 7/1/2005)

IDAHO

ID State Licensing Board of Professional Counselors and Marriage and Family Therapists

700 W. State St.

Boise, ID 83702

(208) 334-3233

(208) 334-3945 (fax)

Deborah.Sexton@ibd.idaho.gov

cou@ibol.idaho.gov

www.ibol.idaho.gov

Title of License: Licensed Clinical Professional Counselor (LCPC)

LPC

Registered Counselor Intern (RCI): a counselor performing under supervision as part of the supervised experience requirement

Educational Requirements: Master's degree or higher in a counseling field from an accredited college or university with 60 semester hours and completion of a 6-semester hour advanced counseling practicum

Experiential Requirements: LPCC: Hold a valid LPC; 2 years/2,000 hours of supervised direct client contact experience accumulated after licensure in any state; 1,000 hours must be under supervision of an LCPC. Minimum of 1 hour face-to-face, one-on-one supervision for every 30 hours of direct client contact. Successful completion of a diagnostic evaluation graduate course or equivalent training/experience is acceptable to the board.

LPC: 1,000 hours is defined as one thousand clock hours of experience working in a counseling setting, 400 hours of which shall be direct client contact. Supervised experience in practica and/or internships taken at the graduate level may be utilized. The supervised experience shall include a minimum of 1-hour face-to-face or one-to-one or one-to-two consultation with the supervisor for every 20 hours of job/internship experience. Face to face may include a face-to-face setting provided by a live video connection between the supervisor and supervisee. As stated under Subsection 150.01.a.iv, counseling practicum experience, as opposed to job or internship experience, shall be supervised at a ratio of 1 hour of supervision for every 10 hours in the settings. **Supervised practicum and/or internship taken at a graduate level may be utilized.**

Exams Required: LPCC: NCMHCE

LPC: NCE

ILLINOIS

IL Professional Counselor Licensing and Disciplinary Board

320 W. Washington St., 3rd Floor

Springfield, IL 62786

(217) 785-0800

(217) 524-6735 TDD

(217) 782-7645 (fax)

www.idfpr.com/profs/ProfCounselor.asp

Title of License: LCPC: holds license authorizing independent practice of clinical professional counseling in private practice

LPC: holds license authorizing the practice of professional counseling

Educational Requirements: LCPC: a master's or higher in professional counseling or a related field from a regionally accredited college/university OR holds a current certified clinical mental health counselor (CCMHC) credential issued by the NBCC (meets all requirements for licensure as an LCPC)

Note: Certain other certifications meet all or part of the LPC or LCPC licensure requirements; please contact the board for more information.

LPC: master's degree or higher in professional counseling or related field of at least 48 semester hours from a regionally accredited college/university in a program approved by the IL Dept. of Professional Regulation.

CACREP- and CORE-accredited programs in professional counseling are approved programs for both LPC and LCPC licensure

Experiential Requirements: LCPC: 2 years/3,360 hours of full-time, satisfactory, supervised employment experience working as a clinical professional counselor in a professional capacity under the direction of a qualified supervisor, subsequent to degree.

Of these, 1,920 hours must be direct face-to-face service to clients.

One year = maximum of 1,680 hours, including 960 hours of direct face-to-face service to clients

If applicant holds a doctoral degree, 1 year must be subsequent to the degree and internships may count toward professional experience.

Exam Required: LCPC: NCE and NCMHCE or ECCP or CRCE

LPC: NCE or CRCE

INDIANA

IN Behavioral Health and Human Services Licensing Board

402 W. Washington St., Rm. W072

Indianapolis, IN 46204

(317) 234-2064

(317) 233-4236 (fax)

pla5@pla.in.gov

www.in.gov/pla/social.htm

Title of License: LMHC

Licensed Mental Health Counselor Associate (LMHCA): a counselor performing under supervision as a part of the supervised experience requirement (required after July 1, 2014)—cannot apply for until AFTER degree is conferred

Educational Requirements: Master's degree or higher in an area related to mental health counseling from a CACREP- or CORE-accredited program or equivalent program from a regionally accredited institution, which includes 60 semester hours of graduate coursework in counseling in 12 specified content areas

Completion of a practicum (100 hours), internship (600 hours), and advanced internship (300 hours) with at least 100 hours of face-to-face supervision is required.

An area related to mental health counseling includes counseling, clinical social work, psychology, human services, human development, family relations, or programs accredited by CACREP or CORE.

Experiential Requirements: 3,000 hours of postgraduate supervised clinical experience over a 21- to 48-month period. Does not start to count until approved as an LMHCA.

100 hours of face-to-face supervision under an LMHC or equivalent supervisor is required.

Exams Required: LMHC: NCMHCE

LMHCA: NCE

Note: If a passing score is achieved on the initial try, the applicant can apply up to 1,500 hours accrued. If a passing score is not achieved, the applicant can no longer accrue hours until a passing score is achieved.

IOWA

IA Board of Behavioral Science Examiners

Lucas State Office Building, 5th Floor

321 E. 12th St.

Des Moines, IA 50319-0075

(515) 281-4422

(515) 281-3121 (fax)

Judith.Manning@idph.iowa.gov

https://idph.iowa.gov/Licensure/Iowa-Board-of-Behavioral-Science

Title of License: LMHC

Note: Can get a temporary license while meeting supervision requirement—expires in 3 years

Educational Requirements: Master's degree or higher in mental health counseling from a CACREP-accredited program or the content equivalent with at least 60 semester hours (or equivalent quarter hours). For applicants who entered the program of study

386 • APPENDIX B: STATE LICENSURE BOARDS AND REQUIREMENTS

prior to July 1, 2010: 45 semester hours (or 60 quarter hours) are required. Degree must be from a nationally accredited college/university; or hold a current CCMHC credential issued by the NBCC (meets educational and experience requirements). Applicants who did not graduate from a CACREP-accredited mental health counseling program as of July 1, 2012, will need to submit to an education review.

Experiential Requirements: 2 years/3,000 hours of full-time, supervised postgraduate work experience in mental health counseling, including 1,500 hours of direct client contact and 200 hours of clinical supervision concurrent with the work experience

At least 100 of the 200 hours of clinical supervision must be individual supervision.

For applicants who entered a program of study prior to July 1, 2010: 2 years of full-time supervised postgraduate work experience in mental health counseling, including 200 hours of clinical supervision concurrent with 1,000 hours of mental health counseling conducted in person with individuals, couples, and families.

At least 100 of the 200 hours of clinical supervision must be individual supervision or hold a current CCMHC credential issued by NBCC (meets experience requirements).

Exam Required: NCE, NCMHCE, or CRCE

KANSAS

KS Behavioral Sciences Regulatory Board

712 S. Kansas Ave.

Topeka, KS 66603

(785) 296-3240

(785) 296-3112 (fax)

www.ksbsrb.org

Title of License: LCPC: may diagnose and treat mental disorders independently

LPC: may practice under the direction of an LCPC, a licensed psychologist, a person licensed to provide mental health services as an independent practitioner and whose license allows for diagnoses and treatment of mental disorders, or a person licensed to practice medicine and surgery

Educational Requirements: LCPC: in addition to or as part of the graduate degree completion of 15 credit hours of supporting diagnosis and treatment of mental disorders with use of the American Psychiatric Association's *Diagnostic and Statistical Manual of Mental Disorders (DSM)* and a graduate-level supervised clinical practicum of professional experience

LPC: 60 graduate semester hours, including a master's degree in counseling from a university approved by the board that consists of 45 graduate semester hours distributed among 10 core categories (this includes a supervised practicum)

Experiential Requirements: LCPC: licensed as an LPC or meets all requirements to be licensed as an LPC, and have 4,000 hours of supervised clinical professional counseling experience under an approved clinical training plan, which includes 1,500 hours of direct client contact and 100 hours of clinical supervision (50 must be individual supervision)

Exams Required: LCPC: NCMHCE

LPC: NCE

KENTUCKY

KY Board of Licensed Professional Counselors

P.O. Box 1360

Frankfort, KY 40602

Diana Jarboe, Board Administrator: Diana.Jarboe@ky.gov

(502) 564-3296

(502) 564-4818 (fax)

lpc.ky.gov

Title of License: LPCC

Licensed Professional Counselor Associate (LPCA): credential holder who has met all qualifications to engage in the practice of professional counseling under an approved clinical supervisor authorized by the board

Educational Requirements: Master's degree or higher in professional counseling or a related field from a regionally accredited institution, with a minimum of 60 semester hours in nine specified areas and a 400-hour practicum/internship. As of May 31, 2020, counselor licensure applicants must graduate from a CACREP-accredited counseling program.

Experiential Requirements: No experiential requirements for LPCA.

LPCC: 4,000 hours of post-master's experience in the practice of counseling under approved supervision, which includes 1,600 hours of direct counseling and 100 hours of individual, face-to-face clinical supervision. Applicants are encouraged to include 10 hours of direct counseling with individuals in a jail or a correctional setting as part of the 4,000 hours. Kentucky requires annual continuing education credits in the areas of domestic violence and suicide assessment.

Exams Required: NCE or NCMHCE

LOUISIANA

LA Department of Licensed Professional Counselors Board of Examiners

8361 Summa Ave.

Baton Rouge, LA 70809

(225) 765-2515

(225) 765-2514

lpcboard@eatel.net

www.lpcboard.org

Title of License: LPC

Counselor Intern: Those with a master's degree in counseling while practicing counseling under the board-approved supervision of an LPC. (There are three parts to registration and hours cannot begin to be accrued until all three are complete.)

Counselor interns have up to 7 years to complete their internship from the date of registration.

Educational Requirements: Master's degree or higher, the substance of which is professional mental health counseling in content, from a regionally accredited institution, with 60 semester hours and coursework in eight content areas. Completion of a supervised practicum (100 hours) and a supervised internship (300 hours) in mental health counseling.

Beginning September 1, 2015, all applicants whose academic background has not been previously approved by the board must have accumulated at least 60 graduate semester hours as part of the graduate degree plan containing the eight required areas, the supervised mental health practicum, and supervised internship in mental health counseling. Applicants may apply post-master's counseling courses toward licensure if their degree program consisted of less than 60 hours. Louisiana requires a grade of "C" or better in all post-master's courses; a grade of "A", "B", or "P" is required for all field experience.

Experiential Credentials: 2 years/3,000 hours of post-master's supervised experience in professional mental health counseling under the clinical supervision of a board-approved supervisor, to be completed in no more than 7 years. Hours to include 1,900 to 2,900 hours of direct client contact in individual or group counseling; a maximum of 1,000 hours additional client contact, counseling-related activities, or education at the graduate level in the field of mental health; and a minimum of 100 hours of face-to-face supervision. Only 50 hours may be group supervision. Up to 25 of the hours can be synchronous videoconferencing. 500 hours of supervised experience may be gained for each 30 graduate semester hours beyond master's degree but must have no less than 2,000 hours of supervised post-master's experience.

Exam Required: NCE or NCMHCE

MAINE

ME Board of Counseling Professionals Licensure

35 State House Station

Augusta, ME 04333

(207) 624-8674

(888) 577-6690

(207) 624-8637 (fax)

www.maine.gov/pfr/olr

Title of License: LCPC

        LPC

Conditional LCPC: a license granted to an applicant for licensure as an LCPC who has met all the requirements except for the supervised clinical experience; valid for 2 years

Conditional LPC: a license granted to an applicant for licensure as an LPC who has met all the requirements except for the supervised clinical experience; valid for 2 years

Educational Requirements: LCPC/Conditional LCPC: Master's degree or higher from a regionally accredited institution that consists of 60 semester hours and is CACREP accredited or consists of coursework in 10 core areas, three additional areas, and a practicum and internship of 900 clock hours

LPC/Conditional LPC: Master's degree or higher from a regionally accredited institution that consists of 48 semester hours and is CACREP or CORE accredited or consists of coursework in 10 core areas and a practicum and internship of 600 clock hours

Experiential Requirements: LCPC: 2 years/3,000 hours of post-master's supervised clinical counseling experience (4,000 hours if qualifying degree did not have practicum/internship). To include 1,500 hours of direct client contact and 1 hour of clinical supervision per 30 hours of client contact with an approved supervisor

LPC: 2 years/2,000 hours of post-master's supervised counseling experience. To include 1,000 hours of direct counseling and 67 hours of supervision with an approved supervisor

Exams Required: LCPC: NCMHCE; LPC/Conditional LCPC/Conditional LPC: NCE

MARYLAND

MD Board of Examiners of Professional Counselors and Therapists

4201 Patterson Ave.

Baltimore, MD 21215

Anna.sullivan@maryland.gov

(410) 764-4732

(410) 358-1610 (fax)

www.dhmh.state.md.us/bopc

Title of License: LCPC

        Licensed Graduate Professional Counselor (LGPC): title used while fulfilling the supervised clinical experience requirement

Educational Requirements: (Same for both license tiers.)

Master's degree or higher in professional counseling or related field from an accredited educational institution, with a minimum of 60 graduate semester hours in specific coursework, including completion of an alcohol and drug counseling course, and supervised field experience.

OR

Doctoral degree with a minimum of 90 graduate semester hours in counseling training approved by the board.

Experiential Requirements: 3 years/3,000 hours of supervised clinical experience in professional counseling (2 years/2,000 hours must be post-master's). 1,500 hours must be direct face-to-face client contact and 100 hours minimum of face-to-face clinical supervision. Supervision must be under a board-approved supervisor. At least half of hours need to be accumulated under the supervision of an LCPC approved by the board. If obtained a doctoral degree: 2 years/2,000 hours of supervised clinical experience in professional counseling (1 year/1,000 hours must be post doctorate). 1,000 hours must be face-to-face client contact and 50 hours minimum of face-to-face clinical supervision. Supervision must be under a board-approved supervisor.

Exams Required: NCE and MD Professional Counselors and Therapists ACT Exam

MASSACHUSETTS

MA Board of Registration of Allied Mental Health and Human Services Professionals
100 Washington St. Suite 710
Boston, MA 02118-6100
Board Administrator: leija.t.meadows@state.ma.us
(617) 727-3080
(617) 727-1627 (fax)
www.mass.gov/dpl/boards/mh

Title of License: LMHC

Educational Requirements: Minimum of 60 graduate semester hours in counseling or a related field from a regionally accredited institution of high education. This includes a minimum of 48 semester credit hour master's degree in mental health counseling or a related field, including a practicum (100 hours), an internship (600 hours), and coursework in each of the 10 content areas as defined by the board; or hold a current certified clinical mental health counselor (CCMHC) credential issued by the NBCC.

Experiential Requirements: 2 years/3,360 hours of full-time post-master's supervised clinical experience in mental health counseling after obtaining 60 graduate semester hours. To include 960 hours of direct client contact (250 hours may be group client contact) and 130 hours of supervision (75 hours must be individual supervision and 25 hours must be under an LMHC). These hours do not include the pre-master's practicum and internship supervision requirements.

Exam Required: NCMHCE

MICHIGAN

MI Board of Counseling
P.O. Box 30670
Lansing, MI 48909

(517) 335-0918

(517) 373-2179 (fax)

bhphelp@michigan.gov

www.michigan.gov/healthlicense

Title of License: LPC

Limited Licensed Professional Counselor (LLPC): A limited license is issued to those who have not yet completed the 3,000-hour supervised counseling experience; valid for 1 year and may be renewed.

Educational Requirements: (Same for both licenses.)

Master's degree or higher in professional counseling from a program that reflects the CACREP curriculum, including a minimum of 48 semester hours and 600 clock hour internship

Experiential Requirements: 2 years/3,000 hours of post-degree supervised counseling experience. To include a minimum 100 hours under immediate physical presence of the supervisor. Supervision must be under an LPC. For persons with 30 semester hours or 45 quarter hours beyond the master's degree: 1 year/1,500 hours of post-degree supervised experience. To include a minimum of 50 hours under immediate physical presence of the supervisor. Supervision must be under an LPC. *Note:* Supervisors of LLPCs are required to have training in supervision.

Exam Required: NCE or CRCE

MINNESOTA

MN Board of Behavioral Health and Therapy

2829 University Ave. SE, Suite 120

Minneapolis, MN 55414

(612) 617-2178

(800) 627-3529 TTY

(612) 617-2187 (fax)

Bbht.board@state.mn.us

www.bbht.state.mn.us

Title of License: Licensed Professional Clinical Counselor (LPCC)[3]

Licensed Professional Counselor—independent designation

Licensed Professional Counselor—supervision designation (LPC), working on supervision hours toward LPC

Educational Requirements: LPCC: Meet all LPC educational requirements, and in addition to or as part of the graduate degree in counseling or a related field—completion of 24 graduate-level semester credits in six clinical content areas

---

[3] Has completed supervision experience for LPC licensure.

392 • APPENDIX B: STATE LICENSURE BOARDS AND REQUIREMENTS

LPC: Master's degree or higher in counseling or a related field from a CACREP-accredited program or regionally accredited institution recognized by the CHEA, which includes a minimum of 48 semester hours and supervised field experience of not fewer than 700 hours that is counseling in nature

The degree must include specific coursework in 10 core content areas.

Experiential Requirements: LPCC: Already has LPC credential; 4,000 hours of post-master's supervised professional practice in the delivery of clinical services in the diagnosis and treatment of mental illnesses and disorders in both children and adults. Supervision must comply with the board's Supervision Contract for LPCC applicants. Practice must include 1,800 hours of clinical client contact. At least 50% of supervision must be individual supervision. Supervisor must have independent CLINICAL license.

LPC: 2,000 hours of post-master's supervised professional practice that is acceptable to the board OR submission of supervision plan for the first 2,000 hours of professional practice. Supervision must be completed in not less than 1 year and not more than 3 years. Practice must include 100 hours of supervision under a board-approved supervisor.

Exams Required: LPCC: NCMHCE. *Note:* The Examination of Clinical Counseling Practice (ECCP) is no longer offered by the NBCC.

LPC: NCE or other national exam that is determined by the board to be substantially similar to the NCE.

MISSISSIPPI

MS State Board of Examiners for Licensed Professional Counselors

239 North Lamar St., Suite 402

Jackson, MS 39201

LeAnn Mordecai, Executive Director: LPMordecai@lpc.ms.gov

(601) 359-1010

(888) 860-7001

(662) 716-3021 (fax)

infor@lpc.ms.gov

Title of License: LPC

> Licensed Professional Counselor: an applicant who has satisfied experience and educational requirements but still needs to pass the exam

Educational Requirements: Master's degree or educational specialists degree in counselor education or a related program from a regionally or nationally accredited college/ university program, subject to board approval, with 60 semester hours (or 90 quarter hours) and completion of coursework in 10 content areas, or doctoral degree primarily in counseling, guidance, or related counseling field from a regionally or nationally accredited college/university program, subject to board approval, with 60 semester hours (or 90 quarter hours) and completion of coursework in 10 content areas

Experiential Requirements: 2 years/3,500 hours of supervised counseling experience in a clinical setting (1,750 hours must be post-master's experience). 1,167 hours must be direct counseling service to clients to include counseling-related activities. Minimum of 100 hours of supervision required (50 hours may be group supervision). Supervision must be under an LPC that has met the requirements to be a MS Board Qualified Supervisor.

Exam Required: NCE; will accept the NCMHCE but not required

MISSOURI

MO Committee for Professional Counselors

3605 Missouri Blvd.

P.O. Box 1335

Jefferson City, MO 65102

profcounselor@pr.mo.gov

Loree.Kessler@pr.mo.gov

pr.mo.gov/counselors.asp

Title of License: LPC

> Counselor-in-Training: issued automatically when supervision is registered and approved and all other requirements are met

Educational Requirements: Master's degree or higher in counseling, counseling psychology, or school psychology from a regionally accredited college or university, with at least 48 semester hours reflecting the CACREP or CORE curriculum, and a practicum, internship, or field experience consisting of 6 semester hours in the practice of counseling

Experiential Requirements: 2 years/3,000 hours of post-master's continuous experience (full or part time), to be completed within 60 months. 1,200 hours must be direct client contact. 30 hours of post-master's study may be substituted for 1,500 of the 3,000 hours.

If a doctorate or specialist's degree: 1 year/1,500 hours of counseling experience (full or part time), to be completed within 36 months; 600 hours must be direct client contact

For both degree paths: 15 hours of supervised counseling experience per week are required, with 1 hour a week of face-to-face supervision. If electronic supervision is continuously interactive, it can count toward required hours. Supervision must be under an LPC or licensed psychologist or psychiatrist approved and registered with the board.

Exam Required: NCE

MONTANA

MT Board of Social Work Examiners and Professional Counselors
301 S. Park 4th Fl.
P.O. Box 200513
Helena, MT 59620
dlibsdswp@state.mt.us
www.swpc.mt.gov

Title of License: LCPC

Educational Requirements: A 60-semester hour (or 90-quarter hour) counseling-in-nature graduate degree from an accredited institution that includes specific coursework and a 6-semester hour advanced counseling practicum, or applicants may apply for licensure with a minimum of 45 semester hours (67.5 quarter hours) master's degree in counseling that includes specific coursework and a 6-semester hour advanced counseling practicum. Applicants must complete the remaining hours within 5 years of the original application approval date. Applicants are not eligible for full licensure, nor are they eligible to test until the hours are completed.

Experiential Requirements: 3,000 hours of supervised counseling experience, 1,500 hours of which must be post-degree. 1,000 of the 1,500 hours must be direct client contact (250 can be group). Must have 1 hour of supervision for every 20 hours. Supervision must be under a licensed professional counselor or licensed allied mental health professional who has had 20 clock hours of supervision training and an agreement approved by the board.

Exam Required: NCE

NEBRASKA

NE Board of Mental Health Practice
P.O. Box 94986
Lincoln, NE 68509
(402) 471-0185
(402) 472-3577 (fax)
Program Manager: kris.chiles@nebraska.gov
http://dhhs.ne.gov/licensure/Pages/Mental-Health-and-Social-Work-Practice.aspx

Title of License: Licensed Mental Health Practitioner-Certified Professional Counselor (LMHP-CPC) or Licensed Professional Counselor (LPC): This additional appellation is available for LMHPs who have a graduate degree from a CACREP-accredited program or a program with equivalent coursework.

Licensed Mental Health Practitioner (LMHP): an individual who is qualified to engage in mental health practice or offers or renders mental health practice services

Provisional Licensed Mental Health Practitioner (PLMHP): an individual beginning the 3,000-hour experience requirement; valid for 5 years

Educational Requirements: Master's degree or higher from an approved educational program that is primarily therapeutic mental health in content, in a CACREP-accredited program (or complete equivalent coursework), from a regionally accredited institution. Completion of a practicum or internship with a minimum of 300 clock hours of direct client contact under the supervision of a qualified supervisor.

Experience Requirements: LMHP-CPC/LPC, LMHP: 3,000 hours of post-master's supervised experience in mental health practice accumulated during the 5 years immediately preceding application for licensure. To include 1,500 hours of direct client contact (not more than 1,500 hours of nondirect service). Supervision must be under an LMHP, LIMPH, a licensed psychologist, or a licensed physician with mental health treatment training.

Exams Required: LIMHP and LMHP with CPC credential: NCE or NCMHCE

NEVADA

The Board of Examiners for Marriage and Family Therapists and Clinical Professional Counselors

P.O. Box 370130

Las Vegas, NV 89134-0130

(702) 486-7388

(702) 486-7258

nvmftbd@mftbd.nv.gov

www.marriage.state.nv.us

Title of License: Licensed Clinical Professional Counselor (LCPC)

Licensed Clinical Professional Counselor Intern

Educational Requirements: (Same for both licenses.)

Master's degree or higher in mental health counseling or community counseling from a program approved by CACREP or equivalent program of at least 48 semester hours and completion of the minimum required coursework, including 3-semester hour courses or 4-quarter hour courses in supervised clinical practice by way of either practicum or internship in mental health counseling, accomplished over a period of 1 academic year

Experiential Requirements: 2 years/3,000 hours of post-master's supervised counseling experience. To include 1,500 hours of direct client contact; 1,200 hours in the practice of clinical professional counseling; and 100 hours of direct supervision under an approved supervisor of which at least 1 hour per week was completed for each work setting at which the applicant provided counseling

Note: Nevada had expanded its scope of practice for LCPCs to include the assessment or treatment of couples or families with demonstration of competence to work with them through education, training, and experience.

Exam Required: NCMHCE

NEW HAMPSHIRE

NH Board of Mental Health Practice

121 S. Fruit St.

Concord, NH 03301

mlynch@dhhs.state.nh.us

(603) 271-6762

(800) 735-2954 TDD

(603) 271-3950

www.oplc.nh.gov/mental-health

Title of License: LCMHC

Educational Requirements: All applicants shall have a master's degree or doctoral degree in clinical mental health counseling from a CACREP-accredited institution or have a 60-credit degree in clinical mental health counseling or its equivalent from an institution which has received regional accreditation from the Association of Secondary Schools and Colleges. A minimum of 1 academic year of full-time graduate study in mental health counseling should be completed in residence at the institution granting the college degree. There are 11 content areas. New Hampshire requires applicants who receive a degree after January 1, 2022, to graduate from a CACREP-accredited program.

Experiential Requirements: 2 years/3,000 hours of paid post-master's supervised clinical work experience in a mental health setting, to be completed in no more than 5 years. Each year shall not be less than 1,500 clock hours. 100 hours of face-to-face supervision provided by a state-licensed, board -approved, mental health professional is required. Nevada also requires 3 units of continuing education in suicide prevention.

Exam Required: NCMHCE and an essay exam provided by the board

NEW JERSEY

NJ Board of Marriage and Family Therapy Examiners, Professional Counselor Examiners Committee

P.O. Box 45007

Newark, NJ 07101

(973) 504-6415

(973) 648-3536 (fax)

www.state.nj.us/lps/ca/medical/procounsel.htm

Title of Credential: LCMHC, LPC

Licensed Associate Counselor (LAC): after acceptable documentation of the satisfaction of the LPC education and examination requirements, an individual may be granted licensure as an associate counselor to practice counseling under the direct supervision of an LPC or a supervisor acceptable to the committee.

Educational Requirements: Minimum of 60 graduate semester hours, which include a master's degree in counseling from a regionally accredited institution of higher education (45–60 hours must be distributed in eight of the nine defined course content areas)

As of April 20, 2006, an acceptable graduate degree means that the word "counseling" or the word "counselor" appears in the title of the graduate degree awarded and that the institution offering the degree states in the catalog or in another format acceptable to the committee that the purpose of the graduate degree is to prepare students for the professional practice of counseling.

Experiential Requirements: LCMHC: Already holds an LPC. Certification by the Academy of Certified Clinical Mental Health Counselors or any successor thereto; passage of a comprehensive qualifying examination prepared by the Academy; evidence satisfactory to the committee that the clinical mental health counselor has satisfied the continuing education requirements of the committee; and evidence satisfactory to the committee that certification of the clinical mental health counselor has been renewed by the Academy. 2 years/3,000 hours of post-master's degree supervised field experience, with 100 hours of face-to-face supervision.

LPC: 3 years of full-time supervised counseling experience in a professional counseling setting, 1 year of which may be obtained prior to the granting of the master's degree. 1 year/1,500 hours of the experience may be eliminated by substituting 30 graduate semester hours beyond the master's degree. In no case may an applicant have less than 1 year of post-master's supervised work experience.

LAC: No experiential requirements

Exam Required: NCE

NEW MEXICO

NM Counseling and Therapy Practice Board

2550 Cerrillos Rd.

Santa Fe, NM 87505

(505) 476-4610

(505) 476-4633 (fax)

counselingboard@state.nm.us

www.rld.state.nm.us/boards/counseling_and_therapy_practice.aspx

Title of License: LPCC

LMHC: an individual who is pursuing the LPCC license but still needs to complete the supervised experience requirement

Educational Requirements: Master's degree or higher in counseling or a counseling-related field with no less than 48 graduate hours from an accredited institution. Related field degree must meet the clinical core curriculum. Counseling-related field is mental health, community counseling, agency counseling, psychology, clinical psychology, family studies, art therapy, or education.

Experiential Requirements: 2 years of postgraduate professional clinical counseling experience, with 3,000 hours of clinical client contact and a minimum of 100 hours of face-to-face supervision. 1,000 hours of clinical client contact may come from the applicant's internship/practicum. Supervision must come from an LPCC or licensed MFT, professional art therapist, psychiatrist, clinical psychologist, or independent social worker.

Exam Required: LPCC: NCE and NCMHCE

LMHC: NCE

NEW YORK

NY State Education Department

State Board for Mental Health Practitioners

Office of the Professionals

89 Washington Ave., 2nd Floor

Albany, NY 12234-1000

(518) 474-3817 x450

(518) 486-2981 (fax)

mhpbd@mail.nysed.gov

www.op.nysed.gov/prof/mhp/mhpcontact.htm

Title of License: LMHC

> Limited Permit: Applicants who have met all requirements except experience and/or exam may apply for a 2-year permit to practice under supervision; may be renewed for one year, upon new application and permit fee.

Educational Requirements: Master's degree or higher in counseling that includes 60 semester hours and completion of specific coursework. *Note:* If counseling degree was completed prior to January 1, 2010, 48 credit hours were required. Completion of a 1-year/600 clock hours supervised internship or practicum in mental health counseling. Completion of coursework or training approved by the education department in the identification and reporting of child abuse.

Experiential Requirements: Completion of a minimum of 3,000 hours of post-master's supervised experience providing mental health counseling in a setting acceptable to the department. 1,500 of the hours must be direct client contact.

Exam Required: NCMHCE (Must be passed without ESL accommodations)

NORTH CAROLINA

NC Board of Licensed Professional Counselors

P.O. Box 1369

Garner, NC 27529

(919) 661-0820

(919) 779-5642 (fax)

ncblpc@mgmt4u.com

www.ncblpc.org

Title of License: LPC

> Licensed Professional Counselor Associate (LPCA): Individuals who are pursuing the LPC license but still need to complete the supervised experience requirements.

Educational Requirements: Master's degree or higher in counseling from a regionally accredited institution of higher education that includes coursework in nine areas of study and meets the following additional requirements:

- If enrolled prior to July 1, 2009, 48 semester hours (or 72 quarter hours) are required.
- If enrolled prior to July 1, 2013, but after June 30, 2009, 54 semester hours (or 81 quarter hours) are required.
- If enrolled after June 30, 2013, 60 semester hours (or 90 quarter hours) are required.
- A practicum and internship must be completed as part of the graduate course of study:
  - must cover at least a combined total of 17 hours of graduate counseling supervision
  - must consist of a combined minimum of 300 hours of supervised graduate counseling experience at a rate of not less than 1 hour of clinical supervision per 40 hours of graduate counseling experience

At least 60% of this counseling experience shall be direct graduate counseling experience.

Experimental Requirements: 3,000 hours of supervised professional practice; 2,000 hours must be direct counseling. No hours can be applied from the practicum/internship. Not less than 8 hours per week but no more than 40 hours per week. 100 hours of clinical supervision required. 75 hours must be individual supervision. Must have a minimum of 1 hour of clinical supervision for every 40 hours of professional practice. Supervision shall be based on direct (live) observation, co-therapy, audio and video recordings, and live supervision. Supervisor must be approved by the board.

Exam Required: LPC/LPCA: NCE, NCMHCE, or CRCE and NC jurisprudence exam
  LPCA: NCE, NCMHCE, or CRCE

NORTH DAKOTA

ND Board of Counselor Examiners

2112 10th Ave. SE

Mandan, ND 58554

(701) 667-5969

(701) 667-5969 (fax)

ndbce@btinet.net

www.ndbce.org

Title of License: LPCC

> LPC: Full professional license after LAPC criteria are met and supervised experience has been completed.

> Licensed Associate Professional Counselor (LAPC): A 2-year license, which allows for completion of the supervised experience. A 2-year plan of supervision and passage of the NCE required.

Educational Requirements: Licensed Professional Clinical Counselor (LPCC): Master's degree in counseling from an accredited college or university, including 60 semester hours, core clinical coursework (a minimum of 15 contact hours in each of three categories determined by the board), and 800 hours of clinical training in a supervised practicum and internship

LPC/LAPC: Master's degree in counseling or closely related field from an accredited college or university including 60 semester hours and specific core counseling coursework within the master's degree

Experiential Requirements: LPCC: Must already possess the first-level LPC credential and 2 years/3,000 hours of post-master's supervised clinical counseling experience in a clinical setting. Experience to include 100 hours of direct supervision (60 hours must be individual, face-to-face supervision) by a board-approved supervisor.

LPC: 400 hours of direct client counseling contact during the 2-year LAPC supervisory period. Experience to include 100 hours of direct supervision (60 hours must be individual, face-to-face supervision) by a board-approved supervisor.

Exams Required: LPCC: NCMHCE and a videotaped clinical counseling session of at least 30 minutes

LPC/LAPC: NCE

OHIO

OH Counselor, Social Worker, and Marriage and Family Therapist Board

50 W. Broad St., Suite 1075

Columbus, OH 43215

(614) 466-0912

(614) 728-7790 (fax)

Cswmft.info@cswb.state.oh.us

www.cswmft.ohio.gov

Title of License: LPCC

> Professional Counselor/Clinical Resident (CR): title used while completing the 3,000 hours of supervised experience required for the LPCC license

> LPC: title used after completing coursework including practicum and internship

> Registered Counselor Trainee (RCT): title used while enrolled in a practicum or internship in a counselor education program

Educational Requirements: Master's degree or higher in counseling from an accredited program, with 60 semester (or 90 quarter) hours, from an accredited institution. 20 hours (or 30 quarter hours) must be in clinical content areas. 100 hours practicum and 600 hours internship required. Ohio, for in-state applicants submitting after January 1, 2018, requires graduation from a CACREP-accredited program.

Experiential Requirements: LPCC: Must already possess the first-level LPC credential and 2 years/3,000 hours of post-master's clinical counseling under the supervision of an LPCC holding the supervision credential. Fifty percent must be clinical experience. The supervision must include the diagnosis and treatment of mental and emotional disorders; 50% of the time must be face-to-face contact delivering clinical counseling services. Supervisor will fill out an evaluation to evaluate competence to diagnose and treat mental and emotional disorders. No experiential requirements for LPC, CR/RCT

Exams Required: LPCC: NCMHCE

LPC: NCE

OH jurisprudence exam

OKLAHOMA

OK State Board of Licensed Professional Counselors

1000 N.E. 10th St.

Oklahoma City, OK 73117

(405) 271-6030

(405) 271-1918 (fax)

nenaw@health.ok.us

pcl.health.ok.gov

Title of License: LPC

> LPCC: An individual may be granted licensure as a licensed professional counselor candidate to practice counseling under the direct supervision of an approved LPC supervisor.

Educational Requirements: Master's degree or higher in counseling or a related mental health field with 60 graduate semester hours (or 90 quarter hours) from a regionally accredited college or university. Completion of coursework in 10 areas and a counseling practicum/internship of 300 clock hours. The board will define what qualifies as counseling related.

Experiential Requirements: 3 years/3,000 hours full-time postapplication professional counseling experience supervised by an approved LPC supervisor. For each 1,000 hours, 350 hours must be direct face-to-face contact. Face-to-face supervision must be 45 minutes for every 20 hours of experience. Up to 2 years of required experience may be gained at a rate of 1 year for each 30 graduate semester hours beyond the master's degree, provided that such hours are clearly related to the field of counseling and acceptable to the board. The applicant shall have no less than 1 year of supervised-time experience in counseling.

Exam Required: NCE and Oklahoma Legal and Ethical Responsibilities Exam (as pertains to LPCs)

OREGON

OR Board of Licensed Professional Counselors and Therapists

3218 Pringle Rd., SE, Suite 250

Salem, OR 97301-6312

(503) 378-5499

(503) 373-1427 (fax)

Lpc.lmft@state.or.us

www.oregon.gov/oblpct/Pages/index.aspx

Title of License: LPC

Registered Intern: an applicant registered to obtain post-degree supervised work experience toward licensure

Educational Requirements: Master's degree or higher in counseling, with 48 semester hours in a CACREP- or CORE-accredited program, or the content equivalent, from a regionally accredited institution. Completion of an internship/practicum consisting of 600 clock hours. If graduating after October 1, 2014: Master's degree or higher in counseling, with 60 semester hours (or 90 quarter hours) in a CACREP- or CORE-accredited program or the content equivalent, from a regionally accredited institution

Experiential Requirements: 3 years of full-time supervised experience in counseling, to include 2,400 hours of direct client contact. The supervision must take place concurrently with the direct client contact hours and must total no less than 2 hours of supervision for months where 45 or fewer direct client contact hours are completed, or total no less than 3 hours of supervision for months where 46 or more direct client contact hours are completed. Up to 75% of the individual supervision can be electronic and 50% of total supervision can be group. An approved supervisor must provide supervision. 600 (from 48 credit hours) or 700 (from 60 credit hours) client contact hours may be obtained during the clinical portion of the qualifying degree program.

Exams Required: NCE, CRCE, NCMHCE, or other exam as approved by the board and Oregon Law and Rules (open book)

PENNSYLVANIA

PA State Board of Social Workers, Marriage and Family Therapists, and Professional Counselors

One Penn Center

2601 N. 3rd St.

Harrisburg, PA 17110

(717) 783-1389

(717) 787-7769 (fax)

ra-socialwork@pa.gov

stsocialwork@state.pa.us

www.dos.state.pa.us/social

Title of License: LPC

Educational Requirements: Successful completion of a planned program of 60 semester hours (or 90 quarter hours) of graduate coursework in counseling or a field closely related to the practice of professional counseling, including a 48 semester hours (or 72 quarter hours) master's degree in professional counseling or in a field closely related to the practice of professional counseling

OR a doctoral degree in counseling or in a field closely related to the practice of professional counseling

AND for both: Completion of coursework in nine core areas including a supervised practicum (100 hours) and internship (600 hours). The supervised internship experience shall begin after completion of the supervised practicum experience.

Experiential Requirements: 3 years/3,000 hours of supervised clinical experience after completing 48 graduate-level credits (or 72 quarter hours). (The applicant has to complete at least 600 hours a year and no more than 1,800 a year.) If obtained a doctoral degree in counseling: 2 years/2,400 hours of supervised clinical experience. 1 year/1,200 hours must be obtained post-degree.

Supervision must be provided by a qualified supervisor. At least 1,800 hours must be completed under an LPC that has 5 years of experience within the last 10 years as a professional counselor. There should be 2 hours of supervision for every 40 hours of client hours. The remaining hours may be completed under an individual that holds a license and has at least a master's degree in a related field and 5 years of experience within the last 10 years in that field.

Exams Required: Any one of the following: NCE, CRCE, Art Therapy Credentials Board (ATCB), Certification Board for Music Therapists (CBMT), Practice Examination of Psychological Knowledge (PEPK), Advanced Alcohol and Other Drug Abuse (AAODA), Examination for Master Addictions Counselors (EMAC)

PUERTO RICO

PR Office of Regulation and Certification of Health Professions

Board of Examiners of Professional Counselors

P.O. Box 10200

San Juan, PR 00908

(787) 723-0102

www.salud.gov.pr

Title of License: LPC

Professional Counselor with Provisional License (PCPL): a person who is granted a temporary/provisional authorization by the board to offer counseling services under supervision to meet the experience requirement; valid for 3 years

Certified Mentor (CM): a licensed PC who has been certified by the board to supervise those who wish to obtain licensure

Educational Requirements: Master's degree or higher in counseling from an institution accredited by the Council of Higher Education of Puerto Rico. Specific coursework required in 8 out of 10 areas with a minimum of 45 semester graduate credits.

Experiential Requirements: Completion of a minimum of 500 hours of practice supervised by a CM. Upon approval of the exam required, the board shall issue a provisional license.

Exam Required: NCE

RHODE ISLAND

RI Board of Mental Health Counselors and Marriage and Family Therapists

3 Capitol Hill, Rm. 104

Providence, RI 02908

(401) 222-2828

(401) 222-1272

www.health.ri.gov/licenses/detail.php?id=228

Title of License: Licensed Clinical Mental Health Counselor (LCMHC)

Educational Requirements: Master's degree or higher specializing in counseling/therapy from a college/university accredited by the New England Association of Schools and Colleges or an equivalent regional accrediting agency OR master's degree, certificate in advanced graduate studies, or a doctoral degree in mental health counseling or allied field from a recognized educational institution.

For all options: Completion of 60 semester hours (90 quarter hours; master's must be 48 semester hours or 72 quarter hours) within the graduate counseling/therapy program, coursework in eight core areas, a supervised practicum (12 semester hours), and 1 calendar year of a supervised internship consisting of 20 hours per week in counseling

Experiential Requirements: 2 years/2,000 hours of direct client contact offering clinical or counseling or therapy services with emphasis in mental health counseling. To include 100 hours of post-master's supervised casework spread over a 2-year period. Supervision must be under a board-approved supervisor.

Exam Required: NCMHCE

SOUTH CAROLINA

SC Board of Examiners for the Licensure of Professional Counselors, Marriage and Family Therapists, and Psychoeducational Specialists

P.O. Box 11329

Columbia, SC 29211-1329

(803) 896-4658

(803) 896-4719 (fax)

www.llr.state.sc.us/pol/counselors

Title of License: LPC

> Professional Counselor Intern (LPC/I): an applicant who has met the education and exam requirements but not the 2-year supervised experience requirements

Educational Requirements: Master's degree or higher in professional counseling or a related discipline from a regionally accredited institution that includes at least 48 graduate hours, coursework in 10 content areas, and 150 hours of supervised counseling practicum

Experiential Requirements: Must already possess the first-level LPC/I credential and 2 years/1,500 hours of full-time, post-master's supervised clinical experience in the practice of professional counseling. The 1,500 hours must be direct counseling with individuals, couples, families, or groups. A minimum of 150 hours of the 1,500 hours must be clinical supervision provided by a board-approved LPC supervisor (100 hours must be individual supervision).

Exam Required: NCE or NCMHCE

SOUTH DAKOTA

SD Board of Examiners for Counselors and Marriage and Family Therapists

P.O. Box 2164

Sioux Falls, SD 57101

(605) 331-2927

(605) 331-2043 (fax)

sdbce.msp@midconetwork.com

https://dss.sd.gov/licensingboards/examiners.aspx

Title of License: Licensed Professional Counselor-Mental Health (LPC-MH)

> LPC

Educational Requirements: Master's degree or higher with an emphasis in mental health counseling from a CACREP-accredited program or equivalent program from an accredited institution that includes specific coursework and a supervised practicum (100 hours) and internship (600 hours). 48 semester hours required for LPC licensure; 60 semester hours or completion of all required coursework for LPC-MH licensure

Experiential Requirements: LPC-MH: Must already possess the first-level LPC credential. 2 years/2,000 hours of post-master's direct client contact in a clinical setting and 100 hours of direct supervision, at least 50 hours of which shall be face to face. 1,000 hours of post-master's direct client contact hours, and 50 hours of face-to-face supervision earned under the LPC credential may be counted toward these requirements if LPC-MH supervision conditions were met.

LPC: 2,000 hours of post-master's counseling experience, with 800 hours of direct client contact and 100 hours of direct supervision, at least 50 hours of which shall be face to face.

Exams Required: LPC-MH: NCMHCE

LPC: NCE

TENNESSEE

TN Board for Professional Counselors, Marital and Family Therapists, and Clinical Pastoral Therapists

227 French Landing, Suite 300

Nashville, TN 37243

(615) 532-3202, ×25138

(800) 778-4123, ×25138

(615) 532-5369 (fax)

www.tn.gov/health/health-program-areas/health-professional-boards/pcmft-board.html

Title of License: Licensed Professional Counselor-Mental Health Service Provider (LPC/MHSP)

LPC

Educational Requirements: LPC/MHSP: In addition to or as part of the graduate-degree completion of 9 graduate semester hours of coursework related to diagnosis, treatment, appraisal, and assessment of mental disorders

LPC: 60 graduate semester hours in professional counseling or a related field from an institution accredited by the Southern Association of Colleges and Schools, CACREP, or a comparable accrediting body, which includes a master's degree in professional counseling and a supervised 500-hour practicum or internship (300 hours of which must be completed in a clinical setting)

Experiential Requirements: LPC/MHSP: 2 years of post-master's professional experience consisting of 3,000 hours of direct clinical experience (not less than 10 hours per week); 1,500 hours have to be direct client contact and 1,500 hours need to be clinically based. Must have 150 hours of supervision

LPC: 2 years of post-master's professional experience consisting of 3,000 hours of direct clinical experience (not less than 10 hours per week). *Note:* As of January 31, 2013, supervisors had to be licensed for 5 years, conform to section F of the *ACA Code of Ethics,* and have at least 12 clock hours of supervision training.

Exams Required: LPC/MHSP: NCMHCE, NCE, and TN jurisprudence exam all required

LPC: NCE and TN jurisprudence exam

TEXAS

TX State Board of Examiners of Professional Counselors

P.O. Box 149347, MC 1982

Austin, TX 78714

(512) 834-6658

(512) 834-6677 (fax)

lpc@dshs.state.tx.us

www.dshs.state.tx.us/plc

Title of License: LPC

Licensed Professional Counselor Intern (LPC-I): an applicant practicing under supervision; valid for 5 years

Educational Requirements: Master's degree or higher in professional counseling or related field from an accredited college/university consisting of 60 graduate semester hours (for degrees conferred after August 1, 2017). Completion of specific coursework and a 300 clock hour supervised practicum with at least 100 hours of direct client contact. Counseling-related field: a mental health discipline utilizing human development, psychotherapeutic, and mental health principles including, but not limited to, psychology, psychiatry, social work, marriage and family therapy, and guidance and counseling. Non counseling related fields include but are not limited to sociology, education, administration, dance therapy, and theology.

Experiential Requirements: 3,000 hours of post-master's supervised experience, including 1,500 hours of direct client contact. Supervision must be provided by a board-approved LPC. Texas requires 4 units of continuing education in ethics and 6 units of supervision for those acting in a supervisory capacity every 2 years.

Exams Required: NCE and Texas jurisprudence exam

UTAH

UT Professional Counseling Licensing Board

P.O. Box 146741

Salt Lake City, UT 84114

(801) 530-6628

(866) 275-3675 (Utah toll-free number)

(801) 530-6511 (fax)

https://dopl.utah.gov/cmhc

Title of License: LCMHC

Licensed Associate Clinical Mental Health Counselor: LACMHC credential required before starting the supervised experience requirement; valid for 3 years

Educational Requirements: Master's degree or higher in mental health counseling from a CACREP-accredited program, including a minimum of 60 graduate semester hours (or 90 quarter hours) in specific coursework. A minimum of 3 semester hours or 4.5 quarter hours of a practicum. A minimum of 6 semester hours or 9 quarter hours of an internship.

Experiential Requirements: Must already possess the LACMHC. 4,000 hours of post-master's supervised professional counseling experience. 1,000 hours must be supervised experience in mental health therapy. 100 hours of face-to-face supervision required. Supervision must be under a licensed mental health therapist on site with a contract.

Exams Required: NCE; NCMHCE; and the Utah Professional Counselor Law, Rules, and Ethics Exam

VERMONT

VT Board of Allied Mental Health Practitioners
89 Main St., 3rd Floor
Montpellier, VT 05620
(802) 828-2390
(802) 828-2465 (fax)
dlafaill@sec.state.vt.us
www.sec.state.vt.us/professional-regulation/list-of-professions/allied-mental-health.aspx

Title of License: LCMHC

Educational Requirements: Master's degree or higher in counseling from an accredited institution, with a minimum of 60 semester hours and 1,000 hours of a supervised practicum, internship, or field experience in a clinical mental health setting. (Master's degree must be 48 semester hours.)

Experiential Requirements: 2 years/3,000 hours of post-master's experience in clinical mental health counseling, including 2,000 hours of direct client contact. 100 hours of face-to-face supervision required. Supervision should be 1 hour per 30 client hours and 50 must be individual supervision. Supervision must be under a board-approved LMHP.

Exams Required: NCE and NCMHCE and VT jurisprudence exam

VIRGINIA

VA Board of Counseling Perimeter Center
9960 Mayland Drive, Suite 300
Richmond, VA 23233
(804) 367-4610
(804) 527-4435 (fax)
coun@dhp.virginia.gov
www.dhp.virginia.gov/counseling

Title of License: LPC

Licensed Professional Counselor Resident: an applicant practicing under supervision

Educational Requirements: Master's degree or higher in counseling that includes 60 semester hours (or 90 quarter hours) of graduate study in counseling. Completion of a supervised internship consisting of at least 600 hours. Programs that are approved by CACREP or CORE are recognized as meeting the definition of graduate degree programs that prepare individuals to practice counseling and counseling treatment intervention.

Experiential Requirements: 3,400 hours of postgraduate supervised counseling experience, including 2,000 hours of direct client contact. 200 hours of supervision required (100 hours must be under the supervision of an LPC approved by the board). Graduate-level internship hours may count toward the 4,000 hours.

Exam Required: NCMHCE

WASHINGTON

WA Licensed Mental Health Counselors, Marriage and Family Therapists, and Social Workers Advisory Committee

P.O. Box 47877

Olympia, WA 98504-7877

(360) 236-4700

(360) 236-4818 (fax)

hpqa.csc@doh.wa.gov

www.doh.wa.gov/licensing

Title of License: LMHC

> Licensed Mental Health Counselor Associate (LMHCA): a prelicensure candidate who has a graduate degree in mental health counseling or related field and is working toward meeting the supervised experience requirements (may renew annually up to six times)

Educational Requirements: LMHC/LMHCA: Master's degree or higher in mental health counseling or related field from a regionally accredited college or university that includes a supervised counseling practicum or internship. Individuals who are certified as NCC or CCMHC are considered to meet educational requirements.

ALL professionals must complete 4 hours of HIV/AIDS education training.

Experiential Requirements: 3 years of full-time counseling or 3,000 hours postgraduate supervised mental health counseling in an approved setting. To include 1,200 hours of direct counseling with individuals, couples, groups, or families and 100 hours of immediate supervision by a board-approved supervisor. Graduates from CACREP-accredited programs can count up to 50 hours of supervision and 500 hours of experience from their practicum/internship.

Exam Required: LMHC: NCE or NCMHCE

LMHCA: None

WEST VIRGINIA

WV Board of Examiners in Counseling

815 Quarrier St., Suite 212

Charleston, WV 25301

(800) 520-3852

(304) 558-5496 (fax)

counselingboard@msn.com

Roxanne Clay: RCLAY27@msn.com

www.wvbec.org

Title of License: LPC

Provisional Licensed Professional Counselor: an applicant who has met the education and exam requirements but not the 2 years supervised experience requirement

Educational Requirements: Master's degree or higher from a program accredited by CACREP or CORE or a comparable accrediting body that includes 60 graduate semester hours (or 90 quarter hours) and a practicum and internship. Acceptable graduate degrees include a specialization in community agency counseling, mental health counseling, pastoral counseling, rehabilitation counseling, school counseling, and substance abuse or addictions counseling. Similar degrees that include the word "counseling" and include specific coursework and are determined by the board by a closely related field are also acceptable.

Experiential Requirements: Must already possess provisional license. 2 years/3,000 hours of post-master's supervised professional counseling experience. If obtained a doctoral degree: 1 year/1,500 hours of post-degree supervised professional counseling experience. At least 50% of the supervised counseling experience must be in the direct provision of counseling services to clients. A minimum of 1 hour of direct individual supervision is required for every 20 hours of practice. Supervision must be under a board-approved professional.

Exam Required: NCE, CRCE, or NCMHCE

WISCONSIN

WI Examining Board of Marriage and Family Therapists, Professional Counselors, and Social Workers

P.O. Box 8935

Madison, WI 53708

(608) 266-2112

(608) 261-7083 (fax)

drl.wi.gov/prof/coun/def.htm

Title of License: LPC

Licensed Professional Counselor Trainee: an applicant who has completed the degree requirements but not the supervised experience; valid for 48 months

Educational Requirements: Master's degree or higher in professional counseling or equivalent program approved by the board, from a regionally accredited institution that includes a minimum of 42 semester hours (or 63 quarter hours). 3 semester hours of counseling theories and 3 semester hours of a supervised counseling practicum are required.

Experiential Requirements: 2 years/3,000 hours of post-master's supervised professional counseling practice, including 1,000 hours of face-to-face client contact. Supervision must include 1 hour per week of face-to-face supervision and must be provided by a board-approved mental health professional.

Exams Required: NCE, CRCE, or equivalent exam approved by the board, and Wisconsin jurisprudence exam

WYOMING

WY Mental Health Professions Licensing Board

2001 Capitol Ave., Room 104

Cheyenne, WY 82002

Michelle M. Lamorie, Executive Director: Michelle.lamorie@wyo.gov

(307) 777-7788

(307) 777-3508 (fax)

plboards.state.wy.us/mentalhealth/index.asp

Title of License: LPC

>Provisional Professional Counselor (PPC): an applicant who has received a master's degree but has not passed the NCE exam or completed the supervised experience requirement; valid for 36 months

Educational Requirements: Master's degree or higher in counseling, with a minimum of 60 semester hours (or 90 quarter hours) from a CACREP- or CORE-accredited program or a regionally accredited college or university which meets the CACREP criteria for coursework, instructor qualification, and supervision

Experiential Requirements: 3,000 hours of supervised post-master's clinical experience (1,200 must be direct client contact and 100 hours must be face-to-face supervision). Supervision must be provided by a licensed mental health professional.

Exam Required: NCE, NCMHCE, or CRCE

DISTANCE COUNSELING, TECHNOLOGY, AND SOCIAL MEDIA INFORMATION

Current guidelines regarding technology in counseling are cited in the text that follows:

Nineteen states (Alaska, Arizona, Arkansas, California, Colorado, Iowa, Louisiana, Massachusetts, Minnesota, Nebraska, Nevada, New York, North Carolina, Ohio, Oregon, South Carolina, Texas, Utah, and West Virginia) regulate electronic communications for counselors, but only within their particular state. The general rule is counselors providing distance education should be licensed in the state where they practice.

Nineteen state counseling boards (Alabama, Connecticut, Delaware, Florida, Georgia, Hawaii, Kentucky, Maine, Michigan, Missouri, New Hampshire, North Dakota, Oklahoma, Pennsylvania, Rhode Island, South Dakota, Vermont, Washington, and Wyoming) and the District of Columbia report an absence of any law, rule, or regulation addressing the use of the Internet with clients.

- One (1) state (Arkansas) has an addendum to its licensure requirements specifically geared toward technology-assisted therapy: The Technology Assisted Counseling Specialization license requires additional education and supervision.
- Six (6) states (Indiana, Maryland, New Mexico, South Dakota, Tennessee, and Virginia) specifically state they do not support electronic communications under their scope of practice for professional counselors.
- One (1) state (Kansas) allows distance supervision provided that the supervision is conducted via confidential electronic communications.
- One (1) state (Louisiana) allows for 25 of the required 100 clinical supervision hours to be conducted via videoconferencing.
- One (1) state (North Carolina) allows video supervision as long as it is synchronous.
- One (1) state (Indiana) allows at least half of their continuing education hours to be taken online and/or through distance learning.
- Iowa, Ohio, and South Carolina consider distance learning continuing education hours as live continuing education hours if they are interactive (Iowa requires a certificate/verification that the CE is offered by the NBCC, CRCC, or AAMT as well).
- As of July 20, 2012, Colorado allows electronic supervision. The initial 2-hour supervision meeting must be face-to-face and supervisor and supervisee must meet face-to-face every 6 months. Electronic supervision must be audio and visual in nature.

Acronyms in the list of state licensure requirements refer to the following:

AAODA	The Advanced Alcohol and Other Drug Abuse Counselor Examination (administered by the International Certification and Reciprocity Consortium/Alcohol and Other Drug Abuse, Inc.)
ATCB	The Art Therapy Credentials Board Certification Examination
CACREP	The Council for Accreditation of Counseling and Related Educational Programs (an organizational affiliate of ACA that provides professional counselor-training accreditation)
CBMT	The Certification Board for Music Therapists Examination
CCMHC	The Certified Clinical Mental Health Counselor (an NBCC professional counseling specialty title; not a required credential)
CORE	The Council on Rehabilitation Education (an independent rehabilitation counselor-training accreditation board)

CRC	The Certified Rehabilitation Counselor (a CRCC professional counseling specialty title; not a required credential)
CRCC	The Commission on Rehabilitation Counselor Certification (an independent, nongovernmental rehabilitation counselor-credentialing board)
CRCE	The Certified Rehabilitation Counselor Examination (administered by CRCC for the certification of rehabilitation counselors; also administered by some states for their own credentialing process as an alternative to their clinically oriented exam)
EMAC	The Examination for Master Addictions Counselors (administered by the NBCC)
NBCC	The National Board for Certified Counselors (an independent, nongovernmental professional counselor-credentialing board and an organizational affiliate of ACA)
NCE	The National Counselor Examination (administered by the NBCC for national certification of professional counselors; also used by most states for their own credentialing process)
NCMHCE	The National Clinical Mental Health Counselor Examination (administered by the NBCC for national certification of mental health counselors; also administered by some states for their own licensure process)
PEPK	The Practice Examination of Psychological Knowledge (administered by the North American Association of Masters in Psychology)

Exam acronyms listed because of a number of different examinations:

AAODA	The Advanced Alcohol and Other Drug Abuse Counselor Examination (administered by the International Certification and Reciprocity Consortium/Alcohol and Other Drug Abuse, Inc.)
ATCB	The Art Therapy Credentials Board Certification Examination
CBMT	The Certification Board for Music Therapists Examination
CRCE	The Certified Rehabilitation Counselor Examination (administered by the CRCC for the certification of rehabilitation counselors; also administered by some states for their own credentialing process as an alternative to their clinically oriented exam)
EMAC	The Examination for Master Addiction Counselors (administered by the NBCC)
NCE	The National Counselor Examination (administered by the NBCC for national certification of professional counselors; also used by most states for their own credentialing process)
PEPK	The Practice Examination of Psychological Knowledge (administered by the North American Association of Master in Psychology)

Appendix C: Documents for Practicum and Internship

Old State University
Mental Health Counseling Program
Practicum and Internship Contract

This agreement is made on _____ by and between _____

                              (Date)   (Practicum/Internship Site)

and the Old State University Mental Health Counseling Program. The agreement will be effective for a period from

_____ to _____ for 100/300[1] semester clock hours for _____.

                                                         (Name of Student)

PURPOSE

The purpose of this agreement is to provide a qualified graduate student with a practicum/internship experience in the field of counseling.

THE UNIVERSITY PROGRAM AGREES

To assign a university faculty liaison to facilitate communication between the university and site;

To provide weekly classroom supervision and instruction for the practicum/internship student through EDU 679, EDU 685/686/687;

---

[1] Practicum requires a minimum of 100 clock hours. Internship requires 300 clock hours. For practicum, 40 of the 100 hours must be direct contact hours. For internship students, 120 of the 300 hours must be in direct service. *Direct service* is defined as individual, group, couples, or family counseling; co-counseling; clinical intakes; phone crisis counseling; team counseling and observation through a two-way mirror; running psychoeducational groups; and so forth.

415

To provide to the site, prior to placement of the student, the following information: profile of the previously named student and an academic calendar that shall include dates for periods during which the student will be excused from field supervision;

To notify the student that they must adhere to the administrative policies, rules, standards, schedules, and practices of the site;

That the faculty liaison shall be available for consultation with both site supervisors and students and shall be immediately contacted should any problem or change in relation to the student, site, or university occur; and

That the university supervisor (or practicum/internship instructor) is responsible for the assignment of a fieldwork grade. Grades are the S/U type.

THE PRACTICUM/INTERNSHIP SITE AGREES

To assign a practicum/internship supervisor who has appropriate credentials, time, and interest for training the practicum/internship student;

The clinical site must provide minimum weekly supervision for 1 hour per week;

To provide opportunities for the student to engage in a variety of counseling activities under supervision and for evaluating the student's performance (suggested counseling experience included in the "Practicum/Internship Activities" section);

To provide the student with adequate workspace, telephone, office supplies, and staff to conduct professional activities;

To provide supervisory contact that involves some examination of student work using audiovisual tapes, observation, and/or live supervision;

To provide written evaluation of the student based on criteria established by the university program; and

To not involve students in any form of billing for professional services.

Within the specified time frame will be the primary on-site practicum/internship site supervisor. The training activities (checked in the text that follows) shall be provided for the student in sufficient amounts to allow an adequate evaluation of the student's level of competence in each activity.

_____ will be the faculty liaison/supervisor with whom the student and practicum/internship site supervisor will communicate regarding progress, problems, performance evaluations, and grading.

PRACTICUM/INTERNSHIP ACTIVITIES

The following is a list of possible clinical activities for the practicum/internship student. It is not necessary that field sites have the student counselor complete all or even most of these. Check all areas that seem to apply. Additional areas of responsibility may be added in the future.

1. **Individual Counseling/Psychotherapy** _____

   Personal/Social Nature _____
   Occupational/Educational Nature _____

2. **Group Counseling/Psychotherapy** _____

   Co-leading _____
   Leading _____

3. **Intake Interviewing** _____

4. **Couples or Family Counseling** _____

   Leading _____
   Co-leading _____

5. **Testing and Assessment** _____

   Administration and Interpretation _____

6. **Report Writing** _____

   Recordkeeping _____
   Treatment Plans _____

7. **Consultation** _____

   Referrals _____
   Team Consultation and Case Staffing _____

8. **Community/Psychoeducational Activities** _____

   Family Conferences _____
   Community/Campus Outreach In-Service
   Presentations _____
   In-Service Presentations _____

9. **Career Counseling** _____

10. **Others (please specify):**

    _____

    _____

    _____

Type of supervision student will receive: Individual _____ Group _____

(Needs 1 hour of formal supervision per week)

Clinical Site Supervisor:_____ Date_____

Student: _____ Date _____

Faculty Liaison: _____ Date _____

FIELD SUPERVISION

As per the Council for Accreditation of Counseling and Related Educational Programs' (CACREP) guidelines, on-site supervisors must hold a minimum of a master's degree earned in counseling or a closely related field. Closely related fields include clinical social work, counseling or clinical psychology, marriage and family therapy, psychiatric nursing, and psychiatry. On-site supervisors must have a minimum of 2-year post-master's degree experience and must be appropriately licensed in their field (e.g., LMHC, LCSW, LP).

On-site supervisors also provide individual or group supervision for 1 hour each week the practicum/internship student accrues hours. The on-site supervisor submits a written evaluation of the student's performance at the end of each semester. On-site supervisors also sign off on the student's time logs.

EVALUATION OF PRACTICUM STUDENT/INTERN'S PERFORMANCE

At the conclusion of each semester, the field supervisor will complete an evaluation of the student practicum/internship student. The evaluation form can be copied from the NU MHC manual. The site supervisor should return the evaluation to:

Coordinator, Mental Health Counseling Program

College of Education

Old State University, NY 14190

712-285-8327

ssegdoh@oldstate.edu

CONCERNS REGARDING THE STUDENT INTERN

The Field Site Supervisor

If the field supervisor has concerns regarding the student's abilities to meet the goals and objectives of the agency, the supervisor has the following options:

The field supervisor apprises the university supervisor of the concern.

The field supervisor discusses the concern with the student.

If resolution does not occur, the field supervisor should notify the university supervisor.

The university supervisor will schedule an appointment with the field supervisor and the student to facilitate the resolution.

If no resolution occurs, the field supervisor may terminate the placement.

For the student, in the event the placement is terminated, the student must find another placement and repeat the practicum or internship.

The University Supervisor

If the university supervisor has a concern regarding the student's performance:

The university supervisor will inform the student that the field supervisor will be notified.

The university supervisor will seek feedback regarding the student's performance at the site.

If the concern cannot be resolved, the university supervisor will decide if the student will be placed in another setting.

If the student will receive an unsatisfactory grade, they will inform the student and the field supervisor that the student will need to repeat the class.

If the student does not pass the classroom or the on-site portion of the practicum/internship, the student will need to repeat the class.

> Because of the nature of student practicum/internships, either the clinical site or the counseling program reserves the right to dissolve this contract should concerns arise.

Note: The agency hosting the placement, the graduate program representative, and the practicum/internship student should all keep a copy of this agreement.

420 • APPENDIX C: DOCUMENTS FOR PRACTICUM AND INTERNSHIP

Sample Consent to Audiotape or Videotape Permission Form

Sample university and the agency provide counseling opportunities for individuals, couples, families, and groups. Signing this form provides the counselor-in-training the opportunity to record your counseling session and to play the recording for the counselor's supervisor and graduate students in the practicum/internship class, all of whom are held to confidentiality. The recording will not be made available to anyone outside the agency or the practicum/internship cohort. Feel free to ask your counselor any questions about the purpose of recording and use of the recording.

Your signature indicates that you give _____ (name of your counselor-in-training) permission to be recorded (audiotaped or videotaped; circle one or both) and that you understand the following:

1. I can request the recorder be turned off at any time and may request the recording be erased.

2. The purpose of recording is for use in training and supervision. This will allow the counselor-in-training to consult with their supervisor(s) in an individual or group format.

3. The contents of these recorded session(s) are confidential and will not be shared outside the context of individual and group supervision.

4. The recording will be stored in a secure location and will be used only for training and supervision purposes as previously stated.

5. The recordings will be erased after they have served their purpose.

_____

Name of Client (Please Print)

_____

Signature

Weekly Practicum/Internship I Hours Log
300 Hours (120 Direct/180 Indirect Needed)

Dates	Direct Hours[a]	Clock Hours[b]	Supervisor Signature

(continued)

422 • APPENDIX C: DOCUMENTS FOR PRACTICUM AND INTERNSHIP

(*continued*)

Dates	Direct Hours[a]	Clock Hours[b]	Supervisor Signature

Note: Practicum requires a minimum of 100 clock hours, which include 40 hours of direct contact. Internship requires 300 clock hours, which include 120 hours as direct contact.

[a]Direct Hours = Individual, group, couples, family counseling, co-counseling, intakes, assessment, phone crisis counseling, psychoeducational or support groups, and any direct contact with clients.

[b]Total Clock Hours = any work activity that does not involve direct contact with clients.

Total Direct Hours _____   Total Clock Hours Completed _____

_____   _____
Student Signature   Date

_____   _____
On-Site Supervisor Signature   Date

_____   _____
On-Site Supervisor Signature   Date

424 • APPENDIX C: DOCUMENTS FOR PRACTICUM AND INTERNSHIP

Sample School Counseling Referral Form

Student name: _____

Date of birth: _____

Teacher referring: _____

Parent/guardian: _____

Home address: _____

Home phone: _____ Cell phone: _____

Please check the behaviors indicated in the list that follows that serve as a reason for the referral:

___ Unable to sit still   ___ Fails to complete homework

___ Impatient   ___ Wastes time

___ Easily distracted   ___ Appears inattentive in class

___ Peer conflicts   ___ Withdrawn during class

___ Noncompliant with rules   ___ Appears worried/preoccupied

Estimated level of classroom functioning: Scale of 1 to 100. Higher scores indicate greater functioning.

___ Math   ___ Reading   ___ Language Arts

___ Science   ___ Social Studies   ___ Physical Education

Please cite any remedial services presently being rendered:

_____

_____

_____

Briefly describe the issue(s) placing the student at risk. Be as specific as possible:

_____

_____

_____

Briefly specify the desired behaviors you would like to see from this student in your classroom:

_____

_____

_____

Teacher making this referral:

_____

Signature:

_____

Title:

_____

Date:

_____

APPENDIX C: DOCUMENTS FOR PRACTICUM AND INTERNSHIP

Mental Status Checklist

	Check	Circle	Counselor's Note
1. Posture	Normal ___	Rigid, slouches	_____
2. Grooming	Normal ___	Well-groomed Disheveled, dirty	_____
3. Dress	Appropriate ___	Ragged Too revealing	_____
4. Facial expression	Appropriate ___	Poor eye contact, stares, downcast	_____
5. Speech			
a. Pace	Normal ___	Pressured, slow	_____
b. Volume	Normal ___	Loud, low	_____
c. Tone	Normal ___	Monotone, angry, low	_____
d. Content	Normal ___	Profane, hostile, illogical	_____
e. Clarity	Normal ___	Scattered, stutters Loose associations	_____

Affect and Mood

	Check	Circle	Counselor's Note
1. Attention	Normal ___	Brief, unable to sustain attention	_____
2. Affect	Normal ___	Inappropriate, flat	_____
3. Mood	Normal ___	Irritable, labile, depressed, euphoric	_____

Perception and Thought Content

	Check if applies	Description
1. Hallucination		
a. Auditory	_____	_____
b. Visual	_____	_____
c. Tactile	_____	_____
d. Taste	_____	_____
e. Smell	_____	_____

2. **Delusion**

   Paranoid _____   Grandeur _____   Persecutory _____   Thoughts _____

   Control _____   Broadcasting _____   Other (name) _____

3. **Phobias** (name): _____

4. **Obsessions** (name): _____

5. **Compulsions** (name): _____

6. **Suicide/homicide**

   Ideation: _____ Plan: _____

   Timetable to carry out suicide plan (e.g., immediate or future):

   _____

Orientation: This client/student is oriented to (check all that apply):

    a. Time _____   **b.** Place _____   **c.** Person _____

Judgment: Good _____   Impaired _____

Memory/Ability to Concentrate

    1. Immediate recall   Good _____   Poor _____

    2. Reversals   Good _____   Poor _____

    3. Serial sevens   Good _____   Poor _____

Abstract Reasoning

    1. Similarities: Good _____   Poor _____   Bizarre _____

    2. Absurdities: Understands _____   Does not understand _____

    3. Proverbs: Normal _____ Literal _____ Concrete _____ Bizarre _____

Insight

    Good _____   Fair _____   Poor _____

Mental Status Exam (Brief Version)

Now, I'm going to ask you a series of questions to test your concentration and memory. Answer to the best of your ability. Okay, any questions before we begin?

1. Orientation to time:
   a. What year is this? (1 point)
   b. What season is this? (1 point)
   c. What is the month and date? (1 point)
   d. What day of the week is it? (1 point)
      (Maximum of 4 points)

2. Orientation to place:
   a. What is the name of this institution/school/agency? (1 point)
   b. What floor are we on? (1 point)
   c. What city and state are we in? (1 point)
   d. What country is this? (1 point)
      (Maximum of 4 points)

3. Immediate recall:
   I am going to say three objects. After I say them, I want you to repeat them. They are "ball," "flag," and "tree." Now say them. Remember them because I will ask you to repeat them later. (Interviewer: **1 point** for each; maximum of **3 points**)

4. Attention: (Serial 7s or spelling. Choose from either of the following items but not both.)
   a. Subtract 7 from 100 and continue until I tell you to stop. (Interviewer, continue until subject makes an error. **1 point** for each correct answer; up to a maximum score of **5 points**)
   b. Spell the word "world" backwards. (**1 point** for each correct letter; maximum of **5 points**)

5. Delayed recall:
   What are the three words I asked you to remember? (**1 point** for each; maximum of **3 points**)

6. Naming:
   Show subject a pen and wristwatch and ask them to name them. (**1 point** for each; maximum of **2 points**)

7. Repetition:
   Repeat the following sentence exactly as I say it. "No ifs, ands, or buts." (**1 point** for each word; maximum of **3 points**)

8. Stage command:

"Now I want to see how well you can follow instructions. I'm going to give you a piece of paper. Take it in your right hand, use both hands to fold it in half, and then put it on the floor." (**1 point** for each command; maximum of **3 points**)

9. Reading:

Show the subject this headline and ask them to read it: "The rain in Spain falls mainly on the plain." (**1 point**)

10. Copying:

Give subject a clean sheet of paper and ask them to draw two interlocking geometric figures (e.g., triangles and squares). If necessary, draw an example for the client. (**1 point**)

11. Writing:

On the same sheet of paper, ask the subject to write a complete sentence. (**1 point**)

Scoring Procedures:

Total (Maximum Score) = 30

Note: Scores of 23 to 30 indicate expected or "normal" functioning. Scores under 23 suggest the presence of cognitive impairment.

23 to 30 = no cognitive impairment

18 to 22 = mild cognitive impairment

0 to 17 = significant cognitive impairment

MSE scores may be invalid if the subject has less than a ninth-grade education, is intoxicated, or is under the influence of drugs.

Adapted from Folstein, M. F., Folstein, S. E., & McHugh, P. R. (1975). "Mini-mental state." A practical method for grading the cognitive state of patients for the clinician. *Journal of Psychiatric Research, 12*, 189–198. https://doi. org/10.1016/0022-3956(75)90026-6

430 • APPENDIX C: DOCUMENTS FOR PRACTICUM AND INTERNSHIP

Intake and Psychosocial Case History Interview

Name of Client[2]: _____

Date of Interview: _____

Place of Interview: _____

Purpose of Interview: _____

Name of Interviewer: _____

I. Introduction:

Introduce yourself, your role, explain the nature of the interview (to assist with treatment), and ask if the client has any questions.

II. Childhood:

Where were you born and raised? (Did you move? When and why did you move?)

Were your parents married?

Did your mother have problems while she was pregnant with you?

Did you reach your developmental milestones, such as walking, talking, and potty training, on time?

With whom did you live while growing up?

Who did you feel closest to?

Who in the family was most affectionate to you?

How did you get along with_____ (whoever raised you)?

Who made the rules and enforced discipline?

Were the family rules clearly and consistently applied?

Do you believe the rules were fair?

How often did you get punished?

How did they usually discipline you?

Were you ever spanked? (If **"yes,"** were there ever bruises? Did you have to see a doctor?)

Did you witness violence in the family (verbal, physical, sexual)?

Did anyone sexually abuse you or a sibling? (If "yes," what happened? How much did this upset you? How upset are you now?)

How would you describe your personality as a child?

How would peers have described you?

---

[2] Pseudonym.

Did you have many friends as a child? (Any close friends? Best friends?)

Were you a leader or a follower?

III. School:

At what age did you begin school?

Did you go to special education classes or regular classes?

(If special classes, why?)

Were you a good student?

Did you ever repeat a grade? (If "yes," what was the last grade you repeated?)

Were you involved in school activities? (If "yes," what types?)

What did you do after you graduated (or dropped out) of school?

Did you attend college or get advanced technical training? (If "yes," did you graduate from college, tech school, etc.?)

Did you like school? (Explain whether "yes" or "no.")

IV. Parenthood:

Do you have any children? (If "yes," how many? What are their ages and sexes? How well do you get along with them?)

V. Friendships and Marriage:

Do you have many friends now? (Any close friends you can trust with secrets? Do your friendships tend to be long-lasting?)

Have you ever been married? (If "yes," how many times? How would you describe your marriages? If divorced, why did you divorce? If never married, why?)

Almost all couples argue or fight at times. I'd like to know a little bit about what happens when you and your partner argue or fight. Do you or your partner ever get pushed, grabbed, or hit? Ever throw things?

If "yes": Describe the most recent or most serious time this happened. How often does this happen? Have one of you ever had to go to the doctor after an assault?

If "no": Did the previous situation ever happen in previous relationships? Are you ever afraid you will be physically hurt during an argument with your spouse/partner?

VI. Relationships With Other Family Members:

Who is your immediate family? Extended family? Do you have in-laws? Grandparents? Grandchildren? Any other family?

Are your parents still alive?

If "yes": Are you close?

How do you get along with them?

How often do you visit them?

How often do you speak with them?

Have you had any recent arguments with them?

When you get angry with them, how long do you stay angry?

Do you have siblings?

If "yes": Are you close?

How do you get along?

Have you spoken with them recently?

Have you argued with them recently?

When you argue, how long do you stay angry with them?

VII. Occupation:

Are you employed?

If "yes": What type of work do you do?

How long have you worked there?

Do you like the work?

Why did you leave?

What is the longest job you have ever held?

If "no": When was the last time you worked?

What kind of job was it?

What other jobs have you had?

What is the longest job you have had?

VIII. Living Situation:

Where do you live? (A house? Apartment? Condominium?)

How long have you been living there?

Where did you previously live?

Why did you move? (Have you moved often?)

Have you ever been homeless or lived in a shelter?

How long were you homeless (or lived in a shelter)?

With whom do you currently live?

IX. Health:

Do you have any serious health problems? (If "yes," describe.)

Has your illness/condition impacted your close relationships? (If "yes," how?)

Have you been more withdrawn?

Do you argue more or less due to your health concerns?

X. Spirituality and Religious Beliefs:

Do you consider yourself a spiritual/religious person?

How important are your beliefs to you?

Would you say your spiritual/religious beliefs assist you in dealing with stress, anxiety, and health concerns? (If "yes," briefly explain how.)

XI. Satisfaction in Life:

Are you generally satisfied with your life?

　　If "no": Which areas of life are you dissatisfied with?

　　　　How much are you dissatisfied?

　　　　If "yes": What areas are you satisfied with?

　　How could you develop more satisfaction in your life?

　　Would you say your life has been meaningful?

　　　　If "yes": What accounts for the meaning in your life?

　　　　If "no": How could you develop meaning in your life?

School Counseling Intake Interview

Date:_____

Student: _____

Age: _____ GPA: _____ Band: _____ Sports: _____

Honor Society: _____ Other Organization: _____

Reason for interview (circle): Academic, Social, Personal, Career, Other

Briefly explain reason cited in the previous line: _____

_____

Discipline history (e.g., suspensions or fighting):

_____

Student's family:

Mother's name: _____

Father's name: _____

Sibling's names and ages: _____

_____

_____

Parents married or living together: Yes _____ No _____

Has student had previous counseling? Yes _____ No. _____ If "yes," reason for previous counseling:_____

Any history of physical/emotional/sexual abuse? Yes _____ No _____

What community resources is the student involved with? (e.g., religious community, YMCA/YWCA, Youth League sports)

Has this student ever been removed from their home? Yes___ No___. If so, for what reason?

_____

Has the student been arrested? Yes _____ No _____. If "yes," what was student arrested for?

_____

_____

Is the student currently taking medication(s): Yes _____ No _____. If "yes," what medications?

_____

What are the student's strengths? _____

_____

How does the parent/guardian describe the student's behavior at home (if known)? _____

_____

_____

Has the student acted out in socially unacceptable ways? Yes _____ No _____ If so, describe.

_____

Does the student have friends? Yes _____ No _____

Has the student made a suicide threat? Yes _____ No _____. If "yes," how long ago? _____

Is the student suicidal? Yes_____ No_____. If "yes," you must activate school plan to notify parent/guardian and appropriate authorities for mental health assistance.

Does the student have a history of alcohol or drug use? Yes _____ No _____. If "yes," what type?

_____

_____

Student: What are your future goals? _____

_____

Student: What are you happiest about? _____

Student: What are you most concerned about? _____

Student: What would you most want the counselor to know? _____

_____

Student: On a scale of 1 to 10, with 1 being *low* and 10 *high*, how optimistic do you feel regarding your life (or school performance or whatever seems appropriate depending on type of student concern)? Score: _____. How could you raise that score one number in the next week?_____

_____

Student: On a scale of 1 to 10, with 1 being *low* and 10 *high*, how effective was today's time?

Score _____. How could the session improve one point next time? _____

_____

436 • APPENDIX C: DOCUMENTS FOR PRACTICUM AND INTERNSHIP

SOAP Progress Note

SOAP stands for **S**ubjective, **O**bjective, **A**ssessment, and **P**lan. Some people prefer DAP notes—DAP stands for **D**escription, **A**nalysis, and **P**lan.

SOAP Notes

Subjective	Subjective experience of the client as related/reported by the client. Often direct quotes from the client of their problems or complaints. Examples include the following: "I had an awful week," "I'm feeling really depressed," "I hate my mother," "I can't seem to stop worrying about my grade," and "I haven't slept in two days." Also, there can be statements made by the client that you summarize without using quotes.
Objective	An objective account of the client's appearance and behaviors. May include client dress/clothing, posturing, eye contact, timeliness to session, affect, activity, speech, and so on. All the information in this section should be objective in the sense that it could be verified by observers and contains no analysis/judgment on your part. The objective section should provide a behavioral picture of the client.
Assessment	Your **theory-specific** analysis or interpretation of the client's issues and the session. Examples include the following: "The client seemed to accept his anger" or "The client's thinking was irrational in the following ways. . . ." This is your chance to hypothesize and define your conceptualization of your client's issues.
Plan	What you plan to do in the next session. Includes homework assignments, planned exercises or techniques, and so on. When writing this section, ask yourself, "Following this theory, what is it I want to remember to do with this client?" or "What do I want to cover with the client next week?" **A plan should always be theory specific.**

APPENDIX C: DOCUMENTS FOR PRACTICUM AND INTERNSHIP • 437

Client's Evaluation of Counseling Session

Date: _____

_____   _____
Counselor   Client

Rate each of the following statements on a 10-point scale, where 1 = Strongly Disagree, 10 = Strongly Agree, and 5 = Neutral.

1. This session assisted you in developing a better understanding of your issue(s) and the primary problem(s).

Strongly Disagree   Neutral   Strongly Agree

1   2   3   4   5   6   7   8   9   10

2. This counselor seemed to have listened very well and understood my concerns.

Strongly Disagree   Neutral   Strongly Agree

1   2   3   4   5   6   7   8   9   10

3. Through this counseling session, I have gained a better understanding of myself.

Strongly Disagree   Neutral   Strongly Agree

1   2   3   4   5   6   7   8   9   10

4. This interview helped me identify new strategies to address my issues and concerns.

Strongly Disagree   Neutral   Strongly Agree

1   2   3   4   5   6   7   8   9   10

5. This session assisted me in identifying strengths and resources to address my concerns.

Strongly Disagree   Neutral   Strongly Agree

1   2   3   4   5   6   7   8   9   10

6. Because of this session, I am more inclined to change my thinking and behavior.

Strongly Disagree   Neutral   Strongly Agree

1   2   3   4   5   6   7   8   9   10

7. The counselor was instrumental in making today's session productive.

Strongly Disagree   Neutral   Strongly Agree

1   2   3   4   5   6   7   8   9   10

8. I would rate today's session as: (Scale 1–10. 1 = *Unhelpful*, 10 = *Very Helpful*)

Circle the appropriate score.

1   2   3   4   5   6   7   8   9   10

438 • APPENDIX C: DOCUMENTS FOR PRACTICUM AND INTERNSHIP

9. What could you and the counselor do to raise your score by one point during the next session? (Write your answer on the following line.)

_____

10. What is one cognitive or behavioral change I can begin using today? (Write on the following line.)

_____

APPENDIX C: DOCUMENTS FOR PRACTICUM AND INTERNSHIP • 439

Student Counseling Session Rating Form

Date:_____ /_____/_____

Student: _____ Evaluator: _____

Audio Recording: _____ Video Recording: _____ In-Class Role Play: _____

Brief Summary of Session Content: _____

_____

_____

Specific Criteria: Rating (1 = *Least*; 5 = *Best*)

1. Opening: 1   2   3   4   5

Was the informed consent thorough and professional? Was confidentiality covered?

2. Rapport: 1   2   3   4   5

Did the counselor establish a good therapeutic alliance (e.g., voice tone, appropriate eye contact, paraphrasing, and summarizing)?

3. Attending Skill: 1   2   3   4   5

Did the counselor use minimal encouragers and refrain from unnecessary interruptions? (Also, was the counselor skilled in using therapeutic silence?)

4. Open-Ended Questioning: 1   2   3   4   5

Did the counselor make appropriate use of open-ended questions?

5. Affective Domain: 1   2   3   4   5

Did the counselor demonstrate appropriate empathy?

6. Challenging/Confrontation: 1   2   3   4   5

Did the counselor confront the client (if necessary)?

7. Solution Skills: 1   2   3   4   5

Did the counselor offer appropriate solution-seeking input?

8. Cultural Issues: 1   2   3   4   5

Did the counselor appear to understand and respect cultural issues? (Culture would include race, ethnicity, gender, sexual orientation, religion/ spirituality, etc.)

9. Goal Setting: 1   2   3   4   5

Did the counselor set effective goals for a follow-up session?

10. Closing: 1   2   3   4   5

Was closing well orchestrated? (Or, was it abrupt?)

440 • APPENDIX C: DOCUMENTS FOR PRACTICUM AND INTERNSHIP

On the following 1-to-10 scale, how effective was the student counselor in facilitating the counseling session (1 = *lowest score*, 10 = *highest score*)? Circle the appropriate number in the following list:

1   2   3   4   5   6   7   8   9   10

Constructive comments for the student counselor's further development:

_____

_____

_____

_____

_____

_____

_____

_____

_____

_____

_____

Signature of Evaluator

APPENDIX C: DOCUMENTS FOR PRACTICUM AND INTERNSHIP • 441

Diagnostic and Statistical Manual of Mental Disorders, **Fifth Edition** *(DSM-5)* **and SOAP Client Case Notes Format**

Name(s) and Age(s) of Client(s): _____

_____

_____

Date: _____/_____/_____ Code(s): _____ Session #:_____

Presenting Problem: _____

_____

_____

_____

_____

Medications:

DSM-5[3]:

Diagnosis: (Cite principal *DSM-5* diagnosis and diagnostic criteria)

Subjective (S): _____

_____

_____

_____

_____

_____

_____

---

[3] Prescriptive. Not intended as a final diagnosis.

442 • APPENDIX C: DOCUMENTS FOR PRACTICUM AND INTERNSHIP

Objective (O): _____

_____

_____

_____

_____

_____

_____

Assessment (A): _____

_____

_____

_____

_____

_____

_____

Plan (P): _____

_____

_____

_____

_____

_____

_____

_____

Counselor's Signature

_____

APPENDIX C: DOCUMENTS FOR PRACTICUM AND INTERNSHIP • 443

Client Initial Intake Form

Name: _____ Date: _____/_____/_____

Address: _____ City: _____ State: _____

Zip Code: _____ Phone: _____ (H) _____ (W/C)

Identifying Information:

Age: _____ Date of Birth: _____/_____/_____ Place: _____

Sex: Female _____ Male _____ Height: _____ Ft. _____ In. Weight: _____ Lbs.

Marital Status: M _____ S _____ D _____ Sep. _____ Other: _____

Ethnicity: Caucasian:___ Hispanic/Latinx:___ Asian: ___ African American: ___
American Indian: ___ Multiethnic: ____

Spouse's/Partner's Name: _____ Age: _____

Occupation: _____ Employer: _____

Name(s)/Age(s) of Children (If applicable)

_____

_____

Referral Source: _____

Address of Referral Source: _____

Treatment History:

Are you currently taking medication?   Yes: _____   No: _____

If "yes," name of medication(s): _____

Provider of medication(s): _____

Have you received previous psychiatric/psychological treatment?

Yes: _____ No: _____

If "yes," name the psychiatric treatment provider: _____

_____

Dates of counseling/psychiatric treatment: _____

_____

Has any close relative ever had psychiatric treatment or been committed to a psychiatric hospital? Yes: _____ No: _____. If "yes," please explain.

_____

_____

What factor(s) led you to seek counseling services?

_____

_____

Symptoms: _____

_____

_____

Family History:

Father's name: _____ Living: _____ Deceased: _____

Occupation: _____

Mother's name: _____ Living: _____ Deceased: _____

Occupation: _____

Brother(s)/Sister(s):

Name: _____ Age: _____ Living: _____ Deceased: _____

Name: _____ Age: _____ Living: _____ Deceased: _____

Name: _____ Age: _____ Living: _____ Deceased: _____

Educational History:

(Name of institution, location, dates attended, degree)

High School: _____

College/University: _____

Technical School: _____

Graduate/Professional: _____

Military Information (if applicable):

Branch of Military: _____

Dates of Active Service/Reserve Commitment: _____

Were you in a combat zone? Yes: ___ No: ___

Did you receive any medical treatment as a result of injuries? Yes: ___ No: ___

If "yes," what injuries were you treated for? _____

_____

_____

Index

AAC. *See* Association Argentina de Counselors
AADA. *See* Association for Adult Development and Aging
AAPC. *See* American Association of Pastoral Counselors
AARC. *See* Association for Assessment and Research in Counseling
AAS. *See* American Association of Suicidology
AASCB. *See* American Association of State Counseling Boards
AATA. *See* American Art Therapy Association
abandonment of clients, 237, 314–316
aboriginal Australians, 40–42, 96
ACA. *See* American Counseling Association; Australian Counselling Association
ACAC. *See* Association for Child and Adolescent Counseling
academic counseling, 23–25
ACC. *See* Association for Creativity in Counseling
ACCA. *See* American College Counseling Association
Accreditation Manual for Rehabilitation Counselor Education Programs, 19
accreditations and affiliations of sites, 57–59
ACES. *See* Association for Counselor Education and Supervision
ACS. *See* Approved Clinical Supervisor
ACT exam, 123
active listening, 178, 229
acute stress disorder (ASD), 269, 270
Adapted SAD PERSONS scale (A-SAD), 224–225, 234
addiction counseling, 70–72, 228
administrative supervision, 167

adolescents
  flashbacks, 282
  Mental Status Examination for, 117–120
  at risk for violent behavior, identifying, 252
  and self-injurious behaviors, 218
  suicide assessment in, 224, 228–231
ADTA. *See* American Dance Therapy Association
advocacy, 29, 34, 36
aggressive behaviors, dealing with, 252–253
AHC. *See* Association for Humanistic Counseling
Alabama Board of Examiners in Counseling, 373–374
Alaska Division of Occupational Licensing, 374
Alcohol Use Disorders Identification Test (AUDIT), 123, 223, 286, 287–289
ALGBTIC. *See* Association for Lesbian, Gay, Bisexual, and Transgender Issues in Counseling
all-or-nothing thinking (negative self-talk), 273
AMCD. *See* Association for Multicultural Counseling and Development
American Art Therapy Association (AATA), 368
American Association for Marriage and Family Therapy, 10
American Association of Pastoral Counselors (AAPC), 58, 59
American Association of State Counseling Boards (AASCB), 6, 368
American Association of Suicidology (AAS), 244
American Board of Genetic Counselors, 17

445

446 • INDEX

American College Counseling Association (ACCA), 365
American Counseling Association (ACA), 2, 3, 7, 8, 9–10, 11, 16, 28, 77, 338, 340, 365
   Code of Ethics, 4, 5, 9, 29, 34, 36, 39–40, 75, 76, 78–79, 88, 89–90, 91, 93–94, 95, 97, 99–100, 102, 132, 133, 135, 141, 154, 165, 185, 206, 221, 233, 302, 314–315
   Counseling Today, 8, 77, 365
   divisions and affiliates of, 13
   Governmental Affairs Officer, 8
   Licensure Requirements for Professional Counselors, 15
   membership, 2, 3, 7, 8–9, 67–68, 101, 141, 365
American Dance Therapy Association (ADTA), 368
American Foundation for Suicide Prevention, 244
American Mental Health Counselors Association (AMHCA), 2, 3, 7, 8, 9, 67–68, 77, 101, 141, 338, 368
American Music Therapy Association (AMTA), 369
American Personnel and Guidance Association (APGA), 5, 9
American Psychological Association (APA), 58, 131
American Rehabilitation Counseling Association (ARCA), 8, 9, 365
American School Counselor Association (ASCA), 2, 3, 8, 9, 68, 141, 338
American Society of Group Psychotherapy and Psychodrama (ASGPP), 369
AMHCA. *See* American Mental Health Counselors Association
AMTA. *See* American Music Therapy Association
angry clients, calming, 254–257, 263
antipsychotics, 250
APA. *See* American Psychological Association
APCS. *See* Association of Psychotherapists and Counsellors of Singapore
APGA. *See* American Personnel and Guidance Association
application, practicum/internship, 60–61
   cover letter, 62
   formal interview, 65–66
   résumé/curriculum vitae, 61–62, 63–65
Approved Clinical Supervisor (ACS), 12
APRCCC. *See* Asia Pacific Rim Confederation of Counsellors Conference
APT. *See* Association for Play Therapy
ARCA. *See* American Rehabilitation Counseling Association
Arizona Board of Behavioral Health Examiners, 374–375

Arkansas Board of Examiners in Counseling, 375
artwork, 121
A-SAD. *See* Adapted SAD PERSONS scale
ASCA. *See* American School Counselor Association
ASD. *See* acute stress disorder
ASERVIC. *See* Association for Spiritual, Ethical, and Religious Values in Counseling
ASGPP. *See* American Society of Group Psychotherapy and Psychodrama
ASGW. *See* Association for Specialists in Group Work
Asia Pacific Rim Confederation of Counsellors Conference (APRCCC), 9
assessment/testing information, 123
assisted suicide, 134, 135–136
Association Argentina de Counselors (AAC), 13, 369
Association for Adult Development and Aging (AADA), 365
Association for Assessment and Research in Counseling (AARC), 366
Association for Child and Adolescent Counseling (ACAC), 366
Association for Counselor Education and Supervision (ACES), 9, 28, 366
Association for Creativity in Counseling (ACC), 366
Association for Humanistic Counseling (AHC), 366
Association for Lesbian, Gay, Bisexual, and Transgender Issues in Counseling (ALGBTIC), 366
Association for Multicultural Counseling and Development (AMCD), 28, 36, 38, 54, 367
Association for Play Therapy (APT), 369
Association for Specialists in Group Work (ASGW), 367
Association for Spiritual, Ethical, and Religious Values in Counseling (ASERVIC), 367
Association of Non-White Concerns in Personnel and Guidance, 28
Association of Psychotherapists and Counsellors of Singapore (APCS), 13
attorney, 84, 87–88, 92, 101, 103, 142, 236
AUDIT. *See* Alcohol Use Disorders Identification Test
Australian Counselling Association (ACA), 9, 13, 16, 369

BACP. *See* British Association for Counselling and Psychotherapy
BAI. *See* Beck Anxiety Inventory
bartering, 94, 99

BCA. *See* Botswana Counselling Association
BCC. *See* Board Certified Coach
BDI-II. *See* Beck Depression Inventory-II
Beck Anxiety Inventory (BAI), 123
Beck Depression Inventory-II (BDI-II), 123, 153, 225–226
behaviors, 148, 238. *See also* suicide
   behavioral history, 237, 249, 254
   changes, 143–144
   dealing with aggressive behaviors, 252–253
   managing, and client violence, 251
   self-injurious, 218
   unusual, 253
beneficence, 75
Bernard's discrimination model of supervision, 173
BLS. *See* U.S. Bureau of Labor Statistics
Board Certified Coach (BCC), 12
body language, 254, 260–261
body work, 293
Botswana Counselling Association (BCA), 13
boundary issues, 93–97, 99–100, 311
Boynton v. Burglass (1991), 86
breath work, 292–293
British Association for Counselling and Psychotherapy (BACP), 13, 16, 369
bullying, 253
burnout, 190–191, 209

CACREP. *See* Council for Accreditation of Counseling and Related Educational Programs
CAGE (Cut-Down use, Annoyed when questions regarding substance use, Guilt at abuse, and needs an Eye-opener to start day) questionnaire, 286–287
California Board of Behavioral Sciences, 376–377
California Senate Bill 788, 6
calm, remaining, 122, 218, 221, 222, 227, 228, 238, 253, 254, 257
Canadian Counselling and Psychotherapy Association (CCPA), 9, 13, 141, 369
career center, 60, 337
career counselors, 66, 341, 346, 354
career visioning, 333–337
   action plan, 334–336
   goals, 334
   personal history, 333
   professional identity, 334
   techniques for, 336–337
   values, 333–334
CARF. *See* Commission on Accreditation of Rehabilitation Facilities

CASA. *See* The Counselling Association-South Africa
case management programs, 309
case notes, 123, 131–132, 137, 138, 142
   behavioral changes, 143–144
   being judicious and supportive, 144
   brevity of, 144–145
   and clinical management, 133–134
   concise comments, 143
   disclosure of, 138
   errors, 153
   format, *DSM-5*/SOAP, 441–442
   in-session notes, 145
   legal implications, 136
   location of, 138
   objective *vs.* subjective information, 142–143
   risk management strategy, 139–141
   SOAP format, 138, 145–154
   and transfer of clients, 136
CAT. *See* Counseling Association of Taiwan
catastrophizing (negative self-talk), 273
CBT. *See* cognitive behavioral therapy
CCE. *See* Center for Credentialing and Education
CCMHC. *See* Certified Clinical Mental Health Counselors
CCPA. *See* Canadian Counselling and Psychotherapy Association
CDC. *See* Centers for Disease Control
Center for Credentialing and Education (CCE), 11–12, 15, 370
Centers for Disease Control (CDC), 247
certifications, 11, 12, 370–371
Certified Clinical Mental Health Counselors (CCMHC), 11, 15, 70–72
Certified Rehabilitation Counselor (CRC), 11
Certified Rehabilitation Counselor Examination (CRCE), 11, 15
Certified Substance Abuse Counselors (CSAC), 12
CF. *See* compassion fatigue
CGAS. *See* Children's Global Assessment Scale
child abuse/neglect, 239–240
   and flashbacks, 282
   reporting, 84–85, 240–241
children
   Mental Status Examination for, 117–120
   minor clients, and confidentiality, 88–89
   at risk for violent behavior, identifying, 252
   suicide assessment in, 228–231
Children's Global Assessment Scale (CGAS), 123
class, counseling practicum/internship, 21, 160, 165–167
   recordings of counseling sessions, 165–166
   sample syllabus, 160–165

448 • INDEX

client records, 122–123, 131, 133
    and clinical management, 133–134
    HIPAA compliance, 137
    legal implications, 136–137
    record keeping, 138, 139, 141–142
    risk management strategy, 139–141
    and technology, 92–93
    and transfer of clients, 136
client's evaluation of counseling session,
    437–438
clinical impressions, 149
clinical issues, 109
    client records, 122–123
    closing the session, 123–124
    counseling techniques, 120–122
    fear of making mistakes, 126
    initial assessment, 111, 114–120
    initial intake form, 111, 112–114
    suggestions, 125
    teletherapy, 109–110
    therapeutic alliance, 110–111, 115
clinical rehabilitation counseling, 19
Clinical Rehabilitation Standards, 19
clinical supervision, 159–160, 167–168, 173–178.
    See also supervision
clinical writing, 131–132, 155–157
    case notes, 138–141, 142–154
    client records, 133–134, 136–137
    documentation of complicated end-of-life
        issues, 134–136
    record keeping, 138, 139, 141–142
closing, counselling session, 123–124
COAMFTE. *See* Commission on Accreditation
    for Marriage and Family Therapy
    Education
Code of Ethics, ACA, 4, 5, 9, 29, 34, 36, 39–40,
    75, 76, 78–79, 88, 89–90, 91, 93–94, 95, 97,
    99–100, 102, 132, 133, 135, 141, 154, 165,
    185, 206, 221, 233, 302, 314–315
cognitive behavioral supervision, 176
cognitive behavioral therapy (CBT), 176, 274,
    295, 296
cognitive self-care, 209–210
collage making, 336
College of Registered Psychotherapists of
    Ontario (CRPO), 16
colonialism, 41
Colorado Division of Professions and
    Occupations, 377–378
Columbia-Suicide Severity Rating Scale
    (C-SSRS), 225
Commission on Accreditation for Marriage and
    Family Therapy Education (COAMFTE),
    10, 19, 58, 59
Commission on Accreditation of Rehabilitation
    Facilities (CARF), 58, 59

Commission on Rehabilitation Counselor
    Certification (CRCC), 11, 15, 370–371
Commission on Rehabilitation Education, 19
communicable diseases, clients with, 89–90
compassion fatigue (CF), 190, 191, 209
competent ethical practice, 76–77
complex trauma, 268, 270
confidentiality, 82–83, 134, 136, 137, 218–219,
    238, 240
    client release of information, 88
    clients planning future crimes, 87
    clients with serious communicable diseases,
        89–90
    danger to self and others, 85–87
    of deceased clients, 142
    exceptions to, 84–91
    in group/family/couples counseling, 77
    legal proceedings, 87–88
    limits/conditions, written protocol about, 89
    minor clients or legally incompetent clients,
        88–89
    recommendations, 92
    and suicidal clients, 221
    suspected abuse, 84–85
    terminally ill clients, 90–91, 134
    unintentional violations of, 82
conflict management skills, 203–205, 348
conflict resolution
    practice, 206
    styles, 204–205
Connecticut Department of Public Health, 378
constructive criticism, 324
constructivist questions and responses, 177
consultation, 76, 99, 160
    with colleagues, 94, 99, 106, 135, 236, 254
    with supervisors, 87, 140, 150, 217, 227, 310
contact hours, 20–21
continuing education, 57–58, 77
continuity of care, 136
contract, practicum/internship, 66–67
co-occurring relationships. *See* dual
    relationships in counseling
CORE. *See* Council for Rehabilitation
    Education
Council for Accreditation of Counseling and
    Related Educational Programs (CACREP),
    3, 6, 10–11, 47, 54, 55, 67, 101, 159, 207, 330,
    371
    internship requirements, 19
    practicum requirements, 18
    requirements for on-site supervisors, 55
Council for Rehabilitation Education (CORE),
    10
counseling, definition of, 3
Counseling Association of Taiwan (CAT), 369
counseling practicum/internship, 1–2, 8, 47, 323

academic and on-site supervision, 22
application, 60–66
class, 21, 160–167
contact hours, 20–21
contract, 66–67, 415–419
documents for, 415–444
encountering violence during, 247–248
hours log, 421–423
issues to consider in, 67–70
practicum vs internship, 17–18
requirements, 18–22
search checklist, 68–69
selection, 47–59
site information form, 50–51
counseling profession, 2, 3–4, 27, 39–40, 47, 76, 247
20/20: A Vision for the Future of Counseling initiative, 2, 3, 6
ethical practice, 4
licensure, 5, 14–16
maturation of, 5–7
Medicare reimbursement, 6, 7–8
occupational outlook, 16–17
professional counseling organizations, 8–14
titles, 15
counseling techniques, 120–122, 189–190
Counseling Today, 8, 77, 365
The Counselling Association-South Africa (CASA), 14
counselor-client relationship. *See* therapeutic relationship
Counselor Preparatory Comprehensive Examination (CPCE), 15
Counselors for Social Justice (CSJ), 367
cover letter, 62, 69, 337, 341, 342, 345–346
CPCE. *See* Counselor Preparatory Comprehensive Examination
CRC. *See* Certified Rehabilitation Counselor
CRCC. *See* Commission on Rehabilitation Counselor Certification
CRCE. *See* Certified Rehabilitation Counselor Examination
creative arts therapy, 16
creative self-care, 211
crisis, definition of, 217, 218
crisis intervention, 217–218
assessment of danger to others, 233–239
child abuse and neglect, 239–241
crisis management plan, 230–231
duty to warn and protect, 218–220
suicidal clients, 220–233, 241–243
tips, 238–239
critical race theory (CRT), 4
cross-disciplinary collaboration, 56
CRPO. *See* College of Registered Psychotherapists of Ontario

CRT. *See* critical race theory
CSAC. *See* Certified Substance Abuse Counselors
CSJ. *See* Counselors for Social Justice
C-SSRS. *See* Columbia-Suicide Severity Rating Scale
cultural awareness, 32
cultural competence. *See* multicultural competence
cultural humility, 33, 40
culture, 251. *See also* multiculturalism/ multicultural counseling
and conflict management, 204
cultural encapsulation, 27
definition of, 28
and dual relationships, 96
and gifts from clients to counselors, 100
and pause time, 122
and scheduling, 124
curriculum vitae (CV), 61–62, 339, 340–342, 354, 359
CV. *See* curriculum vitae

daily gratitudes, 292, 293
danger to others
assessment of, 233–239
and confidentiality, 85–87
potential for violence, 234–235
risk management suggestions, 235–238
danger to self, 85–87. *See also* suicide
DCC. *See* Distance Credentialed Counselor
deceased clients, confidentiality/privacy of, 142
decision tree, 356–357
Delaware Board of Mental Health and Chemical Dependency Professionals, 378–379
demographics, 28
Department of Veterans Affairs (VA), 6, 10, 11, 19
depression, 35, 121, 153–154, 225, 228, 232
Diagnostic and Statistical Manual of Mental Disorders, Fifth Edition, Text Revision (DSM-5-TR), 4, 78, 123, 149, 150, 167, 174, 269–270, 441–442
dialogue, 8, 32, 38, 255–256, 303, 306, 308, 313
discrimination model of supervision (Bernard), 173
dissociation, 272
distance-based supervision, 18–19
distance counseling, 411–412
Distance Credentialed Counselor (DCC), 12
District of Columbia Board of Professional Counseling, 379–380
doctoral interns, 55

450 • INDEX

documentation, 82, 92, 132, 217, 237. *See also*
case notes
of absence of counselors, 315
adequate, 132, 139
of assault, 259
client records, 133–134
of complicated end-of-life issues, 134–136
counseling practicum/internship, 415–444
in crisis situations, 86
for high-risk cases, 139–140
HIPAA compliance, 137
of informed consent, 78
legal implications, 136–137
during termination, 311
and transfer of clients, 136
domestic violence, 151–152, 274
dream journal, 284, 286
dreams, 283, 296–297
drug and alcohol assessment, 123
*DSM-5-TR. See Diagnostic and Statistical Manual
of Mental Disorders, Fifth Edition, Text
Revision*
dual relationships in counseling, 93–97, 99,
237, 310
duty to warn and protect, 86–87, 218–220

EAC. *See* European Association for
Counselling
ECCP. *See* Examination for Clinical Counselor
Practice
Educational and Vocational Guidance
Practitioner (EVGP), 12
EEOC. *See* Equal Opportunity Employment
Commission
EFT. *See* Emotional Freedom Therapy
electronic records, 77, 137, 141, 154
emotional abuse, signs of, 240
Emotional Freedom Therapy (EFT), 270, 293,
295, 296, 297
emotional regulation, 251
emotional self-care, 209
empathy, 33, 205, 207, 222
empty chair technique, 25, 121, 290, 297
end-of-life decisions, 91, 134–136
environmental stressors, 187
Equal Opportunity Employment Commission
(EEOC), 350
ethical and legal issues, 75–76
boundary issues, 93–97, 99–100, 311
competent ethical practice, 76–77
confidentiality and privileged
communication, 82–92
counselor–client attraction, 98–99
exceptions to confidentiality, 84–91

Health Insurance Portability and Accountability
Act (HIPAA), 76, 77, 78, 84, 90, 93
informed consent, 77–81
liability insurance, 101–102
sexual relationships, 93–94, 97–99
suicide, 221–222
technology and client records, 92–93
ethics, 4, 75, 133. *See also* client records; self-care
ACA *Code of Ethics*, 4, 5, 9, 29, 34, 36, 39–40,
75, 76, 78–79, 88, 89–90, 91, 93–94, 95, 97,
99–100, 102, 132, 133, 135, 141, 154, 165, 185,
206, 221, 233, 302, 314–315
codes, 9–10, 53, 56, 75, 92, 94, 122, 235
and multicultural counseling, 36–39
nondiscrimination laws, 39
and religious beliefs, clash between, 36–37
European Association for Counselling (EAC),
13–14, 369
euthanasia, 135
EVGP. *See* Educational and Vocational
Guidance Practitioner
Examination for Clinical Counselor Practice
(ECCP), 15

Facebook, 337
faculty advisors, 19, 48, 49, 56, 60, 61, 67, 70, 92,
179, 337
fading technique, 307
faith-based communities, 35
feedback, 168, 169
from clients to counselors, 306–307, 314
from interns to supervisors, 330, 331
to peers, 171–180
from supervisors to interns, 125, 324, 327
written, 169–171
feminist model of supervision, 174
field supervisor–intern relationship,
termination of, 323–324
internship evaluation form, 324, 325–326
internship evaluation process, 324, 327
self-evaluation by interns, 324, 328–329
self-reflection exercise, 332
student counselor's evaluation of on-site
supervisor, 330–332
fight-flight-freeze response, 187
financial self-care, 210
5-senses grounding technique, 295
flashbacks
definition of, 282
interruption of, 283, 284
managing, 281–283
Florida Board of Clinical Social Work,
Marriage and Family Therapy, and Mental
Health Counseling, 380

follow-up, 140, 313–314
forgiveness, 190
formal interview (practicum/internship application), 65–66
fortune telling (negative self-talk), 274
foster care, 85, 231
4-square breathing technique, 296
future crimes, clients planning, 87

GAF. *See* Global Assessment of Functioning
GCDF. *See* Global Career Development Facilitator
genetic counseling, 16–17
genogram, 32
Georgia Composite Board of Professional Counselors, Social Workers, and Marriage and Family Therapists, 381
gifts from clients to counselors, 99–100
Global Assessment of Functioning (GAF), 123
Global Career Development Facilitator (GCDF), 12
good faith, 85, 86, 240
Guam Board of Allied Health Examiners, 381–382

hate talk, 251
Hawaii Department of Commerce and Consumer Affairs—Professional and Vocational Licensing, 382
health assessment, 123
Health Insurance Portability and Accountability Act (HIPAA), 76, 77, 78, 84, 90, 93, 136, 137, 138, 236
HIPAA. *See* Health Insurance Portability and Accountability Act
Hippocratic Oath, 75
HKPCA. *See* Hong Kong Professional Counselling Association
homework, 81, 121, 304
Hong Kong Professional Counselling Association (HKPCA), 14, 369
hourly practicum/internship activities log, 20–21
hours log, practicum/internship, 421–423
HS-BCP. *See* Human Services-Board Certified Practitioner
Human Services-Board Certified Practitioner (HS-BCP), 12
humility of counselors, 27

IAAOC. *See* International Association of Addictions and Offender Counselors

IAC. *See* International Association for Counselling
IACP. *See* Irish Association for Counselling and Psychotherapy
IACS. *See* International Accreditation of Counseling Services
IAMFC. *See* International Association of Marriage and Family Counselors
IASP. *See* International Association for Suicide Prevention
ICA. *See* Indonesian Counseling Association
Idaho State Licensing Board of Professional Counselors and Marriage and Family Therapists, 383
IDM. *See* Integrated Developmental Model
IKA. *See* Indonesian Counselor Association
Illinois Professional Counselor Licensing and Disciplinary Board, 383–384
Indiana Behavioral Health and Human Services Licensing Board, 384–385
Indonesian Counseling Association (ICA), 370
Indonesian Counselor Association (IKA), 14
informational interview, 59–60, 337
informed consent, 77–79, 124, 136, 142, 237, 258, 313
   consent to audiotape or videotape permission form, 420
   form, 79–81, 99
   for recording of counseling sessions, 165, 420
initial assessment, 111, 114–120
initial intake form, 111, 112–114, 443–444
initial interview with clients, 110, 234, 286, 430–433, 434–435
inner voice, listening to, 122
inpatient placements, 53
in-session notes, 145
Institute of Medicine (IOM), 6
intake and psychosocial case history interview, 430–433
intake information, 122
Integrated Developmental Model (IDM), 174–175
International Accreditation of Counseling Services (IACS), 58, 59, 370
International Association for Counselling (IAC), 14, 370
International Association for Suicide Prevention (IASP), 244
International Association of Addictions and Offender Counselors (IAAOC), 367
International Association of Marriage and Family Counselors (IAMFC), 367
international counseling internships, 34
international counseling organizations, 12–14
International Society for the Study of Self-Injury, 218

452 • INDEX

IOM. *See* Institute of Medicine
Iowa Board of Behavioral Science Examiners, 385–386
Irish Association for Counselling and Psychotherapy (IACP), 14, 370

Jaffee v. Redmond et al. (1996), 83, 136
Jed Foundation, 244
job interview, 346–347, 360
  inappropriate questions, 350–351, 360
  sample questions, 347–350
job offer, 354, 356–358
job search preparation, 333, 360–362
  career center, 337
  career visioning, 333–337
  cover letter, 341, 342, 345–346
  dealing with rejection, 351–354, 360, 362
  job interview, 346–351
  job offer, 354, 356–358
  professional networking, 337–338
  requesting references, 338–340
  résumé/curriculum vitae, 340–342, 343–345
The Joint Commission (TJC), 58, 59
journaling, 280–281, 284, 286, 336
Journal of Counseling and Development, 365

Kansas Behavioral Sciences Regulatory Board, 386–387
KCA. *See* Korean Counseling Association
Keeton v. Anderson-Wiley (2011/2012), 39
Kentucky Board of Licensed Professional Counselors, 387
Korean Counseling Association (KCA), 14, 370

learning contract. *See* contract, practicum/internship
least restrictive setting, 134
legally incompetent clients, and confidentiality, 88–89
legal proceedings, 236
  and case notes, 133, 142
  and client records, 136
  and confidentiality, 87–88
  and privileged communication, 83–84
  and termination, 307
A Letter to My Traumatized Self exercise, 290–291
LGBTQ persons, 251
liability insurance, 8, 67–68, 101–102, 140–141, 237
Licensed Mental Health Counselors (LMHC), 4
licensure, 14–16

boards, 14, 373–413
examinations, 15
laws, 5, 14
process for obtaining, 15
regulations, 7
standards, for supervision, 56–57
Licensure Requirements for Professional Counselors (ACA), 15
lifestyle, healthy/mindful, 186–203
LinkedIn, 337, 359
litigation against counselors, 76, 101–102, 136, 142
LMHC. *See* Licensed Mental Health Counselors
lobbying, 7, 8, 36
locus of control, internal, 272
logistics of counseling, 79
Louisiana Department of Licensed Professional Counselors Board of Examiners, 387–388

Maine Board of Counseling Professionals Licensure, 388–389
malpractice, 94, 101–102, 131, 133
Malta Association for the Counselling Profession (MAPC), 14
managed care, 303
mandated clients, 79, 111, 136, 142, 143, 144, 151–152, 236, 247, 303, 304, 307
mandated reporting, 84–85, 89–90, 220, 239, 240
MAPC. *See* Malta Association for the Counselling Profession
Maryland Board of Examiners of Professional Counselors and Therapists, 389–390
Massachusetts Board of Registration of Allied Mental Health and Human Services Professionals, 390
MAST. *See* Michigan Alcohol Screening Test
Master's in Psychology and Counseling Accreditation Council (MPCAC), 10–11
MBTI. *See* Myers-Briggs Type Indicator
MCI. *See* Multicultural Counseling Inventory
meaning in life, 104, 105, 106, 202–203, 232, 233, 242, 243, 272, 318, 320
Meaning in Life Questionnaire (MLQ), 203
Medicaid, 10
medical history, 237
medical neglect, 239
Medicare, 6, 7–8, 10
medication(s)
  noncompliance, 251
  psychopharmacologic, ceasing taking, 250
  screening, 227
meditation, 292–293, 336
memory(ies)

flashbacks, 281–283
and trauma, 272–273
Mental Health Access Improvement Act, 7
Mental Health Parity Act and Addiction Equity
Act of 2008, 6
mental status checklist, 426–427
Mental Status Examination (MSE), 114–115,
143, 167
brief version, 115–117, 428–429
for older children, adolescents, and adults,
117–120
mentors, site supervisors as, 179–180
MGCA. *See* Military and Government
Counseling Association
Michigan Alcohol Screening Test (MAST), 123,
223
Michigan Board of Counseling, 390–391
microaggressions, 27
Military and Government Counseling
Association (MGCA), 367
mind-body-breath work, 296, 297
mindfulness, 238, 335
mindfulness self-care, 210
mind reading (negative self-talk), 274
Mini-Mental Status Examination, 167
minimization (negative self-talk), 273
Minnesota Board of Counseling, 391–392
Minnesota Multiphasic Inventory-2/A
(MMPI-2/MMPI-A), 123
minor clients, and confidentiality, 88–89
miracle questions, 121, 177, 182
Mississippi State Board of Examiners for
Licensed Professional Counselors, 392–393
Missouri Committee for Professional
Counselors, 393
MLQ. *See* Meaning in Life Questionnaire
MMPI-2/MMPI-A. *See* Minnesota Multiphasic
Inventory-2/A
Monitoring and Revising My Self-Talk
exercise, 291–292
Montana Board of Social Work Examiners and
Professional Counselors, 394
MPCAC. *See* Master's in Psychology and
Counseling Accreditation Council
MSE. *See* Mental Status Examination
multicultural competence, 28, 29, 31–34, 36,
38–39, 54
Multicultural Counseling Competencies and
Standards, 28, 36
Multicultural Counseling Inventory (MCI), 32
multiculturalism/multicultural counseling, 40,
349
ACA *Code of Ethics*, 29, 34, 36, 39–40
cultural assumptions, 32, 33
cultural conflicts, 38–39

culturally appropriate skills, 34–35
ethics, 36–39
exploring resources available to clients, 35
importance of, 27–29
oppressed cultures, 37–38
religious beliefs, 36–37
self-awareness, 29–31
multiple relationships in counseling, 93–97, 99
Myers-Briggs Type Indicator (MBTI), 123

NASW. *See* National Association of Social
Workers
National Association of Social Workers
(NASW), 58, 94
National Board for Certified Counselors
(NBCC), 3, 6, 11, 15, 16, 338, 370, 371
National Career Development Association
(NCDA), 368
National Certified Counselors (NCC), 11
National Clinical Mental Health Counselor
Examination (NCMHCE), 11, 15
National Counselor Examination (NCE), 11, 15, 19
National Employment Counseling Association
(NECA), 368
National Institute for Occupational Safety and
Health (NIOSH), 252
National Organization for People of Color
Against Suicide (NOPCAS), 244
National Society of Genetic Counselors, 17
NBCC. *See* National Board for Certified
Counselors
NCC. *See* National Certified Counselors
NCDA. *See* National Career Development
Association
NCE. *See* National Counselor Examination
NCMHCE. *See* National Clinical Mental Health
Counselor Examination
Nebraska Board of Mental Health Practice,
394–395
NECA. *See* National Employment Counseling
Association
neglect
child, 84–85, 239–241
definition of, 239
signs of, 240
networking questionnaire, 338–339
Nevada Board of Examiners for Marriage
and Family Therapists and Clinical
Professional Counselors, 395
New Hampshire Board of Mental Health
Practice, 396
New Jersey Board of Marriage and Family
Therapy Examiners, Professional
Counselor Examiners Committee, 396–397

New Mexico Counseling and Therapy Practice Board, 397–398
New York, 4
New York State Education Department, 398
New Zealand Association of Counsellors (NZCA), 14, 370
nightmares, 283, 284–285, 296
NIOSH. *See* National Institute for Occupational Safety and Health
nonsuicidal self-injury, 218
NOPCAS. *See* National Organization for People of Color Against Suicide
North Carolina Board of Licensed Professional Counselors, 398–399
North Dakota Board of Counselor Examiners, 399–400
NZCA. *See* New Zealand Association of Counsellors

objective information (case notes), 142–143, 148
Occupational Outlook Handbook (OOH), 371
Occupational Safety and Health Administration (OSHA), 261
Ohio Counselor, Social Worker, and Marriage and Family Therapist Board, 400–401
Oklahoma State Board of Licensed Professional Counselors, 401
on-site supervision/supervisors, 18, 22, 55–57, 59, 66, 132, 159, 168, 178–179, 179–180, 258. *See also* field supervisor–intern relationship, termination of
OOH. *See* Occupational Outlook Handbook
open-ended questions, 120, 336
oppressed cultures, 37–38
Oregon Board of Licensed Professional Counselors and Therapists, 402
OSHA. *See* Occupational Safety and Health Administration
outpatient placements, 53
overgeneralization (negative self-talk), 273

PACFA. *See* Psychotherapy and Counselling Federation of Australia
paraphrasing, 120
pastoral counselors, 93
patient-centered supervision, 173
Peck v. Counseling Services of Addison County, Inc. (1985), 87
peers, feedback to, 171–172
Pennsylvania State Board of Social Workers, Marriage and Family Therapists, and Professional Counselors, 402–403
Pennsylvania State University child sexual abuse scandal, 240

Perceived Stress Scale-4 (Pss-4), 208
personal biases worksheet, 30
person-centered supervision, 176–177
person-centered therapy, 176
PHI. *See* protected health information
physical abuse
    definition of, 239
    signs of, 239
physical activity, 208, 353
physical self-care, 209
physician-assisted suicide, 134
Pilates, 293
placement coordinators, 22, 47, 48, 59, 60, 61, 66, 70, 179
placements, practicum/internship, 47, 48
    homework of students, 49
    lack of help from faculty, 48–49
    variations in settings, 57–58
positive assets, acknowledging, 279–280
post-traumatic stress disorder (PTSD), 269–270, 295
prejudice, 251
pressure points, 295
Principles for Unifying and Strengthening the Profession, 2
privacy, 77, 82, 83. *See also* confidentiality
    of clients with serious communicable diseases, 90
    of deceased clients, 142
    HIPAA Privacy Rule, 137
    and multiple relationships in counseling, 93
privileged communication, 83–84. *See also* confidentiality
pro–con exercise for job search, 356
professional counseling, definition of, 3
professional counseling organizations, 8–14, 340, 349, 365–371
professional goals, 348, 359
professional liability insurance, 101–102, 237
professional networking sites, 337–338. *See also* networking questionnaire
Professional Quality-of-Life Scale (ProQOL), 191, 192–195
propriety of dual relationships, 96
ProQOL. *See* Professional Quality-of-Life Scale
protected health information (PHI), 137, 138
Pss-4. *See* Perceived Stress Scale-4
psychodynamic supervision, 173–174
psychologists, 55–56
psychopharmacologic medications, ceasing taking, 250
psychosocial family assessment, 123
Psychotherapy and Counselling Federation of Australia (PACFA), 14, 370
PTSD. *See* post-traumatic stress disorder
PTSD checklist, 272

Puerto Rico Office of Regulation and Certification of Health Professions, 403–404
purpose in life, 105, 106, 202–203, 232, 233, 242, 243, 269, 320

Qi-gong, 293

racism, 54
   and culture, 31–32
   unintentional, 28
rational emotive behavior therapy (REBT), 181, 274
RC. *See* Registered Counsellor
REBT. *See* rational emotive behavior therapy
record keeping, 138, 139, 141–142. *See also* client records
record retention policy, 93
references/reference letters, 8, 60, 337, 338–340
referral(s), 91, 122, 135, 237, 303, 308, 311, 312–313, 424–425
reflection of feelings, 120
reframing, 121, 189–190, 203–204, 272, 273–274, 282, 295, 297, 335, 354
Registered Counsellor (RC), 16
Registered Psychotherapist (RP), 16
release of information by clients, 88, 303
religion, 251
   addressing in counseling sessions, 150, 153
   clash between religious beliefs and ethics, 36–37
remembering, 272
remote communities, counseling in, 96–97
residential treatment settings, 248, 261–264
   assault by clients, 259
   boundary issues, 93
   and termination, 303
resilience, 232, 233, 268, 272
respondeat superior doctrine, 140
résumé, 61–62, 63–65, 68, 337, 339, 340–342, 354, 359
Rhode Island Board of Mental Health Counselors and Marriage and Family Therapists, 404
right to die, 106, 134
right to self-determination, 135
Roe v. Wade (1973), 4
role-plays, 121, 302, 330
Rønnestad and Skovholt's model of supervision, 175–176
RP. *See* Registered Psychotherapist

SAAC. *See* The South African Association for Counsellors
SAC. *See* Singapore Association for Counselling; Suicide Assessment Checklist

safe areas for interns, 179
safe spaces for trauma survivors, 274, 276–277, 296
safety, 247–248, 261–264
   actions to take after an assault, 259–260
   contracts, 227
   dealing with aggressive behaviors, 252–253
   defusing violence, 254–257
   plan, 247, 249, 252–253, 257
   predictors of client violence, 249–252
   self-defense training, 254, 257–258, 261
   workplace violence prevention plan, 258
SASSI-4. *See* Substance Abuse Subtle Screening Inventory-4
SAT exam, 123
SAVRY. *See* Structured Assessment of Violence Risk in Youth
scaling questions, 121, 123, 178, 196, 281, 295, 306–307
school counseling, 18, 33, 48, 52, 55, 114, 132, 145
   and confidentiality, 89
   and dual relationships, 93, 96
   forms, 167
   intake interview, 434–435
   referral form, 424–425
   suicide assessment, 228–231
   supervision in, 55
selection, practicum/internship, 47–52
   agreements, 49
   clinical populations, 52–54
   faculty advisors, 48, 49, 56, 61
   level of responsibility, 54–55
   placement coordinators, 47, 48
   practicum/internship site information form, 50–51
   professional practices and resources, 59
   role of supervisor, 49, 52
   site accreditations and affiliations, 57–59
   site supervisor, 55–57
self-awareness, 29–31
self-care, 125, 185–186, 211–213. *See also* stress
   compassion fatigue and burnout, 190, 191
   conflict management skills, 203–205
   counseling student as client, 205–207
   healthy and mindful lifestyle, 186–203
   meaning and purpose in life, 202–203
   plan, 209–211, 360
   Professional Quality-of-Life Scale (ProQOL), 191, 192–195
   reflective questions, 191–192
   regarding major successes and failures in your life, 196
   self-monitoring system, 196–201
   stress management, 189–190, 201–202
   suggestions for, 207–211
self-compassion, 128, 196
self-defense training, 254, 257–258, 261

456 • INDEX

self-disclosure, 229
self-evaluation by interns, 324, 328–329
self-injurious behaviors, 218. *See also* suicide
self-medication, 42, 267, 270, 282, 286–289, 294
self-reflection, 76, 121, 126, 128, 186, 190, 232, 312, 316, 324, 332, 354, 355
self-talk, 121, 122, 126, 128, 268, 272, 273–274, 282, 291–292, 297, 335, 354
sexual abuse, 95, 241
  signs of, 240
  trauma, 294–297
sexual relationship, counselor–client, 93–94, 97–99
SGSM. *See* Structured Group Supervision Model
Singapore Association for Counselling (SAC), 370
single episode trauma, 268
site-based supervision. *See* on-site supervision
SMHAI. *See* Suicide and Mental Health Association International
SOAP. *See* Subject Object Assessment Plan notes
social activism, 34
social networking sites, 337, 353, 359
social readjustment rating scale (SRRS), 272
social relationships, counselor–client, 99
social self-care, 210
social workers, 55–56, 65, 83
software programs for counselors, 92
solution-focused brief therapy, 177
solution-focused supervision, 177–178
somatic stress, 187
The South African Association for Counsellors (SAAC), 370
South Carolina Board of Examiners for the Licensure of Professional Counselors, Marriage and Family Therapists, and Psychoeducational Specialists, 404–405
South Dakota Board of Examiners for Counselors and Marriage and Family Therapists, 405
spirituality
  addressing in counseling sessions, 150, 153–154
  spiritual self-care, 210
SRRS. *See* social readjustment rating scale
stress, 186–187
  assessment of, 208
  burnout, 190–191
  and client violence, 251
  compassion fatigue, 190, 191
  effects of, 188–189
  environmental stressors, 187
  manageable level of, 187

  management, 189–190, 201–203
  somatic, 187
  from thoughts, 187–188
Strong Interest Inventory, 123
Structured Assessment of Violence Risk in Youth (SAVRY), 234
Structured Group Supervision Model (SGSM), 168
student counseling session rating form, 169–171, 439–440
student liability insurance, 8, 67–68, 101–102, 140–141
Subjective, Objective, Assessment, Plan (SOAP) notes, 138, 145, 150, 153–154, 436, 441–442
  assessment section, 149–150
  case studies, 151–153
  examples, 151
  objective section, 148
  plan section, 150
  subjective section, 145, 148
subjective assessments, 140
subjective information (case notes), 142–143, 145, 148
subjective units of disturbance scale (SUDS), 274, 277–278, 296, 297
subpoena checklist, 236
substance abuse, 294
  and client violence, 250
  self-medication, 286–289
  and suicide, 223
Substance Abuse Subtle Screening Inventory-4 (SASSI-4), 123, 143, 223
SUDS. *See* subjective units of disturbance scale
suicide, 85, 102–106, 134, 220–221, 241–243
  after-crisis counseling, 231–233
  appropriate measures to prevent, 221
  discussing with clients about, 221
  ethical and legal mandates regarding, 221–222
  intent, 222, 223
  lethality, 223, 229
  means, 222–223, 227
  myths, 220
  organizations for prevention of, 244
  physician-assisted, 134
  plan, 221, 222, 227
  prior attempts, 223
  rational suicide, 90–91
  risk assessment, 222–226, 228
  risk factors, 226
  risk in schools, assessment of, 228–231
  steps to take when a client is contemplating, 226–228
  and substance abuse, 223
  talking with suicidal clients, 222

tips for managing emotions and behavior
when addressing, 238
warning signs of, 226–227
Suicide and Mental Health Association
International (SMHAI), 244
Suicide Assessment Checklist (SAC), 234
suicide contracts, 229
suicide watches, 229
summarizing, 120–121, 124
supervisee-centered supervision, 173–174
supervision, 22, 134, 159–160, 181–183, 237
administrative, 167
clinical, 159–160, 167–168
vs. consultation, 160
counseling practicum/internship class,
160–167
feedback to peers, 171–180
licensure standards, 56–57
models and critique, 167–168
round-robin format, 168–169
style, 172–179
triadic model of, 18–19, 22
video recordings of counseling sessions,
165–166
written feedback, 169–171
supervisors, 49, 52, 69, 87–88, 92, 100, 159, 160,
222, 237, 337. *See also* field supervisor–
intern relationship, termination of
checklist of questions to ask, 180
consultation with, 87, 140, 150, 217, 227, 310
feedback, 125, 168, 169, 178–179
and Medicare reimbursement, 7–8
reporting assault to, 259
and responsibility of students, 54–55
site, 55–57, 59, 66, 132, 159, 178–179, 179–180,
258
theoretical orientation of, 57, 172
supervisory-matrix-centered supervision, 174
support groups
for clients, 308, 309
for counselors/students, 125, 207, 208
support systems for trauma survivors, 276,
278–279
suspected abuse, reporting of, 84–85
syllabus, practicum/internship class, 160–165
systems approach to supervision, 178

T4C. *See* Thinking for a Change-Certified
Facilitator
Tai Chi, 293
*Tarasoff v. The Regents of the University of
California Berkeley* (1976), 75, 85–87, 136,
219–220, 256
technology, 92–93, 167, 335, 411–412

teletherapy, 109–110, 335
Tennessee Board for Professional Counselors,
Marital and Family Therapists, and
Clinical Pastoral Therapists, 406
terminally ill clients, 90–91, 134–136
termination, 67, 301–303, 316–320
abandonment, 314–316
circumstances, 302
client resistance to, 307–310, 315–316
clients in crisis, 237
client's readiness for, 304
counselor resistance to, 310–312
discussion with clients about, 305–307
drop outs, 303
and life process, 302
plan, 307
record, 123
referrals and follow-up, 312–314
and time-limited counseling approaches, 302
when to terminate, 303–305
Texas State Board of Examiners of Professional
Counselors, 406–407
thank-you letter, 66
Thapar v. Zezulka (1999), 87, 136, 239
theoretical orientation/approaches, 57, 69, 79,
120, 122, 172, 348, 359
therapeutic alliance, 110–111, 115, 233, 242
therapeutic relationship, 1, 27, 77, 82, 86,
109, 110, 125, 253, 301–302. *See also*
confidentiality; sexual relationship,
counselor–client; termination
dual/multiple relationships in counseling,
93–97
and feminist model of supervision, 174
and gifts from clients to counselors, 100
Thinking for a Change-Certified Facilitator
(T4C), 12
time-limited counseling, 302
TJC. *See* The Joint Commission
training opportunities, 54, 69
transfer of clients, 136, 154
trauma, 42, 191, 267–268, 294–298
acknowledging positive assets, 279–280
acute stress disorder, 269, 270
assault by clients, 259
assessment of, 272–286
body work, 293
breath work/meditation, 292–293
complex, 268, 270
creating safe spaces, 274, 276–277, 296
daily gratitudes, 292, 293
definition of, 268–269
dream journal, 284, 286
dreams, 283, 296–297
empty chair technique, 290, 297

458 • INDEX

trauma (*conti*)
    factors of, 270–272
    impact of, 269
    journaling, 280–281, 284, 286
    A Letter to My Traumatized Self exercise,
        290–291
    managing flashbacks, 281–283, 284
    Monitoring and Revising My Self-Talk
        exercise, 291–292
    nightmares, 283, 284–285, 296
    post-traumatic stress disorder, 269–270
    remembering, 272–273
    self-medication, 286–289
    self-talk, 273–274
    single episode, 268
    subjective units of disturbance scale, 274,
        277–278
    support systems, 276, 278–279
trauma beliefs inventory, 275
trauma history screen (TRS), 272
trauma symptom inventory (TSI), 272
treatment plan, 123, 150, 227, 268, 302, 320
triadic model of supervision, 18–19, 22
TRICARE, 6, 10, 11
TRS. *See* trauma history screen
TSI. *See* trauma symptom inventory
20/20: A Vision for the Future of Counseling
    initiative, ACA, 2, 3, 6

UA. *See* urinalysis
urinalysis (UA), 71
U.S. Bureau of Labor Statistics (BLS), 16, 165,
    371
Utah Professional Counseling Licensing Board,
    407

VA. *See* Department of Veterans Affairs
values, 53
    and culture, 32
    and job search, 333–334
    value-based referrals, 122, 135
Vermont Board of Allied Mental Health
    Practitioners, 408
victimization, history of, 249–250, 254
Victim–Offender Reconciliation Programs
    (VORP), 260
video recordings of counseling sessions,
    165–166, 420

violence, 86
    assessment of potential for, 234–235
    client, predictors of, 249–252
    dealing with aggressive behaviors, 252–253
    de-escalation training, 254
    defusing, 254–257
    domestic, 151–152, 274
    and duty to warn and protect, 219–220
    encountering during practicum/internship,
        247–248
    identifying children/adolescents at risk for
        violent behavior, 252
    against mental health professionals, 248
    workplace, 247, 248, 252
    workplace violence prevention plan, 258
violent behavior, history of, 249, 254
Virginia Board of Counseling Perimeter Center,
    408–409
Virginia Substance Abuse Counselors, 12
voice tone, 221, 255
VORP. *See* Victim–Offender Reconciliation
    Programs

Ward v. Wilbanks (2010), 39
Washington Licensed Mental Health
    Counselors, Marriage and Family
    Therapists, and Social Workers Advisory
    Committee, 409
weapons, access to, 250–251, 254
West Virginia Board of Examiners in
    Counseling, 409–410
Wisconsin Examining Board of Marriage
    and Family Therapists, Professional
    Counselors, and Social Workers, 410–411
working relationship, 56, 327
workplace violence, 247, 248, 252
workplace violence prevention plan, 258
World Health Organization, 287
written feedback, 169–171
Wyoming Mental Health Professions Licensing
    Board, 411

yoga, 293
Youth Suicide Prevention, 244
Youth Suicide School-Based Prevention Guide,
    244